RED, BLACK, AND JEW

Jewish History, Life, and Culture
Michael Neiditch, series editor

RED, BLACK, AND JEW

New Frontiers in Hebrew Literature

STEPHEN KATZ

UNIVERSITY OF TEXAS
Austin

The Jewish History, Life, and Culture Series is supported by the late Milton T. Smith and the Moshana Foundation, and the Tocker Foundation.

Printed in the United States of America

First edition, 2009

♾ The paper used in this book meets the minimum requirements of ANSI/NISO Z39.48-1992 (R1997) (Permanence of Paper).

LIBRARY OF CONGRESS CATALOGING-IN-PUBLICATION DATA
Katz, Stephen, 1947–
Red, Black, and Jew : new frontiers in Hebrew literature / Stephen Katz. — 1st ed.
p. cm. — (Jewish history, life, and culture)
Includes bibliographical references and index.
ISBN 978-0-292-71926-2 (cloth : alk. paper)
1. Indians in literature. 2. African Americans in literature. 3. Hebrew literature, Modern—United States—History and criticism. 4. Hebrew literature, Modern—American influences. 5. Jews—United States—Intellectual life. I. Title.
PJ5013.I53K38 2009
892.4'09352997—dc22

2008053124

To Eileen
for
Mimi, Haddie, Kendrick, Abby, and Megan
Libby and Josh
for
Kobi, Maya, Simon, and Charlotte

CONTENTS

ACKNOWLEDGMENTS ix

INTRODUCTION 1

Chapter One 13
ENCOUNTERING NATIVE AMERICANS:
B. N. SILKINER'S *MUL OHEL TIMMURA*

Chapter Two 31
FACING THE SUNSET:
ISRAEL EFROS ON NATIVE AMERICANS

Chapter Three 49
TO BE AS OTHERS: E. E. LISITZKY'S
REPRESENTATION OF NATIVE AMERICANS

Chapter Four 77
FANTASY OR PLAIN FOLK:
IMAGINING NATIVE AMERICANS

Chapter Five 91
CHILD'S PLAY: HILLEL BAVLI'S "MRS. WOODS"
AND THE INDIAN IN AMERICAN HEBREW LITERATURE

Chapter Six 109
RED HEART, BLACK SKIN: E. E. LISITZKY'S ENCOUNTERS
WITH AFRICAN AMERICAN FOLKSONG AND POETRY

Chapter Seven 137
FROM PROP TO TROPE TO REAL FOLKS:
BLACKS IN HEBREW LITERATURE

ACKNOWLEDGMENTS

The germ idea of this study was planted by my teachers Harry Blumberg and Milton Arfa, who in the course of introducing me to the greats of modern Hebrew literature would comment on the relative paucity of study of the contributions made by America's Hebraists to the field.

It later took more concrete shape in my readings of the contributions of the likes of Eisig Silberschlag, Jacob Kabakoff, and, more recently, Alan Mintz. The latter has been instrumental in his scholarly attainments and by encouraging others to follow his lead in probing the scope and quality of a largely unexplored landscape of Hebrew belles lettres in America.

Actual work on this study could not have been done without the cooperation and assistance of many good people. I wish to recognize them and express my appreciation for all they have done.

My gratitude goes to the Gnazim bio-bibliographical archives in Tel-Aviv, to Dr. Ḥedva Roḥel, its director, and to Dvora Stavi and her able staff; to the manuscript division of the National and University Library of the Hebrew University of Jerusalem, its director, Mr. Rafi Weiser, and his staff; and to the library staff of the Jewish Theological Seminary; to the various publishing houses for permission to use copyrighted materials, including Am Oved, the Bialik Institute and Kinneret, Zmora-Bitan, and Dvir Publishing.

My thanks also go to Ghela Efros Scharfstein and Ben-Ami Scharfstein for their hospitality and for allowing me to read some of Efros's manuscripts, and for the gift of his many writings. Also, I am indebted to Professor Zephyra (Halkin) Porat for her permission and help with S. Halkin's materials. Likewise to my friend, mentor, and teacher, Hillel Barzel, whose walking conversations have been invaluable in helping me to flesh out my thoughts and contextualize the subject within the greater scope of the Hebrew literary tradition.

I also wish to express my thanks to Professors Gustav Bayerle and Ron Sela, of the Department of Central Eurasian Studies at Indiana University, for acquainting me with studies about the Vogul people, as well as to my colleagues Hasan El-Shami and Henry Glassie of Indiana University's Department of Folklore and Ethnomusicology. I also thank Professor Michael Weingrad for allowing me to read early versions of some of his studies of American Hebrew literature, and Dr. Tim Jon Semmerling. My thanks go to the various anonymous readers of the manuscript, to Stanley Nash, and to the able staff of the University of Texas Press.

For financial support in the course of research for this book, I am indebted to the Memorial Foundation for Jewish Culture, the American Jewish Archives for its 1997–1998 Bernard and Audre Rapoport Fellowship of American Jewish Studies, and various offices of Indiana University, among them: the Indiana University President's Arts and Humanities Initiative Award, the Indiana University Office of Research and Graduate Development for its Emergency Grant in Aid of Research, the Indiana University College of Arts and Sciences Summer Faculty Fellowship, the Department of Near Eastern Languages and Cultures, the Middle Eastern Studies Program, and the Borns Jewish Studies Program for their annual research grants and awards and for the Borns Individual Research Grant. I also wish to thank Melissa Deckard of the Borns Jewish Studies Program for all her expert help with computer files and software.

And, most important, gratitude goes to my family and friends: the Maayans, who have always been so hospitable during my frequent trips to Israel; the Goldfishers, who opened their home to me during my research trips to New York; and above all, to Eileen.

This study is also dedicated to the memory of my father, Zoltan Katz, and family members Olga Eizler, Mike and Netty Feldman, and Iosif Leb. I also remember my departed teachers, mentors, and friends, Ḥayim Abramowitz, Milton Arfa, Harry Blumberg, Henry A. Fischel, and A. Z. Halevy.

RED, BLACK, AND JEW

INTRODUCTION

This is not a history of Hebrew literature in America. Instead it relates a fascinating chapter of that literature's preoccupation with America's indigenous minorities, African Americans and Native Americans. The uniqueness of this interest stems from the fact that at no time in the annals of Hebrew literature and in any land of the Jewish Diaspora have writers demonstrated such a curiosity about other groups, out of sympathy with how other marginalized peoples have fared compared to the way Jews have fared in America. And while some of the ensuing interest is a consequence of the onset of modernity and a fostering of pluralism in Jewish, and Hebrew, culture, the American cultural factor is more significant than others have been. The spectacle of Hebrew writers preoccupying themselves with the ways of other minorities is, but for literature composed in English, unique in its scope among all minority literature on the American stage.

Though Hebrew writers in Europe did delve into encounters between Jewish protagonists and Gentiles, they foregrounded the former, often presenting them in superficial, stereotypical fashion.[1] Few if any works were composed about the Gentile world without Jews as relevant factors in the plot. By the late nineteenth century, Hebrew literature about Jewish women and their lot began to become *de rigueur*. Later, Hebrew literary projects included translations of national epics of other groups out of motives other than interest in marginalized minorities. In tracing the Americanization of Hebrew literature, then, one of my concerns will be the examination of the works by American Hebrew writers who became inordinately enamored of the non-Jewish cultural landscape, including that of Native and African Americans.[2]

Having reached its zenith in the middle of the twentieth century as it grew commensurately with the influx of immigrants, American Hebrew literature is a little-tapped record of the newest wave of Jewish immigration, cultural adaptation, and transformation in the New World. Though little may be attained by probing the meager Hebrew literary legacy of the handful of Jews who populated the United States before the middle of the nineteenth century, when fifty thousand or so augmented the few living there before 1850,[3] later immigration waves changed all that. The truly significant influx of Jews occurred only a decade later, when, by 1860, America's Jewish population swelled to two hundred thousand. Between 1890 and 1920, there were over three million, laying the foundation for a new center of Jewish life. This growth constituted the basis upon which, within only a few decades, one of the most thriving and culturally rich Jewish communities in history took root.[4]

Among the millions of Jews to land in the New World, not a few regretted having made the journey. The attractions, potentials, and promises of life in the Golden Land seemed Faustian to some. While most may have missed the quaintness and familiarity of life in the Old Country, some were quick to realize that life in the New World extracted a higher price in terms of group identity, cohesiveness, and culture. Though many were prepared to bear the cost—to live in America but also to set up a new ghetto existence in order to stem the onslaught of the host culture—others turned back. Not even the thrill of crossing the East River from Manhattan to Brooklyn over the newly constructed bridge kept the most disenchanted or culturally alienated from returning home—as evidenced by an anecdote preserved in my family of the experiences of one grandparent who turned and returned, only to be swept up by the emerging horror of the Holocaust.

Yet the lure of new beginnings in America was a potent force. The masses that landed in the New World made their choice clear by voting with their steerage tickets. Reality trumps idealism; cold existential calculation overwhelms the dream. It was inevitable, then, that among those who arrived there were also talented young, literate Jews who constituted the nucleus of what became a thriving Hebrew (and Yiddish) culture. Among them were those who found the nexus of spiritual values and material temptations a fertile ground upon which to write satirically of Jewish life. In the early years, Gershon Rosenzweig composed a parody of the Talmud, *Talmud Yanka'i* (Yankee Talmud),[5] and deformed the New World's image by calling it *'Amireika* (or *'Amareika*), literally "My good-for-nothing people" (or "A good-for-nothing people"). This tendency to satirize American Jewish life did not abate. L. A. Arieli (Orloff) set the tone of measuring American Jewry's preoccupation with itself, Zion, and progress only to find them wanting.[6]

The waves of immigration bore along a number of established Hebrew and Yiddish literati, among them Y. D. Berkovitch (1885–1967), Sholom

Aleichem (1859–1916), Shimon Ginzburg (1890–1944), and Menachem Mendel Dolitzky (1856–1931), who pulled up roots, immigrated, and catalyzed the emergent literary center in the New World. The arrival of each set off a flurry of expectations among America's Jewish intelligentsia. Younger immigrants, many coming with an education from the traditional East European *ḥeder* and *yeshivah*, landed in the New World to be transformed by the American experience. Of these, some took up the pen, realizing their literary talents or mission to become American-educated writers of Hebrew literature. They participated in what became the heyday of American Hebrew (and Yiddish) literary activity in the first half of the twentieth century. Most, inevitably, embellished the Hebrew tradition by introducing new forms and themes as they drew upon and melded Jewish with American culture.[7]

In an attempt to preserve itself, Hebrew literature in the United States adopted the paradoxical posture of advocating separateness by the very nature of being the expression of a uniquely exploited and distinct cultural group. Yet its engagement with America and its themes belies an impulse to acculturate, to undergo what an astute observer, Yaʿakov Rabinowitz, termed "Americanization."[8] By this he meant to call on Hebrew literature to distinguish itself as American. In some measure, by instigating, supporting, and promoting the Americanization of Hebrew culture, writers were sowing the seeds of their own demise. Inevitably, then, this study charts Hebrew literature's collusion and mirroring of an unprecedented Jewish acculturation into its host society. America was to Jewish civilization the crucible in which its insular particularism was met by threats of acculturation and assimilation in the maelstrom of hyphenations.

In America we can chart the divide between mere Hebraists and Zionists who wrote Hebrew literature. Not all actors on the stage of America's Hebrew literary center's brief flowering were dyed-in-the-wool Zionists, ready to emigrate from the Golden Land and exchange its material comforts for the rigors of a Jewish state-in-the-making. Some, much like their forebears of the *Haskalah* (Jewish Enlightenment), were ardent devotees of the Hebrew language, separating themselves and their pursuits from any Zionist program to which the Hebrew language became a consort by nearly unanimous consent. What becomes patently obvious is the bifurcated response to the prospects of realizing the founding of the Jewish state. As these improved, the ranks of Hebrew writers divided along the lines of those unwilling or the actively engaged in the project of supporting the creation of the political Zionist program and even settling in the state that will eventually arise. Of the latter, a good number—among them S. Halkin, R. Avinoam (Grossman), A. Regelson, and I. Efros—left to settle in Israel. Others, among them S. L. Blank, E. E. Lisitzky, and D. Persky, exhibited an ambivalence in the face of a realized Jewish national dream, justifying their decision to remain in America in a host of ways.

The literature produced by these authors and poets foregrounds questions of group identity as a subtext. Writers were patently conscious of the new course upon which they had launched Hebrew literature in the Golden Land, altering its programmatic agenda to engage with things American in place of those of Europe and Eretz Israel (the Land of Israel, as distinct from the later-established state as a political entity). Having to a great extent abandoned the shaping of Jewish national identity as a leading paradigm, America's Hebrew writers also lost their own raison d'être. To be sure, they did not abandon all encounters with the Land of Israel. Yet an examination of the themes and forms preoccupying American Hebrew writers indicates that they were more absorbed with personal and regional matters of society and landscape. The turn inward, though not shunned even by the greatest of the Zionist poets of the day, became a mark of the fragmentation of American Hebrew literary culture. In place of a uniform enlistment to the Jewish national cause, American Hebraists pursued other courses. Whether out of personal need or as representing the malaise of the generation, they chose to express the sense of the times they or their readers harbored.

In place of toeing the European Hebraists' line, writing of America and its other minorities becomes an act of inscribing the self onto and alongside America's marginalized groups, principally by delving into the lives of Native Americans or Blacks. In so doing, the literary works of these writers exemplify a reimagining of the self in the guise of the Other. It contextualizes the experience of oneself or one's group within a larger milieu. The indirect way of defining themselves became a measure of the depth of the gaping chasm opening between Hebrew writers and the centers of Hebrew literature in Europe and Israel.

Their preoccupation with other minority groups is also a measure of a deep-seated psychological condition these writers shared. Whether because of an inability to come to terms with their own transmuted collective (or individual) identity in the New World, or the lack of a clear vision of what to advocate—beside the obvious topic of the Holocaust and a few others—they wrote of other minorities. In so doing, their subjects became the repositories of issues which continued to engage them. Yet it is likely that by examining other marginalized groups in American culture, Hebrew writers found a means of indirectly writing about themselves.[9]

Hebrew literature's fate in America is also a story of a missed opportunity for Hebraists to transmute their new land into another viable literary center. As early as 1922, the Pittsburgh, Pa., activist in the *Histadrut 'Ivrit*, Chaim Bronstein, observed that "America is the sole place to serve as a haven for the Hebrew movement." The sentiment in favor of establishing a new center of Hebrew life and culture in the New World was supported by M. Ribalow's observation of its necessity for Hebraists in the United States.[10] Yet this abortive attempt is an exemplary chapter in the history of Modern Hebrew literature and deserving of scrutiny. At the time, this incipient center had an independent cadre of Hebrew poets, essayists, and novelists working to engender a literature that failed to propagate itself beyond the generation of its immigrant founders. Nonetheless, the thematic and formal contributions of this half-century of Hebrew literary activity deserve our attention.

That which befell Hebrew literature during its half-century in the New World is a consequence of its confrontation with decidedly more insidious forces of modernism, with a culture unlike those among which it developed and thrived in Eastern Europe. Its demise left Israel as the sole flourishing center of Hebrew letters. What follows, then, is a testimonial to those largely obscure Hebrew writers whose literary activity centered in whole or in part on the New World. Though the effort of most to secure a slice of immortality has been thwarted, their volumes of mostly marginalized prose, poetry, and essays await to be added to the greater edifice of the Hebrew literary tradition, to be accepted as part of the continuum between its East European Hebrew and Yiddish ancestors, though also standing as a bridge to the Bellows, Malamuds, Roths, Gershwins, and Brookses of American culture. As of now, much of these writings remain forgotten, lost to readers whose eyes, minds, and hearts turned to Zion. However, America's Hebrew writers have imprinted on the pages of their literary tradition previously absent themes, forms, and insights that enlarged its scope.

THE PROBLEM OF DEFINITION

Most American Hebrew writers were born in Europe and immigrated at an early age to the United States.[11] Others arrived at a later station in their careers. The question of who among them deserve the appellation "American-Hebrew writer" is obscured by more than their place of birth. Some complicated the question by emigrating at one time or another, as did Y. D. Berkovitch, I. Efros, and S. Ginzburg. Of those, some even returned, either to remain or to depart once again, as was the case with S. Halkin.

A related matter is the number of Hebrew writers in America, which differs with the criteria used for definition. Daniel Persky counted them as a hundred and ten by 1927.[12] The American Jewish Archives (Cincinnati) contains a list, prepared by S. Shiḥor in October of 1962, of 175 writers. Other lists tend to be narrower, as in anthologies representing the writings of a select group of Hebraists. The one compiled by the author of a history (more like a list with short biographies) of American Hebrew literature, Jacques Mikliszanski, amounts to some seventeen poets and twenty-three prose writers in the first period (1860–1914), and at least twenty-nine poets and twenty-four writers in the second (1914–1967).[13]

The compound designation "Jewish American" or "American Jew" signifies the hybridized nature of the Jew in America. If the second term in a compound identity is the leading one, with the first merely modifying it, then the logical process of assimilation is from American Jews to Jewish Americans. The latter of the two is the more Americanized, denoting the last stop before a complete loss of ethnic identity and culture. As in the case of others, not a few Jews strove to merit the label of Jewish Americans. Others, like Mary Antin, recollecting in her book *The Promised Land*, sought to lose even that identity by fully assimilating, erasing one's former self to emerge as a full-fledged American.[14]

Happily, since the following does not endeavor to embrace the full gamut of Hebrew writings in America, it inevitably and out of expediency overlooks or minimizes the contributions made by some of the most important writers. The issues before us are sufficiently demarcated so as to ignore seminal works by writers who did not address themselves to the representation of marginalized minorities in America. My examination of any writer from a particularly thematic or even ideological perspective is an act of isolation, detaching it from the complete oeuvre of that writer. Regrettably, the separated issue, while enabling me to focus on its features, also means a decontextualization. This fact will not be fully remedied below, out of consideration for the scope and size of such a work.

That the writers discussed in this study have become, by and large, unknown to American Jews and most Hebrew readers is a consequence of their works being rarely afforded the resuscitating gesture of a dusting off. As any cursory examination of historical, social, religious, or cultural studies of Jews in the New World reveals, few writers have even been deemed worthy of mention or relevant to the life and culture of American Jewry. Those who were the essential players in American Hebrew culture—H. Bavli, S. L. Blank, I. Efros, M. Feinstein, A. Z. Halevy, S. Halkin, E. E. Lisitzky, B. N. Silkiner, or R. Wallenrod, for example—have been forgotten, individuals without whom the inclusivity of these histories falls short of their proclaimed purpose. Like the authors themselves, their literary enterprise had fallen between the cracks, neglected in Israel as irrelevant and ignored in the United States, where new generations have forsaken their Hebrew reading skills.

HEBREW LITERARY THEMES IN AMERICA

In its heyday, the mainstream of American Hebrew literature—poetry or prose, realistic, modern, or neo-romantic—preoccupied itself with four overriding themes.[15] The first was a revisiting of Jews' European roots, selectively reimagining the home left behind. It is the environment of material values over the intangible spiritual ones that promoted this sense of alienation and loss in the New World. Protagonists who encountered anxieties of adjustment in America figured centrally in works that measured the chasm between the past and the present.

The second leading theme covers the encounter with America, and represents the struggle of Jews with the exotic and mundane in the New World, its physical and social landscape and culture. The ever-present affinity for the Promised Land and Zionism represents the third tier of themes; its absence in many Hebrew works in America is a mark of ambivalence writers displayed about Jewish nationalism. It is also an indication of the rise of a center of American Hebrew literature whose agenda was not directed as wholeheartedly toward a national program. Finally, the fourth theme is the preoccupation with the distant past, revisiting episodes in biblical and later episodes of Jewish history.

This inquiry into Jews' accommodation with America will focus principally on the second of the above. Yet in addressing any of the themes, one cannot but note that while changing in some ways, Hebrew literature remained for many decades a prisoner of a conservatism upholding a high literary style that depended on its classical roots. Many of its followers tenaciously adhered to the Ashkenazi dialect, which affected poetic diction, meter, rhyme, and rhythm. Alternatively, seeming to assert their independence from a newly evolving center in Eretz Israel, American

Hebraists insisted on coining new words and modes of expression to suit local needs in place of looking up to any authority.

All the while that the American Hebrew writer strove to preserve a classical mode of expression, however, another trend precipitated greater concerns: a diminished education that failed to inculcate the next generations with a competence in Hebrew texts. Hebrew proficiency—always a mainstay in the perpetuation of the tradition—declined in America as the immigrant generation gave way to the new, whose diminished interest in traditional learning and its accompanying culture meant a marginalization of Hebrew resources.

INDIANS AS JEWS

Distinguishing themselves from Hebrew literati abroad, and underscoring their assimilation of local life and attitudes, writers focused on American themes. By the years of the Jews' mass migration, the preoccupation with indigenous minorities, Native Americans and Blacks, was of paramount interest in American (English) literature, and it is from this that Hebraists took their cue. Although some common themes characterize much of immigrant literature composed by contemporary Italian, Irish, Polish, and even Yiddish writers, Hebrew poetry carved out for itself new space by delving into the issues hitherto never explored—the life, culture, and experience of underprivileged Others. And while American Hebrew writers did not lend much credence to the theories of the nexus between Native Americans and the Lost Ten Tribes of Israel, their interest in America's marginalized Indian and Black minorities is a concern that runs through many of their works.

Yet it was in this environment that Mordecai Manuel Noah (original name Mendel Gershon Glembotzky), writing in 1837, reached what to him was the logical conclusion. Marshalling evidence from William Penn, Manasseh ben Israel, and Montesini pointing to the Jewish origins of America's Indians, he proposed repatriation, en masse, of the Hebrew nation to the Promised Land. Those returned would include American Indians who, he argued, were a remnant of the Ten Lost Tribes. Making his case by appealing to British interests, he argued that the measure would make good geopolitical sense in order to keep a check on Russian, Turkish, and Persian incursions into their (British) spheres of interest. "By restoring Syria to its rightful owners . . . by the purchase of that territory from the Pacha [*sic*] of Egypt," Britain could also help Providence restore all these Jews to the Promised Land, asserted Noah.

Noah's activities were later viewed as proto-Zionist, spawning works of fiction, ideology, and scholarship in Hebrew, Yiddish, and English—such as Isaac Goldberg's *Major Noah*, Israel Zangwill's "Noah's Ark," and Harry Sackler's play *Messiah American Style* (*Mashiaḥ Nosaḥ America*).[16] Though Noah did not lack for critics, among them S. Dubnov, his role in promoting a refuge for Jews in the New World (on Grand Island, near Buffalo) captivated the imagination of Zionists, among them Y. M. Pines, Kalman Schulman, and Y. Klausner.[17]

The exoticism of the American Indians has not abated even today. In addition to identifying with the history of neglect, abuse, and domination to which they were subjected, Israeli readers remained enchanted by their exoticism as part of a greater fascination with Eastern religions and Buddhism.[18] Recent works by Israeli writers underscore in Israeli culture the continued interest in America's Blacks and Indians that exists in many other corners of the world.[19]

Presumably an outgrowth of this interest, the English-writing successors of the immigrant generation continued to represent Blacks and Indians in their art. Prominent Jewish writers abound, with Bernard Malamud in the lead. His work often focuses on the Black-Jewish encounter, as in his *The Tenants* and "Angel Levine," among others. His posthumously published *The People*[20] also contemplates the Jewish–Native American encounter. In music, the participation of Jews in jazz represents a subject for large studies, nor can one ignore numerous films, among them *Blazing Saddles*, the satirical film by Mel Brooks depicting Jews, Blacks, and Native Americans in a multi-layered mix.[21] Interest in American Black and Indian culture was not restricted to Jews. The composer Dvořák immersed himself in Black and (Algonquin) Indian songs, incorporating them in his compositions.[22]

The following probes the interest exhibited by Hebrew writers in Indians and African Americans. Part of their motive is founded on their desire to lend their work a measure of *Amerikaniyut*, the Hebrew term designating an Americanization of their literary forms and themes. Reading these works from an ethnic perspective, one construes that they serve as a means for writers to imagine the national self projected through others.

Yet the matter is more complex in that Israeli Hebrew literature has also taken part in this encounter. The fiction of Yoram Kaniuk, as will be illustrated, is replete with references to and images of American culture, particularly those arising from his familiarity with Black musicians of New York. Recently, Shuki Ben-Ami published a quasi-fictional tale whose Israeli protagonist escapes his Orthodox Jewish upbringing to rediscover his Native American maternal roots, only to come full circle as he learns of the affinities between his Judaism and elements of Lakota religion. More recently, Nava Semel's novel, *Eesra'el* (IsraIsland), set in America, is preoccupied with the nexus between Mordecai Noah's enterprise and Israeli current events.[23]

In the past, Hebrew literature avoided illuminating other civilizations without making of the poem, story, or essay an arena for the encounter between the Other and the Jew. No work is composed in Hebrew[24] in which an alien society is exposed in and of itself, much as Longfellow's "Song of Hiawatha"—which was certainly a model, acknowledged or not, for American Hebrew poets to follow—is regarding Native Americans. As they emulated Longfellow, America's Hebraists also avoided references to Jews or Judaism, engendering a corpus of poems and short stories which, though written in Hebrew, are devoid of the conventional markings of the writer's ethnic origins.[25]

This phenomenon in American Hebrew letters begs the question of what is the significance of literature posing as if originating from "within" the culture about which it tells. A more familiar though inadequate analogue would be Gershwin's *Porgy and Bess*, which also omits markers of the composer's ethnic identity. In many instances, some mode of interaction between Jews and these Others is the work's preoccupation. But why, we ask, were Hebraists so interested in other minorities? Why was the intended audience only the Hebrew reader—since these works remained untranslated, in whole or large part, into English?[26]

No evidence exists of extensive or direct contact between Hebrew writers and Native Americans. Any acquaintance with them issued primarily from these writers' American schooling, from their readings about Indian life and culture, or by hearsay. Most likely these factors affected their representation of Native Americans in a romanticized vein, as leading a bucolic existence that is corrupted by invading Europeans. As a trope, the Indian became a convenient and latent vehicle for writers to think about Western life and values. As they depicted the rape of Native American culture and lands by the White men, Hebrew writers adhered to their conventional regard for the dangers inherent in Europe for their people. By writing of Indians, Hebrew authors identified with them as mirrors of the Jews' fate, and as signposts of what may be awaiting their coreligionists who drop all guard in the Golden Land and succumb to its cultural and materialistic allures.

Though contact with Native Americans was tenuous at best, Hebraists' encounter with America's Blacks was more immediate, intimate, direct, and many-sided. Within a few decades of each other, Jews and Blacks made their own great migrations to America's major urban centers. While the greater mass of Jews arrived in America before the First World War, it was during and immediately thereafter that Blacks moved en masse north from the rural south. The encounters between them occurred principally against the city landscape, in adjacent streets and neighborhoods. With some exceptions, the tone of these writings is more realistic, particularly those in prose, representing Blacks in isolation as well as in contact with Jews.

The fascination of these writers with the experiences and culture of Blacks is more plausible as an outgrowth of their frequent encounters. However, the experience of Blacks in America has also been a model for Jews. Blacks are treated in Hebrew literature in ways more complex than Indians. The most glaring example is their romanticized treatment in rural America by the poet E. E. Lisitzky. Rather than describe things as they are—in the vein of the realistic literature being written in his days—Lisitzky composed poetry that romanticized them. As in his and others' works about American Indians, no Jews at all are visible among southern Blacks. Other Hebrew writers, however, wrote more realistically, most notable among them S. L. Blank and A. Z. Halevy, even recording conflicts between Blacks and Jews or Whites, representing the former in a less complimentary light.

Representation of marginalized Others carries with it a salutary effect on readers. For whether it is the author's declared goal or not, such writing recognizes the Other as human, analogous or similar to the self. To be more accommodating than the observations by Mentor L. Williams, the humanizing consequences are a product of presenting the Other, with Blacks and Indians possessing traits familiar to readers. Representation of Others as bearers of recognizable human qualities corrects prejudicial stereotypes which otherwise demonize, alienate, or dehumanize those outside the ego or one's cultural circle.[27]

Writing in sympathy with oppressed minorities became an expected and accepted programmatic norm in twentieth century literature. This sentiment, and the desire to open oneself up to greater issues permeating world literature, was also a feature of the Haskalah that in nineteenth century Jewish history raised the banner advocating a more liberal and equitable treatment of the powerless and disenfranchised. To attain this goal, one of its central tenets was the education of the Hebrew reader about the surrounding world. Readers were to be moved to take part in matters beyond those affecting their coreligionists, among which was the insistent advocacy for the downtrodden, particularly those affected by established patriarchal authorities. Within Jewish society proper this included the community's regards for those on the socio-economic margins, or its internal socio-legal system, the practice of matchmaking, marriage, and divorce, traditional education, the treatment of women, social outcasts, and rebels.

Though issues of the marginalized within Jewish society featured centrally in many works of the Haskalah and post-Haskalah age, Hebrew literature's interest in marginalized non-Jewish groups did not flourish in Europe. To be sure, translation of other nations' literatures was a norm among writers of the age, done primarily to familiarize readers with other civilizations and, to a lesser degree, to introduce them to others' plight. In America, interest in the non-Jew became a feature in the works of many immigrant Hebrew writers. American Hebrew literature took its own path by adding non-Jewish protagonists, Blacks and Native Americans principally, as representatives of those in need of justice in the New World.

ENCOUNTERING NATIVE AMERICANS: B. N. SILKINER'S *Mul ohel Timmura*

Chapter One

Every particular Thou *is a glimpse through to the eternal* Thou.

MARTIN BUBER, *I AND THOU*

With the arrival of the masses of Jewish immigrants at America's shores came also a number with an inclination or educational background to form a small nucleus of Hebraists intent on forming a new literary center. The leading figure of the early years was Benjamin N. Silkiner (1882–1933). He not only had a deep immersion in traditional textual studies, but melded these with a love for modern literature and the Haskalah.

Influenced by the Odessa literary circles of Bialik and Aḥad-Haʿam, Silkiner brought their habits, attitudes, and ideological inclinations along when, in 1904, he arrived in the United States to launch a new era of modern Hebrew letters. Though he was preceded by a number of poets and other literary types—among them Gershon Rosenzweig, Jacob Sobel, Moshe Israel Garson, M. Dolitzky, and N. H. Imber[1]—his literary output marks a qualitative and thematic watershed in American Hebrew literature that set him apart from his predecessors. Like Bialik in Odessa, Silkiner drew around him a small coterie of followers who would hold regular meetings and inspire each other by discussing and producing new Hebrew literature.

Though Silkiner was a prolific poet whose output is primarily sensitive lyrical works, his longevity owes much to his single epic poem, *Mul ohel Timmura* (Before Timmura's tent, 1910)—the first sustained long Hebrew poem composed in America.[2] Considered the launching of a modern Hebrew literary sensibility in America in the twentieth century, the poem was dedicated to the Hebrew essayist A. D. Markson, Silkiner's cousin, friend, and translator of Twain's *The Prince and the Pauper.* In form and content it heralds a departure into new spheres, setting new paradigms and archetypes other than those established in Europe, though its style remained very much rooted in the past.

Silkiner's epic poem may have served as the impetus behind a call by

Y. Ḥ. Brenner on America's Hebraists to incorporate local themes and forms into their writings. Brenner perceived in the nascent American center an opportunity to revitalize old Hebrew literary conventions in keeping with his poetic sense and practice at the *fin-de-siècle.*[3] Some years later, this call catalyzed a debate around Ya'akov Rabinowitz's call for the Americanization of modern Hebrew literature. The latter's critique of Silkiner's work issued out of an apprehension that it lacked authenticity. Rabinowitz found *Timmura* an artificial imitation gleaned from extant works in place of a story and images emerging more originally and authentically out of the author's intimate experience of America. And while Rabinowitz did not treat Silkiner's epic kindly in his call for an authentic *American'iyut*,[4] his critique catalyzed and focused the debate on the nature of Hebrew belles lettres and their capacity to capture America for Hebrew readers. Young Hebraists at the time, including Simon Halkin, joined the debate that merits a separate chapter to trace out.

Regardless of Rabinowitz's views, however, Silkiner's epic was a groundbreaking work in many ways, setting the trend for others to follow—whether by emulating or negating its paradigms. Led by this long poem, Hebrew literature in the New World acquired a new hue as it introduced its readers to the exotic theme of Native Americans' demise by European invaders.

THE HEGEMONY OF AMERICAN HEBREW CULTURE

The publication history of *Mul ohel Timmura* illuminates an episode in the effort to establish an American center to rival those in other parts of the world. As American as this project was, Silkiner strove to publish his poem in Jerusalem in order to help its literary community, and also demonstrate the influence—financial and cultural—of an emerging Hebrew center in the New World.[5]

Other publishing ventures lend credence to this effort. As evidenced by some of his correspondence in the same years, Silkiner was also the lynchpin behind an effort to establish Asaf, a publishing house in Eretz Israel for the express purpose of making available to readers the best of Hebrew and world literature in translation, an enterprise reminiscent of Ben-Avigdor's in Europe. Among others, Silkiner's epic poem, and at least two works by R. Brainin—who authored introductions to a number of other books—were published by Asaf. Later, Silkiner was also instrumental in a cooperative venture between America's Hebrew writers' publishing concern, Ḥaverim, and that of Dvir in the Land of Israel. The first of the two was subsequently replaced by M. Newman's Mitzpeh.[6] Had it come to pass, Silkiner's project would have established a significant American imprint on publishing concerns in Eretz Israel and, presumably, would have affected its literary culture.[7]

Additional evidence to this effect is preserved in Silkiner's correspondence. Writing on 10 August 1909, to Yitzḥak Elazar Volcani, head of the agricultural research station in Reḥovot, Silkiner asks him to identify individuals in the profession to help bring about "A new national publishing house (called 'Asaf'), whose goal will be to publish—from time to time—the best creations of Hebrew writers and translations from the best of general literature in our ancestral land and the land of our hopes."[8]

To strengthen American Hebraists' influence on Eretz Israel's literary culture, Silkiner, in a letter to Daniel Persky, wrote that the ties he and his fellows had established included the publication of books, thus exploiting Eretz Israel's book-making infrastructure while also creating a dependence by those dwelling there on American literary activity.[9]

Later, in a letter of 20 October, 1912,[10] Silkiner—still asserting American influence on Hebrew literary circles—invited Y. Ḥ. Brenner, now himself in Eretz Israel,[11] to contribute to a new Hebrew periodical in America, *Ha-toren*, under the auspices of the Aḥiʿever (or Achieber) organization.[12] By then Brenner was among the leading luminaries of Hebrew literary modernism whose ideological and literary contributions had a lasting impact on new paths taken by Hebrew fiction.

The project appears to have borne fruit. In a letter of May 4, 1926, Silkiner writes to the American Hebrew poet and scholar Israel Efros about the dearth of Hebrew prose writing, as opposed to poetry, by American Hebraists. He compliments Efros for his literary fecundity and urges him to take part in a project to publish all Hebrew literary works produced in America, an undertaking that would require two years:

> I am certain that were we to try hard we would be able to publish all the books over two years. Need I add and say that were *all* American "Hebrew prose writings" on one side of the scale they would fail to counterbalance it by a hair against your poetry nor detract anything from the value of your delightful poems?[13]

On a separate note in the same letter, Silkiner informs Efros of the existence of a circle of American Hebraists—Bavli, Halkin, Lisitzky, and Silkiner—calling themselves "Ḥaverim" (Friends), who cooperate with the Dvir publishing house in Eretz Israel. The note documents a measure of American Hebrew literary involvement and attempted influence in the

Land of Israel, though "Ḥaverim" was not an independently dominant concern.

By publishing in Eretz Israel, then, Silkiner was attempting to place his imprint on this nascent Hebrew literary center by Americanizing some of its thematic concerns. Moreover, his affiliation with Eretz Israel may have been an indicator of the import of his work for the Hebrew national enterprise of the times.[14]

As evidenced by many reviewers, *Mul ohel Timmura* carved out a place of honor for Silkiner in the pantheon of American Hebrew writers as the first in line among his fellow literati.[15] Significantly, though, his lyrical poetry was relegated to oblivion while his status among American Hebrew poets was assured because of *Timmura*. It is his epic work that overshadows the rest of his oeuvre more than in the case of Efros or Lisitzky. Following its initial publication in 1910 in a separate volume, *Timmura* was republished with minor stylistic revisions as part of Silkiner's collected work in 1927, assisted by H. Bavli, S. Halkin, and S. Ginzburg.[16] Another version was later published for young readers, edited and rewritten in prose form by A. D. Markson, who was instrumental in the epic's earlier processes of composition and publication.[17]

The genre of choice for *Timmura*, as well as for the other long poems featuring Native Americans, was founded on the long-held tradition of the Hebrew long poem, or *poema*, employed by poets with a varied mix of epic or lyrical intensity. The intersection of lyrical poems within the larger epic poem characterizes these poemas, with Silkiner's and Efros's illustrating the tendency to combine the two modes, while Lisitzky's, as we shall see below, emphasizes epic ingredients. In the same way, these three poets variously intertwine accounts of realistic experience with the mythic, with Efros doing so to a lesser extent than the others. And, as if to underscore the classical feature of the genre and its tale of long ago, the language is suffused with biblical allusions often also set to a familiar and formal meter—Silkiner's is often in amphibrach hexameter (as modeled by Bialik's "The dead of the wilderness"), Efros's varies, and Lisitzky unabashedly follows Longfellow's "Hiawatha" and the *Kalevala*'s trochaic tetrameter.[18]

The Hebrew poema has its origins in the tradition of epic poetry that emerged in Hebrew literature under Russian influences in the first quarter of the nineteenth century. Many bear strong marks of romantic poetry, whose components derive from English and Russian models. This version of the poema appeared in Hebrew literature only in the 1860s and is a composite of many genres, including the neo-classical Hebrew epic.

Other distinguishing marks of the Hebrew poema include its tendency to preserve a lyrical mode and aspects of rhetoric, thought, direct narrative, and generic influence of epic poems, the ballad, and the ode.[19]

Alternatively, the poema is a "lyrical dramatic narrative"[20] originating in the French term *poeme*, "a poem in which a philosophical thought is presented in epic or dramatic form."[21]

Pointedly, Israel Efros avoids the label "poema" in the title for his long poems, *Vigvamim shotkim* (Silent wigwams) and *Zahav* (Gold), preferring the term *shirim*, poems. He also strays from Silkiner's paradigm by shunning the heavy doses of mythic themes, plot, and language. He also limits any strong biblical allusiveness in his language. In many ways, however, his works conform to features of a poema, being long narrative poems that tell a story and are composed in any rhythmic format. However insistent Efros was on avoiding the rubric of a poema in other instances, as in the poem "Man and the void" ("Adam v-tohu"), he acknowledges the genre in the subtitle of his book of poems *Goral u-phit'om* (Destiny and suddenly).[22]

As noted before, Silkiner edited and revised his poem within two decades of its initial appearance. Though a full comparison of the two chief versions of *Timmura*, that of 1910 with the 1927 edition, is beyond the purview of this study, a cursory examination reveals that the revisions were made mostly to enhance clarity, simplicity of syntax, and word choice.[23] Apart from this, Silkiner added and deleted little in his revisions, implicitly recognizing the difficulties posed by the work's language for many a reader.

As the first edition's secondary title, "Shivray po'ema" (poema fragments) indicates, the work strives to resemble a remnant of an ancient tale. To enhance this effect, the poem is embellished with a plethora of ellipses, a deliberately obscure choice of language and syntax, a double-lined hyphen resembling the "equals" sign, and even a font style that bespeaks antiquity. In the revision, the ellipses remain, but the peculiar hyphens and subtitle are dropped, as is any reference to fragments of a larger epic poem. A comparison, for example, of the opening of part three of the 1910 version with that of 1927 is a fitting case in point:

> In the east, the high flint mountains—for eagles of the sky;
> Ancient sea in the west—for violent sea-monsters, progeny of the
> great abyss;
> Primeval forest in the south—for lions, roaring leopards;
> The awesome, great desert in the north—for tempestuous storms;

The blessed precious-stone valley, in the middle, heritage
To the "Rock-Tribe" was given for all eternity.
In the valley, that conceals precious treasures in its depths,
Beneath eternal peaks are concealed buried precious stones,
Revealing but the edge of its beauty tremulously kissing its feet,—
There lived braves, ancient as thunder, nursed by the storm,
Of the Rock-Tribe, and with their mighty Katsika, the brave
Would go out to frighten their adversary tribes in the land
With a hostile fury and pursue them with a fierce stormy battle,
And at evening return to the valley and set out in stormy dance,
With frightful sounds would tear asunder sheets of dew covering the vale
With their clamor put to flight a covert slumber from the crevices of the crags,
And holding up with a mighty hand skulls enshrouded in a blanket of tear-flowers,
They leap upon lions and ride, to the rocks—their ancestors—they rush; (99)

Identical in both, the significance of the opening lines is signaled by the absence of any change. Syntactical modifications clarify and simplify the narrative in its revised version, as in lines 5–6, where redundant synonyms are excised, as are the references to that "something" which is left untold. The elimination of "a gift . . . from ancients" ("li-sgulah . . . mi-kdumim")—to denote that the valley was a gift for some unexplained, special purpose from ancient times or ancient beings—is made less ambiguous by adding instead the words "Me-ʿolam ʿad ʿolam" (Forever), to denote that it was handed down by unspecified sources for all eternity. Likewise, the meaning is illuminated by inserting in line seven of "ba-bikʿah ha-zot" (In this valley) for the earlier "b-vikʿah zu" (In the valley that . . .). Also, changing the verbal form of "yatzʾu" and "yatzaʾu" (went forth) of lines 12 and 14 for "yetzʾu" and "yetzeʾu" (would go forth) enhances the meaning as it denotes a repeated and continuous action.

The revisions testify to a growing trend in Hebrew literature toward a simpler and more lucid expression motivated by the development and refinement of a Hebrew that favored clarity over complexity. Minor as these changes are, they nonetheless indicate Silkiner's compromising gesture with a significantly modernized literary Hebrew that by the second decade of the twentieth century had developed a thriving vernacular. Nonetheless, the conservative impulse to retain a former literary style of the past century is evident in the ponderously obscure linguistic construction of late Haskalah Hebrew.[24]

With these in mind, Silkiner's adherence to the literary conventions of the Haskalah remains evident in the opening of *Timmura*. Its long introduction, numbering over fifty lines, bears the hallmarks of poema conventions in vogue half a century earlier. The emphasis on describing and pondering the scenery of a setting sun is more than a mere exercise in painting a natural phenomenon. A trait adopted by the genre in the 1860s, such as in Goldfaden's "Bat-Sheva" as well as Mandelkern's "Bat-Sheva," this practice was not merely a fitting segue into pathos-laden romanticism but also a means by which to anticipate an analogical theme in the plot.[25]

To that effect all aspects, terms, and images of Silkiner's introduction foreshadow the poema's central plot. For that reason, the preponderance of language associated with silence, "silence" . . . "keep silent" ("dumam . . . shotek"), death, as in "the last beats of the heart of a dying day" ("dfikot aḥaronot shel lev-yom gove'a") and "to the graves of its ancestors, who rest in the vale of shadows, was gathered, / then a pale beauteous-purple enveloped the west in her mourning, / her face turned silvery as she rent her delicate garb" ("v-'el kivray avotav, b-'emek-ha-tzlalim yanuḥu, ne'esaf / yofi-argaman ḥavarvar az he'etah p'at-ma'arav b-'evlah, / hikhsifu panayhah b-kor'ah 'al metah lvushah he-'adin," 81), unspecified mysteries ("v-loḥashot ta'alumot," and they whisper mysteries), and mourning were a conventional means of demonstrating a seamless concordance between nature and human affairs, a fitting feature of romantic literature. They all allude to the upheavals that have ensued, punctuated by the passing of one civilization to be replaced by another, as indicated by the anticipation of a new day.

This gesture, it may be argued, remains in vogue among Silkiner's followers, too, as Efros opens his *Vigvamim shotkim* with a broadly sweeping, almost cinematic, overview of the American map, and Lisitzky begins his work with a prose-poetic introduction observing the demise of Native Americans.

Silkiner's editorial maneuver to update his poema is symptomatic also of his age, a time when the heaviness of Haskalah Hebrew was yielding to a more refined, lucid, exact, and direct expression. Most writers raised on late nineteenth century Hebrew literary conventions sought to modernize their writing in the years following the First World War. Ever the keepers of the flame, however, a significant segment among America's Hebraists were devoted to heightened literary Hebrew rooted in the style of their Haskalah forebears. This tension between the modernist trend in Hebrew belles lettres and the conservative, preservationist tendency to foster the old style continues to play out on the American Hebrew literary scene past the middle of the century.

Before Timmura's Tent: A BRIEF SUMMARY

The story is an account by Timmura to his daughter[26] of the exploits of a wretched old man they notice nearby. This man, Mugiral, was once leader of the "Silent Tribe" who in the sixteenth century confronted a Spanish Conquistador invasion into their valley, located in an imagined landscape somewhere on the Pacific coast of America's Southwest, though the descriptions indicate a setting that resembles the pueblo communities inland from that region. Led by their chief, or *katsika*,[27] Mugiral, they abandon their peaceful ways to massacre the Conquistadors whose leader, Potera, has instigated envy and hostility among them. It is the Spaniard invaders who bring to an end the valley's Edenic existence and arouse the tribe into a series of violent acts which, their temporary victory notwithstanding, precipitate the tribe's eventual demise.

The poem traces the collapse of an ideal existence by a Spanish-instigated ethical disruption which snowballs to the point of the demise of the Indian tribe. In that regard, the tale is reminiscent of a morality play with an unhappy ending.[28] The demise of the good is precipitated by the Spanish Conquistador Potera's greed to possess a noble steed owned by Umilah. To obtain it, he lies to the tribe's *katsika* about the horse's owner. Believing the rumor, the *katsika* selects Umilah to become this year's sacrifice to the Great Spirit.[29]

Because of the wrong motive and the scheme behind it, the Great Spirit refuses the offering and abandons the tribe in an act reminiscent of the kabbalistic notions of *kavanah*—proper intent—and *hester panim*, the hiding of the (Divine) face, which results in drought and famine. The ensuing chaos is part of the poet's preoccupation with the condition of the modern world as a tangled place bereft of Divine grace, oversight, or intervention in personal or national fates.

With the departure of the Great Spirit, Potera assumes its role. He feeds the Indians, but at a price: they are to bring him the precious stones dotting the valley. The desire for food turns the Natives greedy to the point of valuing stones over each other, a serious disruption in the pristine life of the valley (117). The consequence is the appearance of Mugiral, a charismatic though violent leader. He informs the Indians that they have been abandoned by the Great Spirit. To bring back the days of old, Mugiral orders his people to dig in the soil—but this time for the black metal, iron—to fashion tools of war and slaughter the Spaniards. It is during this battle that the statue of *Elnefesh*, their deity of mercy and compassion, is shattered. The bloodbath results in a faux spring, irrigating the soil to bring forth its bounty in a seeming rebirth. However, just as Mugiral is not the same as the *katsika* of yore, so this fecundity and the new image of *Elnefesh* are but a shadow of the past. The attempts to restore the past soon become futile as the Spanish return in numbers and annihilate the Indians.

Silkiner's observation is timely. His poem, composed as it was in the first decade of the twentieth century, bespeaks a modernist dilemma of freedom and violence associated with the demise of Native Americans, recent events in Europe related to the rise of nationalism, or a cautionary word about the dangers that a Jewish national resurgence can bring upon his readers.[30]

RECEPTION AND REACTION TO *Timmura*

As a Hebrew poet, Silkiner was no doubt programmatically engaged in the project of the *teḥiyah*, the Jewish national renaissance of his times. Yet it is significant and characteristic in the case of his and the two other major epics about Native Americans that none is composed as an analogue to the Jewish national question. Nevertheless, readers have made this link by virtue of the juxtaposition of the plot with the leading ideologies preoccupying them as consumers of Hebrew literature. Silkiner's representation of Native Americans, as many saw it, could not but be also an observation of the condition of Jews in the world, be it the depredations of the pogroms,[31] recent wars, or the poet's reflections on the possibility of Jewry's physical or cultural annihilation.

The poet and scholar Eisig Silberschlag observed that "it was the love of romanticized savages for the land of their fathers which turned Silkiner, as Hebrew poet, to the legends of the Indians."[32] *Timmura*, as well as the poem by Silkiner's follower, Israel Efros, tells the story in a mixed fashion, from within the worldview of the Native Americans and also from the perspective of their European adversaries. Unlike them, Ephraim Lisitzky embeds the bulk of his work within the cultural milieu of his subject, the Native Americans, whose point of view he adopts completely and with no regard for alternative perspectives.

Mul ohel Timmura's initial appearance did not meet with great accolades or a sizable reaction, likely because of its obscure Hebrew style, which discouraged many readers.[33] Because many works of the age were characterized by similar linguistic challenges, however, that does not appear to be the chief reason for its lackadaisical reception. It is perhaps the subject of the poem that drew few Hebrew readers at a time when more were interested in representations of the world they left behind or the one into which they entered than a mythic tale of an exotic civilization.

Ostensibly intent on remedying the dearth of review essays about his long poem, and generating some publicity to stimulate reader interest, Silkiner writes from New York, in a letter dated 15 August 1911, to Avraham Leib Jacobovitz that "Mr. Reuven Brainin, editor of '*Ha-dror*' intended to write a large critical essay about my poema, '*Mul ohel Timmura*,' that our literature passed over with almost complete silence." He then asks Jacobovitz to compose an essay about this work that he, Silkiner, will send on to Brainin to be published under Brainin's name. In a later note—Gnazim letter number 54—dated 2 April 1912, Silkiner acknowledges and thanks Jacobovitz for his critique. In the same letter he explains that the betrayal of Mugiral by *Eyn Yonim*—one of the female protagonists—is only feigned.[34]

Those early reviews of *Timmura* that did appear were not all complimentary either. They underscore what critics considered its incompleteness, vague plot, and dense language. One reading, for example, exhibits its author's penchant for comprehending the poem's nuances. The young Tzvi (Harry) Wolfson's insightful review links Silkiner's work with the classical traditions of Byronic epic poetry. Were it judged for any representation of reality, though, Wolfson argues, it would be judged deficient in its limited and formulaic characterizations. Silkiner, out of a lack of intimate familiarity with individual Native Americans of the Southwest, avers Wolfson, resorts to stock, imagined, or documented stereotypes from books about Indians as a group. His strategy, continues the critic, has engendered a poem founded on sweeping, vague, and perhaps erroneous racial characterizations that render its protagonists devoid of individual traits.[35]

Another early critique that identifies a host of deficiencies in the poem is by D. A. Friedman, who in 1927 finds Silkiner's skill inadequate in depicting what he believes to be the epic's major thrust, the struggle of the Natives for existence. However, Friedman recognizes *Timmura*'s importance in expanding Hebrew poetry's literary horizons.[36]

Pointing to influences of the New World and its culture on the composition, Shimon Ginzburg, who assisted Silkiner in completing the poema and was a significant poet who shortly thereafter published "No-York," a briefer, though also myth-laden work that included Native Americans, attempts to justify the poem's shortcomings. He avers that the secondary title of the poem, *shivray poema* (poema fragments), is a mark of its nascence in a chaotic urban environment, meaning New York City, leading to the poet's inability to present a more complete work. Yet, continues Ginzburg, whose review appeared in the mid-1920s, the poem is a unique and definitive American creation. He claims that it was Silkiner's goal to counteract his fellow Jews' nostalgia about the world they left behind by offering them aspects of the new. Moreover, he situates Silkiner's source of inspiration in English poetry, asserting that it is from Tennyson that he learned the technique of conflating lyrical episodes within the epic tale.[37]

Ginzburg also anchors the poem within the Hebraic tradition by noting its affinity with the rage of Bialik's "Scroll of Fire," another poem dominated by supernatural and metaphysical details and interpretations. Another feature that Ginzburg identifies in Silkiner's work—likely a result of the sense of greater freedom of expression in America though couched in the events of the plot—is its message of protest against the lies, deception, and falsehood of modern-day Christianity that permits pogroms to take place.[38] By reading this sentiment into the epic work Ginzburg also shares with Silkiner's composition a definite bias, seeking to expose Europe's colonial complicity in the destruction of the pristine existence of natives. This interpretive tack also affects future allegorical or metaphorical readings of the poem. Ginzburg himself identifies the account of internal strife among the Indians as a metaphor for the struggles between the older generation and young Bundists in the early years of the Russian Revolution of 1905.

Other readers, too, find fault with the work, identifying the incongruity between theme and form. Lachower avers that a work depicting the inner struggles of a people about choices of peace or war, such as the tribe in question, should have been presented in a more lyrical mode rather than in the form of a ponderous, classical epic.[39]

One who finds value in the epic is Y. Y. Geles. He admires the poet's skill at presenting giant figures with an exciting plot to intrigue young readers. And though asserting that the work is made of charming legends, he offers no specific examples to support this contention.[40]

ANTI-EUROPEAN OVERTONES

A thought-provoking metaphorical or allegorical reading is offered by Silberschlag, which is as much a projection of the reader as of the text. He asserts that the poem is motivated by nationalistic forces, concerned as it is with Native American independence. Its protagonist, Mugiral, represents a version of nationalism which gives rise to brute coercive force, whose zeal is a not altogether disguised version of Jewish history. Behind the mask is a story of the people of Israel who, in antiquity, struggled for their independence on the eve of destruction. Moreover, adds Silberschlag, this is also a story of how hatred begets hatred, in that the Spanish Conquistadors engender the likes of Mugiral, whose thirst for revenge is the poem's leading message. Allegorizing the work, he offers that the confrontation with the Spanish also represents the struggles of Jews against the Inquisition.[41]

Silberschlag's reading is characteristic of the first generation of American Hebrew writers who, having internalized the principles of freedom of expression in the United States, are settling scores with Europe for its long tradition of anti-Semitic persecutions. But, as will be explored in a separate chapter, they also demonstrate a moderate nationalism affected by their comfortable lives in America and the ambivalence that has arisen about their regard for an independent Jewish state. To be sure, the juxtaposition of the lot of Indians with the Jewish experience is not made explicitly by the texts. Also, none of the representations of Native Americans—in this work as in the others—gives an unblemished picture of Indians. Intra-ethnic conflicts arise, as do harrowing and cruel treatments of one Indian by his fellows. Nevertheless, these pale in comparison to the horrors wrought by Whites as they eradicated one race and subjugated the other. The Jews' experience with Europe, and the centuries-long suppressed anger at their lot, can be released in America's atmosphere of tolerance and freedom of speech, allowing writers to contemplate a shared experience between what their people, Blacks, and Indians have suffered under Europe's treatment of the Other. It is this force that intrigues Hebrew writers who raise the prospect of cultural annihilation, assimilation, or acculturation before their Jewish readers as a possible consequence of the freedom that America has to offer.

All three epics—*Timmura*, and later *Vigvamim shotkim* and *Mdurot doʿakhot* (Dying campfires)—represent the White man as greedy, self-centered, and aggressive, as do a number of shorter works discussed in later chapters. The lives of Natives are of little value beyond furthering the material good of the invaders. Also in all three, the poets enunciate a strong anti-Western bias. Though no Jews populate these stories, their White protagonists harbor prejudicial attitudes reminiscent of anti-Semitic myths resonant of the European experience.

Silkiner's work sets the tone for subsequent poems in this regard as well. It is the greed for the precious stones buried in the soil of the valley that drives the Spanish Conquistadors to foment hatred, jealousy, and division among the Natives. In Efros's *Vigvamim*, the myth is made more poignant in that the Englishman, Tom, believes that the Natives have concealed their gold from the eyes of Whites—reminiscent of anti-Semitic myths. Too late, he learns that the only treasures are those in a beached Spanish galleon that the Indians have never plundered. Other Whites in the past have introduced alcohol to the Natives, promoting their addiction and subsequent dependence to the detriment of their lives.

Another motive by which Silkiner vents a particularly anti-Spanish bias as the destroyer of Indian civilization may be grounded in contemporary events. Prompted by strong Jewish popular reaction in 1898 to the American intervention to liberate Cuba from Spanish rule, Silkiner's demonization of Spain is affected by the image conveyed by the Jewish press at the time. Specifically, the Spanish were labeled as the ones to have trampled under foot Cuba and other lands in the New World with their Catholicism and Inquisition; it was Spain that cast Jews out and tortured many through its notorious Inquisition. The anti-Spanish mood in the United States before the time of Silkiner's writing helped him identify a fitting nemesis for his story. For the same reason, Silkiner's avoidance of any mention of the depravity of English colonialism in the same light is because of England's support at the time for the United States against Spain's policies and in favor of expelling it from Cuba.[42]

The identity of the White man is conflated with the religion he brings along. Christianity is pitted against the natural religions of Indians as if to underscore the relative barbarity of one against the other. None of the writers postulate an ideal and trouble-free world of the Natives, recognizing its true cruelties. The analogy is particularly strong in the first two works. Silkiner's story, while describing the annual sacrificial rites of the Indians as they offer one of their members to the Great Spirit, underscores the difference with the Conquistadors, whose god demands the slaughter of many:

> The Spaniards already passed through rivers of blood and tears—
> By day with spiraling smoke clouds from burned ruins

By night by the glow of bonfires, set for their god demanding
T h o u s a n d s of offerings—on their way to the valley, whose name
  they heard
From afar . . . (105, emphasis in original)

In the case of Efros, the cruelty of the Christians—possibly Puritans who themselves have fled persecution in their own homeland—is ironic as they shun other Christians for their different ways.

For the sword that clears the way pursued them
Of a faith that brings to sinners salvation and love,
For the society that knows no mercy pursued them . . .[43]

It remains a perplexing phenomenon that this strongly mythologized epic placed Silkiner in the pantheon of American Hebrew poetry at the time when he was best known for his strong lyricism.[44] One suggestion has been that more than an epic work, this is Silkiner's most autobiographical and intimate expression, though much needs to be done to support this contention.[45] It is also his only manifest encounter with Native Americans as a theme.

However, "Me-ʾagadot ha-hodim" (An Indian legend), a posthumously published poem by Silkiner, has been touted as dwelling on an Indian theme.[46] It tells of an Indian, Hambrita, who is searching for the fountain of youth. Silkiner Judaizes the protagonist by representing him on several occasions as pursuing his dream by studiously examining apocryphal scrolls, a fitting image of a maskilic (Enlightened) poet and not a Native American. When he realizes his quest and recognizes a fountain of youth, Hambrita drinks of its waters but continues to age. On his deathbed he learns that the magic works only for those who drink out of a previously unused vessel.

Although cloaked in Indian garb, the tale resonates with a host of other thematic possibilities, and has little to do with a representation of Native Americans. Most likely it was the poet's expression on the nature of art and the anxiety of influence. Its message concerns immortality that cannot be attained by means of worn vessels; innovation is the key. Ironically, such an observation is laid out by an exponent of the Haskalah, its values, themes, and style. As for the representation of the Native American, little can be garnered from this poem in that the protagonist is merely a trope, an exotic rendering of the poet.

SETTING THE PARADIGM

It is *Mul ohel Timmura* that set the paradigm for subsequent long poems whose subject matter was the life, culture, encounters, and conflicts of Native Americans with European Whites: Israel Efros's 1933 long poems, "Silent Wigwams" (*Vigvamim shotkim*) and "Gold" (*Zahav*), of 1942, and E. E. Lisitzky's *Dying Campfires* (*Mdurot doʿakhot*) of 1937. It also has left some imprints on others' engagement with the subject of Native Americans, as well as Lisitzky's single volume of poems addressing African American life and culture, *In the tents of Cush* (*B-ʾoholay khush*) of 1953.[47]

Indeed, a close reading of the subsequent poems can be fertile ground for following up on this discourse among the poets and their works. Though often muted, their conversation breaks into the open in the form of a notable essay by Lisitzky whose critique presents an occasion for self-revelation regarding the proper execution of the genre.[48]

While an exhaustive enumeration of the components introduced by Silkiner's work as paradigms for subsequent long poems is hard to encompass, the following is an attempt to highlight some of the more notable. *Timmura*'s distinctive components were culled variously from the Jewish experience, the Western literary tradition, American cultural resources—literary and ethnographic—and those personal experiences each of the writers had as witness to the experiences of minority groups in their host culture. To be sure, each also had his unique way of addressing any particular component, yet its roots tap into Silkiner's work, as much as his also drew upon extant American models composed in English, the foremost of which was Longfellow's "Song of Hiawatha."

A significant factor is the poet's reliance on Native American legends and folk-themes. This strategy lends a semblance of verisimilitude to each work that exceeds the author's imagination or cultural scope. Readers either sensed or knew of this phenomenon, asserting that Indian themes, stories, or songs are woven into the Hebrew text, though no one has until now identified these thoroughly in the works of Silkiner, Efros, Lisitzky, or the others. In our study of Lisitzky we will do so, thus bearing out the assertions made by Ruth Arazi, one of the few who delved into the matter and came close to identifying specific analogies.

The world of Native Americans before the arrival of Whites is described in near-bucolic terms as suffused by nature and a natural religion bereft of much ritual or ceremony. This observation is more in keeping with the poets' maskilic anti-clerical tradition and romantic longings for a simplified religion than what comprised Indian belief and practice. None of the poems makes a value judgment about the savagery of Indian rituals, even while depicting some. Existence in nature is represented as immediate, unmediated, and harmonious, a relationship disrupted by the incursion of Europeans that introduced conflicts more severe and existentially threatening.[49]

The pristine existence of Native American tribes is often associated with a mythic world. The chief protagonists emerge out of an a-temporal and spatially undefined realm which attributes to them, too, super-human traits. Silkiner's Mugiral emerges out of a red rock, and Lisitzky's Genetaskah is a child of Nemissa, the Star-Maiden and her mortal lover Nanpiwati. The tools they use, such as bow and arrow, are at times also endowed with supernatural powers. In its way, the mythic atmosphere enlarges the scope of the poem as it intersects with ancient tales. This approach, as will be demonstrated, has divided the Hebrew writing community into followers and opponents of this strategy. As in Longfellow's work, some attention is given to etiological questions—the universal questions of origins—and of Indian life, such as the birth of the hero, the emergence of the first medicine man, and the like.

Being more "realistic" and shunning the mythic layers of the poema, Efros's more novelistic work presents protagonists whose origins are more plausible. Lalari, his heroine of *Vigvamim shotkim*, is the daughter of an Indian woman and her White lover. Efros aims more for the human, social, and historical. His work is anchored in specific time and place and provides readers with an abundance of markers for that purpose the early British colonial period in Maryland's Chesapeake Bay area or, in *Zahav*, the California Gold Rush days. He even resorts to Hebraic temporal markers by scattering in the poem the names of Hebrew months.

Representation of Native Americans as victims of Western colonial greed and aggression is a sentiment running through the works of Silkiner, Efros, and Lisitzky, as well as those of other poets, to express sympathy for all victims of European White domination and conquest. As Jacques LeGoff has observed, "The first total confrontation between the antique and the modern was perhaps that between the Indians of the Americas and the Europeans."[50] Hebrew writers whose history includes centuries of such confrontations found it convenient to retell, by analogy, the story of their people's experiences at the hands of Europe, often anticipating the denouement of this collision. Having been totally vanquished, the Native Americans' antiquity had given way to Westernism. By writing of these clashes, Hebrew poets voice their concerns about the form of imperialism that corrupts in place of correcting life, values, and morals. They dwell on the consequences of a confrontation that manifested itself in cultural and physical struggles, in which the lives and heritage of Natives stood little chance of surviving.

Our study of the representation of the marginalized Other is, then, a mirror into which these writers look to understand themselves and the lot of their culture. For Jewish writers who have recently landed in the New World, this sentiment—whether concrete or metaphoric—emerges out of the history of the Jewish ghetto. Their history as victims of Europe is replayed in the guise of Western colonial incursions and devastations of Native American and African cultures, as the lands of the first were expropriated and the bodies of the latter were converted to marketable property. Though these writers, as far as can be ascertained, did not subscribe to the notion of American Indians being of the Ten Lost Tribes of Israel, they re-appropriated the notion in a new way. The fate of Native Americans at the hands of Europeans proved, in a curious way, "that the Indians were Jews."[51]

Convinced that nothing has thus far succeeded in standing up to the overwhelming force of Western will, authors of these works do not harbor much optimism for a better future, only a somber sense of loss of native, pristine, and weaker cultures. As if to foreground the theme, the poems all bear within their titles, chapters, and central imagery metaphors about the end of things as they were, depicted in terms of sunset and darkness, long glances westward at the setting sun, crying, silence, or a stoic acceptance of fate, death, and the like.[52]

This stock of images has powerfully invaded the consciousness of Hebrew writing in America to loom large as one of its dominant tropes, appearing in such diverse works as Israel Efros's *Vigvamim shotkim* (Silent wigwams); E. E. Lisitzky's *Kmo ha-yom rad* (As the day has set) and *Mdurot Doʿakhot*, Gavriel Preil's *Nof shemesh u-khfor* (Sunny vista and frost), *Ner mul kokhavim* (Candle opposite stars), *Ha-ʾesh vha-dmamah* (The fire and the silence), Simḥah Rubinstein's *Nerot doʿakhim* (Dying candles), Reuben Wallenrod's *Ki phanah yom* (For the day has waned), and so forth.[53]

Alternatively, the death of romanticism acknowledges the hopelessness of restoring the generation of the mighty or the innocence and nobility of the native. Death is accepted stoically by all protagonists; a fatalism pervading their worldview as they accept the notion that one mode of existence must of necessity give way to another. Their end corresponds to a disconnect between humanity and nature. By their demise, the Native Americans give way to *homo Americanus*, that artificial, materialistic, techno-industrial self-destructive human whose contact with the world of nature is tenuous.[54] The protagonists' deaths inscribe an end to a world that existed along with them. This posture, too, is evocative of Longfellow's poem in which Hiawatha sails off, abandoning the foreboding here-and-now to return in a more opportune future.

Linguistically, all three poets, and most others, employ a Hebrew reminiscent of the age of the Haskalah, one characterized by an effusively flowery style. By the first decade of the twentieth century this Hebrew was considered passé. It was not in keeping with the Bialikian language of the *teḥiyah*, one characterized either by a flexibility inherited from Mendele's *nusaḥ*, or formula, or by the rise of a vernacular Hebrew in Eretz Israel. Nonetheless, and in spite of the options for clarity and simplicity of expression, most preferred to side with the conservative trend in Hebrew literature out of a conviction that the requisite style should be a high literary Hebrew, one clearly unlike the evolving "compromises" in vogue at the time.[55]

Silkiner's *Timmura* is the first and tentative step in Americanizing Hebrew poetry. Its incompleteness is characteristic of the poet's ambivalent regard for striking out in new directions and creating a model for others to follow. As a mark of their conservatism, those who followed were inclined to build on his work as an archetype, acknowledging its pivotal significance in American Hebrew letters. Whether those who followed were able to improve on the model created by Silkiner is a matter for the following chapters to consider.

FACING THE SUNSET: ISRAEL EFROS ON NATIVE AMERICANS

Chapter Two

In a preface in the manuscript of *Silent Wigwams* (Vigvamim shotkim), Israel Efros's premiere composition about Native Americans—currently in the possession of his daughter, Ghela (Efros) Scharfstein—the poet has left the following lengthy note:

> In 1928 fate robbed me of two dear souls one after the other, souls that forever remain irreplaceable.
>
> I fled from the place of my double calamity to a distant and cold city. But from there I began to greatly miss that parcel of land I left behind, the quiet and sun-drenched Maryland fields.
>
> Long ago I read a legend. It was the tale of an Englishman who happened upon an Indian village in those very fields and whom the head of the village wanted for his daughter, Lalari. And she, too, wanted him, until he revealed to her that his bride awaits him beyond the sea to return with a handful of gold to obtain her noble parents' approval. So Lalari took him to an ancient and wrecked Spanish galleon and showed him the treasures of gold within. After some time, when the Englishman returned to America with his wife, he found a monument upon which was inscribed the name, Lalari.
>
> This legend nestled within my depths as a seed within the earth. It slowly changed form, metamorphosing from within and without, sending roots downward to grow upward in the dark, until the time arrived and my longings began to awaken it and draw it out as the sun would beckon a seed.
>
> And two accompanying feelings dwelled within me at the time of its writing.
>
> The first—that primitivism of culture does not mean a primitivism of the spirit. Suffice it to read the folk songs of Indian tribes to be amazed and be bewildered by the delicacy of its representation, the variety of colors, the art of expression and depth of emotion that is, nonetheless, restrained, checking itself, silent in grief. It seems to me

> that it would be hard to find their like among the folk songs of the Pale Face.
>
> And the second—that the long narrative poem possesses a special value, whether because of its length or because of its narrative quality, whether because of its creator or the reader. Perhaps this genre can return poetry to its ancient glory.
>
> Av [July/August], 1932; Provincetown, Massachusetts.
>
> [part of the second page:] Maryland's fields are sunny and silent. He who loves them but is compelled by a double calamity to flee to a faraway and cold city, who cannot return because the earth burns at his heels, would it be a surprise if he return to them at least by means of a poem?

Though a few of the above lines were retained as a motto, Efros's longer note permits some insight into the story's inception, its transmutation in the artist's imagination, and the subsequent form and content which he gave the tale. It is also a note about the affinity Efros had for the long narrative poem, which he does not term *poema*, but whose qualities he clearly attributes to this genre.

A strain of anti-European and anti-colonial romantic angst about human foibles, coupled with latent Zionism, pervades Israel Efros's (or Efrat's) long poema, *Vigvamim shotkim* (Silent wigwams, 1933). Chronologically it is the second sustained long Hebrew poem focused on Native American life. The author and scholar Reuben Wallenrod averred that Efros initially composed joyous lyrical poems expressive of his spirit while contemplating America's natural and human landscape. However, as the myth of the greatness of America began to tarnish, Efros offered up *Vigvamim shotkim*, a tale of peoples and cultures in collision and the natives' defeat at the hands of Europe's colonial forces. Viewed more broadly, the poem's ceaseless turning back to the past, as if attempting to recapture it, points to the poet's escapist tendencies as being "removed from contemporary movements and conflicts."[1]

Whether by continuity or disjunction, *Vigvamim shotkim* owes a debt to Silkiner's pioneering poema for its leading themes and forms. Most notably, Efros sustains the latent warning of the threat posed by the voraciousness of American materialism. As in the case of Silkiner, this work, too, dwells on the impact of America on Jews-as-Indians, expressed indirectly through the Spanish in the case of Silkiner and the English in Efros's work. In either case, the outcome is the same: the physical or cultural annihilation of the Other and his assimilation into the American mainstream.

In spite of the poet's insistence on calling it and the subsequent *Zahav* (Gold) by the term "shirim," poems, this composition is also a poema, albeit unlike Silkiner's. In place of the latter's emphasis on the mythic, this tale is fixed in a recognizably realistic environment and situation. Efros's language is more lucid, the narrative organized, and the plot accessible. Yet he too intersperses the work with lyrical musings, opening each chapter (or canto) with a poem that either sets the plot in space and time by establishing a narratological perspective from the twentieth century, or ponders abstract principles beyond the immediate plot, such as human nature and its foibles.

BRIEF SUMMARY

The story tells of Tom, an Englishman whose silence and reticence make his fellow colonists of Talbot County, Maryland, suspicious and fearful. Cast out, he is found by the local Indians and is brought back to health only to fall in love with Lalari, the *Sachem*'s (chief's) daughter. One of her suitors is *Harag Namer*, Panther Slayer, the Sachem's deputy and confidant, who shares the secret about Lalari's true ancestry: she is the child of a White man and the Sachem's wife. Dwelling among the Native Americans and closer to nature, Tom regains his artistic drive. He paints pictures that represent scenes of their daily lives against a setting sun. Through his art Tom expresses his bewilderment at the stoic silence with which they accept the prospect of their imminent demise.

To prove his allegiance to the Indians, Tom leads them in battle against the English, in which they attain a temporary victory. Having proved his loyalty to the Indians, he marries Lalari and they move to a neighboring Indian village, in part out of fear of Panther-Slayer.

When their romance wanes, Tom recalls the girl he left behind in London. He asks Lalari about the Indians' gold, of which he has heard many tales. She takes him to the wreck of a galleon, showing him the Spanish gold left untouched by her people, and then leaves him. With riches in hand, Tom returns to England, abandoning a pregnant Lalari to discover that the girl back home did not wait for him.

Lalari gives birth to a stillborn child whom she buries. Tom, who has just returned, attempts to rekindle their relationship, but Lalari takes her own life, leaving Tom to mourn her death and, all too belatedly, regret his ways.

EFROS AND LONGFELLOW

A comparison of Efros's poem with Longfellow's "The Song of Hiawatha" is illuminating. For as much as Efros distanced himself from "Hiawatha,"[2] his reading of the latter has left a number of meaningful imprints on *Vigvamim.* In light of this influence, it might be that it was Longfellow's strategy of presenting the narrative that Efros deemed objectionable, and not the tale itself. Longfellow's meter and integration of Indian lore told in mythic time are clearly absent from Efros's work, but not other aspects of the plot.

A consideration of *Vigvamim* in light of "Hiawatha" highlights the differences of the two in presentation, form, and focus. Nevertheless, Efros does make a significant gesture toward Longfellow's tale. Toward the conclusion of "Hiawatha," for example, we read of the pale-faced "Black-Robe chief" who visits the Indians to bring them a new religion. The black-robed priest also tells the Natives of the Jews, "the tribe accursed."[3]

Hearing his story of "the Master of Life," the Indians depart for their wigwams to relate the Prophet's tale to their families. This event marks the beginning of the end for the pristine life led by Hiawatha and his people. The description of the moment is rife with imagery of war, sunset, and the end of things as they used to be:

> Slowly o'er the simmering landscape
> Fell the evening's dusk and coolness,
> And the long and level sunbeams
> Shot their spears into the forest,
> Breaking through its shields of shadow,
> Rushed into each secret ambush,
> Searched each thicket, dingle, hollow;
> Still the guests of Hiawatha
> Slumbered in the *silent wigwam.*
> From his place rose Hiawatha,
> Bade farewell to old Nokomis . . . (Canto 22, 163b, emphasis added)

This image is intractably inscribed in Efros's poem as it intersects with Longfellow's conclusion. However, the silent wigwams in Efros's work are those of the Indians, who stoically accept their lot as part of a fated existence. The allusion to "Hiawatha" is ironic in that the sense of the Christian guest's secure comfort in Longfellow's work is what ends the peaceful existence of the Native Americans of whom Efros tells.

His choice to title his work by one of Longfellow's concluding images is also telling. The account of the Pale Face Prophet marks the conclusion of mythic time, giving way to historical time. It collapses the idyllic state as ensuing conflicts between Whites and Indians give rise to enmity and death. Efros ushers the story out of its aura of myth and legend and into a pedestrian reality in which magic and the supernatural are ineffective. Much as pointed out in Silkiner's *Timmura*, Efros's long poem taking its signal from Longfellow's "Hiawatha," illustrates the consequences of the encounter with the White Man. Yet unlike his predecessor's poema, Efros's is a thorough treatment of the clash in a language significantly more accessible and realistic.

It is uncertain, though, whether one can actually address the Longfellow-Efros axis as one of influence, since the latter was not overly fond of the former's work. Indeed, Efros did not have to go to Longfellow for inspiration. The two leading Hebrew poets of his day, Bialik and Tschernichowsky, were the leading conduits through whom the long poem or poema passed down within the Hebraic literary tradition, and it is certain that Efros was influenced by their work.[4]

Yet the nexus between Longfellow's closing words and Efros's title begs the question about any affinity between the two. For as the White men are honorably ensconced under the roof of the Indians who obey Hiawatha's teachings to be welcoming, kind, and good to their visitors, the Indians' fate is sealed. This unhappy surmise leaves Efros to write of the consequent developments. In it, the Hebrew poet negates the impression, if there ever was one, that "Hiawatha" ends happily. And as if reinforcing the link between the two, Efros's protagonists look to the West, signifying the setting sun and the concomitant end of Indian existence. Moreover, as if to signal a restoration of an Edenic past in some messianic future, it is also the direction from which Hiawatha is to return someday from "the Land of the Hereafter" to which he has gone (Canto 22, 164). Efros's silent wigwams are the leitmotif of the end of Indian hegemony in the New World.

One of the central images in the poem is the reflexive act of one artist, Efros, representing the work of another, Tom. This strategy allows the poet to express himself about his art, a matter which Efros expanded on in numerous essays as well.[5] Both artists are fascinated by the resignation of Native Americans about their fate, represented by the central image in his art and in the Indians' existence as being "sunset against sunset" ("shkiʿah mul shkiʿah"). Both artists are preoccupied with the emotional power in the scene, one evoked by dwelling on nature as a means of drawing out their inner natures, a theme central for romantic modes of representation of the self and the world about.[6] A revival of Tom's artistic skills among the Indians reflexively illuminates Efros's notion of art inspired by the encounters with nature.[7] The artist in him thrives so long as he does not succumb to greed and a lust for gold.[8]

The intersection of the savage inner spirit and the orderliness of civilized life is a thematic thread that runs through Efros's poetry. This clash between the rational and the intuitive also occupies the protagonists, as the English, representing the former, strive to vanquish the indigenous, "uncivilized," and natural in life, including the Indians. Similarly, Efros, as a Romantic poet, finds inspiration by reflecting on nature, as an alternative to his professional world as a scholar of medieval Jewish philosophy.[9]

The story of the love between Lalari and Tom is reminiscent of a host of archetypal tales. His dwelling on the envy of *Harag Namer* (Panther Slayer) and attempted foiling of the match by him and her father is also psychologically pithy.

The adventure- and action-filled episodes of Tom joining forces with the Indians to fight the English offers a momentary possibility, as in his art, of Tom losing his earlier identity and self by becoming Indian. Considered more broadly, his act is a possibility raised by Efros of an accommodation and co-existence between European and Native Other. Tom's love for Lalari and his becoming a member of Indian society is one means of resolving the tension of the poem. The assimilation of the European into the culture of the Natives is a short-lived attempt to resolve the conflict between nature and all that is European. This prospect is soon foiled as Tom resumes his earlier behavior and seeks the hoard of gold he believes the Indians have been concealing from the White man. It is only upon the loss of the natural, signified by Lalari, and his return to London that he senses the extent of his alienation from all that is valuable, but by then it is already too late. The Indian and his natural existence have already been conquered.

EFROS'S BROADWAY PERSONA

Though some parts of the tale seem to be authentic, such as the song, "Ha-kol yafeh" (All's beautiful), sung by Lalari, much of the plot is of the poet's imagination. This also explains the tight organization and novelistic qualities that contribute to its unity as a "realistic epic," as Lisitzky described it.[10]

Nevertheless, the plot resembles familiar stories, containing elements reminiscent of Puccini's 1904 opera, *Madame Butterfly*, underscoring the special flair Efros had for showmanship and melodramatic plots, also evidenced by his second long poem, *Zahav* (Gold).[11]

Unlike Silkiner's poema, from which Efros seeks to distance his work, "Silent Wigwams" is a lucidly narrated, causally organized, and tightly woven Apollonian composition. It contains surprisingly little in terms of mythology; any secrets it harbors enhance its dramatic pathos and irony. The protagonists possess a psychological individualism better developed than those of Silkiner or even Lisitzky. Such, for example, is the Sachem's difficulty at keeping his word to Lalari's mother. Approached with such assumptions, we can consider the case of the poem's narrator, whose opening observations about the checkered map of the United States from sea to sea, and descriptions of the specific geography of Chesapeake Bay, establish his sentiments and perspective geographically and temporally.

In the checkerboard of sea to sea states
As a broad pavement of conquest and power
Paved by pioneers into end beyond end
Of the new world, there's one state
Where north and south in amity meet,
Where winter wearies not, where summer burns not,
The sun is generous and an abundant harvest fills the earth. (9)

The narrator also offers a brief scientific discourse about the tides (62); describes the sunrise as musical notes (89); and has Lalari explain her voice as sound waves issuing from her mouth (100). He is also unhesitant about identifying his point of view and ethnic identity as Jewish, familiar with the Hebrew months that punctuate the progress of time in the story.[12] The distance between the story teller and the plot is magnified temporally by identifying his perspective in the present, when the states of the United States form a contiguous checkerboard on the North American continent from east to west.

Efros's tale is also contemporary in its broaching of issues such as assimilation and mixed marriage in the formation of one's identity. He also incorporates seemingly authentic Indian songs to lend his work a semblance of reality.

Efros's novelistic tale is not only more "realistic" in plot, but its lucid narrative avoids nearly all semblance of myth. Instead, Efros dwells on the possibility of a romantic relationship between two races as a means of resolving the hostilities that eventually bring about the dissolution of one. *Vigvamim* permits an accurate placement of the Nanticoke tribe geographically, even allowing for an educated determination of the time of the story, details that are supported by a host of specifically ethnic and Indian terms to educate the reader as well as to add to the mimetic qualities of the tale.

Additional prose-like features of this work include a linear plot whose actors are fleshed out, and who interrelate and react to one another. The story is not merely compact in trajectory and uniform in language, but permits substantial character analysis by virtue of the complexity of the protagonists and their psychologically realistic behavior. In addition, the poet's narrative voice remains detached from the story, inviting reader reaction to the behavior or motives of the protagonists. The Sachem is a pensive, philosophical type, not given to violence, and preferring to contemplate intellectual matters. His silence lends an additional dimension to the title of the poema, and a variation on its manifestation in the stoic acceptance of fate by the Indians at their decline. Instead, his silence is motivated by an active and willful gesture to protect Lalari from learning the secret of her White ancestry. The stoicism, as Lalari explains, stems from her people's belief in reincarnation as an affirmation of the endlessness of being:

> We fear not death for we see no death.
> Only Manitu exists, a life force, a wondrous thing
> That flows in all and from eternity to eternity
> In the living, the flower, the tree, the rock,
> And there is no death, only a change of disguises,
> One species willingly surrenders as food for the other,
> And a dying life force to a new life force. (29)

Lalari's envy of Tom's blond hair (Canto 1, part 3, 22) is presented in what appears to be a philosophical contemplation of the heroine on why all races were not heirs to that color. This tendency to philosophize is more in keeping with the poet's predilections than a representation of actual Indians. Her attitude is reminiscent of marginalized individuals who seek to appear like members of the dominant culture. This includes the Jews in America who strove to eradicate many external features that identified them as outsiders. Added to this is another factor of color in the story, stemming predominantly from the notion that local Indians are dark (Canto 1, part 2). By contrast, the poem foreshadows the secret of Lalari's ancestry by observing that her skin is transparent in its hue. Yet, for one not fully knowledgeable of the truth, this detail is inadequate as she wishes to resemble the Whites. Her attraction to the light-skinned

Whites is reminiscent of her mother's feelings, and a sentiment reflecting back to Blacks and Jews.

The complex narrative includes not merely direct speech to supplement the narrator's account but also episodes of an assortment of discourse styles, much as in a novel. In this regard, for example, the episode considered by many the most temptingly reflexive is telling:

> Behind his wigwam in the midst of the field,
> In plowed and furrowed black earth,
> Stood Tom and sowed the autumn seed.
> The young Indians beheld him and smiled,
> Neared the fence and called: for shame!
> How man is debased to be a woman,
> To plow, sow and harvest as she?
> Are there no better chores for a man?
> Behold they're off to the great hunt.
> Let him join and lay in wait for deer,
> And try his strength, tense his muscles
> In battle with a ram fighting for its life—
> That is man's work! For shame to the paleface god!
> He stood listening. Then he neared them
> Leaned on the fence looked them in the face
> Some moments silently and replied slowly:
> "Now, brothers, I understand. I understand why
> The land slips from beneath your feet.
> A nation loving its land, its sons—as saplings
> Embedding themselves within the earth
> Send their roots to subdue the depths
> Entwine their roots 'round stones and rocks—
> Then let the storm come and try to move us!
> Pity! You merited not to be as saplings.
> In forest and field you chase and pursue
> The deer and elk, the antelope and bear.
> So do you hover above the earth, not within.
> So what wonder is it if beneath your feet,
> Your uprooted legs, the earth retreats
> Flees and passes to those, to these
> Yearning to turn their legs into roots?" The silence lingered.
> They knew not what to reply. Him they dearly loved.
> Also they felt the truth and love in his words.

"The hunt you admire, tense the muscles,
The great struggle of man and beast,
Yet look!" The Indians looked.
He turned and took long paces and stood
In mid field that lay cultivated,
Her clods overturned, starved by winter,
As a many open-mawed beast
Roaring: prey! he stood at full height
Alone amidst the lofty and the low, as a god,
And the wild earth as if leaped about him,
His hand he raised: hush! hush! glutton; here's prey!
And in all directions he cast seeds
Letting the famished, dark beast swallow.
And they looked on silently and began to comprehend
The pale-face and essence of his words.
One by one they slipped off and throughout the night
Thought of a people whose sons are as saplings,
And of man as a god mastering the earth-beast.
Next day they forgot all.
Bow and arrow in hand and a feather in their hair,
And off to the hunt they flew. (canto 3, poem 3, 43–45)

Palpably the most "Zionist" scene in the poem, and to which many have previously referred,[13] this account lends itself to analysis from several novelistic standpoints, including its narrative forms, point of view, gender specificity, and ideology. Like most other episodes in this poem, it is presented by an omniscient narrator. As a means to dramatize the situation, the participants' voices intersect the presentation. Significantly, the words of the Native Americans are not presented directly but are mediated by a narrative form known as "experienced speech," "Narrated Monologue," or *Erlebte Rede* that creates the illusion of interpenetrating the narrator's account with what seems to be the protagonist's direct speech.[14] Because none of them is singled out, the Natives constitute a single collectivity, acting as one and easily lending themselves to stereotyping. On the other hand, Tom's words are presented in direct speech, affording a seemingly unmediated and sensory nexus between reader and subject.

The narrators of Longfellow's and Efros's long poems are also not identical. That of "Hiawatha" is an authorial Native American, for Longfellow's method fuses Indian folk-tales into a single narrative,[15] a model emulated by Lisitzky. Instead, Efros's narrator is unabashedly of a Hebrew-Jewish origin. He addresses the story to a postulated audience of Hebrew readers whose familiarity with the American landscape is not always taken for granted. Because of that he strategically intersperses footnotes to explain to the uneducated some of the Indian terms, such as sachem, wigwam, and wampum. Efros also restricts his account to Hebrew readers. For although his talents at composing literary and scholarly pieces in English were proven by then, he did not act to translate and publish this work for those who did not read Hebrew.[16]

Efros retains the Hebraist's perspective in other ways, too. As noted before, he uses the Hebrew calendar as a temporal marker, punctuating the passing of time with a Hebrew month name. He also refers to Sundays as "the Christian Sabbath," and the sunset of those days as "their *mlaveh malkah*," or the escorting of the Sabbath queen (*Vigvamim*, 10–11), a familiar term borrowed from Jewish ritual practice. The silence of Tom among the English residents is given metaphoric embellishment as "ʿatuf b-talit," wrapped in a prayer shawl (*Vigvamim*, 11). Night, too, is described as if enshrouded in a prayer shawl (62). Other references allude to Jewish texts from Hebrew and Aramaic, though the majority is necessary for the narrative of the teller, embedded into his language as metaphors or similes and reminding us of the author's culture.[17] Moreover, the narrative is European in its character, as the long epic poem is interspersed with lyrical episodes to render it a poema.

THE TRILOGY

Efros's composition, though, became more ambitious soon after its publication. Though no evidence is to be found that, from the outset, his plan exceeded the scope of "Silent Wigwams," he followed it up in less than a decade (in 1942) with another long work, *Zahav* (Gold), an account of the California Gold Rush and its impact on his protagonist's rootlessness. Though he did not publish any other long poems of the scope of these two, his archive includes notes for an additional long poem about America, this one centered on the Wall Street financial collapse and the ensuing Great Depression of 1929.[18]

Composed as a poema, *Vigvamim* was Efros's first poetic composition of scale written, and rewritten, as he notes at the opening, over one summer while in Provincetown, Massachusetts.[19] Significantly, Efros's pace in composing this work stopped short of executing the full plan. The Gnazim archive includes rough notes outlining the historical forces and human greed exhibited during the Great Depression, but no trace of the poetic composition exists. No doubt that among the causes cutting short the project is the dramatic turn in the fate of the Jews that led to the Holocaust and Efros's later post-Holocaust mission to Europe to investigate its effects.[20]

The two published long poems, and presumably this would have also applied to the unpublished one, strive to highlight particular episodes in American history. Though each work remains a self-contained creation, with themes localized to the composition in question, as a group they are preoccupied with the deep-seated drives controlling protagonists, their behavior, and their relationships with each other. Against the vast backdrop of exploration, conquest, and subjugation of this continent stands the individual spirit, human greed, the unquenchable thirst for action to occupy the restlessness in the heart of man, even at the cost of jeopardizing human happiness.

Why was Efros so intent on writing his first work to focus on Native Americans, and Nanticoke Indians in particular? No doubt he, like all other Hebrew writers engaged with the subject, was intrigued by their tragic fate and the ebbing of a culture. Their story struck a familiar chord for many Jews who identified the Indians' loss of land and national existence as a metaphor of their own national experience of long ago.[21]

Another explanation emanates from what appear to be Efros's liberal views, perceiving all humans as having one creator, leading to an identity of ancient tribes with each other.[22] His reflections on the subject include expressions about marginalized cultures in America, including memories of cigar store Indians—"a precious gift of England to early America." He also learned of Indians in his history and literature classes, and was influenced by "the sadness of Indian poems, poems resembling modern ones."[23]

The reason for his focus on Nanticoke Indians stems from several considerations. Principally, it was because Efros lived for many years in Baltimore, Maryland,[24] and liked the place—as testified in the above cited and unpublished opening to *Vigvamim.* Also, the history of the Nanticoke may have been especially salient for his purposes. They, as part of the Delaware Indians, suffered many an uprooting following exile from their territory, finally to be settled in Oklahoma. Those who remained were racially discriminated against by Delaware legislation and were treated as "colored." This fate, combined with other indignities, assimilation, oppression and constant maltreatment, and the breaking of treaties made the Nanticokes' history attractive to Efros, who identified the fate of his people with that of the Indians.

Zahav—A BRIEF SUMMARY

Unlike *Vigvamim*, which remained fixed to the Chesapeake Bay region, *Zahav* (Gold, 1942) unveils a sweeping view of coast-to-coast America on a grand scale.[25]

The story focuses on the passion and wanderlust of Ezra Lundt, a New England farmer who was a soldier in the Mexican war. Hearing of the discovery of gold, he is swept up by the California Gold Rush of 1849. Leaving family and farm behind, he dons his soldier's uniform and joins a wagon train in St. Louis headed for California. On the way, Lundt learns of the legends of California and meets Lola, the mesmerizing daughter of the provisions keeper. Her tempestuous and spirited dancing arouses and rallies the demoralized pioneers to continue their journey when conditions become difficult. She also leads them in a battle against the Indians, which Lundt reluctantly joins only to be wounded and tended by her.

Upon arriving in Colorado, the reader learns of the wonders of America's landscape, including the Garden of the Gods and the Humbolt Desert. It is against this backdrop that harsh conditions on the salt flats nearly kill all on the wagon train. Stories of those who did not survive the journey, among them the Donner Party, cast a long shadow over the lot of those daring to make the trek. Their tenacity, though, helps them survive and reach the San Francisco area.

In an episode that underscores a period of time in which Lundt can relax from the passions that push him, we read of how he is hosted and brought back to health by Hutslohan, an Indian. Hutslohan sits facing the sunset before the house he acquired and the land which he farms and tells of his experiences among Whites, and the lessons he garnered about the importance of education, farming, and love of land. While Lundt contemplates a life of tranquility on the farm, even purchasing a few tracts, gold fever soon sweeps him up. He meets up with some of the members of the wagon train, including Lola, who again inspires him to seek ever more efficient ways to find gold. His obsession is not limited to a specific amount of gold to be gathered, or a period of time; it is the very quest that drives him on, leading to a neglect of the promise he made to his wife, Abby, about returning home in a year.

Lola follows Lundt in quest of the Mother Lode. They both spend time in Old Bear (i.e., grizzly bear), or Yosemite Valley, where their Edenic existence is disrupted as they forge ahead to find gold. Lola, who by now yearns to settle down, becomes despondent and takes her life by leaping off a nearby cliff. Her deed occurs at the very time when Lundt discovers the way to the Mother Lode. Though he survives, Lola's death destroys Lundt emotionally, leaving him a homeless wanderer.

Meanwhile, his New England family makes its way to California and Abby, his wife, in her search for him and belief that he died, finds a former admirer with whom she settles down to work some of Lundt's remaining land. The story ends as Lundt's existence wanes. He recognizes her, his son, and her parents, though the concurrent San Francisco fire is a metonym for the finality of things. As he realizes that his quest was for the false gold—her golden hair and the golden grain in the field become the true objects to seek in life—he leaves to face the setting sun alongside his Indian friend Hutslohan.

ANALYSIS

As in the case of "Wigwams," *Zahav* features a male protagonist whose restless spirit urges him to wander, to seek out the new at the risk of losing his present happiness. His roots in the land are tenuous at best as he moves about at will, seeking ever new experiences. His greed is boundless; even the women in his life fall victim to his instability. In place of satisfaction with any specific wealth it is the quest that is at the heart of his action.

Unlike the former poem, *Zahav* is told more "from without" the world of Native Americans as it focuses on the world from the vantage point of the White Man, his needs and motives. The tale begins with Ezra Lundt, whose abandoning of family and farm to find riches in California are evocative of the poems that speak of the people and occupations cast aside by men who took off to find gold.[26]

Efros embellishes this story with many aspects of Americana pertaining to the theme of gold and the difficulties of obtaining it. On the way, Lundt's wagon train encounters Pawnee and Sioux Indians, who threaten the passage of anyone crossing the plains (127, 139–140). He also hears of Calafia, a chief of a land of heroic, Amazon-like women bearing gilded weapons (131–132), and learns of the story of El Dorado, a mythical king whose skin was ritually covered with gold (132).

The poem is studded with elements that lend the imaginary plot a verisimilitude of the times. The protagonists are familiar with and repeatedly sing the popular song "Oh, Suzanna," which Efros translates for his readers.[27] He also embeds other aspects of American culture to underscore its particular flavor, including references to the fate of the Donner Party (135), Sutter's discovery of gold (131), and names former explorers such as Cortez (131), Balboa and Magellan (152), and the Puritans (180). As in the case with "Wigwams," many geographical references fix the narrative into familiar places, among them Salem, New England, Alabama (179), the Missouri territory, the Rockies and Sierras (135), Humbolt Desert (146), Truckee Flats (147), the Pacific Ocean (153), Yellowstone (158), the American River (169), the San Juaquin River (181), Yosemite (209), Sacramento, and other locales (173).

Efros also teaches about methods of gold mining, as by diversion of waterways with dams and extraction by means of mercury (174, 175, 181). Also, reminiscent of the narrative vantage of *Vigvamim*, the temporal markers include Hebrew month names, among them Av (135), Ḥeshvan (157), Tishrei (220), and Shvat (227), as if to remind the reader of the poem's specific perspective.

In both *Vigvamim shotkim* and *Zahav*, Efros's romantic plots pose the individual in the midst of epic conflicts intersecting his life, be they the early settlement of America or the Gold Rush. Events sweep up the protagonists, leaving them vanquished because of their greed and inability to obtain a perspective on the limits of one's abilities against superior forces. The epic event does not lend the individual any luster nor favorably affect his experience. Instead, it makes of him a victim of the greater powers, against which he becomes but a minor player, a victim of little consequence. This fascination with titanic forces is also of interest in the work of E. E. Lisitzky.

As in the case of "Wigwams," the significance of possessing and working the land is a chief concern of the story. So while the land is exploited by goldminers, they quickly also abandon it. The tale underscores the greater value of possessing and farming it permanently, much as Zionist pioneers do in Eretz Israel. So it is Lundt's wife, the symbol of stability, who remains to farm the land and raise the children he abandons. She also establishes a homestead after moving to San Francisco. So does Hutslohan, who has learned from his people's fate and settles to farm his land.

The Native American is portrayed in a greater range of images in *Zahav*, lending nuance and complexity to the monolithic depiction of Indians in many works, including Efros's "Wigwams." Because the story is an account of Lundt, Indians are represented from his and other Whites' perspective. They are observed from afar as stock, faceless savages who stalk and kill Whites crossing their territories. They are hostile to Lundt's wagon train and all Whites.

A more intimate look is afforded in two pivotal instances, however, that contradict the first image. The first is represented by the story of Lola, the leading female protagonist, and the account of her experiences among Native Americans. As is the case with several other components of this poem, she resembles Lalari. Evoking Lalari's mellifluous name, Lola was raised by a Native American, Hutslohan, who rescued her from Nez Perce Indians who attacked and killed her (White) family (190, 217–219). Though not of Indian ancestry, she is also not the daughter of Thomas, the White man on the wagon train (190). Like Lalari, she too dies by her own hand upon contemplating her unstable life.

Unlike Lalari, though, she is more active, assertive, and dynamic, berating the men around her for cowardice when conditions become too difficult. More than the staid and sober Lundt, she is a tempestuous spirit whose appearance and conduct arouse the men to action. Like Lalari before her, she also is the one to tend and heal the wounded White hero (141). She inspires Lundt to seek more daring ways to discover the Mother Lode, and ultimately is the one to bring catastrophe upon both of them. In this she resembles the destructive and self-destructive woman in more than a few romantic works whose allure inspires the hero, but can also be his downfall.

Her education among the Indians includes learning that the evil Manitou is *El-Zahav*, the God of Gold (217), the opposite of Silkiner's benevolent *Elnefesh*, the God of the spirits from before the White men's arrival. She and Lundt are overcome with Gold Fever and are consumed by their madness. In the end, they fall victim to *El-Zahav* in payment for their excessive obsession (223).[28] Resembling him in her restlessness and hunger for taking risks and the obsessive search for new excitement, she transforms Lundt's spirit, drawing out his primal and daring instinct. Her death also precipitates his spiritual downfall, leaving him an empty shell. At the end, Lundt walks away from his family believing that they are happy without him, a theme reminiscent of the ending of many a romantic tale, including Agnon's "V-haya he-ʿakov l-mishor" (And the crooked shall be made straight).

In her self-destructive way, Lola is the opposite of Hutslohan, the Indian who rescued her from the Nez Perce. He is an extension of the Sachem of "Wigwams" in his noble and silent demeanor, justifying his fate and stoically awaiting the end as he sits squinting at the setting sun (154, 155, 248) while harboring a secret about a solitary life (166–167). Hutslohan is the symbol of the defeated Native American. He survives by remaining passive, by forgoing the violence of other Indians who battle with the Pale Face only to be vanquished. His view of the future is pessimistic, though he—unlike the Indians of *Vigvamim*—has learned the importance of land and agriculture as sustaining all life (159–161). Moreover, Hutslohan teaches Lundt that Indians are also nuanced human beings, and not merely savages (157).

The theme remains a vehicle for Efros to imply the fate of his fellow Jews. In this, Efros adheres after a fashion to the image of the *maskil*, the Jew of the Enlightenment, a heritage he embraced in other aspects of his poetry.[29] Writing with the imagery of other poems, Efros allows Hutslohan the words of the seeker of wisdom:

> I went to draw with eye-as-pails
> Light of the life of the Pale-face for my tribe,
> And returned and within my eyes a redoubled darkness . . .
> I returned with empty and feeble arms . . .
> My ancestors did not teach me
> To read and write as you, line by line, so with much effort
> And with endless squinting of eyes,
> My soul strode in the path of wisdom.
> And after many suns and moons
> I found me a book and a path . . .
> The Indian removed his pipe from his lips
> And circled it against the field . . . (158–159)

By contrast, it is Lundt whose passions for material riches consume him and all close to him, as did Tom's in a more muted fashion. Set in the broader context of Efros's poetry, the greed of the Europeans in both works corresponds to the poet's lyrical poems which prize values such as love and transcendence above material gain. Efros is not merely juxtaposing spiritual values against material, but in so doing voices many immigrant Hebrew writers' expressions of disenchantment with the loss of what they considered the metaphysical bases of their culture when embracing America with all her materialism.

The hunt for riches may also be a reflection, at least in part, of Efros's biography. Any cursory perusal of his life illuminates the financial difficulties he frequently faced, a matter which also delayed his eventual settling in Israel. As part of his attempt to do well, and not just an example of entrepreneurial inclinations, he composed a musical play, in English, to be staged on Broadway. Even his academic position at New York City's Hunter College was created by contributions, "soft money" provided perhaps by some wealthy admirers and supporters of his mission.

CONCLUSION

Efros's representation of Native Americans takes on greater depth and complexity than that accomplished by Silkiner. His stories are told in a clear language devoid of his predecessor's obscure style. His more realistic tale, one devoid of much mythic or supernatural details, makes comprehension uncomplicated. Moreover, his poetics about the representation of the Other departs from Silkiner's. Efros's interest is in telling his tale; the medium becomes less significant. His language is decidedly less conservative, flowery, and classical than that of Silkiner or Lisitzky after him. Moreover, his avoidance of the term *poema* when labeling his two long works may have its roots in the same consideration; the poema by Silkiner is clearly more supernatural and lacks the mimetic qualities of a realistic poem of the likes of Efros's.

Efros is also less embedded within his tale. Whereas no identity of the hand composing Silkiner's and Lisitzky's poemas is noted—the latter, as we shall see in the following chapter, refers in at least one instance to his narrator as visiting a New Orleans preacher—Efros embeds a number of distinctly Jewish signs (as in referring to the passing months by their Hebrew names) to set his narrator apart from his subject. This is not to lend quaintness to his poem. It is there to delineate the limits of the introvertedness of the narrative vis-à-vis his subject. So in place of surrendering his identity to the exotic world which he unravels before his reader, as do Silkiner and Lisitzky, Efros consciously sets boundaries between himself and his subject, retaining his identity as separate from that of Native Americans.

Though his works deservedly stand in the foreground of Hebrew literary representation of Native Americans, all signs indicate Efros's pursuit of a greater vision, in which Indians play a lesser role with each subsequent poem. Realizing that his plans included a long poem about the Depression extends the message of the two extant poems beyond the introduction of exotic ethnic groups. Though never realized, Efros's work was to introduce into the Hebrew literary corpus his perception of crucial components making up the American experience, its spirit and values. And, as in the case of many of his literary brethren, he was not reluctant to infuse his Indian poetry with features alluding to specific Jewish national or social concerns.

Chapter Three

TO BE AS OTHERS: E. E. LISITZKY'S REPRESENTATION OF NATIVE AMERICANS

American Hebrew literature, the poetry and prose fiction composed almost exclusively by immigrants, is a tapestry of forms, trends, and genres. It is a testimony documenting early responses of the encounter between Hebraists and the New World. In terms of literary forms and styles, this literature runs the gamut of Hebrew belles lettres, ranging from the traditional European Hebrew literary models to the innovativeness of modernism as affected by American and English literature in the early decades of the twentieth century. In the case of a few exceptional individuals, principally Gavriel Preil, this literature has also given rise to trends which were at the forefront of a Hebrew modernism, paralleling similar developments in Eretz Israel.[1]

However, the criterion of modernism is not the sole yardstick to measure the attainments of American Hebrew literature. Another, though by no means the only alternative, is by its attentiveness to the American socio-cultural scene. It is this feature which governs the present study and which has reached its zenith in the rich and diverse poetical work of Ephraim E. Lisitzky (1885–1962).

Chronologically third among his fellow Hebrew poets to compose a book-length epic poem centered on Native Americans, Lisitzky is arguably the most American. To be sure, other Hebrew writers have also devoted thought, energy, and art to this subject, composing short pieces or, in passing, referring to Indians in their poetry—and, more rarely, in prose.

Lisitzky spent his childhood orphaned of his mother in Slutzk, where he excelled in Talmudic studies. Following his father to Boston in 1900, he resumed his traditional studies, spending a brief time at the Rabbi Yitzhak Elḥanan Yeshiva. Later, he also studied to be a *shoḥet*, a ritual slaughterer, and, some years later, received a degree as a pharmaceutical chemist from Marquette (Milwaukee). Lisitzky also worked for a brief time teaching Hebrew and Judaica in Ontario, Canada, New York State, Milwaukee, and Boston. In 1918, he was recruited to head the New Orleans Communal

Hebrew School, where he became known as *ha-moreh*, the teacher, and where he remained until his retirement. Despite his early plans to immigrate to Eretz Israel, Lisitzky forever exhibited an ambivalence about this dream, visiting there only twice (1934 and 1956). In his later years, he was awarded honorary doctorates from the Jewish Theological Seminary (1949) and the Hebrew Union College–Jewish Institute of Religion (1960).

In terms of sustained interest and quantity, three Hebrew poets—Silkiner, Efros, and Lisitzky—have outdone their fellows in writing about the American Indian. Of them, Lisitzky is conspicuously the most prolific in terms of the absolute number of works on the subject. His *magnum opus* on Native Americans, *Mdurot doʿakhot* (Dying campfires, 1937),[2] also bears the most authentic marks of Indian folktales. Unlike this epic, few works by Hebrew writers explored so intimately a subject so remote from their immediate concerns, a civilization with which Jews had little direct contact. On the other hand, nearly each and every Hebrew poet and author in America has incorporated the subject of African Americans into his work, in large measure or not, of which the most extensive is, again, Lisitzky's *B-ʾoholay Khush* (In the tents of Cush, 1953).

Thematically, it is Lisitzky's oeuvre that makes the definitive contribution on two of the most distinct subjects of the American experience. To be sure, his poetic work falls short of those of his fellows in giving expression to another favorite subject, alienation in the Big City. Yet his work is foremost in expressing quintessential themes set in America's landscape and brought into contact with the Jewish experience. Prior to and in the wake of the above works, he wrote extensively on Blacks, retold other Indian and American folktales—among them Indian legends and the tale of Johnny Appleseed—guiding his readers through New Orleans and the South, North Carolina, Buffalo, and Canada's Ontario province, among other locations.[3]

The following discussion endeavors to evaluate Lisitzky's evolving treatment of and regard for Native American folktales. Unlike his fellow Hebrew poets, it was he who consistently revisited the subject over a considerable literary life span. For that reason alone this study will, of necessity, address most of his writings which pertain to American Indians. But out of its being so central in this endeavor, his epic long poem, *Mdurot doʿakhot*, is our chief subject.

Lisitzky's early poems are a window into strategies which were to distinguish him from others. These steps anticipate the accomplishments of *Mdurot doʿakhot*, which, however, also departs from them in a number of significant ways. Moreover, Lisitzky's post-*Mdurot* poetry goes even further to mark an evolution in the poet's treatment of the subject, while at the same time representing his repeated forays into the realm of the Other.

As the foregoing will demonstrate, Lisitzky's treatment of Native American tales relies heavily on authentic texts that make his work more of a transposition of original works than a product of his imagination—as was the case with Silkiner or Efros. The presence of authentic tales from different Native American tribes, although fused to form a single fabric, also allowed for a representation of the Other in a seemingly unmediated fashion. Nevertheless, Lisitzky altered the tales he so admired in subtle and meaningful ways to reflect his tastes, and to "civilize" them. He makes the tales more palpable to adherents of Haskalah teachings by transmuting them into vehicles of ethical, moral, and intellectual values.

Moreover, to further distinguish himself from his predecessors and avoid the image of an also-ran latecomer on the scene, Lisitzky deflected reader attention from other Hebrew writers by unabashedly crediting Henry Wadsworth Longfellow's "The Song of Hiawatha" as his inspiration in foregrounding Indian lore and legend as primary sources of his narrative, as he notes explicitly in the foreword to his long poem, and the *Kalevala* for the meter of both (*Mdurot*, 3–4).

For decades, we find more than a mere echo of these words reverberating in critical reviews of *Mdurot doʿakhot.* Reception of this long poem is documented in studies representing the gamut of Hebrew scholarship in America and Israel. Nevertheless, few scholars rose to the challenge of reaching beyond an almost mechanical repetition of Lisitzky's own words. Instead, their expressions are general and perfunctory as they either summarize its plot or identify analogical relationships between the poet's biography and his literary output. The fact that readers were unfamiliar with the culture of Native Americans was not ameliorated by critics who, presumably, should or could have done so. In place of reiterating what was readily found in Lisitzky's introduction, scholars could have been more rigorous, analytical, and responsive to the challenges presented by this work and its place in the Hebrew literary canon.[4]

Familiarity with Lisitzky or his oeuvre has generated claims that it proclaims a love and understanding among diverse peoples seeking stability, identity, and a homeland. To be sure, the plot of the story confirms these.[5] However, scholarship and critics have overlooked significant issues in his literary encounters with the American Indian.

Contrary to some observations, Lisitzky's preoccupation with

America's Blacks and Indians should not be dismissed simply as musings of a romantic poet's escapism, nor as mere identification with the lot of people whose fate resembles that of the Jews. It needs to be seen as part and parcel of his engagement with America, as his sympathy for the downtrodden, vilified, and powerless, specifically, and as a metaphor for "the tragedy of the annihilation of the Jewish people."[6] Moreover, although the plot also glosses over cruelties perpetrated by Indians on Whites, a full representation of Indian-White relations—including mutual brutalities—is not the concern of a romantic tale such as this.

Needless to add, it is also true that his poems—in this work as in others—are mirrors of the poet's inner world, temperamentally and in terms of worldview. They reflexively direct the encounter with the Other inward, as an expression of the poet's search for the self through an imagined encounter with his subject. Observed from this perspective, and without regard for the context of numerous other writers' representations of Blacks or Indians, Lisitzky's *Mdurot doʿakhot* is more than an encounter with an exotic subject distant from the poet. Rather, it is a redemptive process of the self in that it is "organic and 'necessary' on his way from himself to himself" (Rabinowitz). It is also possible that poems of this kind liberate Lisitzky from the cumbersome expression of his other works. In other words, this encounter expresses his longing for the authentic primeval in reality; it represents the poet's idealization of the subject, offering up to his readers a molded model—as imagined by the author—in place of the implied model—as imagined by the implied readership.[7]

Departing significantly from those strategies, though engaged with the exotic elements of Lisitzky's poems, is a study by Ruth Arazi. Writing in 1987, she identified common themes between Native American tales and Lisitzky's poetry.[8] Arazi's is the first serious examination of the poet's claims about employing Indian tales and themes in his epic work. Among her findings is that individual tales, woven by Lisitzky into a single fabric, derive their themes from Indian folklore. "From a certain point of view," asserts Arazi,

> Lisitzky's *oeuvre* comprises a kind of Hebrew interpretation of Longfellow's work in that he emphasized and foregrounded those elements deemed significant and crucial in the historical process, which brought about the demise of the Indians.[9]

While not exactly an "interpretation of Longfellow's work," Lisitzky's composition draws on the model set by the latter. Moreover, Arazi's case of the historical processes which contributed to the demise of Native

Americans is not made persuasively by Lisitzky, whose poem is merely a microcosmic presentation of but a single encounter between Europeans and Indians.

Comparing the two, Arazi observes that while Longfellow composed his work

> out of a series of legends and tales of various past eras, . . . Lisitzky . . . clearly distinguishes the mythic layer from that of the plot, introducing the mythic into [his] work as an unambiguous interweaving of tales out of the past, stories passed down *verbatim*, from father to son. In so doing he was careful to present the legends as they appear in the scientific records of Indian legends.[10]

Arazi's claims call for some adjustment and expansion, though they represent a pivotal step in critically interrogating Lisitzky's poetic composition, and illuminating our understanding of the poet and his sources.

An inventory of Native American folktale anthologies published by the first half of the twentieth century confirms that Lisitzky did not merely rely upon themes extant in Indian folktales, but translated many, adapting them into a continuous fabric as the plot of his long work. Lisitzky was not wrong when he declared that he was preserving in, and for, Hebrew literature the vanishing songs of Native Americans. In doing so, he looked to Longfellow's strategies in "The Song of Hiawatha" as the canonical masterwork to emulate.

Lisitzky's interest in Native Americans was doubtless stimulated by the lingering resonance Longfellow's 1854 work[11] had on readers, in addition to his personal proclivity for the romanticism voiced by the pillars of Hebrew literature, Bialik and Tschernichowsky. "Hiawatha" itself emerged out of nineteenth century English Romanticism and Americans' mounting sympathy for and interest in the experiences and culture of Indian tribes that were being decimated at the time. In light of the popularity of Longfellow's poem, and the ongoing inquisitiveness about "primitive" cultures, which helped to spur the sciences of American anthropology and folklore, numerous published compilations and collections of Native American folktales depicted the religious beliefs, lifestyle, and cultures of many of the over five hundred and fifty American Indian tribes in the United States.[12]

By the *fin-de-siècle*, and with the first decades of the twentieth century, numerous anthologies of Indian life were available to readers. The continued popularity of Longfellow's composition no doubt featured centrally in inducing poets, authors, and scholars to offer up their versions in literary or scientific compositions. Longfellow's corruption of the Indian sources, claimed the critics, resulted from his reliance on Western models, among which were the Finnish Eddas and a Western unrhymed trochaic tetrameter in which he wrote his poem.[13] Subsequent anthologies "correct" this shortcoming by presenting folktales in prose or a more "authentic" poetic narrative.

It was in this cultural environment of emergent interest in the exotic Other that immigrant Hebrew writers contributed their unique perception of Native Americans. Most remained unfamiliar with anything more tangible than the verbal representation of Indians. Lisitzky appears to be no different. His activity not merely Westernized the Native Americans—as many English renditions of their myths have also done—but also Americanized the already Westernized Jews. His admission about the influence of Longfellow's epic notwithstanding, though, a closer scrutiny of *Mdurot do'akhot* reveals features which distinguish his work from that of his mentor.[14]

Though influenced by Hebrew poets—such as Tschernichowsky—who presented Hebrew translations of the world's epic tales in poetic form, Lisitzky may have also sampled anthologies in which the Indian tales are presented in poetic form, unlike Longfellow's synthetic approach.[15] Echoed in Lisitzky's introductory opening, Leland's words observe that a vast corpus of Indian poetry was vanishing among the Indians themselves, while Americans remained uninformed of the value of these, which, he adds, "were, in fact, all songs."[16] The intent of his work was to offer up a more genuine version of representative Indian tales in their more pristine state so as to educate American readers about Indian culture.

Also inspired by Lonnrot's *Kalevala* and Homer's great epics, Leland transposed the poetry of the Indians "into English metre,"[17] explaining that the original "Amerindian" song's "primitive rhythm is quite irregular, following only a general cadence rather than observing any fixed number of beats in each line."[18] Unlike Longfellow and Lisitzky, who compiled a disparate collection of tales into a single work, Leland's anthology—while preserving and retaining individual works in a more "authentic" way—also departs from these by centering on one figure, Kuloskap, Lord of Light and Creator of All.

Another indication that the original tales were actually in a form to be sung is found in the *Walam Olum*, a cultural and folkloristic chronicle of the Lanape Indians of Delaware. "The chants of the WALAM OLUM are obviously in metrical arrangement. The rhythm is syllabic and accentual, with frequent effort to select homophones . . . , and sometimes alliteration. Iteration is also called in aid, and the metrical scheme is varied in the different chants."[19]

Given all that, however, some doubt remains about whether Lisitzky was sufficiently informed of the poetic nature of the original tales, and whether he considered preserving the effect for his readers. His preference, obviously, was to emulate his predecessor, the great American poet, to present himself as an analogue among Hebrew literary figures, steadfastly holding on to well-established, and perhaps even out-of-fashion, poetic standards—in terms of meter, (mostly) unrhymed lines, elevated and allusive diction, and familiar Jewish themes—on the one hand, while introducing an exotic, "primitive," and unfamiliar culture on the other.

As in Longfellow's work, Lisitzky's representation of the world of the American Indian blurs the boundaries between a mimetic, concrete reality and the realm of myth. From the opening episode of *Mdurot doʿakhot*, the world in which the chief characters act cuts through that which separates the mythic sphere from reality, with the principal characters remaining undisturbed by this fact, indicating the relative unimportance of realism in his work.

For example, the characters in the poem are never surprised when encountering mythic beings, as in the case of the opening tale, "The Star Maiden" ("Btulat ha-kokhavim"). The hero, Nanpiwati, who abducts the heroine, Nemissah, the mythical Star Maiden,[20] is unperturbed by her supernatural abode, ability to fly, and curious vehicle. Instead, he is struck by her beauty and, true to modern Western fashion, falls in love with her. Additional examples of the mix between myth and reality abound in the composition, including the journey of the hero to the Land of the Spirits (chapter 8); references to a "vision quest," a three-day fast by the hero to bring on a vision of the future of his people when the Whites arrive;[21] and etiological stories of the medicine man, among others.[22]

Moreover, as in the case of Longfellow's story, the force of the mythic sphere fades as the plot reaches its denouement. The intersection of myth and reality, which is intact prior to the arrival of the Whites, dissolves following their appearance. Just as the metaphysical realms and the efficacy of all magic vanish, so the Indians lose the strength to stand up to the conquering Europeans. A new reality, White civilization, invades, disrupts, and supplants the old, unveiling a world of new truths.

Realizing the technological superiority of the Europeans, then, it is no surprise that Todorov's observations, in his *The Conquest of America*, find support in this account (as do Francisco Lopez de Gomara's, note 21 above). Native Americans' authentic perception of their reality is subsumed by an alien, and alienating, actuality bearing inscrutable rules. Neither does this new reality capitulate to their expectations, but is determined by the European Whites. The natives become helpless passive victims of a superior dictum from others and, regardless of any forms of resistance, finally succumb.

Lisitzky's interest in Indian tales does not begin with this long poem. Anticipating this epic work, his earliest known interest in Indians is recorded in several poems published in his 1928 anthology, *Shirim* (Poems).[23] Among them are two incorporating Native American themes and characters; the first is "Maiden of the Falls" ("Btulat ha-ʾashadot"),[24] and the other is "On Niagara Shores" ("ʿAl ḥof Niagara").[25] In both one witnesses Lisitzky's reliance on Native American stories to tell of the vanishing Indians in a romantic mode.

In a letter to the Hebrew poet and editor Yitzḥak Lamdan, Lisitzky described his introduction to *Mdurot doʿakhot* as a prose poem, one which later inspired a similar opening for his *B-ʾoholay Khush*. As if pursuing the thought formulated in his letter,[26] Lisitzky injects into his introduction the metaphor of the birth and creation of the composition, which he terms "a fabric of poetry."[27] The purpose behind creating this fabric is "to rescue and bring into our Hebrew poetry an echo of the sounds of Indian songs that fell silent."[28] Concluding his introduction, he adds that

> with the decline of the Indians, their song, soft-sounding and of delicate majesty, also declined. And if I succeeded in drawing up from the depths of their dimming horizon an echo, be it even flimsy, of this fading song—that would suffice.[29]

Out of a desire to preserve in American Hebrew poetry a rudiment of the original, "an echo of the sounds of Indian songs that fell silent," Lisitzky introduces his readers to his version of the Other. Significantly, and perhaps also ironically, at the very time of writing this work Lisitzky was also cognizant of the challenges confronting Hebrew poetry and culture in America. In the manner that Indian songs were falling into oblivion, so too was Lisitzky's work forgotten. Years later, though, before the publishing date of *B-ʾoholay Khush*, his anthology of poetry inspired by the experiences of African Americans, Lisitzky intertwined the three cultures by observing:

> One people was destroyed and eradicated from America's soil, its land from generation to generation—the Indian people. A second people was down-trodden, oppressed and debased—the Black people; and a

third people is struggling to save a vestige of its being and character within this brand new existence—the Jewish people.[30]

Demonstrating the extent to which Lisitzky depended on authentic Indian folktales is but one path in the evaluation of his compositional strategies for *Mdurot doʿakhot.* An identification of the sources he used can illuminate the extent of the poet's reliance on familiar tales, also indicating the extent of its "Americanization." This approach can also exhibit the poet's reliance on external sources and delineate an effective point of departure for original creativity within the tales, as in fusing them into a single whole. Namely, the measure of how Americanized this work is may be gauged by the degree of its literal adherence to original Indian tales (themselves an adaptation and English translation of the folklorist's record as reported by original Native American oral accounts). In the following, this pursuit will include an examination of what Lisitzky translated as against that which he did not as a demonstration of adaptation of the original to reflect his vision and tastes.

Being third among his fellow poets to publish a long poem on Native Americans, Lisitzky strove to distinguish his art from that of the rest. Nonetheless, his work shares a number of significant features with theirs. Of these the principal one is that all three writers' compositions lack direct and overt expression relating their work to the Jewish world. The works themselves—including Lisitzky's compilation *B-ʾoholay Khush,* and Eisig Silberschlag's "Mi-pi Kushim" (From the mouth of Blacks)[31]—do not indicate any expressed regard for the poets' own ethnic and religious origins, problematics, and culture.

That these works were composed in Hebrew appears coincidental. To be sure, while the poems may illuminate issues pertaining specifically to the Hebrew reader's experience in the New World, these are never stated explicitly. The expectations of the reader, as well as the very mindset of the poets themselves, make this nexus very likely. This analogical relationship is demonstrated in Lisitzky's words, cited above, as in other examples of his tendency to associate the Indian experience with that of Jews, as he did in his farewell speech to his students and community, and see below, in which he struck an analogy between the message in an Indian myth of raising the sky and the Jewish experience in America.[32]

Another common denominator among these works, with the exception of Silberschlag's—which is instructive in itself about this poet's representation of reality—is the somber and pessimistic air pervading each plot. A sense of fatalism governs the protagonists' struggle to avert the physical and cultural destruction of Black and Indian existence by European civilization and might.

Finally, each of the poets—except for Silberschlag, who composed much shorter, and mostly lyrical, poems—opens his work with a description of a seemingly idyllic life of protagonists and tribes preceding their encounter with Whites. Yet, in each instance, the strife among the very tribes anticipates the continued division among them and, with the arrival of the White Man, confirms their eventual demise.[33] The seemingly utopian existence of Native Americans concludes catastrophically as they encounter Europeans and struggle against an inevitable fate.

Lisitzky's composition of *Mdurot doʿakhot* did not arise without prior signs of interest in the subject of the Native Americans. In a review essay of Israel Efros's *Vigvamim shotkim* (Silent wigwams, 1933), dated a year before the publication of his own *Mdurot doʿakhot*, Lisitzky explores his fellow poet's long poem in ways that are more than a critique.[34] The essay offers up more insight into Lisitzky's sense of the proper ways of representing the cultures of Native Americans than about the Efros composition.

Thematically, observes Lisitzky in his essay, telling of the Indian experience presents Hebrew readers with the tragedy of the Native American as an object lesson with which Jews can identify.[35] The episode in *Vigvamim shotkim* that he takes special note of is the Hebrew poet's indirect message to readers of their own existential condition. Efros represents Native Americans as dismissing the significance of land, a detail which readers have noticed as more of a message to Jews than an actual historic fact of Indians' regard for territory, as borne out by published studies of Native American agricultural practices. For that reason, he recognizes the significance of Efros's dwelling on the importance of land possession for the survival of a people. The same criterion seems to be a fair and valid approach in comprehending Lisitzky's *Mdurot doʿakhot* as well. In terms of strategies of interpretation, then, particular Jewish issues may be sought out in the representation by Hebrew writers (and not just Lisitzky) of subjects which otherwise have no direct bearing on Jewish issues.

Among Lisitzky's objections to Efros's poem is the choice of genre made by the latter, which he calls "realistic epic."[36] In it the plot and all its components are directly and unambiguously presented for the reader. Related to this is an excessively prosaic language, accompanied by plot elements which lack a strong causal bond.[37] Lisitzky's preference is that epic works include components that are allusive and, I may add, metarealistic. Such factors lend non-realistic epics a mystery and aura which prompt variant readings issuing out of their multi-layeredness. Lisitzky's opting for Silkiner's and Longfellow's paradigms over that of Efros stems from their reliance on mythic elements which they incorporate into their stories. Mythic components need not be as closely and realistically determined as in the case of the realistic epic presented by Efros.[38]

Mdurot doʿakhot: A BRIEF SUMMARY

The poem tells of the relationship among two neighboring Indian tribes, the Children of the Serpent (Bnay-ha-shfifon) and the Children of the Vulture (Bnay-ha-peres). It begins with the marriage of the Indian chief's son, Nanpiwati, of the Children of the Serpent, with Nemissah, the Star Maiden, who gives birth to their daughter, Genetaskah. When she grows up, Genetaskah frees Midaingah, son of Hutoton, chief of the Children of the Vulture, from her father's prison. As punishment, Nanpiwati condemns his daughter to death by drowning. Tension between the two tribes increases because of a drought, fishing rights, instigations by Yahahadzah, the Medicine Man of the Children of the Vulture, and Midaingah's vision of the coming of the Whites.

Midaingah, who has fallen in love with the dead Genetaskah, seeks her in the Land of the Spirits. Upon finding her, he thinks of remaining there instead of returning to his world, where, unknown to him, his father's death by the White Men's guns has made him the heir apparent. Meanwhile, Yahahadzah, the Medicine Man, attempts to elevate his own son, Hanuhagi, to head the tribe. Hanuhagi's plan includes organizing a group of warriors, after the model of the notorious Clan of the Little Dog, to resist the Whites. His first step is to put to the stake Osnat, a White woman captured by the tribe. Returning in the nick of time from his journey, Midaingah rescues her and advises a diplomatic approach to address the incursion of the Whites, such as by unifying all Indian tribes. He gives Osnat to Nanpiwati, chief of the Children of the Serpent, to replace his dead daughter, Genetaskah. As he does so, he introduces a Lisitzky-esque twist by declaring that Nanpiwati's wife, Nemissah (the Star Maiden), too, was not a Red-Face, but became a Red-Heart. Though he finds in her some resemblance to his dead Genetaskah, Midaingah longs for his departed wife and remains disconsolate.

The Indians are divided between those who advocate a unified resistance to the Whites, and those, like Midaingah, who wish to make peace and learn from them. His pessimism grows when he fails to unify the Indians and hears about the prophesy of doom from a seer. His fears become more acute when Hanuhagi seeks to kill him, and the Whites offer to relocate the tribes farther west. The Indians' independence ends as resistance to relocation results in the suicides of Nanpiwati and Yahahadzah. Though the Indians are victorious in the first battle against the Whites, Midaingah, who comes to them with a peace offer, is imprisoned instead, and his people are driven westward. When Osnat liberates him, Midaingah takes his own life by rowing his canoe over a waterfall instead of having to leave his lands to join his displaced people.

The tale ends as another canoe, bearing Genetaskah, heads in Midaingah's direction to greet him together with the Great Spirit, Gitche Manito, at the entrance to the Spirit World.

Although Lisitzky strove to weave various Indian tales and cultural practices in his tale—including the issue of response to White incursions as treated by Silkiner—he could not completely obliterate the individual identities of some tribal ways over others. His use, for example, of the name Gitche Manito (Manitou or Manitu) for the name of the Great Spirit is indicative of his reliance on woodlands Indians' terminology. The Plains Indians used the name Wakan in reference to the Great Spirit.[39] Moreover, at least some of Lisitzky's protagonists bear names borrowed from heroes of specific groups. The idea of unifying the Indian tribes to resist a greater enemy (or promote peace and harmony), though not necessarily derived from any source, points back to one of the accomplishments of Hiawatha, founder of the Five Nations League.

Most characteristic is that Lisitzky's tale is studded with numerous Indian folktales, some told by his protagonists as object lessons, or narrated by the poet's voice to explain certain phenomena. Together, they lend an air of authenticity to the whole composition. Lisitzky's use and treatment of the original tales, many of which may be identified, is also instructive about the poet and his worldview, as will be illustrated below.

To demonstrate Lisitzky's treatment of extant Native American tales, a number of comparisons between the poet's rendition and the identifiable original accounts follows, beginning with the opening episode of *Mdurot do'akhot.* This account derives from the original Shawnee tale "The Celestial Sisters."[40] It is an account of origins, telling how the protagonist of Lisitzky's tale, Nanpiwati, meets with Nemissah, the Star Maiden, whom he eventually takes for his wife. Both the original and the Hebrew accounts tell of the marriage between the mortal hero and a celestial heroine. The story presents the larger-than-life origins of the protagonist, remotely resembling the biblical tales of Genesis 6:4 about the Nephilim and the sons of the God(s) who take wives from among mortals. In this account, Lisitzky retains a fidelity to the authentic tale, even describing the forest path leading to a clearing in the woods. It is there that twelve celestial maidens descend in a flying basket. Departing from the Indian story, Lisitzky's account dwells more on the beauty of the maidens than one finds in the original:

> It assumed the form of a basket, and was filled with twelve sisters of the most lovely form and enchanting beauty. As soon as the basket touched the ground, they leaped out, and began to dance around the magic ring, striking, as they did so, a shining ball as we strike a drum. Waupee gazed upon their graceful forms and motions from his place of concealment. He admired them all, but was most pleased with the youngest. Unable longer to restrain his admiration, he rushed out and endeavored to seize her. But the sisters, with the quickness of birds, the moment they descried the form of a man, leaped back into the basket and were drawn up into the sky.[41]

The Hebrew version extends the description of the maidens' beauty, embellishing the Indian tale by substituting specific detail in place of the general statement of their appearance. In rendering a fitting translation of the original, I have attempted to retain its rhythm and euphuistic flavor, one which succeeds in transmitting a mood and style resembling an ancient text:

> Then out jump of it so quickly,
> Light footed as are the birds,
> Fair young maidens, twelve, as they
> Were none so beautiful among his people:
> Their faces' hue as of the whiteness
> Of the lily bedewed in morn
> And the crimson of the noon-time rose.
> Their blue eyes, as the color of
> Skies at sunrise as they emerge
> From the darkness of a fading night.
> And as the brown of precious fox skin,
> A ruddy brown pure and clear,
> Was their hair as it cascaded upon
> The blueness of their robes,
> That were transparent as a spider's weave, which
> Enfolded their delicate bodies. (14b)

Further on, Lisitzky alters the account in significant ways. In the case of the latter, the original tale dwells on Waupee's hunting skills as he rushes out of hiding to capture her. By contrast, Lisitzky's hero, Nanpiwati, adopts the familiar *maskilic* (enlightened) pose reminiscent of a protagonist out of the literature of the Hebrew Haskalah period. Though he also leaps at the maidens, Nanpiwati does not attempt to capture the one who strikes his fancy. Rather than brute force, he resorts to words as he strikes the attitude of a rational protagonist to express his feelings:

Then Nanpiwati leaped
Out of his hiding place,
For all of a sudden
He was overwhelmed by a great desire to join
The dancers in their dance.
And as he leaped he cried out
In a wild voice, overcome by savage murmurs:
"Let me, oh, wondrous maidens,
Ere I ask of you who you be
And whence you come,
To whirl with you in your dance
For it be so nice and pleasant—
My heart goes out to your dance,
For a dark spirit it be a salve." (15a–b)

Lisitzky's hero is cultured, polite, and psychologically more genuine than Waupee, hero of the original account. He is initially depressed, for the sight of the young maiden becomes for him "a salve for a dark spirit."[42] The heavenly maidens' dance does not arouse him sexually as much as aesthetically, which explains his wish to join their dance. Any outburst of desire is suppressed by a loquacity, even if it be "a wild voice, overcome by savage murmurs," characterizing his subordination of instinct for intellect. Breaking out in a run toward them, Nanpiwati maintains his eloquence, aiming not to seize but to dance, not to fall upon but to persuade as to his honorable intention.

Nanpiwati also declares that their dance will bring succor to his dark spirit—"marpe bo l-ruaḥ kehah!" Though generally understood, the phrase is also allusive to classical sources, which further illuminate the nuanced expression. In the *Tanakh*, the sole instance combining the two terms, "ruaḥ kehah" ("a dark spirit"), is in Ezekiel 21:12: "v-rafu khol-yadayim v-khihatah khol-ruaḥ" ("and every heart shall melt, and all hands shall be slack, *and every spirit shall be faint*, and all knees shall drip with water"). This nexus begs the conclusion that it is not the hero's physical strength which has been dissolved, but that his spirit is low, and he has lost courage. An attitude of this kind is very much out of character for an Indian hero, though not Lisitzky's, whose anguish is described over several columns.

Also, the physical cause of his spiritual faintness is not depression or sadness, whose raison d'être is absent in this episode, but the very beauty of the maidens, their dance, and the sound of the beating drums. Together, these elements constitute the aesthetic force which engenders his weakness so much so that he loses the courage to capture his heart's desire.

The maidens in both accounts flee their pursuers. But it is the youngest among them in Lisitzky's account, Nemissah, the one who has yet to master her spirit and curiosity, who is drawn back to Nanpiwati and lingers before her sisters draw her away in their escape from the mortal.[43]

While Nanpiwati remains helplessly depressed, Waupee of the folk account resorts to magical measures to cunningly ensnare the one whom he fancies: he disguises himself, first as a possum and later as a mouse. It is this nature of the Indian hero which Lisitzky recasts. Nanpiwati, by contrast, is more anguished, his instincts suppressed. The idea of employing deception to seize his beloved does not even cross his mind. Instead, his parents come to his aid. They offer their advice, cautioning him against attempting to capture a celestial maiden. Their manner is more in keeping with members of an intellectual and enlightened society in which liberal-minded parents resort to verbal persuasion than with parents in a folktale.

When, in the folktale, Waupee captures the nameless celestial maiden, he takes her for his wife. Nanpiwati, Lisitzky's protagonist, does not do so; he is the complete gentleman. After his second attempt, he too succeeds in apprehending the maiden Nemissah,[44] but then resorts to language and logical persuasion to explain his intent to take her for a wife. She, as Lisitzky's cultured and enlightened protagonist, also responds tastefully and logically, accepting his proposal of her own free will:

> Only willingly I shall be subdued to you
> I shall be your wife by my will—
> Hold me, wondrous lad,
> Lead me and bring me
> To your land and people! (20a)

Such manipulations to alter the personal qualities of his protagonists are but a few indications that Lisitzky does not merely translate the Indian stories but adapts them to reflect his culturally determined judgment. For all the critical comment about this composition being an outlet for his passions, Lisitzky mutes the sexually primitive overtones of the folktale, suppressing his protagonists' impulse. Instead, he transforms their relationship to an intellectual discussion based on enlightened, democratic rules of sensitivity, respect, equality, and free choice.

When, after their marriage, the heroine of the tale longs for her parents' home, Lisitzky, foregrounding his romantic and dramatic powers, gives free rein to his imagination to describe effusively and in detail Nemissah's anguish. Such overpowering language heightens the dramatic situation in Lisitzky's work. So when she leaves Nanpiwati to visit her parents, Nemissah wishes to return to him at once. By contrast, the heroine of the folktale prepares at length for her journey, planning to remain with her parents for a protracted period. Nemissah, out of love for him, decides to return to Nanpiwati after only a day's visit, despite her parents' entreaty that she remain longer:

> "Very well"—replied her father
> "On this I shall agree, but
> Do beware: if Nanpiwati
> Will not ascend with you
> To our native land—
> You come up without him
> With the fruit of thy womb that you bear
> For it will be endangered, Nemissah:
> For if to a mortal does conceive
> A maiden of celestial beings—
> If she does not rescue the fruit of her womb,
> If it remain on earth,
> A curse, per chance will be upon it,
> With it and all who join it,
> Thus have I spoken, see, I warn thee!" (25b–26a)

More than in the folktale, Lisitzky's account is sensitive to the values of family integrity and love between husband and wife. Nemissah is concerned for the well-being of her husband and child more than about her parents' wishes. Her desire prevails over their pressure, as her father attempts to block her return to earth by physically locking her up. Though attentive to social norms, Lisitzky places greater import on a woman's feelings than on the values of the authoritarian and patriarchal milieu out of which he came.

The Indian story addresses itself to the celestial sphere, wherein all the mythical creatures are transfigured into familiar animals. Lisitzky, though, remains faithful to the notion that love brings people together, even the celestial woman with her earth-bound husband. Having failed to persuade Nanpiwati to return with her to the heavens, and in the face of his acquiescence that she leave him and return to her parents, Nemissah embraces his world by uttering words evocative of the biblical Ruth's dramatic promise to Naomi:

"No!"—she responded tearfully—
"Whither you settle I shall settle—
Without you what have I, who is for me?
With you I shall stay on earth,
Together with you to share
The good and the bad;
Without you, Nanpiwati,
Sevenfold will every good be bad for me,
Together with you, Nanpiwati,
Sevenfold will every bad be good for me!" (27a–b)

In contrast to the original folktale, Lisitzky's rendition underscores the significance of words. It is by them that the plot progresses, not by actions. Characters affect others by what they say, foregrounding the value of mutual respect, communication, and, above all, logic to affect and persuade. In so doing, Lisitzky modernizes and Westernizes the Indian story, as many American and European writers have done with authentic Indian tales. He humanizes the protagonists of the exotic tale, altering them to mirror his own milieu, in the same way as many Western renditions treated Indian folklore. He also Americanizes and romanticizes Indians in the European sense, making them products of an enlightened, modern world. The reader, who learns to accept the Other by virtue of this account, is also presented with a sanitized version of a world purportedly unlike his own, although as human as his.

Lisitzky relies heavily on Native American folktales extant and available by his day in a number of scientific and popular collections. Though most were in prose form, and we have noted some evidence to support the contention that their originals were either sung or chanted by Native Americans, Lisitzky gave the tales poetic form, much as he witnessed in Longfellow's model. His choice to open his long poem with the above account, which is not first in the Schoolcraft anthology he obviously used, stems from the modern character of his tale. It needed a beginning closer to reality, so he avoided tales of creation or etiology. Instead, he found an account suitable for the introduction of his characters so as to present a unified tale, one focused on the drama of individuals struggling against a fate meted out by a cruel turn of events.

Though Lisitzky appropriated known Native American tales, he not only acknowledged doing so, but used them to ameliorate the image of the Indian. For example, he molded his translation in such ways as to represent a positive image of the hero as a romantic and "modern" individual. His representation of the Other did not emerge out of a desire to accept the exotic for what it is but in order to impose his vision of universal human nature on his protagonist. In place of depicting his subjects in a realistic vein, he favored the allusive, mythical approach, combined with ingredients which converted them to familiar, unthreatening beings.

It is quite likely that the original volumes out of which Lisitzky read, translated, and transposed the tales into Hebrew can be identified, as can the version he selected. This claim may be supported, in part, by the extent to which he retained the details and adhered to the order of original narratives. Though he took some liberties in some instances, as by imposing his own descriptions on the originals, his emendations do not alter the sources. In so doing, Lisitzky set his composition apart from Silkiner's and Efros's and became in effect Hebrew literature's Longfellow. Yet neither the prior cultural affinity (Jewish) nor the language (Hebrew) of the text was instrumental and efficacious in making his compilation as seminal as Longfellow's. For at the very time that he was busily composing *Mdurot do'akhot*, his readership in America continued to wane. America's Jews were becoming assimilated at a rate that deprived Hebrew writers of a significant audience. To be sure, Lisitzky's work was also suitable as a means of acclimating Jews, or readers of Hebrew, to America and its culture, but few needed his guiding hand to make the transition.

One of the overriding issues in *Mdurot do'akhot* is Lisitzky's penchant for the Other, a matter touched upon in many of his poems. This attraction to the outsider no doubt has to do with Lisitzky's personal odyssey from East European Orthodox Judaism to become a liberal, all-inclusive, worldly individual. Discernible in his poetry and prose are his interest in other faiths and sympathy for minorities, evidenced by his personal visits to African American churches and his composition of poetry in the spirit of religious hymns. His inquisitiveness into the early, primitive, and primordial roots of America is in keeping with an affinity he harbored for the ancient, untainted, undisrupted, and ideal in experience.[45] Lisitzky reached the apotheosis of these sentiments in his immense and difficult allegorical poem, *Naftulay Elohim* (Divine struggles, 1934). This ambitious work, presenting a spiritual odyssey in quest of eternal truths, embraced all religions, envisaging races and faiths coming together as a victory of mankind over the forces of evil.

More than just a retelling of Indian tales, however, *Mdurot doʿakhot* illuminates the reciprocal relationship between the Hebrew poet and the exotic, Native American literary and cultural landscape. Through his act of sanitizing and Westernizing the world Lisitzky promoted an acceptance of the authenticity of the Other. On the other hand, contact with Indian tales—altered as they were—Americanized Hebrew literature as much as did street life on the Lower East Side. It brought to the Hebrew reader's attention an awareness of other minorities struggling to retain a modicum of identity in the crucible that is America. Situating the Other, be s/he Black or Indian, in isolation, without contact with Jews, opened Hebrew literature to the Other as much as did many of Moshe Smilansky's Arab romances set in Eretz Israel at about the same time.[46]

More than a few of the borrowed stories contained in *Mdurot doʿakhot* foreground Lisitzky's penchant for locating universal messages in them. It is very likely, indeed, that a chief criterion for selecting some tales over others is their moral, which may be elicited to fit the message of his account. More than a translation, his use of the stories becomes an act of transformation. Lisitzky's sophisticated literary stratagems modify the original account, augmenting it in subtle or manifest ways. His manipulations give rise to a more enhanced tale, embellished and transformed at its deepest layers.

One example concerns the tale of the Young Dog Band (*Mdurot*, 179–189), told by Hanuhagi, son of Yahahadzah the Medicine Man, in support of his plan to form a cadre of elite warriors to thwart the White Man. The reader learns that while in exile from the tribe, Hanuhagi had personally witnessed the Dance of the Young Dog Band among the fictitious "Ree" tribe. Indeed, the source of Lisitzky's tale originated among the Cree Indians, whose identity he slightly altered.[47] Lisitzky even retains the seemingly inconsequential note in the original, describing it as a dance "borrowed from the Crees," by the Pawnee Indians.[48]

The relationship between the two accounts is uncanny. Lisitzky not only adheres to the original, but he also preserves its peculiar details, such as a curious description of the hero lying unclothed in a pit as he waits to trap an eagle.[49] In Lisitzky's account it is his hero, Hanuhagi, who borrows the tale he heard in order to organize a "Young Dog Society" ("Agudat kelev tzaʿir," 188b) within his tribe.

The tale is of a young brave's encounters, in a dream, with a host of magical animals who, every evening, turn into humans. They bestow upon him attributes of their own identity that will make of him a great warrior. It is in imitation of this event that the Young Dog Society is established, incorporating a ritual of the Young Dog Dance to recapture the magical powers granted to the story's hero.[50] Lisitzky retains all the details, even the order in which the animals address the brave—owl, buffalo bull, porcupine, eagle, whooping crane, deer, and bear—as they bestow upon him the same gifts as in the Indian tale.

The significant points of departure include Lisitzky's enhancing of represented discourse. He added more of the protagonists' direct speech, and gave each animal nearly equal space to speak about its traits and gift to the Indian brave. Even in cases where the original account becomes abbreviated, as when the utterances of the buffalo, deer, and bear are only reported in the Indian tale by means of indirect speech, Lisitzky's account alters it to direct discourse, and at a length equal to the others. Another peculiarity in the Hebrew is the mention of Atius Tirawa by the protagonist[51] as the name of the Father-Spirit—explained in a rare footnote by Lisitzky. It is also called "the Great Spirit,"[52] to whom the brave addresses his prayers. Although appearing in the same volume containing the original tale as in Spence's *Myths of the North American Indians*, the name is not mentioned in the same tale but in the book's Glossary, where it is explained as "Principal deity of the Pawnees."[53]

It is by manipulating discourse that Lisitzky's account becomes more dramatic and emotionally nuanced. The same technique underscores my assertion that the tendency to sharpen the psychological dimension of the protagonists is one of the trademarks in Lisitzky's adaptation of Indian stories.[54]

Flood stories abound in many cultures, including those of the New World. Lisitzky's chosen Indian tale tells of a flood that people attempt to outrun by heading to the Coteau des Prairies, the Mountain of the Prairies, Minnesota.[55] The flood waters, however, continue to rise, drowning even those who have reached that haven. In recognition of their act, Gitche Manito, the good Supreme Being, turns them into a red stone, of which peace pipes are fashioned to this day.[56]

A comparison of the folk account with Lisitzky's Hebrew version is revealing. Temporarily cut in half, the first part of the original is told by the principal protagonist, Nanpiwati, who recounts it during the peace pow wow with Hutoton, chief of "Children of the Vulture," the rival neighboring tribe. Nanpiwati tells the tale to complement Hutoton's story of the origins of fire among the Indians.

In the original Indian flood tale, one woman survives the rising waters. She is saved by War Eagle, probably an incarnation of Gitche Manito, and marries him to become the mother of all Indian peoples.[57] The message of the Indians' common ancestry is delayed in Lisitzky's rendition, to be expressed in the second half as it is told by a minor character. In his presentation, Nanpiwati uses the tale to underscore the familial unity of the Indians by observing the symbolic act of sharing a peace pipe, one comprised of the ancestors' bodies:

> We struck a covenant with the pipe:
> For as our ancestors' bodies cleaved,
> By one inseparable union,
> Within the rock of which they were hewn,
> So will cleave together
> Hearts of "Children of the Serpent"
> With "Children of the Vulture,"
> And as they inhale together
> The sweet scent of its smoke
> So will they together aspire
> For peace's delight forevermore. (144a–b)

Lisitzky's interruption of the original folktale is accomplished by inserting this "midrashic" explanation for the act of smoking the peace pipe. The Indian tale, as noted, makes no mention of this interpretation for the ritual. Though both underscore the solidarity among Native American tribes, the poet's insertion interrogates the tale in a new way, reading the physical characteristics of the pipe as symbolic—the stone comprised of the fused bodies of the ancient dead, its redness denoting their blood and bodies—in place of relying on the memory of a common mother to all.

Lisitzky's narrative resumes as Nanpiwati glories in the idea of peace and brotherhood among neighboring tribes, saying, "But sevenfold more splendid [than blue skies or grassy earth] / is the dwelling together of neighboring tribes" ("Ulam yaftah shivʿatayim / shevet shvatim shkhenim gam yaḥad," 144b), echoing the familiar words of Psalm 133:1 that also embodies a rich alliterative consonance.

It is left to Yahahadzah, the Medicine Man, to recall the deleted segment of the folktale. He concludes the original tale and explains its moral as in keeping with the source.[58] As a "man of the cloth" and bearer of memory, it is he who tells of the common ancestry of all tribes by the union of the surviving woman and War Eagle. His observations underscore the mythic or historical function of the peace ceremony. Significantly, he shares Nanpiwati's message, even employing the latter's formula, but in a negative vein. Echoing Nanpiwati's formula of the sevenfold benefit of peace, Yahahadzah's propensity for contrariness is illustrated by his words: "Sevenfold worse is war / for in its wrath it destroys / the victor as the vanquished" ("nor'ah sheva ha-milḥamah / ki tkatzeh vʿevratah / ka-mnatzḥim ka-mnutzaḥim").[59] While Nanpiwati dwells on the beauties of nature and makes peace sevenfold more desirable, Yahahadzah focuses on the calamities wrought by the northern wind and finds conflicts among Indians as sevenfold more pernicious. So while the message he brings reiterates Nanpiwati's, it is subtly different, anticipating his continued treachery as one of Nanpiwati's adversaries. Seeming to complement and complete Nanpiwati's message, Yahahadzah's words allude to his attempted overthrow of Nanpiwati's rule. This sinister quality is anticipated by the negative mindset his words convey, as one in whose imagination war and conflict are at the root of his metaphor.

The episode continues by mimicking the structure of the greater composition. In the same manner as the larger story opens with a mythic plot and concludes on one much more real, this exchange among the participants in the peace talks also opens with accounts out of both tribes' mythology and, when all have had their say, continues as Nanpiwati reports on the arrival of White men and the danger they pose.[60]

One of the most dramatic tales found among many Indian traditions is the hero's pursuit of his beloved to the Land of the Spirits, referred to above. Of all, Lisitzky singled out the Chippewa version of the Orphic tale, which reads like the ultimate expression of love between the protagonists.[61] Recognizing its romantic potential, Lisitzky incorporated it into his composition.

It is the tale of love transcending death, an apt story for a poet whose life story of loss and pain was accompanied by a penchant for emotional literary expression. In this instance, Lisitzky's hero, Midaingah (son of Hutoton, chief of the Children of the Vulture) seeks his beloved Genetaskah (daughter of Nanpiwati, chief of the Children of the Serpent) in the Land of the Spirits. The account follows many of the same details as in the folktale. Unlike in the Indian original, though, where the hero seems to know of the Land of the Spirits and the way there, Midaingah learns of it from the story of Yahahadzah, the tribal Medicine Man.[62] This slight change heightens the tale's drama while offering a reliable authority about the world beyond from one who should know. However, this interjection adds a measure of psychological intrigue as well, for Yahahadzah's motive is to induce Midaingah to take the journey and facilitate his son's rise to leadership.

Unlike the original, Lisitzky's story is simpler in detail and focused on elements that heighten its dramatic features. He creates dialogues where there were none, and extends those which existed, heightening the romantic tension between the lovers as they meet and part.

Arriving at the lake surrounding the Land of the Spirits, Midaingah boards a white stone canoe and notices Genetaskah in a canoe alongside. His anguished heart calls out to her, lending him greater psychological credence in the account by Lisitzky, who adds a particular Hebraic allusion in depicting the white canoe, described as of the whiteness of sapphire, "livnat sapir" (157a). Derived from Exodus 24:10 and Ezekiel 1:26, the words constitute a theophany account. In the poem, the term assigns a metaphysical aura to the canoe, deemed magical in Indian lore.[63]

While the folk story foregrounds the Land of the Spirits as the chief theme of the tale, Lisitzky's emphasizes the hero's great love for Genetaskah, whom he attempts to join prematurely. At their conclusion, both tales preserve the command that the hero return to the Land of the Living to complete his destiny. However, the command to "Go back" of the original account[64] is not motivated as strongly as it is in the case of Midaingah, in his expression of love and desire to remain with his beloved.[65] Unlike in the Indian tale, which ends soon after an inner voice lectures the hero about his obligation to fulfill his destiny, Genetaskah tearfully accompanies Midaingah on his return canoe trip to the lake's shore, promising to be faithful and to await his return "day and night."[66] Underscoring the romantic theme, the Hebrew account also attributes the hero's successful journey to the help of Gitche Manito, the Great Spirit, who "does not scorn / a perfect heart and true love."[67] Even divine help is extended to those who love truly, who are pure of heart.

Lisitzky's story is less an account of heroic prowess than a romantic story of unvanquished love. His tale is less concerned with frightening the reader about the horrors impeding the hero's journey, and more with a nuanced characterization attained by extending the discourse among protagonists. While the original Chippewa hero hears the message of the Master of Life in the wind, urging him to return to the Land of the Living,[68] Lisitzky psychologizes the account as his hero hears an inner voice urging him to go on living, a message soon repeated by Genetaskah as she accompanies his canoe back to shore.[69]

The original folktale is not without its psychological "realism," though. At the folktale's conclusion, the hero appears to awaken from a dream in which he saw and experienced all that has transpired, and did not physically make the journey himself.[70] Lisitzky's hero, however, continues to hear the words of the Great Spirit commanding him to fulfill his destiny before returning again to the Land of the Spirits. The account ends with the voice of the heroine repeating her promise of faithfulness that she will wait, day and night, until he joins her.[71]

It is quite certain that, as declared in his foreword, Lisitzky aimed to preserve Native American tales for his readers. To do so, he remained true to his sources, not inventing new stories, except for the encompassing plot framing the tales in a creative and imaginative way. It is in this process—of composing the frame story, selecting specific tales over others from his sources, and lending protagonists and themes a Western flavor—that Lisitzky rises above the tales he uses.

The strategy of integrating Native American tales into the fabric of his poetry is not an isolated instance for Lisitzky. We witness his preoccupation with Native American themes in the years before and after publication of *Mdurot do'akhot.* Such a broad sweep over time in and of itself distinguishes him from Silkiner and Efros, whose writings on the subject were limited to one or two compositions. Following publication of his long poem, Lisitzky published a number of short works that underscore his ongoing engagement with the subject.

One of these, "At eventide" ("'im 'erev," 1939),[72] focuses on the demise of Indians. In this poem, however, Lisitzky's poetry bears a new emphasis. It departs from the narrow concerns of his subject and points to a parallel experience of Indians and Jews by the poem's analogical structure. In the first part, the poet tells of Indians appearing in an apparition, dancing around a fire, and gathering to hear the words of a wise man. The episode is about the extinction of the Indian nation. The poem's second half focuses on the heroes of ancient Israel, underscoring the nexus which its writer strikes between the fates of the two nations. In conclusion, the poet asks whether the second scene is also fated to never reappear—that the Jews, like the Indians before them, are doomed to cease being.

The poem may be the earliest direct analogy struck by the poet between the fate of Native Americans and Jews. Later, Lisitzky explicitly joins the fates of Indians, Blacks, and Jews in his introductory words to his 1953 autobiography, *Eleh toldot adam.*[73] The poem strikes an analogy between Indians' fate and that of the Jews in America, a theme in the foreground of

Lisitzky's consciousness by this time. Aside from resembling Bialik's long poem, "Mtay midbar" ("The dead of the wilderness"),[74] it is also proof of the poet's longstanding awareness of the analogical possibilities inherent in the subject of the exotic as a mirror of the Jews. Any earlier connection struck by readers between these groups, then, is a legitimate act which Lisitzky left unstated.

Later, in 1947, Lisitzky published an anthology of long poems in which he included "Nightly vision" ("Ḥazon mi-laylah"),[75] a composite of accounts by several characters (artist, violinist, dancer, poet, and philosopher) sharing their life experiences. In the third episode,[76] Lisitzky tells of the dancer's love affair with Winona, an Indian maiden from the American West. "In describing her, the dancer becomes artist and musician," states Menachem Ribalow in his introduction.[77] He also discerns a similarity between the voice of this narrator and that of *Mdurot doʿakhot* as it unfolds a tale of personal loss and scorn reminiscent of Lisitzky's experiences. For the artist, the dancer's death becomes a metaphor for the loss of the primordial force in art. She is the bearer of characteristics reminding the narrator of Venus, nature, and freedom, child-like innocence and spiritual purity.[78]

As they dance together before audiences—with the dancer believing that in so doing he had saved her from a career in cheap saloons—she begins to wither away. Exposed to White civilization, the natural forces in her ebb, very much like the experience of the Indians in *Mdurot doʿakhot.* Similarly, her tribe also wastes away as they sing "a song of dejection, the cry of a vestige of a tribe / the moan of the last generation, survivor of a mighty people / soon will pass and cease to be from the world."[79]

Following her death, his ability to perform comes to an end. He has lost his muse and natural force. As well as a tale of a vanishing Indian, and the loss of the artist's inspiration, the poem is an expression of Lisitzky's fundamental pessimism about life. The unhappy ending is characteristic of the poems of this collection.

The poet's preoccupation with the Niagara landscape continues in his poetry even after publishing *Mdurot doʿakhot* in 1937. In a segment of a 1956 poem, "Niagara Falls" ("Ashdot Niagara"), the poet recalls his walks by the falls as a young man—when he served as teacher in a Buffalo, New York, Talmudic academy, and was facing an emotional crisis. The poem expresses the narrator's personal dejection, a mood suspiciously bordering on a suicidal impulse, evoking similar moods in Lisitzky's own past, as in his *In the Grip of Cross Currents.*[80] As the narrator walks along the falls, his imagination transports him back to the days when the region was populated by Indians and primordial forests. His vision includes the Maid of the Mist, who beckons him to join her in the abyss and there escape his earthly torments.[81]

Another conscious intersection of the Jewish experience with that of the Indians is in an etiological story about pushing up the sky. Citing the Indian tale of people who cooperatively push the sky higher in order to make room for human habitation on earth, Lisitzky states that this is also the destiny of the Jewish nation ever since Sinai.[82]

To tell the tale, Lisitzky uses two available primary sources. His title reflects the account that focuses on the origins of the term "Yahu!" However, the story also foregrounds the motif of pushing up the sky of the other source. Regardless of whether he attempted to meld the two tales, his preference for the first of these is instructive about Lisitzky's revision of the tale's message. As reported, the Indian story is an etiological "why" tale answering the question, "Why do we use the word 'Yahu!' when working in unison?" Though implicit, the second question—"Why is the sky so high?"—remains beneath the narrative surface.

The overriding message Lisitzky finds in the tale is stated explicitly in both renditions, though for different purposes. In his poetic treatment, "The righteous of the world"—"ḥasidim b-ʾumot ha-ʿolam"—the Indian story is placed in the mouth of an old man who, after telling the narrator the story of Johnny Appleseed, closes with the moral of the Snohomish tale.[83] In that tale, the speaker—doubling as the poet's voice—reinterprets the message to represent the lifting of the human spirit along with that of the skies to meet the Almighty who will bestow upon it of the upper spheres: "And as it [the call "Yahu!"] rises, God's glory will descend toward it / And shall impart of His radiance that will emanate from the upper heavenly spheres" ("V-khaʾasher terom el ʿal yered kvod elohim lʿumatah / v-hishrah vah zivo yaʾatzilo mi-sfirot shamayim ʿelyonot."[84] This gift, continues Lisitzky, is granted only to those selected by God in each generation who, by performing acts of goodness and kindness, raise the sky through the love they hold for their Maker and fellow humans.

Lisitzky's conscious misreading of the tale promotes his vision of the human spirit confronted by the persistent onslaught of misery, suffering, and injustice. Though verging on pessimism, the poet's message is of hope, perseverance, and triumph. The Indian tale serves as a vehicle for this message. Read another way, the moral validates the folktale as bearer of universal truths.

In a later pronouncement, delivered on the occasion of his retirement,

Lisitzky used the same tale for a more particular, Jewish purpose: it is the Jews who are entrusted with the responsibility of raising the skies, he adds. The task is attained not by the universal forces of love and kindness but by the force of spirit, of Torah, faith, tradition, and culture.[85] Preceding the retelling of the folktale, he notes that "a moral is concealed within it,"[86] which he proceeds to decipher for his audience:

> This was our historical and fateful destiny ever since Sinai: to uplift the sky with poles, not those of wood as the poles of those Indians but of spirit, which we have fashioned for ourselves. And they possess the strength of the Eternal who will not deceive [a reference to 1 Sam. 15:29]. The one who identified this destiny of ours was Rabbi Yisraʾel Baʿal Shem Tov, who explicated by it the words in Ethics of the Fathers, "Know that which is above you," [namely] know that which is higher than you, that which rises to high spheres because of you, by means of you, by your power it rises. And Rabbi Menaḥem Mendl of Kotzk said it explicitly: man was created to uplift the sky.
>
> And this is my message to you: prepare spiritual poles, those of *Torah*, faith, tradition, and culture, and continue to push the sky with them to lift it up from its baseness. We cannot stand and survive today in a world whose skies have been so debased. "How shall Jacob stand?" [a reference to Amos 7:2,5]—we shall not be renewed [without doing]. Let us be faithful to our fateful and historic destiny—the uplifting of the sky from its baseness.
>
> And with the same Indian call I leave you: "Yahu!"—lift up the sky.[87]

In the above, Lisitzky merely uses the Indian tale in a Jewish context. The Jews have become the larger-than-life protagonists of a story in which the sky itself takes on added significance. The different purposes to which this tale is put are an indication of Lisitzky's "midrashic" propensity. Selecting from a plethora of Indian folktales, he strove to elicit suitable universal or Jewish messages. The midrashic process, so familiar to Lisitzky from his traditional upbringing, provided a creative rereading of those tales to elicit latent meanings which bore the poet's message.

Given Lisitzky's penchant for glossing over the more "authentic" mythical and etiological relevance of Indian tales, his re-presentation of them in a sanitized or literarily enhanced fashion compromised their authenticity. Having identified the sources of a significant portion of these tales, we are challenged to seek out his strategies by interrogating those very texts. One result of this process underscores Lisitzky's penchant for identifying contemporary latent ethical messages in the tales. That is, in place of recognizing Indians as Others, accepting their ways, views, and values as different, he forces upon their tales alien didactic messages which they do not possess. However, it may be that, from the outset, the Indian tales are more sophisticated than their superficial denotations indicate.

In considering a qualitative shift in Lisitzky's regard for and treatment of Indian folktales, at times before and following *Mdurot*, we can propose that it is in such instances that the reader is tempted to perceive the implicit inclusion of the state of American Jewry in the picture. This seems not to be the poet's sole objective, however, for he does not mention Jewry even once in the work, preferring to promote the universal brotherhood of all mankind, a sentiment validated by his other works as well, and in particular his *Naftulay Elohim* (Divine struggles, 1934).[88]

In presenting the lives and experiences of others, Lisitzky also added a new dimension to Hebrew literature, expanding it beyond its narrow, parochial confines. It is this process which, more than anything else, Americanized Hebrew belles lettres and those who contributed to it, giving rise to the Bellows, Malamuds, Ozicks, Potoks, and Roths of later years. In other arts, too, the same interest has yielded fruitful results in the works of such as George Gershwin, Mel Brooks, and Leonard Bernstein, to name but a few. It is through this kind of engagement with non-Jewish lives, experiences, values, and images that Hebrew literature in America distinguished itself from other Hebrew literary centers in the world. It is also through such interests that Hebrew fiction paved the way for Jewish society's ongoing interest in Black, Hispanic, and Indian experiences—be it in conjunction with those of Jews or in isolation from those concerns—in American Jewish literature and arts.

FANTASY OR PLAIN FOLK: IMAGINING NATIVE AMERICANS

Chapter Four

Ever since Silkiner's long poem, Hebrew literature has continued to struggle with the tendency to stereotype Native Americans. The seeming dearth of intimate familiarity and social contact between Jews and Native Americans underlies part of the reason. Representations of First Nations in American Hebrew letters tend to rely heavily on a range of popular stock features of Indian culture, a matter that continued to perpetuate their exoticism and remoteness. Remaining beyond the sphere of a true familiarity, Native Americans continued to be for Hebrew literature the unknown Others, superficial images in place of fleshed-out individuals. Nonetheless their representation as the foremost indigenous and exotic population in America was a matter of necessity for any immigrant literature bent on Americanizing itself. As we have already seen, because of this lack of familiarity some Hebrew writers were led to draw upon extant Indian tales, which they rendered into usable Western generic mediums—verse or prose. However, the patently obvious rendition of original Indian tales into Hebrew perpetuated the chasm between the imagined and real Indian, giving rise to a desire among other writers to offer more realistic portraits of Native Americans.

Because of the few instances demonstrating a desire to capture Indian life in a more realistic fashion, we can assert with confidence that this was not the primary goal of most writers, though for some it was. Instead, most resorted to stock Indian images or themes as metaphors for personal, national, or existential concerns. As will be illustrated in the following, Indians stood for the possibility of co-existence with nature. With the realization of the demise of Native American life, this possibility became an unattainable ideal, or it stood for the loss of some human authenticity crushed by the forces of modernism. In other instances, Indians represented a loss of an authentic culture as Western civilization overtook them, rendering them a fitting projection of the poets' sense of the fate of their own people. Only in a few instances is there any evident desire to represent contemporary Indian life in a mimetically realistic mode.

Incorporating specific ingredients, be they realistic or mythic, about American Indians has distinguished a significant body of Hebrew writings from the greater corpus of modern Hebrew literature, lending it an exotic air. Some of the interest in Native Americans emerges out of pervasive motives in Jewish culture at the time of its encounter with America. This is evidenced, for example, by Lisitzky's maskilic characterizations of his Indian protagonists. Other motives for engaging the Indian theme emerged as Hebrew writers touched upon a range of realities in the New World.

Among the motives, a humanistic empathy for the marginalized and downtrodden Natives constituted a cause sufficiently widespread in America to impact on urbanized twentieth century Hebrew writers as well. This interest intersected in the past with familiar principles in the programmatic ideology of the Haskalah, rendering it an indigenous mission arising also from within the modern Hebraic movement. It included a drive to empathize with the underdog, to lend a voice in the call for justice as applicable to the social, economic, and political well-being of Indian civilization, and to learn more about them. Hebrew writers need not have looked beyond the most superficial factors affecting Indians' marginalization to speak up on their behalf.

The desire to know and support the Other was an ideological given for Hebraists who took up the causes of the Haskalah. To know the Other was to foster individual self-improvement; an appreciation of the diverse attitudes and values among humans meant self-enhancement, hallmarks of the age of liberalism and tolerance. The opportunity to be cognizant of the world beyond the narrow confines of the self, and of Jewish civilization in particular, is also a mark of the Enlightenment, pursued variously by Hebraists seeking modes of representation of wider thematic horizons.

Representation of the world in a romantic vein was and remains one of the dominant currents in Hebrew belles lettres. By this mode authors were equipped to incorporate national, sentimental, and existential themes befitting their era. Similarly, the measure to which a work was romanticized charted the extent to which these writers treated the American Indian more or less realistically. An abiding interest in primitivism, a feature of Western literary art since Rousseau, was also at the root of Hebrew interest in Native Americans. Their culture was depicted as a pristine civilization intimately connected to nature, to whom Western mechanized and industrialized technology was alien, inimical, and artificial. In the clash between Europeans and Native Americans the latter were ultimately crushed by a culture bent on imperialistic voraciousness for dominion, for resources, and for territory. For Jews impacted for centuries by Western hostility, the lot of Native Americans reflected their own experiences reaching back to a time when they, too, led a pristine existence. Their interest in writing of Indians, then, stemmed out of a desire to caution their coreligionists about the fate awaiting any people coming into contact with Western civilization.

Hebrew literature is by no means the sole medium displaying an interest in Native Americans. As in Hebrew, Yiddish culture, too, gave rise to compositions and accounts pertaining to Indians. Among these is I. Y. Schwartz's long poem *Kentucky*, and Sheen Daixel's Indian stories.[1] In Europe, this interest was represented by a host of writers, among them Germany's Karl May (1842–1912), whose contact with Indians was also decidedly limited, indicating the tenuous link between the real and the imagined culture of the Other.[2] Yet his imaginary works engendered the romantic subgenre of Indians in Western literature and catalyzed others to follow in his footsteps. In music, the great composer and lover of nature, Antonin Dvořák (1841–1904), who traveled in the United States between 1892 and 1895, was sufficiently inspired by the music of Blacks and Indians to integrate them into his compositions.

For others, Indians served as emblems of Europeans subjugated by other Europeans. Henryk Sienkiewicz's "Sachem," for example, recounts the tale of German settlers in America who eradicate and supplant an Indian tribe, a not too subtle allusion to German or Prussian treatment of Poles.[3] European curiosity and interest in American Indians has only grown in recent decades, engendering works of literature, social clubs, and a host of activities bespeaking interest in Native Americans' culture and practices.[4]

The particular fecundity of Jewish writings about Indians was perpetuated as they and their heirs took up writing in English and became part of America. Many Jews entered the disciplines of anthropology and folklore to study Native American culture and civilization. In the realm of belles lettres, Bernard Malamud composed a posthumously published novel, *The People*, adding to his writings about African Americans. These endeavors took their place alongside Gershwin's *Porgy and Bess* and descended into popular film culture in Mel Brooks' over-the-top satirical production *Blazing Saddles*.[5]

The following is an exploration of the range of intimacies that Hebrew literature has attained in representing the Indian experience in America, from the most generalized references mentioned in passing, as metaphors or sketched in the barest of outlines, to those where Indians feature prominently, and at times less superficially. The recognition that the White Man played a leading role in the annihilation of First Nations peoples, and the consequent literal or figurative implications, foregrounds a number of more tangible aspects of Native Americans. By turning to the subject of the Indian experience, Jewish writers joined their voices to those in mainstream (English) America as a mark of their acculturation in the New World.

SIMON GINZBURG—NATURE AND CITY

Following chronologically upon Silkiner's major poetic composition, *Before Timmura's tent*, the next poet to make use of the theme of Native Americans was Simon Ginzburg, a member of Bialik's literary circle in Odessa who came to live in America. Incorporating the Indian in a number of shorter—though significant—poems, his references intersect with a strongly lyrical poetry. Ginzburg voices his protagonist's sense of alienation in America's impersonal megalopolis. To counteract the impact of New York, the backdrop of many of his American poems, his hero takes refuge in a remote, imaginary, and idyllic past when Indians populated the landscape, free of the encroachment of Whites, their industrialization, and their subjugation of nature.[6]

Thus the protagonist of Ginzburg's 1916 poem, "On the Hudson River" ("'Al nahar Hudson"), reimagines a pristine world unlike his urban milieu. Feigning an avoidance of this reality, he symbolically faces the Hudson River, ignoring the city spread behind him. The river becomes symbolic of the persistent flow of time, against which his imagination transports him to an age before the European landing, when Native Americans lived in harmony with land and forest. Though the Indians have vanished, the landscape has become the abode preserving their image and song.

> Silently I sit, behind me the city,
> Before me the river; behind it—a great expanse, God's field . . .
> In the forests' hiding places are, certainly, streams,
> In the beginning suns and moons were reflected there.
> In these forest Indians still hunted—
> When the White Skins did not yet rule the land—
> And the song of an Indian man was certainly preserved;

And in the mirror of the stream his image remained
As he'd kneel in hiding drawing his bow
At the face of a White God who came to take his land . . . (p. 92)[7]

Ginzburg's poem does not dwell, as Hillel Bavli will do, on an idyllic life of whites in a landscape free of Indians, but bemoans an unattainable fantasy. For in the process of eradicating the Natives, Whites have cut down forests and dismembered any lingering sounds and signs of Indians. What remains is a barren, unnatural, artificial cityscape in which White residents have lost their true nature and have become clockwork mechanical automatons.

In this system of metaphors the protagonist is alienated from a true existence in nature by choosing to live in the city. The poet's longings for an alternate, presumably more authentic, existence for himself and fellows voices a desire to rediscover a vanished reality. For Jews, this often meant a recapturing of their rural and familiar Eastern European cultural high ground. Taken more extremely, the impulse is a romanticist's advocacy for a life in natural settings.

Ginzburg's more seminal work, "No-York" (1917), composed just a year later, appears more reconciled to city life.[8] Its speaker is ultimately comforted when he discerns signs of spirituality in urban America. However, even here he foregrounds the corrupting features of city life, a frequent theme in American Hebrew poetry and prose. Ginzburg juxtaposes the Big City, enshrouded in myth and personified as a hideous beast that enslaves its citizens to serve its needs.

At that hour
The overlord city-master in the iron-train
With a mocking whistle at the laggards, no mercy, no mercy for them,
Over his mighty iron bridges—as he comes as victor,
As Pharaoh, to command his multitude of slaves arrayed,
Building for him with the sweat of brow storage cities with pyramids.
(274)

Present existence is contrasted with an imaginary, myth-enshrouded past. The tension illustrates the calamity that civilization brought upon the innermost self. The poem's leading image, the lake in Central Park, invokes Bialik's principle symbol for the self in "The Pool" ("Ha-brekhah").[9] Its language, moreover, is an echo of Bialik's socio-political "In the City of Slaughter" ("B-ʿir ha-haregah") by its repeating calls on the reader to bear witness. It also probes deeply into the Hebraic literary tradition of national issues by its resonance with the Bible's Jonah and Ezekiel.[10]

Thematically, the poem bemoans the dehumanizing life in the city. Its deliberate corruption of the city name in the title challenges New York's aura among Jewish immigrants—much as done by G. Rosenzweig's (1861–1914) deliberate misreading of America into "'Ami-reika," meaning "my scoundrel people."[11] This sentiment is underscored by the way the Indian, represented by the spirit of the Brave Katsika, maintains a dialogue with his beloved and personified lake even through the tenuousness of a romanticized imagination.

By its observation of the demise of pristine nature and the triumph of the industrial city, the poem argues against the Futuristic program in art. It takes a stand favoring the more conservative and "natural" existence in harmony with nature. It represents modernism as dehumanizing, turning individuals into spiritless slaves. People's dreary, mechanical, and routine existence, as by daily servicing the Big City, leaves the poet with little hope. As if in response, his imagination transports him to a time when humans and nature were in closer harmony, when the lake was Katsika's[12] beloved and not a prisoner surrounded by the city's towering buildings.

Unlike in his prior poem, however, Ginzburg closes on a conciliatory note. In a mystical experience, his narrator discovers the presence of spirituality in the modern city. Much as in nature, observes the poet, an invisible hand of the divine hovers over the place and its bustle.

Messiah! Messiah! The nation's sovereign appeared unawares—
The hidden God from time immemorial—revealed in His glory. . . .
All around, on both sides of the bridge, afar, at midnight,
As if suspended over an abyss, many fiery chains tremble,
Many lights, lights,
Signaling one another, calling to each other— —
At that moment my spirit, too, sank into the depths of night, . . .
And I thought: who lit these hidden lights,
The Creator concealed long ago—who discovered and drew up God's
mystery,
Embroidering the expanse with lights, as embroidering a divine
canopy with stars?
It is the heart of man, into which the Creator let flow a drop of His
vast knowledge! . . .
And I lifted up my eyes to the stars,
The myriad eyes of the One who sees unseen;

And in my heart I felt His steady, wondrous hand,
Cast upon this metropolis from above . . .
And throughout that night my whole being filled with a new song,
So passed the prophecy of New-York, turning to a hymn of trust.
(284–285)

Born of an epiphany in the observer's consciousness, the mystical experience redefines his attitude. The city, now renamed New-York (p. 285), becomes the locus of worship imagery, indicated by the myriad shimmering lights on the Williamsburg Bridge that inspire the observer. He is also moved by the Brooklyn Bridge, another symbol of connectivity, whose towering cables resemble strings in a divine harp awaiting God's hand.[13]

As before, Native American life and culture is sparse, furnishing little concrete detail beyond stereotypical items presented in a few broad strokes. Such sketchy portrayal underscores the poet's comfort of labeling Indians as metonyms for nature, the Indian as noble and unreal. The Katsika's idealized image leaves no room for qualities that humanize him. Instead, he is an expression of the poet's spirit of longing for a release from modernity's subjugation. Yet the perspective of the poem's narrative is illuminating. The narrator of the account imagines himself alongside the Indian defenders and as inimical to the European ideal of an artificial world: the metropolis in which individualism is lost on the altar of human subjugation to the urban beast. The identity between the Jewish narrator and the Indians, who are held up as denizens of a truly free and natural environment, is sustained.

The sole plausible aspect of Indian reality in "No-York" may be the folkloric germ at its core touching on the relationship of the Brave Katsika with the Lake. Also, in its initial mention of Katsika, the poem tells of his leading the last stand against the invading Whites at this location. The poet explains the event analogously as the Indians' Masada-fortress story (p. 273):

A tradition, recounted to me by an old gardener, of a Masada-fortress
Of desperately fighting Indians, whose shelter was here
And here they fell to the last at the victor's feet, "The White God"
(273)

This is perhaps the first mention of Masada in a work of modern Hebrew literature, later featured more prominently by Y. Lamdan in his epic "Masada."[14] In this instance, though, the story of Masada is transposed to the Indian experience, and calls for a comparison of experiences between the two civilizations. Moreover, as in Lamdan's case, Masada becomes a metaphor for the Indians' fate, though without the heroic, optimistic, and Zionist overtones cultivated by the more famous work. Also, in place of the victorious tone at the conclusion of Lamdan's poem, Ginzburg's is a much starker reference, bemoaning the annihilation of Indians in an act similar to the death at Masada. This treatment of the Masada theme reinforces the utter eradication of Native Americans, for the sole Indian featured in the poem is the hovering ghost of the Brave Katsika who died many years ago.

THE INDIAN AS GHOST

Recognition of some aspects about Native Americans does not imply sufficient knowledge to lead to conclusions about an identity between them and American Jews. On the contrary, the impression of a wholesale eradication of Native Americans has turned them into subjects of mystery and exoticism in Hebrew circles. This lack of familiarity has made of them alien, ghostly images in the imagination of protagonists, opening the way for an attribution of a host of significations that render them less than real.

Such is the case with Yaʿakov Tarkow-Naamani's tales, in which he juxtaposes the Jews' alienation in the New World with a problematic alternative of residence in their national homeland. The protagonist of "Bi-sʿor ha-saʿar" (As the storm blows), who lives in a remote community, abandons his cozy home on a stormy night to participate in a memorial service for a departed fellow Jew, a journey that becomes his last. As he walks through the wailing wind he imagines hearing the voice of Indians emerging out of their graves to avenge the deeds perpetrated by the White man:

> The Red Skins, who were cut down by the pale-faced conquerors leaped out of their graves in a frenzy of revenge to savagely attack the white conquerors' descendants."
>
> ("adumay-ha-ʿor asher niktelu ʿal-yeday ha-kovshim ḥivray ha-panim ḥargu mikivrotayhem v-histaʿaru b-phirʾut umi-tokh shikron-nekamah ʿal tzetzaʾayhem shel ha-kovshim ha-lvanim"—70).[15]

The protagonist identifies himself and fellow Jews with the White conquerors of America. The result is the discomfort, guilt, and fear borne of the knowledge of being complicit in what Europeans have done to the Natives. His awareness leads to an anxiety at being haunted by the ghosts of dead Indians. His lingering awareness of being an alien in America is underscored by his son—a sign of his alter self—who settled in Eretz Israel.

In another story bearing similar views, and whose reading against Bavli's "Mrs. Woods" is a useful exercise, Tarkow-Naamani explores the persistent tension and violence issuing from the European decimation of American Indians. In "Tzlilay shkiʿah" (Sunset shadows) he relates a tale principally "from within," in which Jewish protagonists are nearly absent.[16]

The story is a monologue of an elderly Scottish woman who, with her husband, immigrated to America. She tells of her friends' concern "to live in a strange land among cannibalistic Indians." Soon after settling in the New World, its popular stereotype as the abode of the primitive and savage is realized when Indians, one of whom is shot by her husband, attack and burn down their farm.

The violence, fire, and other images of death conveyed by this experience take on added import when juxtaposed with a Jewish national theme. At the very time of their home's destruction, the Scottish couple's Jewish friends, she recalls, commemorate the ceremonies of the Ninth of Av on the traditional day believed to mark the destruction in antiquity of the Jerusalem Temple and the Jews' national homeland. The nexus is not only an observation on the recurrent violence in human affairs but juxtaposes the loss of a national home to that of a family home. The Indians in this equation are most likely an analogue to the Jews of antiquity, whose role as indigenous natives was disrupted but who now aspire to reestablish their commonwealth. However, the Indians remain faceless and anonymous images imbued with little more than a single idea of resistance.

Revisiting the notion that the Jews are among the invaders of the New World, Tarkow-Naamani's "Shalom ʿal Israel" (Peace upon Israel) juxtaposes the fate of Conversos (or Marranos) in the New World with that of Mexican Indians.[17] Searching for traces of the former Jews in Mexico, the narrator happens upon a synagogue of Indian converts. In the course of his observations, he mentions that the founder of Monterrey, Mexico, who was a Jew, was later executed by the Inquisition. The nexus between the Jews' fate and that of Indians is alluded to in that the converted Indians, too, have not resolved the problem of persecution, much as the Jews have failed to escape the Inquisition. The identity struck between the two groups bespeaks a common fate suffered by them in the New World as in the Old.

Tarkow-Naamani's representation of Native Americans lacks any depth that would distinguish them as individuals. The Indian stands as a metaphor in the author's examination of the American Jew's ambivalence about his own identity. His desire to belong, to be an American, carries with it the consequences of complicity in the conquest of America.

An abiding quest for the ties that bind humanity and nature may not lead to a sober representation of Native Americans. However, it can approximate the Indians' imagination by reproducing some authentic folktales for that purpose. Alternately, they may be a vehicle for the writer's midrashic rereading to instruct readers, as exemplified by Lisitzky's work and, to a lesser extent, by Abraham Regelson's representation of Indians.

Abraham Regelson, an adherent of English poetry and American Transcendentalism, adapted Native American tales and themes to bridge the human longing for a dialogue with nature. His admiration for the Transcendentalist thought of Thoreau inspired him to publish poetry, prose fiction, and other reflections reminiscent of the contributions by the likes of Audubon, Longfellow, Walt Whitman, and Robinson Jeffers.[18] His poetry and prose is romantic and spiritual in its quest to capture the unity between Humanity, Nature, and Universe. It is out of this desire that Regelson introduces myths and folklore of many cultures into Hebrew literature, including those of Native Americans.

Reconstructing the Indian's image under the influence of the likes of D. H. Lawrence,[19] and perhaps at the same time offering up an alternative image than the one presented by Israel Efros (in Silent wigwams), Regelson draws on myth and folktale to romanticize Indian life. In keeping with his philosophical outlook, but one which also adds a realistic dimension to his contribution, he stresses that, contrary to Efros's depiction, America's Natives were occupied with agricultural pursuits in antiquity. Sowing fields cleared of vegetation by lightning, asserts Regelson, they would move on once the soil's nutrition was depleted. Holding dominion over nature, they lived on the move because of the abundance of land, wandering onward and exploring the continent.[20]

Regelson's use of what seem to be original Indian tales also demonstrates the universal wisdom embedded in folk-stories. In a poem evidently drawing on or translated directly from an Indian tale, "Gesher hasela" (The Stone Bridge), the poet includes cosmogonic elements.[21] The tale is an account of Sahal, a divine being who creates a stone bridge over an abyss to foster peaceful cooperation between two tribes, the Umatilla and the Salish. He rewards Old Luvit, the witch and loyal guard of the bridge, by making her young again. Yet as they behold her beauty, the two tribal chiefs vie for her favors and scheme to destroy one another in a war that erupts between them. Sahal punishes the three with death, covering their graves with famous mountains of the Northwest, later known as Mount Adams, Mount Hood, and Mount Saint Helens.

Comprised of more than a kernel of an authentic Northwest Indian folktale, the poem's plot elements and themes resemble many in this genre. Its etiological nature addresses questions pertaining to the origins and purpose of the stone bridge and the three mountains, and perhaps why, like the bridge, they were not destroyed to reverse the inter-tribal animosity. The account also resembles other Native American tales in its magical time setting; a theme of the rejuvenation of a protagonist; and its implicit moral, as well as its specific place and tribal names.

However, the poem's strongly anti-war message—resembling the poet's other work, "'Arafel b-kherem Marta" (Fog in Martha's Vineyard)—also bears a contemporary universal sentiment. An identification of the poem's origins in Indian lore may help address the extent to which Regelson infused the account with his own agenda.

Yet whether derived from a complete or partial folktale, the poem underscores Regelson's observation of nature and a fascination with humanity in a mythical setting. Sadly, like Lisitzky and unlike S. Ginzburg, he does not find any lasting and redeeming qualities among humans living in nature; they all possess deplorable tendencies for envy and war. For Regelson, the mythic past is not an escape; humans remain a destructive force to mar a bucolic order even when the gods endeavor to help them to create an idyllic existence. His pessimism may arise out of a general disenchantment with the prospects of a return to an ideal world.

In place of retreating to utopian speculation, however, Regelson ponders the future. The distance from the ideal past when humans lived in proximity to creation is marked in part by the loss of authentic Indian existence, a theme running through another of his poems. Resembling "Gesher ha-sela" (The stone bridge), his "'Arafel b-kherem Marta" (Fog in Martha's Vineyard) conveys innocence and a folksy perceptiveness derived from life close to nature.[22] Yet it is much more than that. In addition to its resemblance to an Indian tale, it conveys a sobering message in its epilogue about the nature of human bellicosity, much as in the previously discussed poem, foregrounding the account's relevance for twentieth-century readers.

The poem begins as an etiological Indian folktale recounted by a non-Indian New England native, a worthy substitute for the presumably vanished Native Americans. In his tale, the narrator explains the origins of the pervasive fog hovering around Cape Cod, Martha's Vineyard, and

Nantucket. It also presents an account of how Moshop created the two islands and the fog when he took a brief respite for a smoke while pursuing a menacing man-killing bird. The story testifies to its persistent power over humans even when the tale's Indian owners are no longer present to recount it.

The story's apparent goal is left unresolved as its true purpose emerges, in a modern-day gloss. The man-killing bird, declares the tale, is never captured. It escapes across the Atlantic, there to wreak havoc in Europe—presumably a reference to the Second World War and the Holocaust. With the bird's departure, adds the narrator, peace came to the U.S.-Canadian frontier.

Regelson intertwines two functions for his poem. The first is to enrich the Hebrew literary corpus by translating an authentic Indian tale. The second is not just a contemporary coda to the original tale but also explains the persistence of evil in the world by means of a folktale. The nexus between the mythical bird of prey and the raging war and destruction in Europe points to the tale as a metaphor, an apt indication of more than one poet's way with Indian folktales.

The stories, however, barely touch on any direct analogy of Indians with Jews. They leave any juxtaposition to the speculating reader. Instead, Regelson's concern is to present the tale for its contemporary value, as proof of the universal wisdom inherent in seemingly primitive tales. Unlike Lisitzky's, though, his work remains brief and narrow, never seeking to reach the epic scope of the former. In place of fusing them into a single whole, he leaves his renderings of Indian tales isolated from each other. Nonetheless, thematically the individual works share common concerns of human nature, ideals, and regrettable reflections on the pervasiveness of human violence.

The rendering into Hebrew of American tales is a project of Regelson's as he also presents in Hebrew episodes about America's folk-hero, Johnny Appleseed, whose name he translates literally as "Yoni Zera-Tapuaḥ."[23] Regelson represents Johnny Appleseed as the leading American folk-hero and lover of nature that he was, even toying with bear cubs under their mothers' approving gaze. His role in replacing damaged trees brings him into contact and conflict with Indians who seek to forestall the westward progress of the White Man by damaging his agricultural pursuits. Johnny is an ideal hero in his love of nature and Indians, whom he helps and heals. In a fittingly Regelsonian man-in-nature gesture, Johnny is invited to the Indians' village, where he preaches equality and tolerance. However, the poem falls short of adding depth or dimension to the image of the Native

American, whose principal role remains to bridge the Europeans with nature.

Adding to his investigation of exotic civilizations, Regelson also recounts the story of the Mormons on their westward trek to Salt Lake City. In the poem "ʿAmud ha-sheḥafim" (A Pillar of Seagulls)[24]—a title clearly based on the biblical account of the Exodus from Egypt, when God led the Children of Israel by a pillar of cloud by day and one of fire by night (Exodus 13:21–22)—Indians are presented as originating from among the Ten Lost Tribes, a detail preserved in the Mormons' holy book (19), and a subject also noted by Bavli, discussed further on.

Regelson's fascination with the Mormons is a more pronounced issue in this poem than the relation of Jews with Indians. The story's principal concern is with exotic people presented in the most superficial of ways. His discussion remains in the realm of ideas about each rather than presenting actual examples of Jewish behavior or characters resembling Native Americans.

Lastly, when writing in prose fiction, Regelson demonstrates that he, too, can represent Indians more realistically. In a short story, "Avaz afor" (Gray Goose),[25] he presents a more sober and unadorned image of Native Americans—as if illustrating the nadir to which they have descended from their glorious past. In the tale, the narrator observes an Indian couple with a child on a bus (thus the name) from Harrisburg, Pennsylvania, to Buffalo, New York. Lacking the nobility and romanticized ingredient of Indians set in mythic tales, the family is shown in naturalistic light as the husband incessantly reprimands his wife for some deed (39).

Despite his reach for higher spheres of representation, Regelson is not the only one to admit the reality before him. Others, poets included, reach the conclusion about the gap between how Native Americans are imagined and the way they actually exist. The most prominent among these is Hillel Bavli, whose views on the subject have heretofore been overlooked by Hebrew literary scholarship but whose contribution merits the following chapter.

CONCLUSION

The romantic tone was the most widespread mode of representation in Hebrew poetry at the turn of the twentieth century. That the greater part of the literary corpus engaged with representation of Blacks and Native Americans was composed in this vein is an indicator of the limits to which its creators were able to approach and know their subject. On the other hand, Hebraists demonstrated their familiarity with a pursuit of primitivism in representation as well as in admiration of their subjects. This tone also found its resonance among those who sought channels to recapture an imagined dormant antiquity in the national identity of Jews, as they sought their way back to pre-monotheistic times and a mindset believed to be part of the ancient conquerors of Canaan.

Inspired by the experiences of Blacks and Native Americans, Hebrew literature enabled readers to vicariously reimagine their national roots in a distant past. Identification with their subjects reflected indirectly on these writers' search for Jews' national character, dormant though it may have been. At the same time, the representation of the myths of Native Americans in particular taught readers about other groups and facilitated the acculturation of Jews into their adopted land. Against the backdrop of the lost indigenous populations and their culture, Hebrew readers could feel like Americans, being in part also the cause of this eradication, who could also feel haunted by the ghosts of those who were defeated. The fate of the latter could also be read as a cautionary warning to Jews about the power of assimilation in the American crucible.

Part and parcel of the romantic (or neo-romantic) trend in Hebrew belles lettres was that the American experience presented Hebrew literature with new thematic horizons. Its heroes' existence in America's big cities opened up avenues to express their alienation in urban America. Their experience was depicted in terms of the helplessness of the individual in an impersonal environment. The dichotomy struck between nature and city and the sense that the latter represents "modern" America served as a means to redress the balance of those who preferred to imagine the New World in idealistic terms. It also pointed to the destructive nature of city life and existence in the Golden Land, where one's identity—be it personal, national, or ethnic—was altered in the process of acculturation. These works document the loss of one's authentic identity as they became part of the American cultural landscape.

CHILD'S PLAY: HILLEL BAVLI'S "MRS. WOODS" AND THE INDIAN IN AMERICAN HEBREW LITERATURE

Chapter Five

Americans are cognizant of allusions to Indians in their culture. Many use, and some are even familiar with, a few loan words from Indian languages in English. Bearing references to Native Americans are sports teams, train lines, and place names. For these, no actual Indians need be present. The impression left in the minds of some is that Native Americans are missing from the continent.

Such was the impression conveyed in the works of some Hebraists who dwelled on the fate of Native Americans in their critique of the imagined ideal life in the New World. In them they saw reflected their own selves—as Hebraists and Jews—as being at the precipice of extinction in America. The phrase "the last of the Mohicans," borrowed from James Fenimore Cooper's famous novel, has become a figure of speech in reference to themselves, and has even penetrated Israeli Hebrew. The persistent expression, a phrase coined as part and parcel of the language today, underscored the overwhelming threat posed by White America's culture to annihilate and assimilate all minor cultures, absorbing them even as it waxed large on their ruin.[1]

Notwithstanding the existence of over five hundred Indian tribes recognized officially by the federal government, a considerable segment of Americans, Hebraists included, considered Native Americans close to physical extinction. To be sure, the net number of Native Americans is estimated to have decreased precipitously in the early centuries of the European conquest of the New World. According to some, their population declined to an estimated two million.[2] Nonetheless, it seems that the numerical increase of Native Americans in the last century bodes well for their persistence, although it is the quality of life that remains a concern in the case of many.

Because most Native Americans resided away from America's larger cities, whether on the East Coast, in the Midwest, or in the South, few of the Hebrew poets had the opportunity to come into direct contact with them. Most dwelled on reservations, in out-of-the-way locations, or in cities where they were indistinguishable from the colorful population mix and "passed" by virtue of their dress, residence in innocuous neighborhoods, or occupation. The matter of the physical and cultural distance of "authentic" Native American tribes from these writers and their communities reinforced the impression that remained in works of fiction about the continent having been virtually free of native inhabitants by the time of the Jews' great migrations.

Hebrew poets and prose writers who sought to represent Native Americans in their fiction did so out of a host of motives. The most successful were those who studied the lifestyle, belief systems, and exotic culture of marginalized and exploited peoples to immortalize their image in readers' consciousness. Moreover, as Hebrew writers focused attention on the exoticism of Native American life and culture, their writings were read as more authentically "American." More than that, these works were frequently treated by analogy as indirect observations on the Jewish experience as well, even when no implications to this effect existed within the text.

Among the more recognizable strategies of representation has been the incorporation of Native American folktales of various tribes. Carried out most effectively by Lisitzky and Regelson, they exposed the exotic alongside the humane in Native American character. Those more inclined toward a relatively realistic representation insisted on underscoring the Indians' humanity, whose nature differs little from others. The most accomplished representation of the last was by Israel Efros, who—much in the spirit of Puccini's *Madame Butterfly*[3]—tells of the blossoming love between the Indian maiden Lalari and Tom, the Englishman. Others dwelled on the Indians as a people facing total physical or cultural extinction in their struggles against the White Man.

In the first long epic work composed in Hebrew, Silkiner's *Before Timmura's tent*, the issue is raised in the guise of the uprising of the Silent Tribe against the Spanish conquest of their lands. Though they were temporarily successful under Mugiral's leadership, their ultimate demise after the battle that left a mere handful of survivors is an object lesson to anyone who contemplates standing in the way of White will. Other compositions also recount the triumph of Europeans over the inhabitants and include the poet's foretelling of the nearly total extinction of the latter.

Other poets tended to depict the demise of Native Americans, underscoring their absence from the landscape. Of these, though more engaged with America's Blacks than Indians, is I. J. Schwartz's long poem *Ken-*

tucky.[4] Another to do so is A. S. Schwartz, who, in "Mountain Guide" (1939; "Moreh derekh be-harim"), notices a shortcut in a path made by Indians long ago.[5] Representing this somewhat more intimate familiarity with the Indian is Moshe Feinstein's lyrical poem "B-laylot kesef" ("On silvery nights," but also "On nights of longing" or, for the pun on commercialization, "Money nights").[6]

It is a poem open to literal and metaphoric readings. Bemoaning the demise of his imaginary silver eagle, whose feathers will soon adorn the headdresses of haughty women and savage Indians, the poet's observation also permits a figurative interpretation. Reinforcing the latter is the ambiguous title, in which the term for silver or money also denotes yearning or longing. The imaginary eagle is a fitting image of the romantic's muse, whose demise refers to a wholesale marketing of non-lyrical poetry.

The poet's refutation of the commercialized nature of the Indian theme in particular echoes Preil's observation of it being a "pseudo-epic" that a true lyricist—such as Feinstein and Preil—would shun as an escape from the true reality of the self.[7]

Even more exotic and distant, the Aztecs of Central America, much in keeping with the "Last of the Mohicans" theme, evoke a civilization at once remarkable for its attainments and threatening in its horrors. The Aztecs were utterly annihilated by European conquerors; little of their high cultural and religious life remains.[8] Its relics—stone carvings, monuments, jewelry, and material culture—are a vestige of one of the world's great civilizations. Their remoteness made Aztecs a convenient example of a world wiped out by the West. Not familiar with much of that culture, Hebrew writers exploited the subject as a stereotype denoting an unknown, exotic, and anonymous world.

Gavriel Preil treats Aztecs as mere symbols.[9] In his poem "Waiting for the atomic tomorrow" ("Hamtanah la-maḥar ha-ʾatomi") he exhumes Aztec civilization to prefigure the world's annihilation in the nuclear age. Without delving much into Aztec cultural specifics, he cautions readers about the West destroying itself and all existence with its weapons and technology.[10]

Composed with a copious amount of detail—more than in Preil's work—concerning Aztec culture, Silberschlag's poem "Mexico" is a reflection on Zionism.[11] The poem tells of a contemporary Aztec mourning the memory of the mighty city erected by his ancestors at the site of Mexico City. Yet, adds the poet in a gesture meant to redress the balance in the Indians' image, Aztec culture also included human sacrifice. To illuminate his assertion, he graphically illustrates a cruel ancient Aztec ceremony. The Aztec of today, though, also recalls by way of a rejoinder the Spanish Conquistadors' similar cruelties of raping and pillaging his people in the name of a loving god.

However, the poem goes beyond midrashic speculation to comment on Zionism. To establish this nexus, Silberschlag weaves specific references of Jewish culture into aspects of Aztec life. For just as the Aztecs constructed their symbol of serpent and eagle as emblems of identity, values, and aspirations—cunning, courage, earthiness, and flight—so the Jews, asserts the poet, reimagined their past and future as a legacy derived from Sinai, where Judaism's values and future aspirations were inscribed in memory.

The meanings of the Aztec image, partly recalled and partly forgotten, "a piece here and a piece there, as in a vision," refer to a concern of Zionism as regarding Jewish salvation.[12] Moreover, in his account of human sacrifice the poet relies on a narrative form reminiscent of the Mishnaic account describing the priestly rite on Yom Kippur in Tractate Yoma.[13] Though not equating the latter with the barbaric rituals of Aztec culture, Silberschlag relies on the ancient formulaic language of the Jewish rite to establish a resonance of antiquity for his account.

Such pessimistic attitudes are also discernible in a few works of prose fiction. These tend to be more realistic in tone than their poetic counterparts but dwell on similar themes. As if recognizing the finality of Native American life, several writers acknowledge Indians' past, though they do not concern themselves with their lives in the present. The story writer Bernard Isaacs preserves the remnants of Indian culture only in a handful of linguistic terms. Like many Hebraists, he adopts the term "Indian summer" ("kayitz indi'ani") in a tale.[14] Set during an Indian summer, the account signifies a period of seeming respite and normalcy in life following the death of one of his protagonists, Morris, in a post–Labor Day car accident (234). Adding to his readers' education, Isaacs notes that the opposite of Indian summer, a "squaw winter," denotes an especially harsh winter.[15]

Harry Sackler's 1927 play *Messiah, American style* (*Mashiaḥ nosaḥ America*) is an exemplary illustration of prose fiction's representation of Native Americans. The play highlights a historic moment in the life of Mordecai Manuel Noah (1785–1851), who in 1825 acquired a parcel of land on Grand Island, New York, in the middle of the Niagara River near Buffalo. Naming his land "Ararat," Noah planned to make of it a refuge for Europe's persecuted Jews, whom he invited to come and settle there.[16] In the play, Sackler introduces an Indian, Chief Black Hawk, who participates in the opening ceremonies for "Ararat." And while he withholds any close examination of the latter's character, Black Hawk is presented sympathetically as an ally of the Jews. Black Hawk's words are few; his speech is racially stereotypical and syntactically hackneyed. His import, though, is on the non-verbal plane as the requisite noble savage who represents freedom, valor, and purity unattained by White civilization. Both Noah (representing the Jews) and Black Hawk share a fate that challenges their continued perseverance in America.

Part of the ceremony lingers on the gesture by Black Hawk that indicates acceptance of Jews to live alongside his people. But in place of embellishing his play with more Native Americans, the playwright limits himself to but one. Black Hawk is a flat character; lacking originality, dimension, and complexity, an unsatisfactory version of an authentic Indian. Instead, he is sketched out in a few broad strokes that underscore his nobility and is relegated to the background of the play. As a matter of fact, he possesses more European traits than those of an Indian—a minority among the minorities. It is as if his is the personality that emerges out of a confrontation and compromise with European America. Yet Noah labels him in the most positive light as a scion of "pure courage" ("Ha-gvurah ha-tehorah"), a characteristic that he hopes to bestow upon Jewry that stands for "high culture" ("Ha-tarbut ha-gvohah," 301).

Noah's hopes are realized when Black Hawk declares a fraternal fealty with the Jews (301). In return, he is recognized as an equal among Noah's followers, representing a marginal minority. Underscoring this fact is the rationale of one of Noah's fellow ideologues, Rabbi Moshe Pichutto,[17] who rejects the notion favored by Noah that Indians are a remnant of the Lost Ten Tribes. Black Hawk is honored with a participatory role in the ensuing parade to lay the cornerstone of Ararat (317–318). The group's liberal attitude toward Native Americans, though, is equivocal; the Jews are also concerned lest the Indians stage an uprising against White America (322).[18]

In the realm of Hebrew novels, little has been written in America about Indians. In one example, Harry Sackler presents a view in keeping with the notion of the Last of the Mohicans in contemporary America. The narrator of his novel *Between heaven and earth* (*Beyn eretz v-shamayim*)[19] assumes a total dissolution of Indian existence. His is a tale of Abner, a recently immigrated Jewish protagonist who seeks to establish his roots in New York, an alien and alienating world. On one occasion in his wanderings, his gaze falls upon the image of a cigar-store Indian, fixed on the sidewalk in front of a store, advertising its merchandise:

> But most of Abner's walks were in the East Side neighborhood whose center was occupied by Tompkins Square. Most residents of the neighborhood were Germans with a mix of Jews who began to penetrate into it from the lower part of town. The streets were sufficiently tidy though the houses were tattered by time. . . . Most of the residents were grocers, bakers, butchers and owners of delicatessens. . . . Among them were also tailors, shoemakers, plumbers, tinsmiths, upholsterers, haberdashers and launderers (most from China, short, pale and with their hair tied in the back of their heads). Here and there stood an erect wood-carved and multi-hued Indian decorated with a feather to declare that tobacco goods were being sold inside the store . . .
> The quarter was one of those that served as an entrance to the real America. (25)

The scene bears a host of significations: It casts the Indian as a lifeless object deprived of any semblance of humanity. More than that, though, American capitalism has neutralized the threat from Native Americans, absorbed and reformed them as part of its commercial culture. It is as if in the wake of a radical erasure of Native Americans from the landscape, they were recycled only to emerge in a sanitized, harmless and lifeless form, as an object exploited by White America. In this instance Indians have been converted into a grotesque caricature of their former selves to take on an image acceptable to Whites, who have adapted them into a secure and unthreatening facet of their culture. The last sentence of the above quote underscores the cost of acculturation.

Sackler's representation of Native Americans hovers as a muted and superficial background in a number of other instances. In the same novel, the hero samples the life of the Gentiles on Long Island. Because the place is bereft of Native Americans, the children play a game in which a toy train whisks them away to a make-believe land where Indians still dwell. These scenes become occasions for the author to vent some of his displeasure at White society's subjugation of helpless civilizations for its aggrandizement. In place of performing menial tasks, Whites, observes one character, have fashioned a culture of exploitation. The institution of slavery is a direct end result of these attitudes, for when Native Americans refused to work as servants to Whites, they brought in Black slaves instead (212).

The ease with which Whites have vanquished Native Americans leads, in a final reference in this novel, to an ironic analogy. It is easier, asserts one protagonist, for a new immigrant to battle Indians or wolves—namely, to control the forces of nature—than to overcome America's social challenges. Moreover, to be a Zionist pioneer is also easier than America's overcoming her Indians because in the former one need only confront the threat of malaria (443).

In a similar vein, Hillel Bavli (1893–1961), too, pondered the fate of Indians in a number of his poems that survey the American cultural landscape. Born in Lithuania as Hillel Rashgolin,[20] Bavli marked his course of Americanization by a series of name changes—initially Rashgolsky, Rashgalsky, or Roshgolin—that bespeak fluidity in his identity. By 1913, shortly after arriving in America in 1912, he changed his name to Bavli. However, as Persky observes,[21] this did not keep him from continuing to use his former names.

Bavli's use of several names is put to rest by A. R. Malakhi,[22] who explains that though indeed he was born under his father's name, Rashgolin, he altered it (for some unexplained reason) to Rashgolsky upon landing in the United States. Later, and upon his uncle's advice, he changed his name to Price, all the while continuing to use his former names, as evidenced in the signatures bearing his name on some poems. At the same time, adds Malakhi, he "Hebraized his name to Bavli . . . because his family had a tradition that they descended from the exilarch dynasty [exilarch in Hebrew is *rosh-golah*] of the Babylonian Diaspora, the reason for which they were called Rashgolsky." (173)

Bavli's arrival in America in 1912 led him to his first job when, in 1913, he was invited by E. E. Lisitzky, then in Buffalo, to teach at his school. He soon left for New York City, there to pursue his liberal arts studies, but returned to teach again in Buffalo in 1915 while enrolled at Canisius College, a local Catholic school, and received his bachelor's degree.[23] After Buffalo, Bavli continued his graduate studies at Columbia University and taught Hebrew language and literature in New York, principally at the Jewish Theological Seminary of America. As a budding poet, he gravitated to the circle of literati gathered around B. N. Silkiner, the principal poet and leading luminary during the flowering of Modern Hebrew Literature in America.[24]

Bavli's scholarly legacy includes essays and studies on literature, some collected and preserved in a volume of essays, *Ruḥot nifgashot* (Intersecting spirits, 1958). He also edited anthologies of literature and literary scholarship, *Nimim* (1923) and *Masad* (1933, 1936). Among his translations are Dickens's *Oliver Twist* (1924) and Shakespeare's "Antony and Cleopatra" (1952). He gained added distinction for translating American poets, among them Robert Frost, Amy Lowell, Edgar Lee Masters, and Carl Sandburg.[25]

Bavli was among the leading translators eager to introduce his Hebrew readers to African American poetry. He exhibited an interest in New York's Black intelligentsia and its cultural fecundity of the Harlem Renaissance that flowered there in the interwar years. His translations from the works of Black poets include poems by James Corrothers, Paul Laurence Dunbar, W. E. B. Du Bois, and Claude McKay.[26]

As a poet, Bavli is primarily a lyrical composer, addressing issues such as family, nature, and Eretz Israel. In form, language, and technique his poetry is conservative, avoiding "modernist, symbolic or intellectual poetry," as one critic observed.[27] Rather, his work's quest is the intense experiences of reality, be they tangible or metaphoric. As an American Hebrew poet, observes Epstein, he voices the pain and sorrow of the uprooted in a strange land, often defined in terms of exile from his father's house (110–111). Thematically he focuses on the image of "the father as an ideal," as one reader observed,[28] and a longing for an abandoned paternal house and its traditional experiences. It is a theme familiar from the writings of the alienated in the New World whose roots remain across the sea.

However, while Bavli's interest in Black culture is patently evident, his preoccupation with Native American civilization is less so, most likely because of the tenuous contact he had with them. So unlike the plight of African Americans, theirs did not figure prominently in his daily concerns as a resident of New York City, nor did Native Americans exhibit a cultural resurgence in literature, art, or music to attract his attention as did Blacks.

Nonetheless, Bavli's poems do include the image and condition of Indians from time to time. His regard is best expressed in one of his later poems, "In an Indian village" ("Bi-khfar Hodi," 1950), which describes an Indian community. The poem was composed during Bavli's tour of the West, bearing the inscription "Taos," presumably in New Mexico, as its venue. Significantly and strategically, it is sandwiched between one of Bavli's better known works, "The Tale of a Mormon" ("Mormon msaper," 1950), which precedes it and bears the location name of Yosemite Valley, and "Mountain Images" ("Dmuyot be-harim," 1950), which follows, in which he returns to the image of Mrs. Woods, the eponymous heroine of the poem that will be our principal interest in the following.[29]

IN AN INDIAN VILLAGE

No savages seeking war before me,
Legendary heroes, knights of adventure
But innocent humble earthly beings
Who walk in silence as in prayerful whisper.

In their blood are sealed ancient worlds
But their hearts are to their yards, to the field, to the garden;
The windows to their poor homes are sealed
In fear of the spirits that lurk in the corner.

They pour their thoughts and weave their dreams
In cloth, in clods of earth and wool;
Temples shield them on all sides,
The lake, the mountain, and the walls of their place.

I perceived them as monks, tormented and humbled
That live in seclusion awaiting some tidings.
At their sight all veils of wonder scattered
And in the silence I heard a pure human speech.

TAOS, 1950

From beginning to end, the poem negates the stereotypical, romantic image of Indians as noble savages or as thirsty for battle. The encounter has altered the poet's own perceptions, as now, "in the silence I heard a pure human speech." He elevates their silence to a sanctified level by likening them to monks—for they "walk in silence as in prayerful whisper / . . . as monks, tormented and humbled / That live in seclusion awaiting some tidings." The transformation in his perception of these natives is the change within himself. Nothing objective has changed about them between his first and last encounter. Now, however, he has come to know them in a different way, to appreciate the sacred in their existence.

This poem is particularly pithy in light of its strategic framing as it follows immediately on the heels of "The Tale of a Mormon" ("Mormon msaper"). In the latter the poet puts on the stage another exotic American subject for his readers: the image, attitude, and story of Mormons. The Mormon speaker tells of the early history and religious foundations of his faith. Tying his story directly to the people of Israel, he explains that one finds

Wonders in the Book of Mormon: In it were inscribed
Human events generations ago
And first among them—described in it were in true writ
The journeys of ancient Hebrews
From Holy Jerusalem, their glorious city,
To the realms of the new land, America.
Behold the faces
Of our country's dwellers and see
Sons of Shem emerging of the Hebrews' offspring. (126–127)

In this light—that Indians are of the Lost Ten Tribes—the opening lines of "In an Indian village," the poem that follows, take on added significance. Bavli's observation negates the Indians' stereotypical image held by outsiders such as his Mormon narrator. His words underscore the fact that they are merely humans, "innocent humble earthly beings" (135). Without arguing so bluntly, the poem joins the debate begun as early as Silkiner's *Timmura* by challenging the tendency to mythologize Indians in American culture and in the epic works by Silkiner, Efros, and Lisitzky and their ilk. Bavli strikes an unequivocal stance in opposition to the mythologizing strategies of representation that give rise to alienating distancing representations of the Other.

In light of these observations we can now turn our attention to one of Bavli's best known works, the 1924 poem "Mrs. Woods." In it, the poet also devotes a significant part of his art and thought to the matter of Native Americans.[30]

Numbering some two hundred and twenty-four unrhymed lines, the poem is composed in iambic hexameter.[31] Its narrative is largely Mrs. Woods's address to an audience of young visitors from the big city. Ninety-two years old, she claims to have lived out most of her life in the lap of nature cradled by New York's Catskill Mountains. Her longevity and good health, she argues, are directly linked to her lifestyle, for it is her environment that is the ideal locus for human habitation. It is also the abode wherein one can commune with God and learn of the creator's wishes. On the other hand, life in the city is repugnant to her, and she has never been there but for once, and that, too, was in 1863 during the upheavals of the Civil War.[32] All that is evil, polluted, and artificial in life is because of that "bloody monster" (138), the big city. It is there where the young rapidly turn old, while here nature preserves the youthful vitality of a person of her age.

The heroine's monologue focuses on themes that include the superiority and beauty of life in nature, and childhood memories about her friends and family members. In the latter, she recalls three pivotal details: (a) the games she and her friends played, including one she calls "the Red Indian's war," (b) her studies with Miss Virginia, her favorite teacher, and (c) Sundays spent with her family as her father read out of the Good Book. Out of all these episodes she lingers longest and for the greatest number of lines, twenty-eight at least, on the stereotyped image of the Indian with which she grew up, and in describing the game of "the Red Indian's war" that she and her friends played.

The absence in prior critiques of any critical regard for this episode is puzzling in light of its dominance and the attention this popular poem received from American and Israeli readers. A survey of what critics have noted about Bavli's poem demonstrates what drew their attention, including the total disregard in which they held so significant an episode. It is as if the account pertaining to the Indians was as invisible to them as are America's Natives in Hebrew readers' consciousness.

The absence of comments to this effect range from Preil's inability to locate anything American in the poem,[33] to Ribalow's opposite observation and admiration of the true Yankee who lives in harmony with nature and embodies "universal values as she embraces the diversity of American religions, beliefs and ethnic groups."[34] Other reviews include Epstein's and Holtz's esteem for the romantic heroine whose lifestyle is influenced by the Bible.[35]

Readers have been particularly impressed with the heroine's fortitude in standing up to life's challenges. She utters convictions that touch on the romantic notions of life in the lap of nature and exudes an aura of carefree confidence that seems appealing to those who have experienced the challenges of urban life. Curiously, many identify in her the essential characteristics that define the American spirit, though none label her as being among those who subjugated the Indians.[36] Even her innocence and simplicity elicit favorable comment, as readers associate her with the freshness of mountains.[37] She has even been identified as a metaphor for the poet's spirit and abiding respect for traditions and ancestral images.

Observed more broadly against the greater fabric of his oeuvre, and within the context of Hebrew immigrant literature, the poem is understood as a sentimental expression that touches on the past and father's house, voicing Bavli's "admiration for the paternal."[38] In addition, by portraying the heroine as a strong figure, the poem is a celebration of the past as an age of strong women.[39]

It is puzzling that in light of Bavli's oeuvre and the superhuman image readers have, rightfully, attributed to Mrs. Woods, none of them has attended to the problematizing issue raised by one of the poem's principal themes. Her understanding and manner of representing Native Americans and their fate has a decided influence on our fuller comprehension of Mrs. Woods's personality, a matter that will be addressed in the following. This issue not only complicates the image of the heroine but also offers up an implicit view of the poet about America.

As we read "Mrs. Woods" it is important to keep in mind that, except for Bavli's brief introduction that establishes its setting, the poem is presented from its heroine's perspective. This is an invitation that, if acted upon, permits greater insight into her character. The poem is one of those distinctively Americanized Hebrew works—akin to the epic poemas by Silkiner, Efros, and Lisitzky, and some shorter works by Regelson and a handful of others—that depict the world of the Other as if "from within." By this I mean the exoticism of the Other is represented without the Hebrew writer's inclusion of issues pertaining to his own people's characters, identity, or concerns. Instead, he unveils a world about which he writes with the authority of one of those Others.

In the case of Bavli, the sole reference made by his heroine to Jews is in her dismissive regard for any established faith and house of worship as alternatives to her advocacy for a natural religion in encountering the divine; for she believes it is only in nature that true communing with God is possible. This feature, presenting the Other's world from within, defines a subgenre of works I propose to call a "voyage narrative." For just as in an account of a journey, the reader is exposed to new vistas and values in characters and unfamiliar cultures. In this instance—as Bavli would also do in his account of the Mormons and description of an Indian village—the poem unfolds scenes and values of rural Christian America by telling of the heroine's upbringing and attitudes about life among the Catskill Mountains. Whether this picture is a more authentic representation of Americana than the familiar scenes of urban life is debatable, and may have been so even at the time of its composition. However, Ribalow, whose domain was predominantly in New York City, was persuaded that it is so. This detail is further indication of his alienation from the "true" America he seems to seek.

Moreover, as also argued by Epstein, Malachi, and others, "Mrs. Woods" belongs to the genre of the romantic idyll.[40] This is thematically borne out in part by the heroine's stubborn and uncompromising conviction that the pastoral landscape is the answer for those who seek the ideal existence. These convictions are some of the ingredients comprising idyllic romantic poetry. It is also for that reason that Bavli's poem sidesteps descriptions that would bring to the surface indications of tension, so even the words of this stubborn old woman are couched in a humorous tone as she chastises her audience and retells stories of her youth. Idylls by their nature do not tolerate representations of violent acts; as in the case of Tschernichowsky's "Levivot," any such account quickly brings this kind of poem to a conclusion.[41]

One illustration that the poem avoids any descriptions of outright violence is the way Mrs. Woods describes the game she calls "the Red Man's war." This is the one episode in the whole poem described most thoroughly and at great length. The monologue in which she presents her story allows her full control over the narrative, ostensibly without the poet's mediation, intervention, or judgment. That by its very name the game harbors the potential for brutality is obvious. And while it appears that the name of the game is Bavli's invention, it is a mock war between the "Pale Faces" and "Redskins." However, to sustain the conventions of the genre, immediately after first mentioning the game by name she adds a statement that mollifies the violent force implicit in its name: "And at the end of the battle we made peace around the 'tribal rock'" (140):

> At times we played "the Red Indian's war" game,
> And at the end of the battle we made peace around the "tribal rock."
> Elisha was the chief—and so did his title stay with us—
> Decorated with head-feathers, his face tanned ruddy
> Then he really looked like an Indian chief
> Commanding his troops, as is drawn in the pictures,
> And the sly "Foxy" and Thomas and Seymour and courageous Martha
> Proudly marched at his right armed with pitchfork and dagger,
> Doing war-dances and singing songs of the braves—
> How wonderful the sight! I and Abigail and Ruthie
> Saw and were afraid, too, and even ashamed of them lest they say:
> America was vanquished and the Pale Faces were beaten so we
>   provoked them
> With stick and pole, with whips or straps or simply with fists,
> And we also sang "My Country 'Tis of Thee" and "The Star Spangled
>   Banner"

And other dear songs until our young hearts pounded
And, with our last strength we defended the honor of our dear land.
And once, when the battle erupted I raised my large stick
Over the head of our enemy Seymour until blood flowed from him
and he fell;
Little Mary who stood from afar saw and stared,
And she cried out loud, in a fearful voice: Help! Save him! Help!
I too became frightened, but nothing happened, we made peace
As was customary, and after some time became Seymour's wife . . .
(141)

The game is a child's replay of the conquest of Native Americans by Europeans, a national myth ingrained from childhood into the consciousness of Americans and rehearsed in many guises. In all instances of this myth, however, the ending is always predetermined, denying any victory to the Indians. It is for this reason that she betrays the seeming innocuousness of the children's play and becomes more violent to confirm the story's outcome. For when the "Pale Faces" appear to be losing out—"[we] were afraid, too, and even ashamed of them lest they say: / America was vanquished and the Pale Faces were beaten" ("v-khen af paḥadnu, akh boshnu mi-pneyhem pen yomru: / america nutzḥah v-huku ha-lvanim")—she, as one of the "Pale Faces," strikes an "Indian" forcibly in order to "win" the battle. By their play, the children, playing both roles, confirm the superiority of the Whites and the necessity that victory be always theirs over the "primitive" Native Americans.

However, the genre of this poem as a pastoral idyll prevents a foregrounding of a truly violent confrontation; such graphic portrayals might do away with the tranquil air pervading the poem and the speaker's nostalgia. For that reason the brief fight in the game is described circuitously and with little detail. Nevertheless, the reality as to the battles and killings that occurred in the vicinity of the Catskill Mountains—indicated as well in the plot of James Fenimore Cooper's *The Last of the Mohicans*—is barely concealed beneath the surface of the narrative or the reader's consciousness.

The irony with which the narrative regards this not-too-distant past, and the heroine's obliviousness of it, adds another dimension to the poem. It is not that this reality cancels out former readings of the poem, but it does complicate it by drawing attention to a matter overlooked by former criticism. Similarly, the heroine's image as one cognizant of these events, some of which took place in her own lifetime—given that she does not address historical events from her past, though she was mature enough to visit the city in 1863—needs to be kept in mind as we read. In this light she appears as one who prefers to avoid recollection of those less-than-glorious days. By her act of avoidance she reconstructs the past by selectively highlighting a paltry number of personal or historical episodes against the backdrop of an all-too-familiar story of America's recent past. This attitude is what has given rise to the supersessionist regard she projects so confidently, and which has mistakenly been taken for resilience and strength by those fictitious and real audiences who have observed her.

The power of the poem's undercurrent derives from the irony embedded in the "happy ending" that the children can create following their game, and that Mrs. Woods believes she had accomplished by her marriage. According to this, the Indian threat is neutralized by resolving the conflict between the "Pale Faces" and "Red Skins" through the peace struck by the children "around the 'tribal rock'" (140). Her husband-to-be, Seymour, is led by Elisha, who played Indian chief because his "face [was] tanned ruddy." Elisha behaves according to a script known to all, and even looks the part, "as is drawn in the pictures" (140). The other solution to the implied violent face-off is the resolution perceived by the heroine, playing as one of the "Pale Faces" who ultimately marries Seymour, who played a "Red Skin." In so doing, the poem establishes a fiction, as does the heroine, that mutual love, cohabitation, and "marriage" between the two races have the power to put to rest the bloody conflict played out in history between Whites and Indians. But even in this union it is White culture that prevails.

However, because both sides of this play are actually White, the solution is but a childhood fantasy. Mrs. Woods, representing the weaker sex and dependent on the stronger male, demonstrates a tolerance toward the purported Other in the resolution she conflates between her game and her life as she assents to this imaginary "inter-racial" or "inter-ethnic" match. Though playing as one who compromises by this marriage, she and her mate, Seymour, are both Whites who belong to the victors.

Moreover, she who learned in Miss Virginia's class about the threat coming from cannibalistic Indians internalized also the solution to this conflict in the guise of the story she learned about Pocahontas:

> She told of Indians and savages, who eat human flesh till full,
> And of lovely Pocahontas, the courageous and generous—
> Of the pioneers and conquerors, ancestors of this beautiful land,
> Who battled wild nature, beasts and men. (142)

Pocahontas, as is known, married a European (John Rolfe) in the early seventeenth century, became assimilated into his culture, and abandoned her father's house and ancestral homeland. That is to say, when it comes to interracial relations, the solution of accommodation was and remains the loss of one's identity, the identity of the Natives, the Others, the Jews, and their annexation under the wings of the Pale Faces. In the same way Mrs. Woods replays the Pocahontas story in her belief that her marriage to Seymour also is a way to solve the Indian Problem.

The absence of Indians from the story, or the region—they exist solely in the stories that the children learn in school and in the accompanying pictures illustrating their story books (140)—situates the heroine in a secure, unthreatening environment, one in which reign a united culture, order, and discipline. In such a reality the Indian has been annihilated or become a White Man. The children's game of the victory of the White Man is also a psychological act of consciously exorcising the "dybbuk," that haunting ghost of the threatening Indian which they have internalized from school. Their education not only confirms this consciousness but also offers up a solution in the guise of the story of Pocahontas.

Literature set against the backdrop of the Catskills forms a small but interesting subgenre in Modern Hebrew literature.[42] And while "Mrs. Woods" is generically of significant difference, comparisons of some of its features with another Hebrew work—Reuven (Reuben) Wallenrod's novel *Ki phanah yom*, (For the day has waned)—is instructive in that it mutually illuminates the two.[43]

In reviewing Wallenrod's decidedly more realistic novel, S. Halkin[44] observes that its narrator avoids assuming an authorial position to comment or guide the reader's views and conclusions. Neither does he take an overt ideological position so as to share with readers any judgment about the protagonist's behavior or responses to the problem at hand. Halkin goes on to state that

> Wallenrod does not wish to bring Leo Halper [the novel's protagonist] to a critique or to a formulation of ideological claims and counterclaims about the American-Jewish condition. Better that against the sunset of his life the Jewish condition should narrate itself—its profoundly inner confusion that does not know how to express itself and its hesitant escape, hesitant though so overwhelmed by a distressing confusion, one bereft of abstract formulation, lacking any ideological critique. (123)

A similar attitude also characterizes Bavli's work, activating the reader to seek, identify, and ponder any implications that are at the core of each work: Jewish physical and cultural persistence in one and the willful amnesia about Native Americans' demise that cleared the way for a bucolic existence for the victors on the other.

Wallenrod's novel, continues Halkin (124), pits the tenuousness of New York Jews' cultural distinction against the rootedness and cultural authenticity of the American non-Jews, the Douglasses and Stevenses who—as does Mrs. Woods—live on and off the land in the Catskills. Wallenrod problematizes the Jewish question, though he does not extend his scope beyond the Jewish and European sphere. Yet American authenticity itself is relativized when one considers the issue raised by Bavli. Bavli leaves Wallenrod's concerns in the realm of the ephemeral, implicit, and unformulated nexus of Indian-as-Jew. Bavli's more immediate, though also largely unstated, issue concerns itself with the root causes: recent historical events that have permitted residents of the Catskills to lead the kind of life they have.

Weighing the significance of this largely overlooked portion of the poem underscores the more complex dimension of the heroine's character. In this light she is heir to European campaigns of annihilation and subjugation of Native Americans, so it is no wonder, then, that she projects such an image of satisfaction, security, and power. Her history has resulted in her people's supplanting of the former natives of the land and created the impression that she, as some reviewers have observed, is the authentic indigenous dweller. Bavli presents his idyll as a status quo of the American nation. She, who, it cannot be denied, is the representative of the victorious side, can now confidently speak about a deeply rooted life of tranquility in the lap of nature, among mountains and streams, forests and fields. She has become the beneficiary of the wars that children now replay with a confidence about winners and losers. Considered from her perspective, life is indeed good. The Good Book serves her and her family well as its promises are reread in light of American geography and a civilization proclaiming its Manifest Destiny to hold dominion over the continent.

Two and a half decades later, and to supplement his latent critique about the secure and tranquil existence of Europeans in an Indian-free America, Bavli becomes more blatant. His "In an Indian Village" places the emphasis on demythologizing Native Americans following his visit to an Indian village. On this occasion he rectifies the implication of "Mrs. Woods" that

Indians no longer exist. He witnesses a world that confirms to him that all threatening attributes about a primitive people are part of the unrealistic representation, or mythologizing, of a tranquil population. He erases the image of Native Americans as exotic or barbaric, says "no" to the mythologizing strategy propounded by Silkiner, Lisitzky, and Regelson, and reinvents them as ordinary folk. In place of the exoticism, he favors a representation of Indian villagers as humans dwelling in nature, speaking "a pure human speech."

It is also out of the same sentiment that Bavli writes in 1924, the same year as "Mrs. Woods," an essay in which he joins the debate to contest Ya'akov Rabinowitz's charge for "*Ameriqa'iyut.*"[45] Bavli understands Rabinowitz's observations as too narrow and geographically confining for American Hebrew literature. By that logic, Hebrew literature in every land should confine itself to writing literature inspired by the specific host culture in which it exists, asserts Bavli. His concern, moreover, is that Rabinowitz's guidelines would yield superficial imitations of indigenous American works. Instead, the ideas driving Hebrew literature from within need to be further nurtured, he avers. These include the national and universal ideals that count the Jewish nation among all while specifying its uniqueness as well.

Bavli's struggle to project what some found absent from his poetry—an authentic American identity—is exhibited metaphorically by the names he tried on as poet and scholar. His search for the proper voice pitted him against his eternal longing for an ancestral world that, as he imagined, was to be a comforting and tranquil island in a turbulent world. Though this quest remains forever in the realm of a reimagined reality, Bavli did correct the inadequacies arising from an imagined reality about a people.

In works such as those discussed above, he calls to account even such a noble institution as the American Dream, whose realization was attempted at the expense of marginalized victims. In these poems he demonstrates an ability to rise above the lyrical to address universal causes that, as in the case of his heroine, stamp his poetry with traits admired by Hebrew poets as American in scope and temperament.

RED HEART, BLACK SKIN: E. E. LISITZKY'S ENCOUNTERS WITH AFRICAN AMERICAN FOLKSONG AND POETRY

Chapter Six

We do not see things as they are; we see things as we are.

TALMUD

The African American population in the United States represented the most immediate indigenous minority with whom Jews had contact upon arriving in the New World. Moving into large cities, they witnessed the concomitant migration wave of Blacks out of the rural South, cresting in the years after the First World War. Many African Americans settled into predominantly poorer neighborhoods of northern cities, often adjacent to those of Jews.[1] Unlike Europeans who had recently made their way from across the ocean, the exoticism of Blacks for Jews was in their being "Americans," but with a difference. For contrary to the utopian messages pertaining to life in the Golden Land, Blacks exemplified an alternate reality, one of discrimination in the Land of the Free, a population singled out for lowly socio-economic and political status stemming from prejudice and stereotype, for being unlike the ruling elite, for being America's Other. They also had their own music, poetry, and affinity to the Hebrew Bible. In many ways their experiences reminded Jews of their own lot as a marginalized culture. Their curiosity issued out of interest in the history, culture, manners of coping, and destiny of Blacks as indications of what awaited them in America.

Relationships among Jews and Blacks intersected at many socio-cultural points, imprints of which were preserved within Jewish literary memory. In addition to Yiddish literature, representations in Hebrew fiction of contact between Jews and Blacks offer a record of the imagining of Blacks by Hebraists. It is a logical outgrowth of the interest in African Americans, and marks a natural consequence of the reality of social contact between the two groups. These literary representations are found in two predominant modes: romantic and realistic prose and poetry.

The realistic approach, composed primarily in prose fiction, endeavors to depict a socially mimetic experience of things as they are. It documents the initial and ongoing impression held by Hebrew writers of Blacks in American social life. The more romantic mode is sentimental, stereotypical, and less concerned with the here-and-now encounter. The discrepancy between the two modes stems more out of individual writers' personal artistic and ideological predilections than geographic location relative to Black communities. Also, it is not incorrect to assert that the romantic representation of Blacks conforms to the individual writers' general tendency to perceive the world in a sentimental vein in other instances as well.

Hebrew literature's realistic works that encounter the Other are primarily concerned with the external aspects of African American society, dwelling on a host of points of contact. As its romantic counterpart, representation in this vein also tends to be superficial perception, depending on stereotypes by an outsider looking at a complex society. Nevertheless, these experiences helped to lend Americanized Hebrew literature a fresh new character.

Unlike nearly all other compositions by Hebrew writers, Lisitzky's collection, *B-'oholay Khush* (In the tents of Cush, 1953) endeavors to depict the African American experience from a uniquely internal perspective, focusing on its folkways as a mirror of the spiritual component of the community. This chapter will focus on his anthology's dependence on stereotypical themes of Black religious and secular songs. The next chapter will survey all remaining works, most of which not just represent Blacks more realistically, but also portray more intimate encounters between them and Jews.

The near absence of any significant Jewish protagonists in the individual poems of this collection, and their resemblance to works emerging out of Black culture, is an indication that *B-'oholay Khush*, too, resembles those long poems that focus on the life, experiences, and practices of the American Indian. These, and a handful of similar but shorter poems,[2] constitute a unique subgenre in modern Hebrew literature, adapting the conceit of portraying a world of others as if from within. Directly or not, these poets are heirs to the archetypal model they found in Longfellow's "Song of Hiawatha."[3]

It is this point of view, as if observing from within, that distinguishes Lisitzky's poetry of African Americans' experience from most poems and stories composed by Hebrew writers. Those other writers, among them E. Silberschlag, A. Z. Halevy, S. Halkin, S. L. Blank, and I. J. Schwartz (in Yiddish and Hebrew), to name a few, incorporated the encounter with the Other as one of the Jewish immigrant's salient experiences in the New World. Lisitzky's encounter with Black culture becomes the most exemplary act of auto-assimilation of Hebrew writers in American life. It probes a host of responses made by his subjects to their new milieu while it educates readers about America's cultural diversity.

Composed from this point of view, it is no wonder that readers found Lisitzky's narratives particularly strange and exotic. Doubtless, many must have wondered of their relevance to Jews' immediate concerns since, observes Dov Sadan, the "life of the immigrant was the central subject of American Yiddish literature, especially of its poetry, which came to express the fate and especially the state of his soul torn between the pain of his yearning for his old homeland and the pains of his absorption into his new homeland."[4]

By attenuating the cultural gap between himself and his subject, Lisitzky effaces his identity and role as narrator, presenting the narrative of each poem in an unmediated, direct fashion. Such intimacy, also exhibited in works by Silkiner and Efros before him, distinguishes the Hebrew poetry composed in the United States about minority groups from all other Hebrew literary products. It is an attitude never embraced before in modern Hebrew literature in the Diaspora, and perhaps through the annals of Hebrew belles lettres. The sole exceptions to this process are modern translations into Hebrew of other national epics, prepared by translators ranging from Bialik and Tschernichowsky to Ḥayim Lensky and others in our days. Principally, however, these were not original compositions in imitation of some other nation's works.[5]

However, Lisitzky went even further than his fellow poets, who have either written little about minorities or focused primarily on Native Americans. The poems of *B-'oholay Khush* echo themes and concerns pervading the works of Black poets, replicating popular subjects and forms of authentic Black folksongs. Though we may question the literary quality of his poems, thematically they support the contention that Lisitzky deserves the title of the most Americanized of Hebrew poets.

Illustrating the rapid and deliberate integration of Jews into the American landscape, Lisitzky recollects one of his earliest experiences as he witnessed Jewish life in turn-of-the-century Boston. In one of the most moving and edifying autobiographies composed by a Hebrew writer, *Eleh toldot adam* (*In the Grip of Cross Currents*), Lisitzky, still a young yeshivah student, tells of his reactions to the street scene in Boston on the first weekend of his arrival in the New World. Stunned, he looks on as Jews scurry about on the Sabbath, working feverishly while ignoring the sanctity of the day of rest in their pursuit of material gain:[6]

> But in Boston very few Jews observed the Sabbath. In the Jewish quarter through which she had just passed they trampled with weekday shoes the train of her bridal gown and interrupted with shrill weekday outcries the music of her angelic escorts on her way to her betrothed. Leaving the synagogue after the Sabbath Eve service, the observant were confronted by a tumultuous Jewish quarter: shopkeepers stood in their shop doorways, peddlers on their wagons shouted their wares. Mournfully I passed through this Jewish quarter that first Sabbath eve. (*In the Grip*, 67; *Eleh toldot*, 66)

Confronted with the scene of cultural and spiritual assimilation—in which Lisitzky would later also participate—awaiting in the New World, Hebrew poets pondered their people's encounter with the allure of America. Their look beyond the Jewish pale sensitized them to the presence of other groups who were facing similar dilemmas. In the course of these explorations, which in themselves represent a measure of "assimilation," Hebrew writers could not but dwell on the fate of others with a degree of fascination and depth heretofore unmatched in their literature's traditions. Whether out of a desire to learn of them in the New World or a curiosity bordering on the morbid about America's absorption of alien cultures, their writing about non-Jews was unmatched in the course of Hebrew letters in terms of quantity and quality.

Lisitzky, like Silkiner, Efros, and others before him, depicted the encounters of Blacks and Native Americans with European civilization. Unlike them, he followed up his publication of *Mdurot do`akhot* (Dying campfires, 1937),[7] a volume-long poem devoted to Native Americans' life, culture, and its confrontation with White civilization, with one pertaining to Black folk culture. Lisitzky admitted that this composition, *B-'oholay Khush*, was planned as a companion volume to the former, though differing from it in significant ways:

> This book, *B-'oholay Khush*, is a complement to my book *Mdurot do'akhot*. In this too, as in the former, I sought to record, in our Hebrew poetry, an echo of American verse at the time of its formation out of a mighty struggle—a struggle of forces uprooted from their homelands and cast into a primordial mix to become a new being. How far did I succeed in what I wanted to do?—let the reader read and judge. (*B-'oholay*, 4)

By this stroke alone Lisitzky unveils a more complete picture of the Other in the New World than his fellow Hebraists. He, who began to publish poetry in America in 1904,[8] was among the first wave of writers to significantly impact the corpus of an evolving Hebrew literature in the twentieth century. Embracing all themes, his poems look back to the Old Country, confront the New World, look inward in lyrical works, and ponder metaphysical conundrums, the Holocaust, and Eretz Israel. As of most New World Hebrew poets, his modernism was founded less on formal poetic innovation than on the scope and depth of American themes he incorporated. As he often admitted, Lisitzky drew inspiration for themes and forms from the premiere Hebrew poets of the modern age, Ḥ. N. Bialik and S. Tschernichowsky, the giants of the National Renaissance, or *teḥiyah*, who inspired most American Hebraists with their classical style.[9] Like Bialik, Lisitzky was preoccupied with the inherent tension between the expansive socio-cultural world without and the poet's lyrical universe within. But unlike him Lisitzky's glances backward are more nostalgic, short on the venom and despair of his mentor's expression.[10]

In poetic terms, too, Lisitzky is a student of the two giants. He is fond of long-lined verses and the long poem known in Hebrew as the *po'ema* (or poema, the long poem).[11] Like theirs, his affinity for the classical style in Hebrew is motivated by a traditional education and attention to the leading Hebrew poetic fashion of his days. Combined, these also account for his attraction to the works of Shakespeare, of which he translated *Julius Caesar* (1933) and *The Tempest* (1941) into Hebrew. It is likely that his affinity for the poema, on the other hand, was also reinforced by the long poems of Edwin Arlington Robinson, who was admired by other Hebrew poets as well.[12]

FORMATION OF *B-'oholay Khush*

In the course of his travels in the New World and ultimate settling in New Orleans, Lisitzky could not but appreciate the fate and lot of America's Blacks, an interest that engendered *B-'oholay Khush.* The more than three-hundred-page volume is totally dedicated to poetry inspired by and resembling genres, themes. and features pervading African American songs and poems. The works emulate the culture, aspirations, beliefs, religious practices, and worldviews of African Americans. It bears the imprints of collections of poems and songs of Blacks, indicating a likely influence on his choices by extant English-language anthologies available in his days. The volume's most striking feature is that the poems are composed as if from within Black culture, with the sole exception proving the rule.[13] Nevertheless, they are entirely original works composed by Lisitzky, inspired, though, by the cultural environment and Black folksong or poetry of the Harlem Renaissance in the decade following the First World War.[14]

The years 1941–1951 were the most intensive in shaping the volume, indicating a determination to write a sufficient number of poems to supplement those composed earlier bearing similar themes. In 1927–1928, the appearance of an early version of one of the poems, "Mrivay khohanim" (Reverend arguments), must have been the impetus for further interest in the subject.[15] However, by the time of the book's publication it, too, was revised and expanded to its current size of 303 lines (171–181).

Writing of *B-ʾoholay Khush*, scholars puzzled over the motives behind Lisitzky's devotion and desire to compose works about Black people's experience in the United States. Testimonies to this effect, however, abound in his own words, as in his introductory note to the volume. In addition, comments by acquaintances have added to the possible motives, all the more to place into doubt any single reason. Of these, however, several figure centrally. Lisitzky's numerous contacts with members of the New Orleans Black community during the years of his residence in the Crescent City (1918–1962) have added a dimension of familiarity and respect for what he learned. The strong bonds he formed with the Black community are underscored by the reception they held years later in his honor to celebrate the publication of *B-ʾoholay Khush*.[16] However, his initial interest and familiarization with the Black community is founded on a sense of shared fate and destiny following his initial acquaintance, since no documented encounters exist between Lisitzky and Blacks during the years of his life in northern states (1900–1918). It is this experienced familiarity, then, that no doubt served as a basis for *B-ʾoholay Khush*.

Alternatively, it is not unlikely that Lisitzky's encounters with southern Blacks merely furnished him with the themes for the expression of what was already a personal predisposition to explore his own and human suffering. Read this way, and in addition to it being his reflection on the lot of others, *B-ʾoholay Khush* is Lisitzky's mirror of the self. The poet's experiences, his mother's death in his childhood, the abysmal privation of his family in Europe, a life marked by personal misfortune, a self-perception as one destined to suffer, his status as an outsider socially and nationally, as an immigrant, and a temperament to display these as features of a personal life fraught by misfortune—for "scratching at his own wounds" as some critics put it—have converged to engender this work.[17]

RECEPTION

It is the sense of a shared fate, identification with the lot of the Other, that readers consider to be the dominant theme in *B-'oholay Khush.* Lisitzky's personal experiences and observations on the human condition were the impetus behind his sympathy with victims of fate, to see him mirrored in cases of oppression and injustice.[18] What distinguish him from many Hebrew poets who have done the same are the measure of his embrace and the depth of his compassion. Whether Jew or Gentile, man or woman, the overarching experience of injustice—by human hands or the inexplicable divine—have been at the root of Lisitzky's proclamation of his brotherhood with all.[19]

Lisitzky's sympathy for African Americans also emanates from his national and personal past. His skills at melding the personal and national experiences with those of others, speaking in the name of his people and humanity at large, have drawn more than a few comments. As a Jew, he shared in the national memory of the Hebrews' slavery in Egypt, a narrative with which Blacks, too, identified in their construction of a collective experience.[20] Also, Lisitzky often told of his father and grandfather who, despite their educational background, were fated to remain water carriers in Slutzk, his home town. They were "Gibeonites," he declared, a reference to the servile peoples told of in Joshua 9. The recollection of this poverty remained a powerful one in the poet's identity, a scar that he repeatedly evoked as a mark of shame and injustice meted out by a capricious fate.[21]

The enslavement and subjugation of Blacks, during slavery and after Emancipation, resonate with the poet's experience. His empathy for the injustices borne by others occasions him to voice his private anguish as a strategy to attain a personal catharsis. So strong is the nexus between the self and the group in his poems that critics could not but assert that *B-'oholay Khush* also includes traces of the Jewish soul. Elaborating on these, some have added that the accounts about Blacks and Native Americans are a reflection of the Jewish experience of subjugation, shame, and an abiding hope for salvation.[22] Readers also acknowledge his introduction of new themes into Hebrew literature as he voiced the Jews' engagement with the exotic in America,[23] or directed his indictment of its subjugation of the downtrodden.[24]

Alternately, the poems are read as a personal expression of Lisitzky's abysmal loneliness and fatalism about a life of failures.[25] The nature of words, and the process of writing, avers one reader, are his therapy as he seeks a modicum of redemption. Also curative on humanitarian levels, Lisitzky's choice to represent the life of Blacks legitimizes them and their worth,[26] rendering them and their experiences familiar to any reader. By this stroke alone, Lisitzky obliterates the distinction between the Hebrew reader and the exotic Other that Blacks stood for.

The style of *B-ʾoholay Khush* is less confined to a classical expression than much of the poet's *oeuvre.* It represents one of the poet's most liberated expressions of identity with his subject. As opposed to the likes of Halkin, the very act of writing is a manifestation of his attaining transcendence, a metaphysical proximity to the Absolute. This poetry is a personal poetry, asserts Rabinowitz, in that it is "organic" and "necessary" in the poet's journey "from himself to himself."[27]

Lisitzky's affinity for Black society, and particularly the rural communities in the South, is not a sudden reaching out to identify another oppressed group in America. Were we to take his claims made in verse as testimony, then the opening of the long poem, "ʿEzra hakohen" (Reverend Ezra)—which is phrased to appear as his personal, though fictionalized, testimony—recalls an early encounter with Blacks. He tells how, as a youth in Europe, his interest in America's Blacks was kindled after reading Harriet Beecher Stowe's *Uncle Tom's Cabin:*[28]

> This is the chapter
> Of Black slavery, which matters also to one whose ancestors
> Were slaves long ago . . . ,
> Out of its pages he envisaged plants
> Of paradise that his imagination conjured up in his youth,
> Thus the foreign book, with the black visage of its Blacks enchanted
> him . . .
> While still a lad,
> Entitled "Tom's Cabin,"
> And its Hebrew garb took on a Hebrew semblance,
> As he took them close to heart and cast them to the distant past,
> And saw them as a Semitic tribe, joined to those of his ancestors
> Subjugated with them in Egypt's bondage. I observed
> As I came South, the Blacks, their ways and manners,
> And said of them: Black are we but comely!
> (*B-ʾoholay*, 204–205)

Melding past and present, the poet portrays himself as simultaneously young and old, and whose sympathies for Blacks and the downtrodden form an unbroken chain in a lifelong experience. To underscore his attitude by a textual stroke, Lisitzky reinterprets the last words—"Sheḥorim anaḥnu v-naʾavim"—of the last line above. Derived from the Song of Songs 1:5, "Sheḥorah ani v-naʾavah," "I am black but comely"—the poet redirects the reference from the beloved woman to affirm a shared historical and even tribal identity with Blacks. He takes some liberty by explicating the biblical text and asserting that Africans joined the Children of Israel in their Exodus out of Egypt, a matter on which he expands in a long poem, "So Miriam Spoke of Moses" ("Va-tdaber Miriam b-Moshe"). In this way he reverses the conventional content of spirituals and gospel songs. For while the latter have relocated the biblical narrative of bondage and the Exodus from the Jewish to the Black experience of enslavement in the New World, his act reassigns them to the Jewish experience.[29]

In an early poem, "Southward" ("Negba"), composed soon after he was hired to work in New Orleans but still dated as Milwaukee, Tammuz [c. July–August] 1918, Lisitzky writes of his plans to head South[30] to dwell in a landscape which includes "Barefoot Blacks here and there" ("Kushim yeḥefim poh v-sham . . ."). Although romanticized, the tone of the poem cannot be but an expression of glee at the prospect of moving to where he would be encountering African Americans—an experience which, presumably, he did not have while residing in the North.

Readers expounding on these poems frequently cite Lisitzky's observation on the relationship between his Jewish identity and America's downtrodden minorities. At the conclusion of his autobiography, he confirms a lingering fascination with the social crucible of America:

> American soil is a vast battleground. A new life is being forged on it, out of a clash of elements violently torn from their context and matrix and wrenched from their ordered categories and equations, so that they might be recreated in a new organic form. There is something sublime in this drama of the struggle of the titans, at once sublime and tragic. One people—the Indians—being extirpated from American soil, its ancient homeland. Another—the Negroes—trampled, pushed around, cast down. And a third—the Jews—struggling to preserve something of its own character in the midst of this new existence. This drama, with its aspect of the sublime and the tragic, holds great promise for American Hebrew poetry and, indeed, for Hebrew poetry in general. (*In the Grip*, 299–300; *Eleh toldot*, 278)

Expounding on his regard for African Americans, Lisitzky, in the foreword to *B-ʾoholay Khush*, offers a brief survey of Black experiences in America, their enslavement, emancipation, religious practices, habits of identification with narratives from the Bible, and communal singing as expressions of their subjugation and aspirations.[31] In presenting such specific insights of African Americans in this instance and Native Americans in another, Lisitzky enriched Hebrew literature with forms and themes of what he perceived to be authentic folk cultures unmarred by secular and cosmopolitan values. For a number of reasons, however, these poems have never found their way into the canon of Hebrew literature. As per the poems of *B-ʾoholay Khush*, they were seldom incorporated into any anthologies,[32] have rarely been published in translation,[33] nor fostered imitators.

The poet's own comments about his work have been the foundation upon which more than a few critics relied to convey their interpretations. Some of the blame, then, for the lack of fruitful comparative examinations of Lisitzky's *B-ʾoholay Khush* with Black folksongs is to be laid at the feet of the poet himself. It was he, after all, who provided the raw material, as in his introduction, that critics paraphrased. Were critics to have exerted themselves, their studies could have illuminated more fully the variety of genres and thematic affinities Lisitzky's work shares with that of African American songs, religious and other. Thus, for instance, most reviewers erroneously term the poems in Lisitzky's volume as "spirituals," instead of recognizing the generic diversity which his collection embraces.

Whereas some critics declare that, out of a sense of identity with Black experience, Lisitzky presents the reader with a sequence of "Black spirituals,"[34] others, seeking to expand the categories, resort to Western poetical topoi to describe his poems as lyrical poems, ballads, or idylls. Hillel Bavli, Lisitzky's longtime friend,[35] focuses on the influence of the ballad as a model for the longer poems of the book, speaking especially about "So Miriam Spoke of Moses" ("Va-tdaber Miriam b-Moshe") and "Israel in Shittim" ("Israel ba-shitim").[36] B. Y. Michali, while asserting that the collection is a composite of sundry categories and poetic genres, identifies only two: "lyrical poems" and "adventure poems."[37]

Adopting a more plausible course, Yariv Margalit seeks known categories of Black art to identify poems in Lisitzky's anthology that resemble them: "spirituals," "blues," and, without explaining why, "jazz" poems. As for the language, Margalit describes it as a *mlitzah*—a narrative formed by a patchwork of biblical fragments employed primarily during the Haskalah—which leads him to conclude sadly that "the voice of Jacob is heard here out of the 'Tents of Cush,' . . . though we do not hear the voice of Cush in this book except in a very muted way."[38]

Grouping the poems by content has led Yitzḥak ʿOgen in a productive direction. He identifies them as representing slave songs, work songs, lynching and hanging songs, songs of the Black maid, the fleeing slave, songs to and about saviors from slavery—Moses and Lincoln.[39] Although his topos is accurate, ʿOgen does not take the added step of bridging his list of categories with the genres of Black songs.[40]

Indeed, determining genres more by content than by form is a characteristic of many collections, as evidenced by volumes appearing in the years following the Harlem Renaissance. Albeit somewhat late, Lisitzky was doubtlessly inspired by the assemblage of a Black poetic record, including folksongs, upon which he drew to shape and organize his own collection.

Inspired by spirituals and gospel songs, Lisitzky strove to compose his version of these and other genres of Black folksongs. Since those "spirituals,"[41] composed in a more formal and structured fashion in the twentieth century by known hands, and in urban settings, are known as gospel songs,[42] some of Lisitzky's poems are more appropriately gospel songs, though they generally avoid references to the Christian gospels. However, as evidenced from the poems presented in *B-ʾoholay Khush*, he relies on many other themes of Black folksongs and poems. In one, "Pete's on his way" ("Holekh l-masaʿo Pete"; 1952, 90–91), he demonstrates an understanding of the multi-layered train song as a vehicle for physical and transcendental salvation:

PETE'S ON HIS WAY

A letter arrived from on high
By hands of a flying messenger,
A letter arrived from on high
This is what the message said:
"Your being on earth is done,
Pack, Pete, your bundle, don't delay,
And on your way
To heavenly pastures make ready!"
Farewell, farewell, cousin and friend,
Pete's on his way!

A ticket was folded in that message
Sent from on high to me,
A ticket was folded in that message
On it my name I could see—

A journey on a train,
To heavenly pastures from the valley of death
It'll carry me on its way
On its wondrous track—
Farewell, farewell, cousin and friend,
Pete's on his way!

No separate seating on the train
For a Blackman of a downcast people,
No separate seating on the train—
There the downcast is as the noble.
Blackman, White, stranger and resident—
Seats in it are equal for all,
As in heavenly pastures,
Whether of the North or South—
Farewell, farewell, cousin and friend,
Pete's on his way!

Here comes the train
To take me to heaven's pastures,
Here comes the train
To this here station—
Pete's ready, loaded with the bundle he packed
Enter he will when the conductor
Give the sign
To all passengers: all aboard!—
Farewell, farewell, cousin and friend,
Pete's on his way!
(New Orleans, Iyar 1952)

To better appreciate the extent of Lisitzky's accomplishment, it is best to examine this poem against an authentic Black spiritual, "De Gospel Train":[43]

DE GOSPEL TRAIN

De gospel train am a-comin',
I hear it just at han',
I hear de car-wheels rumblin'
An' rollin' th'oo' de lan'.

I see de train a-comin',
She's coming' 'roun' de curve,

She's loosen'd all her steam an' brakes
An' strainin' ev'ry nerve.

De fare is cheap an' all can go,
De rich an' poor are dare,
No second class aboa'd dis train,
No diff'rence in de fare.

Den git on boa'd little children,
Git on boa'd little children,
Git on boa'd little children,
Dere's room for many a mo'.

Both poems employ the image of a train, a central feature of many songs and folksongs. It is the train's metaphoric import that gives it a layered nuance in religious songs, spirituals, or gospel songs. An examination of the two works readily reveals that they use the train for similar purposes. On the most literal level, trains are among the vehicles that convey Blacks away from the lands of enslavement. Following the early decades of the nineteenth century, when spirituals are thought to have first emerged,[44] trains became the chief symbol as the vehicle of conveyance out of slavery in the South and into (presumed) freedom in the North, rapidly moving from objects bearing literal to figurative significance.

Whether used as literal object or metaphor, as in the term "underground railroad," the symbolic relevance of the train as a means of deliverance from servitude is paramount in these songs. In the popular folk imagination, trains took on the Industrial Age's metaphysical import of vehicles transporting spirits from this corrupt world to a better one, giving rise to the image of a train to heaven. This addition validates the poem's message even in the post-Emancipation age as a vehicle for deliverance to a true paradise.

The discovery of de facto discrimination even in the North—when the desire for freedom persisted as the chief aspiration of Blacks and other downtrodden peoples in the Land of the Free—cast the metaphor into metaphysical realms. The train's abstraction in "De Gospel Train" and in Lisitzky's poem is an expression of the frustration experienced by the poet with a forestalled move to attain equality in a democratic civilization. In terms of form, too, Lisitzky realized the mesmerizing effect that repeating lines have in these songs, something which he assiduously reproduced in many instances.

In conformity with their metaphysical sentiments, both poems ponder the irony of true equality being only in the world beyond, projecting the ideal to higher spheres. The realization is that justice is not in the United States, nor does freedom reign in America, but only in the domain of the afterlife, where discrimination no longer holds dominion. These sentiments allow Lisitzky to explode the limits of idealism in the Golden Land, much in the same way as Silkiner and Efros have done in venting their resentment at what European civilization has wrought with the culture of the Native Americans.[45]

PERFORMANCE

The most glaring differences between the above poems, as in others, indicate the shortcomings of Lisitzky's execution. One obvious disparity is the implied function of the text. Words of original spirituals were a scaffolding for free expression and dynamic change. Often altered as the need arose, they exhibit the effect of a set sequence of expected phrases which may be moved from song to song, at times even opening the door to new songs. Lisitzky's work, while relatively more free in spirit than a significant portion of his other poetry, is only relatively unencumbered by the rigid, long, and formal poetic lines and meters of his work. His language bears the marks of a formal literary Hebrew devoid of any attempt to simulate a vernacular style.

Spirituals are performance pieces, designed to be sung and amplified upon. Without that dimension, their lyrics are lifeless and sparse. Left unsung, a principal aspect of the spirituals is missed. It is in their performance that the unique impact of gospel songs and spirituals is brought to bear upon listeners, who often also become active participants. The rhythms, cadences, melodic and sonoric qualities of the performance in the execution of these songs affect the audience at metaverbal levels.

It is the performative dimension of the Black spiritual which Lisitzky could not reproduce or recapture. The rhythm, tune, and African American speech patterns imbued the authentic songs with traits beyond Lisitzky's powers to simulate. His work, while true in theme and form, pales in comparison. It is a feeble imitation of the essence which is at the core of many a gospel song and spiritual. If there is a redeeming value to his poems, though, it resides in the representation of only some thematic and formal features of Black songs.

For all their intent to capture Black culture, Lisitzky's poems do not succeed in reproducing the spiritual or gospel song, nor for that matter even the blues or poems of biblical themes. This shortcoming is rooted chiefly in the limitations of his poems. Much as we have witnessed in his rendition of Indian tales, these have also become an intellectualized version of their original models, sanitized in form, content, expression, and colloquialism. His poems were not composed to be sung or performed in other ways. Although the poet attempted to simulate a sense of the rhythm of a spiritual or gospel song, he did not succeed in transcending their simplest formal structure. The singing of an original spiritual by a chorus or a congregation reflects the performance features missing from Lisitzky's work.

Another notable feature which Lisitzky did not accomplish, and does not appear to have even attempted, was to simulate the spoken, folksy language of African American folksongs and poems. The language, or dialect as it has become known, employed in Black folksong distorts expression to affect a distinctive style. The earthy, folk language of the Black spiritual is what lends it life and a uniqueness of texture that Lisitzky's Hebrew never even attempts to reach. Instead, his Hebrew continues to reflect an elevated poetic style, converting the folksong into a formal poem. Nourished by a strict, text-based tradition of Hebrew learning and poetry, Lisitzky makes no attempt to create a style to simulate Black dialect. For Lisitzky, who considered his translation of Shakespeare's *The Tempest* and *Julius Caesar* into a purely biblical Hebrew style a great accomplishment,[46] even the model of Mendele's *nusaḥ*—a creative amalgam of Hebrew of all ages conveyed with a dose of a freer syntax—was unthinkable.[47]

However, it is not altogether for the lack of a fitting and readily accessible model that he does not do so. Writing most of the poems in the 1940s and 1950s, Lisitzky might have looked to the examples of an emerging Hebrew colloquial style or slang forming in Eretz Israel, for example, to simulate what Black dialect does with the English language. Hebrew literature, even before the establishment of the State of Israel, was shedding the classical styles of the Haskalah and legacies of post-Haskalah writers brought up on Mendele's *nusaḥ*. The writings in poetry and prose of the likes of Shlonsky, Rachel, Moshe Shamir, and S. Yizhar, and the emergence of a spoken Hebrew idiom, were not unknown to Lisitzky. His avoidance of these options cannot be but a conscious choice to not represent Black dialect by lowering his poetic style to a spoken, Israeli or Sabra Hebrew. Instead, his language remains laced with biblical allusions which are far beyond what ordinary spirituals contain.[48]

As in "De Gospel Train," the train occupies a significant place in many other Black songs and poems. Other poems in Lisitzky's collection featuring conveyances such as the ferry or train in a fashion similar to the above example include "Hurry, scurry to the ferry" ("Ushu ḥushu el ha-dovrah"), "The train's call" ("Kol kri'at ha-rakevet"), and "To Canaan" ("Knaʿanah"). The train, then, has become a metaphor in the quest for freedom, or even a symbol of liberation from the miseries of this world as it transports the protagonist to a supernatural realm.[49]

Another example illustrating the use of the train as transporting the spirit to the world beyond represents a category of folktales termed the sermon. In it God and Satan are engineers of two trains, the former carrying souls to paradise, while the latter, full of sinners' souls, is headed for hell.[50]

A counterpart to the vehicle is the prison, a realm of confinement and loss of freedom, a return to a condition associated with servitude for the Black hero. The train is liberating in that it leads one away from the isolation of prison to rejoin society and loved ones, principally women: mother, wife, or lover. Without one, the prisoner's longing is for heaven, a metaphysical destination. Prison songs, by nature, are frequently categorized as blues instead of spirituals or gospel songs. For example, Lisitzky's poem "No wife, no daughter nor son have I" ("Lo raʿayah, lo ben v-lo bat li") is one of several of this genre.

A related motif imported by Lisitzky from familiar Black folksongs is that of the Mammy, the beloved mother figure for whom the prisoner pines. As a maternal figure she is the source of compassion, comfort, and love, an abode of an undisturbed childhood. It is to her that the oppressed protagonist attempts to flee from the merciless paternal forces of the establishment. The prisoner's expressed desire to be free, or escape, is a manifestation of his anxiety about the misery of the here-and-now. In the lap, or even womb of the nurturing mother figure one finds unconditional love, forgiveness, and primal comfort, a motif fixed squarely in the realm of Black songs and the image of African American women.

Lisitzky's "A convict's 'chain gang song'" ("Shir asir bi-'gdud-ha-kevel,'" 1942; 29) draws on a number of these themes. Spanning such issues as work on a chain gang, a longing for freedom, and a call to mother, its chief concern is the prisoner's confinement. In tone the poem fittingly illustrates the blues.

A CONVICT'S "CHAIN-GANG" SONG

I hear the train a-calling
And my heart burns with pain:

A Mammy I have far away—
To her my heart longs and pines!
"Mammy, Mammy!" my soul breaks
My head in your lap I will lay—
Mammy's lap will not alienate
Even one rebuffed by God!
"Mammy, Mammy!" to your cabin
I shall make my way in flight—
My legs are chained, and by me
A guard, a gun in his hand!
I hear the train a-calling
It calls not for me, O, not for me—
Take my greetings, train
To my Mammy!

A Black folksong bearing similar themes is "Chain Gang Blues."[51] Although difficult to substantiate any direct connections, it is representative of the kinds of songs from which the poet drew inspiration in composing his work:

CHAIN GANG BLUES

Standin' on the road side,
Waitin' for the ball an' chain.
Say, if I was not shackled down
I'd ketch that wes' boun' train.

Standin' on the rock pile
Wid a hammer in my hand,
Lawd, standin' on the rock pile,
Got to serve my cap'n down in no-man's land.

The judge he gave me sentence
'Cause I wouldn' go to work.
From sunrise to sunset
I have no other clean shirt.

All I got is lovin',
Lovin, an' a-sluggin',
Say I feels just like a stepchild,
Just gi'me me the chain gang blues.

Oh, my captain call me
An' my gal work in white folks' yard.

I believe I'll go there too,
'Cause I got the chain gang blues.

As in Black poetry, the image of the woman in Lisitzky's work, particularly the mother or her surrogate, is held in special reverence. His personal experience of losing his mother at an early age leaves the poet longing to reconstruct her from memory, with bits of images and an unquenched quest to recapture the loss. It is no wonder, then, that Lisitzky's sympathies are aroused in instances when the subject of the song, his own or those he read, becomes the woman. It is in her, and the fate of those who suffer her loss, that the poet discerns the scars of the human condition.[52]

Lisitzky's poem, "Black maid" ("Amah khushit," 1945; 55–57), reviews the experiences of a Black slave woman. As nursemaid to her master's children, she avenges his cruelty to her own by cursing the milk with which she nurses the White babies. Although resembling J. W. Johnson's "The Black Mammy," which also entertains the prospect of the Black maid's revenge against her master's children, this poem departs in its consideration of the prospect of salvation. Her prayer is that in serving the master's child she will facilitate the upbringing of a White redeemer for her people, as was Lincoln.

Another work resembling these poems is Langston Hughes's "The Negro Mother." However, Hughes's poem represents a later sensibility, one in which salvation emerges from within the Black community. In place of praising the Black nurse of White children for bringing up Whites who may eventually facilitate the salvation of Blacks, Hughes finds a model of courage, strength, and valor in the Black woman who stands up to protect her children against their tormentors.[53]

Many poems about the period of slavery survived as folksongs. These were supplemented in the twentieth century with others that revisit and reimagine the experience in light of contemporary circumstance. They underscore a modern response to slavery as a way to inform the spirit of modern-day American Black society.

Touching on some of the cruelest episodes of the African American experience, the premier Black poet Claude McKay and Lisitzky both focus on the American version of pogroms that culminate in the lynching of a Black man. Each exposes the duplicity of Whites who perpetrate the deed. McKay's poem, "The Lynch," foregrounds the inhumanity, indifference, and lack of revulsion even among genteel White women.[54] Lisitzky, for his part, in "When he was tied to the stake" ("Az ki usar el ha-ʿamud," 45), turns to one of his frequent ironies, terming the executioners "black

White-folk." Embellishing his poem with allusions to Judeo-Christian sources, he voices his outrage by observing that such deeds force the coming of the Messiah, a common notion in Jewish mystical tradition.[55] Adding to this from Christian imagery, Lisitzky refers to Jesus offering to undergo a second crucifixion to atone for the White Man's sin.

Poetry of revolt, the voice of what became the storm of the Civil Rights Movement within an emancipated Black society deprived of civil rights, appeared incrementally in works by African American poets. Following the First World War, Black poetry became a tapestry of voices reacting variously to the de facto segregation pervading America. The debate surrounding the measure of anger to be expressed, and the directness with which it is to be represented—whether subtly or by calls for vindictive reprisals—figured centrally in discussions among Black intellectuals and literary figures.[56] Poets, similarly, made their own choices, whether by distancing themselves from the emotional issue, alerting the reader with cautious warnings, or calling for violent response to discrimination and violence.

Lisitzky's more conciliatory tone about rising tensions between Blacks and Whites did not keep up with the evolution of these sentiments. While his poems also bore warnings, his sense of frustration and altered stance in trying to resolve the matter did not take on the extremes one finds even among moderate Black poets. Writers such as Johnson proceeded to exploit ironic and sardonic tones, while others resorted to hostile and violent expressions, some even voicing a reversed racism.

One of Lisitzky's often-cited poems on the subject is "Yes, so black is the Blackman's body" ("Amen shaḥor guf ha-Kushi," 1941; 24–26), in which he not only warns of the rise of Blacks against their oppressors, but also humanizes the hero by underscoring his hard work and productivity:

YES, SO BLACK IS THE BLACKMAN'S BODY

Yes, so black is the Blackman's body, blacker, blacker than the night.
Yes, so black is the Blackman's body, for so made him God.
But black is not the sweat,
The sweat that streams—
From that body so black
No, not black is his sweat,
Sweat of brow and sweat of arm!
The sweat of his brow, the sweat of his arm,
As it gushes to God's good earth

Will bloom and blossom from its clods
Cotton white, cotton pure.

Yes, so black is the Blackman's body, blacker, blacker than all mortals,
Yes, so black is the Blackman's body, for so made him the Eternal!
But black is not the sweat—
Sweat of Blackman's race—
Who shall loathe him, who shall mock?
No, oh no, black is not the sweat
This black body streams;
Sweat of Blackman's black race
As it flows to earth of God
Will bloom and blossom from its clods
Maize, its hue as that of gold.
. . . .
Black, yes, black is the Blackman's body, but in him, too, a red heart dwells.
Red, yes, red is the Blackman's heart and in it a fire flames.
And red, yes, red it is oh so!—
It burns and burns within him so low,
But the day will come, not faraway,
The flame of his red fire
He'll no longer hold at bay!
Bursting, pouring on his masters
His fire's flame, of mutiny,
Fear, saith the black Blackman,
The flush of my flame is kindled within me! (Hendersonville, 1941)

A repeated use of the word *black* (often in conjunction with the prevailing Hebrew term for Black at the time, "Kushi," or Cushite, though used analogically with the English Negro, both of which are currently deemed pejorative) as noun and adjective, indicates the poet's attempt to neutralize the negative connotations associated with the word, especially as he entwines it with other colors. Instead, he underscores the interdependence between the color of the Black laborer and the product of his work. The fact that some people are black, argues the poet, is an act of the Almighty, as are the surprising and consequent products of the Black man's labors—white cotton and golden grain. Yet it is the Black man's sweat through which divine blessings are made manifest. Though the external color of people may vary, that which unifies and blurs all distinctions is the redness of blood and heart, the inner flame of passion, a quest for equal treatment and a resistance to ongoing deprivation. In Lisitzky's poetry, color becomes a matter of morality.

Lisitzky's call to heed the signs of impending troubles resembles in tone the poetry composed by Black poets of the interwar years, though it falls short of the rage contained in their later poems. The inevitable uprising of Blacks to fight for civil rights is a theme occupying many poets. Countee Cullen's "Heritage" (1925) expresses the tension between racial pride and the desire to wreak vengeance, which he tries to control. In "Strong Men," Sterling A. Brown praises physical strength as a means of deterrence or settling a conflict. Langston Hughes, in "Militant," offers a more overt, violent option for retaliation against inequities in the treatment of Blacks. More violent, and even racist, expressions have been voiced by other Black writers since the composition of the latter poem.[57]

One of the African American poems purporting to examine the eternal relationship between Whites and Blacks in America adopts an ironic posture while turning to theological tenets. James W. Johnson's "Saint Peter Relates an Incident of the Resurrection Day"[58] speculates about the condition of African Americans at the time of the Resurrection. In its narrative, the poem dwells on the resurrection of the war dead, including the soldier buried in the Tomb of the Unknown Soldier who, much to the chagrin of Whites, turns out to be Black. The racists react by contemplating reburying him, though they realize that death no longer exists. The poem ends ironically in observing that even far into the future, on resurrection day, bigotry persists in this country.[59]

MIDRASH AND SONG SERMONS

The second part of Lisitzky's anthology, entitled "Priestly sermons" ("Divray masa mi-pi khohanim"), is also based on familiar Black poetic traditions. The term *masa* in the title, in addition to denoting a burden, which also refers to the pronunciation of a prophetic or oracular message, conveys an ethical word to an imagined audience. The "sermons" are presented in eight poems of relatively medium length, each up to twelve pages long. Unlike the poems of the first part, they represent, as their section's title suggests, poems inspired by Black sermons, and not hymns or folksongs. As if to buttress that effect, they sometimes include the narrator's asides or questions to an imagined audience. What they lack, like those before, is the performative component evident in the spirited presentations of Black church sermons, as well as the occasional phrases incorporating popular Black dialect.

In content and character these poems resemble published sermons in verse, or song sermons, a prevalent genre of Black poetry.[60] Many song sermons incorporate elements that they share with the spiritual; chief among them is the fanciful exploitation of biblical narrative. "The spirituals, as the narratives, are a folk product, often influenced by the Bible, though the authority of the Bible is replaced by free paraphrasing so characteristic of folk tales and poems."[61] The observations are just as applicable to song sermons as to spirituals.

A shared tendency of Lisitzky's work and Black poems—though it resonates best within the context of a modern Hebrew text—are allusions to biblical subtexts. This includes James Weldon Johnson's "O Black and Unknown Bards,"[62] in which he refers to Isaiah and other prophets in his praise of Black poets.[63] Also, Roscoe C. Jamison's "The Negro Soldiers" compares Black soldiers to the crucified Jesus, as they gave up their lives so that others may live: "Shedding their blood like Him now held divine./ That those who mock might find a better way!"[64] His language equates the dead soldiers with Jesus in that all reach the divine sphere in the way their blood was shed.

Though Lisitzky might have read some song sermons, it is more likely that he witnessed such services at New Orleans Black churches. Hearing church sermons, as he attests to have done,[65] Lisitzky could easily recognize the Midrash-like liberties taken with biblical narratives by preachers who recast them in a contemporary, familiar context to embellish their homiletic and ethical sermons. In each case, a fanciful story plot is woven around a familiar biblical citation or account, often retelling or embellishing it in terms of the audience's experiences, all the while eliciting a moral applicable to contemporary issues. In the same way, song sermons by the likes of James Weldon Johnson—be they of creation, the parable of the prodigal son, the tale of Noah and the ark, the crucifixion, or Moses before Pharaoh—embellish the original account and are reminiscent of the genre of the Midrash.

Lisitzky, whose upbringing and traditional shtetl education included many years of Talmudic and midrashic literature, was well versed in the genre and its techniques. Inspired by Black sermons about biblical narratives, he composed his own, coupling the art of Midrash writing to that of the song sermon. His version of song sermons in *B-'oholay Khush* is represented by three long poems: the tale of the Children of Israel's sinfulness at Shittim (Numbers 25), Jacob's struggle with a mysterious stranger at the ford of the Jabbok (Genesis 32:23–33), and Miriam's accusation against Moses for having taken a Cushite wife (Numbers 12).

To readers familiar with the biblical account, this retelling is charming in the quaint, naive execution that captures the perspectives and attitudes of folk narrative. Presentation of contemporary cultural features from African American life together with elements drawn from the biblical world bridges the distance between antiquity and the listeners, lending the ancient account an amusing and refreshing immediacy. Thematically, the focus on the persistent weakness of human flesh in the face of worldly temptations is a frequent motif of African American and other folklore. The solution to such foibles, as this account advocates, is physical force instead of words.

Integrating a biblical retelling, whose moral is stated so blatantly with a portrayal of a Black preacher, benefits the poet in several ways. He can foreground an imaginative retelling of a familiar narrative of the Torah to resemble a Midrash as well as a Black sermon in verse. Also, it blurs the lines between the two genres, fusing the two cultural traditions in a way that, presumably, he would have liked their people themselves to come together. As in the case of all his poems, the act also distorts the identity of the narrator, permitting Lisitzky to play all roles concurrently—the Hebrew poet, the moralizing Black preacher, and the crucible of Americanism mixing Jewish and African American identities—all the while allowing each to retain some of its distinct cultural traits. This, no doubt, also satisfies his latent maskilic propensities to disseminate ethical teachings to readers who, as he knew, were in need of education about justice and racial tolerance.

The remaining five poems of this section, while identified as sermons, do not retell biblical narratives but resemble testimonials of spiritual rebirth. Their confessional accounts tell of traumatic events that brought the teller back to true faith. The narratives are directly addressed to a fictitious congregation, one familiar with Americanisms—including terms and cultural features such as doing the "jig," the traveling salesman, card-playing terms, voodoo as part of folk belief, and notions of the world beyond populated by figures such as Saint Peter, Satan, and the angel Michael. Moreover, the last three poems are unified by the voice of a single preacher who refers to his prior sermons, shares identity marks with them, and uses a similar language.

One of these poems, "For I seek kindness" ("Ki ḥesed ḥafatzti," 1952; 145–155, esp. part 8), resembles James Weldon Johnson's "The Train Sermon"[66] in that both represent the soul's otherworldly train journey. In a whimsical conclusion, the preacher of Lisitzky's composition encourages the congregants to make a contribution to the collection plate making its rounds among them, evidently not merely as a means for them to begin their process of salvation but as payment for his services.

The third part of the anthology, "All their ways" ("B-ʾorḥam uv-rivʿam," a reference to Psalm 139:3), contains the longest poems in the collection. Though numbering only four, they range from ten to fifty pages in length and comprise a broader array of themes than the preceding parts. The first, "Reverend arguments" ("Mrivay kohanim," 1927, 1948; 171–181), is charming in its contents but carries a serious warning. Its protagonists, Lincoln and Washington, are two ministers who drink and argue whether Satan is White or Black. In a seemingly typical Jewish Talmudic practice, each relies on prooftexts from the Bible to buttress his argument. Another Jewish element is the time of the action, identified as the Hebrew month Elul, the month of repentance before the Days of Awe. This choice is critical in constructing the poem's ironic message in light of the sinfulness of the protagonists. Their drinking, followed by a game of dice, leads to blows. The tale's moral, while transparent, also amuses the reader, implying that no matter the color of people, Satan resides in all.

The second poem, "Consecration night at a revival meeting" ("B-layl hitkadesh ʿatzeret teḥiyah," 1948; 181–201), depicts a revival meeting to instruct the Hebrew reader about an unfamiliar practice. It includes references to the role of spirituals as a means for transcending the oppression of the master, but avoids descriptions of any church-like service. It would seem that this feature of the revival meeting, of foregrounding the function of spirituals, is the poem's chief consideration. Specialized terms or words heard at revival meetings "Americanize" the Hebrew but also contribute to the alienation of many a Hebrew reader from cultural features as "safsal avelim" (mourners bench), the declaration "dat li matzati" (I found religion), "ba-ḥoshekh or ʿalay nagah" (In darkness light shone on me), and others.[67]

Having dispensed with the introduction, the poem presents the testimony of four speakers in four distinctly labeled cantos, each sharing an experience which led to his repentance and spiritual rebirth. The contents illustrate confessional and testimonial poetry. Much as in prior poems, they also capture the folk flavor of the situation by presenting fantastic descriptions of the world beyond, apocalypse, resurrection, and Judgment Day, a God who is immanent, angels all too human, and an easily attained salvation.

The drawback in the poem, as in a good number of others, illustrates the challenges facing anyone using an obscure Hebrew style. At the poem's opening, for example, readers are offered a description of nature that ought to be inspiring. Yet Lisitzky's language is so obscure, intellectualized, and impenetrable as to render comprehension nearly unfeasible. The difficult language becomes foregrounded in place of what it attempts to signify.

The most impressive of these long poems is "Reverend Ezra" ("'Ezra Ha-kohen," 1949; 203–255). It is also one of the few into which Lisitzky inserts himself as narrator and character, telling of his search for an African American who personally experienced and witnessed slavery. As with other long works found in his oeuvre,[68] it is set in "'Ir saharonah" (Crescent City), the popular appellation given to New Orleans, located as it is along a bend in the Mississippi River.

Speaking in an unmediated first person narrative to the poem's narrator, Ezra recounts his life as a slave, his marriage, the Civil War, and Blacks' continued struggle for equality. Personages such as Lincoln, John Brown, Wendel Philips, William Garrison, and Frederick Douglass anchor the tale in a setting that is mimetically historical and real.[69]

Other historical events lend a credible and very American background to the events. Among them are the notion of the Underground Railroad;[70] songs such as "Swing Low, Sweet Chariot"[71] and "John Brown's Body,"[72] all rendered in Hebrew translation; a summation of Frederick Douglass's ideas;[73] the phenomenon of White preachers' use of religion to promote slavery and assure the loyalty of slaves to the masters;[74] the likening of Blacks to the Children of Israel, as by citing the verse from Amos 9:7;[75] Black slaves' resistance;[76] folk practices such as the legally unsanctioned custom of performing marriages between Black slaves on the plantation, termed "jumping over the broomstick";[77] and the historical Battle of Fort Hudson.[78] The stylized language of the account also adds to the Hebrew flavor in that Ezra, believably acquainted with Scriptures, inserts biblical citations in his monologue.

The depiction of Ezra's first master as an enlightened, liberal, and progressive Jew,[79] and Ezra's message that liberation in the here-and-now is to be attained by an act of auto-emancipation through education,[80] represents a sequence of coded ideas indicative of Lisitzky's own Haskalah sensibilities—optimism that liberalism and education are the antidote to discrimination and marginalization.[81] At times, Ezra poses as the poet's double in terms of a common background and worldview. Though both have experienced much hardship at the hands of man and fate, they remain steadfast believers that no alternative solutions exist in life; neither seeks escape from his existential situation.

The last poem of the series, "Jupiter the gambler repents" ("Kuvyustus Yupiter ḥozer bi-tshuvah," 1949; 257–299), is another in the category of testimonial, confessional poems. It is a tale of a sinner who mends his ways, one in which love figures centrally and music is a means to reveal the soul, folk-ways, beliefs, spiritualism, and fantasy.

B-'oholay Khush closes the volume with a single poem, "America gam lanu" (America is ours, too; 1952, 302–304) in a separate section entitled "Conclusion" ("Ḥatimah"). It is Lisitzky's expression of convictions that resemble those of many Black poets concerning America. It is a poem summarizing African Americans' history and investment in America—by slavery, work, suffering, and discrimination. However, it also proclaims a commitment to democracy, recognition that Blacks, too, worship the same God, to whom they look for salvation and in whose eyes all are equal. Though possibly also writing in imitation of them, Lisitzky as an immigrant is also capable of expressing similar sentiments independently. America belongs to all her citizens, asserts the poet; Blacks, by virtue of their troubled history of enslavement, are just as deserving of an equal share of the American Dream as others. They, too, have invested their energies in the experiment of a democratic society. The assertion that equality is a principal feature in God's eyes, which remains an unrealized goal of America, is an expression of the ideal whose realization must guide all.

Lisitzky's is a unique collection of poems in Hebrew literature. In its embrace of the identity and experiences of American Blacks it effaces any Jewish communal concerns. But in the convergence of identities the collection foregrounds Lisitzky's sense of shared Diasporic experiences of African Americans and American Jews. Running as a sub-current in the book is the hope of realizing the American ideal of equality, all the while recognizing that it threatens one's ethnic or racial identity, culture, and value system. In taking these steps with both Native and African American groups, the poet has intertwined his art within the American literary and social fabric to an extent that—at least quantitatively if not in quality—exceeds all Hebrew poets.

However, an argument can be made in opposition to Lisitzky's seeming effacing of Jews' ethnic concerns. Most of all, the challenge before each minority remains to rescue unique aspects of its cultural identity as it meets head-on the overpowering assimilatory force of an all-embracing America. To retain a measure of uniqueness in a pluralistic society is a point of contention in the experience of a new ethnic group arriving at the shores of the New World and seeking to immerse itself into the mainstream. Yet a preservation of its unique culture should be in and of itself of value in a society that prides itself on tolerance and diversity. The question pertaining to the possibility of becoming totally Americanized, fully losing one's former cultural baggage in the process, is a trying one. For Jews, the realization that the mass of American citizenry remains religiously and thus in part culturally, unlike the fully assimilated Jew, stands as a last barrier that is difficult to cross. To retain one's unique heritage means rescuing a modicum of one's own culture. Though not a comparable experience, this may be an equivalent of the color barrier in the Americanization of Blacks. For as much as a Jew's religious baggage labels Jews as hyphenated Americans, the color of African Americans distinguishes them outwardly.

For Lisitzky to pose as a spokesman for African American society is admirable and problematic at one and the same time. As an active contributor to the Americanization of Hebrew letters, and a pillar of the short-lived American center of Hebrew literature, his oeuvre stands unrivaled. In terms of depth and scope, he charts the landscape of American minority life more fully than any other Hebrew writer.

This immersion in his subject effaces Lisitzky's identity, blurring the gap between himself and the Other. Such a strategy is both effective and thwarting in that he bridges the gap between the self and the Other, identifying his experiences in theirs. It is not too far from the truth to assert that Lisitzky is not confronting the Other, nor reaching out to understand the Other, as much as he strives to become that Other. In much of the poetry he wrote about African and Native American life Lisitzky no longer retains any identifying marks of being who he is, but has become the very Other he writes about. It is as if the fate of his people has already obliterated the distinction between Jews and that other minority subjected to the pressures of American life and culture. To be sure, his representations are also limited, composed as they are in a romantic vein, idealizing immanent qualities and overlooking more realistic factors about his subject.[82] Nonetheless, they present the Hebrew reader with the cultural and spiritual dimensions of African American and American Indian folk life. His contribution humanizes the Other, underscoring shared universal values. Finally, his writing does little to present the situation of these groups in the poet's present day, a task left primarily to writers of Hebrew prose, bolstered with the few exceptional exemplars of poetry, which prove the rule.

A methodological question that has to do with the end purpose of such writing by a Hebrew, and Jewish, poet, also calls for some consideration. First and foremost, the phenomenon of writing Hebrew poems resembling those composed by Blacks is, if nothing else, impressive. Among the rewards for Hebrew letters is an enriched poetic tradition that prior to this time has been reflexively involved with internal, communal, and national issues. It extends the themes touched on by Hebrew literature, and documents an important era in the Jewish experience.

To argue that the poets composing these works were posing as something else, as the Other of which they were writing, is not altogether untenable. The indirectness by which they retained some measure of social identity with their own ethnic and national concerns became so remote as to jeopardize their own (group) identity in their zeal to become Americanized. If anything stands as the last bastion redeeming these Hebrew poets from forfeiting their identity, then it is the Hebrew language. Many of the writers were fluent in English, though they did little to translate these works themselves or have others do so. So it was not a desire to compete with the likes of Longfellow that lay behind their writing. More likely, their fascination was with the processes of assimilation, their own and those of others, as minority cultures as they were coming into collision with Whites and their Western culture.

FROM PROP TO TROPE TO REAL FOLKS: BLACKS IN HEBREW LITERATURE

Chapter Seven

While the traditional attraction of Jews to Black issues was universalistic in tendency, based on comprehensive social outlook, that of Blacks to Jews was originally particularistic, having to do with deep metaphors and images unique to Black culture and to the religiously based understanding of Black history.[1]

As sound as Heyd's observation may be about the representation of Blacks by Jews in painting or sculpture, the issue is more complex in belles lettres. While Heyd's observation applies to some of the latter, other works are nuanced, realistic, and particularistic. In representing African Americans, Hebrew literature runs the gamut from the most superficial references, in which the subjects are mere tropes, all the way to focused, three-dimensional individuals. At times Blacks are portrayed metonymically as a long-suffering people whose pains, travails, and challenges humanize them, while at other times they are mere images in the social background of the protagonists' everyday life.

In the first decades of the twentieth century Jews found kindred spirits among Blacks, a relationship that later suffered from the vicissitudes of proximity, mutual envy, hostility, competition, and feelings of victimization and exploitation. At the time when European Jews were immigrating en masse to the United States, African Americans were making their exodus in droves out of the rural American South, many heading for the cities in the North. Both groups, like others making their way to the Golden Land, sought to discover new opportunities for a better life, freedom from persecution, and a livelihood to sustain self and family—in short, to live the American Dream.

By the second decade of the twentieth century a rising tide among Americans signaled a gradual shift in their perception of Blacks and their culture. Among others, poetry by Blacks drew not just imitators but also translators. Hebraists, freshly arrived in America, were also swept up in this project, bringing to their readers selections of the creative force in the African American community that included folksongs, spirituals, themes of the Harlem Renaissance, fine arts, and music, among others.

Among the more prolific translators of Black poetry and folksong are Hillel Bavli, whose interest was aroused by James Weldon Johnson's collection, *The Book of American Negro Poetry*,[2] and Eliezer David Fridland, who translated "The Congo (A Study of the Negro Race)" (1914) by Vachel Lindsay (1879–1931), as well as "Stinkers" and "Wounded Hawks" by Robinson Jeffers.[3] Other translators of Jeffers were G. Preil and A. Regelson.[4] Jewish composers and musicians inspired by African American sounds are most prominently exemplified by the accomplishments of the Gershwin brothers, Irving Berlin, and Benny Goodman, to note but a handful.[5] This influence continued beyond the middle of the twentieth century, as it does today.

Apart from the regard held by Jewish musicians for Black culture—admired by some to the point of adapting it in lieu of their own—Hebrew writers also produced poems, stories, translations, and essays on the subject. More American Hebrew writers wrote about Blacks than about Indians, because of the intimacy occasioned by immediate and unmediated contact. Jews and Blacks resided in northern and southern cities, often in geographically proximate neighborhoods, if not closer. Unlike with Native Americans, they did not need to learn of Blacks' social standing in America through books or movies. Witnessing their daily lives and also learning of their history of enslavement in America made the cause of African Americans familiar and urgent as experiences which Jews recognized all too well from their own past. More often than that, inclusion of Blacks in the social landscape of their fiction was made because of recognition of the lingering and pervasive effects of the American legacy of slavery and racial discrimination, a matter which remained a festering issue in their minds, too. By acknowledging this unsavory facet of their milieu, they were unraveling the myths of America and psychologically accommodating themselves and their readers to a true reality about life in the Golden Land. When considering social issues with which to augment their works, they also pondered the Black Problem.

The representation of African Americans is pervasive in American Hebrew literature and is made out of a host of motives. In the following I propose to distinguish between works in which Blacks are vehicles for ulterior purposes and those that seek a more realistic depiction. The latter includes works that offer a close-up of the culture, values, or mindset of an outsider. The former, however, makes the African American a vehicle for other ideas, values, themes, or forces that the author or poet finds germane to the image of African Americans. Of these, some common notions about Blacks are also exhibited, including recognition of the African American's roots in and proximity to a primordial world of undisturbed nature and, consequently, an emotional closeness to instinct and unrepressed behavior as perceived by some. In either case, though, Hebrew literature became more American—also recording the course of Jewish assimilation—as it demonstrated a familiarity with African American civilization and a sufficient comfort about incorporating them as metonymic figures into works of greater concern.

By combining African American themes within their work, Hebrew writers could be universal (or American) and particular at one and the same time. This strategy permitted a voicing of the cause of others alongside their own people. For them the agenda of one was mirrored in the circumstance of the other as their social, economic, and political status and agendas intersected. By calling for changes in attitude pertaining to Blacks, they were standing up for those marginalized and unjustly treated segments of their own people as well.

Also, as heirs to the Haskalah, they found the plight of African Americans a social agenda befitting the ideals espoused by many Jews, to struggle for justice for a people who were as severely disadvantaged as their coreligionists, if not more so. They could call for a rectifying of injustices suffered by the socially marginalized among Jews and Gentiles, be it the orphan, the poor, and the woman as woman, as widow, or as *'agunah*. The amelioration of the one, they hoped, would break down barriers for all; and to be American meant to be free to protest, to vent one's outrage at the established order, its roots and present manifestations.

Hebrew literati's mirroring of Black culture sought to identify shared themes in the experiences of both peoples, encouraging greater contacts between them to learn from and sustain each other's struggles in successfully integrating into American life. This contradiction has been a hallmark of both civilizations. Hebrew writings on the subject have, after the prevailing literary fashion of their day, taken to depicting African Americans romantically, expressing admiration for their native origins and a bemoaning of the fate which led to a near eradication of their heritage. This attitude was a none-too-subtle allusion to the Jews' history and destiny in America. On the other hand, bent on presenting a mimetically realistic portrait of the here-and-now, as was the fashion among modernists of the fin-de-siècle, Hebrew writers could not but also include Blacks.

Though Hebrew writers became closely engaged with Black literary expressions, their endeavor was insufficiently internalized to engender a freshened, informal, and different medium out of the wooden, staid, and overly formalized language they inherited from their Haskalah and *teḥiyah* (National Renaissance) forebears.[6] In fact, African American language and literature stood as a counterpoint to their classicism. As we have seen before, Black folksongs, stories, and culture were characterized by a disregard for formal modes of expression, often challenging and wreaking havoc on English syntax, spelling, and usage. Words would be used in unexpectedly innovative contexts, emulating folk, street, and rural language. In their spirit, Black folksongs served as an inspiration to Hebraists for approximating their quest for a modicum of primitivism in their art. Nonetheless, these psycho-social phenomena remained absent by and large from Hebrew in America during most of the period covered by this study.

In many cases, it is the location of Blacks at the margins of twentieth century American White society that is depicted in Hebrew poetry and prose. In works composed in the romantic vein, many poems explored the nexus between the protagonists' mythic past and their present lot. The conjunction of contradictory fates also bespoke a sentiment held by Hebrew writers about their own experiences. As will be demonstrated in the latter part of the following discussion, the lion's share of the realistic representation was expressed in prose fiction, making the socio-economic status of Blacks most prominent and lending Hebrew belles lettres a semblance of documentary materials.

THE ROMANTIC VEIN

Childhood is a metonymic setting in a number of works that portray Black protagonists in Hebrew literature even before encountering them. The early years often signify the Jewish protagonist's incomplete education, a period rife with stereotypes borne of an insular world, in which anxieties about the exotic and unfamiliar are common. The fears of and reactions to the image of a Black man, at times perpetuated into adulthood, bespeak a fear of the outsider as the repository of all that is suppressed and culturally forbidden. As we have seen in the previous chapter, Lisitzky's formative environment was mediated by Harriet Beecher Stowe's *Uncle Tom's Cabin;* other writers use childhood to represent a setting of incomplete, unformed attitudes. Youth is often a passing phase of limited knowledge and a narrow worldview in which Blacks are markers of the formative years that have refashioned the protagonist's attitude about others.

In Bernard Isaacs's "The Three Maneses,"[7] the Black man is an exaggerated and threatening alien in one's imagination. Recollecting his East European childhood and hometown, the narrator tells of a neighbor who made it in America and is employing a frightening Black man as his doorman: "and an African Blackman, black as soot, with white teeth and shiny rolling eyes stands at the gate without taking his eyes off you for even a second" ("v-khushi afriak'i shaḥor k-phiaḥ, ba'al shinayim lvanot v-'eynayim mavrikot u-mitgalglot, 'omed 'al-yad ha-sha'ar v-'eyno gore'a 'ayin mi-mkhaaf al-rega"). Yet, the account continues, this Jewish employer was unafraid of his Black employee because he possessed a gun. Placing himself in the situation, the story's child-narrator declares that he, too, would not have feared the terrifying Black man because he, the child, had on his *arba kanfot*—the four-cornered fringed garment worn by the Orthodox—as protection. By virtue of his point of view, the narrator-as-adult has distanced himself from his youthful, innocent self by smiling at the child's naive trust in the magical properties of an undergarment and at demonizing the Black doorman.

Another to measure the notion of adulthood by staging the chasm between the imagined and real Black in one's childhood is the author S. Damesek. In his tale, *My fate* (*B-gorali*),[8] the narrator recalls an incident during his childhood in eastern Europe when the local duke employed a Black man as his driver. The exoticism of a Black African in Europe must have been a status symbol for the duke. Yet Jews who saw the automobile and its driver were frightened at the sight, believing that the Black man came from beyond the mythical Sambatyon River, a reference often found in folktales and works of fiction by the likes of Mendele Mocher Sforim and S. Y. Agnon, among others. Projecting their inner fears on him, the Jews believed that his glance would be sufficient to harm pregnant women and cause them to bear Black children, and that children who look at him might forget their Torah lessons. The author's account of this episode in the context of his hospitalization in a sanatorium along with Black patients is a measure of the gap between myth and reality, between the world of childhood ignorance and adulthood.[9]

Damesek is insightful about the shared experiences and travails of Blacks and Whites. He portrays them with a few distinctive features but without any intimacy, as if such proximity is beyond his ken. Setting his work in the American countryside, he takes note of the economic poverty of Blacks residing in shacks alongside White palatial mansions.[10] However, most of his account focuses on autobiographical experiences in hospitals or sanatoriums where Black patients are but one group of a host of races and nationalities. They are an integral part of a diversity of patients, personalized by name and distinct medical case, without any untoward or racist attitude. Thus, for example, *B-gorali* arrays a host of Black patients who are either recovering or dying.[11] Most, though, are drawn two-dimensionally, their individualism marked by a distinctive trait, identity, or ailment. One of these, "Chief," is a prankster who plays jokes on his bunkmate,[12] while Hutchins is a man of the world and famous musician who played in the band of the King of Swing;[13] Hobson always argues about equality;[14] while Lunt and Peterson suffer from tuberculosis, to which they eventually succumb.[15] Another is a nameless six-fingered man who has come in for surgery,[16] while Martin is adopted by a young boy who assembles himself a family from among the sick.[17] One nameless Black woman visits a young man whose true personality is only then made known to the narrator.[18]

At other times, the Black man's exoticism leads many to attribute to him powers beyond human capacity, stereotypical qualities often associated with the unfamiliar, threatening Other. At times he is the bearer of excessive sexuality and a lack of civility, as marked by his ability to cause women to bear Black children without being even touched by him, and others to forget their teachings. It is only through knowledge of the Other, as in the sanatorium of Damesek's tales, that a sense of a shared humanity emerges among ethnic and racial groups.

Composed in the year marking the end of the Second World War, *B-gorali* is a document that flies in the face of racism. Focusing on an institution where the ill lay to recover or die, it is a metaphor that marks the shared fates of all humans, personalizing them for the reader by devoting anecdotal details to enrich and engrave each one's face in the reader's memory.

Seemingly bent on reproducing one stereotypical attribute of African Americans as objective correlatives of his moods, the poet Eisig Silberschlag composed a series of lyrical poems dedicated to the human spirit of joy. His lyricism often stands in the way of a faithful probing of the subjects of his poems, though he manages to capture in his Black protagonists qualities that are also universal human attributes. The relative paucity of more realistic representations of Blacks in his poems, particularly in light of his peregrinations, is puzzling. It probably reinforces the impression that Silberschlag's interest is in lyricism more than on sketching social types of his surroundings.

Even in his "From the mouth of Blacks" ("Mi-pi Khushim"),[19] a collection of poems ostensibly representative of African Americans, Silberschlag presents but the most superficially generalized aspects of Black civilization. The eight poems comprising the assemblage are a single expression, though many address such non-ethnic matters as butterflies, the sun, the moon, and a typology of women. Nearly to the last, they are unpersuasive in capturing Black culture or images mimetically. Rather, the poems convey aspects of the innocent spirit that appear to be the poet's understanding of stereotypical moods among Black people, often exhibiting merriment in the face of adversity. Though the collection humanizes African Americans by underscoring universal spiritual qualities they share, it is the poet's sense of injustice toward Blacks that is particularly interesting.[20]

A few of the poems, however, exhibit a more direct engagement with Black themes. The first, "The Black Skin" ("Ha-ʿor ha-shaḥor"), is a folk account—claimed by at least one reviewer to have originated as an Indian tale pertaining to red skin—or etiological tale of how Black people received the color of their skin.[21] The story tells of God bestowing upon each race a color of the rising sun. However the Blacks, because they overslept and did not come to receive theirs, were colored black. For all its folkloristic charm and naiveté, the poem voices a prejudicial attitude about the laziness of Blacks and their inability to comprehend God's command, confusing "draw back" (*hisog aḥor*) for "rot black" (*himok shaḥor*).

Many of Silberschlag's poems attributed to African American themes possess qualities that resemble folktales, or feature folk heroes. Intent perhaps on not being taken for a racist, for some of his poems may be accounts told by Blacks themselves, Silberschlag is critical of White society in his poem "The Lament" ("Ha-kinah"). In it he presents the obverse of Black culture by foregrounding White society's propensity to glorify war and death. By contrast, he praises the life-affirming and joyous ways of African Americans.[22]

Another poem resembling a folktale is "Brotherhood" ("Ha-ʾaḥavah"),[23] an etiological tale about the origins of prejudice and discrimination. Poignantly, it recounts how the innocent Black man received work tools while Whites were given a pen with which they schemed to deceive and swindle others out of their gains. Though sympathetic to the lot of the downtrodden, the poem is also an implicit expression of the victims' helplessness and powerlessness against those seeking to exploit them. However, Silberschlag also presents one poem, "Cleopatra's Voice" ("Kol Cleopatra"),[24] that presents Cleopatra as a multi-talented Black queen in heroic terms.

In another collection, *On lonesome roads* (*Bi-shvilim bodedim*), Silberschlag includes a poem of sympathy for the lot of a Black man. In "On a Blackman's grave" ("ʿAl kever shel Kushi"),[25] purportedly based on an ancient Egyptian inscription, the poet reaffirms what Lisitzky observed about physical versus ethical color, that the soul of the departed, Black though he may have been, was pure and white.

Black among humans
Was the hue of my flesh;
Heavy as the wilderness—life's yoke
That I bore.
But my soul was white
Before its maker
As an almond blossom, as filaments
Of light.
(*Bi-shvilim*, 79)

Characteristic of many Hebrew poets in America is the propensity to flesh out the image of a Black protagonist in a limited two-dimensional fashion. The practice is especially pervasive in the case of poets whose oeuvre is distinctly sparing in their attention to character. When attending to the subject of the African American experience, they do so in a brief poem or two that, for each poet, is associated with a matter tangential to the *realia* of their subjects' culture. This is often accomplished by the conceit of the poet stopping to dwell on an African American who is unaware of the narrator's gaze. The poet's treatment, moreover, refers to the subject as a metaphor of an abstract notion, much as he is wont to do when reflecting on nature or an object—reminiscent of works by the likes of Wordsworth, Keats, and Robert Frost, among others.

One such poem is by Simon Ginzburg. Even before Lisitzky's poetry, and anticipating the debate that was catalyzed by Yaʿakov Rabinowitz about the Americanization of Hebrew literature, Ginzburg was among the first to do so by giving recognition to the social presence of African Americans. His 1915 poem, "Joe,"[26] appears to be the earliest expression by a modern Hebrew poet on Blacks. The title, though, implies a distance from and unfamiliarity with the individual, "Joe" being often a generic term for an anonymous person. However, the poet's sense of identity with his subject as a bearer of metaphoric import is underscored by his declaration that "your dream—is my dream, your despair—my despair." His formulaic words that bond them echo Ruth's declared identity with Naomi and her people.

Ginzburg dwells on his protagonist as the embodiment of past and present, whom he describes as sweeping a store while his eyes stare into the distance. This juxtaposition emphasizes the gap between a mundane act and a richer inner self. Identifying with Joe's lot in the city, the poet calls him "brother" and his double. Both, he believes, belong to another place; share the same heavenly Father, fate, and destiny. Joe may be longing for faraway Ethiopia, for a mother or a sister somewhere in the South, speculates the narrator, or he may be mourning the lynching death of a brother. By these words Ginzburg summarizes the range of the experiences and aspirations of Blacks, generalized through the very distance he maintains from his subject. They, like him, may yearn for an ancestral homeland, the family home; share ambivalence about America; or contemplate the unfortunate history experienced here.

The poem illustrates a regard for the Other as a reflection of the self. His expressed identity and probing questions—"My dream is your dream, your despair is my despair / Tell me please, Joe, who and what are you? Whence do you come? And where are you going?" ("Ḥalomkha—ḥalomi, ye'ushkha—ye'ushi. / haged-na Joe: mi atah—va-mah? / ay mi-zeh hinkha? Ul-'an atah ba?" 83)—seek to establish the identity of the poet's subject as well as himself. This discovery of the self in the Other is the poem's culmination. Its development moves from the alienation of one for the Other, to an affirmation of the identity between the two.

We are brothers, tied by an invisible thread:
We have one Father, and the same dread;
One is the fate to seek and wander
Till we find each other—at this hour.
(S. Ginzburg, *Shirim u-pho'emot*, "Joe," 83–84)

Though not coming to know Joe as a unique individual, Ginzburg attributes to him the fate of all African Americans who have lost their identity as they became American. As for himself, Joe remains unknowing and unresponsive to the poet's contemplation, more an object than an individual. Yet the poem does inscribe into the Hebrew literary tradition the general experience of Blacks in America, leaving other works to present details or other perspectives.

The African American is often perceived as possessed of an unrestrained sexuality about which the White poet, representing a "more civilized" social milieu, exhibits an anxiety. The attitude is derived in part from the notion that African Americans are physically and temporally closer to their native and natural origins than is the (Jewish) poet. It is in the Black protagonist that the poet can find inspiration or a catalyst to arouse his dormant primitivism, at least vicariously and under the control of a rational mind much too strongly affected by the West and its values to truly let go and become a native again.

In a poem, "Night lends an ear" ("Oznay ha-laylah kashuvot"),[27] Silberschlag's narrator imagines glimpsing the image of a Black woman, perhaps a prostitute, though she is more likely a projection of the poet's inner self. In the poem the protagonist describes a night scene in which he notices a window lit in red, a sensual color associated with prostitution, eroticism, and the secretive realm of inner urges. The window frames the silhouettes of a man and woman kissing. For a moment, he notices the woman's breast as if mingling with the darkness of night. The scene, in which even the race of the subject is merely suggested, projects the poet's sensuality on a canvas beyond his reach. The African American is merely a symbol of the sensual aspect of the poet's self. Treatment of this subject lends itself to a more productive reading when considered against A. Z. Halevy's more stark representation of the same theme, as will be illustrated below.

Sensuality is among the first traits that individuals detect in each other, even when otherwise contact between them is tenuous. This is the case when Blacks and Jews work side-by-side or where the focus is only on one, as in a number of stories by B. Isaacs.[28] Sensuality, purity, sanctity, and the human spirit are the chief subjects of Blank's short story "Strange fire" ("Esh zarah"), about two slaughterers.[29] Yeshaya, the *shokhet*, or ritual slaughterer, and Bill, a Black man, work in the same establishment. While Bill performs the slaughter without concern for any religious rules, Yeshaya considers himself closer to the holy as he prepares meat that is kosher. Yet it is he who is aroused carnally by Maria, a Gentile coworker,[30] despite being happily married and under the strictures that prohibit him from giving in to his impulses. She, however, finds Bill, the one whose work is arguably more carnal, more exciting. Their emotions complete the love triangle in which the boundaries of sacred and profane are blurred. Yeshaya, whose emotions are suppressed, merely fantasizes about Maria. Yet he is so taken by her that the daughter born to him and his wife resembles Maria physically and temperamentally, a fitting manifestation of his suppressed emotions. Later, she rebels against her ancestral ways and falls in love with an Italian.

Another for whom the Black individual signifies primordial forces is Simon Halkin, who composed a number of poems that consider African Americans. In the genre of poetry, though, the speaker's tone is unlike Halkin's in prose, a testimony to the author's manifold skills. In a poem entitled “To the Blackwoman” (“El ha-kushit”),[31] he departs from his practice of writing in a realistic vein in prose fiction, as will be seen below, to treat his subject romantically. With a few powerful strokes, he draws his heroine’s image in ways that reflexively illuminate his inner self. The poem is suffused with eroticism and racial and sexual tension as the narrator observes the Black woman dancing before a gloating White audience. Also, the fact that she is being observed by the Hebrew poet from what may be termed a cross-cultural and cross-Diasporic perspective permits the narrator to contrast her primordial origins with the present:

> Why do you need Paris paint to shade your face?
> You, child of forest and wood’s thicket, whose ruddy eyes dwell on a
>   rampart . . .

The poet identifies her as originating from an intimacy with nature, where eye shadow, facial paint, and costume were superfluous. Gazing past her current state, he admires the woman as she must have been: the native who evokes memories of his own roots. To him she personifies the power of unbridled instinct, the immediacy of a natural drive, one that can satisfy the darker, wilder urges of Whites whose inner vitality is stunted:

> Arise, arise, forest’s child, shed the silk dress!
> Let a firm thigh gleam, animated with muscles,
> Till ebony’s blackness blind moist blue northern eyes.

Calling on her to dance and arouse him, too, the poet confesses to having lost this natural self, his instinct, which she can re-awaken. She reminds him of the fetters he bears of the culture of those who built the city. Yet, as victim of this emasculation, he attempts to reimagine and recapture his authentic self. The Jew, prisoner for centuries of Europe’s cold, has suppressed his quasi-African roots. Yet he, as one whose people have been subjected to centuries of the West, urges her not to lose her natural vitality and succumb under the demeaning yoke of Whites.

By seeking to locate traces of his ancient native spirit within himself, Halkin joins the likes of M. Y. Berdychevsky, S. Tschernichowsky, and, later, Yonatan Ratosh, who sought to recover an imagined Jewish national origin by pursuit of a primitive sensibility. His desire to recapture his own (or national) instincts is acted out vicariously by observing the uninhibited Black dancer. Yet this very conceit bares the poet’s inability to be free of cultural inhibitions, to effect a kind of auto-emancipation. Much like Lisitzky in his simulation of Black folksongs, Halkin, too, approaches the exotic and wild from the perspective of the culturally fettered and suppressed Jew who observes from the sidelines. The exercise fails to accomplish its implied purpose as the poet remains fixed in his literary and cultural milieu.

As if to demonstrate his familiarity with Black culture, Halkin offers another poem, one inspired by spirituals or gospel songs.[32] In a 1927–1928 poem entitled "A Black tune" ("Pizmon Kushi"),[33] he offers up his own version of the folk genre. This early poem stands in stark contrast to his usually complex metaphysical poetry and prose. Instead, it resembles African American folksongs in its simplicity of language, form, and primitive, elemental rhythm.[34] Yet, while most spirituals address the Jordan or Mississippi River as the object to be crossed, Halkin's choice is the Jabbok River. This river resonates in Halkin's literary oeuvre and denotes, by analogy with its biblical origins, a momentous crossing, a transformative experience necessitating a struggle that alters the protagonist.

In choosing to make the Jabbok his refrain, which stresses the theme of fording the river, the poem departs from many spirituals. Though not the Jordan River per se, the Jabbok is one of its tributaries.[35] This minor departure from the expected and accepted lends the poem a Hebraic character, for the one to have crossed the Jabbok was the patriarch Jacob, who was transformed there into Israel. Until that crossing, Jacob was the passive object of manipulation and exploitation by others. It was at this crucial juncture, just before the crossing—as he encountered and successfully struggled with a mysterious stranger in the night—that his identity is transformed as Jacob the follower becomes Israel, the God-wrestler (Genesis 32:23–29). Though temptingly metaphysical in this guise, the poem's message is typical of the spiritual: it is a song of hope and confidence by one approaching death, affirming the fearlessness of the singer at what awaits him, for it is a better existence than the present.[36]

A BLACK TUNE

My sword and shield I shall remove—
  As I ford the Jabbok crossing.
No longer shall I learn war—
  As I ford the Jabbok crossing.
My burden I shall lay on the ground—
  As I ford the Jabbok crossing.
There mother to me will come out—
  As I ford the Jabbok crossing.
Father, too, to me will come out—

As I ford the Jabbok crossing.
And I shall appear before my God—
As I ford the Jabbok crossing.

The poem, not being a translation nor one explicitly about a Black protagonist, demonstrates one of Halkin's sources of inspiration and his skills at writing in imitation of a popular and increasingly admired genre of his days, much as Lisitzky does at the time. It also testifies to the poet's familiarity with features of African American culture and the popularity of the spiritual as a medium for expressing their American experience.

Another instance of a Hebrew poet's generalized representation of African Americans is a poem by Reuben (Grossman) Avinoam. Perhaps one of the best known American-born Hebrew writers (apart from T. Carmi) who settled in Eretz Israel (in 1929), Avinoam composed many works about his adopted land. Yet his poems also look back at African Americans to illuminate the subject from a new perspective. Such are "In the shade of the one with the black skin" ("B-tzel sheḥor-ʿor")[37] and the more realistic "Caleb's confession," discussed later.

The first poem is an apt illustration of how Avinoam prefers to locate aesthetic categories in his Black subject in place of human qualities that catalyze any dialogue with the Other. The poem's signal characteristic is its focus on the Black man as a fountainhead of artistic inspiration, as a muse to inspire the poet. Avinoam asserts that the Black man's song is purer and truer than his because it emanates from and is directly tied to his soul. This unmediated authenticity is merely imitated by the White poet, he concludes. His recognition of this fact is signified by the poem's title as an expression of the poet's sense of subordination. The spiritual state of the Black man contributes to the authenticity in his voice, his song emanating in response to daily experiences of anguish. As the waning day casts its shadow, the Black man's experiences inspire the poet to voice his inner self.

The nameless Black man's travails are a litany of poverty, a mother in faraway Alabama, a raped sister, and the desire for a better life in the world to come. In the poet's view, these ingredients affect the Black man's spiritual state; his suffering begets the tone in his song and lends it a purity and authenticity for which the poet also longs. It inspires him to attain a state of mind like that of his subject in order to sing of his own soul in truth and purity.

Other aspects also emphasize the poet's reverence for the Black man. His shanty, termed "a small temple" ("Mikdash mʿat"), a reference to a synagogue, is lowly but sacred. Accepting the Black man as equally human, though not truly free as yet, the poem notes the by now familiar paradox that though he possesses a black skin his heart is white, as one who is a free slave. Though given more nuance and dimension by the detailed description of specific aspects in his life and environment, the poet's subject never rises above the object upon which he reflects. It seems that more than being privileged to observe the Black man in a realistic setting, the reader is witness to the poet's representation of his subject though stereotyped features and characteristics that romanticize and ennoble him.

Another story that focuses on African Americans' roots in an authentic natural milieu, much like Halkin's "El ha-kushit," is S. L. Blank's "Adam [or A man] and his dog" ("Adam v-khalbo"), a realistic short story about Black protagonists in an urban setting. It tells of Adam, an old Black man whose daughter-in-law cast him out of her home with his dog, Dick, to live in the street.[38] Much of the plot focuses on their nearly Edenic existence in Philadelphia's Fairmount Park, where Adam lives out much of his life.

Narrated from Adam's perspective, the tale voices his thoughts phrased at times using Christian religious terminology that lends it some realism. The proximity also exposes Adam's meekness, illustrating the result of the African American experience of enslavement. Adam believes, for example, that Blacks are created as lesser beings than Whites, and must tolerate humiliation. Yet his spirit highlights his humanity. He raises many questions about divine justice and the fate of his people in a world in which Whites thrive. Signifying the lowly social position both occupy, Adam is fated to lead a life similar to that of his dog, mercilessly cast out. As a man of faith, however, he finds comfort in the conviction that his reward will come in the afterlife.

Following his expulsion from "civilization," Adam and his dog find their earthly paradise in the city park, simulating life in nature and surviving by eating food discarded by residents of a nearby affluent neighborhood. As summer gives way to autumn, a relative takes him in but exploits him for the money he collects as a beggar. His fantasies about a return to live in Africa's jungles are cut short as he dies one day, leaving his dog alone in the world.

The story is a social commentary on the loss of innocence and compassion among people driven by greed. It is also a sobering negation of the dream to recapture a bucolic, Edenic existence. Relying perhaps on Y. L. Peretz's "Boncha the Silent," Blank presents a protagonist who, Christlike, is uncomplaining and forgiving of those who exploit him and prays to God to forgive all those who have done him ill. His very silence, like that of Peretz's protagonist, is the author's outcry against the cruelty suffered by social outcasts.

In some instances, the African American protagonist is less threatening if he is a mulatto. Despite his (or her) lowly position, the hybridized protagonist is held up as a scion of a subculture which is "unnatural" and exciting, sexually wild, unrestrained, and exotic, a tempting or irresistible object.[39] The mulatto signifies a hybridized ethnic identity that possesses some flexibility to pass between races, pushing at the boundaries of social structures. This quality is a tempting metonym for the Jew whose cultural and ethnic progression has been one of a loss of an unequivocally singular self, a subject underscored in Halkin's novel *'Ad mashber* (Until breakdown) and its preoccupation with the deterioration of Jewish identity. In Wallenrod's "Morning phantoms" ("Hazayot boker"),[40] one of the women tells of a mulatto who took a fancy to her. Though an incidental character, the mulatto in that work, too, represents a power of sexuality and desire who threatens the male protagonist's sense of self.[41]

For a host of reasons, Black society is represented in Hebrew literature in greater variety and richness than Native American society. The nuanced expression is also more varied and powerful when it comes to the dialogue Hebrew writers had with Black America. On many levels, their experiences were sufficiently similar—each drawing on national or ethnic themes from the other's past, giving rise to a discourse between them.

The proximity of the two peoples engendered numerous compositions in the romantic and realistic mode. The former, as in the case of representing Native Americans, facilitated a vicarious reimagination of one's native tendencies and character. It opened up avenues for Hebraists to dwell on the eternally unfortunate experiences of Blacks in White society, all the while identifying their experiences as mirrored in them as well.

Composing in the realistic mode, Hebrew writers could extend their representation of Blacks to prose literature. Such representation permitted a more credible picture of the condition of Black society in America, and in their relationship to Jews. This was soon to give rise to many more works in English in which writers exhibited an engagement of Jews with Blacks. The injustice meted out to the latter also reminded Jews of their experiences. At times, reaction of Jews and non-Jews to African Americans was indistinguishable, indicating their amalgamation into the greater American social landscape. Alternatively, considering the fate of America's Blacks promoted a greater universal character to Hebrew literature.

Chapter Eight

REPRESENTING AFRICAN AMERICANS: THE REALISTIC TREND

The realistic representation of African Americans is embedded primarily in prose fiction and published contemporaneously with the poetry. This mode is not of a uniform intensity and attention to detail, however. In most cases, references to Blacks are incidental generalizations which omit intimate personal acquaintance, leaving African Americans as a flat background in the plots.

Such is the case when Blacks are mentioned in passing by the poet and short-story writer, Ḥayim Abraham Friedland. His works are marked by a gentle narrative in which the reader is invited to consider the protagonists against their surroundings. He is fond of basing his stories on oppositions in life—light and dark, past and present, good and evil, and the sadness accompanying adjustment to life in a new world.[1] Envisioning a future ideal America, he presents a scene of young people of all races and nationalities dancing with each other, including Blacks.[2]

Another marginal representation is in the lyrical works of A. S. Schwartz, which seldom stray from their introspectiveness. He, too, addresses the subject on at least one occasion to assert that Blacks are beneficiaries of the Torah's light.[3]

Scarcely more personal, Israel Efros's references to Blacks lend historical veracity to his long poem, *Zahav* (Gold). Set during the Gold Rush days about a decade before the end of slavery, the long poem remotely refers to Blacks. In their conversations, prospectors imagine their future as rich men. One plans to return to Alabama to acquire some slaves.[4] Consonant with the poema's overall theme of people's hunger to acquire wealth, the scene represents the desire of Whites to dominate others. Another, a hunter by profession, plans to return home "to skin some Blacks," as a sign of mastery over other humans, or his disregard for the humanity of Blacks.[5] The moral ramifications of these sentiments are not lost on Efros, as we have already observed in his extended expressions about Native Americans.

Though having had the opportunity and cause to offer more in-depth portraits of African Americans, the Yiddish poet—and translator into Hebrew—of the long poem *Kentucky* (1918),[6] I. J. Schwartz is disappointing in his execution. In his defense it must be said that he does not appear to have set out to do so in this work. Focused on telling of the Jewish experience in the Bluegrass State, he let pass the opportunity to probe more deeply, as a resident of Lexington, Kentucky,[7] into the presence of Others. Instead, Schwartz draws attention to the challenges confronting Jews in the Midwest, paramount among them the threat of assimilation as traditional and spiritual Jewish values are abandoned. Played out against a backdrop that harbors echoes of the Civil War of the last century, and the locus of the very geography where Indians were eradicated, the plot unfolds the challenges to Jews and Blacks who face physical, cultural, and spiritual devastation. The past persists in its impact on the Black population, still suffering the "oppression and victimization of Blacks in the South."[8]

Though his representation of Blacks is more than superficial, and he is among the earliest to do so with some care, one reader faults I. J. Schwartz for drawing on stock images as they "grin from ear to ear, their red lips outline their strong white teeth, they roll their eyes so that only the whites show. . . ."[9]

Ephraim E. Lisitzky, who single-handedly wove the largest poetic oeuvre about African Americans, was fascinated by them from an early age. Were we to accept his testimony regarding his youth in Europe, as we've seen above, he was impressed by their story when reading Harriet Beecher Stowe's *Uncle Tom's Cabin.* Among the events that convinced him to make America his home, he testifies, was Lincoln's emancipation of the slaves and the continued commemoration of their liberation, an act, he believes, inspired by the Jewish legacy in the Hebrew Bible.[10] The fact that Lisitzky juxtaposes this act with his decision to remain in America is evidence about his concern for the downtrodden. Though this was affected by personal experiences, it is his admiration for its being an ideal in America's collective memory that impacted his imagination.

Bolstering his extensive composition of poetry inspired by Black religious music and folksongs, Lisitzky incorporated African Americans in many other poems that include indirect expression about Jewry. For just as was the case with Native and African Americans, Lisitzky perceived the Jewish condition as part of his understanding of the persecuted and tormented, their heroic struggles for existence, and the mystery of their demise.[11]

Incipient poetic activity by Lisitzky that attests to the early shaping of

B-ʾoholey Khush, as early as 1928, is evident in his first book of collected poems. Already there we find works such as "The Salvation Boat" ("Sfinat ha-yesha," 1923, 190–191) and part two of "As the Horn Blows" ("Kitkoʿa shofar"), in which he introduces the reverends Washington and Lincoln, protagonists of his "Reverend arguments" ("Mrivay kohanim") of *B-ʾoholay Khush*. The former is a poem resembling poems of prison and heavenly rewards; the latter tells of the debate of two ministers about whether Satan is White or Black, a theme interspersed in some of the early poetry of revolt.

In the same volume, Lisitzky's poem "Coming to New Orleans" ("Boʾakhah New Orleans") offers a cursory description of the Crescent City that holds up a stereotypical picture of Blacks as singing sad songs that bemoan their experience of slavery.[12] He also includes another minority, the Acadians (Cajuns), who fled from the North as Blacks fled to the North, as well as Jean Lafitte and his fellow pirates. It is African Americans, however, who receive most of the poet's attention, depicted as singing while loading ships, in a city whose legacy of slavery lingers in his consciousness.[13]

Bemoaning the evils of urbanization, as he has done in his more romantic depiction of Native Americans, Simon Ginzburg draws Blacks in broad strokes, calling them brothers in fate and victims of the corruption of modernity.[14] He includes them in his long poem, "No-York," as if to indicate the chasm between their dignity in the past and their dehumanization in modern times. Black women are cast into the Big City's houses of prostitution, he adds,[15] which is another by-product of the corruption of urbanism. It draws and promotes debauchery—where basement saloons beckon with their boisterous sounds, and the music of a weeping violin rises from a bordello of drunken Black women—a view later adopted also by A. Z. Halevy.[16]

In his embrace of realism and diversity, Ginzburg includes references to Blacks among those who occupy the urban landscape. In "On the mountain of the house of Columbia,"[17] he pays homage to Columbia University as the Temple of modern times. The title itself is evocative of the *hapax legomenon* of 2 Chronicles 33:15, in reference to the Mountain of the Lord. As in the words of Isaiah 2:2–3, students of all nations ascend to study at Columbia University as if streaming to the Holy Temple. The poet's daily journey to Columbia is part of a procession of a host of ethnic and national groups that includes students from India and Japan as well as Blacks. However, he does not elaborate further to explore the identities of any. Ultimately, the poem focuses on the theme of a revival for his people in their national homeland, a matter which he juxtaposes with the emergent modern Japan.

A near avoidance of the image of Native and African Americans characterizes the poems of Gabriel Preil, the last Hebrew poet of renown in America. While he takes some note of the former, the nearly complete omission of the latter may be due to the lyricism pervading much of Preil's work; this fact has not stopped him from including assorted aspects of the American landscape. Of the few references, the most notable is also poignant in its depth. In "The moon's way through rivers" ("Derekh hasahar bi-nharot"),[18] the personified moon is witness to a number of scenes on earth: a beautiful woman, Jews celebrating the full moon, and the body of a lynched Black man dangling from a tree. The last scene causes the moon to drown its silvery light in the depths of the rivers.

The source of the poem's title in Proverbs 30:19 focuses on wondrous things on earth. It turns ironic in light of the poet's adding another ingredient to those in the sphere of the unknown: inhumanity and moral degeneracy. Adhering to the verse from Proverbs, the poet's inability to know is an expression of his incapacity to comprehend the lynching of a human being. The absence of divine response to this act, particularly in the years following the Holocaust, adds another unknown to one bent on understanding suffering.

Reuven Avinoam's poem, "Caleb's confession" ("Viduyo shel Calev"),[19] tells of an imprisoned protagonist proclaiming his innocence of the murder of a white man. It was his desire to protect Flossy, his beloved, that prompted this violence, he explains. The absence of individualism in the Black protagonists of this poem, as in his more romantic work discussed previously (p. 149), is marked by the tendency to stereotype them in a language that lends the details a semblance of stock phrases. In each instance his reference to their eyes is by terms such as the "butterflies of his eyes" or the "doves of his eyes" ("parperay-ʿeynav," 172; "yonay-ʿeynav," 177). Both poems refer to the wide nostrils of his Black protagonists and their faces that reflect a golden or copper hue. Both also dwell on lingering traces of persecution, as the poet calls one protagonist "a free slave" and the other a victim of White justice. Both have come from the South to reside in the North's ghettos. And as if to underscore its depravity, Caleb hyphenates the city's name as New York–Nineveh, much as Ginzburg effaces it by the corrupted term No-York.

As the narrator of much of the poem, Caleb is a more accessible protagonist than the anonymous voice of "In the shade of the one with the black skin," exhibiting greater depth and individualism. Caleb's humanity and contrary behavior toward Whites and Blacks lends him emotional depth, as is the motive behind the killing, mitigated by a desire to rescue his Flossy from a White man. His deed becomes a double act of revenge as he also recalls the defilement of his childhood friend, Susie, by a White man. Focused as it is on this theme, the poem resembles the subgenre of race consciousness poems, Black resistance and revolt at the injustices of White society.

Avinoam does not excuse his protagonist's deed, however—Caleb goes to his death for his act—but only provides mediating causes. Seen against the background of the rise of Black racial consciousness and militancy, this is an established theme of a host of literary and extra-literary works at the rising tide of the civil rights movement.

Another poet, Moshe Ben-Meir, whose poems fill but a single volume, many of them written while he was still in Europe, dwells in one of his America poems on a Black woman's prayer. Presented as if voicing her musings, much as is Martha's monologue in Halkin's *Until Breakdown* (*'Ad mashber*), the poem, "A Black woman's prayer" ("Tfilat ishah Kushit"; 1957) expresses this poet's reaction to the lot of a people he only recently came to know.[20]

As its subtitle attests, the poem's inspiration was a newspaper article by Ted Poston, the journalist who covered the civil rights movement, including the celebrated Montgomery, Alabama, bus boycott in the wake of the Rosa Parks incident when she refused to surrender her seat in 1955.[21] The poem is an entreaty by the protagonist, who seeks to know the reasons for her torments at the hands of Whites. It is bracketed in the opening and closing lines by a phrase from Psalm 94:3—"For how long, my God, until when?" The fact that Whites find the white milk with which she nurses their children desirable, but not her skin color, is but one of the innocuous questions she raises. They exploit her as a surrogate mother but without the attendant deference, she adds.[22] They, who so depend on her to bake their bread, taste their food, and nurse their children, keep her from sitting next to them.

The poem's repeated movement contrasting the Black woman's body, with which she serves the Whites, and their hand, raised against her, lends poignancy to the situation. Yet she, too, raises her hands, but in a gesture that calls on an all-too-slow divine justice.

More than much of American Hebrew poetry, the works of Abraham Zvi (Avraham Tzvi) Halevy reject any romanticism about the subjects he foregrounds, nor does he treat African Americans—or others for that matter—sentimentally. While the poet Ginzburg, for example, writes pessimistically when observing existence in the big city, his regard is mitigated by a mystical experience, an epiphany, or visions of an alternate world for which he nostalgically yearns or to which he escapes. Halevy's somber naturalistic poems depict an environment devoid of solace, one populated by humans unadorned by the glimmer of civilization. His poems are gray vignettes of a life suffused with loneliness and resignation born of a futility in pursuit of redemption. However, "the human burning bush aflame in the wasteland of loneliness will not be consumed" ("lo ye'ukal sneh ha-'adam ha-bo'er b-midbar ha-bdod"), he asserts in one poem, "Hide in the rock of silence" ("Ḥaveh b-tzur ha-dmi").[23] Much as was reflected in his demeanor,[24] Halevy's perspective, experiences, and worldview coalesce to form a dour conclusion about a humanity enslaved to and unable to rise above its basest drives. Poetically, he is heir to Ginzburg's angst, though bringing less hope for a redemptive conclusion. His perspective unfolds a world of human immorality and corruption more than urbanism could bring forth. He represents life without embellishment, in which even the narrator does not escape the forces of which he writes.[25]

Geographically, much of Halevy's poetry charts human existence against the New York cityscape, including observations of Blacks who populate run-down Harlem streets. Such is the case with "A shoot of righteousness" ("Tzemaḥ tzedek," an evocation of Jeremiah 23:5 and 33:15) and "Lenox Avenue."[26] The latter refers to Blacks as "a multitude of nations / spread as the locust on the hard, broad and dark pavements." They lead a hard life, emblematic of what he witnessed personally about them and, by analogy, experienced in his own existence. Those he features most frequently—prostitutes, winos, and children playing alongside brothels—are faceless individuals existing at the periphery of African American society, people whom he notices and identifies as exemplars of his perception of reality.

In "Lenox Avenue," Halevy describes one of Harlem's central thoroughfares, which he calls Little Africa. There, where even the black night is Black, the tumult is of a plethora of colors and people, of noises, scents, and sweat. The only whiteness on the scene is marked by a few Whites who have come to seek sexual release from their repressed existence. For unlike in Halkin's poem, Halevy's voyeurism is naturalistic, carnal, and deprived of any romance for the primitive.

As a poet weaned on the conventions of the Hebrew literary tradition, Halevy embeds in his works verse fragments detached from their previously sacred biblical contexts. In "Lenox Avenue," the last line describes a wino with language lifted from the Balaam episode of Numbers 22–24:

"And a drunk whose way was offensive (Numbers 22:32), falling open-eyed (Numbers 24:4, 16), discharging his vomit and wrath into the gutter" ("v-shikor yarat darko, nofel u-gluy ʿeynayim, mafrish ki'o v-kitzpo el biv ha-rḥovot"—71). In place of the heroic original, the poem's line is a repulsive account of a drunkard vomiting into a gutter.

The second poem, "Tzemaḥ tzedek" (A shoot of righteousness) dwells on an abandoned Harlem synagogue building, surrounded by footloose Blacks, the sounds of jazz and prostitutes who ply their trade in its shadows. The poem concludes with the death of a White customer whose bleeding body is abandoned on the oblivious street. The scene is played out before the synagogue building whose Ten Commandments are obscured by a layer of black dust. This observation, borne in the last line bearing the words of Exodus 32:16—"And God's inscription on the tablets which are on Tzemaḥ-tzedek is buried beneath a monument of black dust" ("mikhtav Elohim ʿal ha-luḥot asher ʿal tzemaḥ-tzedek kavur taḥat matzevet avak sheḥorah"—73) points an accusatory finger at the immorality and decay in the neighborhood, where prostitution and murder abound, and which has given up on the values represented by the House of God.

As a counterpoint, and a sign of possible hope, the words "and God's inscription on the tablets" ("mikhtav Elohim ʿal ha-luḥot") evoke the description of the Tablets of the Law as handed to Moses (Exodus 32:16). Though enshrouded in dust, the words await being uncovered again. The synagogue's name, "Tzemaḥ tzedek" is also evocative of Jeremiah's words (23:5; 33:15) pronouncing the divine promise about a rule of justice and righteousness. Though still standing, the principles of the Law are blotted out by the human conduct made manifest on the street. Yet the hope remains that the dust may be washed off and justice restored.

BLACKS IN PROSE FICTION: THE MIMETIC MODE

More than in verse, Hebrew prose fiction offers realistic representations of Blacks and their surroundings. Nevertheless, Hebrew prose is not uniformly mimetic on this subject; it is characterized by varying intensities—realistic and metaphoric—in the representation of African Americans. Its models for such realistic representations are the legacy of the rise of realism in Hebrew prose, as propounded by Mendele, Ben-Avigdor, and their followers, as well as the tradition of "semi-documentary" (as Shaked calls them) works among writers of Yiddish and American English fiction of the early twentieth century.[27]

In much of Hebrew literature African Americans are marginalized by role and periphery. Though included in a range of intensities of realism, Blacks constitute the literary foci of writers endeavoring to present a mimetic picture of social reality. So pervasive are the troubles facing African Americans that seldom do Hebrew writers pause to depict other minorities; even those with whom Jewish protagonists journeyed to the New World receive scant attention. These writers are also aware that by incorporating Blacks they are Americanizing their works, contributing a unique theme to the modern Hebrew literary corpus. Contrary to observations that these stories explore strange and exotic people and events from the perspective of an immigrant who sees a disjointed reality,[28] the tales including Black characters are slices of life in America, testifying to ongoing contact between Jews and Blacks.[29]

As if reflecting the socially pervasive condition of the times, Blacks are often noted coincidentally, depicted as nondescript figures at the margins of plots. In addition to generalized references to Black neighborhoods,[30] the landscape of many Hebrew stories is variegated with images of African Americans in an assortment of peripheral roles. In many instances their scant mention is more useful as social than literary commentary about the visibility and nature of African Americans occupying the authors' field of vision. More than mere background, Blacks remain without a distinct individualism, held up as abstracted images serving generalized ideas and principles. As individuals, they inhabit the countryside, cityscape, and private dwellings of protagonists, performing stereotypical roles as maids, domestics, or menial laborers, saying little, though remaining visible in the author's imagination. However, the fact that it is they who fill these niches most frequently attests to the authors' sense of their significance in lending a verisimilitude to their imagined worlds.

As in the case of Blacks marginalized from Jews (and Whites) by virtue of their work and economic station, their adjoining neighborhoods are considered undesirable and uninhabited by Whites. Such is the case of a protagonist who owns three houses "on the Blacks' street," a reference to a nameless Black neighborhood in a nameless city.[31] In another instance, the chief protagonist lives in East Harlem, with the Black neighborhood separating his residence from City College, where he studies.[32]

Black maids in one's home are signs of status among Jews who want to exhibit their economic and social success. Maids often constitute a mute presence as secondary, background characters that perform menial tasks.[33] At times they are foils to their employers, adherents to alternative values, bemoaning the unfortunate social upheavals in the homes of Jews.[34] In one instance, the older maid doubles as the maternal figure for one of the chief protagonists, one whose thoughts or utterances express more than individual opinion.[35] Most Black maids, though, remain of little consequence in the overall scheme of a story.

While female Black protagonists are situated in the homes of Whites, Black males are depicted as doormen who, in literary works, take on profound symbolic significance as metaphors pointing to the nexus between two realms. Jews' socio-economic attainments are represented in terms of the Black man's servile relationship to his employer, yet he is the one to symbolically admit the Jew into American life before he or his fellow Blacks would do so. This relationship bespeaks future tensions as resentments build up or the experience of submission embraces this episode as well.[36]

In one instance, Wallenrod's short story "In the shade of the walls" ("B-tzel ha-ḥomot"), the profession of doorman is so closely identified with Blacks that a White Christian holding the job is treated as if he were Black. His children are ostracized for their father's profession and socially distanced from their playmates so much so that one of them marries a Jew, another outsider in America.[37]

Other means of contact between the groups include Black janitors who work in a Jewish school or synagogue,[38] elevator operators, menial saloon employees,[39] and musicians.[40] On occasion their current condition is juxtaposed with a romantic picture of leading a free life in nature away from the city and the assimilatory forces of America. In a few examples, the lowly economic state of the Black protagonist is improved by contact with the Jew. Such is the case in S. L. Blank's *Mr. Kunis*, where Tom's living condition improves, symbolized by a change in his hunched-over stature as he straightens out and stands tall.[41]

In another novel, *The isle of tears* (*Ee ha-dmaʿot*),[42] Blank's fresh immigrants encounter the first Americans as they reach land. These are Black workers at the port who submissively remove the belongings of the ship's first-class passengers. The scene shatters the rosy perception of the immigrants about life in America. The fate awaiting them is much the same as that of these porters. Contrary to their expectations upon arriving in the land of milk and honey, and as they will shortly discover about others and themselves, the Land of the Free did not fulfill its message when it comes to its Black citizens. The author's use of the term "nikhnaʿim" (submissive) in two of his works[43] reinforces the image of Blacks employed in menial pursuits and alludes to the seething anger they hold at bay beneath the surface of their obsequiousness.

A similar situation arises in the case of a seemingly original analogy by

Ḥ. A. Friedland, whose protagonist, exploited excessively by his father, accuses him of treatment befitting a Black man: "As a Black man you work me fourteen hours a day," he says, echoing the words of Jacob in Genesis 31:41.[44] The Black man is perceived as belonging to the lowest social class, exploited to perform the hardest menial tasks.[45] We find a similar analogy in one of Wallenrod's tales, "In the family circle," an indication of the social reality in which Blacks were relegated to perform the most arduous tasks.[46] This image also appears to be behind a figure of speech coined by the author in his story, where one of the protagonists likens himself to Blacks, asserting that "I worked as a Black man."[47]

Another conception of Blacks on the margins of the working class is in S. L. Blank's short story, "Man, Woman, and Ape."[48] It is told "from within" as its focus is wholly on non-Jewish characters. The principal character, Anthony, himself a recent immigrant, has learned that Blacks do the most degrading jobs when he likens the work his wife, Marina, performs as waitress to that of a Black street-sweeper.[49]

Though he writes less about African Americans than of Native Americans, Regelson tells of a Jewish youth encountering a Muslim. The latter is a Black man who, it is soon learned, is concealing his Jewish identity. Through the youth's intervention the Black man is brought back into the Jewish fold to lead a prayer service. The account presents any number of possible readings about diversity and creolization, of Jew-as-Black-as-Muslim, etc. Understood allegorically, the youth is the emerging generations' empowerment to bring about situations in which multiple identities and differences coexist.[50]

Though it is Blacks who occupy the lion's share of Others represented in American Hebrew writings, a few instances of protagonists of other ethnic groups deserve mention. Of those writing of a host of racial and ethnic groups, S. L. Blank has succeeded in representing America's diversity. His works focus on the challenges encountered by minorities in the overall experience of immigrants encountering the forces of acculturation and adjustment to the anonymity of the Big City.

Blank's short stories and novels that center on the American urban experience bear a pessimistic tone about prospects of reinstating the bucolic pre-Holocaust European life of his characters—Jews and non-Jews—in the New World. In "Man, Woman, and Ape" ("Ish, ishah v-kof"),[51] he illustrates the experiences of Anthony, a recent immigrant from Italy. Shortly after arriving in America, he loses a leg in a work accident. Set against the Philadelphia cityscape, his search for stability in life leads him to work as a street musician with a music box and a monkey, and to marry

Mariana, an immigrant from Rumania. Blank's generally somber view of life in America, as opposed to his Bessarabian pastoral novels (including his *On American soil*, *ʿAl admat America*), is underscored by the dysfunctional life led by immigrants as they encounter the destabilizing flux of America, including divorce and untimely death.

However, Blank is also among the handful of authors of stories fixing Black protagonists more centrally in their plots. These tales are narrated almost exclusively from within the protagonist's perspective, and without any reference to Jewish issues or characters. Of these, the most noteworthy is his "The tale of a Blackman" ("Maʿaseh b-Khushi").[52] Its White protagonists, Dave and Mary Grossman, are not distinguished as members of any particular ethnic or religious group. Josh, the African American, works as a shoeshine by their barbershop and is one of many infatuated with Mary, the barber's young wife.

The narrative illuminates Josh the impoverished husband and beleaguered father of four, whose skills are limited to shining shoes. The generosity extended him by Mary only reinforces his admiration of this kindly and attractive young woman. His downfall begins when he compares Mary to his wife, which leads to a disenchantment with his family and lot in life, an attitude that precipitates the loss of his job.

As conditions deteriorate, Josh's ardor for Mary grows. One night he climbs into her bedroom only to find her asleep, at which he, unable to rein in his passions, kisses her. She wakes up screaming in the belief that his intentions were more violent, and he runs off in fear. The resultant neighborhood search discloses the suppressed violent passions of citizens and police alike. They expose a mistaken view about the Black man as a savage, whose uncontrolled sexuality must be checked. Once found, Josh is summarily killed by the mob, a lingering smile frozen on his face at having kissed the angelic Mary. The denouement turns the tale into a scathing critique of White prejudice, stereotyping, racism, repressed sexuality, mob hysteria, and violence. It is Whites whose behavior exemplifies the nefarious and malevolent qualities they project onto Blacks.

Josh is humanized by Blank's close point of view as it follows his actions and reveals his thoughts that underscore his innocence. While Josh masters his impulse at the sight of the half-naked Mary, neither she nor other Whites can do so. Yet in his humanization comes Josh's demise, as he falls victim to violence which confirms others' convictions of the absence of humanity in him.[53] Seen from a comparative perspective, the tale concurs with the volume title in which it appears, "A time of crisis"

(*Bi-shʿat ḥerum*), a collection of stories that include tales of pogroms and atrocities in Bessarabia in the interwar years.[54]

The nexus between Blank's dual perspective on Jews and Blacks in this anthology is his understanding of their shared fate at the hands of White society, regardless of geography or American idealism. This analogy is reminiscent of a tale by H. Sackler, who observes the fate that awaited America's Jews and Blacks during the Second World War. Members of both groups are deemed uneducated (the Jews because of their limited knowledge of English) and are prevented from serving honorably.[55] At least as concerning Jews, the assumption of their being unfit for military service falls into a racist stereotyping that they are weak, effeminate, and unmilitary.[56]

Hebrew writers have seldom endeavored to imagine the inner world of Black or Indian consciousness. They prefer to voice their regard about general racial issues, adopting an outsider's stance in the expectation of attaining the role of intermediaries with White America, or being "part of a community of 'others of the world' obliged to help each other."[57] By analogy, though, it may be that their reflections also bear an indirect comment on the Jewish condition in America. Their reluctance to represent the inner world of another Other may be out of an inability to know that which lies beyond them.

However, a number of literary works, most in prose, also feature an implicitly shared experience between Blacks and Jews. Of those, one stands out in its intensity, Halkin's novel *Until breakdown* (*ʿAd mashber*). The first volume of an incomplete trilogy,[58] it examines the social and spiritual decay within American Jewish society refracted though the protagonist, Rabbi Professor Reuben Poller, his wife, Neuta, and his children, all on the cusp of American assimilation. Though economically well off, the family's members find themselves in want of a host of spiritual and existential endowments to make them happy.

Martha, a seventy-eight-year-old Black maid and nanny to Neuta, the lady of the house,[59] is the author's vehicle. It is through her point of view that Halkin underscores his seminal observations, all the while striking an aesthetic distance between the narrator, his Jewish chief protagonist and his subject. Presented as an interior monologue, Martha's opinions are voiced without the narrator's obvious intrusiveness as mediator or interpreter in a narrative form called *Erlebte Rede*, or narrated monologue that joins the narrator's observations with those of the protagonist.[60] Her thoughts reinforce the novel's vignettes about the Jewish characters, illuminating the components of a dysfunctional family and society in a deteriorating American Jewish existence seemingly devoid of purpose.

In two significant and lengthy episodes that permit insight into Martha's inner world, the novel invites a comparison between her and her Jewish employers. Martha's thoughts about values and intimate familiarity with Neuta enrich the plot in a host of ways. She, for example, feels it improper to pamper her mistress in the way her second husband, Reuben Poller, does. Surprisingly, her expressions of low opinion of him include attributions of Black features that she considers lowly as opposed to her views of Neuta's first husband, to whom she assigns admirable White (Aryan) qualities.

Having been the nursemaid to a White child, Martha has also been assimilated by the values and standards of beauty and strength of character admired by Whites:

> And it matters not to Old Martha if this time this robust-bodied fool, thick lipped and wide of nostrils as a black Black, may the Lord forgive the sins of her lips, if he should for once hear what she has in mind to tell him for the past few mornings ever since this Black fool began, may the Lord forgive the sins of her lips, to pamper this mad child even though her legs gave her pain from the time she was a babe to this day—she shouldn't be so pampered in bed till such a late morning hour!
>
> It is not for naught that Old Martha fears him all these years, as she feared the Black Baptist preacher, also robust-bodied, thick lipped and wide of nostrils and lips he too, there in the town of her birth in faraway Mississippi, in her even more faraway childhood, more and more faraway, oh, so far away! . . . A face, may the Lord forgive the sins of her lips! a kind of Black Baptist preacher! It is not for naught that Martha refused to hear of this new match that that little madwoman, Neuta her foolish child, after she divorced her first husband, that white-haired, blue-eyed and trim figured gentleman, who was as a grownup fragrant reed stalk on the banks of the Mississippi River . . . after years and years, ten years for sure, of a happily married life she up and divorced him. She did not want to divorce him, that blue-eyed angel, but divorce him she did for some reason! She cried—as he cried, that charming man, yet she divorced him anyhow, left him after years and years, twelve years for sure, of a gloriously blessed marriage! The pampering of this one, this Black Baptist preacher was what she needed, of this rabbi, may the Lord forgive the sins of her lips! . . . she left! . . . took his young daugh-

> ter that she bore him, and left! To whom did she bear this daughter, if not to that tall and fragrant sapling? Whom, if not him, that tall and charming angel, does that daughter resemble? Especially with her trim figure, the figure of this princess? . . . tall and slender as he, even a might thinner than she should be . . . as the girls of these times, may the Lord forgive the sins of her lips, who do not eat nor drink and all they do is wax leaner and thinner, becoming less and less, so they should appeal to those White clowns of our times, who are not unlike some plain and always footloose and squandering Black dandy who wears duds to kill and slay and shows off big horse teeth, as if he were enticing seven she-devils a day, may the Lord forgive the sins of her lips! (14–15)[61]

Her mistress's troubled legs—an unexplained childhood accident—do not, thinks Martha, preclude Neuta from walking about. However, Rabbi Professor Reuben Poller is anxious to pamper his wife, so he brings her breakfast in bed and encourages her to remain there and away from active participation in the household. Curiously, though, Malki, Neuta's artist friend whose opinions resemble Martha's—very likely a symbol of the salutary role of art in a society plagued with spiritual ailments—inspires her to walk without pain.[62]

Martha's thoughts, continued in a later chapter of the novel,[63] also teach the reader about this being Neuta's second marriage. Neuta as a child was the sole Jew (through her father, owner of cotton fields in the South; her mother was a Gentile) in her southern school, where others taunted her as "The Black Jewess" or "Jews' child,"[64] for being in Martha's care, both attitudes equating Jews with Blacks. They tormented her by using anti-Black epithets instead of anti-Semitic ones,[65] again equating Jews and Blacks as objects of prejudicial hatred.

So while there may be longer works focused on Blacks, Halkin's selections are the most accomplished executions of a sustained intimate representation of African Americans in Hebrew literature. Moreover, the juxtaposition of Martha's thoughts—a practical woman whose wisdom is the accumulation of many years' experience—within the plot foregrounds the artificiality surrounding the lives of the Jewish protagonists. Among her insights is the notion that "Blacks never get old . . . they return as children to the Good Lord, as children whose birth is their burial." (94)

Another episode of *'Ad mashber*[66] contrasts Jews' love of New York City—which Halkin terms "Jew York," and earlier describes with a torrent of pejorative adjectives and names, including "horrible," "hellish," "a desert," "cruel," and "satanic"—with that of other inhabitants.[67] The narrator "scientifically" terms the city's immigrants, including Blacks, "*homo Americanus*," a new species of humans transformed by their environment, the idea reminiscent of intellectuals' speculations about the New Jew of Eretz Israel, a term that Halkin may have created as a counterpoint to further the irony of his narrative.[68]

Other segments of the novel, published as individual stories, also include observations about Blacks. In one, "The visiting hour" ("Bi-sh'at bikur"),[69] also a tale of Jewish cultural deterioration in America, the narrator points out the state of African Americans as being on the lowest social rung. He describes them as victims of the ruling classes, among whom are the Jews and the Irish.[70] As if in response, a drunken Gentile exhibits his anxiety by a humorous speculation that the Jews, Blacks, and Italians are taking over in the United States to rule over Whites.[71] Finally, in "A dream made good" ("Hatavat ḥalom"), Blacks are featured as customers of a Jewish peddler woman in Harlem.[72]

Halkin's other novel, *Yeḥi'el ha-hagri* (Yeḥi'el the Hagrite), follows the protagonist's quest for a spiritual experience and contact with the Eternal. Yeḥi'el, in his quest for answers about God's omnipresence, finds an answer when contemplating the sufferings of African Americans. The Almighty is made manifest as the "hurt in the bodies of the Blacks, bent over in the expansive cotton fields, endless and white as sheets under the blue skies of the South . . . you, God, are in the blue and you are the cotton and the pain in the Black man's bent back" ("Atah ko'ev b-gufot ha-Kushim, ha-kfufim bi-sdot-ha-tzemer ha-rḥavim, ha-malbinim kisdinim she-'eyn lahem ketz taḥat shmay ha-darom ha-kḥulim. . . . Atah, ha-'Elohim, ba-tkhelet v-'atah hu ba-tzemer vha-k'ev b-gav ha-Kushi hakafuf," 155).

IN ISRAEL

Israeli writers have also incorporated African Americans—although Israel's Black population is minuscule—in poetry and prose. Most have done so superficially, out of an interest not always related to the oppression of Blacks in America, as by striking analogies between Blacks and Israel's marginalized minorities.[73] A few, however, have had extensive contact with Blacks in the United States, an experience which they exploit in telling their tales. Yet even they do not delve deeply into the African American condition, nor do they endeavor to approach their subjects by foregoing some stock representations. Indeed, while these works present Blacks to Israelis in varying degrees of intimacy, they are explorations from the outside of an exotic aspect of America that stands as an interesting counterpoint to American Jewry.

An insightful, detailed, and partly autobiographical perspective on the lives of African Americans is embedded in a number of Yoram Kaniuk's American tales. To be sure, his representation, preserved and retold in a number of novels and short stories, is narrowly focused in theme and subject, representing a select group of Black artists his *Palmaḥnik* protagonist encounters in New York.[74] His subjects are mostly of the socially upwardly mobile Blacks, famous New York musicians living in the 1950s. They constitute a special group of social elites among White and Black America, those who have made it, at least financially. His Israeli protagonist appears to benefit from the proximity to these celebrities as he associates with them while observing the chasm between their fame and the dismally wretched lives they lead as subjects of discrimination, victims of exploitation, drugs, and violence.

The stories, however, are complicated by the protagonist's identity and background. Narrating in the first person, he is a veteran *Palmaḥ* soldier of Israel's War of Independence. After being severely wounded—a matter that also permits reading on the metaphorical plane—he flees Israel in search of an alternate existence to recuperate, reconstitute himself, and find a life that would offer integrity, tranquility, and stability.

Kaniuk's writings benefit from drawing on the author's biography. In many of his American-based tales he returns to tell an story or portray a character in ways only slightly unlike before. However, the realization that the events are retold differently, or that the protagonists carry new names, poses a question about the extent of the episodes' authenticity. To be sure, this repeated resemblance lends his narratives the force of authority and veracity. Yet the more productive approach would be to treat them as works of prose fiction focused, as they are, on the experiences of the protagonist. That which befalls the hero-narrator in America constitutes part of his self-portrait as an artist and an Israeli seeking to reconstitute an identity rent asunder by his war experiences.

Once in the United States, however, he learns of the turbulent lives of residents in an admired civilization. Wherever he turns, he finds breakdown in family and individual existence. Deciding to make his career as an artist painting canvases, he is drawn to New York's avant-garde social milieu, although, curiously, he is attracted more to the circle of musicians, where he encounters and befriends many African Americans, among them Billie Holiday and Charlie Parker.

Observing the lives of these artists, he discovers that fame brings no stability, tranquility, or satisfaction to him as an alternative existence to his Israeli experience. As an Israeli and a Jew, he is exotic and marginalized at one and the same time, much as are his Black acquaintances. Yet his attempts to succeed fail at every turn, be it as artist, husband, or friend. In the wake of such calamitous defeats he returns to Israel and his family in expectation of finding stability there.

Kaniuk's attraction to Black culture is not out of any desire to legitimate or question his own identity as a White artist or Israeli. On the contrary, his hero appears to be socially and artistically subordinate to the Black celebrities he admires. His association with them is not to obtain access for personal or financial gain.

Kaniuk's traumatized protagonist is in search of a new mode of life outside Israel. His self-representation is often uncomplimentary and focuses on the Israeli as a lost and self-destructive soul among his like in New York. His adventures in America are no less disappointing as the counterpoint to the mythologized image of the New Israeli. The escapist hero ekes out a living in a superficial existence while seeking meaning in a similarly decadent America. So it is no surprise that he finds his kin among socially dysfunctional individuals and artists populating mid twentieth century America.

His admiration of Black musicians is not merely because of their artistic attainments, as opposed to his own shortcomings, but their ability to sustain themselves in a racially hostile environment. So even if his Israeli protagonist seems to have many doors open before him in White America, it is particularly his attraction to Black society that defines his being. It is also out of this realization that his protagonist finds America to be less than the utopian Golden Land and escape from his past traumas. Moreover, Kaniuk's work challenges the canon of *Palmaḥ*-generation fiction by revealing the tattered soul of his hero, including his sense of impending doom and fear of failure.[75]

His dwelling on the lives and failures of people of renown is a way for him to expose his own and the collective deformation of New York's high society.[76] In this instance, the celebrities are also shown at their lowest as they encounter the challenges of a life of fame in a culture of drugs, alcohol, sex, and social dysfunction. The narrator likes to name-drop and tell of witnessing scenes from the lives of Charlie Parker and others. This lends a semblance of plausibility about them, as do the experiences of his Israeli protagonist.

Kaniuk's most insightful story to focus on New York's Black community is "Charlie Parker's Party" ("Ha-msibah shel Charlie Parker").[77]

Like many of his American tales, it is narrated by his Israeli protagonist who, as in most instances, does not pass judgment on his subjects or their ethically dubious behavior.

The story is about a seemingly inconsequential event, a party thrown by and on behalf of Charlie ("Bird") Parker. In terms of narrative technique, tone, and style, this story resembles a jazz composition. As such it is constructed as a compilation of subtle variations on set motifs, repeated and revised as the narrative unfolds.

The account focuses on an event in Charlie Parker's life that allows for the narrator's associative mind to illuminate his subject's past and present. It focuses on the circumstances of Parker's father's death (at the hands of a prostitute who was not paid her fee, equal to the price of a tepid glass of beer, he repeats), his relationship with a White woman, their son, "Little Bird," and Parker's heroin addiction. The elements worth noting include the circumstances behind Parker's father's death, the party and its venue, Parker's heroin addiction, and more. By way of contrast, the sole redeeming aspect in Parker's life is his love for his wife and child, which stands in marked contrast to the troubled life he leads.[78]

Reminiscent of a jazz composition, the repeated variations on a motif or phrase bring dimension to the account, adding emotional and temporal depth. This is the case with a host of phrases, most prominent of which are the circumstances surrounding the death of Parker's father at the hands of a prostitute. In recounting the event, the narrator presents a sequence of recurring phrases that repeat at an obsessive rate over the course of what is a brief eight-page story: In place of the rhythmic cadences of a musical composition, the narrative repeats the details surrounding several episodes by altering their length and varying the details they contain.

1—"his father was slaughtered by a whore" (9)

2—"The whore also slaughtered the bird. With what voracity. Charlie Parker's father invited her to his home and then confessed before her that he had no money." (9)

3—"She slaughtered him with a broken bottle of Old Crow." (9)

4—"He thinks that he plays beautiful birds, splendid slaughtered peacocks—like his father—on the way to Eden." (9)

5—"He injects himself with heroin injections that slowly kill him, ever since his father lay slaughtered on the floor." (10)

6—"He remembered the word *Kushi* from some old song that his father sang before an old whore slaughtered him because he had no money to pay her the whore's money. Beer! Charlie Parker said that her fee was

a price equal to the price of a mug of beer, and because of that he was slaughtered." (10)
7—"It was the look of a father murdered on a bed. An old whore. The price of a bottle of beer. Warm, not even cold." (12)
8—"He sees his black father slaughtered on the floor." (13)
9—"With a voice suffused with cigarettes and night and shame. Her voice grunting. Like an old whore that kills a man with a broken bottle of Old Crow because of warm beer." (13)
10—"She burst out with a loud and ugly laughter. A filthy laugh, as that of old whores who kill men for a piss-warm mug of beer." (15)
11—"She again began to laugh like an old whore who killed an old black man with a broken bottle of crummy Old Crow." (15)

Reading the story is as much an emotional experience as a verbal one. The refraining cadences of key words, mesmerizing phrases, and images interweave through the narrative to create a sensory rhythm which carries the plot to its conclusion. References to Parker's father's death repeat ten times in the course of the story, always different and varied, giving rise to an allusive texture of referentiality. Rhythmically, the account is repeated four times in quick succession at the story's beginning, the fifth following soon thereafter. Following a brief respite addressing other matters, the phrase returns three more times, closing the story with two references at the conclusion, when the narrative shifts focus onto Parker's woman.

In each instance, the account of the death of Charlie Parker's father is modulated by supplementary information that embellishes the account, adding detail and dimension. The narrative moves from a simple assertion of the father's slaughter by a prostitute to details about the murder that highlight the life he led. In this light, it soon becomes evident that the murder of the father, and the pet bird, resonates against the popular name Charlie Parker received, "Bird." In all instances, the theme of death resonates variously as the fate surrounding Parker's life and that of the Israeli narrator.

By the tale's end, however, the narrator's imagination shifts to Parker's White woman. She takes on characteristics of the old prostitute in her hostility to the narrator and Parker, implying her sinister role vis-à-vis both.

Additionally, the image of a slaughtered father cannot but bring up in Hebrew literature a reversal of the theme of the binding of Isaac (the *'akedah*). The lingering image of the dead father is underscored in the imprints it leaves on the memory of the son, or sons, for the vision haunts

Charlie Parker and, in some similar way, the narrator, who—in other works, such as *Rockinghorse*—has to confront his own relationship with his father to understand himself.

The complexity of the narrative becomes more pronounced as other key terms and phrases also repeat, giving rise to a literary fabric punctuated by repeating themes and verbal colors. Of the more pronounced of these are references to Parker's White woman ("ha-ʾishah ha-lvanah"), her pale face ("panayha ḥivrot"), Parker as her Black master ("adonah ha-shaḥor"), and a host of terms related to death, such as dripping blood ("notefet dam"), murdering him slowly ("rotzaḥat oto at at"), and one who belongs in the cemetery ("shayakh/karov l-vayt ha-kvarot").

The recurrence of these interweaving leitmotifs brings about a textual rhythm and cadence that is more than mere verbal association or a heightened expression for emphasis. They convey in words what a composition would do with a musical phrase. Their apparent arrhythmic nature intensifies the message by sheer repetition,[79] but is also evocative of a musical jazz composition in which motifs and leitmotifs recur at unexpected moments and with ever newer variations.

The repetitive nature of this and other works has led critics to attribute to Kaniuk's narrative influences of metarealistic, unrealistic, or surrealistic writers from Hebrew and world literature. His fiction has been variously associated with the technique and tone of writers such as Agnon and Kafka,[80] Berdychevsky and Brenner.[81] Additionally, Kaniuk himself confesses allegiance to Brecht, Stendhal, Faulkner, and Shaw.[82]

The significant thematic elements pertaining to Black-White relations focus on the narrator's Israeli background, his knowledge of Hebrew, the sacred language used by Jesus—with which one can now curse, translate "Lullaby in Birdland" ("Shir ʿeres b-ʿeretz ha-tziporim"), and purchase hashish.[83]

As for himself, as much as he tries to fit in, to be a Black among Blacks, the narrator remains at the periphery, in and out of the crowd—or, as Parker observed, to remain different from him as "day and night of those twenty-four hours."[84] He hovers sufficiently close to the group to be a close and reliable witness, but not one with Parker, whose music he will never comprehend or feel, as he admits. So no matter how much the narrator strives to deny his own whiteness, he fails. "I always tried to chase from my thoughts the White man that I was," he confesses.[85]

The tale is told in hindsight, sometime following Parker's death. It is a recollected episode in the narrator's experience, yet one reminding him and the reader of the futility of attempting to be one with Black culture or individuals. Cognizant of Charlie Parker's fame not just in America but also among Israelis, Kaniuk returns to dwell on him in many of his American tales. His work on Parker, as on other celebrities, offers a treasure trove of anecdotal information through which the narrator achieves importance and defines himself by belonging. Thus, for example, he shares a theory, heard from Lenny Tristano, that jazz was born in Black funerals because they have white souls and only a blind man (like Tristano) can give expression to the Black man's white soul.[86]

Another personage in Kaniuk's tales to appreciate and defend Blacks, and on whom Kaniuk's narrator dwells, is Frank Sinatra. Sinatra not only defended African Americans against racial hatred but was drawn to the Blues because the music possessed qualities of Black funeral songs.[87]

Seeking an alternate abode from the one they fled, Kaniuk's narrators gravitate to African Americans and their history of subjugation in America. They, like Jews in Israel, are at the crest of a new wave that seeks to redefine them. Yet these narrator-protagonists are sensitive to all Black protagonists, even those who are not celebrities, perhaps because their history is rooted in an unhappy past that they cannot cast by the wayside as they attempt to redefine themselves. Whites who come too near pay dearly for this attraction, which turns out to be premature and violent, as there are others wishing to hold them back.

In an episode repeated in several works, Kaniuk tells of a White woman's love affair with a Black man. The affair results in his death at the hand of Whites, while her family rejects her and treats her as if she were dead.[88] A similar tale is an episode of a White woman who is raped by police officers in Louisiana after being caught kissing a Black man.[89]

In "Thirteen Boiler-Makers," Kaniuk idealizes the staying power of two Black protagonists who drink thirteen boiler-makers with no discernible effect on them, though one's awe of the other is shattered after realizing that he had attained the same legendary feat.[90] The account focuses less on the morality of drinking—with which the narrator never struggles as the root of America's social evil, though it hovers unmentioned in the background—and more on an idealization of the Black man in this story.

Kaniuk's propensity for name dropping is often associated with the exposure of the celebrity's humanity, or even failures in life, that also strikes a nexus between the lofty and lowly spheres in his writings. Such is also his recounting of the tragic life of Billie Holiday, which he does in a review essay—summarized as Hollywood "kitsch"—about the movie treatment of her life, *Lady Sings the Blues*.[91] Kaniuk, who claims to have known her when he was in New York in the 1950s, attempts to explain her art. He attributes her talent to an ability "to sing from her blood," her people's history that originated in their heritage of suffering during slavery and the Middle Passage. Her expressive powers are drawn from deep within; she was a singer who was musically untrained and could not read notes (61), but "from the suffering there came a songbird" (60). When he asserts that her pain is also rooted in her people's being cut off from Africa and from its wild and natural milieu, his observations resemble the sentiments expressed in Halkin's poem "El ha-Kushit," Avinoam's "In the Shade of the One with the Black Skin," and the like. It is the suffering which brings forth a torrent of authenticity and facilitates the release of the inner, natural self. So it is not merely the mechanics of singing that imbued Billie Holiday's singing with its magic; it was the release of the inner self that is palpable in her songs. Such attributes deserve analysis in light of their being analogically valid vis-à-vis Jewish history as well.

In other works, too, Kaniuk returns frequently to the encounters he (or his protagonist) has with African Americans. In *Sus'etz* (*Rocking-horse*),[92] in addition to continuing the practice of name dropping of Black avant-garde artists (77–78, 185; in translated version see pp. 89–91, 219), he records the attitude of anti-Semites who conflate African Americans with Jews, one of whom calls Communists "Black Jews" (71, 91; in translated version pp. 82, 104). That novel also bears the distinctive imprints of a willfully altered writing style. The narrative's tendency to incorporate numerous American English terms into the Hebrew, at times even in a corrupted form, as in many of his American-centered tales, is dependent on geography. As the protagonist maneuvers through the American landscape, his Hebrew demonstrates its assimilation by an abundant use of English terms. However, once the protagonist leaves America's shores to sail back to Israel, this linguistic amalgam is almost completely ended. His Israeli orientation at such times is so strong that even while making a stop in Italy his language does not meld Italian terms or expressions into the Hebrew narrative.

CONCLUSION

In a drive to Americanize their works by including the image of Blacks in poetry and prose, immigrant Hebrew writers could not surmount the stereotypes. Although in most instances their sentiments lay on the side of the Other, they had little intimate familiarity with Blacks beyond the conventional and external features which fed their works. Yet Hebrew writers continue to populate their works with Black protagonists in a host of peripheral or metaphoric roles, signifying everything from part of a mimetic representation of their surroundings to unadulterated natural instincts to threatening excess of sexuality and primitivism which they sought to recapture in themselves. Nonetheless, a number of compositions have succeeded in lending a nuanced and dimensional face to Blacks, benefiting Hebrew literature in the process of its becoming an American literature.

More often than not, though, Blacks remained as idealized images, facilitating the writer's quest for inspiration or as sources of authentic suffering. At times Blacks would be the image of the natural and instinctual forces in man that are being shackled and constrained by Western civilization. At other times, Blacks were mere background detail to document and validate the realistic features of prose narratives.

In all of these, Hebrew literature demonstrated flexibility and a sense of ease in references to African Americans for diverse purposes, underscoring an American-ness to their oeuvre. They sought to be like Blacks in retaining a measure of their unique cultural identity, but at the same time strove to be Americans. Ultimately, one of the more effective means has come, strangely enough, in a scene from the Mel Brooks parody of a Western, *Blazing Saddles.* The Yiddish-speaking Chief of the Sioux warriors, played by Brooks, confronts a family of Blacks who have survived their attack:

> Chief: Shvartzes [Blacks].
> No, no, zeit nisht meshugeh [No, no, don't be crazy]. Lozem gayne [Let them go].
> Chief to Blacks: cop a walk, its [*sic*] all right.
> Black woman: thank you.
> Black child: thank you.
> Chief: a bee gezunt. Take off!
> (to one of the warriors): Est dee gezeynt in den layben? [Have you ever in your life seen?] They're darker than us! Woo![93]

His conclusion, uttered by a Jewish writer and actor playing the Indian, is not to invite them to join his people, not to attack them, but to leave them to go their way. The observation of their external appearance, as being "darker than us," prompts him to this gesture while feeling a kindred identity that has brought on this sympathetic regard. His solution is to not interfere in their lives but leave them be. Brooks's treatment of the issue has already passed beyond the sentimental and ignores the realistic.

Chapter Nine

THE LANGUAGE OF ALIENATION: THE ANXIETY OF AN AMERICANIZED HEBREW

Even before the Czernowitz conference of 1908, when Yiddish was proclaimed by some as the Jewish national language, the preference by others for Hebrew distinguished them ideologically from the former. Supporters of the Zionist platform were also adherents of Hebrew and wedded it with the Jews' national and political aspirations. Opponents of Zionism, who favored the Jews' continued Diasporic existence, often allied behind the quintessential Jewish language of the European Diaspora, Yiddish. In this equation, mainline Hebrew literature was presumed enlisted to the national cause. The Hebrew literary canon of the time became replete with works promoting Zionism. Those Hebrew writers who did not submit to this expectation were marginalized in their days and in future years to become a subject of considerable interest in recent decades.[1]

Yet for all the energy and innovativeness invested in engendering a dynamic and self-renewing Hebrew suitable for the modern age, American writers, particularly poets, were loath to compromise the purity of the language. Their ambivalence about Eretz Israel, as detailed below, became an occasion for pondering its place in America. Not a few assumed that Hebrew was a channel for expressing not national issues but local, American concerns pertaining to existential and personal matters. Ironically, while they were rejecting the expectation attributed to the Hebrew literary milieu, they were becoming the American establishment in cultural and socio-political terms. With their active participation, American Hebrew grew sufficiently apart from other regional influences to become the medium for a nascent center of Hebrew literature that, for a time, dared vie for hegemony among Hebraists. But it defined and distinguished itself by specific linguistic and thematic peculiarities that made it American.

The concurrent trend by Hebraists to follow the general Sephardic style adopted in the Land of Israel also fragmented American acolytes of Ashkenazi Hebrew, creating conditions for innovative change while others adhered to tradition. Whether proponents of the former or conservators of the latter, it fell to these writers to transmute not only linguistic issues but also European literary and ideological conventions, emblazoning upon them a distinct mode of Americanism. Nevertheless, all too many imprints of East European Hebrew literary practices remained in force, some to be challenged by a future iconoclastic generation.[2]

Indeed, the early years of the twentieth century harbored much hope for the imminent emergence of an American Hebrew literary center. The expectation was founded on the recognition of a shift in the center of gravity of Hebrew intellectual life away from Europe. Influenced by events in the Land of Israel, American Hebraists envisioned the transmuted immigrant as the New World Jew. This was to be an American Hebrew (as opposed to an American Jew) characterized by an adherence to a unique identity and aspirations, one distinct from a perceived cultural degeneration among the masses. This Hebrew, so the view held, respected his past, including religion, though he was not personally observant. This anticipation, though, faded by mid-century as Jews abandoned their national and religious language en masse in their rush to become full-fledged Americans.[3]

Yet even as they set foot in the New World, Hebraists were occupied with preserving the Old by conserving its themes, forms, and literary modes. As in the case of similar trends in European Hebrew letters, Hebrew writers in America became bound up with the perpetuation of the *mlitzah* style of Haskalah Hebrew and its evolving post-Haskalah *fin-de-siècle* sensibility, termed the *nusaḥ*, a stylistic formula identified with Mendele Mocher Sforim (Shalom Yaʿakov Abramovitch) and perpetuated by the likes of Bialik and his contemporaries. Their Hebrew remained a rarified poetic style which penetrated into prose fiction as well, giving rise to works that were "charged with poetic overtones."[4] An early proponent of this tendency was B. N. Silkiner, who, as we have seen above, set the literary tone and thematic path by promoting a willfully anachronistic Hebrew reminiscent of many European maskilim in the composition of his epic poem, *Mul ohel Timmura* (Before Timmura's tent, 1909). So obscure and ponderous was the Hebrew of the first edition—"his Indian epic . . . is impossible to read," asserts one reader[5]—that Silkiner revised it,[6] condensing and substituting a simpler and somewhat more transparent language.

Though by no means the only one to continue use of this cumbersome Hebrew, E. E. Lisitzky composed what is fittingly the apotheosis of the Haskalah in that it bears and refines many of its hallmarks. Although at times his medium complemented the archaic themes and settings of his compositions,[7] it remains an unpersuasive argument in light of his dizzying variety of subjects, which are rarely met with a commensurate stylistic modulation. In fact, his Hebrew remains uniformly monolithic, leading readers to identify him as "the poet of the *nusaḥ*," the established elevated language of post-Haskalah Hebrew, "and the unrivaled conservator among the poets of our age. Lisitzky does not even succumb to the blinding glitter of the ultimately stressed Sephardic syllable. Self-loyalty is what keeps Lisitzky from deviating, which undermines the spirit of his poetry."[8]

As in language, so in form, Lisitzky adheres to staid, traditional poetic conventions. His long poems in *Anshay midot* (Men of stature, 1958), for instance, are composed in iambic meter whose phrases become more obscure as the poet enfolds idea within idea, slowing down the reading and, ironically, depriving the poems of their intended folk flavor. The scholar in Lisitzky, again, prevails over the man of the people.

Another factor to detract from any affinities with folk origins is the large number of newly coined words. In a letter of 18 January 1959 to Lisitzky, Daniel Persky comments at length on his linguistic exoticism in *Anshay midot* (not *Anshay ma'alot*, as Persky erroneously notes there). As if to enforce a correct form of the classical, Persky, who has not concealed his preference for the conservative, Ashkenazi Hebrew of the Diaspora, appends a list of twenty-one words that, in his judgment, call for correction because they do not follow biblical form.[9]

Comparisons of American Hebrew writers with those in the Land of Israel, especially in the years following statehood, are unanimous about the ever-widening generic, linguistic, and thematic chasms forming between the two groups. The phenomenon is perceived as a mark of the decline of the former, and evidence about its eventual demise. One study compares an Israeli poet, Shlomo Zamir, with Lisitzky as models of treating Hebrew in opposing ways. Lisitzky is held up as exemplifying the classical Hebrew past, poetically a tradition-laden conservative, whereas Zamir—a new poet switching from Arabic to Hebrew—illustrates revolutionary literary and linguistic tendencies of the present.[10]

Conscious of the disparagement of their center primarily by Israeli writers, America's Hebraists strove to defend their attainments and destiny as early as the 1930s. Yet the lack of innovation, linguistic and stylistic, remained a sore point difficult to defend in the ensuing years.[11]

One consequence of this shortcoming was that American Hebraists were losing their audience. In his collection of poems, *Kmo ha-yom rad* (As the day has set, 1960), Lisitzky expresses his pessimism about a future readership of Hebrew American poets. While seeming to accept his own demise as part of the natural order of life, he remains unsure about his audience (83), echoing observations made earlier by one of his mentors, the poet Y. L. Gordon. As is true of many works by American Hebrew writers, his poems bear themes and images of the waning of the day, an inevitable ending which, even when not directly referring to their lot, nevertheless incorporates it.[12]

The call on America's Hebraists by the likes of Y. Ḥ. Brenner and Yaʿakov Rabinowitz to emerge from their self-imposed insularity and sentimental preoccupation with the past and incorporate an American air into Hebrew literature was met with depictions of the social scene and local landscape.[13] But more important, Hebraists also turned to hone a language that distinguished their works from those in other literary centers. By this act, they strove to liberate their work from the confines of Haskalah literature, among whose legacies was the writing of nature poetry of the most generalized kind, typical and abstract, devoid of concreteness about place and time.[14]

The strategies adopted by the novelist and short-story writer S. L. Blank are illustrative of the way many writers have responded to America. Unlike with Hebrew poets who strove to narrow their style by limiting themselves to a classical idiom, the verisimilitude of his idyllic tales set on the Bessarabian tundra was enriched with loan words and depictions of unique cultural practices.[15] These are interlaced within his allusive Hebrew style, a mix of biblical, mishnaic, Talmudic, and rabbinic Hebrew with some Aramaic, whose intertextuality is never sufficiently exploited. The model, including Aramaic terminology, except for the preponderance of European terms, served him well as he replaced European cultural imprints with those of America in his U.S.-centered stories, such as *Mister Kunis*, which also became the stage for newly coined Hebraisms.

It is not unlikely that Blank is also the most prolific in incorporating English terms within his prose, though many writers exhibit similar tendencies. Writing tales set in America, such as *Mister Kunis*, or *ʿEtz ha-sadeh* (The tree of the field) and *B-maʿarbolet ha-ḥayim* (In the whirlpool of life), he introduces English words or expressions, often translated literally or transliterated from the English. Numerous words are interspersed among biblical terms,[16] as are names of current significance—an example is the acronym H.I.A.S. (Hebrew Immigrant Aid Society), an agency whose services are described in some detail in *Ee ha-dmaʿot* (The isle of tears, 1941), or numerous place and people's names, even transcribed as a Jew would pronounce them.

Even more than in *Mister Kunis*, Blank's 1941 novel *Ee ha-dmaʿot*, which speaks volumes, by analogy, of the depredations of the Holocaust, details the despoliation of Europe's Jews in the post–First World War years. It mirrors the rapid assimilation of America's Jews as they strive to differentiate themselves from their immigrant coreligionists. The novel documents the practice of Jews losing themselves, their unique identity, and their linguistic origins in America, a phenomenon heretofore not found among Jews in transit from one land to another.

In many instances he also introduces newly coined words, often depending on archaic forms or adaptation of words from other parts of speech. However, he is best at illustrating the assimilation of Jews with particular effectiveness through interesting linguistic transitions in *Ee hadmaʿot.* So long as the novel's protagonists remain out at sea, out of touch with America, the narrative language is nearly all Hebrew, sprinkled at times with some Europeanisms. The encounter with America, however, introduces protagonists and readers alike to English words interspersed within the Hebrew. The language of narrative and discourse reinforces the immigrants' arrival in the New World, where dockworkers and immigration officials speak English.

The process of distancing oneself from the Old Country and its language increases the pace of acculturation. In Blank's *Mister Kunis*, the words of the woman in whose apartment the protagonist, Leibush Kurki, or Leon Kunis, rents a room are a case in point:

> Instead of saying *gafrur*, it's better to say "match" in English; instead of *b-vakashah* [say] "please," and so forth . . . such is the rule: the more one uses English in speech, the better. Also, one should always carry an English paper along and look at it while traveling on the tram or the subway, and one should not carry a Yiddish paper, lest the Gentiles mock him. (51)

These words, so richly allusive to traditional texts, poignantly and ironically rephrase a familiar utterance from the Passover Seder into the secular domain of America: "The more one uses English in speech, the better." The original wording refers to the increased merit obtained by recounting ever more of the story of the Exodus from Egypt. Blank's formulation reverses the intent to mean that the most meritorious act is to conceal one's national or ethnic identity by resorting to English whenever possible. The allusion turns the ritual of national identity on its head by obliterating the self through the rites of assimilation.

By linguistic turns the author points to the Americanization of recently immigrated Jews, now proud to exhibit their mastery of the new language. When the protagonists' relatives show up on Ellis Island, the novel's language, correspondingly, becomes an arena for transliterated English.[17] Those who have begun to strike root in the New World exhibit the erosion of their ancestral language—illustrated with Hebrew, though it was Yiddish in most instances—as English words encroach upon and replace those of the Old World. Among the first to go are the names of the new arrivals. One changes her name from the Hebrew Hannah to Anna (140), carving out a new distance from her love, David, who remains imprisoned at Ellis Island. She loses her "green" look (140) as she is drawn into alien and alienating circles of Jews who assimilate into the American landscape.

Many writers follow similar stratagems, a tradition that ends (for the time being) in the American fiction of Yoram Kaniuk. Numerous illustrations may be drawn from prose fiction, from works by L. A. Arieli, Moshe Brind, Bernard Isaacs, and B. Rassler, who represent the Americanization of Jews by interspersing their Hebrew narrative or discourse with foreign terms. Highlighting the linguistic mix, English, Russian, and Yiddish terms, expressions, or even sentences are either transliterated into the Hebrew or are printed out in Cyrillic or Latin alphabet within the protagonists' discourse.[18]

By means of these strategies, authors present readers with foreign terms and cultural features. However, these often lack the necessary underpinnings to allow Hebrew readers to comprehend the connotations in the words. So while archaic Hebrew (and Aramaic) terms remain within the province of the Jewish cultural domain, and presumably accessible to educated readers, the case differs when foreign terms are translated or transliterated. In those cases, it is evident that the narrative "speaks" ever more clearly to the Americanized Hebrew reader than to the one in Israel, whom it alienates.

This strategy, as Shaked points out, may be the author's signal of translating the dialogues from other languages, and is an anti-literary device that lends his work a local flavor.[19] While his observation may be valid in the case of Arieli, it is an exaggerated generalization about criteria demonstrating anti-literary tendencies among Hebrew writers in America. Arieli, influenced by Brenner's strategies, shatters literary conventions in his narrative by mimetically simulating the fragmentation of reality, conveying the narrator's tone, often cynical, about American Jews, or recording a reality which is not of one fabric.[20]

Evidence for the free practice of individual authors in coining Hebrew terms is found in the names they give to the Statue of Liberty. Arieli, in

"Emigrantim" (Emigrants), a poignant story of uprootedness composed and set in the mid 1920s,[21] translates it literally as "pesel ha-ḥerut" (137), a term that is current in Hebrew. Harry Sackler translates it as "andartat ha-ḥofesh" (monument, or statue of freedom).[22] By contrast, S. L. Blank, in his *Ee ha-dmaʿot*, calls it variously, and quite literally, "pesel ha-dror" (16) and "andartat ha-dror" (24), echoing, perhaps, the term for liberty, "dror," in Lev. 25:10, and throughout Jeremiah. Also, when his heroine, Hannah, is let out of Ellis Island, she is granted "dror," or liberty. Evidently, each writer sought ways to impress a personal imprint on the Hebrew language, either by "inventing" his own terms or by determining a personal way to depict Americanisms.

Another subject of interest is the term for skyscraper. Silberschlag offers the word derived from sky, "shaḥakon,"[23] while Isaacs prefers "mkartzefay ʿananim," for "cloud-scrapers."[24] Halevy uses a slight variant to that with "markiʿay sheḥakim" and "gorday sheḥakim," and Moshe Brind translates the English more literally as "mkartzefay sheḥakim" in his poetry.[25] Others who follow Brind include A. Regelson[26] and A. S. Schwartz.[27]

The absence of what should have been an intimate dialogue between Hebrew writers (and poets in particular) in America and Israel had its effect. The aging generation of American Hebrew writers became the keepers and defenders of an outmoded Hebrew.[28] Without a younger generation of Hebrew writers to pick up the mantle in America, one poised to struggle against the Hebrew of their forebears, and with the desired know-how to perform the obligatory act of literary patricide by honing a more modern Hebrew—inspired, perhaps, by what was happening at the time in Eretz Israel—the old ways of the Haskalah reigned on until the demise of its writers. In their stead came Jewish writers of a younger, English-speaking generation, giving rise to the ever revitalized generations of Bellows, Ginzbergs, Malamuds, Ozicks, Roths, and Englanders, among others.

The strategies by the likes of Blank and Arieli, however, do not hold for all Hebrew writers. Some poets, as well as many writers of prose fiction, plied their art with a lucid and precise Hebrew stripped of its allusiveness. Practiced most successfully in poetry by Gavriel Preil (though he also translates some locale names and coins new words such as "mḥulan, hitḥalnut, miteḥalen" to denote secularism),[29] it is observable in the works of Israel Efros, though to a lesser degree.[30]

The differing attitude about language in America and Israel has to do with the direction in which Hebrew was headed in each location. At a time when in the Land (and later state) of Israel the Committee for the Hebrew Language (1890s), followed by the Academy for the Hebrew Language (1953), took on the leading role of coining and disseminating new terms, American Hebraists were loath to accept its authority. Instead, and to uphold their independence, they exhibited a disproportionate degree of self-reliance and a blatant disregard for any agency. Moreover, Israeli-coined terms seldom appear in the works of American Hebrew writers, who were keenly aware of the literary output of their Israeli fellows.

As is evident from the activity of many of America's Hebrew writers, the Academy's authority or its decisions were not regarded as binding in America (nor in Israel). In defense of a classical style, the American Hebraist Daniel Persky even claimed that the Sephardic accent, as used in Israel, should not be binding on the Hebrew dialect of the Diaspora.[31] Instead, authors in the New World are characterized by a prolific introduction of new terms into Hebrew, most of which did not take hold, since each writer appears to adhere to his own practices and disregard the others.

American Hebrew writers reacted variously to the change of preferred accentuation in Hebrew. Though some poets acceded to the new trend, others chose to retain the traditional Hebrew of Eastern Europe. Eisig Silberschlag observed that "soon enough, it [Ashkenazi Hebrew] will be a subject for archaeologists."[32] Others wrote in both modes, using footnotes or other methods to alert the reader as to the preferred dialect to follow. One of the principal poets, Israel Efros, acknowledging that his *Silent Wigwams* is composed in the Ashkenazi—for example, by rhyming the words "tif'eres" (glory) and "vha-ḥeres" (and the sun) in the epigraphic opening poem—appends to the volume a bibliographical afterword encouraging readers to read as they prefer.[33]

In terms of adaptation to the local cultural landscape, S. Halkin's novel *ʿAd mashber* (Until breakdown) exemplifies a different approach in American Hebrew. In place of transliterating or printing out foreign words with a non-Hebrew alphabet, Halkin translates many terms into Hebrew, though his rules emerge out of concern for clarity of comprehension. Place names, streets, and neighborhoods often remain transliterated. However, such locations in New York City as Central Park or the East River are translated as "Gan ha-merkazi" and "Nahar ha-mizraḥ."[34] Many other terms, expressions, and figures of speech are also rendered into a usable Hebrew, even in Halkin's short story "Ba-ḥeder ha-pnimi" (The inner room), creating for the reader familiar with English a quaint can-you-guess-what-this-is puzzle.

Though Halkin's technique is more innovative than those practiced by Arieli and Blank (though they also resorted to Halkin's practice, but not as pervasively), the absence of any cultural underpinning to provide the milieu for the expressions leaves the Hebrew hollow. Thus, the expression "mgalah et klafayha" (shows her cards)[35] reproduces an Americanism without correcting the reader's belief that the heroine is engaged in playing cards.[36] The incongruity of the expression, which is, admittedly, sufficiently widespread to the point of not necessitating a card-playing environment, is out of place in the Hebrew.

Halkin's literature may be the first example of a quantitative absorption of Americanisms into Hebrew. It is as if writers such as he have come to terms with the new environment and assimilated English into their works, enriching and distinguishing American Hebrew from the one evolving in Eretz Israel. Meanwhile, their style models but one way in which this Hebrew can mirror the assimilation of its readers (speakers were few) in the New World. While most expressions have never become part of normative Hebrew, the process anticipates more recent developments in Israeli culture as Americanism invades it. The current Israeli preference for loan words such as "hamburger" and "video," as a direct transliteration, or even as composites, as in the case of the Hebrew "telefon selulari" (cellular telephone), or a direct translation, minus the cultural resonance of terms such as "lirot min ha-moten" (to shoot from the hip), etc., echo Halkin's Americanized Hebrew.[37] Another, Aaron Zeitlin, who bemoans his poetry's neglect, writes to Lisitzky that "the trouble is that not only the Sephardic accent is against the last Mohicans" (a reference to American Hebraists preferring the Ashkenazi accent) but grammar itself "has decreed (as it were) an end to our penultimate Ashkenazi accent, and who will stand up to mighty grammar?"[38]

Explaining his departure from Ashkenazi Hebrew, Halkin claims to have acquired during childhood the Sephardic style that, it turns out, has been a factor in the longevity of his poetry. However, "I was forced by the traditional practice of the Ashkenazi accent to return to the 'ḥeder inflection,' [but] . . . when I came to the land [of Israel] in that year [1929] the transition for me to the correct dialect was natural . . ."[39] Indeed, Halkin adapted the accentuation of many of his poems for Israeli readers, for "one who lived in the land and knows how difficult it is for the Eretz Israel reader to appreciate the taste of the accent, and at times the rhyme in Hebrew poetry as written with the penultimate [Ashkenazi] accentuation, will understand the composer's desire to rescue even in a small way the accent of his works . . . [for] the correct accent, the one approximating

Eretz Israel speech, also brings the language of the poem closer to the spoken language."[40]

E. E. Lisitzky remarked frequently on the practice of an altered inflection, although he did not change his own Ashkenazi-influenced accent and meter, adhering steadfastly to his traditional Hebrew, which he held to be the highest model for literary purposes. In 1910, at the beginning of his literary career, he translated a poem by Tennyson, which he entitled "Iyov-Promite'us" (Job-Prometheus) (74–75), for *Snunit*, in which he rhymed "u-mesos" with "mi-mos" (rottenness/death). In a letter to the writer and fellow countryman Y. D. Berkovitch (Berkowitz) in the summer of 1918, Lisitzky asserted proudly that, in translating Shakespeare's *Julius Caesar*, he consciously chose to employ biblical Hebrew and style. When he needed a non-biblical term, he continues, he would rely on Talmudic language only in the most unavoidable case.[41]

The practice of adherence to Ashkenazi Hebrew affected the rhyme and meter sensed by readers, and stood as but one impediment to a favorable reception of American Hebrew poetry in Israel. Many Israeli readers have frequently come to refer to the Hebrew of American poets (in particular) as esoteric, alien, and dissonant to the ear. At times this objection is followed by a condescending observation that while out of date, this language is nevertheless read fluently and warmheartedly.[42]

In the case of Lisitzky's *B-'oholay Khush*, its archaic style is deemed fitting to the subject, for it possesses the right cadence to convey the pain of the children of slaves by an admixture of biblical and voodoo images.[43] The style, while lacking the freshness of the new, was considered a fitting medium for representing an exotic and unfamiliar reality.[44] Y. Klausner, perhaps without irony, crowned Lisitzky the champion of champions of the *Tanakh*.[45]

As seen from the above, Lisitzky's writing received significant criticism from readers in Israel and America who were raised on or cultivated a taste for the new dialect. Recognizing his tenacious insistence on the archaic pronunciation and penultimate stress of Ashkenazic Hebrew, they observe, for instance, that "the language of the poet is very un-Israeli; it reminds one . . . of Haskalah literature," one having an "affinity for Biblical Hebrew, and self-invented words and phrases, even the same grandiloquence," that remind one of Bialik's poetry.[46] Or, as another observed, "The language is somewhat euphuistic and of an Ashkenazi dialect,"[47] modeled on styles ranging from the *Tanakh* to Michal (Lebenson), Y. L. Gordon, and Bialik, adding that its linguistic peculiarities are a mark of Lisitzky's conservative, preservationist tendencies. Such idiosyncrasies have contributed to difficulties of comprehension for contemporary readers.[48]

Yet as if to acknowledge the contributions of American Hebraists in coining Hebrew words, and particularly Lisitzky's role in this endeavor, A. Kariv writes to him, in a letter dated 15 Ḥeshvan 1959 praising his influence on the Hebrew language:

> In the past weeks I have often encountered your name. Every night I examine the Supplements Volume of Even-Shoshan's *New Dictionary* [Hebrew-Hebrew], containing newly coined literary terms and expressions. The author cites many innovations from your book *Eleh toldot adam* [*In the Grip*]. For example, "hitbokek"—"a worn out heart and an emptied [*she-nitbokekah*] soul" . . . and so forth and so on, tens of words . . .[49]

Nevertheless, though tied to their European roots, American Hebrew poets participated in the development of a literary language whose trajectory was unlike that of writers in the Old Country. At the time, the latter were extricating themselves from the *mlitzah*, that cumbersome, formulaic, florid, and artificially classical style of Haskalah Hebrew. American Hebrew was also significantly unlike that emerging concurrently in Eretz Israel.[50] Although it emerges from the style of the European Haskalah—particularly in its tendency to preserve a "pure" high literary style—this Hebrew evolved in its own way even in the United States at a time when writers in Eretz Israel were actively promoting the emergence of a stark, colloquial, and unadorned vernacular. American Hebraist poets continued to prefer obscure words frequently rejected by their European and Israeli counterparts, and created a flood of neologisms unlike those emerging from the Israel center.[51]

For this reason as well, Hebrew writing in America quickly lost the vital readership base so essential for their perpetuation. The extent to which many works of prose fiction in particular became sites for the incorporation of numerous loan (English) words is unprecedented. Though adding a measure of realism to the narrative, these terms taught English to Hebrew readers in America. In addition, they contributed to the narrowing of the readership to those familiar with English, while alienating others. Regrettably, too, these works were often stillborn, lacking any popular readership even in America, where an ever-diminishing audience was turning to Israeli writers, and in Israel, where these works were judged difficult, distant, and alien. Finally, Hebrew writers in America seemed less engaged with the leading issues at the forefront of Israeli or Hebrew readers in any land. Rather, their involvement in the pursuit of meaning to life, in being engrossed in the metaphysical pursuit of the divine, were of little concern in Israel, where local and daily events were deemed of historical significance.

ASHKENAZ IN AMERICA: ISRAELI VS. AMERICAN HEBREW

The amazing tenacity with which American Hebrew writers adhered to a classical style in light of the ever-changing dynamism of Israeli Hebrew engendered an American Hebrew. Adhering to an Ashkenazi accent even after the middle of the century identified them as rooted in a Diasporic culture distant from groundbreaking changes taking shape in Eretz Israel. This had become even more evident by the end of the first quarter of the twentieth century as Eretz Israeli Hebrew literature was generating and mirroring a colloquial style that American Hebrew writers did not represent in their works. While it is obvious from many sources that they were cognizant of the less formal Hebrew—as in their correspondence, in Hebrew prose fiction, and the exceptional language of a handful of poets—Americans clung to a higher literary style.

On occasion, one can even discern the Ashkenazi Hebrew in the untenable lost rhymes of a Sephardic reading of poems. Lisitzky rhymes "resen" (restraint) with "pesen" ("peten" in Sephardic, a serpent), and "l-khalanis" (Sephardic "l-kalanit," to an anemone) with "Adonis," or "amus" (Sephardic "amut," I shall die) with "kamus" (hidden),[52] indicating his stubborn hold on stylistic and formal elements which, even before Israeli statehood, assured his poetry's marginalization. Though some compromised by employing a Sephardic Hebrew, the very fact that they also continued to write in the Ashkenazi vein was nothing but self-destructive for reception.

More than one scholar has observed the difference in the development of Hebrew in America from that of Eretz Israel, explaining the former as a consequence of conservation and the latter as the dynamism of a living language engaged with daily necessities.[53] Their themes, too, revolved about a preservation and depiction of a remembered past, couched in a nostalgia in which memory selectively retained a world of harmony, where order and authority were in patriarchal hands, and where tradition and religious faith remained at the core of life.

The dense, impenetrable styles of some writers, such as Silkiner's and Lisitzky's on the one hand, and the highly allusive though unyielding prose of Blank's Bessarabian novels, foreground language as an impediment to clarity of meaning. Israeli readers, in particular, have encountered the greatest difficulties with this archaic Hebrew,[54] suffused as it is with biblical overtones indicative of the richness of expression, though also of the *mlitzah*, or euphuism, in style.[55]

As in the case of Lisitzky's and even some of Halkin's poems, the difficulty of the Hebrew tends to obscure whatever story or message was contained in the work. It is as if some writers placed the medium before the message—or made the medium the message—by ignoring clarity of expression in preference for a densely idiosyncratic language. Much as in Haskalah literature, the indirectness of the message arising from such an obsessive pursuit of acumen often frustrates the reader, retarding the progress of the idea for the sake of the language. Few readers would tolerate such literary strategies, particularly the Israelis at a time when directness of expression, simplicity of style, and the use of colloquialism were becoming paramount requisites of any work. Their reaction exhibits this distaste, as in Penueli's comment about *Adam ʿal adamot* (Man on earth), to the extent that even when impressed with the power of a work such as *B-ʾoholay Khush*, in which the poet conveys the pain, suffering, and aspirations of Blacks, they find the Ashkenazi accent to be an impediment, an alien feature for contemporary readers.[56]

Isaiah Rabinowitz, who erroneously identifies all of Lisitzky's poems of Blacks as "spirituals," adds perceptively about the poet's language and style:

> The heavy biblical language renders the biographical poetry heavy, but here [in *B-ʾoholay Khush*] it serves a fitting narratological mechanism for the life of Blacks from within and without. The authentic biblical language of *B-ʾoholay Khush* fits well the Black man's ambivalent existential vision: the dire irredeemable poverty in his daily reality and his supreme religious resistance accompanying him at every step. In this manner the biblical ornament does not constitute a sort of a *mlitzah* [euphuism] but a two-sided revolving mirror in which reality and vision function as one. The euphuism does not pose a burden in the poetic narratives of this kind . . . on the contrary: it promotes the poem, its description, meter, rhythm and ambiance. The sense of euphuism in Lisitzky's poetry is completely eradicated in these poems.[57]

CONCLUSION

Even without a systematic linguistic analysis, which remains to be conducted, American Hebrew exhibits traits testifying to its transmutation from its European origins. At a time when imprints of Haskalah Hebrew remained to affect themes, expressions, and word forms in poetry, prose narratives struck out in new ways to emulate the processes of Jews' assimilation (or acculturation) in America. Yet in many instances Hebrew is seen to give way to English. For while some writers, such as Halkin in particular, sought to find equivalent Hebrew modes of expression for the English surrounding them, others did not. Instead, in their works the Hebrew language gives way to English, much as Jews' national hopes were replaced by an acceptance of life in America. English vocabulary, expressions, cultural peculiarities, and even alphabet impinge on the Hebrew. Indeed, the very Hebrew text becomes a means for readers to learn English and, presumably, cross over to read in another language in place of Hebrew.

Hebrew's role as dedicated to the preservation and promotion of a Jewish national agenda, Zionism, was being significantly compromised in America. The marginalization of this mission is not so much a measure of the inability of Hebrew to contain and voice the American experience as much as it is a reflection of the conditions on the ground. America's Hebraists were, at best, "Ḥalutzim sheba-ʿoref," rear-guard pioneers. Their willingness to remain at the margins of the Jewish national experience linguistically and in terms of their expressed regard for the opportunity to settle in the Land of Israel also placed them at the margins of the Hebrew literary canon.

SINGING THE SONG OF ZION: AMERICAN HEBREW LITERATURE AND ISRAEL

Chapter Ten

THE MESSAGE: PAINS OF SEPARATION AND UPROOTEDNESS

Literary representations of the encounter between Jews and America are inevitably portrayed in archetypal, if not cosmic, terms, much like when American Hebrew literature comes into contact with Eretz Israel. In each instance, it is as if authors were cognizant of the significance of the change from their European experience. To mark the encounter between Jews and the United States and Israel, writers resorted to stock archetypes of national mythic dimensions, drawing particularly on the sea crossing to underscore the imagined leap of difference.

The encounters expressed in such passion by some prompted the less enthusiastic of writers to challenge the notion. Summed up by the title of his tale, L. A. Arieli-Orloff's ambivalence in "Emigrants"[1] underscores his uncertainties about America as a fitting haven for his landless protagonists.

Less uncertain, though still ambivalent to the point of eschewing epic analogies, is S. L. Blank's *The Isle of Tears* (*Ee ha-dma'ot*).[2] Unlike Arieli's ambiguous view of America, Blank's can be seen as more positive. Nearly all of his protagonists enter the United States after a hiatus on Ellis Island, though at some cost. Hannah, the leading heroine, is rescued by her family. Yet despite promising faithfulness to her beloved David, who remains on Ellis Island, she soon forgets and surrenders to American cultural expectations. Symbolically, she Americanizes her name (to Anna), replaces her traditional language, and changes her wardrobe. As if to make her transformation final, she befriends a new suitor, Joe, who also recently shed his "greenhorn" self.[3]

The dizzying pace of Jewish assimilation in America is unprecedented. Many traditional Jews readily surrendered their Old World (and shtetl) ways, values, and culture. The new state of affairs mandated a pursuit of materialism and an assimilation regarded by some as a veritable conversion to a secular culture. Jews' tacit acquiescence to the requisites of Americanism is illustrated by E. E. Lisitzky's recollection of his first Sabbath in America, which anticipated his own ultimate surrender:

> But in Boston very few Jews observed the Sabbath. In the Jewish quarter through which she had just passed they trampled with weekday shoes the train of her bridal gown and interrupted with shrill weekday outcries the music of her angelic escorts on her way to her betrothed. Leaving the synagogue after the Sabbath Eve service, the observants were confronted by a tumultuous Jewish quarter: shopkeepers stood in their shop doorways, peddlers on their wagons shouted their wares. Mournfully I passed through this Jewish quarter that first Sabbath eve.[4]

Within two decades of immigration, with roots freshly embedded in American soil, many Jews were soon confronted with the challenge of a nascent Jewish state. For the Hebraists who subscribed to the Zionist mantra of a national rehabilitation in their historic homeland, the new call was for a realization of the dream. Yet as the reality of a Jewish state was about to be crystallized, as the Zionist movement was gathering energy and gaining followers in Europe and America, Hebrew poets and authors took advantage of their enhanced material condition and the increased comforts of travel by sea to visit the object of their yearning. Their writings preserve—explicitly or indirectly—their impressions of the journey and encounter.

Among America's Jewish intelligentsia of the early twentieth century, many of whom were rapidly assimilating into its secularized, material culture, Hebrew writers faced an additional conundrum: as keepers of the flame of the national language, the one identified as the *sine qua non* emblem of the Jewish national movement, they took upon themselves to uphold the Zionist agenda in the hearts and minds of their coreligionists.[5] And though many did so unhesitatingly, and with all the requisite energy and commitment, it was soon becoming evident that those who conveyed the Zionist message were themselves of two minds about practicing what they preached, a tone that permeated and beclouded their voice, characterizing it as ambiguous and ambivalent.

That Hebraists everywhere should add their expression of a hoped-for return to Zion was a given, a matter rooted in a longstanding tradition. But following the First World War and the Balfour Declaration, what were they to do as they witnessed the dream about to be realized? Conditions on the ground had turned the hope into an imminent reality and their call would be expected to be followed by personal example. Soon enough travel to Eretz Israel became easier, inviting America's Jews to behold the object of their centuries-old longings directly or otherwise.

For America's Hebraists who made the journey, the experience must have been physically and emotionally trying, perhaps more so than when emigrating from Europe to the Golden Land a brief decade or two earlier. They no doubt sought ways to express the experience of the voyage, the encounter with the Land of Israel and subsequent return, of the impression that this meeting left on them and the journey itself. Of the possible images, they frequently resorted to the poems by and popular tale concerning the pilgrimage of the medieval poet-philosopher Yehudah Halevi (c. 1075–1141) as a fitting story that for them took on archetypal stature.

However, the literary critic and editor Menaḥem Ribalow was not far off the mark when he observed that too few of America's Hebrew literati devoted any significant attention to Eretz Israel. It is only literary critics and writers of current events, he adds, that were affected significantly, so much so that "the authors of Eretz Israel are evaluated and illuminated in American critiques much more than are the American (Hebrew) writers critiqued and illuminated by critics of Eretz Israel." Concluding on a telling observation, Ribalow notes that America's Hebraists "are capable of better observing the greatness of the mountain and the might of the sight from afar. At a distance they love to draw an abundance of enthusiasm and sanctity from that place that is holy to all Israel in its Diaspora."[6]

A measure of ambivalence penetrated the expression of most writers as they observed the rapidity with which Jews were assimilating in America. Even before Lisitzky was to note his experience at the pace of assimilation, the sardonic tone of Gershon Rosenzweig challenged America's promise when he cynically named the new land "*ʾAmi-reika*," my scoundrel nation, in the first decade of the twentieth century.

A similar attitude pervaded about Zionism and the ongoing adherence of Hebrew writers to the idea of Eretz Israel. Though Hebrew was adopted as the official language of the Zionist Movement at an early stage, the poetry and prose that constituted American Hebrew literature did not always exhibit a devotion to the ideals expected from devotees of the language of the national movement.

For while a handful of writers did make their choice by emigrating to Eretz Israel, those more comfortable with life in America no longer considered the alternative as cogent. Rather, in view of the First World War's destruction of East European Jewish communities, the ensuing pogroms, and, ultimately, the Holocaust, the Land of Israel became a haven they proffered to their coreligionists seeking refuge in an unwelcoming world.

Early in the twentieth century American Hebrew poets and authors plied their art in the shadows of more dominant East European literary centers. Many identified Bialik and Tschernichowsky, who were also the chief luminaries in voicing Jewish national aspirations, as their inspiration in form and content, though somewhat selectively. These writers behaved very much as did their European counterparts. As I have described before, they settled in the New World and engendered a new center of Hebrew literature with its own themes, forms, and linguistic idiosyncrasies. Though poets maintained a tenacious adherence to a classical, conservative, and high literary language, writers of prose fiction developed a unique and more realistic Hebrew sprinkled with Englishisms.[7]

The American landscape broadened these writers' thematic horizons but also posed a number of challenges to complicate their allegiance to the mission they presumably bore. The lines to a continued adherence to the past, precipitated also by American Jewry's physical and ever-greater psychological distance from the European centers, were exacerbated by powerful assimilatory forces in the New World. The resultant ambiguous stand on the issue of the Zionist agenda facilitated the repositioning of American-Hebrew writers to the margins of a coalescing canon of programmatically mainstream nationalist, Zionist Hebrew belles lettres.

LURE OF THE LAND: FASCINATION WITH THE LAND OF ISRAEL

A decided ambivalence and even outright repudiation of the Zionist program stand out as paradoxical curiosities in American Hebrew belles lettres. After all, this was the language enlisted for and expected to bear the banner of a Jewish nationalism that some literati grew to resent. Poetry and prose composed in it had to meet, as a precondition, the expectations of a national program before becoming part of the canon. Not all works, to be sure, exhibit this uncertainty. A favorable tone, even a chorus of enthusiastic hallelujahs about Zionism and Eretz Israel, is a counterpoint to those who questioned the Jewish national program and their participation in its realization. Yet even the authors of laudatory expressions do so in multifaceted and at times unconventional ways that call for scrutiny. The motives behind their affirmative regard can range from an ideological identity with the Promise to plans to immigrate to the Land of Israel, or more lukewarm attitudes and well-rehearsed justifications for remaining in the Diaspora.

Such a vantage point characterizes the work by Harry Sackler, who, in his 1927 play, "Messiah American style,"[8] underscores the nexus between the Native American and Jew as marginalized groups and offers a reappraisal of Noah as a proto-Zionist.

In an afterword essay on the subject, Sackler shares his thoughts about the motives for composing the play. He does not wish readers to surmise that his desire was to stimulate American Jewry's dormant nationalistic revival while he himself was not intent on heeding the call. Rather, he avers that his play voices the Jews' ancient aspiration, of which Zionism is but a contemporary expression.[9]

While Sackler focuses principally on historical works that retell the Jewish national past, one, *Between heaven and earth* (*Beyn eretz v-shamayim*), is a novel set in modern times and follows the experiences of contemporary Jewish protagonists who recently immigrated to America.[10] Set in pre–First World War years, the plot, among other things, depicts Zionist activity in a culturally decaying Jewish America as a romantic ideology calling on Jews to realize the building of a new nation and a revival of its ancient language (387–390). Later, the Balfour Declaration prompts a number of protagonists to leave for the Land of Israel to help its pioneers or to join the British army's Zion Mule Corps (founded in 1915; 408–409). However, much like Sackler himself, his chief protagonists do not abandon the American scene but find a way to reconcile themselves to an ongoing Diaspora existence.

Other favorable expressions abound, including Abraham Goldberg's (1883–1942) sketch "Despair" ("Ha-mitya'esh") about a Zionist protagonist who ultimately redeems himself by returning to Zion.[11] Shlomo Damesek's narratives are filled with positive expressions, such as one of a heroine whose visits and experiences include meeting surviving children of the Holocaust, and for whose benefit she solicits financial contributions.[12] Damesek voices similar sentiments in *There, too, the sun shined* (*Gam sham zarḥah ha-shemesh*).[13] One character, Mr. Gershoni, is sympathetic to any event that takes place there. In another account, "Days of trial,"[14] Damesek tells of a man who sells some paintings to contribute toward the building of the State of Israel. Yet in none of these tales does the protagonist make a personal commitment of settling in Israel but calls for assistance for those residing there instead.

Not all literati were so undecided about the prospect of encountering or even moving to Israel. As one whose shuttling between America and the Land of Israel is emblematic of the condition, Simon Halkin's works are relatively sparse in bearing the Zionist message to his readers. Paradoxically, his prose fiction refrains from mentioning the Land of Israel, though his poetry includes descriptions of its scenery. In an ideological gesture, he preferred publishing his poetry in Israeli periodicals and publishing houses.[15]

Halkin's earliest (undated) poem about the Land of Israel, "Stranger" ("Zar"), voices a longing for the Promised Land out of a sense of an unrealized bond, depicting himself as the outsider who has not consummated his yearning by settling there.[16] Similar sentiments are expressed in his "Yaʿakov Rabinowitz in Yarmouth" ("Yaʿakov Rabinowitz b-yarmut"),[17] in which the Land of Israel is the solution to the Jew's identity crisis.

In "Home" ("Bayit"),[18] the poet's joy at the rise of each new building in Israel is likened to man's partnership with God in creation and recreation of the land. However, in "Here anger abounds" ("Poh rav ḥori-ha-ʾaf"),[19] his impressions are not all rosy, as he discerns enmity among the dwellers in the Land of Israel.

Halkin's "Great days" ("Yamim gdolim")[20] is the poet's joyous embrace of the Land of Israel. He is enthralled at witnessing the Great Days, presumably the impending birth of the State of Israel, though as a poet he feels inadequate at capturing and conveying the germ of those events to future generations.

> As fat golden seeds,
> Without the merciful land, thirsty
> For impregnation below—were you poured
> Upon me, you great quaking days
> In the land of God Almighty, and a bottom
> My trembling heart has not
> To contain your goodness for the coming generation
> As in the granary of eternity.[21]

Later, he identifies himself at the apex of a long ancestral chain who longed to unite with the Land of Israel. Among others, he includes his immediate family, especially his grandmother, as the driving force behind his personal realization of their yearnings.

Halkin's enthusiasm is not unbounded, though; he witnesses some of the deficiencies that contradict the idealism of the Zionist enterprise and writes of them in a number of poems. In one, "In the Diaspora" ("Ba-nekhar"),[22] he describes himself variously as a wanderer, an alien bird, and a stranger out of place and alone in the Diaspora. In the poem that follows, "In this land" ("B-ʾeretz zot"),[23] as he observes the Land of Israel (the poem is dated 1929, the year of his first visit), Halkin is overcome at perceiving what he considers the divine in its landscape.

Ever since his first journey, the vistas of Eretz Israel occupy center stage in Halkin's poetry.[24] Yet, as in this poem, his quest for the metaphysical transmutes the landscape into an array of allusive signs confirming that God's kindness and anger are both bound up in the land. He finds in it forces that attract and repel, its qualities being at the root of Jonah's escape, a theme Halkin uses often to represent a personal and national lot.

When in Israel, his ambivalence is expressed in terms of the story of Jonah, representing himself as drawn to flee for Tarshish, the biblical land of gold and Halkin's imaginary Elsewhere, often associated with America.[25] This movement is best illustrated in the poem "To Tarshish" ("Tarshishah"),[26] in which Halkin-Jonah refers to himself as fleeing in place of heeding the call to remain.

Being caught between two worlds is a plight encountered by more than Halkin. As we shall see below, the poet Avraham Zvi Halevy has much to say about his condition, as does Avraham Solodar (1890–1936), who, in his poem "Hymn" ("Himnon"),[27] bemoans his departure from Eretz Israel in 1926 (to which he immigrated in 1911) for the United States, where he passed away a decade later:

> As a priest,
> As a pale gloomy priest I stand,
> Scattering my tears,
> With my palms open to my land I bow.
> How have I left you? And you are ablaze as an altar,
> In my nightly diadem you are exalted as the moon.

Solodar's poem elevates the Land of Israel to realms of the sacred in which he, posing as the high priest, performs the rite of bemoaning the gulf that stands between them.

Another to express his affinity for the land, and who ultimately settled in Israel, was Israel Efros. Evident in his poems is Efros's intimate engagement with Israel's social and political upheavals before and following statehood. Prior to moving, however, Efros was not known for many descriptive poems of Eretz Israel. His poems detailing the journey to the Land of Israel are, however, allusive and bear epic elements.[28]

Yet his affirmative regard for Eretz Israel is enunciated at an early stage of his literary career in "My land's melody" ("Nginat artzi").[29] Though never stated so explicitly, the reference to "artzi" (*my* land) underscores the contention that the referent is not America, or Europe, but the Land of Israel. This is borne out by the theme of the land awaiting the return of its beloved—its "dod"—an image charged with biblical connotations as twentieth century Zionism anticipated the conclusion of the Jews' endless years of night.

Following his immigration, Efros composed many more poems about Israel, at times reflecting on landscape as historical or metaphoric object. In some poems, his representation of the vistas of Israel is deeply rooted in its history and rebirth.[30] Yet in other instances his poetry expresses the dilemma of one who has uprooted himself from his American home to journey to Israel and experience the pangs of absorption.[31]

Whether on his initial journey of 1934 or later, Efros focuses on Jerusalem at length. In "Jerusalem" ("Yerushalayim"),[32] dedicated to S. Y. Agnon, Efros captures episodes of the Jews' resistance, lauding the spirit of those who dare to challenge the British mandatory authority.

Topical as it is, the lengthy poem is of more historical than literary value; its form is of interest, as it is composed as a rhymed poetic narrative of events. It is a form he later employs in documenting his encounter with Holocaust refugees at Lake Oswego.[33] Its four parts bear the names of four Kabbalistic attributes or spheres (*sfirot*) of the divine: sovereignty, eternity, valor, and loving-kindness. The adaptation expresses the poet's elevation of Jerusalem to the realms of the metaphysical and the sacred, though in ways more intricate than attempted by Solodar. For as much as the divine is indescribable by words or signs—especially to the mind of Efros, a scholar of medieval Jewish philosophy—so, too, Jerusalem defies the same, requiring instead an indirect referential apparatus.

Yet as the poet strives to capture the ineffable, he locates its manifestations in concrete, historical factors experienced in specific space and time. Composed in the turbulent years of the British Mandate, the poem records a number of events that express the poet's sympathies, such as in describing Jews as being pulled from the sea ("Mshuyay yam"); reporting the Jewish attack on a British outpost; the curfew at sunset; or the imminent time of independence.

In "Valor" ("Gvurah"), the poem captures a moment of violent confrontation between Jewish militants and a British outpost, and one about the poster-paster, whose contribution is more verbal. In "Eternity" ("Netzaḥ"), the poem strikes a temporal analogy between the present curfew and confrontations with the Romans in antiquity as if to underscore its recurrence in the Jewish experience.[34] The final episode, "Sovereignty" ("Malkhut"), depicts Holocaust survivors arriving on Israel's shores wreathed in blood, a mark by which the poet crowns them and the emerging settlements. The image resembles that in Alterman's 1947 poem "The Silver Platter" ("Magash ha-kesef"), composed concurrently and bearing a similar theme of the young generation sacrificing themselves for a state.

Efros also composed a cycle of poems entitled "In sovereignty's sphere" ("Bi-sfirat malkhut," 1949),[35] into which he integrates Kabbalistic principles. The poem's first part, entitled "Morning in Tel-Aviv," foregrounds the vast openness of the city's shores, its waves embracing the hulk of the *Altalena* as they bear surfers on their backs. The poem underscores the identity of a people who have until recently been subjugated but have now cast off their shrouds to don royal vestments in celebration of the return to Zion. It also refers to Israel's first year of independence, embellishing it with citations from Psalm 126.

The poem's second part focuses on the celebration of "Herzl Day"—likely the first Independence Day celebration, since it is also called "the first year of the count," evocative of the religious rite of counting days before *Shavu'ot* (Pentecost). The poet dwells on the transformation of Holocaust survivors who now embody the notion of Hebrew (as opposed to Jewish) power; its new heroes are members of the resistance against the British Mandate who are hanged at the Acco prison.

The poem is replete with images and references to salvation, messianism, and an affirmation of national existence. The poem also dwells on the glories of Jerusalem and the Burma Road, paved to reach the besieged city. The final part, "Judgment," frames the account as it returns to Tel-Aviv, where the parade ends as new immigrants bring with them salvation and judgment.

In the early 1950s Efros composed a series of poems whose theme was the Ingathering of the Exiles, a topic addressed by many contemporary writers. His fascination with the diversity of Jewish ethnicity bespeaks an ongoing enthusiasm for the return to the Promised Land from places as diverse as Babylon, Egypt, Yemen, or America. Preceding these, Efros sets the poem "Ezra," which reaches back to biblical times to depict the Ingathering of the Exiles from Babylon. The nexus is telling in the poet's habit of linking and revisiting historical themes in the present.[36]

The Israel-centered poetry of Efros continues into the years of his residence there, as he takes on the perspective of an insider. Following his settlement, Efros' poetry becomes more natural, less affected by polemic or the infatuation with an idealized landscape. Israel becomes a backdrop to his revived, lyrical poetry, which takes on modern forms and modes of expression.[37]

AFFIRMATION AND AMBIVALENCE IN POETRY AND PROSE

Writers represent Israel as an antidote to America's eradication of Jewish identity. Ḥ. A. Friedland, whose prose expresses such sentiments[38] as when he compares Israel to a sonnet, his favorite poetic form: "And what is my beloved land, lamentably tiny / if not a compact sonnet, a dear golden poem?"[39]

Considered the premier modernist poet of American Hebraists, Gavriel Preil also reflects on the inspiring natural and national landscape of Israel, though he never settled there permanently.[40]

Another to share an affirmative expression of Israel is the poet Aaron Zeitlin, who resided in the Land of Israel shortly after the First World War but returned to Poland only to escape to America while most of his family was exterminated during the Holocaust. That trauma is evident in his representation of Israel as a refuge. In two long poems, "To Zikhron Ya'akov: a dramatic poema" ("L-Zikhron Ya'akov: po'emah dramatit," 1959) and "The world's dream: a dramatic poema" ("Ḥalomo shel ʿolam: poʾemah dramatit"), he intertwines personal experiences with the dilemmas of his generation.[41] Another who immigrated to Israel but could not fully extricate himself from the influence of American poets and culture, Abraham Regelson, nonetheless is a spirited partisan of life in his chosen land, presenting enthusiastic vignettes of the land's vistas.[42]

Among the leading American Hebraists is Eisig Silberschlag, whose ambivalence about the Land of Israel is a characteristic illustration of the culture in which he lived. In a letter from the late 1920s, when Tschernichowsky—mentioned therein—made his visit to the States (between November 1928 and March 1929), Silberschlag makes his anxiety explicit. Writing to Halkin of his impending trip to Europe and plan to visit the Land of Israel, Silberschlag declares that he plans to do so only incrementally: ". . . I am afraid of the Land. I'll stay for a time in Paris, in Berlin, before I dare to make *ʿaliyah*" [immigrate], he writes."[43]

Yet his concern is soon laid to rest, turning to a strong affection that becomes a refrain in his correspondence. In a letter to Yitzḥak Lamdan of 21 August 1933, he confesses to a burning thirst for Israel.[44] Having overcome his initial fears, Silberschlag managed to strike a balance between his continued residence in the States and his love of Israel. For him, the possibilities of the Land of Israel are a palliative to the deteriorating conditions for Hebrew writers in America. In the fall of 1933, he again writes to Lamdan that "a pleasant feeling that I never had before is that someone waits impatiently for my words. The state of orphanhood that eats us up here accustomed me to one terrible thought that has become as an axiom: we are not needed."[45]

As if to confirm the above, Silberschlag's poems also offer affirmative views of the Land of Israel. In a prophetic poem, "From Poland to America,"[46] Israel is his assurance against America's ruination of Judaism's rich legacy, turning Jews "from the culture of desire to the culture of the dollar" (a play on words: "mi-tarbut ha-kosef el tarbut ha-kesef," 6). He takes comfort in the Land of Israel as the arena of new possibilities that, according to another poem, "The stars of Canaan" ("Kokhvay knaʿan," ibid., 62) dwarf him.[47]

Another affirmative voice about the Land of Israel is Barukh Katznelson, who (in 1934) settled there to become a farmer.[48]

A PERSISTENT AMBIVALENCE

Readers of American Hebrew fiction have taken note of the flirtatious, if complicated, relationship its writers had with Eretz Israel. "There is no Hebrew poet among those in the New World who has not sung the song of Zion on America's soil," observes Jacob Kabakoff. Often, however, these negotiations were manifestly ambivalent. As the song of Zion persisted on American soil, few of its writers practiced what they called for. It is as if the subject has become a requisite, a conventional trope, or merely a conceit to satisfy a readership that, in itself, was not inclined to consummate that which words expressed. "In the case of most of our poets, one senses a sort of duality with regard to Zion. They sing hymns to her [Israel] yet envisage themselves here in the Diaspora," continues Kabakoff.[49]

One of the ways in which this duality became reinforced over the decades was by the Americanization of Hebrew literature. Thus, for example, the preoccupation of writers with Native Americans or Blacks may be more of an escapist manifestation than a mark of their striking roots in the United States. Yet any such gesture implied a willful exchange of Zion for America.[50]

Almost to the last, Hebrew writers express an ambiguity about the beckoning call of Zion and the ideology they embraced. Even among those who eventually settled there before or following statehood, one cannot escape the impression of an anxiety in having made such a fateful step to become immersed in a new culture. Such an attitude may either voice a personal experience or represent attitudes harbored by American Jews.

I FLEE FROM MY LAND

Whether residents of the Land of Israel or not, Hebrew writers have been cognizant of their special role to make Hebrew the voice of Jewish national aspiration. While many adhered to this expectation out of personal conviction, more than a few exhibited an ambivalent regard stemming from motives that are personal, artistic, or ideological. As in the case of Lisitzky, those who emigrated from or paid visits to the Land of Israel before or after statehood characteristically found themselves voicing contrary opinions. While their compositions admired the Zionist pioneers and resonated spiritually with the land, most were unable to tear themselves away from America.

A considerable corpus of responses to the prospects of a Jewish state mirrors this ambivalence. The most extreme reactions include an abandonment of their calling to write in Hebrew and turn to alternative languages. Such is the case of the Hebrew poet Menaḥem M. Dolitzky. Though it was not a choice made easily, he compromised his literary ideals by abandoning Hebrew to write cheap, "shund" literature in Yiddish in order to make a living in America.[51]

More extremely, Reuven Brainin abandoned Hebrew for Yiddish and advocated the settling of Jews in Birobidjan, the eastern province of the Soviet Union, against the mounting wave of Zionist calls for settling Eretz Israel. In 1926, Brainin, who earlier resided in America, left the Land of Israel to settle in the Soviet Union, a move that raised a storm among his fellow Hebraists.[52]

S. L. BLANK'S DISREGARD OF ERETZ ISRAEL

More than simple ambivalence about the Land of Israel pervades S. L. Blank's fiction. Though he was settled in the United States since 1923, Blank's novels remained nostalgic about his Bessarabian homeland.[53] They served as an antidote to the turbulent, chaotic, and uprooted experiences of the author in the New World. In place of repeating the tale of shtetl life and culture, Blank tells, mostly from the vantage point of his Philadelphia home, of protagonists who trade urban landscapes for the comfort of the plains of Bessarabia, where they farm the land and coalesce into a small agrarian town.

Composed in the first half of the twentieth century, the novels inescapably pose a counterpoint to Zionism, pioneering, and farming in Eretz Israel. In them, the imperative to settle and work the land is evocative of the utterances, mottoes, and ideals of Zionist pioneers intent on establishing *kibbutzim* and *moshavim* in Eretz Israel at the very same time. Yet Blank appears to consciously disregard the Zionist enterprise and its ideals to depict protagonists who are mysteriously drawn out of village life to become farmers. This is not merely a nostalgic hindsight; it is also the author's implicit claim to an alternate, anti-canonical, reality of Eretz Israel. His protagonists who lack farming experience nevertheless succeed in realizing their agrarian ambitions through dedication and sheer persistence. Their ability to establish themselves successfully as farmers, without the need to be educated about agriculture—as if it was second nature or even an instinct in their very fabric—is a mark of the idealistic air enshrouding these novels. Their emphasis on self-reliance and a tenacious hold on the soil as an ideal pursuit of humankind is reminiscent of kibbutz ideology, as is the representation of all members of the farming community as one family, with each sacrificing for the other. These traits of kibbutz society are transferred by Blank onto the Bessarabian landscape where, unlike in much of Europe, Jews were able to hold and farm land.

Blank's protagonists' motives also evoke those of kibbutz dwellers: to be renewed by contact with the soil and life close to nature. One of them, Boaz, whose name evokes the rich biblical romance of the story of Ruth, even delivers a Tolstoyan lecture reminiscent of the ideology propounded by A. D. Gordon pertaining to the Religion of Labor.

The absence of the Israeli (and Zionist) option and its impact on Jewry is, at best, an expression of Blank's ambivalence about the viability of the former. Instead, he presents his protagonists with two Diasporic options, Europe and America, while ignoring the Zionist movement as a factor. This is most blatant in two of his novels, *Naḥalah* (Patrimony) and *Adamah* (Land). The protagonist of both, Akivah, is a bookish, maskilic scholar, son of the miller Matit and his wife, Dvorah. All of Akivah's attempts to take the plough or perform any physical labor underscore his unsuitability for life on the farm. If Akivah represents the Haskalah, during which the story appears to take place, and implicitly—or by analogy, for he reads the journal *Ha-tzfirah* (1860–1936; or 1862–1931)[54]—of the nascent Zionist movement, then he is indeed a grotesque caricature of that culture.[55]

The absence of any mention of the Jewish national enterprise in these novels, as in much of Blank's oeuvre, cannot be an oversight. In place of ambivalence, he strikes an indifferent (or apathetic) attitude with regard to the Zionist alternative for his protagonists, either as they seek a proper refuge as farmers away from urban life or as an escape from racist persecution. Only toward the end of his literary career, in what appears to be one of Blank's last works,[56] does his American-Jewish hero contemplate stopping off on his trip to Europe to see what the *ḥalutzim* (pioneers) of Eretz Israel have attained in the Promised Land. And, if things appeal to him he would then perhaps also leave something of himself there as a sign of having visited the State of Israel.[57]

AMBIVALENCE AND SATIRE: BERNARD ISAACS AND L. A. ARIELI

Unlike in Blank's prose, the Implied Author's regard for Eretz Israel in the stories of Bernard Isaacs and L. A. Arieli (Orloff) is decidedly stronger than that of most of their American protagonists. This ideological difference between character and Implied Author allows Isaacs to unfold the ambivalence harbored by American Jews for Israel and their reluctance to carry out the goals of Zionism. In stories such as "Nameless" ("Bli shem") and "Ascent and descent" ("Ba-maʿaleh uva-morad"),[58] he foregrounds the risks of life in America as Jewish culture continues its dissolution. His response is by satirizing his protagonists or holding out Eretz Israel as an antidote to the anti-Semitism and materialistic excesses dominating America.[59]

More judgmental than Isaacs, L. A. Arieli (Orloff) offers little hope in his observation of the foibles of America's Jews. His narrator is decidedly sardonic about the Americanized culture of Jews in the New World. He exposes their superficial regard for the Zionist enterprise. Zionism for them is a convenient conversational topic that they use to further their social status. This attitude takes center stage in his "New York" (1926),[60] while in "Emigrantim" (Emigrants, 1925), one of Arieli's more accomplished short works, he portrays the chasm between the Land of Israel and what awaits immigrants to the New World.[61]

HILLEL BAVLI

Despite an affirmative tone, Hillel Bavli's and A. S. Schwartz's (who resided there in 1953–1954) poetry of the Land of Israel is obscured by a veil of uncertainty. Though Bavli often pauses to sing the praises of Israel's locales, among them Jerusalem, Tsfat, and the Jezreel Valley, the reader is witness to the poet's dilemma. Though appreciating historic vistas, Bavli conveys a personal alienation about the impact of the encounter on his art. "You have crushed me" ("Dike't oti," 1938) expresses a loss of words at encountering the land, reducing his light and colorful verse to dim broken lines:

> You have stopped up all my life's abundant wells
> And behold, the world's splendor had dimmed about me
> And my heart in me is injured, crushed and shattered is my song.[62]

Both poets resort to enumerating the forces keeping them from a total commitment. Bavli's enthusiasm for Eretz Israel rings hollow in response to leaving after a visit. Instead of blaming himself for having to abandon Israel, however, he accuses God in "Crying, I left you" ("Bi-vkhi mi-mekh yatzati").[63] This outlook contradicts the notion of will in Zionist dogma, or the sense of belonging to Joshua's generation of conquerors, which the poem evokes. Bavli exposes the bankruptcy of all expectations for the miracle that he himself could have performed—to remain in Israel:

> Crying, I left you, my land, with prayer and trembling.
> God did not allow me to settle in you as one of your sons
> And to carry, day and night, day and night the burden of all your
> sorrow and splendor;
> I was merely a wretched wayfarer in you, merely a miserable wanderer
> Who came to explore to roam about look and vanish with the
> winds. . . .
> As if I was a first possessor-subduer of this land of Canaan. . . .
> At times I felt deep within: it was only yesterday that I was born in the
> land
> And till now all my life was mere light echo of good tidings
> For these joyous moments. . . .
> And at times I prayed: Were it that of a sudden a miracle would
> happen
> And my legs and body would be bound to the heart of the land
> So that I will be unable to leave.

Yet—alas!—the miracle did not happen. My life's joy ended at its beginning.
And on one of the last days of autumn I was uprooted, as a tender sapling,
From the bosom of land that I love, ere I took root in it,
And cast out beyond its boundaries. (186–187)

The poet's effusive use of the passive form, as if powers beyond him conspired to frustrate his desire to remain in Eretz Israel, flies in the face of the affirmative Zionist message. It is as if he is mocking himself for his inadequacy, for not being more assertive, an attitude we find characterizing the works of Lisitzky and others as well.

Schwartz allies himself more with those Hebraists who find value in Eretz Israel for the survivors of the Holocaust. However, following his encounter with Israel as a reality while residing there, he becomes sardonic and embittered. His sympathy for Holocaust survivors, and the State of Israel as their refuge, turns to criticism of those citizens who represent themselves as deserving in light of having been in the vanguard of national salvation.[64]

AVRAHAM ZVI HALEVY

The Land of Israel is the object of longing for A. Z. Halevy, voiced in tones that differ from the dour depiction of his New York experiences. In a letter of 1 January 1947, to Yitzḥak Lamdan, Halevy calls his departure from Eretz Israel in 1938 a blunder, an abandoning of a thriving literary milieu only to join the graveyard of America's Hebrew world presided over by Menaḥem Ribalow.[65]

Halevy lays out his relationship to the Land of Israel in six poems. In a section entitled "Motherland wounds" ("Pitzʿay moledet"),[66] he repeatedly accuses himself of treason for, while impatiently seeking material rewards, abandoning the Land of Israel in time of need. As a latter-day Jonah, he writes, he has guilt feelings for fleeing his land that are magnified by a realization that any return (or repentance, the Hebrew word for both being identical) is impossible, leaving him to contend with the existential conditions of a fate meted out to him in America.

Brimming with a vocabulary encoded with references to a host of biblical verses, the poet, in "Can't you help, motherland?" ("Ha-yadekh tiktzar, moledet?"),[67] seeks consolation and refuge in the Land of Israel. The first stanza is a catalogue of sins for having left, only to find emptiness and restlessness abroad. Life in New York is death-like, its skyscrapers like tombs, its skies heavy, and its land unsupportive.

The second stanza presents the alternative that he so desires: the Land of Israel's skies would be a welcoming *sukkah* (booth) of peace—a reference to the *hashkivenu* prayer, in which one implores God for a restful sleep. The stars above would shower him with their nectar, he asserts, much as do the hills in the visions of Amos 9:13 and Joel 4:18 that the poem invokes. Much as in the medieval Yehudah Halevi's dream, his hope is to tread the land's clodded earth where his barren life will be enriched, he avers, by the blessed first and last rains of the season—a reference to their coming at appointed times in Deuteronomy 11:14.

In other poems, too, Halevy revisits the issue of having left Israel. In "I flee from my land" ("Mi-pnay artzi anokhi boreaḥ"),[68] he identifies with the prophet Jonah, though unlike him, he is without a haven, a Tarshish—a reference to a land of gold or the Golden Land—to which he can flee. His sense of betrayal is also featured in "You're wounded, my land" ("Ptzuʿah at artzi"),[69] in which the poet takes on the guise of a rootless wanderer, also repeated in "Cactus" ("Tzabar").[70] He shares a similar sentiment in "Your expectations were frustrated" ("Lo kam bi ḥazonekh"),[71] blaming himself for having abandoned his undefended land, which he now implores to come to his aid and accept him. In his search for shelter from the prison that is America he finds ruins around his old home, an outcome of his absence at a time when he needed to help defend the land and its familiarity. By escaping to find a better place he contributed to the ruins he discerns upon return, leaving him with no safe harbor. This is the response in "My shattered landscape" ("Nofi ha-shavur").[72] It is an account of a belated return to his Jerusalem neighborhood. Much as in Bialik's "ʿAl saf beyt ha-midrash" (At the threshold of the house of study), the act of capturing the past is frustrated by the ruins he encounters in the present, a decay that frustrates any attempted preservation of the familiar. Halevy recognizes the impossibility of resolving his imprisonment in America by responding in the negative about altering his New York existence.

Halevy's poetry of the Land of Israel lacks the euphoria or glee of one who has returned. His existential state is not alleviated by what he finds, nor can he obtain relief from the images of physical and moral decay that shadow him in New York. This poetry can also be directed at the all-too-familiar condition of the American Zionist torn between the good life and the call to fulfill the ideological imperative.[73]

AMBIVALENT ACCOMMODATIONS WITH ERETZ ISRAEL: YEHUDAH HALEVI IN AMERICA

America's Hebraists, in the search for thematic means of contextualizing their experiences of the journey to the Land of Israel, have found it fitting to emulate the works of the medieval poet Yehudah Halevi. Halevi, whose poetry was rediscovered in the middle of the nineteenth century (primarily through the efforts of S. D. Luzzato), was long identified by his poetry of love of Eretz Israel and the ensuing legends that gathered about his journey to behold the land. Although many of his poems were available by then for them to emulate, it was the story of his journey that struck a chord with America's Hebraists, who saw themselves following in his wake.

Examining American Hebraists' poetry about their journey to the Promised Land, one is drawn to the manner in which they signaled these connections with the medieval poet. While some analogies are overt, as through direct reference to him by name, the less obvious ones cite a key term or a brief phrase from Halevi's Love of Zion poems. More coincidental are general references made to the sea voyage, to the image of waves, or the longing to behold and caress the soil of Eretz Israel, ingredients that could presumably also arise independently out of the personal experience of each writer.

Whether with unabashed enthusiasm or ambivalent intentions, Hebrew poets inscribed their journey to and encounter with the Land of Israel by resorting to the popular and mythic archetype accounts that coalesced about Yehudah Halevi. Like him, they were more than ready to express their longing for Zion, a theme that also linked them up with fellow Hebrew literati in Europe. Like him, they were poets who wrote of a yearning to realize a centuries-old dream of Zion, to embrace her stones and be tender to her dust and convince others about the veracity of this, one now formalized within the ideological infrastructure of the Zionist movement. Like him, they lived the good life in the far reaches of the West with hearts directed East. And despite his classical expression in the medieval period, they identified in him Romantic qualities that fittingly embodied their sentiments. So when the opportunity presented itself to travel to Eretz Israel—most making the journey by sea—they could not but identify with Halevi's dream and the tales that gathered about him in the popular imagination. Ever since Yehudah Halevi's poetry of sailing to the Land of Israel, including poems expressing his anticipation and expectations to finally realize his yearnings,[74] the imagery of the voyage by sea to the Promised Land has taken on an epic equivalence to the crossing of the Red Sea by the Children of Israel.

American Hebrew literati left a considerable oeuvre documenting and reflecting upon their journeys to Eretz Israel.[75] Some of this bears explicit references to Halevi as a *leitmotif* that cements the nexus between the medieval journey and the modern. By revisiting this centuries-old motif writers invited a reading of their own expressions in light of the archetype. By reimagining Halevi, they gave recognition to the opportunity to encounter the beloved object of their yearnings. Whether set before or during the early years of Israel's statehood, the poems, stories, and other memoirs of American Hebraists testify to the imminent encounter between them and the Promised Land, made more poignant in an age of Zionist resurgence. Halevi's poetic output and even the legends that coalesced about his journey—his purported arrival and beholding of Jerusalem, and then being struck down by an Arab horseman[76]—are the yardstick by which we shall measure a number of writers, their attainments marking the extent to which they, by their deeds, retraced or reread the tales about him.

Many a poet's expression of longing for Eretz Israel includes a catalogue of causes forestalling an earlier journey. In most instances, it is the distance that leaves poets pining. Once they initiate the journey, American writers insert in their works metaphors framed in biblical language and imagery embellished by Halevi's phrasing, as they emulate themes evoked by him also.

As if forming a preamble to the celebrated trip, they at times evoke the medieval bard's poems of his anticipated voyage. The latter in turn arouses contradictory and anxiety-laden reactions as the prospect of one's yearnings is about to be realized. At other times, the analogy is less intimate, the American writer leaving but the barest and possibly coincidental analogies for the reader to ponder. In most cases, however, the very analogy they attempt to strike is ironic in that the contemporary poet was not committed to fulfill Halevi's plan of moving to settle in the Land of Israel.

Cognizant of Halevi's Love-of-Zion poems, and his celebrated collection of works about his sea voyage in fulfillment of this longing, modern poets select but the most familiar and superficial themes. One of America's leading Hebrew poets, Ephraim E. Lisitzky, does not fail to demonstrate this identity. In poems composed on the eve of sailing to Eretz Israel in 1934,[77] he emulates Halevi's formula—whether in imitation of the latter or as a natural development of the personal journey—by tracing his experiences from setting sail to journey's end. As if punctuating the distance covered, his poems record specific sights on the way, followed by scenes and encounters in the Land of Israel. Unlike Halevi's, however, Lisitzky's journey was to be a round trip, a visit concluded upon return to his New Orleans home. Significantly, this also enabled him to include personal reflections on coming home again.

In "To my land" ("L-ʾartzi," *Ascents*, 156–158), Lisitzky relies on a typical love-of-Zion motif when addressing his longing for an imagined Eretz Israel. Though wishing to behold the land, he writes, he is barred from doing so by the great divide separating them. Initially, his poem invokes a questionable analogy with Moses beholding the Promised Land from afar, as he blames his absence upon a divine command keeping him from reaching the object of his desire despite his cherished dream to be there just once before he dies:

A)
For a lifetime on imagined Nebo's summit
I stood and beheld you, land of glory—
In my vision I beheld you, my heart yearning
. . . but a voice rang in my ears—destiny's command:
"From afar shall you behold the land
But enter there you shall not." (*Ascents*, 156–157)

The analogy with Moses is soon shattered when Lisitzky observes that for him the journey *is* possible. By overturning this initial correspondence, Lisitzky renders the prior parallel with Moses ineffectual as he finds himself on his way to behold the Land, and not from afar, before he dies. Yet a palpable undercurrent of anxiety at the prospect of realizing his dreams anticipates the poet's ambivalence as he imagines the encounter for which he has been pining for so long:

B)
So why, then, does my heart faint [Gen. 45:26] and my soul,
Why does it fall silent? and what do
The fear and trembling which have overcome me mean?
Do I fear the interpretation of my choicest dreams
And best visions on earth?
Does my hand fear to remove the veil
From the last sanctuary, from the holy-of-holies,
Lest the glory of God rise from the hiding place of His power? (Ibid., 158) [The verb is in reference to Num. 10:11, Ezek. 9:3; the noun

is in Hab. 3:4 and is a *hapax legomenon*, appearing but once in the Bible.]

As if to underscore his longing for Eretz Israel, Lisitzky raises the specter of Yehudah Halevi, who, according to legend, realized his dream only to die upon reaching Jerusalem:

C)
I pray, my land: may it be that as I fall
Upon your holy land, satiating its soil
With kisses from my mouth and tears of my eyes, together,
May Halevi's lot be my lot—
May my lifeblood flow to your eternity [Isaiah 63:3], and my body
In your bosom, the bosom-of-immortality, shall rest! (Ibid., 158)

Beyond the explicit reference to Moses in excerpt A, Lisitzky alludes to additional texts whose juxtaposition adds to the poem's meaning. In passage B, the quotation from Genesis 45:26 corresponds to the poet's circumstances. The source text concerns Jacob's learning of his long-lost son Joseph being alive and ruling over Egypt. Now, Lisitzky replaces Joseph with the Land of Israel, the object of his longing. In the biblical narrative it is Jacob who leaves the Promised Land to behold his son, while the present situation offers Lisitzky the opportunity to return.

Excerpt C embeds Halevi's expressed desire to shed tears in Zion—as in "Ode to Zion" ("Tziyon halo tish'ali")[78]—a powerfully resonant image associating Lisitzky with past Mourners of Zion. He also makes another indirect nod to medieval literary practice in employing both meanings of the word "netzaḥ," which denotes eternity and also lifeblood in Isaiah 63:3. Here the term is used in the latter and more obscure meaning. By using the root twice in the same line, the poet re-creates a form of punning that resembles the medieval literary convention of exploiting homonyms to elicit assonance through elegant wordplay. Though it initially pretends to be a wasteful repetition of the more common reference to eternity, the realization of a second meaning adds dimension and acumen to the poem's meaning. Less obvious, though not unlikely, is the poem's use of another rare term, "will abide" ("tishleh"), the last verb in Lisitzky's poem. It echoes Halevi's use of the same root, though in a different form, "shleh u-shlam b-no'am,"—". . . rest and be pleasantly at peace"—in his poem "For whom did burst out . . ." ("l-mi bak'u").[79]

Ironically, Lisitzky also embeds an ambivalent tone about Eretz Israel in a poem entitled "Yehudah Halevi."[80] Referring to the Great Bard's arrival in the Promised Land, Lisitzky reimagines the scene and reinterprets the legend. In place of prostrating himself, Halevi is dumbstruck at the sight of the land's desolation. In contrast with the fecundity back in Andalusia that he recalls, the Holy Land's state of deprivation is disenchanting:

> Is this the beauteous vista that gladdens the world? Did he
> Long for this from the vistas of Andalusia?
> What was it that his hand choked when covering his mouth,
> Was it a mocking smile or a lament? (*Ascents*, 169)

It is this shock, asserts Lisitzky, that brings on Halevi's depression before his death, prompting the question: "was it a horse-rider who dispatched [his body] / Or did the weight of his sorrow subdue it?"

Shock at the sight of the landscape underscores Lisitzky's disenchantment, too, undercutting his romantic expectations about the object of his dreams. The observation is a transparent projection of his emotional state, here attributed to Halevi's response, presented using the narratological technique of reported speech in which poet and subject share a voice. Contextualizing it in the tale about Halevi's sojourn in Eretz Israel effectively undermines the legend, overturning the ostensible joy of the medieval poet's response upon reaching Zion and his purported death at Jerusalem's gates. Just as before when striking an analogy with Moses that is soon exploded, he also renders the parallel with Halevi's story ineffectual by deflating the myth.

HEART AND BODY, EAST AND WEST: THE POETRY OF MOSHE FEINSTEIN

Through his correspondence as in his poetry, Moshe Feinstein (1896–1964), like other American Hebrew poets, expresses the ambivalence and anguish of one torn between foci of love and disaffection with America and Israel in more poignant extremes than Lisitzky. Feinstein, founder and long-standing chief administrator of the Hertzliah Hebrew Teachers Institute in New York, composed little of substance on Eretz Israel. He was principally a lyrical poet whose work at Hertzliah may have been a factor limiting his literary output; his few Eretz Israel poems merit scrutiny nonetheless.[81]

As if to illuminate and supplement his few poems on the subject, Feinstein's correspondence opens a window on his affirmative regard for life in Israel and the prospect that awaits those who move there. However, his is an eternal ambivalence, always yearning for the place where he is not.

In an early letter he writes of the emotional and physical toll of administering Hertzliah while longing instead for the streets of Tel-Aviv.[82] This sense does not leave him. A typical letter of 2 October 1958, to Shlomo Shenhod, becomes an occasion to write of his isolation in America, where he is surrounded by few acquaintances and harbors a decreasing tolerance for its lifestyle. "I sit here in the Diaspora and my heart is in the East," he asserts, paraphrasing Yehudah Halevi.[83] Yet in early 1964, in a letter to Moshe Maizlish, Feinstein writes from Israel complaining that "my longing to see my children, grandchildren and Hertzliah drives me crazy."[84]

In a poem that refers to Halevi's famous lament for Zion, Feinstein injects a complicating factor that the medieval poet glosses over, representing a variation on the *leitmotif.* In "My heart and body in the east" ("Libi v-gufi ba-mizraḥ"),[85] Feinstein underscores the ambivalence of one who cannot uproot himself and settle in Israel:

My heart and body in the east.
My heart and body in the west.
I hear my heart sigh.
I see my body offered up
Upon the pyre that consumes
All remaining strength, vigor.
Doubtless a curse lingers
And my whole being is a disgrace. (Tel-Aviv, 1959)

Evoking Halevi's famous lament, the poem departs from it by underscoring the predicament facing an exilic Jew: in place of facing a single challenge, the poet is in a state of flux, his body and soul shuttling between East and West. His sense of imbalance transmutes the poem from a focus on the speaker's yearnings for Zion to a lyrical outpouring of personal inadequacy and lost vigor. Composed in Tel-Aviv in 1959, the theme loses further resonance with Zion as he is already in the land of his desire, leaving him instead to yearn for his home in the distant West. The binary locus of today's protagonist reinforces the impression that his lament is concerned with a spiritual state of exhaustion rather than with national or religious issues. The turnabout is not totally a betrayal of the communal for the individual, for this feeling of a dual allegiance is a pervasive one among many Americans for whom Feinstein also speaks.

In a much longer poem, "The Great Moment" ("Ha-rega ha-gadol," ibid., 19–25), Feinstein combines the experience of arriving in Israel with his spiritual state. His imagination creatively revises Yehudah Halevi as theme for ulterior purposes; the divided self and impossibility of locating one's resting place become a mark of the contemporary protagonist. It is this arena that continues to be Feinstein's major preoccupation as he departs from the Zionist purposes to which others have put the medieval poet.

ISRAEL EFROS AND THE PAIN OF UPROOTING

Also one to identify with Halevi's experience as he sailed for the first time to Eretz Israel in 1934 and on subsequent journeys was Israel Efros (1890–1981), the poet and scholar of medieval Jewish thought. Though not mentioning the medieval bard explicitly in many of his voyage poems, Efros evokes similar motifs that, arguably, could also arise independently. Among these are his anticipation, attention to other passengers, seascape, and geography as markers of his approach. Also of significance are the historic stations to which he attends, beginning with Spain and concluding as the boat approaches Israel's shores. Presented in several poems,[86] his voyage is not just geographical but also an inward journey of exploration as he nears Eretz Israel.

Yet Efros does make direct reference to Halevi in a four-poem sequence, "Sights on the Mediterranean Sea" ("Mar'ot ʿal ha-yam ha-tikhon"; 24–26)[87] that dramatize the ship's approach to Israel. The first, "At the gate" ("Ba-shaʿar," 24), announces the ship's entry into the Mediterranean upon passing through the Straits of Gibraltar. On the port side he beholds the gallows-like pyramidal rock, an apt metonym for the history associated with Spain and Europe for Jews. On the starboard side he sees the unthreatening image of a slumbering African whose bare outline identifies him as Black—curly hair, flat nose, and thick neck. These images capture the poet's imagination as the ship slips through the Straits as "the gallows upon the blood-soaked gateway awaits."

The second and third poems, "Noon" ("Tzohorayim," 24–25), and "Anvil" ("Sadan," 25), describe the ship sailing on, as if drawn by the waves likened to horses, beneath which a rainbow appears in the deep. The imagery strongly expresses a progression in the direction of the poet's desired goal, the rainbow holding the promise of a covenant. Also, Efros represents the ship as fixed in the center of a universe whose pleasurable simplicity will soon be missed once they lay anchor.

The last poem directly refers to Halevi by its title. Halevi is identified as accompanying the ship, guiding it confidently to safe harbor while singing a song. It is his song that brings the shore into close proximity, as if Halevi is the vehicle facilitating the encounter. Initially, it is Halevi alone who sings, until Efros, identifying with him, joins in. Significantly, this is the first reference to the contemporary poet's silence, a state that is ended by inspiration, or memory of the medieval bard's spirit.

While other poems allude to the themes and experiences of Halevi's works about the journey, they could have emerged independently of the medieval model and do not otherwise raise any direct analogy with it. Among these are poems surrounding the various journeys Efros took to Eretz Israel. The first poem, "José" (*Dorot*, 78), is a ballad in which a toreador longs for the love of his *señorita*. Though relating an aspect of Spanish culture, the poet's choice of subject is a re-encounter of a Jew with Spain. Indirectly, it invites a metonymic reading that expresses his longing for Zion. In another, "Vesuvius," he characteristically goes beyond a superficial and geological observation. The volcano becomes a metaphor for a repressed force which, while held at bay, has not surrendered to fate. Read against the poet's journey, it is a temptingly allusive comment on Jewish aspirations and national expectations. Reinforcing this is his ascent to its peak to witness the tension as the primordial force is about to erupt. Read on another plane, the image may be an apt metaphor for the resurgence of Jewish nationalism that Efros identifies as a dominant *leitmotif* of his journey.

A characteristic of American Hebrew poets is that they often neglect geographical specificity for a general or lyrical scene. The upshot is that they detract from concrete American landscapes or experiences as they strive for the universal. The same may be said of some poems pertaining to the journey to the Promised Land. Like others, Efros also reduces the landscape of ancient Rome to lyrical objective correlatives. It is no longer the occasion for a historical re-encounter between the present-day Jew and the descendants of his former oppressors. Later, as he nears shore, he also represents the land of Israel in broad strokes that leave little of the concrete image. While it is the land of his aspirations, and one which he anticipates to encounter soon, he offers the barest of tangible evidence to represent his imminent response. Instead, the sole focus aboard ship is on an Arab passenger with whom he shares a preference for poetic styles. Otherwise, the distance to Eretz Israel is indirectly noted by mentioning the sights of sea and sky surrounding him. These are not only a beautiful distraction but denote the poet's veiled ambivalence about the ultimate encounter, as in his poem, "The path is so attractive" ("Yif koh ha-shvil," 85).

Whether taking his cue from Halevi or voicing a deeply held conviction, the poet's idealism persists. In "On the golden bridge" ("'Al gesher ha-zahav," 86), Efros compares his ship's wake to a golden bridge over the sea, bringing him and others to the Promised Land. Notable among the missing ingredients is an effusive language or lyrical and emotional outpouring of what he feels or how he, historically, is linked to the sites or personages he mentions. Instead, he makes the vaguest reference to Eretz Israel being the land of his ancestors, who stand to welcome all alongside the metaphoric bridge. A few decades later, as we shall see, Efros will record some of the most intimate and poignant poetry about his immigration to Israel. Though circumspect about being overly effusive when he first encountered the Land of Israel in 1934, Israel Efros becomes abundantly more specific once he reaches shore. He offers five poems tangibly concrete in title and contents—"On the Yarkon River," "To the Hebrew driver in Canaan," "Hills," "Crowns," and "To the land" ("ʿAl pnay ha-Yarkon," 88; "La-nehag ha-ʿivri bi-Khnaʿan," 89; "Gvaʿot," 90; "Ktarim," 91; "El ha-ʾaretz," 92)—in which he documents the sights and recent historical events that have affected the emergence of the state of Israel.[88]

These poems sum up his first encounter with the Land of Israel and represent images and themes Efros has heretofore left unexplored. He notes geographical features—among them the Yarkon River, mountains, and hills—and discerns details that, in his eyes, transform the Jew. In "To the Hebrew driver in Canaan" (89), he asserts that soon after landing the immigrant is purged of his Diasporic chaff. The move transmutes him from Jew to Hebrew and crowns him as master of the roads and guardian of his taxi. These contemporary duties are so phrased as to be made analogues to and replacements for the rites pertaining to the ancient temple.

His choice of naming the Land of Israel Canaan is also telling in that he projects the Jew back to antiquity, a feature of many poets who at the time preferred the term *Hebrew* in place of *Jew*. Another poem, "To the land" (92), illustrates the poet's emotional response at the Promised Land, pouring out effusive sentiments attributing all yearning to Eretz Israel.

In "On Manhattan's shore" ("ʿAl ḥof Manhattan," 93), Efros re-encounters the life waiting for him in America upon returning from Eretz Israel. Like Lisitzky, he is dejected at having to return to his adopted land to experience the alienation and isolation of life in the Big City. New York is inhospitable; Manhattan is denuded of greenery; and high angular buildings pierce the sky as chimneys belch forth black smoke. The city's sounds are frightful and its inhabitants are swallowed up within cavernous spaces. More than a love-of-Israel poem, the expression falls into Efros's anti-urban sentiments that harbor a romantic's fondness for nature. On the other hand, the Land of Israel satisfies one's longings for spiritual and physical comforts, for a sense of familiarity and belonging.

Some two decades after his initial visit to Israel, Efros joined other Hebraists by making the move (in 1955) to reside there. Unlike Noah Stern, S. Halkin, R. Avinoam (Grossmann), and T. Carmi, his move was made only following Israel's statehood. Leaving a relatively comfortable life in America (as teacher at Hunter College of the City University of New York and Philadelphia's Dropsy College), he took on the mantle of rector of the newly emerging Tel-Aviv University (where in 1960 he was appointed honorary president). The move marked a radical leap in his life, as he now made the commitment to surrender the secure life in America for the upheavals of Israel.

Reflecting on this fateful move, Efros—by now in his mid-sixties—published a series of poems that give voice to the spiritual challenges inherent in the move, *How deep he is planted* (*Meh ʿamok hu shatul*).[89] The title, comparing him to a sapling whose roots must be pulled up and transplanted into the soil of a new land, sums up his anticipation and angst. In poems that introduce the voyage and follow him on his journey (pp. 11–27), Efros struggles with a loss of identity again—as a youth he immigrated in 1905 to the States from Volhynia (Ukraine). Unknown to him at the time, and despite the evidently heavy toll the transplantation took, he was to undergo an artistic renaissance. For until his first trip, his poetry gives but the slightest indication of an evolving transformation in the poet's art. The contact with the new environment revitalized his poetry, lending it nuance, sophistication, and linguistic vigor as it shed its Americanized conservatism.[90]

More sobering, candid, and realistic, the poems unfold the pains of uprootedness. The opening poem of *How Deep*, "Sapling" ("Ilan," 11), says it all: "Man knows not how deep he is planted, / Till the hour of wandering" (11). The poems underscore the chasm between the idealistic literary theme as imagined in Halevi's work and the actual emotional toll the move exacts from the individual self. In "Roots" ("Shorashim," 12), he is bewildered about his uprootedness and seeks to ameliorate the problem of his roots left so exposed. However, his resolve about the move is evident in the poem's concluding lines as the poet makes of his transition another subject of introspection: "One needs to hold up a lucid mirror to the pain of crossing over, / One needs to cross the river of mutabilities neck-deep" (12). The cycle of poems then follows the uprooted speaker as he symbolically takes his leave from his home by locking its door. His uprooted condition is defined by the sea journey to an unknown destination, one that would, presumably, end as he strikes roots in the historic crucible of his personal and national soil. The ensuing poems record his journey, the stops he makes on the way, and his encounter with Israel's shore.

The journey of one who is committed to settle in the land differs from that of a visitor. While the latter is secure in the knowledge of having a safe refuge of home and familiar life routines following the journey, the former is uprooted—physically, emotionally, spiritually, and artistically. He is separated from a familiar home, anxiously seeking to relocate them in new ground. This is the archetypical Wandering Jew, one for whom a home is a fluid entity lacking a cohesiveness. For this individual there always is another home within the self, different from the one in which he is located. This divided identity is what continued to define American Hebraists throughout their lives, affecting even those who resettled in the Promised Land.[91]

Efros's identity has been molded by such experience. His poems follow an uprooting from America and describe how with considerable trepidation he began the journey. Similar to Halevi's mixed emotion about leaving home, Efros mitigates the momentous event by registering the physical pain and spiritual angst at the uncertain future awaiting him at the end of the road. Nonetheless, he does sense the mystery in the historic return. To him it is an occasion of great expectations for renewal or as he phrases it in "Lamb" ("Seh," 18) by finding "water and a pail" while making his way toward the searing sun.

His poetry recounts the journey in ways reminiscent of Halevi's sea voyage, observing the waves that accompany him in "Aboard ship" ("Bo-ʾoniyah," 17–18), and the emotions that overtake him. The voyage reverses his age, he asserts, returning him to an infancy that retraces the journey of the souls of all who preceded him, as he turns into the vessel bearing them all on his journey to Israel, "to right a great error."

The sea voyage is also described in the poems that follow. In "Desolation" ("Tohu," 19) the observer off the side of the ship imagines a host of forms in the waves, the sea being the setting for a dynamism of creation and destruction. Three other poems follow, bearing the rubric of "Three Songs of the Sea" ("Shloshah shiray-yam," 21–23), charting themes and titles that facilitate his undeclared imitation of Halevi. All three, though, are more engaged with metaphysical pursuits of signs of the divine in nature. They hold up the possibility that by contemplating the metaphysical, contact with the ultimate Other would be attainable.

Of all America's Hebraists, Efros is one of the few who, like Halevi, made the journey so as to settle in Eretz Israel. And while other writers have immigrated as Efros had, including Reuben Avinoam (Grossmann), T. Carmi, and Reuven Ben-Yosef, few exploited the imagery of Halevi to highlight their affinity for him or to resurrect his image as a medieval version of present-day Zionist aspirations.

While direct reference to Halevi by name is the most indisputable avenue for establishing analogies, other references are struck by less direct means. Although the latter forms of allusion are debatable, the character of some seems less coincidental simply by the confluence of more than one element that is part of the medieval bard's identity.

The poetry of Reuben Avinoam (Grossmann; 1905–1974) is a case in point. In many poems he addresses unambiguously the prospects of life in Israel, and while not citing Halevi directly, they are replete with idylls in praise of a return to Zion.[92] As part of his personal move to put down roots he composed poems grouped together around his sea voyage in 1929, which deserve a separate study.[93] Such an early record makes him the first known American Hebraist to write of his journey—and in "real time," as he labels his poems "on the way to" or "at the gate of" the Land of Israel—during which he, as Lisitzky will do later, makes a number of stops to visit historic sites before reaching Eretz Israel.[94]

In the latter collection, his poems echo key terms from Halevi's, including a reference to the proximity of "East" and "my heart" in "To the kind wind" ("La-ruaḥ ha-ḥasudah," 96); the encounter with stormy weather, as in "From within sea and night" ("Mi-tokh yam va-layl,"; 92–93); and the reference to his impending arrival, phrased in terms of being at Zion's gates. They betray the poet's primary quest to reach out to the divine, a theme abandoned by most poets in the Land of Israel at the time but which is also part of Halevi's quest.[95] On the other hand, however, the references to the eastern and western winds may be read as symbolic—with the former representing the ancient past—thus putting into doubt the analogy for which I argue.

The sentiment is enhanced in "To the kind wind," in which the poet is grateful for the wind heralding the approaching shore, "Lo, the East nears us! / We near the East!" This is the measure of the poem's allusion to Halevi's assertion of being torn, with heart in the East and body in the West. Yet the poem traces its creator's predilections for seeking the transcendental as it appears to use this image for metaphysical purposes. The image of reciprocity offered is reminiscent of the notion of divine grace, for as one repents by approaching God, God comes halfway to man.[96] The poet associates the eastern wind with the message of freedom and salvation from cold and dark northern climes, a return to the longed-for past, and the warmth of one's nest.

One to embed a note of anxiety behind nearly every line pertaining to his journey is the poet A. S. Schwartz. Like others, he foregrounds the message about the Ingathering of the Exiles while envisaging himself as re-enacting Yehudah Halevi's journey in his 1954 poem, "In the heart of the sea" ("B-lev yam"),[97] a term that also evokes Halevi's poem "Ha-tirdof naʿarut . . ."[98] Like Wallenrod (1899–1966) in prose,[99] Schwartz's poem focuses on the diversity of Jewish passengers, their origins and experiences—a theme harboring the unknown lurking among them, since they are strangers. And while referring to the dangers lurking beneath the beauty of the blue waves, he is comforted by the sense of mutual fate of the immigrants, as well as by his anticipated arrival in the land of prophecy and messiahs. Though not mentioned explicitly, Halevi's spirit hovers over the poet as he resorts to a familiar theme of the threatening abyss juxtaposed with the exhilaration at arriving in the historical homeland.[100]

So of what significance is the uncovering of tokens, as superficial as some may be, of Halevi's poetry and story in American Hebrew literature? It is likely that in him they identified their own plight professionally, geographically, and culturally. The irony, of course, was that most of them failed to carry out fully his agenda of settling in the Land of Israel. Halevi's religious quest and sensibilities notwithstanding, for most American Hebraists were not religious in his way, they most likely detected the irony of their Americanness holding them back from fulfilling the Zionist program of immigration. They preferred to remain as "rear-guard pioneers" to borrow Lisitzky's self-described raison d'être, "rear-guard pioneering" ("ḥalutziyut sheba-ʿoref").[101] This nuanced expression of guilt at "betraying" Halevi's archetypal pilgrimage is an issue left for a separate study.

Since his rediscovery, Halevi's shadow hovered over European Hebraists even before affecting American Hebrew literati. The pathos in his story permitted them to identify him as an anachronistic bearer of the love of Zion, a matter that has made Halevi a popular figure of the Haskalah and *Teḥiyah* (Revival) periods. He was the great medieval poet whose aspirations for Zion were deemed as anticipating contemporary nationalist aspirations. Of added import was his philosophical work, which, while also germane literarily, became the subject of numerous studies in the realm of Jewish thought.

Halevi's poetic expression was of particular value to poets of the *Ḥibat Tziyon* (Love of Zion) movement. Poets of the Haskalah composed poems about him or modeled his sentiments. Most notable of them were Michal (Micha Yosef Cohen Lebenson), the poetess Elisheva, N. H. Imber—composer of Israel's national anthem but who also wrote (while in the Land of Israel) of Halevi's journey—M. M. Dolitzky, S. Mandelkern, Y. Rabinovitch, Y. L. Landau, Z. Yabetz, D. Frischmann, Sarah Shapira, A. Leibushitzky, D. Shimoni, A. Hameiri, Y. Rimmon, Y. Burla, and U. Z. Greenberg.[102]

References to Yehudah Halevi are but one emblem of America's Hebrew literati's ambivalence about answering Zion's call of personally making the move to Israel.[103] My reading is based on the lyrical nature of these poets' oeuvre, indicating that the dilemmas they express are personal experiences. Yet their expressions also represented the collective, and appear to hold true today.

In a comparison of European and American belles lettres' appropriation of Halevi's image, it is evident that decidedly fewer of the former were composed by writers on their way to the Land of Israel. American Hebraists, on the other hand, resorted to this motif on the occasion of an actual journey they had taken. In most instances, the affinity of the Europeans for Halevi is thematic, drawing on the temper he exudes in his lament over Zion, with poets identifying more with his longing than the journey itself. The American Hebraists' affinity is—for all their divergence from Halevi's act—stronger in their re-enactment of the voyage of encounter, whether for visiting or to settle. Emotionally, nearly all are drawn to his lyricism and the romanticism surrounding the tale of his journey—a sentiment also discernible among other than Hebrew writers, as in Heine's poetry—when voicing his longing to behold Eretz Israel. The story as to the tragic death he met upon arrival was a perfect complement in a life-imitates-art situation for romantic poets.

In some instances, in place of deep-seated expressions of longing for Zion, the insertion of Halevi into poetry appears more as an expected stock intertext by European and American writers. Often enough they resort to it without intent to fully realize Halevi's pilgrimage themselves. As such, the motif underscores the Diasporic nature of many a poet and his difficulties of accommodation with the reality of the incipient state. So while many may have wanted to bring the story of Halevi full circle by highlighting a spiritual realization of his longing, few of the Americanized writers could bring themselves to physically emulate the bard. Most have never cut the cord with their American base, preferring to reread Halevi's story as an account of a tourist's journey that would conclude upon returning home.

The literary expressions discussed above stand in marked contrast to the enthusiasm with which canonical works sing the praises of the Land of Israel. Yet the times appeared to have resonated significantly less in America. These were the interwar years of the second and third *'aliyot*, with Eretz Israel representing a haven for Jews who dared to run the blockading cordon of British naval vessels seeking refuge from the rising tides of persecution in Europe. Yet at least a number of America's Hebrew writers clearly did not toe the line, their hesitation and uncertainty mirroring not only personal qualms about risking the comforts of America but on a deeper level harboring ambiguous regard for the Zionist project as perceived by their coreligionists in the Golden Land. In so doing, America's literati were adding but another stone to the gradually rising wall separating them from their Israeli fellows, marginalizing themselves as outsiders to the Zionist enterprise. As if in response, contemporary readers of Hebrew literature ignored the output of much of their literary corpus, consigning it to oblivion.

CONCLUSION

Whether by linguistic strategies, conservatism, or personal innovation, America's Hebrew writers distanced themselves from the dynamism of an awakening language. Their attainments alienated them from the mainstream of Hebrew innovation and mass consumption that would have presented them with a chance at rescuing the American center from oblivion.

Ideologically, the considerable uncertainty about joining forces with the innovators of a modern, Land of Israel–centered Hebrew in cultivating the message of ethnic and national identity widened the chasm between the two continents. Hebraists in the Land of Israel were increasingly distanced from those in the American center as each delved into the meaning of their environment, or mirrored their inner selves with lyrical works. As opposed to the Diasporic centeredness in America, literature in the Land of Israel focused on promoting the collective experience of a renascent society set on constructing its own social and political structures.

The encounters between the two camps only highlighted the widening chasm opening between them. Communication between the sides only sharpened the reality that shattered the popular myth of a unified corpus of Hebraist expression. The literature of America's Hebrew authors and poets admits insight into the painful realization of the emerging differences and the all-too-certain recognition of the death knell of the last of these "Mohicans."

CONCLUSION

Glancing back from the vantage point of the twenty-first century at what transpired in American Hebrew letters, we witness a chapter that has now reached its conclusion. Circumstances within and beyond the pale of Jewish society have coalesced to efface any prospects for a lasting imprint of Hebrew culture's flowering in America. Of all the Hebrew literary talent that populated the American landscape, little has remained. The contribution by America's Hebraists was consigned to oblivion, falling mostly by the wayside of the canon.

The very center that it begat has also come to an end, facilitated by Hebraists whose conservatism increasingly limited their audience. Most readers of Hebrew literature in America turned to the colloquial and contemporary uses of the language as exhibited by Hebrew writers in Israel. Others were lost as they shifted allegiance to English literature. American Jewry failed to establish a Hebrew educational system of sufficient breadth and depth to replace those losses with new talent and readers of a secularized Hebrew. Thematically, too, American Hebrew literature's primary preoccupation with lyrical poetry, and even its romanticism about Blacks and Indians, did not satisfy a readership drawn by contemporary issues and more realistic depictions of the here-and-now.

Ideologically, readers became detached from Zionist and Israel-centered literature produced by American Hebraists. Instead, a significant proportion of American Jews sought ways to assimilate and "pass" as citizens of their new land. Those who remained devotees to Hebrew and a Jewish national cause rapidly decreased in numbers, to be replaced by few new readers. The closing of America's doors to new immigrants limited the prospects of infusing fresh talent and energy to replace authors who died or left for the Land of Israel. Later, as Israelis began to appear on the American scene, they read the literature published in Israel, or turned to English.

Was the encounter with America so unlike those with Europe's cultures to eradicate Hebraism within half a century? Though similar phenomena of the demise of specific centers of Hebrew literature have occurred in Europe, they did not bankrupt Hebrew culture as happened in America. Continued education and the accompanying fidelity to a rich array of cultural practices sustained the population of Jews throughout Eastern Europe. The move to the New World must have been accompanied by tidal changes that facilitated and encouraged Jewish accommodation to a new culture.

The end to the Hebrew literary center in America stems in part from the inertia exhibited by its own members. For in their rush to Americanize Hebrew belles lettres, authors and poets risked casting aside their national agenda as Zionists. To be sure, were they to retain a strong hold on that ideology, any ties to their adopted land would have been tenuous. Yet their identity with and ties to Israel may have continued their center in ways that can only be surmised. However, time and circumstance promoted a greater intimacy and familiarity with America even by the most ardent of Zionists. The eventual separation of some as they left for Israel was a painful experience that few could sustain. Those less ideologically committed never even gave a thought to abandoning the Golden Land. Instead, they let their ideologies and particular identities fade into the American cultural landscape.

Though gone, Hebrew writers in America have left behind a vast and unique literary corpus that bears some distinctive traits. Their exploration of the lives, culture, and experiences of Native and African Americans is unmatched by any other immigrant group. To be sure, and unlike some more contemporary reflections on the subject, theirs was a one-sided discourse, directed at but not expecting a response from Blacks or Indians. Yet this phenomenon represents a profound turn in Hebrew culture from being a separatist ethnocentric movement to a willing integration into the diversity that is America. In writing of America's minorities, Hebrew authors and poets have added new images and drawn wider vistas supplementing the reach of a limited—but ancient—literary tradition as theirs, enriching it and extending its scope. It may also be that in so doing they laid the ground for a consciousness among their readers of becoming more open and accommodating to the diversity that comprises American culture.

The desire of Hebrew writers to represent Native American and Black folkways must have a number of motives. Hebraists reached out to exotic cultures deemed more authentically American than those who settled in America but whose European origins were evident. In a modern and liberal age, this interest characterized Hebrew (and to some extent Jewish) intellectuals as having developed an interest in the Other in ways that surpassed their fellows' earlier attempts to engage with European culture. Unlike the latter, this turn was marked by interest and identification with the downtrodden and by attempts to examine cultures other than those from Back There. The process was not concerned so much with reaching out to act for the betterment of these groups, though it included that as well, as much as a desire to form a new amalgam that would give rise to a Jewish American culture, as these very writers were imagining their national and ethnic concerns through the experiences of the other.

The move to conflate Jewish culture with something perceived as indigenously American stood against separatist tendencies in Jewish civilization that advocated retention of Judaic ways within America. By introducing their readers to these civilizations, Hebraists held up a challenge to their followers to recognize alternate, non-Jewish ways, values, and modes that would prompt them to seek solutions to the challenges of survival in a pluralistic society.

This phenomenon, promoted by a sizable cadre of Hebrew literati, created the climate befitting a literary center in its own right. Yet just as in a number of European arenas, the American center was short-lived. In America, however, it was affected more by its internal dynamics as people shifted from Hebrew to English language and culture. Yet as much as these Hebraists strove to become as American as others, to shed their particularistic tribalism for the sake of the heterogeneous diversity of the New World, circumstances mounted to thwart this very impulse as the Holocaust reminded them that their identities do not always depend only on how they seek to define themselves, but also on how others do. This, however, is a subject for another book.

This study followed some of the stages in the Americanization of Jews as mirrored in the words of some of their literature as it regarded a number of specifically American themes. Native and African Americans served as a means to measure the extent to which immigrant Jews sought ways to identify with and become Americans.

Hebrew writers also attempted to pave the way for their followers by modeling strategies of giving voice to their Jewishness, or Hebrewness, through the American prism. Nonetheless, their failure is marked by the absence of any literary progeny—be they Hebraist and even Yiddishist—who took up their model to promote the survival of Jewish civilization and culture in the New World.

As in some of the earliest English writings by immigrant Jews, such as the fiction of Mary Antin, Hebrew writers documented the rapid assimilation of Jews into the American cultural landscape. Unlike her, though, they did not encourage the process. Theirs was a failed attempt at a rescue of Hebraism within America as most of Hebrew educational systems focused more on religious education than on a secular literary proficiency.

Realizing the futility of their attempts, those Hebrew writers who survived into the middle of the twentieth century (and who chose to remain in America) satisfied themselves with Lisitzky's formulated notion of rearguard pioneerism. Whether this was sufficient to convince them of the lasting value of their role in America remains to be explored in future studies. The fact that the works of most were left by the wayside as American Jewry pursued its cultural metamorphosis—in place of a greater number of them immigrating to the Jewish State—is sufficient evidence as to the little recognition they received for their self-sacrifice.

Much like Abraham Cahan's protagonist, David Levinsky, Hebrew writers have also been conscious of the inverse relationship between material gain and spiritual bankruptcy in the lives of American Jews. Unlike the former, though, many protagonists of Hebrew literature remain immersed in their past, upholding its riches as a buffer against America's onslaught. Nonetheless, most Hebraists had to reinvent themselves into an amalgam of Hebraism and American ways and values, emerging as visionaries of a pluralism that would permit the salvaging of their cultural and spiritual values. This hope remained a dream unfulfilled in light of the emptiness of American Jews' lives of the Jewish cultural legacy and experience.

In pursuit of representing their affinity for America, Hebrew writers struggled with a fitting means of doing so. The choice of focusing on America's marginalized natives and former slaves was in itself a radical new thematic turn for Hebrew literature. Generically, it was the poetic form that retained hegemony in this arena too, though the output testifies that its creators, too, were divided over modes of representation. For while the lead was marked by Silkiner's romanticizing and mythologizing bent, not all poets did so. Another approach to representing the marginalized can be best described as more realistic, even novelistic in some of its representative pieces. In observing this dichotomy, one cannot but consider these categories as some proposed criteria toward a history of Hebrew literature in America.

The ultimate demise of American Hebrew literary life is indebted as well to the daring of its literati in clearing new thematic directions for themselves. By attending to their immediate challenges in the New World and focusing on subjects seemingly tangential to the Hebrew national cause, many wrote themselves out of the canon, becoming, instead, marginal curiosities of little relevance to the greater existential challenges faced by Jews. At a time when the prevailing and desirable issues involved the challenges of settlement in Eretz Israel, American Hebrew belles lettres offered up a contradictory oeuvre of concern for the Other, diversity, assimilation, and suggested strategies for survival in a Diasporic existence.

American Hebrew literature inscribed its own identity before its demise. Toward that goal, it shunned total allegiance to an Israel-centeredness or a set of literary themes or group behavior expected by the Zionist national agenda. Whether the latter was motivated out of a desire to separate itself from the larger national program in order to morph into another form of American literature is not altogether evident. It might just as well have been driven by its all-too-conservative tendencies in the sphere of Hebrew language and literary mission. The American Hebraic experience is a willful desire to remain in exile, to retain a Diasporic identity within the Diaspora, to remain marginalized among the marginalized. As such, American Hebrew literature wrote itself out of the Hebrew literary continuum to leave behind a more Americanized, and decidedly less Jewish, literary legacy in English.

NOTES

INTRODUCTION

1. For instance, Shmuel Werses, *Relations between Jews and Poles in S. Y. Agnon's Work* (Jerusalem: Magnes Press, 1994); Dan Miron, "German Jews in Agnon's Work," *Leo Baeck Institute Yearbook* 33 (1978): 265–280.

2. Though I often use them interchangeably, I prefer acculturation as a term designating a partial replacement of one's own culture by that of another, whereas assimilation represents the total loss of self-identity within another culture. John Bodnar, in his *The Transplanted: A History of Immigrants in Urban America* (Bloomington: Indiana University Press, 1985), 214, employs other terms to depict the same dynamic: the "accommodationists" sought and promoted rapid Americanization among immigrants, whereas the traditionalists were interested in the preservation of aspects of their communal identity and separateness despite America.

3. E. Silberschlag, "Hebrew Literature in America: Record and Interpretation," *Jewish Quarterly Review* 45, no. 4 (April 1955): 413. These years of massive immigration augmented the increasing population of Jews already settled in America, among them the Sephardim and German Ashkenazim who had been arriving in America since 1654. See Stephen Birmingham, *"Our Crowd": The Great Jewish Families of New York* (New York: Dell, 1967); also his *The Grandees: The Story of America's Sephardic Elite* (New York: Dell, 1971); Irving Howe, *World of Our Fathers* (New York: Harcourt Brace Jovanovich, 1976).

4. For the numbers I rely on Jonathan Sarna, *American Judaism: A History* (New Haven, Connecticut: Yale University Press, 2004), 375. For comparison, a mere eighty thousand Jews immigrated to Eretz Israel in the years 1880–1920.

5. First published in Vilna in 1894; Gershon Rosenzweig, "Masekhet America" (Tractate America), in *Talmud Yanka'i* (Yankee Talmud) (New York: S. Druckerman, 1907). For a published sample in English see Silberschlag, "Hebrew Literature in America," 421.

6. Philip A. Hollander, "Between Decadence and Rebirth: The Fiction of Levi Aryeh Arieli" (Ph.D. diss., Columbia University, 2004). For Arieli's work, see *Kitvay L. A. Arieli* (Writings of L. A. Arieli), 2 vols., ed. Micha'el (Milton) Arfa (New York and Tel-Aviv: Keren Israel Matz and Dvir), 1999.

7. Avraham Holtz, "Dyokan—Lisitzky: ish midot" (Portrait—Lisitzky: a man of stature). *Niv: kli mivta l-sofrim tzʿirim* (New York) 24, no. 1 (Iyar 5720; May 1960): 5–7. Jacob Kabakoff, "Hebrew Literature on American Soil," *Modern Hebrew Literature* 2 (Summer 1975): 17–25. Alan Mintz, "Hebrew Literature in America," in Michael P. Kramer and Hana Wirth-Nesher, eds. *The Cambridge Companion to Jewish American Literature* (Cambridge, UK: Cambridge University Press, 2003), 92–109. Moshe Pelli, *Ha-tarbut ha-ʿivrit ba-ʾAmerica: 80 shnot ha-tnuʿah ha-ʿivrit b-ʾartzot ha-brit—5676–5758 (1916–1995)* (Hebrew culture in America: 80 years of Hebrew culture in the United States 1916–1995). Tel-Aviv: Rshafim, 1998.

8. See Yaʿakov Rabinowitz, "Rshimot: Americaʾiyut" (Notes: Americanism) (New York). *Miklat* 2, no. 4–6 (Tevet–Adar 5680; 1920): 463–465; "Americaʾiyut" (Americanism). *Hadoʾar*, year 3, vol. 4, no. 34 (8 Av 5684; 18 August 1924): 9–11; "Americaʾiyut (maʾamar 3)" (Americanism: third essay). *Hadoʾar*, year 4, vol. 5, no. 38 (1 Elul 5685; 21 August 1925): 10–12. Also see Ezra Spicehandler, "ʾAmeriqaʾiyut in American Hebrew Literature," in Alan Mintz, ed., *Hebrew in America: Perspectives and Prospects* (Detroit: Wayne State University Press, 1993), 68–104.

9. Yeshayah Rabinowitz, "Yetzirato shel Ephraim E. Lisitzky" (E. E. Lisitzky's work). *Bitzaron* 41, no. 4 (Adar 5720; February–March 1960): 188–200.

10. Pelli, *Ha-tarbut ha-ʿivrit*, 100.

11. A few notable exceptions who prove the rule include the poet Reuven Avinoam (Grossman). Born in Chicago and educated in New York, he immigrated to Eretz Israel in 1929. Others include T. Carmi, born in New York in 1925, educated and settled in Israel in 1947, and Reuven Ben-Yosef, born in 1937, immigrated to Israel in the late 1950s.

12. *Sefer ha-yovel shel Hadoʾar* (Hadoʾar jubilee volume) (New York: 1927), 346–352, cited in Ezra Spicehandler, "Ameriqaʾiyut," in Mintz, ed., *Hebrew in America*, 69.

13. S. Shiḥor (unpublished manuscript), "Rshimat ha-sofrim she-ḥayu ba-ʿAmerica o she-ḥayu bah" (List of authors who were or lived in America), American Jewish Archive misc. file; Jacques Miklishansky, *Toldot ha-sifrut ha-ʿivrit ba-ʾAmerica* (History of Hebrew literature in America) (Jerusalem: Reuven Mass/ʿOgen, 1967.

14. Mary Antin, *The Promised Land* (Boston: Houghton Mifflin Company, 1969).

15. I rely on M. Ribalow's analysis of themes, which he terms "colors." Menaḥem Ribalow, "Eretz Yisraʾel vha-prozah ha-ʿivrit ba-ʾAmerica" (The land of Israel and Hebrew prose in America). *Hadoʾar*, year 32, vol. 33, no. 25 (1 Sivan 5713; 15 May 1953): 520–521. E. Silberschlag, in his "Hebrew Literature in America" enumerates three phases of Hebrew literature in America (413): "The period of oddities," "The period of belated beginnings," and "The period of emergent achievements." And see his article "Hebrew Literature in America: Record and Interpretation."

16. H. Sackler, *Sefer ha-maḥazot* (Book of plays) (New York: ʿOgen, 1943), 269–330; years later he published an imagined dialogue between himself and Noah on his contribution to Zionism, *ʿOlelot* (Gleanings) (Tel-Aviv: Yavneh, 1966), 89–97. More recently, a novel by the Israeli Nava Semel, *Eesraʾel* (*IsraeIsland*) also incorporates depictions of Noah, and see below. A recent study on Noah in literature is by Michael Weingrad, "Messiah American Style: Mordecai Manuel Noah and the American Refuge," *AJS Review* 31, no. 1 (April 2007): 75–108.

17. On Mordecai Noah, see Yaʿakov (Jacob) Kabakoff, "Noaḥ ba-sifrut ha-ʿivrit," *Niv: kli mivta l-sofrim tzʿirim* (New York) 1, no. 6 (Sivan 5697; May 1937): 14–17; Jonathan D. Sarna, *Jacksonian Jew: The Two Worlds of Mordecai Noah* (New York: Holmes and Meier, 1981).

18. The discourse was stimulated and supported by verses from the *Tanakh*, including Exod. 28:30, Lev. 8:8, Neh. 7:65, Ezra 2:63. For particulars on the debate see Tzvetan Todorov, *The Conquest of America: The Question of the Other*, trans. Richard Howard (New York: Harper and Row, 1987), 11–12; Captain G. Palmer, *The Migration from Shinar* (London, 1879), cited in Lewis Spence, *The Myths of the North American Indians* (New York: Dingwall-Rock Limited, c. 1927), 3–4; George Catlin, "Letter—No. 14: Mandan Village, Upper Missouri," "Letter—No. 58: North Western Frontier," in *Letters and Notes on the Manners, Customs, and Condition of the North American Indians*, vols. 1 and 2 (Minneapolis: Ross and Haines, 1965), 104, 223–256, accordingly. Also see Richard Popkin, "The Rise and Fall of the Jewish Indian Theory," in Shalom Goldman, ed., *Hebrew and the Bible in America: The First Two Centuries* (Hanover, NH: Brandeis University Press and Dartmouth College/University Press of New England, 1993), 7–90.

19. Such are the novels and stories of Yoram Kaniuk, some of which will be discussed below; also Shuki Ben-Ami, *Notzah shsuʾah: ish ha-rfuʾah ha-ʾindiʾani* (Split feather: the Indian medicine man) (Tel-Aviv: Ha-kibbutz Ha-mʾuḥad, 2003), 256; and Nava Semmel, *Eesraʾel* (IsraIsland) (Tel-Aviv: Yediʿot Aḥaronot/Sifray Ḥemed, 2005). Also see Colin G. Calloway, Gerd Gemunden, and Susanne Zantop, eds. *Germans and Indians: Fantasies, Encounters, Projections* (Lincoln: University of Nebraska Press, 2002).

20. *The People and Uncollected Stories*, edited by Robert Giroux (New York: Farrar Straus Giroux, 1989).

21. I wish to express my thanks to the Lilly Library at Indiana University for making their copy of the screenplay available to me.

22. For example, see John Clapham, "Dvořák and the American Indian," and Jean E. Snyder, "'A Great and Noble School of Music': Dvořák, Harry T. Burleigh, and the African American Spiritual," in John C. Tibbetts, ed., *Dvořák in America* (Portland, OR: Amadeus Press, 1993), 113–122, 123–148.

23. Shuki Ben-Ami, *Notzah shsuʾah* (Split feather) (Tel-Aviv: Ha-kibbutz Ha-mʾuḥad, 2003); Nava Semmel, *Eesraʾel* (IsraIsland). In part, Semmel's reimagined history forms a thematic bond with a novel by Michael Chabon, *The Yiddish Policeman's Union* (New York: HarperCollins, 2007).

24. And little in Yiddish, as they also tell of the encounter of Jews with Indians. For example, see Sheen (Shmu'el) Daixel, *Indianishe dertseylungen* (Indian stories) (New York: S. Daixel bukh-komitet, 1959). My thanks to my colleague Dov-Ber Kerler for bringing this example to my attention.

25. Matthew Frye Jacobson, in *Special Sorrows: The Diasporic Imagination of Irish, Polish, and Jewish Immigrants in the United States* (Cambridge, Mass.: Harvard University Press, 1995), 285, n. 96, identifies a number of Polish works describing or involving Native Americans, such as Adam Mickiewicz's "Potato" and Henryk Sienkiewicz's "Sachem." The comparison is inadequate not only due to the sheer quantity of Hebrew works on Black and Native American life, but they differ also in that the Polish works exploit Native Americans as characters in works which otherwise focus on issues of their own Polish socio-cultural concerns to perpetuate anti-German bias motivated by Poland's treatment by Germany at the *fin-de-siècle*. Hebrew literature differs in that its vast number of works on Blacks and Native Americans exclude the Jews totally, similar to Longfellow's "Song of Hiawatha," which also appears to be composed from within the focus group, as if told by a member of the tribe. The Hebrew writers do not insert Jews into these works. It is this perspective that distinguishes their specific compositions from others done by them or other immigrant writers, Jews or gentiles. Sienkiewicz's "Sachem" is in *Lillian Morris, and Other Stories* (Boston: Little, Brown and Co., 1894), 155–176.

26. The poet E. E. Lisitzky did plan to publish an English version of his long poem *Naftulay Elohim* (Divine struggles). Housed at the American Jewish Archives is a typewritten synopsis of this work in English, prepared, presumably, in order to interest publishers in the enterprise: "Synopsis of Divine Struggles—A Poetic Drama." Lisitzky Collection. American Jewish Archives, Cincinnati.

Elliott Rabin explains that to write in Hebrew is an indication of the author's attachment to and strong identity with Jewish civilization; even when they rejected religious components of Judaism, these writers continued to identify themselves as part of the community of Israel, even when that meant financial loss or loss of the prestige of writing for a larger audience: "Why write in a language that lacked a significant readership . . . ? The answer must lie in the fact that they possessed an extraordinary attachment to Jewish identity and community; when they had lost the bond of religious practice, Hebrew literature itself became their primary medium of attachment . . . Hebrew literature was the locus of a new, secular Jewish identity . . . [sufficiently] powerful to compensate for the inevitable loss of prestige and money that would come by writing in such a marginal language. By the very act of adapting European literary fashions to a language of prophets and rabbis, Hebrew writers were expressing their ardent nationalist aspirations . . ." Elliott Rabin, "Idolatrous Fictions: Art and Religion in Modern Hebrew Literature" (Ph.D. diss., Indiana University, Bloomington, 1997), 10.

27. Mentor L. Williams, ed., *Schoolcraft's Indian Legends* (East Lansing, Michigan: Michigan State University Press, 1956), 299.

CHAPTER ONE

1. I rely on Eisig Silberschlag's list, in "Ha-shirah ha-ʿivrit ba-ʿolam he-ḥadash" (Hebrew poetry in the new world). *Aḥisefer*. Ed. S. Niger and M. Ribalow (New York: Keren Louis LaMed, 1944), 216.

2. N. B. Silkiner, *Mul ohel Timmura: shivray poʾema (mi-zman shilton-hasfardim ba-ʾAmerica)* (Before Timmura's tent: poema fragments [from the time of Spanish rule in America]) (Jerusalem: Asaf, 1910).

3. Brenner's review of *Mul ohel Timmura* appeared on the heels of the work's publication, in *Ha-poʿel Ha-tzaʿir*, Kislev 1910; reproduced in Yosef Ḥayim Brenner, *Ktavim*, vol. 3: *publitzistikah*, *bikoret* (Writings, vol. 3: Current affairs, criticism) (Tel-Aviv: Ha-kibutz Ha-mʾuḥad and Sifriyat Poʿalim, 1985), 517–520.

4. See Introduction, n. 8.

5. M. Ribalow, ed. *Sefer zikaron l-B. N. Silkiner* (Memorial book for B. N. Silkiner). New York: ʿOgen, 1934), 60–61.

6. Yaʿakov (Jacob) Kabakoff, "Binyamin Naḥum Silkiner ʿal-pi igrotav (B. N. Silkiner according to his letters), *Mahut* (Summer 1989), 63–70.

7. Confirmed in Ribalow, ibid., 63. For an alternate view on these publishing endeavors, see Jacob Kabakoff, "B. N. Silkiner and His Circle: The Genesis of the New Hebrew Literature in America," *Judaism* 39, no. 1 (Winter 1990): 97–103.

8. Gnazim, no. 23/7428-alef.

9. 28 December 1911, Gnazim, no. 21/4119/1.

10. Gnazim no. 20/18614-alef.

11. Also invited was F. Lachower, in a separate letter of 8 November 1912; Gnazim, no. 16/11366/8.

12. On *Ha-toren*, see Mintz's seminal article, "A Sanctuary in the Wilderness: The Beginning of the Hebrew Movement in America in *Hatoren*," in *Hebrew in America: Perspectives and Prospects*, ed. A. Mintz (Detroit: Wayne State University Press, 1993), 29–67.

13. "Btuḥani ki im nishtadel nukhal l-hotzi et kol ha-sfarim b-meshekh shel shnatayim. Haʾim naḥutz li l-hosif, lomar, ki im gam yihyu *kol* ʿkitvay ha-prozah ha-ʿivritʾ ba-ʾAmerica ʿal kaf moznayim aḥat lo yukhlu l-hakhriʿa ki-mlo nima et kaf ha-moznayim shel shiratkha v-ligroʿa bi-mʾumah meʿerekh shiraykha ha-neḥmadim?" Gnazim, no. 91/40138/1 (emphasis in original; all translations are mine, unless otherwise indicated).

14. A similar motive would be behind a later project by Menaḥem Ribalow in establishing ʿOgen, the publishing arm of the Histadrut Ivrit of America, and see Menaḥem Ribalow, "Sofrim u-sfarim: ʿOgen'" (Authors and books: ʿOgen), *Hadoʾar* year 19, vol. 20, no. 18 (28 Adar alef 5700; 8 March 1940).

15. D. A. Friedman, "ʿAl sfarim v-sofrim: kniyat ʿolam b-shirah aḥat" (Of books and authors: immortality with one poem), *Ktuvim* 61, no. 2 (30 November 1927): 2; also see incidental remark by Yaʿakov Tzuzmer, letter of 13 September 1910 (6 Kislev 5688), Gnazim, no. F/19426: "Ha-mshorer—rishon she-raʾuy

l-shem zeh ʿal admat America—B. Silkiner, ʿa"h" (The poet—the first to deserve this designation on American soil—B. Silkiner).

16. See Silkiner's foreword to the 1927 edition, N. B. Silkiner, *Shirim* (Poems) (New York: Ḥaverim; Tel-Aviv: Dvir, 1927).

17. N. B. Silkiner, "Mul-ohel Timmura: poemah mi-zman shilton ha-sfardim ba-America" (Before Timmura's tent: a poema from the time of Spanish rule in America), *Shirim* (Poems), 73–186. B. N. Silkiner, "Mul ohel Timmura: me'et B. N. Silkiner: mʿubad li-vnay ha-nʿurim bi-yday Aharon David Markson" (Before Timmura's tent by B. N. Silkiner, reworked for young readers by A. D. Markson), in *Kitvay A. D. Markson* (The works of A. D. Markson), edited B. Isaacs and D. Persky (Detroit: Ha-kvutzah Ha-ʿivrit, 1938), 139–170.

An additional example of its early inception exists in manuscript form, bearing the title "Ki-ntot ha-layl (balada)" (As night falls [a ballad]), Gnazim, no. 188/4122. It bears the segment telling of the parents of Etzima, who sculpts the new *Elnefesh*, from the beginning of the ninth chapter.

18. Moshe Steiner, "Motivim indi'aniyim ba-shirah ha-ʿivrit-Americanit" (Indian motifs in American-Hebrew poetry). *Divray ha-kongres ha-ʿolami ha-shishi l-madaʿay ha-yahadut* (Proceedings of the sixth world congress of Jewish studies). Vol. 3. Ed. Avigdor Shin'an. Jerusalem: Ha-'igud Ha-ʿolami L-madaʿay Ha-yahadut, 1977, 505, 508.

19. Yehudit Bar-El, *Ha-po'emah ha-ʿivrit: me-hitehavutah v-ʿad reshit ha-me'ah ha-ʿesrim—meḥkar b-toldot janer* (The Hebrew long poema from its emergence to the beginning of the twentieth century: a study in the history of a genre) (Jerusalem: Mosad Bialik, 1995), 17, 19, 20, 21, 22, 26, 58, 62, 75, 88. The *po'ema* (or "po'emah"), derived from the French *poeme*, describes a genre of the long poem which is a "Lyric-dramatic narrative," (Hrushovsky) ". . . in which a philosophical thought is presented in epic or dramatic form" (Shipley, n. 21 below). The debate about its constituent components continues into the present. Lisitzky's works in this genre adhere to a conventional form and content. More daring, Abba Kovner redefined and extended the parameters of the genre. His works ceaselessly challenge the balance between the lyrical and the historical components. For discussions, see articles by Hrushovski, Luria, and Miron in Shalom Luria, ed., *Abba Kovner: mivḥar ma'amaray bikoret ʿal yetzirato* (Abba Kovner: a selection of critical essays on his writings) (Tel-Aviv: Ha-kibbutz Ha-m'uḥad, 1988), 7–88, 192–280; Hillel Barzel, *Ha-shir he-ḥadash: sgirut u-phtiḥut* (The new poem: open and closed structures) (Tel-Aviv: ʿEked, 1976), 46–56; Dan Miron, "Mivneh u-vinah b-kovtzay shirah shel Natan Alterman" (Structure and sense in N. Alterman's poetry anthologies), *Moznayim* 32, no. 4–5 (1971): 305–319. Also, see Hrushovsky's interpretive comments to "Opening," *The Modern Hebrew Poem Itself*, ed. Stanley Burnshaw, et al. (New York: Schocken Books, 1966), 148. Also see Joseph Shipley, ed., *Dictionary of World Literature* (Totowa, New Jersey: Littlefield, Adams and Co., 1968), 311. In the manuscript chapter entitled "The Poetry of an Upturned

World," in his forthcoming study of American Hebrew literature, Michael Weingrad also focuses on the affinities between America's Hebraists and *maskilim.*

20. Benjamin Hrushovski, "Abba Kovner," in Burnshaw, *The Modern Hebrew Poem*, 148.

21. Shipley, *Dictionary of World Literature*, 311. For additional discussion see Luria, *Abba Kovner.*

22. Israel Efrat (Efros; all his Hebrew works will bear the former, while our discussion and any English works will use the latter), *Goral u-phit'om: shirim u-pho'emot* (Destiny and suddenly: poems and poemas) (Jerusalem: Mosad Bialik, 1954), 9–25; also see Ilana Elkad-Lehman, "Tmurot po'etiyot b-shirat Israel Efrat" (Poetic changes in Israel Efrat's poetry) (Ph.D. diss., Bar-Ilan University, Ramat-Gan, Israel, December 1995), 128–134.

23. See also S. Ginzburg, "Bi-kh'ev dmamah dakah" (In the pain of still silence), *Sefer zikaron Silkiner*, 24–32, esp. 28, 30.

24. On the conservatism in American Hebrew see Uzi Shavit, "The New Hebrew Poetry of the Twenties: Palestine and America," *Prooftexts* 12, no. 3 (1992): 213–230; S. Ginzburg observes that the early Hebrew writers in America were Haskalah writers who adhered to its precepts in the New World long after it fell out of favor back in Russia. And see Shimon Ginzburg, "Shirah ʿivrit ba-'America" (Hebrew poetry in America), *Ha'aretz*, vol. 21, no. 5539, 17 Ḥeshvan 5698; 22 October 1938, 9–10. For one perspective (of many) on the language struggle see Gershon Shaked, *Ha-siporet ha-ʿivrit 1880–1970, [A]: Ba-golah* (Hebrew Narrative Fiction 1880–1970, [A]: In Exile) (Tel-Aviv/Jerusalem: Ha-kibbutz Ha-m'uḥad and Keter, 1977), 40–48.

25. Here I follow Bar-El's discussion and typology of the poema in the age of the late Haskalah. Yehudit Bar-El, *Ha-po'emah ha-ʿivrit*, 80–85.

26. A summary with commentary is also provided by Michael Weingrad, "Lost Tribes: The Indian in American Hebrew Poetry," *Prooftexts* 24, no. 3 (Fall 2004): 291–319. The following summary relies on the 1927 edition.

27. It is also possible that the plot represents the fateful Coronado expedition of 1540, in which the Zuni Indians were among the earliest to encounter Europeans. The popular mystique of the Zunis may have still been in the air when Silkiner composed of his story; and see Fergus Bordewich, *Killing the White Man's Indian: Reinventing Native Americans at the End of the Twentieth Century* (New York: Doubleday, 1966), 185. The term, also spelled *cacique*, or *Kasique*, denotes a leader or chief of Native Americans; and see Tzvetan Todorov, *The Conquest of America*, 103, 112, etc; also in M. L. Marks, *Jews among the Indians: Tales of Adventure and Conflict in the Old West* (Chicago: Benison Books, 1992), 112, 122; and a book in which the term *Katsika* is explained to mean a minister or prince, by Francisco Lopez de Gomara, *Sefer ha-'indi'ah ha-ḥadashah v-sefer Fernando Cortes [1553] nosaḥ ʿivri shel toldot Peru u-Mexico bi-yday Yosef Hakohen [1568]* (The new India book and the book of Fernando Cortes [1553] a Hebrew version of the history of Peru

and Mexico by Yosef Hakohen [1568]), ed. Moshe Lazar (Lancaster, California: Labyrinthos, 2002), 158, 195, 231, 233, 235.

28. For one familiar with Agnon's fiction, this tangle, proceeding domino-like from one act to the next, is also reminiscent of "Agunot," first published in 1908.

29. Silkiner intuitively grasps the force behind schemes and lies as the root of a greater collapse, perhaps modeling his on earlier Haskalah tales. Historically, lying was a potent (verbal) weapon employed by the Spanish conquerors to weaken Native Americans by dividing them. Moreover, lying aids those who seek power over others to foment envy, a practice frowned upon by (Aztec) Indians. See Todorov, *The Conquest of America*, 90–91.

30. For a similar suggestion by M. Weingrad in his article, an idea derived independently in both of our works on this topic, though preceded by Silberschlag, "Ha-shirah ha-ʿivrit," 217–218, see M. Weingrad, "Lost Tribes," 295.

31. Suggested by S. Ginzburg, "B. N. Silkiner," *Hadoʾar* 4, no. 4 (1 Kislev 5685; 28 November 1925): 12–13, and Weingrad, "Lost Tribes," 297.

32. E. Silberschlag, *From Renaissance to Renaissance I: Hebrew Literature from 1492–1970* (New York: Ktav, 1973), 280.

33. S. Ginzburg, "Shirah ʿivrit ba-ʾAmerica," 9–10.

34. Abraham Schwadron Collection at National and University Library at the Hebrew University of Jerusalem, Lisitzky folder 2, letter no. 53. I also have a photocopy of letter no. 52, of June 7, 1909, wherein Silkiner calls himself "Silk"; its number is Fi 1203 PHOT337. Confirming this name is Efros's eulogy, "Meshi va-ḥalomot" (Silk and dreams), in *Sefer zikaron Silkiner*, 65.

35. Tz. H. Wolfson, "Mul ohel Timmura (bikoret)," *Ha-dror* 1, no. 6 (14 Tishrei 5672; 6 October 1911): 107–108.

36. D. A. Friedman, "ʿAl sfarim," 2.

37. Shimon Ginzburg, *Sefer zikaron Silkiner*, n. 23 above, 28, 30; also see his essay, "Binyamin Naḥum Silkiner," *B-masekhet ha-sifrut: masot u-rshamim* (In the web of literature: essays and observations) (New York: Vaʿad L-hotzaʾat Kitvay Shimon Ginzburg, 1945), 223–234; it first appeared as "B. N. Silkiner," *Hadoʾar*, year 4, no. 4 (1 Kislev, 5685; 28 November 1924): 12–13.

38. Ginzburg, *Sefer zikaron Silkiner*, 28.

39. Thus Lachower in F. Lachower, "B. N. Silkiner," *Moznayim* 1, no. 3 (Kislev 5694/December 1933): 99–101.

40. Y. Y. Geles, "Shirim" (Poems), *Ha-ʿolam* 16, no. 27 (18 Tammuz 5688; 6 July 1928): 517–518.

41. Silberschlag, "Ha-shirah ha-ʿivrit," 216–245, esp. 217–219; for a similar view, see S. Ginzburg, "Shira ʿivrit ba-ʾAmerica."

42. Matthew Frye Jacobson, *Special Sorrows: The Diasporic Imagination of Irish, Polish, and Jewish Immigrants in the United States* (Cambridge, Mass.: Harvard University Press, 1995), 141–176.

43. Israel Efrat, "Vigvamim shotkim," *Kitvay Israel Efrat: sefer rishon: min*

ha-ʿolam he-ḥadash—shnay shirim (The writings of Israel Efros: book one: from the new world—two poems) (Tel-Aviv: Dvir, 1966), 9. S. Ginzburg, "Bi-kh'ev dmamah dakah," 29. Weingrad also takes note of this irony in "Lost Tribes," 315.

44. However, the tendency is anticipated by a number of Silkiner's other works. And see Avraham Epstein, *Sofrim ʿivrim ba-ʾAmerica* (Hebrew writers in America) (Tel-Aviv: Dvir, 1952), 31–38, esp. 35–36. Many Hebrew poets wrote lyrical poems as part of their *oeuvre.* One to have adhered to this mode is Avraham (Arnold J.) Band, and see his *Ha-rʾee boʿer ba-ʾesh* (The mirror burns with fire) (New York: ʿOgen; Jerusalem: Ogdan, 1963).

45. Also Weingrad, "Lost Tribes," 309.

46. B. N. Silkiner, "Me-ʾagadot ha-hodim" (An Indian legend), in *Sefer zikaron Silkiner,* 82–83; also appeared in *Hadoʾar* 13:6 (20 Kislev 5694; 1933).

47. Israel Efrat, "Vigvamim shotkim" (Silent wigwams), 9–118; E. E. Lisitzky, *Mdurot doʿakhot* (Dying campfires) (New York: ʿOgen, 1937); E. E. Lisitzky, *B-ʾoholay Khush* (In the tents of Cush) (Jerusalem: Mosad Bialik, 1953).

48. See the essay he writes on Silkiner's and Efros's notion of poema, discussed below in Chapter Three. E. E. Lisitzky, "Vigvamim shotkim" (Silent wigwams), *Bi-shvilay ḥayim v-sifrut* (In the paths of life and literature) (Tel-Aviv: Maḥbarot L-sifrut and ʿOgen, 1961), 60–72.

49. A similar impression is obtained from many Native American tales, and see, for example, Charles A. Eastman and Elaine Goodale Eastman, *Wigwam Evenings: Sioux Folk Tales Retold* (Lincoln: University of Nebraska Press, 1990).

50. Jacques LeGoff, *History and Memory,* trans. Steven Randall and Elizabeth Claman (New York: Columbia University Press, 1992), 37.

51. M. Weingrad, "Lost Tribes," 296.

52. One to note this about Silkiner is S. Y. Pineles, who notes that the sunset is also an observation of the poet's own condition in America. See S. Y. Pineles [Penueli], "Sifrutenu ha-ḥadashah ba-ʾAmerica: shirat B. N. Silkiner" (Our new literature in America: The poetry of B. N. Silkiner), *Gilyonot* 15, no. 4 (Tishrei 5704; 1943): 189–192.

On silence as a culturally respected trait among the Crow and other tribes, see Fergus Bordewich, *Killing,* 289. In a poem about the impending Holocaust, "By the Rivers of Babylon" ("ʿAl naharot bavel"), Efros also employs the image of the setting sun. Israel Efrat, *Anaḥnu ha-dor* (We are the generation) (New York: ʿOgen, 1944), 11–14. Also see Elkad-Lehman, "Tmurot poʾetiyot," 96.

53. Israel Efrat, *Vigvamim shotkim* (Silent wigwams); Reuven Wallenrod, *Ki phanah yom* (For the day has waned) (New York: Ohel; Tel-Aviv: M. Newman, 1946); E. E. Lisitzky, *Mdurot doʿakhot* (Dying campfires); *Kmo ha-yom rad: shirim* (As the day has set: poems) (Tel-Aviv: Maḥbarot L-sifrut, 1960); B. N. Silkiner, *Mul ohel Timmura* (Before Timmura's tent); Gavriel Preil, *Nof shemesh u-khfor: shirim* (Sunny vista and frost: poems) (New York: Ohel, 1944); and *Ner mul kokhavivm: shirim* (Candle opposite stars: poems) (Jerusalem: Mosad Bialik, 1954); and *Ha-ʾesh vha-dmamah: shirim* (The fire and the silence: poems) (Ramat-Gan:

Agudat Ha-sofrim and Massada, 1968); Simḥa Rubinstein, *Nerot doʿakhim: sipurim* (Dying candles: stories) (New York: Hadoʾar, 1966).

54. Using a term coined by S. Halkin, *ʿAd mashber: roman* (Till breakdown: a novel), the narrator "scientifically" terms those who dwell in New York, including Blacks, "*homo Americanus*," those humans who through their life in the New World have been altered from their previous character to become something new. S. Halkin, *ʿAd mashber* (Until breakdown) (Tel-Aviv: ʿAm ʿOved, 1944), 134.

55. Uzi Shavit, "The new Hebrew Poetry"; Zohar Shavit, "Ha-nisayon ha-koshel l-hakim merkaz shel sifrut ʿivrit ba-ʾAmerica" (The failed attempt to establish a center of Hebrew literature in America). *Migvan: meḥkarim ba-sifrut ha-ʿivrit uv-giluyeha haʾAmericaniyim—mugashim l-Yaʿakov Kabakoff* (Migvan: Studies in Hebrew Literature in Honor of Jacob Kabakoff), ed. Stanley Nash (Lod, Israel: Makhon Haberman L-meḥkray Sifrut, 1988), 433–449.

CHAPTER TWO

1. Reuben Wallenrod, *The Literature of Modern Israel* (New York: Abelard-Schuman, 1956), 237.

2. According to his daughter, Ghela Efros Scharfstein, he disliked Longfellow's work. I wish to express my thanks to Ghela for allowing me to examine some of the manuscripts still in her possession.

3. Henry Wadsworth Longfellow, "The Song of Hiawatha," in *The Poetical Works of Longfellow: Cambridge Edition*, trans. George Monteiro (Boston: Houghton Mifflin Company, 1975), 113–164, esp. 163. All subsequent quotations and references are to this edition.

4. See Ilana Elkad-Lehman, "Tmurot poʾetiyot b-shirat Israel Efrat" (Poetic changes in Israel Efrat's poetry), Ph.D. diss., Bar-Ilan University, Ramat-Gan, Israel, December 1995. According to Ghela Efros Scharfstein, Efros was fond of the long poetic form of Edwin Arlington Robinson, such as his "Cavender's House."

5. Israel Efrat, *Kitvay Israel Efrat: sefer ʿasiri: ha-rʾee ha-yotzer—masot ktanot 1971–9* (The writings of Israel Efros: book ten: the creative mirror: short essays, 1971–9) (Tel-Aviv: Dvir, 1980); *Yalkut masot* (An anthology of essays), ed. B. Y. Michali, Y. Orpaz, et al. (Tel-Aviv: Yaḥdav, 1980).

6. For a masterly analysis of these tendencies, see Ilana Elkad-Lehman, "Tmurot poʾetiyot."

7. Ibid., 25ff.

8. Ibid., 61.

9. For a study of Efros's transitions from Romanticism to Expressionism and to Lyricism see Elkad-Lehman, "Tmurot poʾetiyot."

10. Here I rely on Lisitzky's claim; he even adds that the translation is not faithful. And see Ephraim E. Lisitzky, "Vigvamim shotkim" (Silent wigwams) *Masad: maʿasef l-divray sifrut 2* (Masad: an anthology of literary issues, 2), ed.

Hillel Bavli (New York: Ḥaverim; Tel-Aviv: Mitzpeh, 1936), 340–341. I have added Efros's observation with some trepidation in light of his testimony, whose veracity I was unable to substantiate thus far, that he read a similar tale in an unspecified source.

11. Also noted by Steiner, who mistakenly attributes the opera to Verdi: Moshe Steiner, "Motivim indi'aniyim ba-shirah ha-ʿivrit-Americanit" (Indian motifs in Hebrew-American poetry), *Divray ha-congres ha-ʿolami ha-shishi l-madaʿay ha-yahadut* (Proceedings of the sixth world congress of Jewish studies), vol. 3, ed. Avigdor Shin'an (Jerusalem: Ha-'igud Ha-ʿolami L-madaʿay Ha-yahadut, 1977), 506. M. Weingrad has noted the story's movie-like qualities in "Lost Tribes: The Indian in American Hebrew Poetry," *Prooftexts* 24, no. 3 (Fall 2004): 310. While I could not locate an exact version of the name Lalari outside of Efros's work, it resembles similar-sounding extant mellifluous names of Indians that may have also inspired his construction, such as "Leelinau"; see Henry Rowe Schoolcraft, *Schoolcraft's Ojibwa Lodge Stories*, ed. Philip P. Mason (East Lansing: Michigan State University Press, 1997), 5, 171 n39, and "Leelinau: A Chippewa Tale," in Henry R. Schoolcraft, *The Myth of Hiawatha and Other Oral Legends* (Philadelphia: J. B. Lippincott and Company, 1856), 299–301; or "Lelawala," the name of the last maiden sacrificed by being sent over the Niagara Falls in 1679; see Charles M. Skinner, ed., *Myths and Legends of Our Own Land*, 4th ed., vol. 1 (Philadelphia: J. B. Lippincott Company, 1896), 61.

12. Mentioned are the months of Kislev (68), Shvat (72), and Iyar (77).

13. Including most recently Michael Weingrad, "Lost Tribes," 311. Possibly for the same reason, it was excerpted for instruction in a Hebrew day-school text: in Tzvi Scharfstein, ed., *Shaʿar la-sifrut* (Gateway to literature) (New York: Shilo, 1947), 135–137. Also see Barukh Katznelson, "Vigvamim shotkim," *Hado'ar*, year 14, vol. 15, no. 7 (8 Tevet 5695; 14 December 1935), 125–126; M. Steiner, "Motivim indi'aniyim," 506.

14. For discussion and a useful though somewhat dated bibliography of this mode of represented speech, see my Hebrew study, *Ha-gibor b-ʿeynay ruḥo: omanut ha-siper shel ʿAgnon b-'oreaḥ nata la-lun* (The hero in his own eyes: narrative art in Agnon's *A Guest for the Night*) (Tel-Aviv: Eked, 1985), 107, 132–133.

15. For example, Stith Thompson, "The Indian Legend of Hiawatha," in Carleton Brown, ed., *Publications of the Modern Language Association of North America* 37 (1922), 128–140; Cornelius Matthews, ed., *Hiawatha and Other Legends of the Wigwams of the Red American Indians* (London: W. Swan Sonnenschain and Co., n.d.).

16. See his early play, *The Bloody Jest: A Drama in Four Acts* (Boston: Gorham Press/Richard G. Badger, 1922).

17. Readers have pointed to analogical language between episodes in "Vigvamim" and Mishnaic discussion: Ephraim E. Lisitzky, "Vigvamim shotkim," 334–343; Avraham Epstein, *Sofrim ʿivrim ba-'America* (Hebrew writers in America), 2 vols. (Tel-Aviv: Dvir, 1952), 76; reprinted in Yitzḥak Orpaz, et al., eds., *Israel*

Efrat: mshorer v-hogeh (Israel Efros: poet and thinker) (Tel-Aviv: Tel-Aviv University, 1981), 50.

18. Notes about this chapter are housed at Gnazim; Ghela Efros Scharfstein, the poet's daughter told me that he had plans to compose additional works that survey the history of the United States; interview notes from July 1996 in her Tel-Aviv residence.

19. *Kitvay Israel Efrat: sefer rishon: min ha-ʿolam he-ḥadash—shnay shirim* (The writings of Israel Efros: book one: from the new world—two poems) (Tel-Aviv: Dvir, 1966), 5.

20. Efros took an active role in several capacities during and immediately following the Holocaust. He was among the delegates to visit Jewish refugees rescued and brought to Fort Ontario in Oswego, New York, which inspired a number of poems in his large collection about the Holocaust. He also was among the delegates investigating DP camps immediately following the Holocaust, serialized in *Hadoʾar* and published in Yiddish as *Heimlose Yidn* (Homeless Jews) (Buenos Aires, 1947), as testified by Jacob Kabakoff in "Israel Efros: Poet-Philosopher (On the Occasion of His 80th Birthday)," *Jewish Book Annual* 28 (1970–1971), 107. On the Jews at Fort Ontario, see Ruth Gruber, *Haven: The Unknown Story of 1,000 World War II Refugees* (New York: Coward-McCann, 1983). A comprehensive study of American Hebrew writers' response to the Holocaust is beyond the scope of the present work and is currently in preparation to be published separately.

21. S. Y. Penueli, "Shirah ʿivrit rḥokah-krovah—ʾVigvamim shotkimʾ v-ʾZahavʾ l-Israel Efrat" (Close-distant Hebrew poetry: "Silent wigwams" and "Gold" by Israel Efros), *Ha-galgal* (29 Tammuz 5704; 20 July 1944): 21–22.

22. Imanuʾel Bin-Gurion, "Shirah v-lashon" (Poetry and language), *Davar*, 25 March 1955.

23. Ibid.: "ʿogmat shirav ha-liriyim-ʿamamiyim, b-ḥayay shirim kimʿat moderniyim."

24. Efros was ordained as a Conservative rabbi and held pulpits in Baltimore, Buffalo, and Chicago.

25. Israel Efrat, *Zahav* (Gold) (New York: Sfarim, and Keren L-Tarbut B-Cincinnati, 1942)—due to the greater accessibility of this long work in the poet's collected works issued later, all references will be from the latter, Israel Efrat, "Zahav" (Gold) in *Min haʿolam he-ḥadash*, 119–249.

26. See "Yellow Fever" (1848), O.P.Q. (anonymous), 92–93, and "Westward," by Velma Caldwell Melville, in Alfred Powers, ed., *Poems of the Covered Wagons* (Portland, Oregon: Pacific Publishing House, 1947), 92–94.

27. "Zahav," 125, 134, 195; as part of their Americanization, many authors and poets presented full or partial translations of American popular songs. Among these, for example, are: "Old Folks at Home" ("Way Down upon the Swanee River") in Reuben Avinoam (Grossman), *Av u-vito: sipur* (Father and daughter: a tale) (Tel-Aviv: Mitzpeh, 1934), 132. In "Zahav," Efros also adds lullaby songs, which may be translations, 176–177, 239. Bavli mentions American songs by name

without translating them—"My Country 'Tis of Thee" and "The Star Spangled Banner"—in "Mrs. Woods," and see Hillel Bavli, *Shirim* (Poems), in 2 vols. (Tel-Aviv: Dvir, 1938), 136–145, esp. 141.

28. In another poem, "The Young Sailor," Efros strikes an analogy to his long poems as well. His protagonist who goes out in quest of hills of gold is destroyed by the same greed that dwells in the hearts of Tom and Lundt. Also see Elkad-Lehman, "Tmurot po'etiyot," 92.

29. For more details see Elkad-Lehman.

CHAPTER THREE

1. T. Carmi and Robert Friend, "By Way of a Preface," and "Introduction," in Gabriel Preil, *Sunset Possibilities and Other Poems*, trans. and with an intro. Robert Friend (Philadelphia: Jewish Publication Society, 1985), xiii–xv, xvii–xxiii; Yael Feldman, *Modernism and Cultural Transfer* (Cincinnati: Hebrew Union College Press, 1985); and Dan Miron, "Beyn ha-ner la-kokhavim: ʿal shirat Gavriel Preil" (Between candle and stars: on the poetry of Gavriel Preil), in Gavriel Preil, *Asfan stavim: shirim 1972–1992* (Collector of autumns: collected poems 1972–1992) (Jerusalem: Mosad Bialik, 1993), 273–381.

2. *Mdurot doʿakhot* (New York: ʿOgen, 1937); translated also as "Dying Embers," in A. R. Malachi, "Ephraim Lisitzky—Pioneer Poet," trans. Rose Brener, *Jewish Ledger* (New Orleans) 1, 51 (c. 1954); and as "Smouldering [and Smoldering] Fires," under "Lisitzky, Ephraim E.," in John Simons, ed., *Who's Who in American Jewry* (New York: National News Association, 1938), 3:671; and in "Ephraim Lisitzky, Hebrew Poet, Translator and Educator, Dies," *New York Times*, 27 June 1962, Obituary section.

3. Discussion of his other poems is in a number of locations in this study. The story of Johnny Appleseed is incorporated into his poem, "Ḥasidim b-'umot ha-ʿolam" (The righteous of the world), in *Kmo ha-yom rad: shirim* (As the day set: poems) (Tel-Aviv: Maḥbarot L-sifrut, 1960), 72–204, esp. 283–300; as to this, see Daniel Persky, "Mi-zimrat America ha-ʿivrit . . . B.) b-shevaḥ yetzirato shel Ephraim E. Lisitzky" (From the song of Hebrew America . . . B. in praise of E. E. Lisitzky's work), *Hado'ar*, year 41, vol. 42, no. 10 (29 Tevet 5722; 5 January 1962): 148. A translated excerpt of Lisitzky's poem of Native American origins, "On the banks of the Niagara," appears in A. R. Malachi, "Ephraim Lisitzky—Pioneer Poet," 51; the article is a translation of A. R. Malakhi, "Ephraim E. Lisitzky (l-yovlo)" (E. E. Lisitzky: on his anniversary), *Hado'ar*, year 33, 34, no. 12 (18 Shvat 5714; 22 January 1954): 221–222.

4. S. Bass, "Mdurot doʿakhot," *Gilyonot*, year 3, no. 5 (29) (Tammuz 5697; 1937): 441–443; a similar view, reflecting Lisitzky's own words as phrased in his introduction, is presented in articles by Agaf, Dar, Kariv, and Silberschlag. In these, they describe, without further elaboration, Lisitzky's work on the Indians as being founded on folkloristic sources. And see: M. Agaf, "E. E. Lisitzky (shmo-

nim shanah l-huladeto)" (E. E. Lisitzky: Eighty years since his birth), *Ḥazut* (21 January 1965); Y. A. Dar, "Shnay kolot ba-shirah ha-ʿivrit ('kmo rad ha-yom' [*sic*] l-Ephraim E. Lisitzky v-'ha-kol mi-baʿad la-ʿanaf' l-S. Zamir)" (Two voices in Hebrew poetry ["As the day set" by E. E. Lisitzky and "The sound through the branch" by S. Zamir]), *Yediʿot Aḥaronot* 8670, 12 August 1960, "Shivʿah Yamim," p. 6; Avraham Kariv, "ʿIm sfarim—Ephraim E. Lisitzky: Mdurot doʿakhot" (Among books—E. E. Lisitzky: dying campfires), *Davar* no. 3789 (5 November 1937), p. 7; Eisig Silberschlag, "L-ʿEphraim E. Lisitzky ben ha-shivʿim va-ḥamesh: saba shel shiratenu ba-ʾAmerica" (To the seventy-five year old E. E. Lisitzky: grandfather of our poetry in America), *Hadoʾar*, year 39, vol. 40, no. 22 (11 Nisan 5720; 8 April 1960): 400. Abraham Epstein, in his survey of Hebrew writers in America, also repeats Lisitzky's introductory words that *Mdurot doʿakhot* is a collection of folk-tales, legends, beliefs, and Indians' ways that the poet collected and combined into a single whole. Epstein, however, does not amplify or specify beyond this generalization. Avraham Epstein, *Sofrim ʿivrim ba-ʾAmerica* (Hebrew writers in America) (Tel-Aviv: Dvir, 1952), 39–65, esp. 56, 57, 63.

Adir Cohen repeats similar words in his survey of Lisitzky's literary contributions. Lisitzky, asserts Cohen, "draws on Indian mythology and blends reality with legend, idyll with dramatic plot": Adir Cohen, "ʿOlam yetzirato shel Ephraim E. Lisitzky (bi-mlot lo shivʿim va-ḥamesh shanah)" (E. E. Lisitzky's creative world: upon his seventy-fifth birthday), *Gazit* 18, no. 1–2 (May 1960): 16–18; also Yaʿakov Miklishansky, *Toldot ha-sifrut ha-ʿivrit ba-ʾAmerica* (History of Hebrew literature in America) (Jerusalem: Reuven Mass and ʿOgen, 1967), 48; and Yaʿakov Kabakoff, *Shoḥarim v-neʾemanim: masot u-meḥkarim ʿal ha-sifrut vha-tarbut ha-ʿivrit ba-ʾAmerica* (Seekers and stalwarts: essays and studies on American Hebrew literature and culture) (Jerusalem: Reuven Mass, 1978), 172. For the latest example of this ongoing propensity to echo the poet's words see Sarah Feinstein, "Ephraim E. Lisitzky—dyokan ha-moreh vha-mshorer ha-ʿivri b-ʾartzot ha-brit" (Ephraim E. Lisitzky—portrait of the Hebrew teacher and poet in the United States), *Hador: Hebrew Annual of America* 2 (2008): 126–131.

5. S. Y. Pineles, "Sifrutenu ha-ḥadashah ba-ʾAmerica: shirat Ephraim E. Lisitzky" (Our new literature in America: the poetry of E. E. Lisitzky), *Gilyonot* 15, no. 3 (Av–Elul 5703; 1943): 138–141; S. Y. Penueli, "Bi-sdeh sefer: adam ʿal adamot" (In the field of books: man on earth), *Gilyonot* 22, no. 7–8 (Adar–Nisan 5708; 1948): 62–64.

6. Yaʿakov Kabakoff, "Mi-shirat mhagrim l-shirah Americaʾit (li-mlot 10 shanim li-ftirato shel E. E. Lisitzky)" (From immigrant to American poetry: ten years since the death of E. E. Lisitzky), *Hadoʾar*, year 51, vol. 52, no. 28 (27 Sivan 5732; 9 June 1972): 473; also his seminal study, *Shoḥarim v-neʾemanim*, 167–172; Shmuʾel Blumenfeld (Samuel Blumenfield), "L-zikhro shel Ephraim E. Lisitzky: klil kotzim—klil tifʾeret" (In memory of E. E. Lisitzky: a crown of thorns—a crown of glory), *Hadoʾar*, year 42, 43, no. 27 (23 Iyar 5723; 17 May 1963): 495–496; Eisig Silberschlag, "Ha-shirah ha-ʿivrit ba-ʿolam he-ḥadash" (Hebrew poetry in

the new world), *Aḥisefer*, ed. S. Niger and M. Ribalow (New York: Keren Louis LaMed, 5704; 1944), 240. Also, Samuel Blumenfield, "Ephraim Lisitzky—American Hebrew Bard," *Chicago Jewish Forum* (Spring 1964): 204–207.

7. Gershon Shaked, *Panim aḥerot bi-ytzirato shel S. Y. Agnon* (Another aspect in the writing of S. Y. Agnon) (Tel-Aviv: Ha-kibbutz Ham'uḥad, 1989), 91 etc.; Yeshayah (Isaiah) Rabinowitz, "Yetzirato shel Ephraim E. Lisitzky" (E. E. Lisitzky's work), *Bitzaron* 41, no. 4 (Adar 5720; February–March 1960): 188–200, esp. 196; for a similar idea see Zvulun Ravid, "'Elbon ha-yaldut she-lo nitkaper (l-zekher Ephraim E. Lisitzky: 23 Sivan 5722–23 Sivan 5732)" (An unforgiven childhood shame: in memory of E. E. Lisitzky, 23 Sivan 1962–23 Sivan 1972), *Hado'ar*, year 51, 51, no. 28 (27 Sivan 5732; 9 June 1972): 474–475.

8. Ruth Arazi, "The American Indian in American Hebrew Poetry" (Ph.D. diss., New York University, 1987) (in Hebrew). Although a similar generalization is made by Silberschlag, in his "Ha-shira ha-'ivrit," 240, it merely echoes the poet's words. Silberschlag does not illustrate his assertion that Lisitzky's work is "an adaptation of raw Indian folktales."

9. Arazi, "The American Indian," 94 (all translations from Arazi are mine).

10. Ibid., 96.

11. Henry Wadsworth Longfellow, "The Song of Hiawatha," in *The Poetical Works of Longfellow* (Boston: Houghton Mifflin Co., 1975), 113–164.

12. Susan Williams, "Inaugural pow wow to bring remembrance, renewal, awareness" (Bloomington, Indiana), *IU Home Pages* 6, issue 10, Friday 1 March 2002, p. A1; Fergus M. Bordewich, *Killing the White Man's Indian: Reinventing Native Americans at the End of the Twentieth Century* (New York: Doubleday, 1966), 19.

13. Arazi, "The American Indian," 97; Ernest J. Moyne, *Hiawatha and Kalevala* 80, no. 2 of *FF Communications* (Helsinki: Soumalainen Tiedeakatemia Academic Scientiarum Fennica, 1963). The meter is also recognized by M. Steiner, who, without identifying any specific Indian folktales as being at the root of this composition, notes the powerful link in the plot between love and death. He also notes another link to Longfellow's work in that Lisitzky's composition, too, is comprised of twenty-two chapters (or cantos) and an introduction: Moshe Steiner, "Motivim indi'aniyim ba-shirah ha-'ivrit-Americanit" (Indian motifs in Hebrew-American poetry), *Divray ha-congres ha-'olami ha-shishi l-mada'ay ha-yahadut*, 3 (Proceedings of the sixth world congress of Jewish studies, vol. 3), ed. Avigdor Shin'an (Jerusalem: Ha-'igud Ha-'olami L-mada'ay Ha-yahadut, 1977), 509. The Ashkenazi rhyme is not merely assumed to retain the Longfellow-esque similarity, as he employed a trochaic dimeter, or tetrameter of Schoolcraft (p. 314), but it was needed to establish Ashkenazi rhymes such as "peres" (vulture) with "tif'eres" (glory)—for example (p. 66).

14. All evidence indicates that Lisitzky read Longfellow's poem in the original prior to preparing his own, which he also acknowledges in his introduction.

However, his first encounter with it may have been in the 1913 Hebrew translation prepared by S. Tschernichowsky, one of the Hebrew poets he admired most. Tschernichowsky, who together with Ḥ. N. Bialik comprised the two pillars of Hebrew poetry in the period known as *teḥiyah*, the national renaissance, had significant impact on Lisitzky, as on other American Hebrew poets. Tschernichowsky, more than most Hebrew poets, prepared translations of world masterpieces, epic poetry in particular, for Hebrew readers. And though not fully in imitation of his work in this sphere, Lisitzky and his predecessors may have been inspired by his attainments to pursue their depiction of other life and cultures of Indians and Blacks in the New World. To judge from the prolific literary and critical reaction to Tschernichowsky's translation of "The Song of Hiawatha," the resonance to his rendition lasted many decades in Hebrew letters. The impact of this work, then, may have been more inspirational on Lisitzky than the accolades to Longfellow in English, which by the early twentieth century became gradually diluted by harsh criticism and a new modernism in American poetry. Lisitzky's admiration of Longfellow is also discernible by an observation he made in a letter to the Hebrew poet Gabriel Preil, dated 15 August 1954, in which Lisitzky tells of a visit he made to his brother-in-law (no name provided) in St. Paul, Minnesota, noting that "his home stood not far from the Minnehaha waterfall" ("V-lo raḥok beyto mi-mapal Minnehaha") (Gnazim, no. 4966/11).

15. Charles G. Leland and John D. Prince, eds. and trans., *Kuloskap the Master and Other Algonquin Poems* (New York: Funk and Wagnalls Co., 1902); Charles G. Leland, *The Algonquin Legends of New England* (Boston: Houghton, Mifflin and Co., 1885).

16. Leland and Prince, *Kuloskap*, 11.

17. Ibid., 12.

18. Ibid., 16.

19. Daniel G. Brinton, *The Lenape and Their Legends* (New York: AMS Press, 1969), 159–160. For more on the Walam Olum (or Wallum-Olum), see Lewis Spence, *The Myths of the North American Indians* (New York: Dingwall-Rock Limited, 1927?), 77–78. For a more general work, see George W. Cronyn, ed., *American Indian Poetry: An Anthology of Songs and Chants* (New York: Liveright, 1962).

20. *Mdurot*, 13–20.

21. On vision quests—also performed by Hiawatha, in canto V of "The Song of Hiawatha"—see Henry Rowe Schoolcraft, *Schoolcraft's Indian Legends*, ed. Mentor L. Williams (East Lansing, Michigan: Michigan State University Press, 1956), 36, 47, 49; the same text is also preserved in the reprint of the 1839 edition: Henry Rowe Schoolcraft, *Algic Researches: Indian Tales and Legends*, 2 vols. (New Introduction by W. K. McNeil. Baltimore: Clearfield Company, 1992); and Charles M. Skinner, *Myths and Legends of Our Own Land*, vol. 2, 4th edition (Philadelphia: J. B. Lippincott Co., 1896), 158; compare these to Lisitzky, *Mdurot*, 97–98. For an alternate account of the practice see Lame Deer, "The Vision Quest," in *The*

Sound of Flutes and Other Indian Legends, ed. Richard Erdoes (New York: Pantheon Books, 1976), 63–67; or Richard Erdoes and Alfonso Ortiz, eds., *American Indian Myths and Legends* (New York: Pantheon Books, 1984), 69–72. However, the practice of calling forth a dream, or an explanation of one, is a familiar theme among observant, especially Hasidic, Jews. On the practice, termed "Sh'elat ḥalom," see Shmu'el Yosef Agnon, "'Agunot," *Elu v-'elu* (These and those) (Tel Aviv and Jerusalem: Schocken, 1966), 415; English version in Alan Mintz and Anne Golomb Hoffman, eds., *A Book That Was Lost and Other Stories* (New York: Schocken, 1995), 46. These folkloristic practices are borne out also by early explorers of the Americas. See, for example, Francisco Lopez de Gomara, *Sefer ha-'indi'ah ha-ḥadashah v-sefer Fernando Cortes [1553]: nosaḥ 'ivri shel toldot Peru u-Mexico bi-yday Yosef Hakohen [1568]* (History of New India and Mexico [1553] Hebrew version [1568] by Yosef Hakohen), ed. Moshe Lazar (Lancaster, California: Labyrinthos, 2002).

22. For variant tales of the origins of the Medicine Man see Spence, *Myths*, 230–232, 249–251, 354; James Mooney, *James Mooney's History, Myth, and Sacred Formulas of the Cherokees*, New Introduction by George Ellison (Ashville, N.C.: Historical Images/Bright Mountain Books, 1992), 25–52; William T. Corlett, *The Medicine-Man of the American Indian and His Cultural Background* (Baltimore: Charles C. Thomas, 1935); "The Grizzly Bear's Medicine," in George Bird Grinnell, *The Punishment of the Stingy and Other Indian Stories* (New York: Harper and Brothers Publishers, 1901), 87–113, esp. 107–109; and "How Medicine Began," in Hitakonanu'laxk (Tree Bear), ed., *The Grandfathers Speak: Native American Folk Tales of the Lenape People* (New York: Interlink Books, 1994), 60–62.

23. *Shirim* (Poems) (New York: Ḥaverim; Tel-Aviv: Dvir, 1928); these, too, may have been preceded by published poetry in periodicals. Lisitzky's early treatment of Indian tales mirrors his lyrical, poetic inclinations, as the poet considers his own condition by recollecting those ancient tales. A case in point is the immediate discussion on his "Maiden of the Falls." However, he also published a direct translation of an Algonquin creation story which, unlike the former comment, does not address any aspect of the poet himself. This translation, soon after publication of "Maiden of the Falls," indicates how the effect of an unmediated presentation of the exotic world is attained, and may have been a step in the poet's evolving strategy of presenting that world as if from within, which led to the next logical step, constructing a fictitious scaffolding upon which to suspend many authentic tales. And see Ephraim Lisitzky, "Agadat ha-bri'ah asher la-'Alganquinim (min ha-mitologya ha-hodit)" (The Algonquin creation legend: from Indian mythology), *Hado'ar*, year 9, 10, no. 10 (3 Tevet 5690; 3 January 1930): 163.

24. "Maiden of the Falls," *Shirim* (Poems), 90–91. In Indian lore, the sacrificed maiden is deemed the Bride of Manitou, and see Charles Skinner, *Myths and Legends*, 61–62; the account is retold as "The Sacrifice at Niagara Falls," in Margot Edmonds and Ella E. Clark, eds., *Voices of the Winds: Native American Legends* (New York: Facts on File, 1989), 336–337.

25. "On Niagara's shore," *Shirim* (Poems), 92–98.

26. Ephraim Lisitzky to Yitzḥak Lamdan, 5 June 1951, Gnazim, catalogue number 17841/1.

27. *Mdurot*, 3.

28. Ibid.

29. Ibid., 4.

30. *Eleh toldot adam* (These are the tales of man) (Jerusalem: Mosad Bialik, 1949), 287.

31. In his anthology *ʿAleh, ʿolam, b-shir* (Rise, O world, in song) (New York: ʿOgen; Boston: Boston Hebrew College, 1946), 107–122.

32. Composed in poetic form in his *Kmo ha-yom rad*, 300–304; retold in prose form in his *Bi-shvilay ḥayim v-sifrut* (In the paths of life and literature) (Tel-Aviv: Maḥbarot L-sifrut and ʿOgen, 1961), 190–191.

33. So noted by Menaḥem Ribalow, *Ktavim u-mgilot* (Writings and scrolls) (New York: ʿOgen, 1942), 183–189, esp. 187–188.

34. *Bi-shvilay*. 60–72.

35. Ibid., 70.

36. Ibid., 60.

37. Ibid., 62.

38. Ibid.

39. Daniel Leeming and Jake Page, *The Mythology of Native North America* (Norman, Oklahoma: University of Oklahoma Press, 1998), 16.

40. Henry Rowe Schoolcraft, *Indian Legends*, 31–33. For a discussion of variants and revisions of the account, see there, n. 1, p. 33. The folktale is similar to the Shawnee tale "The Star Family or Celestial Sisters," in Henry R. Schoolcraft, *The Myth of Hiawatha and Other Oral Legends* (Philadelphia: J. B. Lippincott and Co., 1856), 116–120. In the same source (335–339), the author presents the original Indian song on which the tale in prose is based. Another variant is the "Chippeways" [*sic*] story "The Star Maiden," in Spence, *North American Indians*, 152–156, which has an attractive color illustration, p. 154.

41. Schoolcraft, *Indian Legends*, 31; similar in his *Algic Researches*, 68.

42. Schoolcraft, *Indian Legends*, 15.

43. The name Nemissah is taken from the name of the Star Maiden in Spence, *North American Indians*, 156–159, though Lisitzky does not use the story of the Star Maiden as told there. Moreover, Lisitzky uses the name of the hunter of the Star Maiden, Algon, for another purpose, and replaces it with Nanpiwati, and see Spence, 152–156. Lisitzky's Algon is a tribal elder who tells the stories of the Sacred Bear Spear (229–231) and of Kwakigala (231–233).

44. *Mdurot*, 18–21, esp. 18–19.

45. Preil called Lisitzky the most American of Hebrew poets, presumably in thematic rather than formal terms, and see Gavriel Preil, "Nosaḥ-America ba-shirah ha-ʿivrit" (American style in Hebrew poetry), *Mtzudah* 7 (1954): 498.

46. On Smilansky, see Gila Ramras Rauch, *The Arab in Israeli Literature* (Bloomington: Indiana University Press, 1989).

47. Compare Spence, *North American Indians*, 190–193, with Lisitzky's *Mdurot*, 179–189.

48. Spence, 190.

49. Compare Spence, 191, with Lisitzky, *Mdurot*, 180b.

50. Thus, Dog Soldiers are "older warriors of high standing," according to Natalie Curtis [Burlin], *The Indians' Book* (New York: Harper and Brothers Publishing, 1923), 31. Compare also to the account concerning the White Dog Feast in William M. Beauchamp, ed., *Iroquois Folk Lore: Gathered from the Six Nations of New York*, Empire State Historical Publications, no. 31 (Port Washington, N.Y.: Ira J. Friedman, Inc., 1965), 182–189, as an Iroquois (Onondaga) ceremony. A similar ritual, among Lakota (Sioux) Indians, is described in Curtis, ibid., 58–59. Finally, a reference to the practice of sacrificing a white dog as part of the New Year ceremonies, though said to be relatively modern, as noted by Beauchamp, ibid., 39, is retained by Lisitzky, *Mdurot*, 82ff.

51. *Mdurot*, 182a.

52. Ibid., 308.

53. Spence, *North American Indians*, 377, 122.

54. Another version of the story is "The Grizzly Bear's Medicine," in Grinnell, *The Punishment*, 87–113, esp. 107–109. It is the same as the poet's tendency in the episode concerning the bringing of fire to the Indians, and see my article "To Be as Others: E. E. Lisitzky's Re-presentation of Native Americans," *Hebrew Union College Annual* 73 (2002): 249–297.

55. Chapter 11, 143–144.

56. The poet has based his account on a tale of the Knisteneaux Indians recorded in Katharine B. Judson, *Myths and Legends of the Mississippi Valley and the Great Lakes* (Chicago: A. C. McClurg and Co., 1914), 94. The very presence in this collection of the two tales, of the origins of fire and the flood story, in accounts whose details parallel closely those presented by Lisitzky, is strong evidence that the poet had this anthology in hand while working on his poem. For variants on the flood account as here presented, see there, 90–91, 93; in addition, see also Charles M. Skinner, "Pipestone," in *Myths and Legends*, 2: 162–164; Katherine B. Judson, *Myths and Legends of the Great Plains* (Chicago: A. C. McClurg and Co., 1913), 26–27; Albert B. Reagan, *Some Flood Myths of the Indians*, vol. 2 of *The Sun God—Moccasin Tales* (Provo, Utah: Albert B. Reagan, 1936); on the prevalence of the use of pipestone from Red Pipe-stone Rock, a site located in Minnesota, see Spence, *North American Indians*, 116–118. It is from this location that the peace pipes of many tribes have been fashioned, a sacred location to which many adults have made pilgrimage. According to an Ojibwa tale, the peace pipe is made in imitation of the pipe originally fashioned by Gitche Manito, as per Judson, *Great Lakes*, 90–91. In "The Song of Hiawatha," the redness of the rock is attributed

to the blood of the buffalo hunted there by Gitche Manito. This pipestone bears the scientific term Catlinite, named after the discoverer of the location, George Catlin.

57. Judson, *Great Lakes*, 94; also see Curtis, *Indians' Book*, 4–7; for a Mojave-Apache version of the story, see Curtis, 330–331.

58. *Mdurot*, 144–145.

59. Ibid., 145. For a similar stylistic formula compare Nemissah's oath of faithfulness to Nanpiwati, discussed above, *Mdurot*, 127.

60. Ibid., 145–152.

61. Compare "The White Stone Canoe," in Schoolcraft, *Indian Legends*, 246–248, with Lisitzky, *Mdurot*, chapter 12, 155–161. Similar accounts include "The Journey to the Island of Souls," in W. W. Gibbings, ed., *Folklore and Legends, North American Indians* (London: W. W. Gibbings, 1890; reprint, Felinfach, Wales: Llanerch Publishers, 1993), 129–133; a similar Algonquin tale is in Spence, *North American Indians*, 162–165. Also see Schoolcraft, *The Myth of Hiawatha*, 223–227; a variant to this tale is "The Man Who Went to Spirit-Island," in George A. Dorsey, *The Pawnee Mythology* (Lincoln, Nebraska: University of Nebraska Press, 1997), 411–413.

62. *Mdurot*, 155.

63. The white stone canoe appears to have its origins in the image of the birch bark canoe of Canadian or upper New York State Indian tales, the color often also signifying peace. Hiawatha steps into a white canoe as he begins his last journey and rises to heaven. See Beauchamp, *Iroquois Folklore*, 85–86, 98–99; also Schoolcraft, *The Myth of Hiawatha*, 223–227. The Hebrew term *livnah* indicates "whiteness" or "clearness." And see Reuven Avinoam (Grossmann), *Compendious Hebrew-English Dictionary*, ed. M. H. Segal (Tel Aviv: Dvir, 1962), 167. The term, combined as "livnat ha-sapir," is also the title of an early (1328) Kabbalistic work, according to Gershom Scholem, *Major Trends in Jewish Mysticism* (New York: Schocken Books, 1941), 386, n. 14. The term is also associated with representations of the celestial throne among mystics, inspired, no doubt, by Exodus 24:10.

64. Schoolcraft, *Indian Legends*, 247.

65. *Mdurot*, 159b.

66. Ibid., 161a.

67. Ibid., 159a.

68. Schoolcraft, *Indian Legends*, 247.

69. *Mdurot*, 160–161.

70. Schoolcraft, *Indian Legends*, 248.

71. *Mdurot*, 162.

72. Ephraim E. Lisitzky, *B-ma'alot uv-moradot* (Ascents and descents) (Tel-Aviv: Dvir, 1954), 30–31.

73. *Eleh toldot adam*, 287; translation, *In the Grip of Cross Currents*, trans. Moshe Kohn and Jacob Sloan, and revised by the author (New York: Bloch Publishing Co., 1959, 2001), 300.

74. The English translation of this poem, by Maurice Samuel, is in *Complete Poetic Works of Ḥ. N. Bialik*, vol. 1, ed. Israel Efros (New York: Histadruth Ivrith of America, 1948), 103–119.

75. *Adam ʿal adamot: poʾemot* (Man on earth: poemas), intro. M. Ribalow (New York: ʿOgen, 1947), 155–223.

76. Ibid., 184–194.

77. Ibid., xiv.

78. Ibid., 186–187.

79. Ibid., 191.

80. Ibid., 281; *In the Grip*, 290.

81. Lisitzky, *Kmo hayom rad*, 204–211, esp. 206.

82. The tale originated among the Snohomish Indians, drawn from a report by Chief William Shelton, "Pushing Up the Sky," in Ella E. Clark, ed., *Indian Legends of the Pacific Northwest* (Berkeley: University of California Press, 1953), 148–149. An earlier source for this tale is in Hermann Haeberlin, "Mythology of Puget Sound," *Journal of American Folk-Lore* 37, nos. 143–144 (January-June 1924): 371–438, especially "Origin of the Exclamation 'Yahu!,'" 417. It seems that Lisitzky used the more accessible version, though the greater brevity of the latter is matched by his account as well, indicating that he had access to both. The similarity of the first source to the Lisitzky rendition is in the resemblances of the two accounts, though the Hebrew version omits place names and secondary details. For a more distant variant, where the sky is pushed up magically as the hero rubs tobacco into a fine powder, see the Dieguenos Indian tale, "The Story of Creation," in Edmonds and Clark, *Voices of the Winds*, 145–146, drawn from Constance G. Du Bois, "The Story of Creation," *Journal of American Folk-Lore* 14 (1901): 181. Ephraim E. Lisitzky, "Yaha! harimu ha-shamayim (divray pridah mi-tokh prishah)" (Yahu! lift up the sky: parting words at retirement), *Hadoʾar*, year 39, 40, no. 23 (2 Iyar 5720; 29 April 1960): 435–436, 441; Lisitzky, *Bi-shvilay ḥayim v-sifrut*, 177, 191, esp. 190–191; reprinted in "Ḥasidim b-ʾumot ha-ʿolam" (The righteous among the world's nations), *Kmo ha-yom rad*, 272–304, esp. 300–304.

83. "Ḥasidim b-ʾumot ha-ʿolam," 303–304.

84. Ibid., 301–303, esp. 303.

85. Lisitzky, *Bi-shvilay*, 191.

86. Ibid., 190.

87. Ibid., 191.

88. Lisitzky, *Naftulay Elohim* (Divine struggles) (New York: ʿOgen; Tel-Aviv: Dvir, 1934). An undated fifty-six-page English abstract of this work is located at the American Jewish Archives. Possibly prepared as a proposal for publishing a translation of this unusual work in English, this carbon copy of a lost typed original is entitled "Synopsis of *Divine Struggles*—A Poetic Drama." From its appearance, it seems to have been home-made, though no evidence exists from the text itself as to the identity of the one who prepared this synopsis, when, or whether it was ever considered by a publisher. See Ephraim Lisitzky, [?], "Synopsis of

Divine Struggles—A Poetic Drama," Lisitzky Collection MSS, American Jewish Archives, Cincinnati.

CHAPTER FOUR

1. Israel Yaʿakov Schwartz, *Kentucky* (Yiddish) (New York: Shlomo Rabinovitch, 1936); I. Y. Schwartz, *Shirat Kentucky* (Kentucky song), intro. Dov Sadan (Jerusalem: Mosad Bialik, 1962). Parts of the latter appeared in print as "Me-ʾidilyot Kentucky" (Kentucky Idylls), *Ha-tkufah* 32–33, ed. Y. Silberschlag and A. Zeitlin (1948): 254–283; ibid., 34–35, ed. A. Zeitlin (1950): 288–305; *Sefer Hadoʾar: li-mlot lo 35 shanah* (The Hadoʾar Jubilee Volume: upon its 35th year) (New York, 1957): 173–175. I. J. Schwartz, *Kentucky*, trans. Gertrude W. Dubrovsky (Tuscaloosa: University of Alabama Press, 1990); also, Alan Trachtenberg, *Shades of Hiawatha: Staging Indians, Making Americans, 1880–1930* (New York: Hill and Wang, 2004). My thanks to Rachel Rubinstein for bringing the latter to my attention and to Dov-Ber Kerler for alerting me about the Yiddish volume, Sheen (Shmuʾel) Daixel, *Indianishe dertseylungen* (Indian stories) (New York: S. Daixel bukh-komitet, 1959).

2. Colin G. Calloway, Gerd Gemunden, and Susanne Zantop, eds., *Germans and Indians: Fantasies, Encounters, Projections* (Lincoln: University of Nebraska Press, 2002); Nitza Ben-Ari, "Mitos ha-yaḥid" (Myth of the loner), *Yediʿot aḥaronot*, 4 March 1974, 31.

3. See in *Lillian Morris and Other Stories* (Boston: Little, Brown, and Co., 1894), 155–176; Matthew Frye Jacobson, *Special Sorrows: The Diasporic Imagination of Irish, Polish, and Jewish Immigrants in the United States* (Cambridge, Mass.: Harvard University Press, 1995).

4. For details, see Calloway, Gemunden, and Zantop, *Germans and Indians.*

5. Bernard Malamud, *The People and Uncollected Stories*, ed. Robert Giroux (New York: Farrar Straus Giroux, 1989). Bernard Malamud, *Ha-ʿam v-sipurim aḥerim* (*The people and other stories*), trans. Ruth Livnit (Tel-Aviv: Zmora Bitan, 1993). My thanks to the Lilly Library, at Indiana University, Bloomington, for allowing me to examine the film script of Mel Brooks, producer, "Blazing Saddles."

6. Menaḥem Ribalow, *ʿIm ha-kad el ha-mabuʿa: masot bikoret* (With the pitcher to the spring: critical essays) (New York: ʿOgen, 1950), 269.

7. Shimʿon Ginzburg, "ʿAl nahar Hudson," *Shirim u-phoʾemot* (Poems and poemas) (Tel-Aviv: Aḥim/Dvir, 1931), 91–93.

8. S. Ginzburg, "No-York," ibid., 263–285. Michael Weingrad, "Lost Tribes: The Indian in American Hebrew Poetry," *Prooftexts* 24, no. 3 (Fall 2004): 293.

9. Ḥayyim Naḥman Bialik, "Ha-brekhah" (The Pool), in *Modern Hebrew Poetry: A Bilingual Anthology*, ed. and trans. Ruth Finer Mintz (Berkeley: University of California Press, 1968), 2–19.

10. Ḥ. N. Bialik, "In the City of Slaughter," see text translation and discus-

sion in Alan Mintz, *Ḥurban: Responses to Catastrophe in Hebrew Literature* (New York: Columbia University Press, 1984), 130–155; for the same translation, by A. M. Klein, see Israel Efros, ed., *Complete Poetic Works of Ḥayyim Naḥman Bialik* (New York: Histadruth Ivrith of America, 1948), 1: 129–143; another translation, "City of Killing," in Atar Hadari, ed. and trans., *Songs from Bialik: Selected Poems of Ḥayim Naḥman Bialik* (Syracuse: Syracuse University Press, 2004), 1–9.

11. Gershon Rosenzweig, *Talmud Yanka'i* (Yankee Talmud) (New York: S. Druckerman, 1907).

12. This is an authentic title of leadership among many Indians and is used by Hebraists since Silkiner's composition. Hebrew documentation to its use goes back to the sixteenth century: Francisco Lopez de Gomara, *Sefer ha-'indi'ah ha-ḥadashah v-sefer Fernando Cortes [1553]: nosaḥ Ivri shel toldot Peru u-Mexico bi-yday Yosef Hakohen [1568]* (History of new India and Mexico [1553], Hebrew version [1568] by Yosef Hacohen), ed. Moshe Lazar (Lancaster, California: Labyrinthos, 2002), 158 and others.

13. The imagery is reminiscent of Shlonsky's long poems "Jezreel" ("Yizr'el") and "Toil" ("'Amal"). And see Ruth Finer Mintz, *Modern Hebrew Poetry*, 170–187.

14. "Masada" was composed in 1923–1934 and published in 1927: Leon Yudkin, *Isaac Lamdan: A Study in Twentieth-Century Hebrew Poetry* (Ithaca: Cornell University Press, 1971), 15, 49; for a translation of "Masada," see there, 199–234. Scholars have thus far identified Lamdan's work as the first treatment of Masada in a modern Hebrew literary medium—implying, at least, that he was first to use it in a work of literature as a metaphor for a contemporary issue. On this see, for example, Baila R. Shargel, "Evolution of the Masada Myth," *Judaism* 28, no. 3 (1979): 357–371; Barry Schwartz, Yael Zerubavel, and Bernice M. Barnett, "The Recovery of Masada: A Study in Collective Memory," *Sociological Quarterly* 27, no. 2 (Summer 1986): 147–164, in which we read: "Precipitating the 1927 recovery of Masada was the appearance of a very popular poem which used the ancient battle as an allegory of the Jewish settlers' struggle [in the Land of Israel]" (147), and "The event that most effectively mobilized interest in Masada was the publication in Palestine of a poem by a Ukrainian immigrant, Yitzḥak Lamdan . . . 'Masada,' enjoyed immense popularity when it first appeared in 1927" (148); Yael Zerubavel, "The Death of Memory and the Memory of Death: Masada and the Holocaust as Historical Metaphors," *Representations* 45 (Winter 1994): 72–100. Also see Yael Zerubavel, *Recovered Roots: Collective Memory and the Making of Israeli National Tradition* (Chicago: University of Chicago Press, 1995), 60–76, 114–137, 192–213. The theme of Masada appeared in Hebrew literature on more than one occasion following Lamdan's work, among them being the play *Masada* by Avigdor Hameiri. On that, see, for example, Hillel Barzel, *Shirat Eretz Israel, kerekh shvi'i—romantikah ide'ologiyah mytologiyah* (The poetry of the land of Israel, vol. 7: romanticism, ideology, mythology) (Tel-Aviv: Sifriat Po'alim, 2006), 263–265.

15. Ya'akov Tarkow-Na'amani, "Bi-s'or ha-sa'ar," *Rsisay ḥayim (mivḥar sipurim*

u-rshimot) (Fragments of life: selected stories and sketches) (New York: ʿOgen, 1951), 69–75. The twentieth century American poet and former (1995–1996) poet laureate, Robert Hess, writes of the ongoing ghost-like presence of Indians hovering over the California landscape.

16. Ibid., 85–88. As noted in Chapter One above, any works of the period contain terms having to do with darkness, shadows, and loss of hope: Benjamin Sackler's play "Lights out of Darkness" ("Orot me-ʾofel"); the three parts of Ḥaya (Claire) Levy's poetic anthology, *Kisufim* (Longings): "Ba-ʿarov ha-yom" (As the day sets), "Manginot laylah" (Night melodies), and "Toḥelet ha-shaḥar" (Hope of sunrise); G. Preil's translated anthology, *Sunset Possibilities and Other Poems;* and his other works, including *Nof shemesh u-khfor: shirim* (Sunny vista and frost: poems); *Ner mul kokhavim: shirim* (Candle opposite stars: poems); *Mapat ʿerev: shirim* (An evening map: poems); *Ha-ʾesh vha-dmamah: shirim* (The fire and the silence: poems); *Asfan stavim: shirim 1972–1992* (Collector of autumns: collected poems 1972–1992); Simḥa Rubinstein, *Nerot doʿakhim* (Dying candles); Lisitzky, *Mdurot doʿakhot* (Dying campfires); Wallenrod, *Ki phanah yom* (For the day has waned); Efros, *Vigvamim shotkim* (Silent wigwams); and Silkiner, *Mul ohel Timmura* (Before Timmura's tent).

17. Tarkov-Naʿamani, "Shalom ʿal Israel" (Peace unto Israel) *Rsisay ḥayim*, 169–171.

18. Avraham Regelson, "Elohay ha-teva ba-shirah ha-ʾAmericaʾit" (The gods of nature in American poetry), *Mlo ha-talit ʿalim: masot v-siḥot* (A shawl full of leaves: essays and discourses) (New York: Vaʿad L-hotzaʾat Kitvay A. Regelson, 1941), 9–12, 25; reprinted in Regelson, *Rvivim va-tal: siḥot v-ʿolelot shir* (Spring showers and dew: discourses and poetry gleanings) (Tel-Aviv: ʿEked, 1980[?]), 43–60.

19. Regelson, *Rvivim va-tal*, 59–60; *Mlo ha-talit*, 23.

20. Regelson, *Rvivim va-tal*, 48; "Elohay ha-teva," 9.

21. Yet the one to identify this phenomenon, M. Steiner, does not identify any of its sources, as he avoids them in his discussions of other Hebrew poets. Regelson, "Gesher ha-sela" (The stone bridge), in *Ḥakukot otiyotayikh: shirim* (Your letters are inscribed: poems) (Tel-Aviv: Maḥbarot L-sifrut, 1964), 179; Moshe Steiner, "Motivim indiʾaniyim ba-shirah ha-ʿivrit-Americanit" (Indian motifs in Hebrew-American poetry), in *Divray ha-congres ha-ʿolami ha-shishi l-madaʿay ha-yahadut* (Proceedings of the sixth world congress of Jewish studies), vol. 3, ed. Avigdor Shinʾan (Jerusalem: Ha-ʾigud Ha-ʿolami L-madaʿay Ha-yahadut, 1977), 503–509, esp. 508–509.

22. Regelson, "ʿArafel b-kherem Marta," *Ḥakukot otiyotayikh*, 176–8; Avraham Epstein, *Sofrim ʿivrim ba-ʾAmerica* (Hebrew writers in America) (Tel-Aviv: Dvir, 1952), 145.

23. Regelson, *Beyt ha-nitzotz: marʾot v-ʾagadot* (The spark's dwelling: visions and legends) (Ramat-Gan: Dvir, 1972), 22–27.

24. Regelson, "ʿAmud ha-sheḥafim" (A pillar of Seagulls), *Ḥakukot otiyotayikh*, 12–21.

25. Regelson, *Kitvay Avraham Regelson, Sham ha-bdolaḥ: marʾot v-ʾagadot* (There is the crystal: visions and legends). New York: Vaʿad L-hotzaʾat Kitvay A. Regelson, 1942), 35–45.

CHAPTER FIVE

1. Witness a recent statement by the Israeli pop singer, Ḥavah Alberstein, describing herself as the last of the Mohicans in reference to publishing her songs in CD format: Sagi Ben Nun, "200 shirim yeshanim shel Ḥavah Albershtein roʾim or la-rishonah ʿal diskim" (200 old songs by Ḥavah Alberstein are issued for the first time on CDs), *Haʾaretz*, "Galeriyah," 5 September 2003, D2.

2. Fergus Bordewich, *Killing the White Man's Indian: Reinventing Native Americans at the End of the Twentieth Century* (New York: Doubleday, 1996), 19, 55.

3. Michael Weingrad observes the affinities between the Efros poem and cinematic images in his "Lost Tribes: The Indian in American Hebrew Poetry," *Prooftexts* 24, no. 3 (2004): 309–310. Moshe Steiner discerns a semblance of the heroine's and that of Y. L. Gordon's female protagonists. He also notes the plot's resemblance to Puccini's opera (though he erroneously attributes it to Verdi): Moshe Steiner, "Motivim indiʾaniyim ba-shirah ha-ʿivrit" (Indian motifs in Hebrew poetry), *Divray ha-congres ha-ʿolami ha-shishi l-madaʿay ha-yahadut* (Reports of the sixth world congress for Jewish studies), vol. 3 (Jerusalem, 1977), 506.

4. Yisrael Yaʿakov Schwartz, *Kentucky* (New York: Shlomo Rabinowitz, 1936); I. J. Schwartz, *Kentucky*, trans. Gertrude W. Dubrovsky (Tuscaloosa: University of Alabama Press, 1990). For more, see n. 1 in Chapter Four.

5. Avraham Shmuel Schwartz, *Shirim* (Poems) (Tel-Aviv: M. Newman, 1958), 112–114.

6. Moshe Feinshtein, *Shirim v-sonetot* (Poems and sonnets) (New York: ʿOgen, 1935), 29–30.

7. Dan Miron, "Beyn ha-ner la-kokhavim: ʿal shirat Gavriel Preil" (Between the candle and the stars: on the poetry of Gavriel Preil) in *Gavriel Preil, asfan stavim: shirim 1972–1992* (Gavriel Preil, collector of autumns: collected poems 1972–1992) (Jerusalem: Mosad Bialik, 1993), 276–288. Kabakoff, too, observes that the writing on Black and Indian themes was considered by many critics as a superficial gesture offered up by Hebrew poets in America to "pay" for the emblem of being called American: Yaʿakov Kabakoff, *Shoḥarim v-neʾemanim: masot u-meḥkarim ʿal ha-sifrut vha-tarbut ha-ʿivrit ba-ʾAmerica* (Seekers and stalwarts: Essays and studies on American Hebrew literature and culture) (Jerusalem: Reuven Mass, 1978), 173.

8. Tzvetan Todorov, *The Conquest of America: The Question of the Other*, trans.

Richard Howard (New York: Harper Torchbooks, 1987); Francisco Lopez de Gomara, *Sefer ha-ʿindia ha-ḥadashah v-sefer Fernando Cortes, nosaḥ ʿivri shel toldot Peru u-Mexico bi-yday Yosef Hakohen [1568]* (History of New India and Mexico, [1553], Hebrew version [1568] by Yosef Hakohen, edited by Moshe Lazar) (Lancaster, Calif.: Labyrinthos, 2002).

9. Miron, "Beyn ha-ner," 316.

10. Ibid.; Gavriel Preil, "Hamtanah la-maḥar ha-ʾatomi" (Awaiting the atomic tomorrow), *Yalkut shirim* (An anthology of poems), ed. Reuven ben Yosef (Tel-Aviv: Yaḥdav, 1978), 34.

11. Yitzḥak Silberschlag, "Meksiko," *ʿAleh ʿolam, b-shir* (Rise, O world, in song) (New York: ʿOgen; Boston: Boston Hebrew College, 1946), 125–128.

12. Ibid., 125. The line "zeʿeyr sham zeʿeyr sham, kiv-ḥazon" (A bit there a bit there, as in a vision) is a citation from Isaiah 28:13, often understood as a coded reference to the End of Days.

13. For example: (1) "vha-kohanim vha-ʿam" (the priests and the people) (127)—as repeated in the Ha-ʿavodah account of Yom Kippur, to refer to the rite of the High Priest, and the response of the bystanding priests and people (as in Yoma 6:2); (2) "az ʿalah b-maʿalah" (then he ascended the stairs) (127) has no clear source, though is an echo of Ezekiel 40:22, as a depiction of the Temple or altar, or just associative with a sacred place and rite. In Yoma, it is alluded to in the frequent use of "az ʿalah . . ." (then he ascended)—as in Yoma 7:3, 7:4; (3) "yekod" (flame) (127)—both as a noun derived from Isaiah 10:16; its accompanying symbol as an abbreviation is a traditional way to indicate a number, as in this poem to designate the number 114; (4) "kohen zariz v-ragil" (an adroit and experienced priest) (127) is a slight rephrasing of the "hineni" prayer of the cantor on the High Holydays; though the term *experienced* is one frequently used in Yoma.

14. As do Wallenrod, Halkin, Amichai and many others: Reuven Wallenrod, *Ki phanah yom: sipur* (For the day has waned: a story) (New York: Ohel; Tel-Aviv: M. Newman, 1946), 251–252; Shimʿon (Simon) Halkin, "Tarshishah" (To Tarshish), *ʿAl ha-ʿee: shirim* (On the island: poems) (Jerusalem: Mosad Bialik, 1946), 300–305; Yehuda Amichai, "Kayitz hodi b-Princeton" (Indian summer in Princeton), *ʿAkhshav ba-raʿash* (Now in the quake) (Jerusalem: Schocken, 1975), 145.

15. B. Isaacs, "Hi lo baʾah" (She did not come), *ʿAmos mokher tapuzim v-ʿod sipurim* (Amos sells oranges and other stories) (Tel-Aviv: M. Newman, 1953), 56–65.

16. H. Sackler, *Mashiaḥ nosaḥ America (Major Noah), Sefer ha-maḥazot* (The book of plays) (New York: ʿOgen, 1943), 269–330; also Jonathan D. Sarna, *Jacksonian Jew: The Two Worlds of Mordecai Noah* (New York: Holmes & Meier, 1981). Ararat and Noah have recently become the subject of a new novel by Nava Semmel, *Eesraʾel* (or IsraIsland), (Tel-Aviv: Yediʿot Aḥaronot, 2005). Michael Weingrad, "Messiah American Style: Mordecai Manuel Noah and the American Refuge," *AJS Review* 31, no. 1 (April 2007): 75–108.

17. Likely a reference to Moses Levi Maduro Paixotto, a "layman" and friend

in Noah's Congregation Shearith Israel, where he served as the "appointed minister," Sarna, *Jacksonian Jew*, 55.

18. In his dedication ceremony of Ararat, Noah included the decree that "Indians, 'being in all probability the descendants of the lost ten tribes of Israel,' must be made sensible to their condition and reunited with their brethren." He also labeled the Indians as "the lineal descendants of the Israelites." Cited in Sarna, *Jacksonian Jew*, 67, 70. Sackler's Black Hawk is perhaps modeled after an Indian chief by that name who was paraded around White communities in the first half of the nineteenth century, and see David Philipson, ed., *Letters of Rebecca Gratz* (Philadelphia: Jewish Publication Society of America, 1929), 166–167, 183–184.

19. Harry Sackler, *Beyn eretz v-shamayim* (Between heaven and earth) (Tel Aviv: Yavneh, 1964); the following and all subsequent translations of poetry and prose are mine.

20. See Yaʿakov Kabakoff's Hebrew article: "Hillel Bavli ha-mshorer vha-ʾadam" (Hillel Bavli: The poet and the man), *Jewish Book Annual* 20 (1962–1963): 76; restated in his study *Shoḥarim v-neʾemanim*, 174. As for Bavli's use of various names on his poetry, see testimony in his signature H. A. Rashgolin on an article "Shimshon" (Samson), *Miklat* 2, vol. 4–6 (Tevet–Adar 1920): 462; also see Aharon Ben-Or (Urinovsky), *Toldot ha-sifrut ha-ʿivrit b-dorenu: mshorerim* (History of Hebrew literature in our generation: poets) (Tel-Aviv: Izreel, 1968), 1:121. The same fact is noted by Eisig Silberschlag, *From Renaissance to Renaissance: Hebrew Literature from 1492–1970* (New York: Ktav, 1973), 1:291.

21. Corroboration and additional information available in various locations add to the confusion about his identity. The card catalogue of the National and University Library at the Hebrew University of Jerusalem also points to several names, as do the signatures accompanying several poems. Also see Selig Adler and Thomas E. Connolly, *From Ararat to Suburbia: The History of the Jewish Community of Buffalo* (Philadelphia: Jewish Publication Society of America, 1960), 241, 250. Hebrew documents regarding this plethora of identities abound, as in Hillel Bavli, "Hadoʾar lifnay shivʿim va-ḥamesh shanah: shirim—Hillel Bavli" (Hadoar 75 years ago: poems—Hillel Bavli), *Hadoʾar* 83, no. 1 (Ḥeshvan; fall 2003): 34; also Daniel Persky, *Kitvay Daniel Persky—vol. 1: ʿIvri anokhi* (The writings of Daniel Persky—vol. 1: I am a Hebrew) (New York: Ha-mḥaber, 1948), 162; G. Kressel, *Leksikon ha-sifrut ha-ʾivrit ba-dorot ha-aḥaronim* (Lexicon of Hebrew literature in recent generations) (Merḥaviah: Sifriyat Poʿalim Hakibutz Ha-ʾartzi Ha-shomer Ha-tzaʿir, 1965), 1:196; also see the card catalogue of the National and University Library of the Hebrew University of Jerusalem's manuscripts division, Shevadron Collection. Lisitzky's correspondence indicates that Bavli also went by the name of Aaron Ely Price or Prince, attested in some of his poems, such as no. 22 in A. R. Malakhi, ed., "Yetzirotav ha-piyutiyot shel Bavli" (Bavli's poetic works), and also part 5 of *Zekher l-Hillel: bibliyographiyah shel yetzirot Hillel Bavli b-shirah u-phroza u-rshimat ha-maʾamarim she-nikhtvu ʿalav v-ʿal sfarav* (In memory of Hillel: a bibliography of the poetic and prose writings of Hillel Bavli and a list of essays written

about him and his books) (New York: Alumni Association of the Teachers Institute and Seminary College of Jewish Studies of the Jewish Theological Seminary of America, 1962), 17, 54.

22. A. R. Malakhi, "L-toldot Hillel Bavli" (Biography of Hillel Bavli), parts 1–3, *Bitzaron* 44, no. 7 (Av–Elul 5721; 1961): 166–173; 45, no. 2 (Kislev–Tevet 5722; 1961): 67–75; no. 3 (Shvat–Adar 5722; 1962): 137–148.

23. Hillel Bavli, "B-mikhlalah katolit b-Buffalo" (In a Catholic college in Buffalo), *Gilyonot* 31, no. 8–10 (Av–Elul 5714; 1954): 122–126; also Lisitzky's testimony in "Hillel Bavli—Darko ba-sifrut uva-ḥayim" (Hillel Bavli: His way in literature and life), *Bitzaron* year 22, vol. 44, no. 7 (225) (Av–Elul 5721; September 1961): 161.

24. Malakhi, *Zekher l-Hillel*, 7–8; Kressel, *Leksikon*, 196.

25. From his essay of 1923, "Shirat ha-cushim" (Poetry of Blacks), *Ruḥot nifgashot: divray masah* (Intersecting spirits: essays) (New York: ʿOgen; Jerusalem: M. Newman, 1958), 280–291.

26. Also called the "New Negro Renaissance," the "Black Renaissance," and the "New Negro Movement," the Harlem Renaissance is characterized by a cultural revitalization in African American civilization in the interwar years, and see Sterling Brown, "Contemporary Negro Poetry, 1914–1936," in *Anthology of American Negro Literature*, ed. Sylvestre C. Watkins (New York: Modern Library/Random House, 1944), 243–244. Other studies include Arna Bontemps, ed., *The Harlem Renaissance Remembered* (New York: Dodd, Mead and Co., 1972); John H. Franklin and Alfred A. Moss, *From Slavery to Freedom: A History of African Americans* (New York: Alfred A. Knopf, 1994), 361–380; Mark Helbling, *The Harlem Renaissance: The One and the Many* (Westport, Conn.: Greenwood Press, 1999); Victor A. Kramer and Robert A. Russ, eds., *Harlem Renaissance Re-Examined* (New York: Whitston Publishing Co., 1997).

27. Especially A. Epstein, "Hillel Bavli," *Sofrim ʿivrim ba-ʾAmerica* (Hebrew writers in America) (Tel-Aviv: Dvir, 1952), 104–124. Confirmation of Bavli's conservatism is also made by Yitzḥak Silberschlag, "Kavim li-dmuto shel Hillel Bavli" (Outlines of Hillel Bavli's image), *Bitzaron*, year 22, vol. 44, no. 7 (225) (Av–Elul 5721; September 1961): 163. On the literary conservatism of America's Hebraists, see Uzi Shavit, "The New Hebrew Poetry of the Twenties: Palestine and America," *Prooftexts* 12, no. 3 (1992): 213–230.

28. S. Pineles, "Shirat Hillel Bavli (bi-mlot lo ḥamishim shanah)" (The poetry of Hillel Bavli: upon reaching fifty), *Gilyonot* 14, no. 12 (Nisan 5703; 1943): 291.

29. Bavli's poems "Bi-khfar Hodi," "Mormon msaper," and "Dmuyot beharim," in his *Aderet ha-shanim: shirim* (A mantle of years: poems) (Jerusalem: Mosad Bialik, 1955), 135, 124–134, 136–142.

30. "Mrs. Woods," *Shirim* (Poems), 2 vols. (Tel-Aviv: Dvir, 1938), 136–145.

31. Yeshaya Rabinowitz, "ʿAl shirat Hillel Bavli" (On Hillel Bavli's poetry), *Hadoʾar* year 37, vol. 38, no. 13 (3 Shvat 5718; 24 January 1958): 233.

32. Her views about the big city are close to Bavli's heart. They are also

echoed in the opinions of her son, featured in "Dmuyot be-harim" (Mountain images). The sentiment is also projected in Bavli's critique of S. Ginzburg's poetry in which he finds the poet's disdain for and demonization of existence in urban life represented in his "No-York" and other poems, and see Hillel Bavli, "Shimʿon Ginzburg," *Bitzaron*, year 5, vol. 10, no. 9–10 (Sivan–Tammuz 5704; June–July 1944): 168–173.

33. Gavriel Preil, "Al ha-ʾAmericaniyut shel Hillel Bavli" (Hillel Bavli's Americanism), *Bitzaron* 45, no. 2 (227) (Kislev–Tevet 5722; November–December 1961): 76–77.

34. M. Ribalow, "Hillel Bavli," *Ktavim u-mgilot* (Writings and scrolls) (New York: ʿOgen, 1942), 204–208.

35. Avraham Holtz, "Hillel Bavli—ha-ʾadam vi-ytzirato" (Hillel Bavli—The man and his work), *Niv: kli mivta l-sofrim tzʾirim* (New York) year 26, vol. 7, no. 1 (Kislev 5722; November 1961): 10–17; A. Epstein, *Sofrim ʿivrim ba-ʾAmerica*, esp. 118–119.

36. As, for example, does Kabakoff, "Hillel Bavli," 76.

37. Yitzḥak Silberschlag, "Ha-shirah ha-ʾivrit ba-ʿolam he-ḥadash (Hillel Bavli)" (Hebrew poetry in the new world [Hillel Bavli]), *Aḥisefer*, ed. S. Niger and M. Ribalow (New York: Keren Louis LaMed, 1943), 223.

38. S. Y. Pineles, "Shirat Bavli" (Bavli's poetry), 290–293. For similar views see Epstein, "Hillel Bavli," *Sofrim ʿivrim ba-ʾAmerica*, 110–111; Silberschlag, *Aḥisefer*, 221; Aharon Zeitlin, "Asefah rabat-ʿam l-zikhro shel Hillel Bavli" (Large gathering in memory of Hillel Bavli), *Hadoʾar*, year 41, vol. 42, no. 9 (24 Tevet; 19 December 1961): 139; Rabinowitz, "ʿAl shirat Hillel Bavli"; Ribalow, *Ktavim u-mgilot*, 205.

39. S. Pineles, "Shirat Bavli," 292; Ribalow, *Ktavim u-mgilot*, 207.

40. A. R. Malakhi, "L-toldot Hillel Bavli" (Biography of Hillel Bavli), part 3, esp. 137. As for Bavli's affinity for idylls see Silberschlag, "Kavim li-dmuto," 163.

41. Isaiah Rabinowitz also notes Bavli's affinity for this poet in his "ʿAl shirat Bavli," 232–233. The atmosphere is reminiscent of Tschernichowsky's idylls that also mask turbulent events by understatement, effacement, and humor, as in Ruth Finer Mintz, ed., *Modern Hebrew Poetry: A Bilingual Anthology* (Berkeley: University of California Press, 1968), 44–67. Another to point to the poem as an "exemplary idyll" is Ben-Or, *Toldot ha-sifrut*, 123–124.

42. On the interest in the Catskills as a subgenre see Myrna Frommer, *It Happened in the Catskills* (San Diego: Harcourt Brace, 1996); Phil Brown, *In the Catskills: A Century of Jewish Life in "The Mountains"* (New York: Columbia University Press, 2002); Phil Brown, *Catskill Culture: A Mountain Rat's Memories of the Great Jewish Resort Area* (Philadelphia: Temple University Press, 1998). Interest in this venue lingers among scholars, as evidenced by speakers at one session (5.4) of the 2000 and several speakers (sessions 3.9 and 5.8) of the 2007 annual conferences of the Association for Jewish Studies. Also set in these mountains are Herman Wouk's *Marjorie Morningstar* and an episode in Art Spiegelman's *Maus*.

43. Reuven Wallenrod, *Ki phanah yom;* R. Wallenrod, *B-harey ha-Catskil*

(maḥazeh) (In the Catskill Mountains: a play) act 1, *Hado'ar*, year 42, vol. 43, no. 23 (11 Nisan 5723/5 April 1963): 419–420; act 2, no. 24 (2 Iyar 5723/26 April 1963): 448; act 3, no. 25 (9 Iyar 5723/3 May 1963): 467; act 4, no. 26 (16 Iyar 5723/10 May 1963): 486; epilogue, no. 27 (23 Iyar 5723/17 May 1963): 504. English translation: Reuben Wallenrod, *Dusk in the Catskills* (New York: Reconstructionist Press, 1957).

44. S. Halkin, "Ha'arakhot v-divray bikoret: ki phanah yom" (Criticism and evaluations: for the day has waned), *Bitzaron*, year 8, vol. 15, no. 2 (86) (Ḥeshvan 5707/November 1946): 121–127. The objective or neutral perspective is a trait of Bavli's that has been discerned also by A. Z. Halevi; see Zeitlin, "Asefah rabat-ʿam" (Large gathering): 139.

45. See Bavli's essay, "Yashan v-ḥadash b-sifrutenu" (Old and new in our literature), *Sefer ha-do'ar: mivḥar ma'amarim l-yovel ha-shishim 5682–5742* (Hadoar yearbook: selected essays on its sixtieth anniversary 1922–1982), ed. Y. Miklishanski and Y. Kabakoff (New York: Histadruth Ivrith of America, 1982), 4–5. On the debate surrounding Rabinowitz's call for "Ameriq'aiyut," the Americanization of Hebrew letters, see Introduction, n. 8. Rabinowitz's 1924 essay also appears in the abovementioned *Sefer Hado'ar*, 52–54. For a recent summary of the debate, see Ezra Spicehandler, "*Ameriqa'iyut* in American Hebrew Literature," in *Hebrew in America*, ed. Alan Mintz (Detroit: Wayne State University Press, 1993), 68–104.

CHAPTER SIX

1. On the movement of Blacks to the North—which took place in a number of waves, some coinciding with the mid-nineteenth century wave of German Jewish immigration, and others with East European Jews' arrival prior to the First World War and after the Second World War—see John Hope Franklin and Alfred A. Moss, Jr., *From Slavery to Freedom: A History of African Americans*, 7th ed. (New York: Alfred A. Knopf, 1994), 235, 310–311, 340–341, 364, 424, 493, 519–520, 561–562.

2. Hillel Bavli, "Mrs. Woods," *Shirim* (Poems), 2 vols. in one (Tel-Aviv: Dvir, 5698; 1938), 136–145; Eisig Silberschlag, "Mi-pi khushim" (From the mouth of Blacks), *ʿAleh, ʿolam, b-shir* (Rise, O world, in song) (New York: ʿOgen; Boston: Boston Hebrew College, 1946), 107–122.

3. Ephraim E. Lisitzky, *B-'oholay Khush: shirim* (In the tents of Cush: poems) (Jerusalem: Mosad Bialik, 1953). By the time these poets were exposed to Longfellow, they had access to "Hiawatha" in the original, as many of the U.S.-educated were well versed in much of English literature. Those whose command of English was not firm had at their disposal the 124-page Hebrew translation of "The Song of Hiawatha," prepared by the Hebrew poet Saul Tschernichowsky in Odessa in 1913, and see Zivah Golan and Ḥavivah Yonai, eds., *Shaul Tschernichowsky: bibliographiyah* (Saul Tschernichowsky: a bibliography) (Tel-Aviv: Makhon Katz L-ḥeker Ha-sifrut Ha-ʿivrit B-'universitat Tel-Aviv, U-merkaz Ha-

hadrakhah L-sifriyot Tziburiyot, 1981), 40, n. 174. An examination of the origins, models, and influence of Longfellow's long poem on Hebrew literature is beyond the scope of this study. A few more observations have been made in this regard in Chapter Three, addressing Lisitzky's *Mdurot do'akhot.*

4. Dov Sadan, "Mavo" (Introduction), I. Y. Schwartz, *Shirat Kentucky* (Kentucky poem) (Jerusalem: Mosad Bialik, 1962), 12.

5. Bialik, for example, translated S. Ansky's *Dybbuk*, Cervantes' *Don Quixote* (1912), and Schiller's *Wilhelm Tell.* See Israel Efros, ed., *Complete Poetic Works of Ḥ. N. Bialik* (New York: Histadruth Ivrith of America, Inc., 1948), 266. Among Tschernichowsky's numerous translations are selections of the Finnish epic, or edda, *Kallevalah*, selected Serbian epics, Homer's *Iliad* and *Odyssey*, poems by Goethe, Longfellow, Pushkin, and others. For a more complete listing, see Golan and Yonai, *Tschernichowsky: bibliographiyah*, 188–189. In 1933, Lensky published a creative translation, one as yet awaiting study, of the Vogul (or Mansi) people's epic, the "Yangal Ma'ah." He claims to have reworked the epic, which appeared in Moscow, entitling it "Sefer ha-tundrah"—the Tundra Book. And see Ḥayim Lensky, "Sefer ha-tundrah," *He-'anaf ha-gadu'a: kitvay sofrim 'ivrim shebi-vrit ha-mo'atzot, 1, Ḥayim Lensky: shirim rshimot u-mikhtavim, Elisha Rodin, shirim v-hegyonot* (The severed branch: Hebrew writers' works in the Soviet Union, vol. 1, Ḥayim Lensky: poems, notes, and letters, Elisha Rodin: poems and musings), ed. Avraham Kariv (Jerusalem: Mosad Bialik, 1954), 123–157. The Vogul were an Ob Ugrian people whose territory was incorporated into the Russian state in the sixteenth century. In the years 1714–1722, they were converted to Russian Orthodoxy, with opponents killed off under a directive of Czar Peter the First (this being the content of the epic). A full study of this fascinating preoccupation by a long-neglected, though not forgotten, Hebrew poet awaits the scholar with the proper linguistic skills. On the Vogul (or Mansi), see G. F. Cushing, "Ob Ugrian (Vogul and Ostyak)," in *Traditions of Heroic and Epic Poetry*, vol. 1, *The Traditions*, ed. A. T. Hatto (London: Modern Humanities Research Association, 1980), 211–235. My appreciation to Professors Gustav Bayerle and Ron Sela of Indiana University's Department of Central Eurasian Studies for their help in directing me to some of the literature on the Vogul. Information is also available on web sites such as: http://www.suri.ee/eup/mansis.shtml; and http://www.eki.ee/books/redbook/mansis.shtml.

An example of a similar Hebrew literary project in antiquity may the Book of Job, were we to accept Tur-Sinai's thesis that it was a translation from the Aramaic, and see N. H. Tur-Sinai (Torczyner), *The Book of Job: A New Commentary* (Jerusalem: Kiryath Sepher, 1967), xxx–xl; Marvin H. Pope, introduction to *Job*, vol. 15 of *The Anchor Bible* (New York: Doubleday and Company, 1965), xlii–xlv.

6. *Eleh toldot adam* (Jerusalem: Mosad Bialik, 1949); English version, Ephraim E. Lisitzky, *In the Grip of Cross-Currents*, trans. Moshe Kohn and Jacob Sloan and revised by the author (New York: Bloch Publishing Company, 2001). All translations will be from the 2001 edition. A critical biography of this most

interesting Hebraist, his life in Europe, America, and Canada, remains to be written.

7. Ephraim E. Lisitzky, *Mdurot do'akhot* (Dying campfires) (New York: 'Ogen, 1937).

8. His first published poem, "Lullaby," appeared in *Ha-le'om*, in 1904, according to A. R. Malachi, "Ephraim Lisitzky—Pioneer Poet," trans. Rose Brener, (New Orleans) *Jewish Ledger*, c. 1954, 1, 51–52; for the original Hebrew article see A. R. Malakhi, "Ephraim E. Lisitzky (l-yovlo)" (E. E. Lisitzky: on his anniversary), *Hado'ar*, year 33, 34, no. 12 (18 Shvat 5714; 22 January 1954): 221–222.

9. And see Lisitzky's letter of 1906 to Brenner in this regard, cited immediately below. Lisitzky also wrote about Bialik on a number of occasions, among them an essay entitled "Ḥayim Naḥman Bialik mi-tokh tzfiyah retrospectivit" (A retrospective view of Ḥ. N. Bialik), *Kneset* (Tammuz 5720; 1960); reprinted in E. E. Lisitzky, *Bi-shvilay ḥayim v-sifrut* (In the paths of life and literature) (Tel-Aviv: Maḥbarot L-sifrut and 'Ogen, 1961), 158–176. One of the many critics noting Lisitzky's affinity for Bialik is Yeshurun Keshet, "'Al Ephraim Lisitzky ha-mshorer" (On the poet E. E. Lisitzky), in *Havdalot* (Distinctions) (Tel-Aviv: Agudat Ha-sofrim and Dvir, 1962), 258. Exceptions to most Hebrew poets in America are the works of Gabriel Preil and Eliezer D. Fridland, who exhibited a decidedly modernist poetic sensibility, and see Yael S. Feldman, *Modernism and Cultural Transfer: Gabriel Preil and the Tradition of Jewish Literary Bilingualism* (Cincinnati: Hebrew Union College Press, 1986); Dan Miron, writing on Preil, includes Fridland as an exceptional poet among his peers, and see his essay "Beyn ha-ner la-kokhavim: 'al shirat Gavriel Preil" (Between the candle and the stars: on the poetry of Gavriel Preil), in Gavriel Preil, *Asfan stavim: shirim 1972–1992* (Collector of autumns: collected poems, 1972–1992) (Jerusalem: Mosad Bialik, 1993), 273–381.

10. In a letter dated December, 1906, Lisitzky writes to Y. Ḥ. Brenner: "Bialik, too, stood at the threshold of the House of Study, but Bialik's response is not my response. He returned to it in order to rebuild and improve it, so as 'to revive the walls and ash heaps' [a reference to Bialik's formulation in the last stanza of his poem "At the Threshold of the House of Study": "Of your ash heaps I'll revive the walls"]. His optimism reaches such a level that he comes to believe fully that 'You will not fall, tent of Shem! I'll rebuild you and you'll be rebuilt / . . . Still will you outlast palaces as you have outlasted . . .' For Bialik's soul is despairing-consoling; even when his despair overcomes him he finds consolation . . . but I myself know that my House of Study is in ruins 'and it has no chance of being repaired so it must be destroyed . . . nevertheless I return to it because I found nothing else in the world of deceit, I return to it because it was the cradle of my youth . . . the lap into which my tears flowed.' It is a ruin whose ultimate end is to fall. But nevertheless I like the sublime beauty of ruins, especially the 'shadows.'" Gnazim, no. alef20/18561–alef

The subject is also broached in a study by Yitzhak (Irving) Finkl, "Pgishot 'im

Ephraim E. Lisitzky" (Meetings with E. E. Lisitzky), *Bitzaron*, year 29, vol. 58, no. 6 (Sivan–Tammuz 5728; May–June 1968): 102. Other evidence of Lisitzky's special affinity for Bialik includes examples of his early poetry, wherein the latter's influence is evident in his use of images and themes. Among these is unrequited love, which leads the poet to inquire of the waves, clouds, or birds; a depiction of his return to faith only to find everything in ruins; the self as "a soul cut off from its God" ("Nefesh she-nikhrtah me-ʾelah!" 74), or a description, in the same location, of the woods and stream that is strongly evocative of Bialik's "Ha-brekhah"—"The Pool"—and see E. E. Lisitzky, "Ḥavok, nashok—maḥar namut" (Embrace, kiss—tomorrow we shall die) and "Ḥorshah" (A wood), *Shirim* (Poems) (New York: Ḥaverim; Tel-Aviv: Dvir, 1928), 68–74. The critic M. Ribalow also traced out this influence, identifying themes of poverty in Lisitzky's autobiographical poetry which are similar to Bialik's, especially between *Adam ʿal adamot* (Man on earth) of the former and Bialik's works, identifying some by name, as in "La-mnatzeaḥ ʿal ha-mḥolot," "Tzartzar mshorer ha-dalut," and "B-shirati" (To the director of dances, Cricket poet of poverty, and In my song), and see Menaḥem Ribalow, "Ephraim Lisitzky v-shirat ḥayav" (E. E. Lisitzky and his life's song), in *ʿIm ha-kad ʾel ha-mabuʿa: masot bikoret* (With the pitcher to the spring: critical essays) (New York: ʿOgen, 1950), 295–296. One difference between the two is rooted in the physical and cultural distance between Lisitzky and his hometown of Slutzk, which he often painted sympathetically, despite his acknowledgment of the dire poverty in which he lived. This tension characterizes many of his poems, and also those of other Hebrew poets in America, a place bereft of authentic *batey midrash* and shtetls. Keshet, in his study, also notices the influence of Bialik on Lisitzky, though he also includes the Hebrew poet Zalman Shneour: Y. Keshet, *Havdalot*, 271. Epstein finds Bialik's (and M. Z. Feierberg's) influence in Lisitzky's portrayal of the impact of fate on his life by questioning his tradition and ancestral values and by portrayal of a God in his own image—a miserable and powerless God, and see Avraham Epstein, *Sofrim ʿivrim ba-ʾAmerica* (Hebrew writers in America) (Tel-Aviv: Dvir, 1952), 40–41. Blumenfield finds that the kinship between Bialik and Lisitzky is characterized by many literary and biographical issues, though he does not detail them. And see Samuel Blumenfield, "Ephraim Lisitzky—American Hebrew Bard," *Chicago Jewish Forum* (Spring 1964), 206. More specific is S. Y. Penueli, who notes that Bialik's influence on Lisitzky was clearest in his early literary career, in Bialik's "Mgillat ha-ʾesh" (The scroll of fire), the representation of the Holy Presence (*Shekhinah*) imagined as a bird with a broken wing, Bialik's "Safiaḥ" ("Aftergrowth") on the rendering of Lisitzky's autobiography, among others. Emerging later from under that influence, Lisitzky was affected by Anglo-Saxon works, among them Richard Wright's *Black Boy* (1937) and Alan Paton's *Cry, the Beloved Country* (1948). Lisitzky's career of revolt against established values returns him to a resignation about the way things are, asserts Penueli, a message inspired by African American and Native American literature. Lisitzky, however, continues Penueli, remains always in Bialik's shadow in that he retains a practice of imitating the great bard's forms without their uniqueness, resulting in static images and inanimate motifs, and see his "Me-ʾalef ʿad heh" (From "alef" to "heh"), *ʿAl ha-mishmar,* 31 August 1956, n.p.

11. On the Hebrew *poʾema*, see Chapter One, nn. 18–20.

12. In a conversation with Ghela (Efros) Scharfstein, I learned that, despite the prevailing tendency to compare his long poems about Indians with "The Song of Hiawatha," Israel Efros was fond of E. A. Robinson's poetry, and shunned that of Longfellow.

13. That being the opening of "Reverend Ezra" ("ʿEzra ha-kohen," *B-ʾoholay Khush*, 204–211), in which the poet recounts his own childhood readings about Blacks, his arrival in the South, and a search for a member of the Black community to tell him of his experiences in slavery. These seem to be actual, verifiable events in Lisitzky's experiences, as attested by people who have heard tales of his habits when living in New Orleans. Lisitzky's earliest published works about Blacks, some of which were to form part of *B-ʾoholay Khush*, include "The salvation boat" ("Sfinat ha-yesha," *Shirim* [Poems]), 190–191).

14. See Chapter Five, n. 26. For possible models guiding Lisitzky, see, for instance, Howard W. Odum and Guy B. Johnson, *Negro Workaday Songs* (1926; reprint, New York: Negro University Press, 1969). The blues, more than any other genre, are "the song of a single singer," expressing an individual's reaction, usually one of depression. "They stressed melancholy, love, misfortune, complaint, homelessness . . ." Newman I. White, *American Negro Folk-Songs* (Hatboro, Pennsylvania: Folklore Associates, Inc., 1965), 387.

15. Lisitzky, *Shirim*, 266–277.

16. Foreword to *B-ʾoholay Khush*, vii; and I heard of his practices indirectly from others who knew or heard of him, among them Professor Anne Brener, a New Orleans native, in February 2002.

17. Zevulun Ravid, "ʿElbon ha-yaldut she-lo nitkaper (l-zekher Ephraim E. Lisitzky: 23 b-sivan 5722–23 b-sivan 5732)" (The childhood shame that was not expiated: in memory of E. E. Lisitzky, 23 Sivan 1962–23 Sivan 1972), *Hadoʾar,* year 51, vol. 51, no. 28 (27 Sivan 5732; 9 June 1972): 474–475. Menaḥem Ribalow, "Ephraim E. Lisitzky v-shirat ḥayav," 295–313; Adir Cohen, "ʿOlam yetzirato shel Ephraim E. Lisitzky (bi-mlot lo shivʿim va-ḥamesh shanah)" (E. E. Lisitzky's creative world: upon his seventy-fifth birthday), *Gazit* 18, nos. 1–2 (May 1960): 16; Yeshurun Keshet, *Maskiyot: masot vikoret* (Ornaments: critical essays) (Tel-Aviv: Agudat Ha-sofrim Ha-ʿivrim and Dvir, 1953), 282. An oft-cited self-revelation is "All my life I bore a crown of thorns upon my head and I devised to set a Sabbath hat over it to conceal it from all eyes. I now remove this Sabbath hat. I no longer shy from revealing my crown of thorns—it is a crown of glory that was set upon my head." (Epigram to *In the Grip.*)

18. Reuven Avinoam, "ʿIm shirato shel E. E. Lisitzky" (With E. E. Lisitzky's poetry), *Moznayim* 3, no. 4 (Av 5716; July 1956): 247–252; Hillel Bavli, "Ephraim E. Lisitzky," *Gilyonot* 31, no. 8–10 (Av–Elul 1954): 92–100; Shmuel

Blumenfeld (Samuel Blumenfield), "L-zikhro shel Ephraim E. Lisitzky: klil kotzim—klil tif'eret" (In memory of E. E. Lisitzky: a crown of thorns—a crown of glory), *Hadoʾar*, year 42, vol. 43, no. 27 (23 Iyar 5723; 17 May 1963): 495–496, reprinted in *Mshorerah shel yahadut America: kovetz l-zikhro shel E. E. Lisitzky Z"L* (Poet of American Jewry: a collection in memory of E. E. Lisitzky), ed. Reuven Avinoam and Yitzhak Finkl (Tel-Aviv: Maḥbarot L-sifrut, 1966), 63–71; Shlomo Damesek, "Ha-zaken sheba-ḥavurah" (The senior in the group), *Hadoʾar*, year 42, vol. 43, no. 27 (23 Iyar 5723; 17 May 1963): 497.

19. As Lisitzky declares in his poem, "Li adam aḥ" (Man is my brother), a poem dated 1937 and often taught to schoolchildren; *B-maʿalot uv-moradot* (Ascents and descents) (Tel-Aviv: Dvir, 1954), 92–93; it was anthologized in George Epstein and Max Zeldner, eds., *Modern Hebrew Literature* (New York: Hebrew Publishing Company, 1948), 53. A similar message pervades many of Lisitzky's poems, including his gargantuan *Naftulay Elohim* (Divine struggles, 1934), and the poem "V-ʾulay" (Perhaps, 1942) in *Kmo ha-yom rad: shirim* (As the day set: poems) (Tel-Aviv: Maḥbarot L-sifrut, 1960), 21; *Naftuley Elohim* (Divine struggles) (New York: ʿOgen, and Tel-Aviv: Dvir, 1934); Keshet, *Havdalot*, 258–261.

20. The identification of Black slaves with the story of the Hebrews' enslavement in Egypt is noted as early as 1839 by Fanny Kemble. She asserted that "the slaves considered their case analogous to that of the oppressed Israelites of song and sermon." White, *American Negro Folk-Songs*, 11–12.

21. References to this self image, indicating a troubled inner soul, abound in his poetry and prose. Interestingly, it appears as Lisitzky's version of Bialik's self-reference as the hewer of wood, "ḥotev ʿetzim," used in his poem, "Shaḥah nafshi" (My spirit sank): Ḥayim Naḥman Bialik, "Shaḥah nafsi," *Hadoʾar*, year 3, vol. 3, no. 239 (28 Adar 5683; 16 March 1923): 2. See for example, Ribalow's observations in his introduction, p. viii, as well as Lisitzky's own poem, "ʿAl kever av" (On a father's grave), *Adam ʿal adamot: poʾemot* (Man on earth: poemas), introduction by M. Ribalow (New York: ʿOgen, 1947), 33–48; Reuven Avinoam, "ʿIm shirato shel E. E. Lisitzky" (With E. E. Lisitzky's poetry), 248; Hillel Bavli, "Ephraim E. Lisitzky," 92. He explores the same theme at length in his autobiography, *Eleh toldot adam*, 9; *In the Grip*, 5. Also Keshet, *Havdalot*, 268.

22. Avraham Epstein, "Ephraim E. Lisitzky (l-yovel ha-shishim shelo)" (E. E. Lisitzky: on his sixtieth anniversary), *Sefer ha-shanah li-yhuday America*, 8–9 (American Hebrew Yearbook, 8–9) (New York: Ha-histadrut Ha-ʿivrit Ba-ʾAmerica, 1948), 56–57; also see his study, *Sofrim ʾivrim ba-ʾAmerica*, 10; also Mordekhai Nadav, "Shirat ha-Kushim l-ʾEphraim E. Lisitzky" (E. E. Lisitzky's poetry of Blacks), *Zmanim* 47 (28 Ḥeshvan 5714; 25 February 1953); Yedidyah Menosi, "ʿIm shiray Lisitzky" (With Lisitzky's poetry), *Hadoʾar*, year 34, vol. 35, no. 17 (3 Adar 5715; 25 February 1955): 325; Avraham Broides, "Ephraim E. Lisitzky," *Ha-poʿel Ha-tzaʿir*, 10 July 1962, n.p.

23. B. Y. Mikhali, "Mshorer ʿivri 'B-ʾoholay Khush'" (A Hebrew poet in the tents of Cush), in *Mshorerah shel yahadut America*, 34; also see Yaʿakov Kabakoff,

"Mi-shirat mhagrim l-shirah America'it (li-mlot 10 shanim li-ftirato shel E. E. Lisitzky)" (From immigrant to American poetry: ten years since the death of E. E. Lisitzky), *Hado'ar* year 51, 51, no. 28 (27 Sivan 5732; 9 June 1972): 473.

24. M. Z. Levinson-Lavi, "'B-'oholay Khush' shirim" ('In the tents of Cush: poems'), *Bitzaron*, year 15, vol. 30, no. 6 (Iyar–Sivan 5714; May 1954): 127.

25. Y. Rabinowitz, "Yetzirato shel Ephraim E. Lisitzky" (E. E. Lisitzky's work), *Bitzaron* 41, no. 4 (Adar 5720; February–March 1960): 188, 191.

26. Ibid., 191.

27. Ibid., 196. As to the conservatism of American Hebraists, see Uzi Shavit, "The New Hebrew Poetry of the Twenties: Palestine and America," *Prooftexts* 12, no 3 (1992): 213–230.

28. Initially published in installments, 1840–1852, the novel first appeared in 1852. Lisitzky must be referring to the Hebrew translation, *Ohel Tom* (Warsaw, 1896), by the author and translator Abraham Singer (1864–1920). This version appeared in a number of editions until 1901. The novel was also translated in 1927 by the author and translator Asher Barash (1889–1952) as *Ohel ha-dod Tom*, and again by the poet and translator Eliahu Meitus (1892–1977), whose title is more accurately rendered as *Biktato shel ha-dod Tom* (Tel-Aviv, 1952). The availability of an edition in Hebrew during Lisitzky's youth lends credence to his claim and helps in bonding the poetic voice with the poet. Another to refer to having read the 1896 version is Hillel Bavli, "Shirat ha-Kushim ba-'America" (Black poetry in America), *Nimim: ma'asef l-divray sifrut yafah ul-divray bikoret*. Ed. H. Bavli. 1 (New York: Ḥaverim, 5683; Summer 1923), 108; revised version in his *Ruḥot nifgashot: divray masah* (Intersecting spirits: essays) (New York: 'Ogen; Jerusalem: M. Newman, 1958), 280.

29. Elsewhere, Lisitzky demonstrates a similar proclivity toward reinterpreting biblical verse, as by citing the words of Amos, 9:7, "Are ye not as the children of the Ethiopians unto Me, . . . ?" wherein the children of the Ethiopians (the "bnay khushim") are considered unremarkable in God's view, as one of many nations. The poet, instead, uses the words to express his identification with them, placing himself in the role of uttering these words. Also, his long poem, "Va-tdaber Miriam" (So Miriam spoke . . .), is represented as a sermon on the biblical episode in Numbers 12, with the protagonists as Blacks. For Lisitzky's poem, see Stephen Katz, trans. and commentary, "'So Miriam Spoke of Moses' by E. E. Lisitzky," *CCAR* [Central Conference of American Rabbis] *Journal* (Fall 2008): 59–89. On the idea of Blacks joining the Hebrews out of Egypt and the use of the verse from Amos (esp. see there chapters 2–3); see also Abraham Melamed, *The Image of the Black in Jewish Culture: A History of the Other* (New York: RoutledgeCurzon, 2003), 40; or in Hebrew, *Ha-yahafokh Kushi 'oro: ha-adam ha-shaḥor k-"aḥer" b-toldot ha-tarbut ha-yehudit* (Can the Cushite change his skin: the Black man as "Other" in Jewish cultural history) (Haifa and Lod: Haifa University and Zmora-Bitan, 2002), 53.

30. In a telephone conversation on 3 February 1997, I learned from Mrs. Rosalie Cohen of New Orleans of her father's hiring of Lisitzky away from his Milwaukee

position in that year to teach (and be administrator) in the New Orleans Communal Hebrew School.

31. Another case in point is Nat Turner of the novel by William Styron, *The Confessions of Nat Turner* (New York: Random House, 1967), who often cites from the Bible to remake himself as a free man, as by identifying with heroes of the Bible, among whom are Moses preaching about slavery (307–311); Joshua and David are cast as Black heroes (331) or expressed identification with the likes of Gideon, Saul, and David as warriors (382 and elsewhere).

32. "Amen shaḥor guf ha-Kushi" (Yes so black is the Blackman's body), *Prozdor: mikra'ah l-veyt-sefer tikhon* (Prozdor: a high-school reader), ed. M. Steiner and Y. K. Miklishansky (Mikliszanski) (Tel-Aviv: Maḥbarot L-sifrut, 1967), 31–32; "Li adam aḥ" (Man is my brother), n. 19 above.

I am not familiar with any study surveying anthologies of Hebrew literature with attention to the qualitative and quantitative, or rising and declining representation of American Hebrew literature in them, published in the United States, Israel, or elsewhere. For a recent study of the dynamics surrounding canon-formation see Michael Gluzman, *The Politics of Canonicity: Lines of Resistance in Modernist Hebrew Poetry* (Stanford: Stanford University Press, 2003).

33. Some of the translations include: excerpts of "Man is my brother" ("Li adam aḥ") in Samuel M. Blumenfield, "Ephraim Lisitzky: Poet Educator," in *Philip W. Lown: A Jubilee Volume*, ed. Judah Pilch (New York: Bloch Publishing Co., 1967) 83–87, esp. 84; the same poem, as well as excerpts of "God Spake to Moses," "Yes So Black is the Blackman's Body," and "Ezra the Preacher," in Samuel M. Blumenfield, "Lisitzky—Bard," 204; another offers excerpts from "Flames," "Tom Comes Home," "Freedom," and "Amen, Black is the Body of the Negro," in James B. Rosenberg, "Negro Life in Hebrew Poetry," *Jewish Spectator* 40, no. 2 (summer 1975): 34–36; "New Orleans Countryside," trans. I. M. Lask, in *New Orleans Ledger*, c. 1955, 15.

34. See, for example, Samuel Blumenfield, "Lisitzky—Bard," 204; Shmuel Blumenfeld, "L-zikhro shel Lisitzky," 495.

35. Bavli, among the leading Hebrew poets in America, was originally called Rushgalski, or Rashigolski, though he also went by the English name of Prince. On the latter, see Selig Adler and Thomas E. Connolly, *From Ararat to Suburbia: The History of the Jewish Community of Buffalo* (Philadelphia: Jewish Publication Society of America, 1960), 241; also 250. For more on Bavli and his name changes see Chapter Five. Others documenting Bavli's teaching with Lisitzky in Buffalo include A. R. Malakhi, "Lisitzky ki-mḥanekh" (Lisitzky as educator), *Bitzaron*, year 21, vol. 41, no. 4 (Adar 5720; February-March 1960): 205; Hillel Bavli, "B-mikhlalah katolit b-Buffalo" (In a Catholic college in Buffalo), *Gilyonot* 31, nos. 8–10 (Av–Elul 5714; 1954): 122–126.

36. Hillel Bavli, "Ephraim E. Lisitzky," 98. The latter poem was previously published as "Israel ba-shitim: Mi-drashotav shel komer Kushi" (Israel in Shittim: A Black minister's sermon), in E. E. Lisitzky, *Adam 'al adamot*, 245–255.

37. B. Y. Mikhali, "Ephraim E. Lisitzky: B-'oholay Khush," [Buenos Aires] *Darom* 3–4 (198–199) (5704; 1944): 47–48.

38. "Kol Ya'akov nishma kan mi-tokh oholey khush,' . . . akh et kolo shel Kush 'atzmo lo nishma b-sefer zeh ki im b-'im'um me'od, me'od." Yariv Margalit, "Kol Ya'akov me'oholay Khush" (Jacob's voice from within the tents of Cush), *Ha'aretz* ("Tarbut v-sifrut"), 36, no. 10409, 28 Ḥeshvan 5714; 6 November 1953, p. B.

39. A common practice of American Blacks was to identify Lincoln as Moses, both being divine messengers to free slaves. And see James Weldon Johnson, *Saint Peter Relates an Incident: Selected Poems by James Weldon Johnson* (New York: Viking Press, 1935), 93.

40. Yitzhak 'Ogen, "Ephraim Lisitzki: B-'oholay Khush" (Ephraim Lisitzky: in the tents of Cush) *La-kore ha-tza'ir: 'alon l-vikoret ul-hadrakhah sifrutit*, 11–12 (Elul–Tishrei 5714; September–October 1953): 1–2.

41. Often confused with each other, spirituals and gospel songs share many attributes—such as biblical or religious themes, or the notion of death as salvation—though they also differ. Having their origins in African and Western musical traditions, they are related in that the gospel song is chronologically a more modern version of the former, and of known authorship. Thematically, spirituals express a message of optimism about individual salvation, telling of a process of repentance for one who harbored doubts about the values of piety. Spirituals emphasized the notion of justice, rewards, and retribution for sins, a message of deliverance from slavery in this world and the world to come.

42. For more details on the history, development, and themes of spirituals and gospel songs, see James Weldon Johnson, "The History of the Spiritual," *Anthology of American Negro Literature*, edited by Sylvestre C. Watkins (New York: Modern Library/Random House, 1944), 125–126; for illustration, see also Richard M. Raichelson, *Black Religious Folksong: A Study in Generic and Social Change* (Ann Arbor, Michigan: University Microfilms, 1982), 88. Howard Thurman, *Deep River and the Negro Spiritual Speaks of Life and Death* (Richmond, Indiana: Friends United Press, 1975). Langston Hughes and Arna Bontemps, eds., *The Book of Negro Folklore* (New York: Dodd, Mead and Co., 1958). James Weldon Johnson, ed., *The Book of American Negro Poetry* (New York: Harcourt, Brace and Company, 1931). Clement Wood, ed., *Negro Songs: An Anthology* (Girard, Kansas: Haldeman-Julius Co., n.d.). James Weldon Johnson and J. Rosamond Johnson, eds., "The Second Book of Negro Spirituals," *The Book of American Negro Spirituals* (New York: The Viking Press, 1940). James Weldon Johnson, *God's Trombone: Seven Negro Sermons in Verse* (New York: Penguin, 1976). Raichelson, *Black Religious Folksong*, 242, notes that they are called "evangelical songs," "book hymns," or merely "hymns," 12, 315–316.

43. Wood, *Negro Songs*, 11–12.

44. See note 42 above.

45. In a poem entitled "Ba-masa" (On the way, 12–17 of vol. 2), Israel Efros refers to the train as a marvel of modern technology, ferrying passengers out of

the heat of the big city and into the lap of nature, a technology which democratizes all. Though he also refers to the theme of equality, his expression is more universal and without relation to any particular racial group. The poem is more about anti-urban sentiments of the poet than about others in America.

46. Avraham Holtz, who calls Lisitzky the Hebrew Vachel Lindsay, also observes this disparity, though he proposes that in place of performance directions Lisitzky "satisfies himself with the assonance reserved in the letters of the poems," and see, Avraham Holtz, "Dyokan—Lisitzky: ish midot" (Portrait—Lisitzky: a man of stature) *Niv: kli mivta l-sofrim tz'irim* (New York) 24, no. 1 (Iyar 5720; May 1960): 6. For a more thorough discussion of the conservatism of American Hebrew poetry, see Shavit, "The New Hebrew Poetry," 213–230.

47. See the list of Shakespeare's plays and their American Hebrew translators in Spicehandler's "*Ameriqa'iyut* in American Hebrew Literature," *Hebrew in America: Perspectives and Prospects*, ed. Alan Mintz (Detroit: Wayne State University Press, 1993), 103–104.

48. See, for example, Benjamin Harshav, *Language in Time of Revolution* (Stanford: Stanford University Press, 1993). Studies on the development of Hebrew slang and its representation in literature include Moshe Shamir, *B-kolmos mahir* (A quick pen) (Tel-Aviv: Sifriyat Po'alim, 1960), esp. 11–30, 59–71; Moshe Steiner, "Parashat gvurah b-lashon 'agah (b-shulay ha-maḥazeh 'b-'arvot ha-negev' l-Yig'al Mossenson, hotza'at Twersky, Tel-Aviv, 5709)" (A heroic chapter in slang: at the margins of the play "On the plains of the Negev," by Y. Mossenson, Twersky Publishers, Tel-Aviv, 1949), *Bitzaron*, year 11, vol. 22, no. 5 (125) (Nisan 5710; April 1950), 60–62.

49. Later, the same image was extended to liberation from prison, as in the song "The Midnight Special."

50. Johnson, *God's Trombone*, 1.

51. Odum and Johnson, *Negro Workaday Songs*, 78.

52. The woman as a projection of the mother he lost at an early age reappears in his poetry, particularly in his immense and allegorical *Naftuley Elohim* (Divine struggles). Lisitzky's translation of the title is part of what seems to be his own manuscript, "Synopsis of Divine Struggles—A Poetic Drama," a manuscript in the Lisitzky files of the American Jewish Archives, Cincinnati. Another crisis in Lisitzky's life, to which he barely alludes in his autobiography, is a divorce from his first wife in Milwaukee, and which appears to be the motive behind an attempted suicide about which he writes—conflating wife with mother—in the above, part 4 chapter 2. Concerning his mother, see his autobiographical work, *Eleh toldot adam* (*In the Grip*). In his last years he also composed a poem for his father, with whose fate he seemed to identify as he himself was dying of cancer.

53. Langston Hughes, *The Collected Poems of Langston Hughes*, ed. Arnold Rampersad and David Roessel (New York: Alfred A. Knopf, 1994), 155–156.

54. Johnson, *Book of American Negro Poetry*, 168. On the history of lynching, see Franklin and Moss, *From Slavery to Freedom*, 312–317.

55. See "*Dehikat hakets*" (hastening the "End") in Gershom Scholem, *Major Trends in Jewish Mysticism* (New York: Schocken Books, 1941), 246ff.

56. For example, see Sterling Stuckey, introduction to Sterling A. Brown, *Southern Road: Poems by Sterling A. Brown* (Boston: Beacon Press, 1974), xii–xxx; Sterling A. Brown, "Contemporary Negro Poetry, 1914–1936," in *Anthology of American Negro Literature*, 243–261, and especially his identification of "protest voices" as a category; White, in *American Negro Folk-Songs*, also identifies the category of "race consciousness" (376–386) in the same manner as in J. W. Johnson, *Book of American Negro Poetry*, 4, 6, 28ff.

57. For a study of mutual representations of Jews and Blacks in prose fiction see Ethan Goffman, "Imag(in)ing Each Other: Black and Jewish Literary Representations" (Ph.D. diss., Indiana University, 1997); or his *Imagining Each Other: Blacks and Jews in Contemporary American Literature* (Albany, N.Y.: State University of New York Press, 2000); Countee Cullen, "Heritage," in *Color* (New York: Harper and Brothers, 1925), 36–41. Lisitzky had the opportunity to witness some of the ideological tensions emerging among Blacks in the debate about increasing militancy in Black poetry. Among these was W. E. B. Du Bois's departure from Booker T. Washington's moderate approach, as well as the rising activism and race consciousness among Blacks. And see Franklin and Moss, *From Slavery to Freedom*, 274–275, 317–322, 326–327, 329–330, 350, 352, 354–360, 386–394, 400.

58. Johnson, *Saint Peter*, 13–22.

59. The same tone also characterizes his "Fifty Years," as Johnson testifies, which he composed so it "ended on a note of bitterness and despair" (91), even though the poem was composed in honor of the Emancipation Proclamation's fiftieth anniversary. The poet also notes that he excised the pessimistic lines to avoid marring the spirit of the occasion, and see Johnson, *Saint Peter*, 91–97.

60. Johnson, *God's Trombone*, 10, and his *Saint Peter*, 13–22; Raichelson, *Black Religious Folksong*, 358–360.

61. Johnson, "History of the Spiritual," 142–143.

62. Johnson, *Saint Peter*, 25.

63. Ibid., 25–26.

64. Wood, *Negro Songs*, 51.

65. Foreword to *B-'oholay Khush*, vii.

66. So also attested in ibid., 343.

67. Ibid., 186.

68. For example, ibid., 280–281.

69. In his autobiography, Lisitzky tells of Truex, a Canadian he met while in Ahmic Harbor, northern Ontario, who was a soldier in the Union Army, met Lincoln, and was witness to the Gettysburg Address. And see his *Eleh toldot adam*, 222; *In the Grip*, 223ff.

70. *B-'oholay Khush*, 220; reference to the spiritual "Go Down Moses" is in ibid., 215.

71. Ibid., 255.

72. Ibid., 239.
73. Ibid., 223–227, 234–238, 254.
74. Ibid., 223–227, 234–238, 254.
75. See also Thurman, *Deep River*, 39–40.
76. *B-ʾoholay Khush*, 219.
77. Ibid., 217; Styron, *Nat Turner*, 343.
78. *B-ʾoholay Khush*, 240.
79. Ibid., 213.
80. Ibid., 251–252.
81. Lisitzky seems to be making a point in this case, particularly in light of studies concluding that an insignificant number of slaveholders were Jews, and see John Hope Franklin, *From Slavery to Freedom;* Hugh Thomas, *The Slave Trade: The Story of the Atlantic Slave Trade, 1440–1870* (New York: Simon and Schuster, c. 1997); Saul S. Friedman, *Jews and the American Slave Trade* (New Brunswick, N.J.: Transaction Publishers, c. 1998).
82. See also Holtz, n. 46 above, 6.

CHAPTER SEVEN

1. Milly Heyd, *Mutual Reflections: Jews and Blacks in American Art* (New Brunswick, N.J.: Rutgers University Press, 1999), 6.
2. According to Silberschlag, though this contention is challenged because, "Yet it was not the [Black] per se who interested Bavli but the [Black] as a symbol of Jewish destiny." Eisig Silberschlag, *From Renaissance to Renaissance I: Hebrew Literature from 1492–1970* (New York: Ktav, 1973), 291.
3. Eliezer David Fridland, *Shirim b-sulam minor* (Poems in a minor key) (Jerusalem: M. Newman, 1966), 59ff.
4. Yael S. Feldman, *Modernism and Cultural Transfer: Gabriel Preil and the Tradition of Jewish Literary Bilingualism.* Cincinnati: Hebrew Union College Press, 1986), 191; for Regelson, see his essay: Avraham Regelson, "Elohay-ha-teva ba-shirah ha-ʾAmericaʾit" (The gods of nature in American poetry), *Mlo ha-talit ʿalim: masot v-siḥot* (A shawl full of leaves: essays and discourses) (New York: Vaʿad L-hotzaʾat Kitvay A. Regelson, 1941), 9–25, esp. 12.
5. Jeffrey Melnick, *A Right to Sing the Blues: African Americans, Jews, and American Popular Song* (Cambridge: Harvard University Press, 1999). This influence continued beyond the middle of the twentieth century, as it does today. Two Jews, for example, Jerry Lieber and Mike Stoller, wrote popular songs in the late 1950s in the vein of Black musicians which, when heard, amazed African American performers for their insight into their culture and values. The two fused Rhythm and Blues with quotes from classical music to create a new and heightened style appealing to the popular ear. Cited from a PBS program, "Rock and Roll: In the Groove," part 2, aired 16 June 2001.
6. Moshe Steiner, "Shira Kushit ba-ʾAmerica" (Black poetry in America), in

Hagut ʿivrit ba-ʾAmerica (Hebrew thought in America), 2, ed. M. Zahari, A. Tartkover, and H. Ormian (Tel-Aviv: Brit ʿIvrit ʿOlamit/ Yavneh, 1973), 315.

7. Bernard Isaacs, "Shloshet ha-Manesim: tmunah me-ḥayay ha-yehudim b-Lita b-reʾshit meʾah zo" (The Three Maneses: a picture of Lithuanian Jewry at the beginning of this century), *Sefer B. Isaacs* (The B. Isaacs book), ed. Moshe Noble (New York: n.p., 1977), 72.

8. Shlomo Damesek, *B-gorali: rshimot i-beyt ha-ḥolim* (My fate: notes from a hospital) (New York: Bitzaron, 1946).

9. This work is one of several in the subgenre of hospital stories composed by several writers. Damesek's account is retold in several of his works, among them: *Mi-po u-mi-sham* (From here and there) (New York: Talmidim Vi-ydidim, 1956); and *Gam sham zarhah ha-shemesh* (There, too, the sun shined) (Tel-Aviv: Sifray Gadish, 1960). Other works belonging to this subgenre are: S. L. Blank, "Tehom" (Abyss), in *B-maʿarbolet ha-ḥayim* (In the whirlpool of life), 122–154; S. L. Blank, "Ḥeder 603" (Room 603), in *ʿEtz ha-sadeh: sipurim* (The tree of the field: stories) (Jerusalem: Kiryat Sefer, 1961), 127–140; Abba Kovner, *Sloan Kettering* (Tel-Aviv: Ha-kibbutz Ha-mʾuḥad, 1987); translation of the latter, *Sloan-Kettering*, trans. Eddie Levenston (New York: Schocken, 2002).

10. Damesek, *Mi-po u-mi-sham*, 32.

11. Damesek, *B-gorali*, 16, 30–31, 32, 71, 113, 114, 124, 126.

12. Ibid., 16.

13. Ibid., 30–31.

14. Ibid., 32.

15. Ibid., 71, 124, 126.

16. Ibid., 87–89.

17. Ibid., 114.

18. Ibid., 113. Some of the same also appear in his *Gam sham zarḥah ha-shemesh*. There, too, the narrative includes Chief (19–20), Martin (62), Lunt (73–74), Peterson (90–91), the six-fingered man (160), a Black nurse named Cleopatra (33), and a comment observing that Blacks and Whites alike share a similar fate at the institution (14).

19. Eisig Silberschlag, "Mi-pi Khushim" (From the mouth of Blacks), *ʿAleh, ʿolam, b-shir* (Rise, O world, in song) (New York: ʿOgen; Boston: Boston Hebrew College, 1947), 107–122.

20. Moshe Steiner, "Shira Kushit," 323.

21. Ibid., 322; Silberschlag, "Ha-ʿor ha-shaḥor" (The Black skin), ibid., 114–116.

22. Silberschlag, "Ha-kinah" (The lament), 121–122.

23. Silberschlag, "Haʾaḥavah" (Brotherhood), 119–120.

24. Silberschlag, "Kol Cleopatra" (Cleopatra's Voice), 132–133.

25. "ʿAl kever shel Kushi" (On a Blackman's grave), *Bi-shvilim bodedim: shirim* (On lonesome roads: poems) (New York: ʿOgen, 1930), 79.

26. Shimon Ginzburg, "Joe," *Shirim u-phoʾemot* (Poems and poemas) (Tel-

Aviv: Aḥim/Dvir, 1931), 83–84; also appeared in Menaḥem Ribalow, ed., *Antologiyah shel ha-shirah ha-ʿivrit ba-ʾAmerica* (Anthology of Hebrew poetry in America) (New York: ʿOgen, 1938), 161–162.

27. Silberschlag, *Kimron yamay: shirim* (My days' curve: poems) (Jerusalem: Kiryat Sefer, 1959), 44.

28. B. Isaacs, "Bli shem" (Nameless), in *ʿAmos mokher tapuzim v-ʿod sipurim* (Amos sells oranges and other stories) (Tel-Aviv: M. Newman, 1953), 38–43, also "Yadayim" (Hands) and "Beyno l-veynah" (Between him and her) in *Beyn shnay ʿolamot: sipurim v-tziyurim* (Between two worlds: stories and sketches) (New York: ʿOgen, 1949), 135–161, 162–188.

29. S. L. Blank, "Esh zarah" (Strange fire), in *ʿEtz ha-sadeh*, 174–190. The story first appeared as part of Blank's 1958 novel *ʿAl admat America* (On American soil) (Tel-Aviv: Avraham Tziyoni, 1958), 94.

30. "Esh zarah," ibid. 179.

31. S. Halkin, "El ha-kushit" (To the Blackwoman), *ʿAl ha-ʾee: shirim* (On the island: poems) (Jerusalem: Mosad Bialik, 1946), 234–235. The poem appeared initially under the poet's pseudonym, Dobsky, *Hadoʾar*, year 5, vol. 6, no. 17 (25 Adar 5686; 11 March 1926): 306; and testimony by B. Shakhevits (Shahevitch), *Yeʿarot mtohamim: epizodot ba-biyografia literariyah shel Shimʿon Halkin* (Abyssed forests: episodes in Simon Halkin's biographia literaria) (Tel-Aviv: Katz Research Institute for Hebrew Literature, Tel-Aviv University, 1982), 77, 167.

32. S. Y. Penueli, *Ḥuliyot ba-sifrut ha-ʿivrit ha-ḥadashah* (Segments in modern Hebrew literature) (Tel-Aviv: Dvir, 1953), 61.

33. Halkin, "Pizmon Kushi" (A Black tune), *ʿAl ha-ʾee*, 245.

34. Shaḥevitch, ibid., 167.

35. The Jabbok also features in the title of another of Halkin's anthologies of poems, *Maʿavar Yabok* (Jabbok Crossing: poems) (Tel-Aviv: Am ʿOved, 1965), also noted by Shaḥevitch, 167.

36. Penueli, *Ḥuliyot*, 61.

37. Reuven (Grossman) Avinoam, "B-tzel sheḥor-ʿor" (In the shade of the one with the black skin), *Shirim u-phoʾemot* (Poems and poemas) (Tel-Aviv: Yavneh, 1950), 172–173.

38. Blank, "ʾAdam v-khalbo" (Adam and his dog), *ʿEtz ha-sadeh*, 201–221.

39. S. Halkin, *ʿAd mashber* (Until breakdown) (Tel-Aviv: ʿAm ʿOved, 1945), 38–39, 59–60.

40. Wallenrod, "Hazayot boker" (Morning phantoms), *Ba-dyotah ha-shlishit: sipurim* (On the third floor: stories) (Tel-Aviv: Dvir, 1937), 60–71.

41. Ibid., 70.

CHAPTER EIGHT

1. Menaḥem Ribalow, "Ḥ. A. Friedland," *Ktavim u-mgilot* (Writings and scrolls) (New York: ʿOgen, 1942), 230–245; *ʿIm ha-kad el ha-mabuʿa: masot biko-*

ret (With the pitcher to the spring: critical essays) (New York: ʿOgen, 1950), 247–250.

2. Ḥ. A. Friedland, "Ha-peraḥ ha-ḥay" (The living flower), *Shirim* (Poems) (Tel-Aviv: ʿOgen, 1940), 150.

3. Avraham Shmu'el Schwartz, "El Tanakh-kis" (To a pocket Bible), *Shirim* (Poems) (Tel-Aviv: M. Newman, 1958), 152; also see Menaḥem Ribalow, "ʿAl shirato shel A. S. Schwartz," *ʿIm ha-kad*, 286ff.

4. Israel Efrat (Efros), *Zahav* (Gold) (New York: Sfarim, 1942). All citations from *Kitvay Israel Efrat: sefer rishon: min ha-ʿolam he-ḥadash—shnay shirim* (The writings of Israel Efros: book one: from the new world—two poems) (Tel-Aviv: Dvir, 1966), 179, 238.

5. Ibid., 197.

6. Testimony to this effect is evident, among other sources, in a letter by his brother, A. S. Schwartz, to Avraham Kariv: "My brother, I. J. Schwartz: he is currently completing the translation into Hebrew of Kentucky, several chapters were published in special issues of Hado'ar and perhaps even in the Yearbook, and the translation is very good." Gnazim, no. 61/50712-alef. S. Halkin also translated a part of this epic work in *Aḥisefer*; ed. S. Neiger and M. Ribalow (New York: Keren Louis LaMed, 1943), 420–425; also see Bo'az Shakhevitz (Shaḥevitch), *Yeʿarot mtohamim: epizodot ba-biyografiyah literariyah shel Shimʿon Halkin* (Abyssed forests: episodes in Simon Halkin's biographia literaria) (Tel-Aviv: Katz Research Institute for Hebrew Literature, Tel-Aviv University, 1982), 133.

7. Tzvi (Harry) Sackler, "Darko shel mshorer du-lshoni" (A bilingual poet's way), *Hado'ar*, year 42, vol. 43, no. 29 (15 Sivan 5723; 7 June 1963): 548–549.

8. Gertrude W. Dubrovsky, "Introduction," in Israel Jacob Schwartz, *Kentucky*, trans. Gertrude W. Dobrovsky (Tuscaloosa: University of Alabama Press, 1990), 11–12.

9. Ibid., 13.

10. Ephraim E. Lisitzky, *Eleh toldot adam* (These are the tales of man) (Jerusalem: Mosad Bialik, 1949), 82; translation in Ephraim E. Lisitzky, *In the Grip of Cross-Currents*, trans. Moshe Kohn and Jacob Sloan and revised by the author (New York: Bloch Publishing Co., 1959, 2001), 82 ff.

11. Avraham Epstein, "E. E. Lisitzky," *Sofrim ʿivrim ba-ʾAmerica* (Hebrew writers in America) (Tel-Aviv: Dvir, 1952), 39–65, esp. 10, 56; Yeshurun Keshet, "ʿAl Ephraim Lisitzky ha-mshorer" (On thepoet E. E. Lisitzky), *Havdalot* (Distinctions) (Tel-Aviv: Agudat Ha-sofrim and Dvir, 1962), 266–268; Menaḥem Ribalow, *ʿIm ha-kad*, 306; Reuven Avinoam, "ʿIm shirato shel E. E. Lisitzky" (With E. E. Lisitzky's poetry), *Moznayim* 3, no. 4 (Av 5716; July 1956): 247–252, esp. 251; Shmu'el Blumenfeld, "L-zikhro shel Ephraim E. Lisitzky: klil kotzim—klil tif'eret" (In memory of E. E. Lisitzky: a crown of thorns—a crown of glory), *Hado'ar*, year 42, vol. 43, no. 27 (23 Iyar 5723; 17 May 1963): 495; Shlomo Damesek, "Ha-zaken sheba-ḥavurah" (The senior of the group), *Hado'ar*, ibid., 497.

12. Lisitzky, "Bo'akhah New Orleans" (Coming to New Orleans), *Kmo ha-*

yom rad: shirim (As the day set: poems) (Tel-Aviv: Maḥbarot L-sifrut, 1960), 169–184, esp. 171. He also includes another minority, the Acadians (Cajuns) (173), who fled the North, and Jean Lafitte and his fellow pirates (174–175). It is African Americans, however, who receive most of the poet's attention. He repeatedly describes them as singing while loading ships (174), yet does not overlook the region's deficiencies as he takes note of the slave trade, which was a thriving industry in the city (175).

13. Ibid., 173, 174–175, 177, 181.

14. Eisig Silberschlag, "Ha-shirah ha-ʿivrit ba-ʿolam he-ḥadash" (Hebrew poetry in the New World") *Aḥisefer,* 235.

15. Shimʿon Ginzburg, "No-York," *Shirim u-phoʾemot* (Poems and poemas) (Tel-Aviv: Aḥim/Dvir, 1931), 268; Menaḥem Ribalow, *ʿIm ha-kad,* 272.

16. "From across the alley / The sound of wild rejoicing rises slowly from a cellar / And the tune of a violin cries in a house where the love / of drunken Black women is sold . . ." ("uv-simtah mi-neged / at nisa mi-martef kol mitzhalot pruʿim / u-neginah shel kinor mityapeaḥ b-veyt mimkar ahavah / shel kushiyot svuʾot"), Ginzburg, ibid., 268).

17. "B-har beyt Columbia" (On the mountain of the house of Columbia), *Shirim u-phoʾemot,* 94–101.

18. Gavriel Preil, "Derekh ha-sahar bi-nharot" (The moon's way through rivers), *Asfan stavim: shirim 1972–1992* (Collector of autumns: poems 1972–1992) (Jerusalem: Mosad Bialik, 1993), 240; also in Gavriel Preil, *Nof shemesh u-khfor: shirim* (Sunny vista and frost: poems) (New York: Ohel, 1944), 55.

19. Reuven (Grossman) Avinoam, "Viduyo shel Calev" (Caleb's confession, 1942) *Shirim u-phoʾemot* (Poems and poemas) (Tel-Aviv: Yavneh, 1950), 177–182.

20. Moshe Shlomo Ben-Meir, "Tfilat ishah Kushit" (A Black woman's prayer, 1957), *Tzlil va-tzel: shirim v-ʾagadot* (Sound and shadow: poems and legends) (New York: ʿOgen; Tel-Aviv: M. Newman, 1958), 94–95; appeared earlier in *Hadoʾar,* year 36, vol. 37, no. 14 (30 Shvat 5717; 1 February 1957), 256.

21. The event energized the Black civil rights movement and brought to the fore leaders such as Martin Luther King, Jr., and Malcolm X.

22. As a poem by James Weldon Johnson, "The Black Mammy," *Saint Peter Relates an Incident: Selected Poems by James Weldon Johnson* (New York: Viking Press, 1935), 40; Langston Hughes's "The Negro Mother," in *Selected Poems of Langston Hughes* (New York: Vintage Books, 1959, 1974), 288–289, and others, a topic also engaging painters, who saw in the role of the nursing woman a symbol of salvation which will come once a White woman nurses a Black child; and see Milly Heyd, *Mutual Reflections: Jews and Blacks in American Art* (New Brunswick, N.J.: Rutgers University Press, 1999), 79–81.

23. Avraham Tzvi Halevy, *Mi-tokh ha-sugar: shirim* (From within the prison: poems) (New York: Ohel, 1948), 24.

24. Such, too, was the mood in his classes during my years of study with him. This did not keep him from being ironically humorous. In one letter he com-

ments, "And I, may you be spared, have contracted diabetes. Imagine, a bitter person such as I with an excess of sugar in his disobedient blood"—letter from A. Tz. Halevy to Yaʿakov David Avramsky, 10 July 1965, Gnazim, no. 4/48558.

25. Shimʿon Halkin, "Haʿarakhot v-divray bikoret: Avraham Tzvi Halevy" (Criticism and evaluations: A. Z. Halevy), *Bitzaron*, year 10, vol. 19, no. 3 (Kislev–Tevet 5709; December 1948–January 1949): 194–200.

26. A. Tz. Halevy, *Mi-tokh ha-sugar*, 71–72.

27. Gershon Shaked, "The Beginnings of Hebrew Literature in America," in *The New Tradition: Essays on Modern Hebrew Literature* (Cincinnati: Hebrew Union College Press, 2006), 83–84; but see my essay on the limited realism practiced by Ben-Avigdor, "History, Memory, and Ideology: Ben-Avigdor and *Fin-de-Siècle* Hebrew Literature," *Jewish History* 12, no. 2 (Fall 1998): 33–49.

28. Epstein, *Sofrim ʿivrim*, vol. 2, 334–351, esp. 347.

29. Shaked endeavors to assert that many works of prose fiction are less fiction and more documentary in their content in his essay, "The Beginnings," 85.

30. Ḥ. A. Friedland, "Mḥol ha-praydah" (Farewell dance), *Sipurim* (Stories) (Tel-Aviv: ʿOgen, 1939), 169–175.

31. Ḥ. A. Friedland, "Miss Rauz" (Miss Rose), ibid., 84–87.

32. Reuven (Reuben) Wallenrod, "Traditziyot u-minhagim" (Customs and traditions), *Ba-dyotah ha-shlishit: sipurim* (On the third floor: stories) (Tel-Aviv: Dvir, 1937), 136–143, esp. 139–140; also in *Me-ʾotzar ha-sifrut ha-ḥadashah* (From the treasure of modern [Hebrew] literature), ed. M. Zeldner and G. L. Epstein (New York: Hebrew Publishing Company, 1965), 76–85.

33. See Blank's "Neder" and "Ha-rishon" (Vow, and The first), *B-maʿarbolet ha-ḥayim* (In the whirlpool of life) (New York: ʿOgen, 1954), 17–25, 25–30, accordingly, 24; 25, 28; *ʿEtz ha-sadeh: sipurim* (Tree of the field: stories) (Jerusalem: Kiryat Sefer, 1961), 50, 68, 129, 139; "Ḥeder 603" (Room 603), 127–140, 143, esp. 129, and in "Mother" (Em), *ʿAl admat America*, (13, 33, 81); also Sackler's *Beyn eretz v-shamayim*, 431; Israel Efros, "Zakharti lakh" (I recall), *Kitvay Israel Efrat: sefer slishi: Meh ʿamok hu shatul* (The writings of Israel Efros: book three: how deep he is planted) (Tel-Aviv: Dvir, 1966), 72; and S. L. Blank's novel, *Mister Kunis*, 94–96.

34. S. L. Blank, "Snaʾim" (Squirrels), *B-maʿarbolet ha-ḥayim*, 88–89; in Halkin's *ʿAd mashber* (Until breakdown) (Tel-Aviv: ʿAm ʿOved, 1945), 290–300; Neuta, Martha's "child," also reviews her relationship with her nanny.

35. As in Halkin's *ʿAd mashber*, 34, and *Yeḥiʾel ha-hagri* (Yeḥiʾel the Hagrite) (Tel-Aviv: A. Y. Stybel, 1935/6), 34, 149, 156.

36. S. L. Blank, "Snaʾim," 88–89.

37. Reuven Wallenrod, "B-tzel ha-ḥomot" (In the shade of the walls), *Beyn ḥomot New York: sipurim* (Between New York's highrises: stories) (Jerusalem: Mosad Bialik, 1952), 193–245; appeared earlier in *Sefer ha-shanah li-yhuday America* (The American Hebrew Year Book), vol. 6, ed. Menaḥem Ribalow (New York:

Ha-histadrut Ha-ʿivrit Ba-ʾAmerica, 1942), 296–329, reference is from p. 302 there.

38. Wallenrod, ibid., 151, 156–157; L. A. Arieli, "Kaytzad naʿaseti ʾantishemi" (How I became an anti-Semite), *Kitvay L. A. Ariʾeli* (Collected works of L. A. Arieli: Stories, Plays, Legends, Essays, Letters), vol. 1, ed. Michael (Milton) Arafa (New York and Tel-Aviv: Keren Israel Matz and Dvir, 1999), 509–540, esp. 517.

39. *ʿAd mashber* 255; Blank, *Mister Kunis*, pp. 110–113, 132, 139.

40. B. Isaacs, "Bar-Mitzvah: hed-siaḥ" (Bar-Mitzvah: echo of a conversation), *Mivḥar sipurim* (Selected stories) (Tel-Aviv: Maḥbarot L-sifrut, 1968), 14.

41. S. L. Blank, *Mister Kunis*, 112.

42. S. L. Blank, *Ee ha-dmaʿot* (The isle of tears) (New York: ʿOgen, 1941), 17.

43. Ibid., and his "K-ʾesh kotzim (monit mesaperet)" (As a fire among thorns: tale of a taxi), *ʿEtz ha-sadeh*, 95.

44. Ḥ. A. Friedland, "Ḥov" (Debt), *Sipurim*, 123–129: "k-khushi atah maʿavideni arba-ʿesreh shaʿot l-yom," 129; Friedland, "Mumḥeh min ha-ḥutz," ibid., 151–164, esp. 151, 156–157; also in B. Isaacs, "Amos mokher tapuzim" (Amos sells oranges), *Amos mokher tapuzim v-ʿod sipurim* (Amos sells oranges and other stories) (Tel-Aviv: M. Newman, 1953), 5–17, esp. 11.

45. Tarkow-Naamani, "Yehudi ba-golah" (A Jew in Diaspora), *Rsisay ḥayim (mivḥar sipurim u-rshimot)* (Fragments of life: selected stories and sketches) (New York: ʿOgen, 1951), 76–81; also Blank's "Eshet nʾurim" (Wife of one's youth) and "Leḥem" (Bread), *B-maʿarbolet ha-ḥayim*, 156, and 245, 248, 251–254, accordingly.

46. Reuven Wallenrod, "B-ḥug mishapḥah" (In the family circle), *Sefer ha-shanah li-yhuday America* (The American Hebrew yearbook), vol. 4, ed. Mnaḥem Ribalow (New York: Ha-histadrut Ha-ʿivrit Ba-ʾAmerica, 1939), 38–77.

47. "ʿAvadeti k-khushi" (I worked as a Black man), 41; also see Sackler, *Beyn eretz v-shamayim*, 289, 378.

48. S. L. Blank, "Ish, ishah v-kof," *B-maʿarbolet ha-ḥayim*, 186–241.

49. Ibid., 215.

50. Regelson, "B-ʿod Moshe naʿar" (When Moses was a youth), *Kitvay Avraham Regelson: sham ha-bdolaḥ: marʾot v-ʾagadot* (Works of Avraham Regelson: There is the crystal: visions and legends) (New York: Vaʿad L-hotzaʾat Kitvay A. Regelson, 1942), 71–79.

51. S. L. Blank, "Ish, ishah v-kof," 186–241.

52. Blank, *B-maʿarbolet ha-ḥayim*, 59–88.

53. Ethan Goffman, "Imag(in)ing Each Other: Black and Jewish Literary Representations," Ph.D. diss., Indiana University, Bloomington, 1997, esp. 287–319. Published as *Imagining Each Other: Blacks and Jews in Contemporary American Literature* (Albany, N.Y.: State University of New York Press, 2000).

54. Blank, *Bi-shʿat ḥerum* (A time of crisis) (Philadelphia: Har-Zion, 1932).

55. H. Sackler, *Beyn eretz v-shamayim*, 422.

56. The best known work of fiction illustrating this is Mendele's *The Brief*

Journeys of Benjamin the Third. The notion is discussed by Sander L. Gilman, *The Case of Sigmund Freud: Medicine and Identity at the Fin de Siècle* (Baltimore: Johns Hopkins University Press, 1993), 31–32, 119, 142; also see S. Gilman, *The Jew's Body* (New York: Routledge, 1991), 40, 52–53; on the notion of Jewish soldiers in Poland, see also Israel Bartal, "Giborim o mugay lev: yehudim b-tziv'otayha shel Polin (1794–1863)" (Heroes or cowards: Jews in Poland's armies, 1794–1863), in *Kiyum va-shever: yehuday Polin l-dorotayhem* (Existence and breakup: Polish Jews through the generations), ed. Israel Bartal and Israel Gutman (Jerusalem: Merkaz Zalman Shazar, 1997), 353–367. My thanks to Professor Derek Penslar for the reference.

57. Goffman, 159.

58. Halkin, *'Ad mashber.* Only one of the novels, which were planned as a trilogy, was published in full. Individual chapters of the other parts were published as stories, among them "Bi-sh'at bikur," "Hatavat ḥalom," "Ba-ḥeder ha-pnimi," and "Torat ha-geza" (At the visiting hour; A dream made better; In the inside room; and Theory of race, accordingly) in his collection of short stories, *Nekhar: sipurim* (A foreign country: stories) (Jerusalem: Mosad Bialik, 1972), 134–161; 162–173; 174–194; 195–225; also see interview of Halkin by Moshe Dor, "Rshut ha-dibur li-professor Shimon Halkin" (Professor S. Halkin's turn to speak), *Ma'ariv,* 3 September 1971, 33–34; also Shahevitch, 49, 167, 177–182, 188, among others.

59. *'Ad mashber,* 292.

60. Many studies have been made on this narrative mode, also known as "Style Indirect Libre," "Narrated Monologue," and, in Hebrew, "dibur ḥavuy." For some discussion see my study of narrative in Agnon's *Oreaḥ nata la-lun* (*A Guest for the Night*), in Shmu'el (Stephen) Katz, *Ha-gibor b-'eynay ruḥo: omanut ha-siper shel 'Agnon b-Oreaḥ nata la-lun* (The hero in his own eyes: Narrative techniques in S. Y. Agnon's Oreaḥ nata la-lun) (Tel-Aviv: Eked, 1985), 132–133, n. 44, 135–162.

61. In another work the author also strikes an analogy by claiming that a resemblance exists between his Jewish protagonist and a Black man. R. Schochat, in an account of the pioneers in Eretz Israel, tells of one who, because he resembles a Black man, is called by all Jeep. Adding to this similarity is the habit of this pioneer to be the clown in the camp, one who imitated Blacks and knew that it is his duty to keep his fellow pioneers in a cheerful mood. Refa'el Shoḥat (Schochatt), *Kitvay Repha'el Shoḥat* (Writings of R. Schochatt), ed. A. R. Malakhi (New York: Yedidim, 1942), 193.

62. *'Ad mashber,* 338.

63. Ibid., 292–300.

64. Ibid., 300–301.

65. Ibid., 301–302.

66. Ibid., 101.

67. Ibid., 46, 56; 46; 46, 49, 71; 41, 42; 58, accordingly.

68. Ibid., 335; also "Torat ha-geza," in *Nekhar,* 195–225, esp. 224.

69. *Nekhar,* 134–161.

70. Ibid., 140.

71. Ibid., 150–151.

72. Ibid., 162–173.

73. Natan Shaḥam, "Daber el ha-ruaḥ" (Speak to the wind), in Itamar Ya'oz Kest, ed., *Mivḥar sifrutenu bi-shnat 5735* (Selected Israeli literature from 1975) (Tel Aviv: Misrad Ha-ḥinukh Vha-tarbut / Yaḥdav, 1976), 193–200, esp. 196–197. David Shaḥar, "Moto shel ha-'elohim ha-katan" ("The death of the Little God"), *Moto shel ha-'elohim ha-katan: sipurim* (The Death of the Little God: stories) (Jerusalem and Tel-Aviv: Schocken, 1970), 233–243, esp. 241; English translation in *News from Jerusalem: Stories* (Boston: Houghton Mifflin Co., 1974), 300–310. Shuki Ben-Ami, *Notzah shesu'ah: ish ha-rfu'ah ha-'indi'ani* (Split feather: the Indian medicine man) (Tel-Aviv: Ha-kibbutz Ha-m'uḥad, 2003).

74. Among them are works by Yoram Kaniuk, *Ha-yored l-ma'alah* (The acrophile) (Jerusalem: Schocken, 1963); *Sus'etz: masa* (Rockinghorse: a journey) (Tel-Aviv: Sifriyat Po'alim, 1973); *Ḥayim 'al nyar zkhukhit* (Life on sandpaper/I did it my way) (Tel-Aviv: Yedi'ot Aḥaronot/ Sifray Ḥemed, 2003); and some of the short works in *Mot ha-'ayir* (The donkey's death) (Ramat-Gan: Sifriyat Makor, 1973); *'Afar u-tshukah* (Dust and lust) (Tel-Aviv: Sifriyat Po'alim, 1975); *Kmo sipurim* (As-if stories) (Tel-Aviv: Kineret, 1983. The English versions include: *The Acrophile* (New York: Atheneum, 1961) and *Rockinghorse* (New York: Harper and Row, 1977). His work is productively illuminated by studies of the Jewish encounters with Black musicians, narratives that may be deemed supplementary to Jeffrey Melnick's *A Right to Sing the Blues: African Americans, Jews, and American Popular Song* (Cambridge: Harvard University Press, 1999), 12, 95ff, 120.

75. Hillel Barzel, "Ḥavayah b-livyat mitos—'Timber,' 'Ha-ḥayim ha-yafim shel Clara Shi'ato'" (Experience with myth—"Timber," "Clara Shiato's beautiful life"), *Mgamot b-siporet ha-hoveh: ha-sipur he-ḥavuy* (Major trends in contemporary Hebrew prose: Tales of experience), ed. Hillel Barzel (Tel-Aviv: Yaḥdav, 1979), 171–172; Gershon Shaked, *Sifrut az, kan v-'akhshav* (Literature then, here and now) (Tel-Aviv: Zmora Bitan, 1993), 29.

76. Barzel, ibid., 171; H. Barzel, "Yoram Kaniuk: ha-mromam vha-naḥut" (Yoram Kaniuk: the elevated and the low), *Msaprim b-yiḥudam* (Authors in their uniqueness) (Tel-Aviv: Yaḥdav, 1981), 217–248.

77. Yoram kaniuk, "Ha-msibah shel Charlie Parker" (Charlie Parker's party), *Mot ha-'ayir*, 9–16.

78. Barzel, "Yoram Kaniuk: ha-mromam," 226.

79. Shaked, *Sifrut*, 47.

80. Also Camus; Barzel, "Yoram Kaniuk: ha-mromam," 217–248.

81. Ortziyon Bartana, *Tlushim va-ḥalutzim: hitgabshut ha-mgamah ha-neoromantit ba-siporet ha-'ivrit* (The torn and the pioneers: crystallization of the neoromantic trend in Hebrew narrative) (Jerusalem: Dvir, 1983), 80, 116, 117.

82. Eilat Negev, "B-khol adam ḥavuy korban v-rotzeaḥ" (In every man lurks a victim and a killer), *Yedi'ot Aḥaronot: "7 yamim,"* 17 November 1995, 36–38.

83. Kaniuk, "Ha-msibah shel Charlie Parker," 10.

84. Ibid., 16.

85. "Tamid nisiti l-hanis mi-maḥshavotay et ha-ʾish ha-lavan she-hayiti," 16.

86. Yoram Kaniuk, "Leni Tristano ha-ʿiver" (Blind Lennie Tristano), *Mot ha-ʿayir*, 20.

87. Yoram Kaniuk, *Kmo sipurim.*

88. "Ha-tinok ha-ʾavud shel naʾarat ha-telefon" (The lost child of the telephone girl), *Kmo sipurim*, 52; retold from "Maʾaseh b-motah shel Brenda-Jeans Dewitt" (Story of the death of Brenda-Jeans Dewitt), *Afar u-tshukah*, 38–39; and in *Ha-yored l-maʾalah* and *Ḥayim al nyar zkhukhit.*

89. "Ha-diskjockey lokhed rotzḥim" (The killer-catching diskjockey), *Kmo sipurim*, 110.

90. *Kmo sipurim*, 171–173; partially retold in *Ḥayim ʿal neyar zekhukhit.* The episode, which is preceded by one regarding Billie Holiday, is available in translation: Yoram Kaniuk, "Killers: Excerpted from *I Did It My Way*, trans. Anthony Berris, *Zeek: A Jewish Journal of Thought and Culture* (Fall/Winter 2007): 70–76.

91. Kaniuk's review of *Lady Sings the Blues*, in *ʿAfar u-tshukah*, 56–64.

92. For *Susetz* and *Rockinghorse*, see n. 74 above.

93. Mel Brooks, "Blazing Saddles: Mel Brooks' Black Bart," an original screenplay by Mel Brooks (et al). Based on a story by Andrew Bergman—draft (Burbank, California: Warner Brothers, 1972), 49–50. I wish to express my thanks to the Lilly Library of Indiana University for allowing me to examine this archived draft. The dialogue cited is from the actual movie. Also see, Patricia Erens, *The Jew in American Cinema* (Bloomington: Indiana University Press, 1984), 328.

CHAPTER NINE

1. See, for instance, Michael Gluzman, *The Politics of Canonicity: Lines of Resistance in Modernist Hebrew Poetry* (Stanford: Stanford University Press, 2003).

2. Nurit Govrin, "Ha-tviʿah la-ʾAmericaniyut' v-hagshamatah ba-sifrut ha-ʿivrit ba-ʾAmerica" (The call for 'Americanism' and its realization in Hebrew literature in America), in *Migvan: meḥkarim ba-sifrut ha-ʿivrit uv-giluyeha ha-ʾAmericaniyim—mugashim l-Yaʿakov Kabakoff* (Migvan: Studies in Hebrew Literature in Honor of Jacob Kabakoff), ed. Stanley Nash (Lod, Israel: Makhon Haberman L-meḥkray Sifrut, 1988), 83–84.

3. Moshe Pelli, *Ha-tarbut ha-ʿivrit ba-ʾAmerica: 80 shnot ha-tnuʿah ha-ʿivrit b-ʾartzot ha-brit—5676–5756 (1916–1995)* (Hebrew culture in America: 80 years of Hebrew culture in the United States, 1916–1995) (Tel-Aviv: Rshafim, 1998), 21, 45.

4. Eisig Silberschlag, "Development and Decline of Hebrew Letters in the U.S.," *The American Jew: A Reappraisal*, ed. Oscar I. Janowsky (Philadelphia: Jewish Publication Society of America, 1964), 179, 182.

5. Alan Mintz, citing B. Friedman in "A Sanctuary in the Wilderness: The

Beginnings of the Hebrew Movement in America in *Hatoren*," in A. Mintz, ed., *Hebrew in America: Perspectives and Prospects* (Detroit: Wayne State University Press, 1993), pp. 29–676; citation from p. 51.

6. With assistance of Simon Ginzburg, and see Menaḥem Ribalow, ed., *Sefer zikaron l-B. N. Silkiner* (Memorial book for B. N. Silkiner) (New York: ʿOgen, 1934), 30; Shimʿon Ginzburg, *Kitvay Shimʿon Ginzburg: b-masekhet ha-sifrut—masot u-rshamim* (In the web of literature—essays and impressions) (New York: Vaad L-hotzaʾat Kitvay Shimon Ginzburg, 1945), 232; N. B. Silkiner, "Petaḥ davar" (Introduction), *Shirim* (Poems) (New York: Ḥaverim; Tel-Aviv: Dvir, 1927).

7. S. Bass, "Mdurot doʿakhot," *Gilyonot*, 3rd year, no. 5 (29) (Tammuz 1937): 443.

8. Elḥanan Indelman, "Anshay midot" (Men of stature), *Hadoʾar*, year 38, vol. 39, no. 11 (14 Shvat 5719; 23 January 1959): 192, 197.

9. Indelman, 192; and see letter by Persky to Lisitzky, 18 January 1959, Genazim no. 19752-13. Also Shlomo Haramati, "Daniʾel Persky—ish ha-lashon" (Daniel Persky: the language man) *Hadoʾar* 83, no. 1 (Fall 2003): 26–28.

10. Y. A. Dar, "Shnay kolot ba-shira ha-ʿivrit ('kmo rad ha-yom' [*sic*] l-Ephraim Lisitzky v-'ha-kol mi-baʿad la-ʿanaf' l-Sh. Zamir)" (Two voices in Hebrew poetry ['As the day set' by E. E. Lisitzky and 'The sound through the branch' by S. Zamir]), *Yediʿot Aḥaronot*, "7 Yamim" (7 Days), no. 8670, 12 August 1960, 6.

11. Pelli, *Ha-tarbut ha-ʿivrit*, 165.

12. The titles alone of many works bespeak this pessimism as imagined through the image of a setting sun, darkness, or silence. For specifics, see above, Chapter Four, n. 16.

13. See Introduction, n. 8.

14. Govrin, in *Migvan*, 84; also see Abraham Epstein, *Sofrim ʿivrim ba-ʾAmerica* (Hebrew writers in America) (Tel-Aviv: Dvir, 1952), especially on the poetry of A. S. Schwartz, p. 21.

15. Shmuʾel Leib Blank's novels include: *ʿAravah* (Prairie) (New York: Ha-histadrut Ha-ʿivrit Ba-ʾAmerica, 1926); *Tzon* (Sheep) (Berlin-Charlotburg: A. I. Stybel, 1929); *Adamah* (Land) (Tel-Aviv: Mitzpeh, 1931); *Naḥalah* (Patrimony) (Tel-Aviv: A. I. Stybel, 1933); *Mister Kunis* (New York and Tel-Aviv: A. I. Stybel, 1934); *Moshavah* (Colony) (Tel-Aviv: A. I. Stybel, 1936); his post-Bessarabian-life novels and short stories, many much more pessimistic and stark, include *Bi-shʿat ḥerum* (A time of crisis) (Philadelphia: Har Zion, 1932); *Ee ha-dmaʿot* (The isle of tears) (New York: ʿOgen, 1941); *Mister Kunis; B-yad ha-goral: shloshah sipurim* (In the hand of fate: three stories) (New York: ʿOgen, 1944); *B-maʿarbolet ha-ḥayim* (In the whirlpool of life) (New York: ʿOgen, 1954); *ʿAl admat America* (On American soil) (Tel-Aviv: Avraham Tziyoni, 1958); *ʿEtz ha-sadeh: sipurim* (Tree of the field: stories) (Jerusalem: Kiryat Sefer, 1961). A similar attitude, perhaps influencing Blank, is evident in Moshe Siko's idyllic tales of Bessarabia.

16. Blank, *ʿEtz ha-sadeh*, 199, 151, 208.

17. Ibid., 84, 85, 86, 87, 90, 94, 97, as examples.

18. Arieli's "New York," *Kitvay L. A. Arieli* (Collected works of L. A. Arieli: Stories, Plays, Legends, Essays, Letters), vol. 1, ed. Michael (Milton) Arfa (New York and Tel-Aviv: Keren Israel Matz and Dvir, 1999), 425–437; 425, 431. B. Isaacs, *'Amos mokher tapuzim v-'od sipurim* (Amos sells oranges and other stories) (Tel-Aviv: M. Newman, 1953); English version, "Amos the Fruit Seller," in Bernard Isaacs, *Selected Stories by Bernard Isaacs*, trans. Shoshana Perla (Bat-Yam, Israel: E. Lewin-Epstein, Ltd., 1968), 19–28; although he also uses "r'ino'a" for moving pictures, a more common term in early Hebrew, and see there, p. 130. Binyamin Rasler, *Naḥlat tzvi: roman* (Tzvi's patrimony: a novel) (New York: 'Ogen; Tel-Aviv: M. Newman, 1958), 151.

19. Gershon Shaked, *Ha-siporet ha-'ivrit 1880–1980 (B): ba-'aretz uva-tfutzah* (Hebrew fiction 1880–1980 (B): In the Land and the Diaspora) (Tel-Aviv/Jerusalem: Ha-kibbutz Ha-m'uḥad/Keter, 1983), 126.

20. For this practice by Brenner, see Todd Hasak-Lowy, "Between Realism and Modernism: Brenner's Poetics of Fragmentation," *Hebrew Studies* 44 (2003): 41–64.

21. First published in 1925, *Hashiloaḥ*, 43, and see Arieli, vol. 2, 209; the story is reproduced there, vol. 1, 119–141.

22. See H. Sackler, *Beyn eretz v-shamayim* (Between heaven and earth) (Tel-Aviv: Yavneh, 1964), 18.

23. Eisig Silberschlag, "Rish tif'artenu" (The poverty of our glory), *Kimron yamay: shirim* (My days' arch: poems) (Jerusalem: Kiryat Sefer, 1959), 31.

24. In B. Isaacs, *Beyn shnay 'olamot: sipurim v-tziyurim* (Between two worlds: stories and sketches) (New York: 'Ogen, 1949), 192.

25. Moshe Brind, "Eynam ohavim l-hipazer ha-'ananim" (The clouds refuse to scatter), *Bi-tzvat ha-goral: shirim liriyim v-sipuriyim, sonetot, shninot u-baladot tanakhiyot* (In the grasp of destiny: lyrical and narrative poems, sonnets, witticisms, and biblical ballads), kinus shlishi (third compilation) (New York: Merḥav, 1941), 119, also 124; Halevy, in "Yonim 'al pasay 'ilit" (Pigeons on the el tracks) and "'Asarah cent ha-rikud" (Ten cents a dance), *Mi-tokh ha-sugar: shirim* (From within the prison: poems) (New York: Ohel, 1948), 67, 68–69.

26. Avraham Regelson, "Hodah shel 'ir" (A city's glory), *Kitvay Avraham Regelson: sham ha-bdolaḥ: mar'ot v-'agadot* (The works of Avraham Regelson: there is the crystal: visions and legends) (New York: Va'ad L-hotza'at Kitvay A. Regelson, 1942), 50.

27. Avraham Shmuel Schwartz, "Ma'atayim va-ḥamishim" (Two hundred and fifty), *Shirim* (Poems) (Tel-Aviv: M. Newman, 1959), 179.

28. Uzi Shavit, "The New Hebrew Poetry of the Twenties: Palestine and America," *Prooftexts* 12, no 3 (1992): 213–230; also see related articles in *Migvan*, n. 2 above.

29. Gavriel Preil, *Asfan stavim: shirim 1972–1992* (Collector of autumns: col-

lected poems 1972–1992) (Jerusalem: Mosad Bialik, 1993), 61, 181, 161, 64, 115, 226.

30. Aharon Shabtai, ed., *Gavriel Preil: mivḥar shirim u-dvarim ʿal yetzirato* (Gavriel Preil: selected poems and comments on his work) (Tel-Aviv: Maḥbarot L-shira, 1965), 11. Similar observation is made by D[ov] S[htok] [Dov Sadan], "'Vigvamim shotkim' meʾet Israel Efrat" ("Silent wigwams" by Israel Efros), *Gilyonot* 1, no. 1 (2) (Kislev 5694; 1933): 84.

31. Haramati, "Daniʾel Persky." Also see Daniʾel Persky, *Kitvay Daniʾel Persky—vol. 1, ʿivri anokhi* (The writings of Daniel Persky, vol. 1, I am a Hebrew) (New York: Ha-mḥaber, 1948), 54–59.

32. "Ani ʿover la-havarah ha-sfaradit. Ha-davar kasheh, kasheh mʾod, akh l-hamshikh b-ʾashkenazit ee efshar. ʿod mʿat v-tihyeh ʿinyan l-ʾarkheʾologim." Letter of Eisig Silberschlag, no addressee or date (though likely to Halkin in the early 1930s), Gnazim no. 85533-alef.

33. Israel Efrat (Efros), *Kitvay Israel Efrat: sefer rishon: min ha-ʿolam he-ḥadash—shnay shirim* (The writings of Israel Efros: book one: from the new world—two poems) (Tel-Aviv: Dvir, 1966), 251.

34. S. Halkin, *ʿAd mashber* (Until breakdown) (Tel-Aviv: ʿAm ʿOved, 1945), 257, 206, 209, 210, 241, and more.

35. In "Ba-ḥeder ha-pnimi" (The inner room), *Nekhar: sipurim* (A foreign country: stories) (Jerusalem: Mosad Bialik, 1972), 174–194, esp. 185.

36. Not to be outdone, other writers fall into the same pitfall, including Yaʿakov Tarkow-Naamani, who translates "foxhole" literally as "ḥor ha-shuʿalim," *Rsisay ḥayim (mivḥar sipurim u-rshimot)* (Fragments of life: selected stories and sketches) (New York: ʿOgen, 1951), 93.

37. Others included A. Z. Halevy, Solomon (Shlomo) Damesek, Harry Sackler, Yaʿakov Tarkow-Naamani, Abraham Soyer, Avraham Regelson, and Ḥ. A. Friedland, whose rhymes include "tikhʿasi" / "basi" / "ḥatasi" (you'll be cross / I came / I sinned; in "Havah nitpaysah" (Let's reconcile) or "u-migbaʿas"/ "taʿas" (and hat / loss) in "Shloshim yom meʿata" (Thirty days hence, 47); Ḥ. A. Friedland, *Shiray-ʿam (meʿezvono)* (Folk-poems: from his bequest), ed. Israel Efros, and Ḥayim Orlan (Tel-Aviv and Jerusalem: ʿOgen, M. Newman and Lishkat Haḥinukh Ha-yehudi b-Cleveland, 1963); Aharon Zeitlin, *Shirim u-phoʾemot* (Poems and poemas) (Jerusalem: Mosad Bialik, 1949), 73, 216, 242–244, 272, 273.

38. Letter of Aharon Zeitlin to E. E. Lisitzky, 30 March 1954, Gnazim no. 14/8694/33.

39. Epstein, *Sofrim ʿivrim*, 183. The observation is in his afterword in *ʿAl haʾee: shirim* (On the island: poems) (Jerusalem: Mosad Bialik, 1946), 336; reprinted in his *Shirim: 5677–5733* (Poems: 1917–1973) (Jerusalem: Mosad Bialik, 1977), 435.

40. Ibid.; also Boʾaz Shakhevitz [Shaḥevitch], *Yeʿarot mtohamim: epizodot babiyografiyah literariyah shel Shimʿon Halkin* (Abyssed forests: episodes in Simon

Halkin's biographia literaria) (Tel-Aviv: Katz Research Institute for Hebrew Literature, Tel-Aviv University, 1982), 119, 166.

41. Y. D. Berkowitz (Berkovitch), "Beyn adam la-ḥavero" (Between man and his fellow), in R. Avinoam and Y. Finkle, eds., *Mshorerah shel yahadut America: kovetz l-zikhro shel E. E. Lisitzky Z"L* (Poet of American Jewry: a collection in memory of E. E. Lisitzky) (Tel-Aviv: Maḥbarot L-sifrut, 1966), 9.

42. P. ʿAzaʾi, "Ngohot ba-ʿarafel" (Brightness through the fog), *Ha-ʿoved Ha-tziyoni* (Sivan 5717; May 1957): 31–32.

43. Yeshurun Keshet, "Mshorer ʿivri ʿal enut ha-kushim" (A Hebrew poet on Black suffering); no further bibliographical data, though published following Lisitzky's death in 1962; M. Ungerfeld, "Ngohot me-ʿarafel" (Brightness through the fog), *Ḥerut* (Elul 5717; 6 September 1957): n.p.

44. P. Lander, "Shirat Efraim E. Lisitzky" (E. E. Lisitzky's poetry), *Haʾaretz* 43, no. 12521, 7 October 1960, 13.

45. Y. D. Abramsky, "Al tdaber elay yehudit . . ." (Don't speak Yiddish to me . . .), no additional details.

46. I. M. Lask, "An American Hebrew Poet's Dilemma," *Jerusalem Post* vol. 31, no. 8108, 4 March 1955, p. 8; reprinted in M. A., "Round the Bookshops," *Jerusalem Post* vol. 36, no. 9716, 29 April 1960, p. iv.

47. On Lisitzky's *B-maʿalot uv-moradot*, see Yedidya Menosi, "ʿIm shiray Lisitzky" (With Lisitzky's poems), *Hadoʾar*, year 34, vol. 35, no. 17 (3 Adar 5715; 25 February 1955): 325.

48. K. A. Bertini, "Mi-konanit ha-sfarim: kmo ha-yom rad" (From the bookshelf: as the day set), *Moznayim* 12, no. 1 (Kislev 5720; December 1960): 63. Eisig Silberschlag, "Ha-shirah ha-ʿivrit ba-ʿolam he-ḥadash (Hillel Bavli)" (Hebrew poetry in the New World [Hillel Bavli]), *Aḥisefer*, ed. S. Niger and M. Ribalow (New York: Keren Louis LaMed, 1943), 238; Refaʾel Shoḥat, "Ha-ʾeyn be-ʾemet kore ʿivri ba-ʾAmerica?" (Is there indeed no Hebrew reader in America?), *Kitvay Refaʾel Shoḥat* (Writings of R. Shochatt), ed. A. R. Malakhi (New York: Yedidim, 1942), 264.

49. Avraham Kariv letter to E. E. Lisitzky, 13 February 1960, Gnazim no. 45/15727.

50. Robert Alter, *The Invention of Hebrew Prose: Modern Fiction and the Language of Realism* (Seattle, 1988), 23–24; Alter describes the style of *melitzah* as a "pastiche," in *After the Tradition: Essays on Modern Jewish Writing* (New York: E. P. Dutton, 1969), 80.

51. Part of the above is based on "Maʿamad ha-ʿivrit b-ʾarhab" (The status of Hebrew in the U.S.A.), *ʿAlon Elah: Ha-ʾagudah Li-rkhishat Ha-ʿivrit Ul-horaʾatah* (The Hebrew Language Association [HELA] Newsletter) (Tel-Aviv University), pamphlet 2 (no date, c. 1993), 6.

52. In his poems in *Kmo ha-yom rad: shirim* (As the day set: poems) (Tel-Aviv: Maḥbarot L-sifrut, 1960), 148, 149, 161, accordingly.

53. See, for example, Nurit Govrin, "Beyn ʿolim li-mhagrim: kivunim

mnugadim b-hitpatḥut ha-merkazim ha-sifrutiyim vha-ʿivriyim b-ʾeretz Yisraʾel uv-ʾartzot ha-brit" (Between immigrants to Israel and other immigrants: contradictory movements in the development of the Hebrew literary centers in Eretz-Israel and the U.S.), *Bitzaron*, 8, no. 31–32 (Summer–Fall 1986): 29; also Govrin, in *Migvan*, n. 2 above, 83; Zohar Shavit, "Ha-nisayon ha-koshel l-hakim merkaz shel sifrut ʿivrit ba-ʾAmerica" (The failed attempt to establish a center of Hebrew literature in America), *Migvan*, 433–449. Also, Yeshurun Keshet, "ʿAl Ephraim Lisitzky ha-mshorer" (On the poet E. E. Lisitzky), *Havdalot* (Distinctions) (Tel-Aviv: Agudat Ha-sofrim and Dvir, 1962), 257; Uzi Shavit, "The New Hebrew Poetry."

54. Avraham Kariv, "ʿIm sfarim—Ephraim E. Lisitzky: Mdurot doʾakhot" (Among books—E. E. Lisitzky: dying campfires), *Davar* no. 3789, 5 November 1937, 7.

55. M. Nadav, "Shirat ha-kushim l-ʾEfraim Lisitzky" (E. Lisitzky's poetry of Blacks), *Zmanim* 47 (28 Ḥeshvan 5714; 6 November 1953), n.p.

56. S. Y. Penueli, "Bi-sdeh sefer: adam ʿal adamot" (In the book field: man on earth), *Gilyonot* 22, no. 7–8 (Adar 2–Nisan 5708; 1948), 64; Dan Pagis, "Bikoret sfarim—*B-ʾoholay Khush: shirim* meʾet E. E. Lisitzky" (Book review: In the tents of Cush: poems by E. E. Lisitzky), *Davar* 128, no. 8632, 30 October 1953, 4; Yeshayahu Rabinowitz, "Yetzirato shel Ephraim E. Lisitzky" (E. E. Lisitzky's work), *Bitzaron* 41, no. 4 (Adar 5720; February–March 1960): 191.

57. Rabinowitz, ibid., 198.

CHAPTER TEN

1. For examples of the mythical approach, see the work of Mendele Mocher Sforim, "Shem and Japheth on the Train," in Robert Alter, ed., *Modern Hebrew Literature* (New York: Behrman House, 1975), 16. Another to do so was Sholom Aleichem, *Adventures of Mottel the Cantor's Son*, trans. Tamara Kahana (New York: Collier Books, 1953), 147. L. A. Arieli, *Kitvay L. A. Arieli* (Collected Works of L. A. Arieli: Stories, Plays, Legends, Essays, Letters), Volume 1, ed. Milton Arfa (New York and Tel-Aviv: Israel Matz and Dvir, 1999), 119–141.

2. S. L. Blank, *Ee ha-dmaʾot* (The Isle of Tears) (New York: ʿOgen, 1941).

3. Ibid., esp. 137–145.

4. Ephraim E. Lisitzky, *In the Grip of Cross-Currents*, trans. Moshe Kohn and Jacob Sloan and revised by the author (New York: Bloch Publishing Co., 1959, 2001), 67; the Hebrew original is *Eleh toldot adam* (These are the tales of man) (Jerusalem: Mosad Bialik, 1949), 66.

5. Much has been written about the subject; for a brief overview see Gershon Shaked, *Ha-siporet ha-ʿivrit 1880–1970 (A): ba-golah* (Hebrew narrative fiction 1880–1970: [A]: in exile) (Tel-Aviv/Jerusalem: Ha-kibbutz Ha-mʾuḥad/Keter, 1977), 40–48. Also see Gershon Shaked, *Modern Hebrew Fiction* (Bloomington: Indiana University Press, 2000), 1–10. Although no equivalent event to the 1908

Czernowitz conference declaring Yiddish as the Jews' cultural language can be pointed to about Hebrew, the Zionist conference in December 1906 in Helsingfors (Helsinki) appears to have gone a long way to confirm the priority of Hebrew. It is even likely that the Czernowitz conference was a response to this event. And see, for example, Michael Berkowitz, *Zionist Culture and West European Jewry before the First World War* (New York: Cambridge University Press, 1993), 40. My thanks to Professor Jeffrey Veidlinger for his help on this issue. For a study replete with statistical and ideological evidence of American Jews' ambivalence about immigration to Eretz Israel, much of which bears out the specifics noted in this study, see Joseph B. Glass, *From New Zion to Old Zion: American Jewish Immigration and Settlement in Palestine 1917–1939* (Detroit: Wayne State University Press, 2002), 47–49.

6. Menaḥem Ribalow, "Eretz Israel vha-proza ha-ʿivrit ba-ʾAmerica" (The land of Israel and Hebrew prose in America), *Hado'ar*, year 32, vol. 33, no. 25 (1 Sivan 5713; 15 May 1953): 520–521.

7. Demonstrated by Zohar Shavit, "Ha-nisayon ha-koshel l-hakim merkaz shel sifrut ʿivrit ba-ʾAmerica" (The failed attempt to establish a center of Hebrew literature in America), *Migvan: meḥkarim ba-sifrut ha-ʿivrit uv-giluyeha ha-ʾAmericaniyim—mugashim l-Yaʿakov Kabakoff* (Migvan: Studies in Hebrew Literature in Honor of Jacob Kabakoff), ed. Stanley Nash (Lod, Israel: Makhon Haberman L-meḥkray Sifrut, 1988), 433–449. See there for additional essays on the subject.

8. Tzvi (Harry) Sackler, "Mashiaḥ nosaḥ America" (Messiah American style), *Sefer ha-maḥazot* (The book of plays) (New York: ʿOgen, 1943), 269–330. For a recent review of Noah's place in American literature, including Sackler's work, see Michael Weingrad, "Messiah American Style: Mordecai Manuel Noah and the American Refuge," *AJS Review* 31, no. 1 (April 2007): 75–108.

9. H. Sackler, "Tnu'ah u-manhigeha" (A movement and its leaders) *Sof pasuk: simanim v-samemanim l-otobiyografiyah* (Full stop: signs and signals for an autobiography) (Tel-Aviv: Yavneh, 1966), 47–50.

10. H. Sackler, *Beyn eretz v-shamayim* (Between heaven and earth) (Tel-Aviv: Yavneh, 1964).

11. Avraham Goldberg, *Kitvay Ab. Goldberg—srigim: shirim, tziyurim, sirtutim u-filitonim* (The writings of Abe Goldberg—Grids: poems, portraits, sketches and feuilletons) (New York: ʿOgen, 1930), 68–72.

12. Shlomo Damesek, *Mi-po umi-sham* (From here and there) (New York: Talmidim Vi-ydidim, 1956), 58–59.

13. Shlomo Damesek *Gam sham zarḥah ha-shemesh* (There, too, the sun shined) (Tel-Aviv: Sifray Gadish, 1960), 147.

14. "Bi-ymey nisayon," *Mi-po umi-sham*, 73–79; also appears in *Gam sham zarḥah ha-shemesh.*

15. Bo'az Shakhevitz [Shaḥevitch], *Yeʿarot mtohamim: epizodot ba-biyografiyah literariyah shel Shimʿon Halkin* (Abyssed forests: episodes in Simon Halkin's bio-

graphia literaria) (Tel-Aviv: Katz Research Institute for Hebrew Literature, Tel-Aviv University, 1982), 107, 171.

16. Shimʿon Halkin, *ʿAl ha-ʾee: shirim* (On the island: poems) (Jerusalem: Mosad Bialik, 1946), 205.

17. Halkin, *Maʿavar yabok: shirim* (Jabbok crossing: poems) (Tel-Aviv: ʿAm ʿOved, 1965), 119–176.

18. Halkin, *ʿAl ha-ʾee*, 255–256.

19. Ibid., 257.

20. Ibid., 261–263.

21. Ibid., 261.

22. Ibid., 251.

23. Ibid., 252–254.

24. Shaḥevitch, 108.

25. Ibid., 110–111.

26. Ibid., 300–305.

27. Menaḥem Ribalow, ed., *Antologiyah shel ha-shirah ha-ʿivrit ha-ʾAmerica* (Anthology of Hebrew poetry in America) (New York: ʿOgen, 1938), 313. Also see Avraham Solodar, *Shirim (Poems)*. Ed. M. Ribalow (Chicago: Ha-histadrut Ha-ʿivrit B-Chicago, 1939).

28. See the 1948 essay "Israel Efrat" (Israel Efros), in Avraham Epstein, *Sofrim ʿivrim ba-ʾAmerica* (Hebrew writers in America) (Tel-Aviv: Dvir, 1952), 66–91, esp. 72.

29. Efrat, "My land's melody" ("Nginat artzi"), *Kitvay Israel Efrat: sefer sheni: dorot* (The writings of Israel Efros: Book Two: Generations) (Tel-Aviv: Dvir, 1966), 29.

30. Shalom Kramer, "Israel Efrat—ḥatan pras Brenner" (Israel Efros—Brenner prize laureate), in *Israel Efrat: mshorer v-hogeh* (Israel Efros: poet and thinker), ed. Yitzḥak Orpaz, et al. (Tel-Aviv: Katz Research Institute for Hebrew Literature, Tel-Aviv University, 1981), 29–31.

31. Israel Zmora, "Shirat Israel Efrat" (Israel Efros's poetry), in *Israel Efrat: mshorer v-hogeh*, 70–78. On the loss of home among Iraqi Jewish writers, see Nancy Berg, *Exile from Exile: Israeli Writers from Iraq* (Albany, N.Y.: State University of New York Press, 1996).

32. Efrat, *Dorot*, 181–188; appeared earlier in Israel Efrat, *Goral u-phitʾom: shirim u-phoʾemot* (Destiny and suddenly: poems and poemas) (Jerusalem: Mosad Bialik, 1954), 56–63.

33. Efrat, *Goral u-phitʾom*, 35; also *Dorot*, 162, and poetical record of his visit, 144–152.

34. Similar effects occur, though in reverse, in Efros's poem "ʿAd matay atah moser . . ." (For how long will you turn in . . .), *Dorot*, 203–216, in which the tension between nationalism and religious orthodoxy is cast back to a confrontation in Roman times between Rabbi Yehoshua ben Karkḥa and Rabbi Elazar ben Rav Shimon bar Yoḥai, his pupil.

35. *Goral u-phit'om*, 189–195. The poem appeared initially in *Hado'ar* 28, no. 28 (Iyar 5709; 27 May 1949): 659–661.

36. In the following, all in vol. 3, according to order: "Three sacks" ("Shloshah sakim," 1950, 33–34); "Sa'adiah" "Se'adyah," 1951, 38–43); "Yahyah" ("Yaḥyah," 45), and "Ezra" (31–32). *Kitvay Israel Efrat: sefer shlishi: meh 'amok hu shatul* (The writings of Israel Efros: book three: how deep he is planted) (Tel-Aviv: Dvir, 1966).

37. Ilana Elkad-Lehman, "Tmurot po'etiyot b-shirat Israel Efrat" (Poetic changes in Israel Efrat's poetry) (Ph.D. diss., Dept. of Literature of the Jewish People, Bar-Ilan University, Ramat-Gan, Israel, 1995.

38. "When her husband left" ("Ba-'azov ba'alah"), "Disappointment" ("Akhzavah") and "On a wedding eve" ("B-layl ḥatunah"): Ḥ. A. Friedland, *Sipurim* (stories) (Tel-Aviv: 'Ogen, 1939), 176–182, 196–206, 212–216. Also Ḥ. A. Friedland, "Ten left 'Eyn ha-kovesh" ("Me-'eyn ha-kovesh yatz'u 'asarah") and "The crucible" ("Kur ha-mivḥan"), *Shirim* (poems) (Tel-Aviv: 'Ogen, 1940), 34–36; 76–89.

39. "Sonnet" ("Soneta"), Ibid., 172. The analogy to gold is based on the Hebrew numeric value of the word *zahav*, gold, which is numerically equal to fourteen, the number of lines of a sonnet.

40. It is ironic in some ways, then, that Preil died on a visit to Jerusalem. For a sampling of his poetry on Eretz Israel, see "To my land a confession" ("el artzi viduy"), Gavriel Preil, *Mapat 'erev: shirim* (An evening map: poems) (Tel-Aviv: Dvir, 1961), 106; or "The miracle of the things: 1967" ("Ha-nisiyut sheba-dvarim: 5727"), *Ha-'esh vha-dmamah: shirim* (The fire and the silence: poems (Ramat-Gan: Agudat Ha-sofrim and Masada, 1968), 119; or "Hebrew painter" ("Tzayar 'ivri"), in Gavriel Preil, *Mi-tokh zman v-nof: shirim mkubatzim* (Out of time and vista: collected poems) (Jerusalem: Mosad Bialik, 1972), 134. "A rose will spring from the wormwood" ("Mi-la'anah ta'aleh ha-shoshanah"), Jerusalem and Athens in "In the city of song, two people" ("'Ir ha-shir, shnay anashim"), or Athens with New York in "Robot in autumn" ("Robot ba-stav"). In "Let the East verify" ("Ye'amet ha-mizraḥ") he identifies the Orient reflected within. His expressions about Israel are favorable and full of praise, whether at its ability to stand up in battles or at hearing the Hebrew accent in the mouth of a child in "To the Hebrew child" ("el ha-yeled ha-'ivri"), or "A face in a Jerusalem mirror" ("Panim b-mar'ah yerushalmit"), *Asafan stavim: shirim 1972–1992* (Collector of autumns: collected poems 1972–1992) (Jerusalem: Mosad Bialik, 1993), 213–215.

41. Aaron Zeitlin, *Min ha-'adam va-ma'alah: shtay po'emot dramatiyot* (Above man: two dramatic poemas) (Tel-Aviv: Yavneh, 1964), 124–125, 125–229. A. Zeitlin, *Shirim u-pho'emot* (Poems and poemas) (Jerusalem: Mosad Bialik, 1949), 213–232.

42. See, for example, his poems "Plums in the desert" ("Shezifim ba-midbar"), "Adamit, a nest in the clouds" ("Adamit: ken be-'avim"), and "The hut that outlives palaces: according to a lost notebook" ("Ha-sukah ha-mvalah heykhalot: 'al pi maḥberet ne'elamah"), Avraham Regelson, *Beyt ha-nitzotz: mar'ot v-'agadot*

(The spark's dwelling: visions and legends) (Ramat-Gan: Dvir, 1972), 82–90, 91–101, 102–104; or "The stone remover" ("Ha-msakel"), *Kitvay Avraham Regelson: sham ha-bdolaḥ—mar'ot v-'agadot* (The works of Avraham Regelson: there is the crystal: visions and legends) (New York: Va'ad L-hotz'at Kitvay A. Regelson, 1942), 61–69.

43. "'Od me'at avo le-'Eropah, muvteḥani she-tihyeh 'od b-'Eretz Israel. Ashraykha[?]Ani yare et ha-'aretz. Ani eshheh zman-mah b-Paris, b-Berlin, terem ahin la-'alot." Gnazim, n.d., no. 175/85534-alef.

44. Gnazim, no. 196/51019/1. Further notes of affection are expressed in letters 196/51039/1 of 6 July 1936, and 171/71139/1 of ḥol ha-mo'ed Sukkot (approximately October) 1974.

45. Gnazim, 7 Tishrei 1933, no. 196/51026/1.

46. Eisig Silberschlag, "Mi-Polin 'ad America," in *'Aleh, 'olam, b-shir* (Rise, O world, in song) (New York: 'Ogen; Boston: Boston Hebrew College, 1946), 5–8.

47. Similar sentiments are expressed, and extended, in his later volume, Eisig Silberschlag, *Kimron yamay* (My days' arch: poems) (Jerusalem: Kiryat Sefer, 1959), in poems such as "1947" ("TShZ," 15), "Jerusalem" ("Yerushalayim," 24–25), "To the Sharon" ("La-sharon," 26), "My land, your width is as a pinky" ("Artzi, roḥbekh ka-zeret," 89), and "Decade" ("'Asor," 97–99).

48. Barukh Katznelson, *Mi-lev el lev: shirim* (From heart to heart: poems) (Tel-Aviv: Agudat Ha-sofrim Ha-'ivrim L-yad Dvir, 1954).

49. Ya'acov (Jacob) Kabakoff, "Li-dmutah shel ha-sifrut ha-'ivrit ba-'America" (Image of Hebrew literature in America), *Jewish Book Annual* (*Shnaton ha-sefer ha-yehudi*) 13 (1955–1956): 9–19; quoted from p. 16.

50. See, for example, B. Y. Mikhali, "Mshorer 'ivri b-'oholay khush" (Hebrew poet in the tents of Cush), in Reuven Avinoam and Yitzḥak Finkle, eds., *Mshorerah shel yahadut America: kovetz l-zikhro shel E. E. Lisitzky Z"L* (Poet of American Jewry: a collection in memory of E. E. Lisitzky) (Tel-Aviv: Maḥbarot L-sifrut, 1966), 33–40.

51. See Lisitzky's *In the Grip*, 175–176; Zohar Shavit, n. 7 above. On "shund" literature see, for example, Choneh Shmeruk, "L-toldont sifrut ha-'shund' b-Yiddish" (On the History of Yiddish "Schund" Literature) *Tarbitz: riv'on l-mada'ay ha-yahadut* (*Tarbitz: A Quarterly for Jewish Studies*) 52, no. 2 (Tevet–Adar 5743; January–March 1983): 325–354. My thanks to Professor Dov-Ber Kerler for bringing this article to my attention.

52. Shlomo (Stanley) Nash, "'Ivrit v-Yidish bi-ytzirato shel Reuven Brainin" (Hebrew and Yiddish in the works of Reuven Brainin), *Migvan*, 281–297.

53. For Blank's works, see above, Chapter Nine, n. 15.

54. *Moshavah (Colony)*, 152; *Naḥalah (Patrimony)*, 192.

55. The journal *Ha-tzfirah* was established as a voice of Russian maskilim in the middle of the nineteenth century by Slonimsky, and edited also by Naḥum Sokoloff. *Ha-tzfirah* began its publication in Warsaw in 1862, with the goal of disseminating knowledge of the natural sciences. The publication did not dwell

on current events pertaining to Jews in Russia or Poland. Only after 1870 did it emphasize a political agenda. *Ha-tzfirah* was a conservative and accommodating periodical as regarding new trends in Jewish national issues and did not serve as a platform for debates on new ideologies. And see on this Yosef Klausner, *Historiyah shel ha-sifrut ha-ʿivrit ha-ḥadashah* 4 (A history of modern Hebrew literature, vol. 4) (Jerusalem: Aḥi'asaf, 1963), 123–125.

56. S. L. Blank, "Hon" (Riches), in *ʿEtz ha-sadeh: sipurim* (Tree of the field: stories) (Jerusalem: Kiryat Sefer, 1961), 141–152, esp. 151. Another tale in the same anthology also contains some affirmative views of Israel, and see "Ruḥot msaprot (bayt-ha-kneset msaper)" (Tell-tale spirits: the synagogue's story), ibid., 199.

57. Now explicitly termed a state, a medinah, "Hon" (Riches), ibid., 151. Blank's regard for the State of Israel is significantly more positive than implied in his fiction, though, as is evident in his correspondence of the 1950s. He envies those who have emigrated to live there from the States, a location he calls "A bitter Diaspora" and a "mire." See Gnazim, 221/4522-alef, a letter from Blank to Mordecai Halevy of 16 April 1956. And see there for other letters of similar views.

58. Bernard Isaacs, "Bli shem" and "Ba-maʿaleh uva-morad" (Nameless; On the ascent and the descent), in *ʿAmos mokher tapuzim v-ʿod sipurim* (Amos sells oranges and other stories) (Tel-Aviv: M. Newman, 1953), 38–43, 66–95.

59. For examples, see B. Isaacs, "Ha-ḥalutzah," in *Ḥoter mi-geza: sipurim* (A branch off the stem: stories) (Tel-Aviv and Jerusalem: ʿOgen and M. Newman, 1960), 125–147; English translation, "A Modern Chalutzah," in *Selected Stories by Bernard Isaacs*, trans. Shoshana Perla (Bat-Yam, Israel: E. Lewin-Epstein, 1968), 95–111. Other stories in the above and in his *Mivḥar sipurim* (Selected stories) (Tel-Aviv: Maḥbarot L-sifrut, 1968).

60. L. A. Arieli, *Kitvay Arieli*, vol. 1, 425–437.

61. For a study of the author's tales prior to arriving in America, see Philip Hollander, "Between Decadence and Rebirth: The Fiction of Levi Aryeh Arieli" (Ph.D. diss., Columbia University, 2004). Though Hollander's study covered Arieli's seminal works not composed in America, the latter call for a separate evaluation.

62. Ribalow, ed., *Antologiyah*, 185. Recently, Tamara Hess pointed to the ambivalence in Bavli's "As a golden tiara" ("Ka-ʿateret zahav"), in which the narrator is awed by the Jerusalem landscape all the while that it terrifies him. It is threatening "as an overturned tub over me," he asserts, referencing the Midrash on the imposition of the Ten Commandments on the Children of Israel. Tamara Hess, "'B-ʿeretz lo li': The Sense of Home and Poetic Legacy in Hillel Bavli's Poems," session 6.9 of the Thirty-Eighth Annual Conference of the Association for Jewish Studies, 18 December 2006, San Diego, California.

63. Ibid., 186–187. For Schwartz's response see Shimʿon Halkin, "Shirat A. S. Schwartz" (The poetry of A. S. Schwartz), in A. S. Schwartz, *Shirim* (Poems) (Tel-Aviv: M. Newman, 1959), 352–354.

64. Compare *Shirim*, ibid., 171–172, with Halkin, ibid., 358. Another poet,

Moshe Ben-Meir, writes little of Israel, though he expresses some ambivalence about the prospect of making his home there. Moshe Ben-Meir, *Tzlil va-tzel: shirim v-ʾagadot* (Sound and shadow: poems and legends) (New York: ʿOgen; Tel-Aviv: M. Newman, 1958).

65. Gnazim, no. 196/51389/1; Ribalow's part in American Hebrew culture still awaits a full study.

66. Avraham Zvi Halevy, *New York: shirim v-ʿiyunim b-sifrutenu ha-ḥadashah* (New York: poems and studies of our new literature), ed. Yaʿakov Rimon (Tel-Aviv: Ha-mnorah, 1968), 65–72.

67. Ibid., 67.

68. Ibid., 68.

69. Ibid., 69.

70. Ibid., 71.

71. Ibid., 72.

72. Ibid.

73. Shimʿon Halkin, "Haʿarakhot v-divray bikoret: Avraham Tzvi Halevy" (Criticism and evaluations: A. Z. Halevy), *Bitzaron*, year 10, vol. 19, no. 3 (Kislev–Tevet 5709; December 1948–January 1949): 194–200.

74. Ḥaim Schirmann, *Ha-shirah ha-ʿivrit bi-Sfarad uvi-Provence*, sefer 1, kerekh 2 (Hebrew poetry in Spain and Provence, book 1, vol. 2) (Jerusalem and Tel-Aviv: Mosad Bialik and Dvir, 1954), 485–513, esp. 494–513; stormy seas are reported in poem 2, 502–503; and in poem 212, 494–497; also included are descriptions of storm at sea in poem 9, 506–510. For a new study on Halevi's voyage to Eretz Israel, the surrounding legend, and relevant poems in the original and English translation, see Raymond P. Scheindlin, *The Song of the Distant Dove: Judah Halevi's Pilgrimage* (New York: Oxford University Press, 2008), 4, 150.

75. Later, air travel would replace the longer and more dramatic crossing by sea, as in the case of Saul Bellow's journey, *To Jerusalem and Back: A Personal Account* (New York: Viking Press, 1976).

76. Told by the sixteenth century Italian Jewish scholar Gedalia Ibn Yaḥya, discussed in Scheindlin, 249–252.

77. Ephraim E. Lisitzky, *B-maʿalot uv-moradot* (Ascents and descents) (Tel Aviv: Dvir, 1954), 128–154; 155–193. All translations from the Hebrew are mine, unless otherwise stated.

78. Schirmann, 485–489, and Scheindlin, 172–176, repeated in Halevi's "Beauteous vista . . ." ("Yefeh nof"), Schirmann, 489, translated as "O lovely hill" in Scheindlin, 166–167, in which the cluster of terms is closer to Lisitzky's, especially line 6. The translations by Nina Salaman of the Hebrew titles are from Heinrich Brody, ed., *Selected Poems of Jehudah Halevi* (Philadelphia: Jewish Publication Society of America, 1952).

79. Ḥayim Brody, ed., *Divan: v-hu sefer kolel kol shiray abir ha-mshorerim Yehudah ben Shmuʾel Halevi* (Diwan des Abu-l-Hasan Jehuda ha-Levi) (Reprint, England: Gregg International Publishers Ltd., 1971), 1:53–55; citation is from

p. 55, line 59. The poem is also reproduced in Israel Zmora, ed., *Shiray rabbi Yehudah Halevi*, kerekh 1, sefer 3 (The poems of Rabbi Yehudah Halevi. Vol. 1, book 3), "Poems of friendship: for Rabbi Yehudah Ben-Giyat—6 poems" (Tel-Aviv: Maḥbarot L-sifrut, 1946), 99–101. Strategically, Lisitzky's poem bears an intertextual relationship to the medieval bard's in more than mere word usage. In Halevi's work, the poem raises the issue of harboring two loyalties, the love for two places. Halevi also includes a discourse—perhaps imaginary—with Ibn Giyat, the subject of this panegyric on the possibility of sustaining a dual loyalty to east and west, among other dichotomies.

80. "Rabbi Yehudah Halevi," *Ascents*, 168–169.

81. Avraham Epstein, "Moshe Feinstein," *Sofrim ʿivrim ba-ʾAmerica*, 125–141.

82. Gnazim, 16 October 1932, catalog number 21/21841.

83. Gnazim, catalog number 412/10994/2.

84. Gnazim, catalog number 374/78925/1.

85. Moshe Feinstein, *ʿAl saf ha-sof: shirim v-sonetot* (On the edge of the end: poems and sonnets) (Jerusalem: M. Newman, 1964), 84.

86. Israel Efrat, *dorot*, n. 29 above.

87. Israel Efrat, *meh ʿamok hu shatul*, n. 36 above, 24–26.

88. Ibid. The anthology also carries a number of long poems set in and addressed to the matter of Eretz Israel, 181–203. These works appeared originally in *Goral u-phitʾom*, 56–63, 64–77, 90–125: "Jerusalem" ("Yerushalayim"), composed between 1945–1954, "In the sphere of royalty" ("Bi-sfirat malkhut") (1948), and "I remember" ("Zakharti lakh") (1945–1954). The last was later moved into *Meh ʿamok hu shatul*, 49–85.

89. Ibid.

90. Elkad-Lehman, "Poetic changes." On the conservatism of American Hebrew poetry see Uzi Shavit, "The New Hebrew Poetry of the Twenties: Palestine and America," *Prooftexts* 12, no. 3 (1992): 213–230.

91. For insight into the paradoxical states of home and exile among oriental Jewish literati see Berg, *Exile.*

92. Reuven (Avinoam) Grossmann, *Idilyot* (Idyls) (Tel-Aviv: Ḥavurah/ Dvir, 1934).

93. Reuven (Avinoam) Grossmann, *Shirim* (Poems) (Tel-Aviv: Ḥavura/ Dvir, 1930), 92–98, 119–128.

94. Reuven (Avinoam) Grossmann, *Shirim u-phoʾemot* (Poems and poemas) (Tel-Aviv: Yavneh, 1950).

95. Scheindlin, 31–35, 64, 72–78, 156–162, and elsewhere, although the nature of their quest differed. Though interesting in itself, a consideration of this subject is beyond the scope of the present study.

96. A similar formula on the reciprocity between man's act and God's response is expressed by Halevi, and see Scheindlin, 44–7, 81.

97. A. S. Schwartz, *Shirim*, 257–259.

98. Schirmann 494–497; for the Hebrew and English, translated as "Equipped

for Flight," see Brody, 10–13; or "Still Chasing Fun," also used by Halevi in "Trapped in the Heart of the Sea," Scheindlin, 184–189 and 234, accordingly. The title also resonates with S. Y. Agnon's novella, "In the Heart of the Seas."

99. Reuven Wallenrod, *Drakhim va-derekh: pirkay masa* (Roads and byways: chapters of a journey) (New York: 'Ohel; Tel-Aviv: M. Newman, 1950), 10–11. On the occasion of the State of Israel's first anniversary, Tarkov-Na'amani draws attention to American Jewry by borrowing Halevi's words as a title for his essay: Ya'akov Tarkov-na'amani, "Tziyon halo tish'ali" (Zion, won't you ask), *Hado'ar* 28, no. 28 (Iyar 5709; 27 May 1949): 703–704.

100. Halevi in Schirmann: "To You is my soul . . ." ("Lekha nafshi btuḥah . . ."), 502–503, "The western wind" ("Zeh ruḥakha, tzad ma'arav . . ."), 504; "Considers and upholds . . . ," ("Yo'etz u-mekim . . ."), 506–510; in Scheindlin, 230–233, 226–229, and 242–247, accordingly. That Halevi was also beset by ambivalence and anxiety, see Scheindlin, 148–149, 217, 228.

101. Ephraim E. Lisitzky, *Eleh toldot*, 285. English version, *In the Grip*, 296. On the contentiousness and varied means of support for the Zionist enterprise, see Joseph Glass, *From New Zion*, 47–49.

102. Hillel Barzel, *Toldot ha-shirah ha-'ivrit mi-ḥibat tziyon 'ad yameynu—kerekh alef: shirat ḥibat tziyon* (A History of Hebrew poetry, volume 1: The Ḥibat Tziyon period) (Tel-Aviv: Sifriyat Po'alim, 1987), 102, 123, 167–170, 184, 199, 222, 286, 358, 374; Hillel Barzel, *Toldot ha-shirah ha-'ivrit mi-ḥibat tziyon 'ad yameynu—kerekh dalet: shirat ha-teḥiyah: omanay ha-janer* (A History of Hebrew poetry from the Ḥibat Tziyon period to our times, volume 4: masters of genre) (Tel-Aviv: Sifriyat Po'alim, 1997), 643–644; Hillel Barzel, *Toldot ha-shirah ha-'ivrit mi-ḥibat tziyon 'ad yameynu—kerekh heh: shirat Eretz Israel: Avraham Shlonsky, Natan Alterman, Leah Goldberg* (A history of Hebrew poetry from the Ḥibat Tziyon period to our times, volume 5: the poetry of the Land of Israel: A. Shlonsky, N. Alterman, L. Goldberg) (Tel-Aviv: Sifriyat Po'alim, 2001), 207; Avraham Sha'anan, *Ha-sifrut ha-'ivrit ha-ḥadashah li-zramayha—kerekh ḥamishi: ha-nosaḥ u-mitos ha-ḥipus b-nigudayhem* (Trends in Modern Hebrew Literature—5: The nosaḥ and quest myth opposed) (Hebrew; Tel-Aviv: Sifriyat Davar and Bar-Ilan University, 1977), 174; Gershon Shaked, *Hasiporet ha-'ivrit 1880–1980 [G] ha-modernah beyn shtay milḥamot ha-'olam mavo l-"dor ba-'aretz"* (Hebrew narrative fiction 1880–1980: 3. The "moderna" between wars—introduction to "generation in the land" (Tel-Aviv/Jerusalem: Hakibbutz Ha-m'uḥad and Keter, 1988), 88; Eisig Silberschlag, *From Renaissance to Renaissance: Hebrew Literature from 1492–1970*, vol. 1 (New York: Ktav, 1973), 36, 54, 203, 339.

103. The obscure poet Yehudah Goldman also composed a number of poems of his travels by sea, though his work does not make it clear as to the origins or destination of the trip. However, other poems in the collection testify to residence in the Land of Israel and familiarity with its landscape. Yehudah Goldman, *Nimim (shirim)* (Chords: poems), vol. 1 (New York: Agudat Sofrim 'Ivriyim Tz'irim, 1932).

BIBLIOGRAPHY

ARCHIVES

American Jewish Archives (Cincinnati)
Gnazim Bio-Bibliographical Archive (Tel-Aviv)
National and University Library Archives at the Hebrew University of Jerusalem (Jerusalem)

ENGLISH-LANGUAGE SOURCES

Abramson, Glenda, ed. *The Oxford Book of Hebrew Short Stories.* New York: Oxford University Press, 1997.

Adler, Selig, and Thomas E. Connolly. *From Ararat to Suburbia: The History of the Jewish Community of Buffalo.* Philadelphia: Jewish Publication Society of America, 1960.

Aleichem, Sholom. *Adventures of Mottel the Cantor's Son.* Trans. Tamara Kahana. New York: Collier Books, 1953.

Alexander, Michael. *Jazz Age Jews.* Princeton: Princeton University Press, 2001.

Alter, Robert. *After the Tradition: Essays on Modern Jewish Writing.* New York: E. P. Dutton, 1969.

———. *The Invention of Hebrew Prose: Modern Fiction and the Language of Realism.* Seattle: University of Washington Press, 1988.

———, ed. *Modern Hebrew Literature.* New York: Behrman House, 1975.

Antin, Mary. *The Promised Land.* Boston: Houghton Mifflin Co., 1969.

Avinoam (Grossmann), Reuben. *Compendious Hebrew-English Dictionary.* Edited by M. H. Segal. Tel Aviv: Dvir, 1962.

Bavli, Hillel. *The Growth of Modern Hebrew Literature.* New York: Hebrew P.E.N. Club, 1939.

———. *Some Aspects of Modern Hebrew Poetry.* New York: Theodor Herzl Foundation, 1958.

Bachman, Merle Lyn. "American Yiddish Poetry's Encounter with Black America." *Shofar* 21, no. 1 (2002): 3–24.

Beauchamp, William M., ed. *Iroquois Folk Lore: Gathered from the Six Nations of*

New York. Empire State Historical Publications, no. 31. Port Washington, N.Y.: Ira J. Friedman, Inc., 1965.

Bellow, Saul. *To Jerusalem and Back: A Personal Account.* New York: Viking Press, 1976.

Berg, Nancy. *Exile from Exile: Israeli Writers from Iraq*. Albany, N.Y.: State University of New York Press, 1996.

Bergman, Leo A. "Dr. Ephraim E. Lisitzky." (New Orleans) *Touro Synagogue Bulletin* 12, no. 5 (16 January 1959).

Berkowitz, Michael. *Zionist Culture and West European Jewry before the First World War.* New York: Cambridge University Press, 1993.

Bialik, Ḥayyim Nachman. *Complete Poetic Works of Ḥayyim Nachman Bialik.* Vol. I. Edited by Israel Efros. New York: Histadruth Ivrith of America, 1948.

———. *Selected Poems.* Edited by Israel Efros. Rev. ed. New York: Bloch/ Histadruth Ivrith of America, 1965.

Bilik, Dorothy Siedman. *Immigrant-Survivors: Post-Holocaust Consciousness in Recent Jewish American Fiction.* Middletown, Conn.: Wesleyan University Press, 1981.

Birmingham, Stephen. *"Our Crowd": The Great Jewish Families of New York* (New York: Dell, 1967).

———. *The Grandees: The Story of America's Sephardic Elite* (New York: Dell, 1971).

Black History Museum Committee, ed. *Sterling A. Brown: A UMUM Tribute.* Philadelphia: Black History Museum UMUM Publishers, 1976.

Blumenfield, Samuel M. "Ephraim Lisitzky—American Hebrew Bard." *Chicago Jewish Forum* (Spring 1964): 204–207.

———. "News and Views: American Hebrew Bard, Negro Lover, Singer of National Beauty—Ephraim Lisitzky." *Der Tog* (New York), 5 August 1964, 1–2.

———. "Ephraim Lisitzky: Poet-Educator." In *Philip W. Lown: A Jubilee Volume.* Edited by Judah Pilch, 83–87. New York: Bloch Publishing Co., 1967.

Bodnar, John. *The Transplanted: A History of Immigrants in Urban America.* Bloomington: Indiana University Press, 1985.

Bontemps, Arna. "Rock, Church, Rock!" in Langston Hughes and Arna Bontemps, eds., *The Book of Negro Folklore.* New York: Dodd, Mead and Co., 1958.

———, ed. *The Harlem Renaissance Remembered.* New York: Dodd, Mead and Co., 1972.

Bordewich, Fergus M. *Killing the White Man's Indian: Reinventing Native Americans at the End of the Twentieth Century.* New York: Doubleday, 1966.

Bourgeois, Arthur P., ed. *Ojibwa Narratives of Charles and Charlotte Kawbawgam and Jacques LePique, 1893–1895.* Detroit: Wayne State University Press, 1994.

Brawley, Benjamin, "The Negro in American Fiction," in *Anthology of American Negro Literature*, edited by Sylvestre C. Watkins. New York: Modern Library/ Random House, 1944, 108–116.

Brinton, Daniel G. *The Lenape and Their Legends.* New York: AMS Press, 1969.

Brody, Heinrich, ed., *Selected Poems of Jehudah Halevi.* Philadelphia: Jewish Publication Society of America, 1952).

Brooks, Mel, et al. "Blazing Saddles: Mel Brooks' Black Bart." An original screenplay based on a story by Andrew Bergman—draft. Burbank: Warner Brothers, 1972.

Brown, Joseph Epes. *The Sacred Pipe: Black Elk's Account of the Seven Rites of the Oglala Sioux.* Norman: University of Oklahoma, 1953.

———. *The Spiritual Legacy of the American Indian.* New York: Crossroads, 1982.

———. *Animals of the Soul: Sacred Animals of the Oglala Sioux.* Rockport: Elements, Inc., 1992.

Brown, Phil. *Catskill Culture: A Mountain Rat's Memories of the Great Jewish Resort Area.* Philadelphia: Temple University Press, 1998.

———. *In the Catskills: A Century of Jewish Life in "The Mountains."* New York: Columbia University Press, 2002.

Brown, Sterling A. "Contemporary Negro Poetry, 1914–1936." In *Anthology of American Negro Literature,* edited by Sylvestre C. Watkins, 243–261. New York: Modern Library, Random House, 1944.

———. "The Blues as Folk Poetry." In *The Book of Negro Folklore,* edited by Langston Hughes and Arna Bontemps, 371–385. New York: Dodd, Mead and Co., 1958.

———. "The Spirituals." In *The Book of Negro Folklore,* edited by Langston Hughes and Arna Bontemps, 279–289. New York: Dodd, Mead and Co., 1958.

———. *Southern Road: Poems by Sterling A. Brown.* Boston: Beacon Press, 1974.

———. *The Last Ride of Wild Bill: And Eleven Narrative Poems.* Detroit: Broadside Press, 1975.

Burnshaw, Stanley, et al., eds. *The Modern Hebrew Poem Itself.* New York: Schocken Books, 1966.

Cahan, Abraham. *The Rise of David Levinsky.* New York: Harper and Row, 1960.

Calloway, Colin G., Gerd Gemunden, and Susanne Zantop, eds. *Germans and Indians: Fantasies, Encounters, Projections.* Lincoln: University of Nebraska Press, 2002.

Catlin, George. *Letters and Notes on the Manners, Customs, and Conditions of the North American Indians.* 2 vols. Minneapolis: Rose and Haines, 1965.

Chabon, Michael. *The Yiddish Policeman's Union.* New York: HarperCollins, 2007.

Choate, Florence, and Elizabeth Curtis. *Indian Fairy Book.* New York: N.p., 1916.

Clark, Ella E. *Indian Legends of the Pacific Northwest.* Berkeley: University of California Press, 1953.

———. *Indian Legends from the Northern Rockies.* Norman: University of Oklahoma, 1966.

———. *Voices of the Winds: Native American Legends.* New York: Facts on File, 1989.

Clark, W[illiam] P[hilo]. *The Indian Sign Language, with Brief Explanatory Notes.* Philadelphia: L. R. Hamersly, 1885.

Coen, Rena. "Longfellow, Hiawatha, and American Nineteenth Century Painters." *Papers Presented at the Longfellow Commemorative Conference*, 1–3 April 1982. N.p. Longfellow National Historic Site, 1982, 68–91.

Coleman, Sister Bernard, Ellen Froguer, and Estelle Eich. *Ojibwa Myths and Legends.* Minneapolis: Ross and Haines, Inc., 1962.

Conelly, Marc. *The Green Pastures: A Fable.* New York: Books, Inc., 1945.

Corlett, William T. *The Medicine-Man of the American Indian and His Cultural Background.* Baltimore: Charles C. Thomas, 1935.

Cronyn, George W., ed. *American Indian Poetry: An Anthology of Songs and Chants.* New York: Liveright, 1962.

Cullen, Countee. *Color.* New York: Harper and Brothers, 1925.

Curtin, Jeremiah. *Creation Myths of Primitive America.* London: Williams and Norgate, 1899.

Curtis [Burlin], Natalie, ed. *The Indians' Book.* New York: Harper and Brothers Publishing, 1907, 1923.

Cushing, G. F. "Ob Ugrian (Vogul and Ostyak)." In *Traditions of Heroic and Epic Poetry.* Vol. 1, *The Traditions*, edited by A. T. Hatto, 211–235. London: Modern Humanities Research Association, 1980.

Davidson, Levette J., ed. *Poems of the Old West: A Rocky Mountain Anthology.* Denver: University of Denver Press, 1951.

Davis, Colin. *Levinas: An Introduction.* Notre Dame, Indiana: University of Notre Dame Press, 1996.

Dorsey, George A. *The Pawnee Mythology.* Lincoln: University of Nebraska Press, 1997.

Dorsey, James O. *A Study of Siouan Indian Cults.* Eleventh Annual report of the Bureau of American Ethnology, Smithsonian Institution, Washington, D.C., 1894.

Dorsey, James O., and Alfred L. Kroeber. *Traditions of the Arapaho.* Field Museum of Natural History, Anthropological Series vol. V, Chicago, 1903.

"Dr. Lisitzky is Poetry Winner." (New Orleans) *Times Picayune*, 18 May 1961.

Du Bois, Constance Goddard. "The Story of Creation." *Journal of American Folk Lore* 14 (1901): 181–183.

Du Bois, William Edward Burghardt. *A W. E. B. Du Bois Reader*, edited by Andrew G. Paschal. New York: Macmillan Company, 1971.

Dunbar, Paul L. *The Complete Poems of Paul Laurence Dunbar.* New York: Dodd, Mead and Company, 1945.

Duncan, Barbara, ed. *Living Stories of the Cherokee.* Chapel Hill: University of North Carolina Press, 1998.

Eastman, Charles A., and E. G. Eastman. *Wigwam Evenings: Sioux Folk Tales Retold.* Lincoln: University of Nebraska Press, 1990. Originally published 1909.

Edmonds, Margot, and Ella E. Clark, eds. *Voices of the Winds: Native American Legends.* New York: Facts on File, 1989.

Efros, Israel. *The Bloody Jest: A Drama in Four Acts.* Boston: Gorham Press/ Richard G. Badger, 1922.

———, ed. *Complete Poetic Works of Hayyim Nahman Bialik.* Vol. 1. New York: Histadruth Ivrith of America, 1948.

Efros, Israel, and Judah Ibn-Shmuel (Kaufman), eds. *English-Hebrew Dictionary: Supplement.* Tel Aviv: Dvir, 1968.

Efros, Israel, Judah Ibn-Shmuel (Kaufman), and Benjamin Silk, eds. *English-Hebrew Dictionary.* Tel Aviv: Dvir, 1955.

"Ephraim Lisitzky, Hebrew Poet, Translator and Educator, Dies," *New York Times,* 27 June 1962.

Epstein, George, and Max Zeldner, eds. *Modern Hebrew Literature.* New York: Hebrew Publishing Company, 1948.

Erdoes, Richard, ed. *The Sound of Flutes and Other Indian Legends.* New York: Pantheon Books, 1976.

Erdoes, Richard, and Alfonso Ortiz, eds. *American Indian Myths and Legends.* New York: Pantheon Books, 1984.

Erens, Patricia. *The Jew in American Cinema.* Bloomington: Indiana University Press, 1984.

Feldman, Yael S. *Modernism and Cultural Transfer: Gabriel Preil and the Tradition of Jewish Literary Bilingualism.* Cincinnati: Hebrew Union College Press, 1985.

Fenkl, Heinz Insu. *Memories of My Ghost Brother.* New York: Dutton, 1996.

Field, Alan G. "Halutziut in New Orleans." *Jewish Spectator* (June 1957), 25–26.

Frank, Gelya. "Melville J. Herskovits on the African and Jewish Diasporas: Race, Culture and Modern Anthropology." *Identities,* volume 8, no. 2 (2001), 173–209.

Franklin, John Hope, and Alfred A. Moss, Jr. *From Slavery to Freedom: A History of African Americans.* New York: Alfred A. Knopf, 1994.

Friedman, Myrna. *It Happened in the Catskills.* San Diego: Harcourt Brace, 1996.

Friedman, Saul S. *Jews and the American Slave Trade.* New Brunswick, N.J.: Transaction Books, 1998.

Gal, Allon, ed. *Envisioning Israel: The Changing Ideas and Images of North American Jews.* Jerusalem and Detroit: Magnes Press, Hebrew University, and Wayne State University Press, 1996.

Gibbings, W. W., ed. *Folklore and Legends, North American Indians.* London: W. W. Gibbings, 1890. Facsimile reprint, Felinfach, Wales: Llanerch Publishers, 1993.

Gilman, Sander L. *The Jew's Body.* New York: Routledge, 1991.

———. *The Case of Sigmund Freud: Medicine and Identity at the Fin de Siècle.* Baltimore: Johns Hopkins University Press, 1993.

Glass, Joseph B. *From New Zion to Old Zion: American Jewish Immigration and*

Settlement in Palestine, 1917–1939. Detroit: Wayne State University Press, 2002.

Gluzman, Michael. *The Politics of Canonicity: Lines of Resistance in Modernist Hebrew Poetry.* Stanford: Stanford University Press, 2003.

Goffman, Ethan. "Imag(in)ing Each Other: Black and Jewish Literary Representations." Ph.D. dissertation, Indiana University, Bloomington, 1997.

———. *Imaging Each Other: Blacks and Jews in Contemporary American Literature.* Albany: State University of New York Press, 2000.

Goldman, Shalom, ed. *Hebrew and the Bible in America: The First Two Centuries.* Hanover, N.H.: Brandeis University Press and Dartmouth College/University Press of New England, 1993.

Goldman, Shalom, and Laurie Patton. "From All Their Habitations—Indian Love Call: Orthodoxy and Indian Culture." *Judaism* 50, no. 3 (Summer 2001): 351–361.

Grinnell, George Bird. *Blackfoot Lodge Tales—The Story of the Prairie People.* New York: Scribners, 1892.

———. *The Punishment of the Stingy and Other Indian Stories.* New York: Harper and Brothers Publishers, 1901.

———. "Some Early Cheyenne Tales." *Journal of American Folklore*, vol. 20, no. 78 (1907).

———. *The Cheyenne Indians—Their History and Ways of Life.* New Haven: Yale University Press, 1923.

———. *By Cheyenne Campfires.* New Haven: Yale University Press, 1926.

Gruber, Ruth. *Haven: The Unknown Story of 1,000 World War II Refugees.* New York: Coward-McCann, 1983.

Grusd, Edward E. "Tale of Two Cultures." *National Jewish Monthly* (November 1950): 11.

Hadari, Atar, ed. and trans. *Songs from Bialik: Selected Poems of Hayim Nahman Bialik.* Syracuse: Syracuse University Press, 2004.

Haeberlin, Hermann. "Mythology of Puget Sound." *Journal of American Folk-Lore* 37, nos. 143–144 (January–June 1924): 371–438.

Halkin, Simon. *Modern Hebrew Literature: Trends and Values.* New York: Schocken Books, 1950.

Hansen, Marcus Lee. *The Problem of the Third Generation Immigrant.* Republication of the 1937 address with introduction by Peter Kivisto and Oscar Handlin. Rock Island, Ill.: Swenson Swedish Immigration Center and Augustana College Library Occasional Paper No. 16, 1987.

Harshav, Benjamin. *Language in Time of Revolution.* Stanford: Stanford University Press, 1993.

Hasak-Lowy, Todd. "Between Realism and Modernism: Brenner's Poetics of Fragmentation." *Hebrew Studies* 44 (2003): 41–64.

Hazen-Hammond, Susan. *Spider Woman's Web: Traditional Native American Tales about Women's Power.* New York: Perigee Books, 1999.

Helbling, Mark. *The Harlem Renaissance: The One and the Many.* Westport, Conn.: Greenwood Press, 1999.

Hess, Tamara. "'B-'eretz lo li': The Sense of Home and Poetic Legacy in Hillel Bavli's Poems." Paper presented at session 6.9 of the Thirty-Eighth Annual Conference of the Association for Jewish Studies, 18 December 2006, San Diego, California.

Heyd, Milly. *Mutual Reflections: Jews and Blacks in American Art.* New Brunswick, N.J.: Rutgers University Press, 1999.

Hitakonanu'laxk [Tree Bear], ed. *The Grandfathers Speak: Native American Folk Tales of the Lenape People.* New York: Interlink Books, 1994.

Hollander, Philip Abraham. "Between Decadence and Rebirth: The Fiction of Levi Aryeh Arieli." Ph.D. dissertation, Columbia University, 2004.

Howe, Irving. *World of Our Fathers.* New York: Harcourt Brace Jovanovich, 1976.

"HUC to Confer Honorary Degree on Dr. Lisitzky: Dr. Lisitzky Awarded Honorary Degree by HUC." *New Orleans Jewish Ledger,* 29 January 1960.

Hughes, Langston. *Selected Poems of Langston Hughes.* New York: Vintage Books, 1959, 1974.

———. *The Panther and the Lash: Poems of Our Times.* New York: Vintage, 1967, 1992.

———. *The Collected Poems of Langston Hughes,* edited by Arnold Ramperrad and David Roessel. New York: Alfred A. Knopf, 1994.

Hughes, Langston, and Arna Bontemps, eds. *The Book of Negro Folklore.* New York: Dodd, Mead and Co., 1958.

Hughes, Langston, and Zora Neal Hurston. *Mule Bone: A Comedy of Negro Life,* edited by George Houston Bass and Henry Louis Gates, Jr. New York: Harper Collins, 1991.

Isaacs, Bernard. *Selected Stories by Bernard Isaacs.* Trans. Shoshana Perla. Bat-Yam, Israel: E. Lewin-Epstein, 1968.

Jacobson, Matthew Frye. *Special Sorrows: The Diasporic Imagination of Irish, Polish, and Jewish Immigrants in the United States.* Cambridge, Mass.: Harvard University Press, 1995.

Janowsky, Oscar I., ed. *The American Jew: A Reappraisal.* Philadelphia: Jewish Publication Sciety of America, 1964.

Jennings, Francis. *The Invasion of America: Indians, Colonialism, and the Cant of Conquest.* New York: W. W. Norton & Co., 1975.

Johnson, James Weldon. *Saint Peter Relates an Incident: Selected Poems by James Weldon Johnson.* New York: Viking Press, 1935.

———. "The History of the Spiritual." In *Anthology of American Negro Literature,* edited by Sylvestre C. Watkins, 117–154. New York: Modern Library, Random House, 1944.

———. *God's Trombone: Seven Negro Sermons in Verse.* New York: Penguin, 1976.

———, ed. *The Book of American Negro Poetry.* New York: Harcourt, Brace and Co., 1931.

Johnson, James Weldon, and J. Rosamond Johnson, eds. *The Book of American Negro Spirituals.* Including "The Book of American Negro Spirituals" and "The Second Book of Negro Spirituals." New York: Viking Press, 1940.

Jones, Jeffrey R. *Noccalula: Legend, Fact and Function.* Collinville, Ala.: Jeffrey and Jones Gang, Inc., 1989.

Judson, Katherine Berry. *Myths and Legends of the Great Plains.* Chicago: A. C. McClurg and Co., 1913.

———, ed. *Myths and Legends of the Mississippi Valley and the Great Lakes.* Chicago: A. C. McClurg and Co., 1914.

———. *Myths and Legends of British North America.* Chicago: A. C. McClurg and Co., 1917.

Kabakoff, Jacob. "Hebrew Culture and Creativity in America." In *Jewish Life in America,* edited by Theodore Friedman and Robert Gordis. New York: Horizon Press, 1955, 170–196.

———. "Hebrew Literature: The Gamut of Emotions." *The JWB Circle—In Jewish Bookland* (May 1955): 7.

———. "The Baring of a Soul Laden with Suffering." *JWB Circle* (January 1965).

———. "Israel Efros: Poet-Philosopher (On the Occasion of His 80th Birthday). *Jewish Book Annual* 28 (1970–1971): 105–109.

———. "Simon Halkin—Man of Letters: On the Occasion of His 75th Birthday." *Jewish Book Annual* 31 (1973–1974): 62–66.

———. "Major Aspects of American Hebrew Literature." *Hebrew Abstracts* 15 (1974): 58–67.

———. "Hebrew Literature on American Soil." *Modern Hebrew Literature* 2 (Summer 1975): 17–25.

———, ed. *Master of Hope: Selected Writings of Naphtali Herz Imber.* London: Herzl Press and Fairleigh Dickinson University Press, 1985.

———. "B. N. Silkiner and His Circle: The Genesis of the New Hebrew Literature in America." *Judaism* 39, no. 1 (Winter 1990): 97–103.

———. "Hebrew Literature: Poems Evoke the Gamut of Memory of People and Places." N.d., n.p.

Kaniuk, Yoram. *The Acrophile.* New York: Atheneum, 1961.

———. *Rockinghorse.* New York: Harper and Row, 1977.

———. *Commander of the Exodus.* New York: Grove Press, 1999.

———. "Killers: Excerpt from *I Did It My Way.*" Trans. Anthony Berris. *Zeek* (Fall/Winter 2007): 70–76.

Karp, Abraham J., ed. *The Jew in America: A Treasury of Art and Literature.* N.p.: Hugh Lauter Levin Associates, Inc., 1994.

Katz, Gideon, and Gideon Nevo. "Two Perspectives on Abraham Regelson's

'Hakukot Otiyotayich' (Engraved Are Your Letters)." *Hebrew Studies* 48 (2007): 317–338.

Katz, Stephen. "History, Memory, and Ideology: Ben Avigdor's Fin-de-Siècle Hebrew Literature." *Jewish History* 12, no. 2 (Fall 1998): 33–49.

———. "To Be as Others: E. E. Lisitzky's Re-presentation of Native Americans." *Hebrew Union College Annual* 73 (2002): 249–297.

———, trans. and commentary. "'So Miriam Spoke of Moses' by E. E. Lisitzky." *CCAR Journal* (Fall 2008): 59–89.

Keiser, Albert. *The Indian in American Literature.* New York: Octagon Press, 1970.

Kilpatrick, J. F., and Anna G. Kilpatrick. *Friends of Thunder: Folktales of the Oklahoma Cherokees.* Dallas: Southern Methodist University Press, 1964.

Kovner, Abba. *Sloan-Kettering.* Trans. Eddie Levenston. New York: Schocken Books, 2002.

Kramer, Michael P., and Hana Wirth-Nesher, eds. *The Cambridge Companion to Jewish American Literature.* Cambridge, UK: Cambridge University Press, 2003.

Kramer, Victor A., and Robert A. Russ, eds. *Harlem Renaissance Re-Examined.* New York: Whitston Publishing Co., 1997.

Lame Deer. "The Vision Quest." In *The Sound of Flutes and Other Indian Legends,* edited by Richard Erdoes, 63–67. New York: Pantheon Books, 1976.

Lask, I. M. "An American Hebrew Poet's Dilemma." *Jerusalem Post,* vol. 31, no. 8108, 4 March 1955, 8.

Learsi, Rufus [pseud. Israel Goldberg]. *The Jews in America: A History.* New York: Ktav, 1972.

Leeming, Daniel, and Jake Page. *The Mythology of Native North America.* Norman: University of Oklahoma Press, 1998.

LeGoff, Jacques. *History and Memory.* Trans. S. Randall and E. Claman. New York: Columbia University Press, 1992.

Leivick, H., and Israel Efros. "They Must Be Rescued." *Congress Weekly: A Review of Jewish Interests* 13, no. 21 (19 July 1946): 6–8.

Leland, Charles G. *The Algonquin Legends of New England: or, Myths and Folk Lore of the Micmac, Passamaquady, Penobscot Tribes.* Boston: Houghton, Mifflin and Company, 1884. Reprint, Detroit: Singing Tree Press, 1968.

———. *The Algonquin Legends of New England.* Boston: Houghton, Mifflin and Co., 1885.

Leland, Charles G., and John D. Prince, eds. and trans. *Kuloscap the Master and Other Algonquin Poems.* Trans. metrically by Charles G. Leland and John D. Prince. New York: Funk and Wagnall's Company, 1902.

Levinas, Emmanuel. *Totality and Infinity: An Essay on Exteriority.* Trans. A. Lingis. The Hague: Martinus Nijhoff Publishers, 1979.

———. *Humanism of the Other.* Trans. N. Poller. Urbana: University of Illinois Press, 2003.

"Life and Letters." *Jerusalem Post.* Vol. 38, no. 10472, 29 June 1962.
Lipstadt, Deborah E. *Beyond Belief: The American Press and the Coming of the Holocaust—1933–1945.* New York: Free Press, 1986.
Lisitzky, Ephraim E. "New Orleans Countryside." Trans. I. M. Lask. *New Orleans Ledger,* c. 1955, 15.
———. *In the Grip of Cross Currents.* Trans. Moshe Kohn and Jacob Sloan and revised by the author. New York: Bloch Publishing Co., 1959, 2001.
———. "I Have No Wife . . ." *Jewish Spectator* (January 1973), 16–17.
———. "Excerpts from Three Poems Written in Hebrew and Translated by the Author." American Jewish Archives, Cincinnati.
———(?). "Synopsis of *Divine Struggles*—A Poetic Drama." MSS, Lisitzky Collection. American Jewish Archives, Cincinnati.
"Lisitzky's New Book Acclaimed in Israel." New Orleans, La.: *Jewish Ledger,* 20 November 1953, 2.
Longfellow, Henry Wadsworth. *The Poetical Works of Longfellow: Cambridge Edition,* trans. and with New Introduction by George Monteiro. Boston: Houghton Mifflin Co., 1975.
M. A. "Round the Bookshops." *Jerusalem Post.* Vol. 36, no. 9716, 29 April 1960, p. iv.
M. H. "Round the Bookshops." *Jerusalem Post.* Vol. 34, no. 9235, 5 October 1958, p. iii.
Macfarlan, Alan A., ed. *Native American Tales and Legends.* New York: Dover Publications, Inc., 2001.
Malachi, A. R. "Ephraim Lisitzky—Pioneer Poet." Trans. Rose Brener. New Orleans, La.: *Jewish Ledger,* c. 1954, pp. 1, 51–52.
Malamud, Bernard. *The People and Uncollected Stories,* edited by Robert Giroux. New York: Farrar Straus Giroux, 1989.
Marks, M. L. *Jews among the Indians: Tales of Adventure and Conflict in the Old West.* Chicago: Benison Books, 1992.
Marriott, Alice, and Carol K. Rachlin. *American Indian Mythology.* New York: Thos. Crowell, 1968.
———. *Plains Indian Mythology.* New York: Thos. Crowell, 1975.
Matthews, Cornelius. *The Indian Fairy Book.* New York: n.a., 1869.
———, ed. *Hiawatha and Other Legends of the Wigwams of the Red American Indians.* London: W. Swan Sonnenschain and Co., n.d.
McKay, Claude. *Selected Poems of Claude McKay.* New York: Bookman Associates, 1953.
Melamed, Abraham. *The Image of the Black in Jewish Culture: A History of the Other.* London: RoutledgeCurzon, 2003.
Melnick, Jeffrey. *A Right to Sing the Blues: African Americans, Jews, and American Popular Song.* Cambridge: Harvard University Press, 1999.
Mintz, Alan. *Ḥurban: Responses to Catastrophe in Hebrew Literature.* New York: Columbia University Press, 1984.

———. *Popular Culture and the Shaping of Holocaust Memory in America.* Seattle: University of Washington Press, 2001.

———. "An American Hebrew Romance: The Indian Epics of Israel Efros and E. E. Lessitzky [*sic*]." Paper presented at the 2001 International Conference on Hebrew Language and Literature of the National Association of Professors of Hebrew, New York City, 10–12 June 2001.

———. "The Persistence of Eros in the Lyric Poetry of Eisig Silberschlag." Paper presented at the 38th Conference of the Association for Jewish Studies, San Diego, California, 17–19 December 2006.

———, ed. *Hebrew in America: Perspectives and Prospects.* Detroit: Wayne State University Press, 1993.

Mintz, Alan, and Anne Golomb Hoffman, eds. *A Book That Was Lost and Other Stories.* New York: Schocken, 1995.

Mintz, Ruth Finer, ed. and trans. *Modern Hebrew Poetry: A Bilingual Anthology.* Berkeley: University of California Press, 1968.

Miron, Dan. "German Jews in Agnon's Work." *Leo Baeck Institute Yearbook* 33 (1978): 265–280.

Mirzoeff, Nicholas, ed. *Diaspora and Visual Culture: Representing Africans and Jews.* New York: Routledge, 2000.

Mooney, James. *The Ghost-Dance: Religion and the Sioux Outbreak of 1890.* Fourteenth Annual Report of the Bureau of American Ethnography, pt. 2. Washington, D.C., 1896.

———. *James Mooney's History, Myth, and Sacred Formulas of the Cherokees.* New Introduction by George Ellison. Asheville, N.C.: Historical Images/Bright Mountain Books, 1992.

Morse, Arthur D. *While Six Million Died: A Chronicle of American Apathy.* New York: Random House, 1967.

Moyne, Ernest J. *Hiawatha and Kalevala: A Study of the Relationship between Longfellow's "Indian Edda" and the Finnish Epic.* FF Communications, vol. 80, No. 2. Helsinki: Soumalainen Tiedeakatemia Academic Scientiarum Fennica, 1963.

Neihardt, John G. *Black Elk Speaks.* New York: Morrow, 1932.

"New Orleans Hebrew Poet Received Kovner Award." (New Orleans) *Times-Picayune* CXX, pp. 1, 6.

Novick, Peter. *The Holocaust in American Life.* New York: Houghton Mifflin Co., 1999.

Odum, Howard W., and Guy B. Johnson. *Negro Workaday Songs.* 1926. Reprint, New York: Negro Universities Press, 1969.

Oz, Amos. *A Perfect Peace.* Trans. Hillel Halkin. New York: Harcourt Brace Jovanovich, 1985.

Pallis, Marco. *The Way and the Mountain.* London: Peter Owen, 1960.

Patterson-Randolph, Carol. *On the Trail of Spider Woman: Petroglyphs, Pictographs, and Myths of the Southwest.* Santa Fe, N.M.: Ancient City Press, 1997.

PBS. *Great Performances,* "From Shtetl to Swing." Aired 5 October 2005.

———. *Great Performances*, "The Story of Gospel Music." BBC, 1996; aired on PBS, c. 1996.

Philipson, David, ed. *Letters of Rebecca Gratz*. Philadelphia: Jewish Publication Society of America, 1929.

Pope, Marvin H., ed. *Job*. Vol. 15 of *The Anchor Bible*. New York: Doubleday and Company, 1965.

Potter, Stephen R. *Commoners, Tribute and Chiefs: The Development of Algonquian Culture in the Potomac Valley*. Charlottesville: University Press of Virginia, 1993.

Powers, Alfred, ed. *Poems of the Covered Wagons*. Portland, Ore.: Pacific Publishing House, 1947.

Preil, Gabriel. *Sunset Possibilities and Other Poems*, edited by Robert Friend. Philadelphia: Jewish Publication Society, 1985.

Rabin, Elliott. "Idolatrous Fictions: Art and Religion in Modern Hebrew Literature." Ph.D. dissertation, Indiana University, Bloomington, 1997.

Raichelson, Richard M. "Black Religious Folksong: A Study in Generic and Social Change." Ph.D. dissertation, University of Pennsylvania, 1975.

———. *Black Religious Folksong: A Study in Generic and Social Change*. Ann Arbor, Mich.: University Microfilms, 1982.

Ramras Rauch, Gila. *The Arab in Israeli Literature*. Bloomington: Indiana University Press, 1989.

Read, William A. *Louisiana Place-Names of Indian Origin*. Baton Rouge, La.: Louisiana State University, 1894.

Reagan, Albert B. *The Sun God—Moccasin Tales*. Vol. 2, *Some Flood Myths of the Indians*. Provo, Utah: Albert B. Reagan, 1936.

Reichard, Gladys A. *Spider Woman: A Story of Navajo Weavers and Chanters*. Glorieta, N.M.: Rio Grande Press, Inc., 1934; 1968.

Ribalow, Harold. "In the World of Books: Life's Fulfillment." *Congress Bi-Weekly*, n.d., 17–18.

Rochlin, Harriet, and Fred Rochlin. *Pioneer Jews: A New Life in the Far West*. Boston: Houghton Mifflin Co., 1984.

Rosenberg, James B. "Negro Life in Hebrew Poetry." *Jewish Spectator* 40, no. 2 (Summer 1975): 34–36.

Rovner, Adam. "'The Politics of Canonicity: Modernist Hebrew Poetry,' Michael Gluzman." *Prooftexts* 24, no. 2 (Spring 2004): 248–257.

Rubin, Sydelle. "There's No Place Like Home?—Two Books on African and Jewish Diaspora Art—Review." *http://www.findarticles.com/p/articles/mi_m0425/is_2_60/ai_773747723/print*

Rubinstein, Rachel. "Nathaniel West's Indian Commodities." *Shofar* 23, no. 4 (2005): 98–120.

Sachar, Howard Morley. *The Course of Modern Jewish History*. New York: Delta Books/Dell, 1958.

Sackler, Harry. *Festival at Meron.* New York: Covici-Friede Publishers, 1935.

Sarna, Jonathan D. *Jacksonian Jew: The Two Worlds of Mordecai Noah.* New York: Holmes and Meier, 1981.

———. "A Projection of America as It Ought to Be: Zion in the Mind's Eye of American Jews." In *Envisioning Israel: The Changing Ideas and Images of North American Jews*, edited by Allon Gal, 41–59. Jerusalem and Detroit: Magnes Press, Hebrew University, and Wayne State University Press, 1996.

———. *American Judaism: A History.* New Haven, Conn.: Yale University Press, 2004.

Scheindlin, Raymond P. *The Song of the Distant Dove: Judah Halevi's Pilgrimage.* New York: Oxford University Press, 2008.

Scherman, Tony. "Chipping Away at the Myths of a Blues Legend." *New York Times* (20 September 1998); reprinted in the *Jerusalem Post* (25 September 1998), 16.

Schiff, Alvin I. *The Mystique of Hebrew: An Ancient Language in the New World.* New York: Shengold, 1996.

Scholem, Gershom. *Major Trends in Jewish Mysticism.* New York: Schocken Books, 1941.

Schoolcraft, Henry Rowe. *The Myth of Hiawatha and Other Oral Legends.* Philadelphia: J. B. Lippincott and Co., 1856.

———. *Schoolcraft's Indian Legends*, edited by Mentor L. Williams. East Lansing: Michigan State University Press, 1956.

———. *Algic Researches: Indian Tales and Legends.* 2 vols. 1839. Reprint, with a new introduction by W. K. McNeil. Baltimore: Clearfield Company, 1992.

———. *Schoolcraft's Ojibwa Lodge Stories*, edited by Philip P. Mason. East Lansing: Michigan State University Press, 1997.

Schwartz, Barry, Yael Zerubavel, and Bernice M. Barnett. "The Recovery of Masada: A Study in Collective Memory." *Sociological Quarterly* 27, no. 2 (Summer 1986): 147–164.

Schwartz, Israel Jacob. *Kentucky.* Trans. Gertrude W. Dubrovsky. Tuscaloosa: University of Alabama Press, 1990.

Shaḥar, David. *News from Jerusalem: Stories.* Boston: Houghton Mifflin Co., 1974.

Shaked, Gershon. *Modern Hebrew Fiction.* Bloomington: Indiana University Press, 2000.

———. *The New Tradition: Essays on Modern Hebrew Literature.* Cincinnati: Hebrew Union College Press, 2006.

Shandler, Jeffrey. *While America Watches: Televising the Holocaust.* New York: Oxford University Press, 1999.

Shargel, Baila R. "Evolution of the Masada Myth." *Judaism* 28, no. 3 (1979): 357–371.

Shavit, Uzi. "The New Hebrew Poetry of the Twenties: Palestine and America." *Prooftexts* 12, no. 3 (1992): 213–230.

Shelton, William. "Origins of the Exclamation 'Yahu'!," 417. In Hermann Haeberlin, "Mythology of Puget Sound." *Journal of American Folk-Lore* 37, nos. 143–144 (January–June 1924): 371–438.

———. "Pushing Up the Sky." In *Indian Legends of the Pacific North West*, edited by Ella E. Clark, 148–149. Berkeley: University of California Press, 1953.

Shipley, Joseph, ed. *Dictionary of World Literature.* Totowa, N.J.: Littlefield, Adams and Co., 1968.

Silberschlag, Eisig. "Hebrew Literature in America at the Tercentenary." *Jewish Book Annual* 12 (1954): 29–33.

———. "Hebrew Literature in America: Record and Interpretation." *Jewish Quarterly Review* 45, no. 4 (April 1955): 413–433.

———. "Zionism and Hebraism in America." In *Early History of Zionism in America.* Isidore S. Meyer, ed. New York: American Jewish Historical Society and Theodor Herzl Foundation, 1958, pp. 327–328.

———. *Hebrew Literature: An Evaluation.* New York: Theodor Herzl Foundation, 1959.

———. "Development and Decline of Hebrew Letters in the United States," pp. 175–191. In *The American Jew: A Reappraisal*, edited by Oscar I. Janowsky. Philadelphia: Jewish Publication Sciety of America, 1964.

———. *From Renaissance to Renaissance I: Hebrew Literature from 1492–1970*. New York: Ktav, 1973.

———. "The Thrust of Hebrew Letters in America: A Panoramic View." *Jewish Social Studies* 38, nos. 3–4 (1976): 277–288.

———. *From Renaissance to Renaissance II: Hebrew Literature in the Land of Israel: 1870–1970*. New York: Ktav, 1977.

Sienkiewicz, Henryk. "Sachem." In *Lillian Morris and Other Stories.* Boston: Little, Brown and Co., 1894.

Simons, John, ed. *Who's Who in American Jewry.* Vol. 3, 1938–1939. New York: National News Association, 1938.

Skinner, Charles M., ed. *Myths and Legends of Our Own Land.* 2 vols. Philadelphia: J. B. Lippincott Company, 1896.

Snowman, L. V. "The American Hebrew Poet." *New Judean* (November 1945): 22–30.

Soyer, Abraham. *The Adventures of Yemima and Other Stories.* New York: Viking, 1979.

Spence, Lewis. *The Myths of the North American Indians.* London: G. G. Harrep, 1914.

———. *The Myths of the North American Indians.* New York: Dingwall-Rock Limited, c. 1927.

Spicehandler, Ezra. "*Ameriqa'iyut* in American Hebrew Literature." In *Hebrew in America*, edited by Alan Mintz, 68–104. Detroit Wayne State University Press, 1993.

Stevens, Carter. "Volumes Written in Hebrew: Orleanian Given Poetry Prize." (unknown newspaper source), 15 November 1948.

Styron, William. *The Confessions of Nat Turner.* New York: Random House, 1967.

Swichkow, Louis J., and Lloyd P. Gartner. *The History of the Jews of Milwaukee.* Philadelphia: Jewish Publication Society of America, 1963.

Tarnor, N. "American Motifs in Hebrew Literature." *Jewish Book Annual* 33 (1975–1976): 33–39.

Thomas, Hugh. *The Slave Trade: The Story of the Atlantic Slave Trade, 1440–1870.* New York: Simon and Schuster, 1997.

Thompson, Stith, ed. "The Indian Legend of Hiawatha." *Publications of the Modern Language Association of America,* edited by Carleton Brown, vol. 37 (1922), pp. 128–140.

———. *Tales of the North American Indians.* Cambridge: Harvard University Press, 1929.

Thurman, Howard. *Deep River and the Negro Spiritual Speaks of Life and Death.* Richmond, Ind.: Friends United Press, 1975.

Tibbetts, John C., ed. *Dvořák in America.* Portland, Ore.: Amadeus Press, 1993.

Todorov, Tzvetan. *The Conquest of America: The Question of the Other.* Trans. Richard Howard. New York: Harper and Row, 1987.

Trachtenberg, Alan. *Shades of Hiawatha: Staging Indians, Making Americans, 1880–1930.* New York: Hill and Wang, 2004.

Tur-Sinai (Torczyner), Nahum. *The Book of Job: A New Commentary.* Jerusalem: Kiryath Sepher, 1967.

Vizenor, Gerald, ed. *Native American Literature: A Brief Introduction and Anthology.* New York: Harper Collins, 1995.

Wagenknecht, Edward. *Henry Wadsworth Longfellow: His Poetry and Prose.* New York: Ungar, 1986.

Wallenrod, Reuben. *The Literature of Modern Israel.* New York: Abelard-Schuman, 1956.

———. *Dusk in the Catskills* (New York: Reconstructionist Press, 1957).

Washington, Booker T. *Up from Slavery: An Autobiography.* School ed. Cambridge, Mass.: Houghton Mifflin Company/ Riverside Press, 1928.

Watkins, Sylvestre C., ed. *Anthology of American Negro Literature.* New York: Modern Library/Random House, 1944.

Weingrad, Michael. "Lost Tribes: The Indian in American Hebrew Poetry." *Prooftexts* 24, no. 3 (Fall 2004): 291–319.

———. "The Last of the (Hebrew) Mohicans." *Commentary* (March 2006): 45–50.

———. "Messiah American Style: Mordecai Manuel Noah and the American Refuge." *AJS Review* 31, no. 1 (April 2007): 75–108.

Werses, Shmuel. *Relations between Jews and Poles in S. Y. Agnon's Work.* Jerusalem: Magnes Press, 1994.

White, Newman I. *American Negro Folk-Songs.* Hatboro, Pa.: Folklore Associates, Inc., 1965.

Williams, Mentor L., ed. *Schoolcraft's Indian Legends.* East Lansing: Michigan State University Press, 1956.

Williams, Susan. "Inaugural Pow Wow to Bring Remembrance, Renewal, Awareness." (Bloomington, Indiana), *IU Home Pages* 6, issue 10, Friday 1 March 2002, p. A1.

Wissler, Clark, and D. C. Duvall. *Mythology of the Blackfoot Indians.* Anthropological Papers of the American Museum of Natural History, 7, 8, 19. New York, 1909.

"Women in Green Recall Treatment of Indians." *Indiana Jewish Post and Opinion,* 10 July 1996, p. 1.

Wood, Clement, ed. *Negro Songs: An Anthology.* Little Blue Book No. 626, edited by E. Haldeman-Julius. Girard, Kans.: Haldeman-Julius Co., n.d.

Woodhead, Henry, et al., eds. *Algonquinians of the East Coast.* Alexandria, Va.: Time-Life Books, 1995.

Wyman, David S., ed. *America and the Holocaust. Vol. 1: Confirming the News of Extermination.* New York: Garland, 1990.

Yudkin, Leon. *Isaac Lamdan: A Study in Twentieth-Century Hebrew Poetry.* Ithaca, N.Y.: East and West Library/Cornell University Press, 1971.

Zerubavel, Yael. "The Death of Memory and the Memory of Death: Masada and the Holocaust as Historical Metaphors." *Representations* 45 (Winter 1994): 72–100.

———. *Recovered Roots: Collective Memory and the Making of Israeli National Tradition.* Chicago: University of Chicago Press, 1995.

HEBREW AND YIDDISH SOURCES

Abramowitz, Ḥaim. "Blimah" (Nothingness). *Niv: kli mivta l-sofrim tzʿirim* (New York) 1, no. 1 (December 1936): 12–18.

———. "Ha-tabaḥ ha-filipinaʾi" (The Filipino cook), *Niv: kli mivta l-sofrim tzʿirim* (New York) 1, no. 2 (Shvat 5697; January 1937), n.p.

———. "Ha-dod Leib" (Uncle Leib). *Niv: kli mivta l-sofrim tzʿirim* (New York) 1, no. 3 (Adar 5697; February 1937): 12–16.

———. "Bar met" (Dead). *Niv: kli mivta l-sofrim tzʿirim* (New York) 1, no. 5 (Iyar 5697; April 1937): 4–8.

———. "Mshorer b-tokhenu" (A poet among us). *Niv: kli mivta l-sofrim tzʿirim* (New York) 1, first issue (12 Sivan 5697; 22 May 1937): 25–27.

———. "Reshit mashber" (First crisis). *Niv: kli mivta l-sofrim tzʿirim* (New York) 1, no. 6 (Sivan 5617; May 1937): 17–22.

———. "B-ʾeyn ashrai" (No credit). *Niv: kli mivta l-sofrim tzʿirim* (New York) 2, no. 7 (Tammuz 5698; June 1938): 6–9.

———. "Yerushah baḥayim" (Life inheritance). *Niv: kli mivta l-sofrim tzʿirim* (New York) 3, no. 2 (Ḥeshvan 5699; November 1938): 6–7.
———. "Jazz" (Jazz). *Niv: kli mivta l-sofrim tzʿirim* (New York) 3, no. 5 (Shvat-Adar 5699; February 1939): 6–7.
———. "Student b-veyt ḥaroshet" (A student in a factory). *Niv: kli mivta l-sofrim tzʿirim* (New York) 4, no. 3 (Tevet 5700; January 1940): 3–4.
———. "Eyneni soḥer" (I'm not a merchant). *Niv: kli mivta l-sofrim tzʿirim* (New York) 4, no. 4 (Shvat-Adar I 5700; February-March 1940): 3–4.
———. "Dam" (Blood). *Niv: kli mivta l-sofrim tzʿirim* (New York) 4, no. 6 (Iyar 5700; May 1940): 6–7.
———. "B-mazal klafim" (Card fortune). *Niv: kli mivta l-sofrim tzʿirim* (New York) 5, no. 1 (Kislev 5701; December 1940): 5–6.
———. *Al haleḥem lvado* (On bread alone). New York: Kadimah, 1944.
———. "Ha-ḥayal" (The soldier). *Niv: kli mivta l-sofrim tzʿirim* (New York) 8, no. 4–5 (Iyar-Sivan 5706; May-June 1946): 13–17.
Aflat, Timuti. "B-ḥipus aḥar ha-hitgalut" (In quest of revelation). *Haʾaretz*, 19 August 1996, B5.
Agaf, M. "E. E. Lisitzky (shmonim shanah l-huladeto)" (E. E. Lisitzky: Eighty years since his birth). *Ḥazut*, 21 January 1965.
Agnon, Shmuel Yosef. *Elu v-ʾelu* (These and those). Tel-Aviv and Jerusalem: Schocken, 1966.
"Ahavah li-yhuday ha-ʿayarah" (Love for the town's Jews). *ʿAyin b-ʿayin*, 29 April 1958, 12.
Amichai, Yehuda. *ʿAchshav ba-raʿash* (Now in the quake). Jerusalem: Schocken, 1975.
Arazi, Ruth. "The American Indian in American Hebrew Poetry." Ph.D. dissertation, New York University, 1987 (in Hebrew).
Arfa, Michael. "'Yemay shnotaynu' shel Pierre Van Passin" ("Days of our years" by Pierre Van Passin). *Niv: kli mivta l-sofrim tzʿirim* (New York) 4, no. 3 (Tevet 5700; January 1940): 10.
———. "Goralah shel sifrut b-yamim eleh" (Literature's fate in these days). *Niv: kli mivta l-sofrim tzʿirim* (New York) 4, no. 4 (Shvat-Adar 5700; February-March 1940): 13.
———. "Lḥeker tafkid ha-tarbut ha-yisrʾelit ba-galut (rashay prakim)" (A study of Israeli culture's role in the diaspora [an outline]). *ʿAlil: bamah l-sifrut, l-maḥshavah ul-divray bikoret, sefer sheni* (Kislev 5708; 1948): 1–21.
Arieli, L. A. *Yeshimon: sipurim u-maḥazeh* (Wasteland: stories and a play). Tel-Aviv: Dvir, 1990.
———. *Kitvay L. A. Arieli* (Collected works of L. A. Arieli: Stories, Plays, Legends, Essays, Letters). 2 vols. Ed. Michael (Milton) Arfa. New York and Tel-Aviv: Keren Israel Matz and Dvir, 1999.
Ash, Shneur Zalman. "L-mikra 'anshay midot' l-E. E. Lisitzky" (Reading 'men

of stature' by E. E. Lisitzky). *Bitzaron*, year 21, vol. 41, no. 4 (Adar 5720; February–March 1960): 213–215.

Avinoam (Grossman), Reuven. *Shirim* (Poems). Tel-Aviv: Ḥavurah/Dvir, 1930.

———. *Arba'ah iyim: min ha-havai ha-'Americani* (Four islands: from Amerian realia). Tel-Aviv: Universal, 1930(?).

———. *Av u-vito: sipur* (Father and daughter: a tale). Tel-Aviv: Mitzpeh, 1934.

———. *Idilyot* (Idyls). Tel-Aviv: Ḥavurah/Dvir, 1934.

———. *Milon 'Ivri-angli shalem* (Compendious Hebrew-English dictionary). Ed. M. H. Segal. Tel-Aviv: Dvir, 1938, 1962.

———. *'Alay-dvai: 'al mut la-ben* (Leaves of sorrow: on the son's death). Tel-Aviv: 'Am 'Oved, 1948.

———. *Shirim u-pho'emot* (Poems and poemas). Tel-Aviv: Yavneh, 1950.

———. "'Im shirato shel E. E. Lisitzky" (With E. E. Lisitzky's poetry). *Moznayim* 3, no. 4 (Av 5716; July 1956): 247–252.

———. *'Etz shatalti: shirim 'al mut la-ben* (A tree I planted: poems on the son's death). Tel-Aviv: Yavneh, 1958.

———. *B-mish'oli: shirim 5711–5731* (In my path: poems 1951–1971). Tel-Aviv: 'Am-Ha-sefer, 1971.

Avinoam (Grossman), Reuven, and Yitzhak Finkle, eds. *Mshorerah shel yahadut America: kovetz l-zikhro shel E. E. Lisitzky Z"L* (Poet of American Jewry: a collection in memory of E. E. Lisitzky). Tel-Aviv: Maḥbarot L-sifrut, 1966.

Avinor, Gita. *B-tzel ha-zikhronot: ma'amarim b-vikoret ha-sifrut* (In memory's shadow: essays in literary criticism). Haifa: Mif'al Sofray Haifa, 1975.

Avni, Beni. "B-'ir ha-migdalim ha-'aforim" (In the city of gray towers) *Musaf Ha'aretz*, 25 August 1989, 28–29.

Avramsky, Y. D. "Al tdaber elai yhudi . . ." (Jew, don't speak to me . . .), N.p., n.d.

'Aza'i, P. "Ngohot ba-'arafel" (Brightness through the fog). *Ha-'oved Ha-tziyoni*, Sivan 5717; May 1957, 31–32.

Band, Avraham. "Ha-psantran" (The piano player). *Bitzaron*, year 19, vol. 38, no. 5 (201) (Nisan–Iyar 5718; April–May 1958): 56.

———. "'Arvit" (Evening prayer). *Niv: kli mivta l-sofrim tz'irim* (New York) 24, no. 1 (Ḥeshvan 5720; November 1959): 6.

———. "Mifras shir" (Poetic sail) and "Piyut" (Liturgical poem). *Niv: kli mivta l-sofrim tz'irim* (New York) 24, no. 2 (Iyar 5720; May 1960): 7.

———. "Be-'ir 'ara'it zot" (In this transient town). *Niv: kli mivta l-sofrim tz'irim* (New York) 25, no. 1 (Shvat 5721; February 1961): 16.

———. *Ha-r'ee bo'er ba-'esh* (The mirror burns with fire). New York: 'Ogen; Jerusalem: Ogdan, 1963.

Bar-El, Yehudit. *Ha-po'emah ha-'ivrit: me-hit'havutah v-'ad reshit ha-me'ah ha-'esrim—meḥkar b-toldot janer* (The Hebrew long poem from its emergence to the beginning of the twentieth century: a study in the history of a genre). Jerusalem: Mosad Bialik, 1995.

Bartal, Israel. "Giborim o mugay lev: yehudim b-tziv'otayha shel Polin (1794–1863)" (Heroes or cowards: Jews in Poland's armies, 1794–1863). *Kiyum va-shever: yehuday Polin l-dorotayhem* (Existence and breakup: Polish Jews through the generations). Ed. I. Bartal and Israel Gutman. Jerusalem: Merkaz Zalman Shazar, 1997, 353–367.

Bartana, Ortziyon. *Tlushim va-ḥalutzim: hitgabshut ha-mgamah ha-neo-romantit ba-siporet ha-ʿivrit* (The torn and the pioneers: crystallization of the neo-romantic trend in Hebrew narrative). Jerusalem: Dvir, 1983.

Barzel, Hillel. "Du-siaḥ l-ʾaḥar ha-mavet" (Dialogue after death). *Ha-boker*, 10 January 1964, pp. 5–6.

———. *Ha-shir he-ḥadash: sgirut u-phtiḥut* (The new poem: open and closed structures). Tel-Aviv: ʿEked, 1976.

———. "Ḥavayah b-livyat mitos—'Timber,' 'Ha-ḥayim ha-yafim shel Clara Shiʾato'" (Experience accompanied by myth—"Timber," "Clara Shiato's beautiful life"). *Mgamot b-siporet ha-hoveh: Ha-sipur he-ḥavuy* (Major trends in contemporary Hebrew prose: tales of experience). Ed. Hillel Barzel. Tel-Aviv: Yaḥdav, 1979, 171–184.

———. "Yoram Kaniuk: ha-mromam vha-naḥut" (Yoram Kaniuk: the elevated and the low). *Msaprim b-yiḥudam* (Authors in their uniqueness). Tel-Aviv: Yaḥdav, 1981, 217–248.

———. *Toldot ha-shirah ha-ʿivrit mi-ḥibat tziyon ʿad yameynu—kerekh alef: shirat -ḥibat tziyon* (A History of Hebrew Poetry from the Ḥibat Tziyon period to our times, vol. 1: the Ḥibat Tziyon period). Tel-Aviv: Sifriat Poʿalim, 1987.

———. *Toldot ha-shirah ha-ʿivrit mi-ḥibat tziyon ʿad yameynu—kerekh dalet: shirat u-teḥiyah: omanut ha-janer* (A History of Hebrew Poetry from the Ḥibat Tziyon period to our times, vol. 4: masters of genre). Tel-Aviv: Sifriat Poʿalim, 1997.

———. *Toldot ha-shirah ha-ʿivrit mi-ḥibat tziyon ʿad yameynu—kerekh heh: shirat Eretz Israel: Avraham Shlonsky, Natan Alterman, Leah Goldberg* (A History of Hebrew Poetry from the Ḥibat Tziyon period to our times, vol. 5: the poetry of the Land of Israel: A. Shlonsky, N. Alterman, L. Goldberg). Tel-Aviv: Sifriat Poʿalim, 2001.

———. *Shirat eretz-Israel, kerekh shviʿi: romantikah, ideʾologiyah mytologiyah* (The poetry of the Land of Israel, vol. 7: romanticism, ideology, mythology). Tel-Aviv: Sifriat Poʿalim, 2006.

Bass, Sh[muʾel]. "B. N. Silkiner (l-yovlo)" (B. N. Silkiner: on his anniversary). *Haʾaretz* 15, no. 3915, 5 Sivan 5692; 9 July 1932, 5.

———. "Mdurot doʿakhot" (Dying campfires). *Gilyonot*, year 3, no. 5 (29) (Tammuz 5697; 1937): 441–443.

"Ba-tarbut ha-ʿivrit: 'tzlil va-tzel' l-Ben-Meir A"H" (In Hebrew culture: sound and shadow by Ben-Meir). *Hadoʾar*, year 38, vol. 39, no. 12 (21 Shvat 5719; 30 January 1959): 216.

Bavli, Hillel [signed as H. A. Rashgolin]. "Shimshon" (Samson). *Miklat* 2, books 4–6 (Tevet–Adar 5680; 1920): 462.
Bavli, Hillel. "Shirat ha-kushim ba-ʾAmerica" (Black poetry in America). *Nimim: maʾasef l-divray sifrut yafah ul-divray bikoret.* Vol. 1. Ed. H. Bavli. New York: Ḥaverim, Summer 5683; 1923): 108–119.
———. "Israel Efrat." *Masad: maʾasef l-divray sifrut. Sefer rishon.* New York and Tel-Aviv: Ḥaverim and Mitzpeh, 1933, 151–163.
———. "ʿAl Tschernichovsky" (On Tschernichowsky). *Hadoʾar,* year 15, vol. 16, no. 20 (26 Adar 5696; 20 March 1936): 363.
———. "ʿAl saf ha-dorot (. . . azkarah l-Naḥum Sokolov)" (On the threshold of generations: eulogy for N. Sokolow). *Hadoʾar,* year 15, vol. 16, no. 30 (29 Sivan 5696; 19 June 1936): 548–549.
———. *Shirim* (Poems). 2 vols. Tel-Aviv: Dvir, 1938.
———. "Peretz smolenskin." *Bitzaron,* year 4, vol. 7, no. 6 (Adar 1–Adar 2 5703; March 1943): 397–405.
———. "Shimʿon Ginzburg." *Bitzaron,* year 5, vol. 10, no. 9–10 (Sivan–Tammuz 5704; June–July 1944): 168–173.
———. *Shirim l-Raḥeleh* (Poems for Rachel). Tel-Aviv: M. Newman, 1950.
———. "ʿAl maʿaseh ʿavel eḥad" (Of one injustice). *Hadoʾar,* year 30, vol. 31, no. 37 (6 Elul 5711; 7 September 1951): 724.
———. "Ephraim E. Lisitzky." *Gilyonot* 31, no. 8–10 (Av–Elul 1954): 92–100.
———. "B-mikhlalah katolit b-Buffalo" (In a Catholic college in Buffalo). *Gilyonot* 31, nos. 8–10 (Av–Elul 5714; 1954): 122–126.
———. *Aderet ha-shanim (shirim)* (The mantle of years: poems). Jerusalem: Mosad Bialik, 1955.
———. "Bi-shliḥut ha-lev" (Mission of the heart). *Hadoʾar,* year 34, vol. 35, no. 39 (28 Tishrei 5716; 14 October 1955): 783.
———. *Ruḥot nifgashot: divray masah* (Intersecting spirits: essays). New York: ʿOgen; Jerusalem: M. Newman, 1958.
———. "Mi-dvarav ha-ʾaḥaronim shel Hillel Bavli." (Hillel Bavli's last words). *Bitzaron* 45, no. 2 (Kislev–Tevet 5722; November–December 1961): 64–65.
———. "Hadoʾar lifnay shivʿim va-ḥamesh shanah: shirim—Hillel Bavli" (Hadoʾar seventy-five years ago: poems—Hillel Bavli). *Hadoʾar* 83, no. 1 (Ḥeshvan; Fall 2003): 34.
———, ed. *Nimim: maʾasef l-divray sifrut yafah ul-divray bikoret* (Chords: a belles lettres and criticism anthology). Vol. 1. New York: 1923.
———, ed. *Masad: maʾasef l-divray sifrut. Sefer rishon* (Masad: an anthology of literary issues). Vol. 1. New York and Tel-Aviv: Ḥaverim and Mitzpeh, 1933.
———, ed. *Masad: maʾasef l-divray sifrut. Sefer sheni* (Masad: an anthology of literary issues). Vol. 2. New York and Tel-Aviv: Ḥaverim and Mitzpeh, 1936.
———, ed. *Sefer ha-yovel li-khvod Tzvi Scharfshtein li-mloʾt lo 70 shanim* (Zvi Scharstein jubilee volume on his 70th aniversary). New York: Ha-moʿatzah Ha-ʾartzit L-maʿan Ha-ḥinukh Ha-yehudi Ba-ʾAmerica, 1955.

"B-halvayato shel M. S. Ben-Meir N"E" (At M. S. Ben-Meir's funeral). *Hado'ar*, year 38, vol. 39, no. 11 (14 Shvat 5719; 23 January 1959): 203.

Behar, Uzi. "Be'or rig'i mitporer" (In a fading momentary light). *Ha'aretz* (sfarim), 28 July 1993, 4.

Ben-Ami, Shuki. *Notzah shsu'ah: ish ha-rfu'ah ha-'indi'ani* (Split feather: the Indian medicine man). Tel-Aviv: Ha-kibbutz Ha-m'uḥad, 2003.

Ben-Ari, Nitza. "Mitos hayaḥid" (Myth of the loner). *Yedi'ot aḥaronot*, 4 March 1974, 31.

Ben-Avigdor (Shalkovitz, Avraham Leib). *Ha-sifrut ha-'ivrit ha-ḥadashah va-'atidotayha* (Modern Hebrew literature and its future). New York: Mfitzay Sfat 'Ever V-sifrutah, 1908.

Ben-Meir, Moshe S. "Sha'ashu'ay-ha-lashon b-shirat-Halevi" (Word play in Halevi's poetry). *Hado'ar*, year 20, vol. 21, no. 10 (4 Tevet 5701; 3 January 1941): 159–161.

———. "Anusim mityahadim (rshimot u-rshamim mitaḥanat- ndudim)" (Converting conversos: notes and impressions from a wandering stop). *Hado'ar*, year 20, vol. 21, no. 27 (12 Iyar 5701; 9 May 1941): 436–437; continued *Hado'ar*, year 20, 21:27 (19 Iyar 5701; 16 May 1941): 455–456.

———. "Nsi ha-'anusim ha-mityahadim" (The converting conversos' chief). *Hado'ar*, year 20, vol. 21, no. 39 (27 Elul 5701; 19 September 1941): 709–710.

———. "Mshorer ha-yofi sheb-dalut Israel (bi-mlot ḥamishim shanah la-'avodato ha-sifrutit shel Avraham Raisin" (Poet of beauty of Israel's poverty: fifty years of Abraham Raisin's literary creativity). *Hado'ar*, year 21, vol. 22, no. 32 (25 Tammuz 5702; 10 July 1942): 529–530.

———. "David Pinsky: (bi-mlot shiv'im shanah l-ḥayav va-ḥamishim li-ytzirato ha-sifrutit)" (David Pinsky: at seventy years of life and fifty of literary creativity). *Hado'ar*, year 22, vol. 23, no. 9 (24 Tevet 5703; 1 January 1943): 146–147.

———. "Moreshet ha-'saba' (Bimlot 25 shanim l-mot Mendele Mokher Sfarim" (Legacy of the "grandfather": 25 years since the death of Mendele Mokher Sfarim). *Hado'ar*, year 22, vol. 23, no. 26 (9 Iyar 5704; 14 May 1944): 448–449.

———. "Sofrim u-sfarim: 'anaḥnu ha-dor'" (Authors and books: "we are the generation"). *Hado'ar*, year 24, vol. 25, no. 29 (27 Sivan 5705; 8 June 1945): 625–626.

———. "Sofrim u-sfarim: 'ḥurban Polin'" (Authors and books: "Poland's demise"). *Hado'ar*, year 26, vol. 27, no. 16 (24 Shvat 5707; 14 February 1946): 391–392.

———. "Sofrim u-sfarim: 'Me'asfim' 6" (Authors and books: "anthologists" 6). *Hado'ar*, year 25, vol. 26, no. 36 (10 Elul 5706; 6 September 1946): 892–893.

———. "Daray matah" (Earthly denizens). *Bitzaron*, year 8, vol. 16, no. 7 (5717; May 1947): 131–134.

———. "Sofrim u-sfarim: 'ki phanah yom'" (Authors and books: "for the day has waned"). *Hado'ar*, year 26, vol. 27, no. 30 (18 Sivan 5707; 6 June 1947): 978–979.

———. "Im sh'erit ha-pletah" (With the surviving remnant). *Bitzaron*, year 9, vol. 17, no. 3 (99) (Kislev–Tevet 5708; December 1947–January 1948): 202–204.

———. "Antologiyah la-shirah ha-ʿivrit" (Anthology of Hebrew poetry). *Hado'ar*, year 28, vol. 29, no. 23 (9 Nisan 5709; 8 April 1949): 548–549.

———. "Israel." *Hado'ar*, year 28, vol. 29, no. 28 (28 Iyar 5709; 27 May 1949): 693.

———. "Ha-rishonim (zikaron la-ʿaliyat Bilu)" (The first: memory of the Bilu immigration). *Hado'ar*, year 28, vol. 29, no. 28 (28 Iyar 5709; 27 May 1949): 748–749.

———. "Shavririm" (Fragments). *Hado'ar*, year 29, vol. 30, no. 27 (3 Sivan 5710; 19 May 1950): 765–766.

———. "Dapim l-vikoret: sifro ha-'aḥaron" (Critical pages: his last book). *Hado'ar*, year 34, vol. 35, no. 17 (3 Adar 5715; 25 February 1955): 232–233.

———. "Dapim l-vikoret: mi-Galicia la-'America" (Critical pages: From Galicia to America). *Hado'ar*, year 35, vol. 36, no. 25 (23 Iyar 5716; 4 May 1956): 501–502.

———. "Dapim le-vikoret: 'ngohot me-ʿarafel'" (Critical pages: "brightness through the fog") *Hado'ar*, year 35, vol. 36, no. 37 (10 Elul 5717; 6 September 1957): 661.

———. *Tzlil va-tzel: shirim v-'agadot* (Sound and shadow: poems and legends). New York: ʿOgen; Tel-Aviv: M. Newman, 1958.

———. "Dapim l-vikoret: shabtotayha shel ima" (Critical pages: mother's Sabbaths). *Hado'ar*, year 38, vol. 39, no. 11 (14 Shvat 5719; 23 January 1959): 191–192.

Ben-Mordecai, Yitzhak. "Bi-r'ee ha-re'alizm ha-tzalul: yezirato shel Reuven Wallenrod" (In lucid realism's mirror: the work of Reuven Wallenrod). *Migvan: Meḥkarim ba-sifrut ha-ʿivrit uv-giluyeha ha-'Americaniyim—mugashim l-Yaʿakov Kabakoff* (Migvan: Studies in Hebrew literature and its American manifestations—presented to Jacob Kabakoff). Ed. Stanley Nash. Lod, Israel: Makhon Haberman L-meḥkeray Sifrut, 1988, 35–51.

Ben-Ner, Yitzhak. *Shkiʿah kafrit: sipurim* (Rustic sunset: stories). Tel-Aviv: ʿAm ʿOved, 1976.

Ben-Nun, Sagi. "200 Shirim yeshanim shel Ḥavah Albershtein ro'im or la-rishonah ʿal diskim" (200 old songs by Ḥavah Albershtein are issued for the first time on CDs). *Ha'aretz*, "Galeriyah," 5 September 2003, D2.

Ben-Or (Urinovsky), Aharon. *Toldot ha-sifrut ha-ʿivrit b-dorenu, 1: mshorerim* (History of Hebrew literature in our generation, 1: poets). Tel-Aviv: Izreel, 1968.

Bergman, Devorah. *Shvilay ha-zahav: ha-sonet ha-ʿivri bi-tkufat ha-renesans vha-barok* (The golden mean: the Hebrew sonnet during the Renaissance and the Baroque). Be'er Sheva: Makhon Ben-Tzvi L-ḥeker Kehilot Ha-mizraḥ V-hotza'at Sfarim shel Universitat Ben-Gurion Ba-negev, 1995.

Berkovitch, Y. D. *Kitvay Y. D. Berkovitch* (Writings of Y. D. Berkovitch). 2 vols. Tel-Aviv: Dvir, 1959.

Bertini, K. A. "Mi-konanit ha-sfarim: kmo ha-yom rad" (From the bookshelf: as the day set). *Moznayim* 12, no. 1 (Kislev 5720; December 1960): 63.

———. "Mi-konanit ha-sfarim: shnay shirim meʾet Ephraim E. Lisitzky" (From the bookshelf: two poems by E. E. Lisitzky). *Moznayim* 12, no. 1 (Kislev 5720; December 1960): 63.

———, David Vinitzky, and B. Mikhali, eds. *ʿAravot ha-ruaḥ: antologiyah shel sofray Bessarabia* (Prairies in the wind: an anthology of Bessarabian authors). 2 vols. Tel-Aviv: Bronfman, 1981.

Bialik, Ḥayim Naḥman. "Shaḥah nafshi" (My spirit sank). *Hadoʾar*, year 3, vol. 3, no. 239 (28 Adar 5684; 16 March 1924): 2.

Bin-Gurion, Imanuʾel. "Shirah v-lashon" (Poetry and language) *Davar*, 25 March 1955, n.p.

Bistritzky, Natan. "Mafteaḥ l-shirat Shimʿon Halkin" (A key to Simon Halkin's poetry). *Maʿariv*, 25 November 1977, 35.

Blank, Shmuʾel Leib. *ʿAravah* (Prairie). New York: Ha-histadrut Ha-ʿivrit Ba-ʾAmerica, 1926.

———. *Tzon* (Sheep). Berlin-Charlotburg: A. I. Stybel, 1929.

———. *Adamah* (Land). Tel-Aviv: Mitzpeh, 1931.

———. *Bi-shʿat ḥerum* (A time of crisis). Philadelphia: Har Zion, 1932.

———. *Naḥalah* (Patrimony). Tel-Aviv: A. I. Stybel, 1933.

———. *Mister Kunis*. New York and Tel-Aviv: A. I. Stybel, 1934.

———. *Moshavah* (Colony). Tel-Aviv: A. I. Stybel, 1936.

———. *Ee ha-dmaʿot* (The isle of tears). New York: ʿOgen, 1941.

———. *B-yad ha-goral: shloshah sipurim* (In the hand of fate: three stories). New York: ʿOgen, 1944.

———. *B-maʿarbolet ha-ḥayim* (In the whirlpool of life). New York: ʿOgen, 1954.

———. *ʿAl admat America* (On American soil). Tel-Aviv: Avraham Tziyoni, 1958.

———. *ʿEtz ha-sadeh: sipurim* (Tree of the field: stories). Jerusalem: Kiryat Sefer, 1961.

Blidstein, Yaʿakov. "B-shevet ha-bikoret: shloshah sifray shirah ʿivriyim . . ." (With the rod of criticism: three Hebrew poetry books . . .). *Niv: kli mivta l-sofrim tzʿirim* (New York) 23, no. 3–4 (Iyar 5719; June 1959): 9.

Blumenfeld, Shmuʾel (Samuel Blumenfield). "L-zikhro shel Ephraim E. Lisitzky: klil kotzim—klil tifʾeret" (In memory of E. E. Lisitzky: a crown of thorns—a crown of glory). *Hadoʾar*, year 42, vol. 43, no. 27 (23 Iyar 5723; 17 May 1963): 495–496.

Brainin, Reuven, ed. *Snunit: kovetz shirim* (Snunit: poetry anthology). Jerusalem and New York: Aḥiʿever, 1910.

———. *Kol kitvay Reuven ben Mordecai Brainin: yeshanim v-gam ḥadashim* (Collected works of R. Brainin: old and new). Vol. 1. New York: N.p., 1922.

Brenner, Yosef Ḥayim. *Ktavim* (Writings). Vol. 3 and 4. Tel-Aviv: Ha-kibbutz Ha-m'uḥad and Sifriyat Po'alim, 1985.

Bril, M. "Lisitzky b-New Orleans" (Lisitzky in New Orleans). *Hado'ar*, year 42, vol. 43, no. 27 (23 Iyar 5723; 17 May 1963): 498–499.

Brind, Moshe. *Bi-tzvat ha-goral: shirim liriyim v-sipuriyim, sonetot, shninot u-baladot tanakhiyot* (In the grasp of destiny: lyrical and narrative poems, sonnets, witticisms and biblical ballads). Third compilation. New York: Merḥav, 1941.

Brody, Ḥayim, ed. *Divan: v-hu sefer kolel kol shiray abir ha-mshorerim Yehudah ben Shmu'el Halevi* (Diwan des Abu-l-Hasan Jehuda ha-Levi). Reprint, England: Gregg International Publishers Ltd., 1971.

Broides, Avraham. "Ephraim E. Lisitzky." *Ha-po'el Ha-tza'ir*, 10 July 1962, n.p.

Chapman, Avraham. "Ha-kushim ha-'America'im v-shiratam ha-ḥadashah" (American Blacks and their new poetry). *Gilyonot* 2, no. 6 (Tammuz 5694; 1934): 59–71.

Cohen, Adir. "Arba'ah sifray shirah" (Four books of poetry). *Ha-boker*, 15 Av 5718; 1 August 1958.

———. "'Olam yetzirato shel Ephraim E. Lisitzky (bi-mlot lo shiv'im va-ḥamesh shanah)" (E. E. Lisitzky's creative world—upon his seventy-fifth birthday). *Gazit* 18, nos. 1–2 (May 1960): 16–18.

———. "Bi-shvilay ḥayim v-sifrut" (In the paths of life and literature). *Hado'ar*, year 13, vol. 4, no. 3 (Shvat 5722; February 1962): 232.

———. "Kmo ha-yom rad" (As the day set). *Ha-boker* n.d., n.p.

D. S. [Dov Shtok/Sadan]. "'Vigvamim shotkim' me'et Israel Efrat" ("Silent wigwams" by Israel Efros). *Gilyonot* 1, no. 1 (2) (Kislev 5694; 1933): 84.

D. Z. "Pit'ḥay sfarim: anshay midot l-E. E. Lisitzky" (Book gateways: men of stature by E. E. Lisitzky). *Davar*, 6 March 1958.

———. "Pit'ḥay sfarim" (Book gateways). *Davar*, 4 April 1958, 6.

Daixel, Sheen (Shmu'el). *Indianishe dertseylungen* (Indian stories). New York: S. Daixel bukh-komitet, 1959.

Damesek, Shlomo. *B-gorali: rshimot mi-beyt ha-ḥolim* (My fate: notes from a hospital). New York: Bitzaron, 1945.

———. *Mi-po umi-sham* (From here and there). New York: Talmidim Vi-ydidim, 1956.

———. "'Negohot me-'arafel'—sefer po'emot l-'Ephraim Lisitzky" ("Brightness through the fog"—a book of poemas by Ephraim Lisitzky). *Bitzaron* 37, no. 2 (Kislev 5718; November–December 1957): 93–97.

———. *Gam sham zarḥah ha-shemesh* (There, too, the sun shined). Tel-Aviv: Sifray gadish, 1960.

———. "Al ha-msaper Reuven Wallenrod (bi-mlot lo shishim shanah)" (On the author Reuben Wallenrod: on his sixtieth birthday). *Bitzaron* 45, no. 2 (Kislev-Tevet 5722; November–December 1961): 91–94.

———. "Ha-zaken sheba-ḥavurah" (The senior of the group). *Hado'ar*, year 42, vol. 43, no. 27 (23 Iyar 5723; 17 May 1963): 496–497, 499.

Dan [Dov Sadan?]. "'Od mashehu 'al 'Vigvamim Shotkim'" (More about "Silent Wigwams"). *Gilyonot* 1, no. 1 (2) (Kislev 5694; December 1933), 85.

Dar, Y. A. "Shnay kolot ba-shirah ha-ʿivrit ('kmo rad ha-yom' [*sic*] l-Ephraim E. Lisitzky v-'ha-kol mi-baʿad la-ʿanaf' l-S. Zamir") (Two voices in Hebrew poetry: ["as the day set" by E. E. Lisitzky and "The sound through the branch" by S. Zamir]). *Yediʿot Aḥaronot*, "7 Yamim," no. 8670, 12 August 1960, p. 6.

Davis, Moshe. *Beyt Israel ba-ʾAmerica: meḥkarim u-mkorot* (American Jewry: sources and studies). Jerusalem: Ha-merkaz L-ḥeker Yahadut America, Beyt Hamidrah L-rabanim Ba-ʾAmerica, 1970.

de Gomara, Francisco Lopez. *Sefer ha-'indi'ah ha-ḥadashah v-sefer Fernando Cortes [1553]: nosaḥ 'ivri shel toldot Peru u-Mexico bi-yday Yosef Hakohen [1568]* (History of New India and Mexico [1553] Hebrew version [1568] by Yosef Hakohen). Ed. Moshe Lazar. Lancaster, California: Labyrinthos, 2002.

"Dmuyot me-ʾetmol" (Images from yesterday). *Yediʿot Aḥaronot*, 9 May 1958.

Deutch, Ḥayim, and Menaḥem Ben-Sason, eds. *Ha-ʾaḥer: beyn adam l-ʿatzmo ul-zulato* (The Other: between man and himself and the other). Tel-Aviv: Yediʿot Aḥaronot/Sifray Ḥemed, 2001.

Di Haz, Karl. *Birinikah: tragediyah ba-ḥamesh maʿarakhot* (Birinika: a tragedy in five acts). Trans. Eisig Silberschlag. New York: Mosad Goslava V-Avraham Yosef Stybel, 1946.

Dor, Moshe. "Rshut ha-dibut l-profesor Shimon Halkin" (Professor S. Halkin's turn to speak). *Maʿariv*, 3 September 1971, 33.

Efrat (Efros), Israel. *Shirim 5671–5688* (Poems 1911–1928). Tel-Aviv: Mitzpeh, 1932.

———. *Zahav* (Gold). New York: Sfarim and Keren L-tarbut B-Cincinnati, 1942.

———. *Anaḥnu ha-dor . . .* (We are the generation . . .). New York: ʿOgen, 1944.

———. "Bi-sfirat malkhut" (In sovereignty's sphere), *Hadoʾar* 28, no. 28 (Iyar 5709; 27 May 1949: 659–661.

———. *Goral u-phitʾom: shirim u-phoʾemot* (Destiny and suddenly: poems and poemas). Jerusalem: Mosad Bialik, 1954.

———. *Beyn ḥofim nistarim* (Between hidden shores). Tel-Aviv: Dvir, 1960.

———. *Kitvay Israel Efrat: sefer rishon: min ha-ʿolam he-ḥadash—shnay shirim* (The writings of Israel Efros: book one: from the new world—two poems). Tel-Aviv: Dvir, 1966.

———. *Kitvay Israel Efrat: sefer sheni: dorot* (The writings of Israel Efros: book two: generations). Tel-Aviv: Dvir, 1966.

———. *Kitvay Israel Efrat: sefer shlishi: meh ʿamok hu shatul* (The writings of Israel Efros: book three: how deep he is planted). Tel-Aviv: Dvir, 1966.

———. *Kitvay Israel Efrat: sefer rviʿi: elegiyot breshit* (The writings of Israel Efros: book one: ancient elegies). Tel-Aviv: Dvir, 1966.

———. *Kitvay Israel Efrat: sefer shmini: sefer ha-masot* (The writings of Israel Efros: book eight: essays). Tel-Aviv: Dvir, 1971.

———. *Elul kulo ḥodesh shel shir: 5726–5731* (Elul a month of poetry: 1966–1971). Ramat-Gan: Massada-Agudat Ha-sofrim, 1972.

———. *Kitvay Israel Efrat: sefer tshi'i: kaytzai ha-srufim ronenim 'al gagi: shirim 5726–5739* (The writings of Israel Efros: book nine: my burnt summers sing on my roof: poems 1966–1969). Tel-Aviv: Dvir, 1980.

———. *Kitvay Israel Efrat: sefer 'asiri: ha-r'ee ha-yotzer* (The writings of Israel Efros: book ten: the creative mirror: short essays 1971–1979). Tel-Aviv: Dvir, 1980.

———. *Yalkut masot* (An anthology of essays). Ed. B. Y. Mikhali, Y. Orpaz, et al. Tel-Aviv: Yaḥdav, 1980.

Efrat (Efros), Israel, B. N. Silkiner, and Y. Ibn-Shmu'el. *Milon Angli-'Ivri* (English-Hebrew dictionary). Ed. Y. Ibn-Shmu'el Kaufman. Tel-Aviv: Dvir, 1929.

Ekroni, Aviv. "'Al sfarim: trioletim u-vnay ha-'elohim" (About books: triolets and the sons of the gods). *'Al Ha-mishmar*, 4 September 1964, 6.

"Eleh toldot adam l-Lisitzky b-tirgum angli" (These are the tales of man in English translation). *Hado'ar*, year 38, vol. 39, no. 28 (28 Iyar 5719; 5 June 1959).

Elḥanani, A. H. "Im ba'al 'eleh toldot adam'—Ephraim Lisitzky" (With the author of "these are the tales of man"—E. E. Lisitzky). *Davar* 43, no. 9463, 20 July 1956, 5.

Elkad-Lehman, Ilana. "Tmurot po'etiyot b-shirat Israel Efrat" (Poetic changes in Israel Efrat's poetry). Ph.D. dissertation, Department of Literature of the Jewish People, Bar-Ilan University, Ramat-Gan, Israel, December 1995.

Epstein, Avraham. *Mi-karov ume-raḥok: pirkay masah u-vikoret* (From near and far: essay and critical chapters). New York: 'Ogen, 1934.

———. *Sofrim: divray masah u-vikoret* (Authors: essays and criticism). New York: 'Ogen, 1934.

———. "Ephraim E. Lisitzky (l-yovel ha-shishim shelo)" (E. E. Lisitzky—on his sixtieth anniversary). *Sefer ha-shanah li-yhuday America*, 8–9 (American Hebrew yearbook, 8–9). New York: Ha-histadrut Ha-'ivrit Ba-'America, 1948), 39–65.

———. *Sofrim 'ivrim ba-'America* (Hebrew writers in America). Tel-Aviv: Dvir, 1952.

Feinstein, Moshe. *Shirim v-sonetot* (Poems and sonnets). New York: 'Ogen, 1935.

———. *'Al saf ha-sof: shirim v-sonetot* (On the edge of the end: poems and sonnets). Jerusalem: M. Newman, 1964.

Feinstein, Sarah. "Ephraim E. Lisitzky—dyokan ha-moreh vha-mshorer ha-'ivri b-'artzot ha-brit" (Ephraim E. Lisitzky—portrait of the Hebrew teacher and poet in the United States). *Hador* 2 (2008): 126–131.

Feldman, Yael. "B-'atid shel lo-ulai l-Gavriel Preil—bi-mlot lo 75 shanah" (In a future of no-maybe by Gavriel Preil—at his reaching 75). *Bitzaron* 8 (Kayitz-Stav 5746–5747; Summer–Fall 1986): 20–5.

Fichman, Ya'akov. "Sefer zikaron l-B. N. Silkiner" (Memorial book for B. N. Silkiner). *Moznayim* 4, no. 1 (Sivan 5695; 1935): 102–104.

Finkle, Yitzhak. "Pgishot ʿim Ephraim E. Lisitzky" (Encounters with E. E. Lisitzky). *Bitzaron*, year 29, vol. 58, no. 6 (Sivan-Tammuz 5728; May-June 1968): 97-102.

Fleisher, Ezra, ed. *Meḥkray sifrut: mugashim l-Shimʿon Halkin* (Literary studies: presented to S. Halkin). Jerusalem: Magnes, 1973.

Fridland, Eliezer David. *Shirim b-sulam minor* (Poems in a minor key). Jerusalem: M. Newman, 1966.

Friedland, Ḥ[ayim] A[vraham]. *Sonetot* (Sonnets). Tel-Aviv: ʿOgen, 1939.

———. *Sipurim* (Stories). Tel-Aviv: ʿOgen, 1939.

———. *Shirim* (Poems). Tel-Aviv: ʿOgen, 1940.

———. *Shiray-ʿam (meʿezvono)* (Folk-poems: from his bequest). Ed. Israel Efros and Ḥayim Orlan. Tel-Aviv and Jerusalem: ʿOgen and M. Newman and Lishkat Ha-ḥinukh Ha-yehudi B-Cleveland, 1963.

Friedman, D. A. "Kisufay sheḥor" (Black longings). *Hadoʾar*, year 3, vol. 4, no. 41 (27 Elul 5684; 26 September 1924): 10-11.

———. "ʿAl sfarim v-sofrim: kniyat ʿolam b-shirah aḥat" (Of books and authors: immortality with one poem). *Ktuvim* 61, no. 2 (6 Kislev 5688; 30 November 1927): 2.

Geles, Y. Y. "Shirim" (Poems). *Ha-ʿolam* (London) 16, no. 27 (18 Tammuz 5688; 6 July 1928): 517-518.

Ginzburg, Shimʿon. "B. N. Silkiner." *Hadoʾar* 4, no. 4 (1 Kislev 5685; 28 November 1925): 12-13.

———. *Shirim u-phoʾemot* (Poems and poemas). Tel-Aviv: Aḥim/Dvir, 1931.

———. "Shirah ʿivrit ba-ʾAmerica" (Hebrew poetry in America). *Haʾaretz*, 21, no. 5539, 17 Ḥeshvan 5698; 22 October 1937, 9-10.

———. *Kitvay Shimʿon Ginzburg: b-masekhet ha-sifrut—masot u-rshamim* (Writings of S. Ginzburg: in the web of literature—essays and impressions). New York: Vaʿad L-hotzaʾat Kitvay Shimʿon Ginzburg, 1945.

———. *Kitvay Shimʿon Ginzburg: ahavat Hosheʿa—poʾemah* (Writings of S. Ginzburg: the love of Hosea—a poema). New York: Vaʿad L-hotzaʾat Kitvay Shimʿon Ginzburg, 1946.

———. *Shirim u-phoʾemot* (Poems and poemas). Jerusalem: M. Newman, 1970.

———. "B. N. Silkiner." *Doʾar ha-yom* (?), n.d., 5-6.

Golan, Ziva, and Ḥavivah Yonai, eds. *Shaul Tschernichovsky: bibliographiyah* (Saul Tschernichowsky: a bibliography). Tel-Aviv: Makhon Katz L-ḥeker Ha-sifrut Ha-ʿivrit B-ʾuniversitat Tel-Aviv, U-merkaz Ha-hadrakhah L-sifriyot Tziburiyot, 1981.

Goldberg, Av[raham]. *Kitvay Ab. Goldberg, ḥelek B: sifrut vo-ʾomanut* (The writings of Abe Goldberg, part II: literature and art). New York: ʿOgen, 1929.

———. *Kitvay Ab. Goldberg, ḥelek A: likrat tkufah* (The writings of Abe Goldberg, part I: toward an era). New York: ʿOgen, 1930.

———. *Kitvay Ab. Goldberg: srigim: shirim, tziyurim, sirtutim u-filitonim* (The writings of Abe Goldberg: Grids: poems, portraits, sketches and feuilletons). New York: ʿOgen, 1930.

———. *Sefer Avraham Goldberg: kovetz maʾamarav v-divray haʿarakhah ʿal ḥayav u-phʿulotav* (The Avraham Goldberg book: collected essays and evaluations of his life and work). Ed. M. Ribalow et al. New York: ʿOgen, 1945.

Goldman, Yehudah. *Nimim (shirim)* (Chords: poems). Vol. 1. New York: Agudat Sofrim ʿIvriyim Tzʿirim, 1932.

Goldshmit, Imanuʾel. "ʿAl shirat ha-ḥurban shel Aharon Zeitlin" (Aaron Zeitlin's poetry of the Ḥurban). *Migvan: meḥkarim ba-sifrut ha-ʿivrit uv-giluyeha ha-ʾAmericaniyim—mugashim l-Yaʿakov Kabakoff* (Migvan: Studies in Hebrew literature and its American manifestations—presented to Jacob Kabakoff). Ed. Stanley Nash. Lod, Israel: Makhon Haberman L-meḥkray Sifrut, 1988, 99–112.

Govrin, Nurit. "Beyn ʿolim li-mhagrim: kivunim mnugadim b-hitpatḥut ha-merkazim ha-sifrutiyim vha-ʿivriyim b-ʾeretz Israel uv-ʾartzot ha-brit" (Between immigrants to Israel and other immigrants: contradictory movements in the development of the Hebrew literary centers in Eretz Israel and the United States). *Bitzaron* 8, nos. 31–32 (Summer–Fall 1986): 26–33.

———. "Ha-tviʿah la-ʾAmericaniyut' v-hagshamatah ba-sifrut ha-ʿivrit ba-ʾAmerica" (The call for "Americanism" and its realization in Hebrew literature in America). *Migvan: meḥkarim ba-sifrut ha-ʿivrit uv-giluyeha ha-ʾAmericaniyim—mugashim l-Yaʿakov Kabakoff* (Migvan: Studies in Hebrew literature and its American manifestations—presented to Jacob Kabakoff). Ed. Stanley Nash. Lod, Israel: Makhon Haberman L-meḥkray Sifrut, 1988, 81–97.

Greenberg, Uri Zvi. *Rḥovot ha-nahar: sefer ha-ʾiliyot vha-koaḥ* (Streets of the river; the book of mourning and strength). Jerusalem: Schocken, 1978.

Gur, Yehudah. *Milon shimushi la-safah ha-ʿivrit* (Functional dictionary for the Hebrew language). Tel-Aviv: Dvir, 1950.

Gurin, Ḥaviv. *Intermetzo: shirim* (Intermazzo: poems). Tel-Aviv: Traklin, 1985.

———. *Hedim u-tzlilim: shirim* (Echoes and sounds: poems). Tel-Aviv: Traklin, 1987.

———. *Ba-ʿayin ha-pnimit: shirim* (With the inner eye: poems). Tel-Aviv: Traklin, 1987.

———. *Ha-lapid vha-sela* (The torch and the rock). Tel-Aviv: Traklin, 1988.

Halevy, Avraham Tzvi (Zvi). *Mi-tokh ha-sugar: shirim* (From witin the prison: poems). New York: Ohel, 1948.

———. "Reʿi ha-ʾilan" (My friend the tree). *Hadoʾar*, year 34, vol. 35, no. 37 (22 Elul 5715; 9 September 1955): 713.

———. "Stav ʿal ha-Hudson" (Autumn on the Hudson). *Hadoʾar*, year 37, vol. 38, no. 16 (24 Shvat 5718; 14 February 1958): 287.

———. "Asefah rabat-ʿam l-zikhro shel Hillel Bavli" (Large gathering in memory of Hillel Bavli). *Hadoʾar*, year 41, vol. 42, no. 9 (22 Shvat 5722; 19 December 1961): 139.

———. *New-York: shirim v-ʿiyunim b-sifrutenu ha-ḥadashah* (New York: poems and studies of our new literature). Ed. Yaʿakov Rimon. Tel-Aviv: Ha-mnorah, 1968.

Halevy, Moshe. *Kitvay Moshe Halevy* (Writings of Moshe Halevy). New York: Keren Israel Matz, 1936/7.

Halkin, Shimʿon (Simon). "Tafkid ha-shirah b-ḥayenu" (Poetry's role in our lives). *Nimim* 1. Ed. Hillel Bavli. New York: Ḥaverim, 1923, 5–12.

———. "Ha-shirah ha-ʿivrit ba-ʾAmerica" (Hebrew poetry in America). *Hadoʾar*, year 3, vol. 4, no. 4 (1 Kislev 5685; 28 November 1924): 10–12.

———. *Yeḥiʾel ha-hagri* (Yeḥiʾel the Hagrite). Tel-Aviv: A. Y. Stybel, 1935/6.

———. *Araʾi va-keva: ʿiyunim b-sifrut* (Temporary and permanent: studies in literature). New York: Ohel, 1942.

———. *ʿAd mashber* (Till breakdown). Tel-Aviv: ʿAm ʿOved, 1945.

———. *ʿAl ha-ʾee: shirim* (On the island: poems). Jerusalem: Mosad Bialik, 1946.

———. "Haʿarakhot v-divray bikoret: ki phanah yom" (Criticism and evaluations: for the day has waned). *Bitzaron*, year 8, vol. 15, no. 2 (86) (Ḥeshvan 5707; November 1946): 121–127.

———. "Haʿarakhot v-divray bikoret: Avraham Tzvi Halevy" (Criticism and evaluations: A. Z. Halevy). *Bitzaron*, year 10, vol. 19, no. 3 (Kislev–Tevet 5709; December 1948–January 1949): 194–200.

———. *Mavo la-siporet ha-ʿivrit: rshimot lfi hartzaʾotav shel prof. Halkin bi-shnat 5712* (Introduction to Hebrew prose: notes according to Prof. Halkin's lectures in 1952). Jerusalem: Mifʿal Ha-shikhpul, 1958.

———. *Maʿavar yabok: shirim* (Jabbok crossing: poems). Tel-Aviv: ʿAm ʿOved, 1965.

———. *Nekhar: sipurim* (A foreign country: stories). Jerusalem: Mosad Bialik, 1972.

———. *Shirim 5677–5733* (Poems 1917–1973). Jerusalem: Mosad Bialik, 1977.

———. *Muskamot u-mashbrim b-sifrutenu: 12 siḥot ʿal ha-sifrut ha-ʿivrit ha-ḥadashah* (Conventions and crises: 12 conversations about modern Hebrew literature). Jerusalem: Mosad Bialik, 1980.

"Ha-mshorer Ephraim Lisitzky" (E. E. Lisitzky the poet). *Haʾaretz*, 8 September 1957(?).

"Ha-msibah shel yameynu" (Today's party). *Yediʿot Aḥaronot*, 25 July 1956.

Haramati, Shlomo. "Daniʾel Persky—ish ha-lashon" (Daniel Persky—the language man). *Hadoʾar* 83, no. 1 (Ḥeshvan 5764; Fall 2003): 26–28.

Hillels, Shlomo. *Taḥat shmay Bessarabia: sipur* (Under Bessarabian skies: a story). New York: Sfarim, 1942.

———. *Artzah: sipur bi-shnay ḥalakim* (Israel bound: a tale in two parts). New York: Sfarim, 1945.

Hinitz, Nahum. "Sofrim u-sfarim: aḥaray mitato shel M. M. Dolitzky (kitʿay zikhronot)" (Authors and books: following M. M. Dolitzky's casket—memory fragments). *Hado'ar*, year 10, vol. 11, no. 18 (24 Adar 5691; 13 March 1931): 286.

Holtz, Avraham. "Dyokan—dmut dyokano shel Hillel Bavli ha-mshorer vha-masa'i" (Portrait: image of Hillel Bavli the poet and essayist). *Niv: kli mivta l-ofrim tz'irim* (New York) 23, nos. 3–4 (Iyar 5719; June 1959): 10, 23.

———. "Beyn ha-shitin: M. Flinker—ha-navokh ha-sho'el" (Between the lines: M. Flinker—the perplexed questioner). *Niv: kli mivta l-sofrim tz'irim* (New York) 24, no. 1 (Iyar 5720; November 1959): 14.

———. "Dyokan—Lisitzky: ish midot" (Portrait—Lisitzky: a man of stature). *Niv: kli mivta l-sofrim tz'irim* (New York) 24, no. 1 (Iyar 5720; May 1960): 5–7.

———. "Neta zar: sipur" (A strange plant: a story). *Niv: kli mivta l-sofrim tz'irim* (New York), ed. M. Pelli, year 25 (Shvat 5721; February 1961): 12–15.

———. "Ha-mashiaḥ: rshimah" (The messiah: a sketch). *Niv: kli mivta l-sofrim tz'irim* (New York) 25, no. 2 (Sivan 5721; May 1961): 25-26.

———. "Hillel Bavli—ha-'adam vi-ytzirato" (Hillel Bavli—The man and his work). *Niv: kli mivta l-sofrim tz'irim* (New York), year 26, vol. 7, no. 1 (Kislev 5722; November 1961): 10–17.

———. "B-tzel be'er ha-mayim: sipur" (In the shadow of the well: a story). *Niv: kli mivta l-sofrim tz'irim* (New York) 25, nos. 1–2 (Tishrei 5725; September 1964): 23–28.

———. "Dmuyot ba-gan (sipur)" (Images in the park: a story). *Niv: kli mivta l-sofrim tz'irim* (New York) 30, nos. 1–2 (Nisan 5726; April 1966): 23–26; continued in *Niv* 30:3.

Holtzman, Avner. *Mle'khet maḥshevet: teḥiyat ha-'umah- -ha-sifrut ha-'ivrit l-nokhaḥ ha-'omanut ha-plastit* (Artful work: national revival—Hebrew literature confronting the plastic arts). Tel-Aviv: Universitat Haifa and Zmora Bitan, 1999.

Hoss, Avraham. "'B-'oholay Khush' l-Ephraim E. Lisitzky" (E. E. Lisitzky's "In the tents of Cush"). *Gazit* 14, nos. 9–10 (May–June 1956): 13–17.

Ḥurgin, Ya'akov. "B-'oholay khush" (In the tents of Cush). *Hado'ar*, year 33, vol. 34, no. 13 (25 Shvat 5714; 29 January 1954): 243–244.

Indelman, Elḥanan. "Sofrim u-sfarim: 'adam al adamot'" (Books and authors: "man on earth"). *Hado'ar*, year 27, vol. 28, no. 28 (19 Iyar 5708; 28 May 1948): 683–684; cont. vol. 28, no. 29 (26 Iyar 5708; 4 June 1948): 707–708.

———. *Even li ekaḥ: shirim* (I'll take me a stone: poems). Jerusalem: Kiryat Sefer, 1956.

———. "Anshay midot" (People of stature). *Hado'ar*, year 38, vol. 39, no. 11 (14 Shvat 5719; 23 January 1959): 192, 197.

———. "Shnay sifray shirah l-Ephraim E. Lisitzky" (Two poetry books by E. E. Lisitzky). *Bitazron* 45, no. 2 (Kislev–Tevet 5722; November–December 1961): 78–85.

Isaacs, B[ernard]. *Beyn shnay 'olamot: sipurim v-tziyurim* (Between two worlds: stories and sketches). New York: 'Ogen, 1949.

———. *ʿAmos mokher tapuzim v-ʿod sipurim* (Amos sells oranges and other stories). Tel-Aviv: M. Newman, 1953.
———. *Ḥoter mi-geza: sipurim* (A branch off the stem: stories). Tel-Aviv and Jerusalem: ʿOgen and M. Newman, 1960.
———. *Mivḥar sipurim* (Selected stories). Tel-Aviv: Maḥbarot L-sifrut, 1968.
———. "Ḥ. A. Friedland—ish ha-ʾeshkolot" (H. A. Friedland—the scholar). *Sefer B. Isaacs*. Ed. Moshe Noble. New York: n.p., 1977, 88–90.
Israel, G. "Naftulay adam veʾlohim shel mshorer: shaʿah kalah ʿim Ephraim Lisitzky" (Human and divine struggles of a poet: a brief while with Ephraim Lisitzky). *Omer*, no. 1555, 30 July 1956, p. 2.
Kabakoff, Yaʿakov (Jacob). "Noaḥ ba-sifrut ha-ʿivrit" (Noah in Hebrew literature). *Niv: kli mivta l-sofrim tzʿirim* (New York) 1, no. 6 (Sivan 5697; May 1937): 14–17.
———. "Beyt Israel ba-ʾAmerica" (American Jewry). *Niv: kli mivta l-sofrim tzʿirim* (New York) 4, no. 7 (Iyar 4699; April 1939): 16–17.
———. "ʿAl Ḥ. A. Friedland" (About H. A. Friedland). *Niv: kli mivta l-sofrim tzʿirim* (New York) 4, no. 1 (Tishrei–Ḥeshvan 5700; October 1939): 10–11.
———. "Bikoret: Reuven Brainin b-zikhronotav" (Criticism: Reuben Brainin in his memoirs). *Niv: kli mivta l-sofrim tzʿirim* (New York) 4, no. 5 (Adar 2–Nisan 5700; April 1940): 7–8.
———. "Li-dmutah shel ha-sifrut ha-ʿivrit ba-ʾAmerica" (Image of Hebrew literature in America). *Jewish Book Annual (Shnaton ha-sefer ha-yehudi)* 13 (1955–1956), 9–19.
———. "Gershon Rosenzweig baʿal ha-parodiyot (l-yovel ha-meʾah l-huladeto)" (Gershon Rosenzweig the parodist: one hundred years since his birth). *Hed ha-kvutzah: bitaʾon ha-kvutzah ha-ʿivrit b-Detroit* 20–21, nos. 23–24 (5720–5721; 1960–1961): 77–82.
———. "Hillel Bavli ha-mshorer vha-ʾadam" (Hillel Bavli the poet and the man). *Jewish Book Annual* 20 (1962–1963): 76–83.
———. "Tzvi Gershoni: me-ḥalutzay ha-sifrut ha-ʿivrit ba-ʾAmerica v-ʾigrotav" (Tzvi Gershoni: pioneer of Hebrew literature in America and his correspondence). *Sura: maʾasef l-meḥkar ul-ʿiyun bi-vʿayot Israel vha-ʿolam ba-ʿavar uvahoveh* 5 (Jerusalem): N.p., 1964.
———. *Ḥalutzay ha-sifrut ha-ʿivrit ba-ʾAmerica* (Pioneers of Hebrew literature in America). Tel-Aviv: N.p., 1966.
———. "Mi-shirat mhagrim l-shirah Americaʾit (li-mlot 10 shanim li-ftirato shel E. E. Lisitzky)" (From immigrant to American poetry: ten years since the death of E. E. Lisitzky). *Hadoʾar*, year 51, vol. 51, no. 28 (27 Sivan 5732; 9 June 1972): 473–474.
———. *Shoḥarim v-neʾemanim: masot u-meḥkarim ʿal ha-sifrut vha-tarbut ha-ʿivrit ba-ʾAmerica* (Seekers and stalwarts: essays and studies on American Hebrew literature and culture). Jerusalem: Reuven Mass, 1978.

———. "Binyamin Naḥum Silkiner ʿal-pi igrotav" (B. N. Silkiner according to his letters). *Mahut* (Summer 1989): 63–70.

Kaniuk, Yoram. *Ha-yored l-maʿalah* (The acrophile). Jerusalem: Schocken, 1963.

———. *Mot ha-ʿayir* (The donkey's death). Ramat-Gan: Sifriyat Makor, 1973.

———. *Susʿetz: masa* (Rockinghorse: a journey). Tel-Aviv: Sifriyat Poʿalim, 1973.

———. *ʿAfar u-tshukah* (Dust and lust). Tel-Aviv: Sifriyat Poʿalim, 1975.

———. *Laylah ʿal ha-ḥof ʿim tranzistor* (Nigh on the beach with a transistor radio). Tel-Aviv: Ha-kibbutz Ha-mʾuḥad, 1979.

———. *Kmo sipurim* (As-if stories). Tel-Aviv: Kineret, 1983.

———. *Ḥayim ʿal nyar zkhukhit* (Life on sandpaper/I did it my way). Tel-Aviv: Yediʿot Aḥaronot/ Sifray Ḥemed, 2003.

Kariv, Avraham. "ʿIm sfarim—Ephraim E. Lisitzky: mdurot doʿakhot" (Among books: E. E. Lisitzky—dying campfires). *Davar* no. 3789, 5 November 1937, 7.

Karol, Tz. "Rshimot bibliographiyot" (Bibliographical notes). *Haʾaretz* 10, no. 2486, 21 Tishrei 5688; 17 October 1927, 4.

Katz, Shmuʾel (Stephen). *Ha-gibor b-ʿeynay ruḥo: omanut ha-siper shel ʿAgnon b-ʾoreaḥ nata la-lun* (The hero in his own eyes: narrative art in Agnon's *A Guest for the Night*). Tel-Aviv: ʿEked, 1985.

Katzman, Avi. "Moto shel asfan stavim" (Death of the collector of autumns). *Haʾaretz*, 6 November 1993, B7.

Katznelson, Barukh. "ʿAl shiratenu ba-ʾAmerica" (About our poetry in America). *Hadoʾar*, year 14, vol. 15, no. 10 (29 Tevet 5695; 4 January 1935): 182.

———. "Vigvamim shotkim" (Silent wigwams). *Hadoʾar*, year 14, vol. 15, no. 7 (8 Tevet 5695; 14 December 1935): 125–126.

———. *Mi-lev el lev: shirim* (From heart to heart: poems). Tel-Aviv: Agudat Ha-sofrim Ha-ʿivrim L-yad Dvir, 1954.

Keshet, Yeshurun. *Maskiyot: masot bikoret* (Ornaments: critical essays). Tel-Aviv: Agudat Ha-sofrim Ha-ʿivrim and Dvir, 1953.

———. "Ha-mshorer ha-humanistan" (The humanist poet). *Hadoʾar*, year 39, vol. 40, no. 22 (11 Nisan 5720; 8 April 1960): 401–403.

———. "ʿAl Ephraim Lisitzky ha-mshorer" (On the poet E. E. Lisitzky). *Havdalot* (Distinctions). Tel-Aviv: Agudat Ha-sofrim and Dvir, 1962.

———. *Amadot: haʿarakhot bikortiyot* (Approximations: essays in literary criticism). Jerusalem: Agudat Shalem, 1969.

———. "Mshorer ʿivri ʿal enut ha-kushim" (A Hebrew poet on the sufferings of Blacks). N.d., n.p.

Klausner, Yosef. *Historyah shel ha-sifrut hʿivrit ha-ḥadashah* (A history of modern Hebrew literature). Vol. 4. Jerusalem: Aḥiʾasaf, 1963.

Kleinman, Moshe. "Bibliographiyah" (Bibliography). *Ha-ʿolam* 17, no. 25 (Sivan 5689; 21 July 1929): 500.

Kopelevitz, Yaʿakov. "Skirat sfarim: sefer ḥayim shel Ephraim Lisitzky" (Survey of books: E. Lisitzky's book of life). N.p., 16 June 1950.

Kovner, Abba. *Sloan Kettering*. Tel-Aviv: Ha-kibbutz Ha-m'uḥad, 1987.
Kramer, Shalom. *Panim va-'ofen: masot 'al shirah ve-'al mshorerim* (Face and modes: essays on poetry and poets). Ramat-Gan, Agudat Ha-sofrim; Massadah, 1976.
Kressel, G[etzel]. *Leksikon ha-sifrut ha-'ivrit ba-dorot ha-'aḥaronim* (Lexicon of Hebrew literature in recent generations). 2 vols. Merḥaviah: Sifriyat Po'alim/ Ha-kibbutz Ha-'artzi Ha-shomer Ha-tza'ir, 1965.
Lachower, F[ischel]. "B. N. Silkiner." *Moznayim* 1, no. 3 (Kislev 5694; December 1933): 99–101.
Lander, P[inḥas]. "Eleh toldot adam" (These are the tales of man). *Ha-po'el Ha-tza'ir* 43, no. 37 (28 Sivan 5710; 13 June 1950): 12–13.
———. "B-taltlat goral va-sevel" (In the pendulum of destiny and suffering). *Ha'aretz* 32, no. 9392, 7 July 1950, 5.
———. "Dyokanay sofrim: Ephraim E. Lisitzky—ben 75" (Author portraits: E. E. Lisitzky—75 years old). *Ha'aretz*, "Tarbut v-sifrut" (Literature and culture) 57, no. 12458, 22 July 1960, 15.
———. "Mi-madaf ha-sfarim: shirat E. E. Lisitzky—bi-ymay sho'ah u-msho'ah" (From the bookshelf: the poetry of E. E. Lisitzky—in the days of destruction and desolation). *Ha'aretz*, 27 Tishrei 5721; 7 October 1960, 13.
———. "Shirat Ephraim E. Lisitzky" (E. E. Lisitzky's poetry). *Ha'aretz* 43, no. 12521, 7 October 1960, 13.
Laor, Dan, ed. *Shim'on Halkin: mivḥar ma'amaray bikoret 'al yetzirato* (S. Halkin: selected critical essays on his work). Tel-Aviv: 'Am 'Oved, 1978.
Leaf, Ḥayim. "Sipuray America l-B. Isaacs" (B. Isaacs' America tales). *Bitzaron* 45, no. 2 (Kislev–Tevet 5722; November–December 1961): 89–91.
———. "Ephraim E. Lisitzky Z"L (tziyunim 'al kivro hara'anan)" (E. E. Lisitzky: remarks over his fresh grave). *Bitzaron* 46, no. 6 (231) (Sivan–Tammuz 5722; May–June 1962): 59–61.
———. "E. E. Lisitzky: ha-'aḥaron mi-dor ha-rishonim ba-sifrut ha-'ivrit" (E. E. Lisitzky: last of the first generation of Hebrew literature). *Ha-po'el Ha-tza'ir* (24 August 1962): 44–45.
———. *Ktavim u-dyokna'ot* (Writings and profiles). Tel-Aviv: 'Eked/ Traklin, 1998.
Lensky, Ḥayim. "Sefer ha-tundra" (The Tundra book). In *Ḥayim Lensky: shirim rshimot u-mikhtavim, Elisha Rodin: shirim v-hegyonot* (Ḥayim Lensky: poems, notes and correspondence, Elisha Rodin: poems and musings). Vol. 1 of *He-'anaf ha-gadu'a: kitvay sofrim 'ivrim shebi-vrit ha-mo'atzot* (The severed branch: Hebrew writers' works in the Soviet Union). Ed. Avraham Kariv. Jerusalem: Mosad Bialik, 1954, 123–157.
Levinson-Lavi, M. Z. "'B-'oholay khush': shirim" ("In the tents of Cush": poems. *Bitzaron*, year 15, vol. 30, no. 6 (Iyar–Sivan 5714; May 1954): 125–132.
Levy, Ḥayah (Claire). *Kisufim* (Longings). New York: Pardes, 1941.
Lisitzky, Ephraim E. "Vegen di vahlen tzum Yiddishen kongres" (Elections for

the Jewish Congress) *Milvoker wokhnblatt*, 4, no. 1, 8 March 1917, 1. [For similar articles in same source, see 4, no. 3, 16 March 1917; 4, no. 9, 4 May 1917, p. 3; 4, no. 12, 25 May 1917; 4, no. 13, 8 June 1917, p. 2; 4, no. 14, 8 June 1917, pp. 1, 3; 15 June 1917; 13 July 1917; 23 November 1917.]

———. *Shirim* (Poems). New York: Ḥaverim; Tel-Aviv: Dvir, 1928.

———. "Agadat ha-bri'ah asher la-'Algonquinim (min ha-mitologyah ha-hodit)" (The Algonquin creation legend: from Indian mythology). *Hado'ar*, year 9, vol. 10, no. 10 (Tevet 5690; 3 January 1930): 163.

———. *Naftulay elohim* (Divine struggles). New York: 'Ogen; Tel-Aviv: Dvir, 1934.

———. "Vigvamim shotkim" (Silent wigwams). *Masad: ma'asef l-divray sifrut* (Masad: an anthology for literature), 2. Jerusalem: New York/Tel-Aviv: Ḥaverim/Mitzpeh, 1936, 334–343.

———. *Mdurot do'akhot* (Dying campfires). New York: 'Ogen, 1937.

———. *Adam 'al adamot: po'emot* (Man on earth: poemas). Introduction M. Ribalow. New York: 'Ogen, 1947.

———. "'Al ha-shirah ha-'ivrit ba-'America" (Hebrew poetry in America). *Hado'ar*, year 28, vol. 29, no. 7 (15 Kislev 5709; 17 December 1948): 164.

———. *Eleh toldot adam* (These are the tales of man). Jerusalem: Mosad Bialik, 1949.

———. *B-'oholay khush: shirim* (In the tents of Cush: poems). Jerusalem: Mosad Bialik, 1953.

———. "Holekh l-masa'o Pete" (mi-shiray ha-kushim) (Pete's on his way: poems of Blacks). *Gilyonot* 29, no. 7 (Iyar–Sivan 1953): 14–15.

———. *B-ma'alot uv-moradot* (Ascents and descents). Tel-Aviv: Dvir, 1954.

———. "Israel b-'artzo v-Israel b-galut America" (Jewry in its land and Jewry in the American diaspora). *Hado'ar*, year 35, vol. 36, no. 37 (24 Elul 5716; 31 August 1956): 703–704.

———. *Anshay midot: po'emot* (Men of stature: poemas). Tel-Aviv: 'Am Ha-sefer, 1958.

———. "Masa nud" (Aimless wanderings). *Bitzaron*, year 20, vol. 40, no. 6 (209) (Iyar–Sivan 5719; May–June 1959): 81–82.

———. *Bi-ymay sho'ah u-msho'ah: maḥazot* (In days of destruction and desolation: plays). Tel-Aviv: 'Ogen/M. Newman, 1960.

———. *Kmo ha-yom rad: shirim* (As the day set: poems). Tel-Aviv: Maḥbarot L-sifrut, 1960.

———. "Ne'um she-lo nin'am" (A speech that was not delivered). *Bitzaron*, year 21, vol. 41, no. 4 (Adar 5720; February–March 1960): 185–187.

———. "Yaha! harimu ha-shamayim (divray pridah mi-tokh prishah)" (Yahu! lift up the sky: farewell words at retirement). *Hado'ar*, year 39, vol. 40, no. 23 (Iyar 5720; 29 April 1960): 435–436, 441.

———. "Ḥayim Naḥman Bialik mi-tokh tzfiyah retrospectivit" (A retrospective view of Ḥ. N. Bialik). *Kneset* (Tammuz 5720; 1960): 26–38.

———. *Bi-shvilay ḥayim v-sifrut* (In the paths of life and literature). Tel-Aviv: Maḥbarot L-sifrut and ʿOgen, 1961.

———. "Hillel Bavli—darko ba-sifrut uva-ḥayim" (Hillel Bavli: His literature and life). *Bitzaron*, year 22, vol. 44, no. 7 (225) (Av–Elul 5721; September 1961): 157–162.

———. *Kokhavim noflim: sefer ha-triʾoletim* (Falling stars: the book of triolets). Tel-Aviv: Maḥbarot L-sifrut, 1963.

Luria, Shalom, ed. *Abba Kovner: mivḥar maʾamaray bikoret ʿal yetzirato* (Abba Kovner: A selection of critical essays on his writings). Tel-Aviv: Ha-kibbutz Ham'uḥad, 1988.

Luz, Tzvi, ed. *La-shemesh: masot ʿal klil sonetot l-Shaʾul Tschernichovsky* (To the sun: essays on S. Tschernichowsky's sonnet cycle). Ramat-Gan, Israel: Universitat Bar-Ilan, 1996.

"Maʿamad ha-ʿivrit b-ʾarhab" (The status of Hebrew in the United States). *ʿAlon Elah: ha-ʾagudah li-rkhishat ha-ʿivrit ul-horaʾatah* (Hebrew Language Association [HELA] newsletter (Tel-Aviv University). Pamphlet 2, c. 1993, pl 6.

Malakhi, A. R. "Ephraim E. Lisitzky (l-yovlo)" (E. E. Lisitzky: on his anniversary). *Hadoʾar*, year 33, vol. 34, no. 12 (18 Shvat 5714; 22 January 1954): 221–222.

———. "Lisitzky ki-mḥanekh" (Lisitzky as educator). *Bitzaron*, year 21, vol. 41, no. 4 (Adar 5720; February–March 1960): 203–212.

———. "L-toldot Hillel Bavli" (Biography of Hillel Bavli). *Bitzaron*, year 22, vol. 44, no. 7 (Av–Elul 5721; 1961): 166–173; continued in year 23, vol. 45, no. 2 (Kislev–Tevet 5722; November–December 1961): 67–75; conclusion in vol. 45, no. 3 (Shvat–Adar 5722; 1962): 137–148.

———. *Zekher l-Hillel: bibliyographiyah shel yetzirot Hillel Bavli b-shirah u-phrozah u-rshimat ha-maʾamarim she-nikhtvu ʿalav vʿal sfarav* (In memory of Hillel: a bibliography of the poetic and prose writings of Hillel Bavli and a list of essays written about him and his books). New York: Alumni Association of the Teachers Institute and Seminary College of Jewish Studies of the Jewish Theological Seminary of America, 1962.

Malamud, Bernard. *Ha-ʿam v-sipurim aḥerim* (The people and other stories). Trans. Ruth Livnit. Tel-Aviv: Zmora Bitan, 1993.

Margalit, Yariv. "Kol Yaʿakov me-ʾoholay Kush" (Jacob's voice from within the tents of Cush). *Haʾaretz*, "Tarbut v-sifrut," 36, no. 10409, 28 Ḥeshvan 5714; 6 November 1953, p. B.

Markson, A[haron] D[avid]. *Kitvay A. D. Markson* (The writings of A. D. Markson). Ed. B. Isaacs and Daniel Persky. Detroit: Ha-kvutzah Ha-ʿivrit, 1938.

Meitus, Eliyahu. "Hagigim" (mi-maḥzor trioletim) (Meditations: from a cycle of triolets). *Moznayim* 1, no. 6 (Av 5715; August 1955): 357.

Meizlish, M[enasheh]. "B-naftulay ḥazon" (In vision's struggles). *Hadoʾar*, year 15, vol. 15, no. 10 (29 Tevet 5695; 4 January 1935): 174–175.

———. "M. S. Ben-Meir." *Hado'ar,* year 38, vol. 39, no. 11 (14 Shvat 5719; 23 January 1959): 187.

Melamed, Avraham. *Ha-yahafokh Kushi ʿoro: ha-ʾadam ha-shaḥor k-"ʾaḥer" b-toldot ha-tarbut ha-yehudit* (Can the Cushite change his skin: the Black man as "Other" in Jewish cultural history). Haifa and Lod: Haifa University and Zmora Bitan, 2002.

Menosi, Yedidyah. "ʿIm shiray Lisitzky" (With Lisitzky's poems). *Hado'ar,* year 34, vol. 35, no. 17 (3 Adar 5715; 25 February 1955): 325.

"Msibah l-Lisitzky" (A party for Lisitzky). *Davar* 47, no. 9467, 25 July 1956, 2.

"Met ha-mshorer Ephraim Lisitzky" (The poet E. Lisitzky is dead). *Haʾaretz,* 27 April 1962.

Mikhali, B. Y. "Ephraim E. Lisitzky: b-ʾoholay khush." (Buenos Aires) *Darom* 3–4 (198–199) (5704; 1944): 47–48.

———. "Israel Efrat: nofim Americaniyim b-shirato" (Israel Efros: American vistas in his poetry). *Dmuyot u-tzdudiyot* (Images and profiles). Tel-Aviv: Hakibbutz Ha-m'uḥad, 1971, 173–186.

Miklishansky, Yaʿakov [Mikliszanski, Jacques]. *Toldot ha-sifrut ha-ʿivrit ba-ʾAmerica* (History of Hebrew literature in America). Jerusalem: Reuven Mass and ʿOgen, 1967.

Miklishansky, Yaʿakov [Mikliszanski, Jacques], and Yaʿakov Kabakoff, eds. *Sefer ha-doʾar: Mivḥar maʾamarim l-yovel ha-shishim 5682–5742* (Hado'ar year book: selected essays on its sixtieth anniversary 1922–1982). New York: Ha-histadrut Ha-ʿivrit Ba-ʾAmerica, 1982.

Miller, Shmuel. "Sofrim u-sfarim: ha-mshorer hayah raʿev" (Authors and books: the poet went hungry). *Hado'ar,* year 10, vol. 11, no. 18 (24 Adar 5691; 13 March 1931): 286.

Miron, Dan. "Mivneh u-vinah b-kovtzay shirah shel Natan Alterman" (Structure and sense in Nathan Alterman's poetry anthologies). *Moznayim* 32, no. 4–5 (Adar–Nisan 5731; March–April 1971): 305–319.

———. "Beyn ha-ner la-kokhavim: ʿal shirat Gavriel Preil" (Between the candle and the stars: on the poetry of Gavriel Preil). In *Gavriel Preil, Asfan stavim: shirim: 1972–1992* (Collector of autumns: collected poems 1972–1992), pp. 273–381. Jerusalem: Mosad Bialik, 1993.

Nadav, Mordecai. "Shirat ha-kushim l-ʿEphraim Lisitzky" (E. Lisitzky's poetry of Blacks). *Zmanim* 47 (28 Ḥeshvan 5714; 6 November 1953).

Nash, Shlomo [Stanley], ed. *Migvan: mehkarim ba-sifrut ha-ʿivrit uv-giluyeha ha-ʾAmericaniyim* (Migvan: studies in Hebrew literature and its American manifestations—presented to Jacob Kabakoff). Lod, Israel: Makhon Haberman L-meḥkray sifrut, 1988.

Negev, Eilat. "B-khol adam ḥavuy korban v-rotzeaḥ" (In every man lurks a victim and a killer). *Yediʿot Aḥaronot,* "7 yamim," 17 November 1995, 36–38.

"Neshef la-mshorer: Y. Y. Schwartz vi-ytzirato" (Ball in honor of the poet: Y. Y.

Schwartz and his work). *Hado'ar*, year 42, vol. 43, no. 29 (15 Sivan 5723; 7 June 1963): 546.

Niger, Shmuel, and M. Ribalow, eds. *Aḥisefer*. New York: Keren Louis LaMed, 1943.

Noble, Moshe. "ʿAl mshorer ʿivri ḥadash ba-ʾAmerica" (A new Hebrew poet in America). *Hed ha-kvutzah: bitaʾon ha-kvutzah ha-ʿivrit b-Detroit* 22–24, no. 25–27 (5722–5724; 1962–1964): 5–10.

———, ed. *Sefer B. Isaacs* (The B. Isaacs book). New York: n.p., 1977.

ʿOgen, Yitzhak. "Ephraim Lisitzky: b-ʾoholay khush" (Ephraim Lisitzky: in the tents of Cush). *La-kore ha-tzaʿir: ʿalon l-vikoret ul-hadrakhah sifrutit* 11–12 (Elul-Tishrei 5714; September–October 1953): 1–2.

Or, Amir. "Kriʾat shir: sendvich msupak" (Reading a poem: a dubious sandwich). *Haʾaretz*, 6 August 1993, 7.

Orah, Sh. "Ḥag 'ha-moreh' b-New Orleans" ("The teacher's" festival in New Orleans). *Hado'ar*, year 38, vol. 39, no. 26 (14 Iyar 5719; 22 May 1959): 492.

Orpaz, Yitzḥak, et al., eds. *Israel Efrat: mshorer v-hogeh* (Israel Efros: poet and thinker). Tel-Aviv: Katz Institute for Hebrew Literature, Tel-Aviv University, 1981.

Oz, Amos. *Mnuḥah nkhonah* (A perfect peace). Tel-Aviv: ʿAm ʿOved, 1982.

Pagis, Dan. "Bikoret sfarim—B-ʾoholay khush: shirim meʾet E. E. Lisitzky" (Book review: In the tents of Cush: poems by E. E. Lisitzky). *Davar* 128, no. 8632, 30 October 1953, p. 4.

Pelgat, Yaron. "Ha-sipur ha-ʿivri ha-katzar ba-ʾAmerica, 1900–1950" (The Hebrew short story in America, 1900–1950). *Hado'ar* 83, no. 1 (Ḥeshvan 5764; Fall 2003): 20–25.

Pelli, Moshe. *Ha-tarbut ha-ʿivrit ba-ʾAmerica: 80 shnot ha-tnuʿah ha-ʿivrit b-ʾartzot ha-brit—5676–5758 (1916–1995)* (Hebrew culture in America: 80 years of Hebrew culture in the United States, 1916–1995). Tel-Aviv: Rshafim, 1998.

———. *Sugot v-sugyot b-sifrut ha-haskalah ha-ʿivrit: ha-janer ha-maskili va-ʾavizarayhu* (Kinds of Genre in Haskalah Literature: Types and Topics). Tel-Aviv: Ha-kibbutz Ha-mʾuḥad, 1999.

Penueli [Pineles], S. Y. "Sifrutenu ha-ḥadashah ba-ʾAmerica: shirat B. N. Silkiner" (Our new literature in America: the poetry of B. N. Silkiner). *Gilyonot* 15, no. 4 (Tishrei 5704; 1943): 189–192.

———. "Sifrutenu ha-ḥadashah ba-ʾAmerica: sipuray Yoḥanan Twersky" (Our new literature in America: the tales of Y. Twersky). *Gilyonot* 15, no. 5 (Ḥeshvan 5704; 1943): 228–232.

———. "Sifrutenu ha-ḥadashah ba-ʾAmerica: shirat Israel Efrat" (Our new literature in America: the poetry of Israel Efros). *Gilyonot* 15, no. 6 (90) (Kislev 5704; 1943): 335–339.

———. "Shirah ʿivrit rḥokah-krovah: 'vigvamim shotkim' v-'zahav' l-Israel Efrat" (Close-distant Hebrew poetry: "Silent wigwams" and "Gold" by Israel Efros). *Ha-galgal* (29 Tammuz 5704; 20 July 1944): 21–23.

———. "Bi-sdeh sefer: adam ʿal adamot" (In the book field: man on earth). *Gilyonot* 22, no. 7–8 (Adar II–Nisan 5708; 1948): 62–64.
———. *Ḥuliyot ba-sifrut ha-ʿivrit ha-ḥadashah* (Segments in modern Hebrew literature). Tel-Aviv: Dvir, 1953.
———. "E. E. Lisitzky b-maʿalotav uv-mordotav" (E. E. Lisitzky in his ascents and descents). *Zmanim: L-sifrut ul-ʾomanut* (10 January 1954): 4.
———. "Me-ʾalef' ʿad 'heh'" (From 'alef' to 'heh'). *ʿAl ha-mishmar*, 31 August 1956.
Perlberg, A. N. *Kitvay A. N. Perlberg* (Writings of A. N. Perlberg). Ed. D. Persky and M. Ribalow. New York: Esther Perlberg, 1939.
Persky, Daniel. *L-ʾelef yedidim* (To a thousand friends). New York: Vaʿad Ha-yovel, 1935.
———. *Kitvay Daniel Persky*. Vol. 1, *ʿivri anokhi* (The writings of Daniel Persky, Vol. 1, I am a Hebrew). New York: Ha-mḥaber, 1948.
———. "Mi-zimrat America ha-ʿivrit . . . B) b-shevaḥ yetzirato shel Ephraim E. Lisitzky" (From the song of Hebrew America . . . B: in praise of E. E. Lisitzky's work). *Hadoʾar*, year 41, vol. 42, no. 10 (29 Tevet 5722; 5 January 1962): 148.
Philips, Yaʿakov and A. Heiman. *Moreh ʿivrit ha-shalem* (The complete Hebrew teacher). New York: Hebrew Publishing Company, 1911.
Pineles [Penueli], S. Y. "Shirat Hillel Bavli (bi-mlot lo ḥamishim shanah)" (The poetry of Hillel Bavli: upon reaching fifty). *Gilyonot* 14, no. 12 (Nisan 5703; 1943): 290–293.
———. "Sifrutenu ha-ḥadashah ba-ʾAmerica: sipuray S. Halkin" (Our new literature in America: the tales of S. Halkin). *Gilyonot* 15, no. 1 (Iyar–Sivan 5703; 1943): 3–11.
———. "Sifrutenu ha-ḥadashah ba-ʾAmerica: shirat Ephraim E. Lisitzky" (Our new literature in America: the poetry of E. E. Lisitzky). *Gilyonot* 15, no. 3 (Av–Elul 5703; 1943): 138–141.
———. "Bikoret sfarim: b-ʾoholay khush—shirim meʾet E. E. Lisitzky" (Book review: In the tents of Cush—poems by E. E. Lisitzky). *Davar* 128, no. 8632 (30 October 1953): 4.
Preil, Gavriel. *Nof shemesh u-khfor: shirim* (Sunny vista and frost: poems). New York: Ohel, 1944.
———. *Ner mul kokhavim: shirim* (Candle opposite stars: poems). Jerusalem: Mosad Bialik, 1954.
———. "Nosaḥ-America ba-shirah ha-ʿivrit" (American style in Hebrew poetry). *Mtzudah* 7 (1954): 498.
———. *Mapat ʿerev: shirim* (An evening map: poems). Tel-Aviv: Dvir, 1961.
———. "Al ha-ʾAmericaniyut shel Hillel Bavli" (Hillel Bavli's Americanism). *Bitzaron* 45, no. 2 (227) (Kislev–Tevet 5722; November–December 1961): 76–77.
———. "Mshorerah shel 'Kentucky'" (The poet of "Kentucky"). *Hadoʾar*, year 42, vol. 43, no. 29 (15 Sivan 5763; 7 July 1963): 546.

———. *Ha-ʾesh vha-dmamah: shirim* (The fire and the silence: poems). Ramat-Gan: Agudat ha-sofrim and Massada, 1968.

———. *Mi-tokh zman v-nof: shirim mkubatzim* (Out of time and vista: collected poems). Jerusalem: Mosad Bialik, 1972.

———. *Shirim mi-shnay ha-ktzavot* (Poems from the two extremes). Jerusalem: Schocken, 1976.

———. *Yalkut shirim* (An anthology of poems). Ed. Reuven ben Yosef. Tel-Aviv: Yaḥdav, 1978.

———. *Adiv l-ʿatzmo: shirim 1976–1979* (Courteous to himself: poems 1976–1979). Tel-Aviv: Ha-kibbutz Ha-mʾuḥad, 1980.

———. "Lo b-diyuk concherto," "ʿal ha-kir" ("Concerto" and "On the wall"). *Yediʿot Aḥaronot*, 5 Sivan 5746; 6 December 1986, p. A.

———. *Ḥamishim shirim ba-midbar: shirim 1980–1985* (Fifty poems in the wilderness: poems 1980–1985). Tel-Aviv: Ha-kibbutz Ha-mʾuḥad, 1987.

———. "Asiya meḥalonah ha-yerushalmi" (Asiya from her Jerusalem window). *Haʾaretz*, "Tarbut v-sifrut," 14 February 1992, p. 8B.

———. *Asfan stavim: shirim 1972–1992* (Collector of autumns: collected poems 1972–1992). Jerusalem: Mosad Bialik, 1993.

Rabinowitz, Yaʿakov. "Rshimot: Americaʾiyut" (Notes: Americanism) (New York). *Miklat* 2, nos. 4–6 (Tevet–Adar 5680; 1920): 463–465.

———. "Americaʾiyut" (Americanism). *Hadoʾar*, year 3, vol. 4, no. 34 (8 Av 5684; 18 August 1924): 9–11.

———. "Americaʾiyut (maʾamar 3)" (Americanism: third essay). *Hadoʾar*, year 4, vol. 5, no. 38 (1 Elul 5685; 21 August 1925): 10–12.

———. *Nduday ʿAmasay ha-shomer: sipur* (Amasi the watchman's wanderings: a tale). 2 parts. Jerusalem: Mitzpeh, 1929.

Rabinowitz, Yeshayah [Isaiah]. *Ha-sifrut b-mashber ha-dor: masot* (Literature in the generation's crisis: essays). New York: Ohel, 1947.

———. "ʿAl shirat Hillel Bavli" (On Hillel Bavli's poetry). *Hadoʾar*, year 37, vol. 38, no. 13 (3 Shvat 5718; 24 January 1958): 232–233, 239.

———. "Yetzirato shel Ephraim E. Lisitzky" (E. E. Lisitzky's work). *Bitzaron* 41, no. 4 (Adar 5720; February–March 1960): 188–200.

Rabinovitch, Yitzhak Ben Mordacai. *ʿAl nahar Kvar* (On the Kvar River). New York: Gaver Brothers Press, 1897.

Ramras-Rauch, Gila. *L. A. Arieli (Orloff): ḥayav vi-ytzirato* (L. A. Arieli [Orloff]: his life and work). Tel-Aviv: Papyrus, 1992.

Raskin, P. M. *Tzafririm: shirim* (Zephyrs: poems). New York: Ramah, 1939.

Rasler, Binyamin. *Naḥlat-tzvi: roman* (Tzvi's patrimony: a novel). New York: ʿOgen; Tel-Aviv: M. Newman, 1958.

Rav Binyamin [Binyamin Radler-Feldman]. "Ephraim Lisitzky: ḥalutziyut sheba-ʿoref" (E. E. Lisitzky: rearguard pioneerism). *Mishpḥot sofrim: partzufim* (Authors' families: portraits). Jerusalem: Ha-vaʿad Ha-tziburi L-hotzaʾat Kitvay R. Binyamin, 1960, 187–188.

Ravid, Zvulun. "Yetzirah ʿal nose lo-yehudi hiniḥah et ha-yesod la-sifrut ha-ʿivrit ba-ʾAmerica (shishim shanah l-tzet la-ʾor 'mul ohel Timmurah' l-B. N. Silkiner)" (A work on a non-Jewish theme laid the foundation of Hebrew literature in America: sixty years since the publication of "Before the tent of Timmura" by B. N. Silkiner). *Hadoʾar,* year 49, vol. 50, no. 22 (11 Nisan 5730; 17 April 1970): 367–368.

———. "ʿElbon ha-yaldut she-lo nitkaper (l-zekher Ephraim E. Lisitzky: 23 Sivan 5722–23 Sivan 5732)" (The childhood shame that was not expiated: in memory of E. E. Lisitzky, 23 Sivan 1962–23 Sivan 1972). *Hadoʾar,* year 51, vol. 51, no. 28 (27 Sivan 5732; 9 June 1972): 474–475.

Raz, Hertzliah. "Anshay midot" (Men of stature). *Ha-poʿel Ha-tzaʿir* 35, 8 Sivan 5718; 27 May 1958.

Regelson, Avraham. *Mlo ha-talit ʿalim: masot v-siḥot* (A shawl full of leaves: essays and discourses). New York: Vaʿad L-hotzaʾat Kitvay A. Regelson, 1941.

———. Kitvay Avraham Regelson: *Sham ha-bdolaḥ: marʾot v-ʾagadot* (The works of Avraham Regelson: There is the crystal: visions and legends). New York: Vaʿad L-hotzaʾat Kitvay A. Regelson, 1942.

———. *Ḥakukot otiyotayikh: shirim* (Your letters are inscribed: poems). Tel-Aviv: Maḥbarot L-sifrut, 1964.

———. *Erʾelay maḥshavah: haʾazanah l-divray aḥaronim* (Angels of thought: listening to the words of the last). Tel-Aviv: Dvir, 1969.

———. *Beyt ha-nitzotz: marʾot v-ʾagadot* (The spark's dwelling: visions and legends). Ramat-Gan: Dvir, 1972.

———. *Shirotayim: la-sulam tzorit—shnay barburim v-nahar* (Two poems: to the Sulam-Tzorit—two swans and a river). Mifʿalim Universitaʾiyim/ Siman Kriʾah, 1972.

———. *Rvivim va-tal: siḥot ve-ʿolelot shir* (Spring showers and dew: discourses and poetry gleanings). Tel-Aviv: ʿEked, 1980(?).

Ribalow, Menaḥem. *Sefer ha-masot* (Book of essays). New York: ʿOgen, 1928.

———. *Sofrim v-ʾishim* (Authors and personages). New York: ʿOgen, 1936.

———. "Sofrim u-sfarim: ʿOgen" (Authors and books: ʿOgen). *Hadoʾar,* year 19, vol. 20, no. 18 (28 Adar 5700; 8 March 1940): 282–283.

———. *Ktavim u-mgilot* (Writings and scrolls). New York: ʿOgen, 1942.

———. "ʾAdam al adamot': ʿal ha-shirah ha-ʾepit shel Ephraim E. Lisitzky" ("Man on earth": E. E. Lisitzky's epic poetry). *Hadoʾar,* year 26, vol. 27, no. 29 (4 Sivan 5707; 23 May 1947): 829–832.

———. *ʿIm ha-kad el ha-mabuʿa: masot bikoret* (With the pitcher to the spring: critical essays). New York: ʿOgen, 1950.

———. "Eretz Israel vha-prozah ha-ʿivrit ba-ʾAmerica" (The land of Israel and Hebrew prose in America). *Hadoʾar,* year 32, vol. 33, no. 25 (1 Sivan 5713; 15 May 1953): 520–521.

———. "ʿAl shirato shel Efrat" (On Efros's poetry). *Hadoʾar,* year 32, vol. 33, no. 32 (12 Av 5713; 24 July 1953): 658–659.

———. *Me-ʿolam l-ʿolam: divray-masah v-rishmay-masa* (From one world to another: essays and travelogues). New York: ʿOgen, 1955.
———, ed. *Sefer zikaron l-B. N. Silkiner* (Memorial book for B. N. Silkiner). New York: ʿOgen, 1934.
———, ed. *Antologiyah shel ha-shirah ha-ʿivrit ba-ʾAmerica* (Anthology of Hebrew poetry in America). New York: ʿOgen, 1938.
———, ed. *Sefer ha-shanah li-yhuday America li-shnat 5699* (American Hebrew year book for 1939) (New York: Ha-histadrut Ha-ʿivrit Ba-ʾAmerica, 1939).
———, ed. *Sefer zikaron l-Ḥ. A. Friedland* (The H. A. Friedland memorial book). New York: Ha-histadrut Ha-ʿivrit, 1940.
———, ed. *Sefer ha-shanah li-yhuday America* (American Hebrew year book) 6 (New York: Ha-histadrut Ha-ʿivrit Ba-ʾAmerica, 1942).
———, ed. *Sefer ha-shanah li-yhuday America* (American Hebrew year book) 7 (New York: Ha-histadrut Ha-ʿivrit Ba-ʾAmerica, 1944).
———, ed. *Sefer ha-shanah li-yhuday America* (American Hebrew year book) 10–11 (New York: Ha-histadrut Ha-ʿivrit Ba-ʾAmerica, 1949).
Ribalow, Menaḥem, and S. Bernstein, eds. *Sefer ha-shanah li-yhuday America* (American Hebrew year book) (New York: Ha-histadrut Ha-ʿivrit Ba-ʾAmerica, 1935).
Rivkind, Yitzhak. "Mshorer lita" (A Lithuanian poet). *Hadoʾar*, year 42, vol. 43, no. 29 (15 Sivan 5723; 7 June 1963): 548.
Rosenzweig, Gershon. *Talmud Yankaʾi* (Yankee Talmud). New York: S. Druckerman, 1907.
Rotblat, H. M. "Vigvamim shotkim meʾet Israel Efrat" (Silent wigwams by Israel Efros). *Dorenu: yarḥon mtzuyar ʿivri* (Chicago) 1, nos. 5–6 (Kislev 5695; December 1934): 53–54.
———, ed. *Ha-sifrut vha-ḥayim: mikraʾah sifrutit l-vatay-sefer tikhoniyim* (Life and literature: literary reader for secondary schools). Book 2. New York: Hebrew Publishing Company, 1943.
Rubinstein, Simḥah. *Nerot doʿakhim: sipurim* (Dying candles: stories). New York: Hadoʾar, 1966.
Sackler, Tzvi (H[arry]). *Sefer ha-maḥazot* (The book of plays). New York: ʿOgen, 1943.
———. *Ha-keshet be-ʿanan: shivʿah sipurim* (The rainbow in the cloud: seven stories). New York: ʿOgen, 1948.
———. *U-sfor ha-kokhavim: roman history* (Number the stars: a historical novel). Jerusalem: ʿOgen and M. Newman, 1961.
———. *Hilula b-Meron: roman history* (Rejoicing in Meron: a historical novel). New York: ʿOgen, 1963.
———. *Beyn eretz v-shamayim* (Between heaven and earth). Tel-Aviv: Yavneh, 1964.
———. *Masakh u-masekhot: arbaʿah maḥazot u-shnay maʿarkhonim* (Curtain and masks: four plays and two sketches). Tel-Aviv: Maḥbarot L-sifrut, 1964.

———. *ʿOlelot* (Gleanings). Tel-Aviv: Yavneh, 1966.
———. *Sof pasuk: simanim v-samemanim l-ʾotobiyographiyah* (Full stop: signs and signals for an autobiography). Tel-Aviv: Yavneh, 1966.
Scharfstein, Tzvi. "Lisitzky ha-mḥanekh" (Lisitzky the educator). *Hadoʾar*, year 42, vol. 43, no. 27 (23 Iyar, 5723; 17 May 1963): 498.
———. "Mtargem oman" (An artful translator). *Hadoʾar*, year 42, vol. 43, no. 29 (15 Sivan 5723; 7 June 1963): 547.
———, ed. *Yesodot ha-ḥinukh ha-yehudi ba-ʾAmerica: kovetz maʾamarim* (Jewish educational principles in America: an anthology of essays). New York: Beyt Hamidrash Le-morim, 1946.
———, ed. *Shaʿar la-sifrut* (Gateway to literature). New York: Shilo, 1947.
Schirmann, Ḥayim. *Ha-shirah ha-ʿivrit bi-Sfarad uvi-Provence, sefer 1, kerekh 2* (Hebrew poetry in Spain and Provence, book 1, vol. 2). Jerusalem and Tel-Aviv: Mosad Bialik and Dvir, 1954.
Schwartz, Avraham Shmuel. *Shirim* (Poems). Tel-Aviv: M. Newman, 1959.
Schwartz, Israel Yaʿakov. *Kentucky* [Yiddish]. New York: Shlomo Rabinovitch, 1936.
———. "Meʾidilyot Kentucky" (Kentucky idylls). *Ha-tkufah* 32–33. Ed. Itzhak Silberschlag and A. Zeitlin. New York: Mosad Goslava v-Avraham Yosef Stybel, 1948.
———. "Meʾidilyot Kentucky" (Kentucky idylls). *Ha-tkufah* 34–35. Ed. Aharon Zeitlin. New York: Mosad Goslava v-Avraham Yosef Stybel, 1950.
———. *Shirat Kentucky* (Kentucky poem). Intro. Dov Sadan. Jerusalem: Mosad Bialik, 1962.
———. "Darko shel mshorer yehudi du-lshoni" (The way of a bi-lingual Jewish poet). *Hadoʾar*, year 42, vol. 43, no. 29 (15 Sivan 5723; 7 June 1963): 548–549.
Segal, A., and S. Safrai, eds. *Hakarat he-ʿavar b-todaʿat ha-ʿamim uv-todaʿat ʿam Israel [kovetz hartzaʾot she-hushmʿu ba-kenes ha-shloshah-ʿasar l-ʿiyun b-historiyah (ḥanukah 5728)]* (Awareness of the past in the conscience of nations and of the Jews: anthology of lectures presented at the thirteenth conference on the study of history, December 1968). Jerusalem: Ha-ḥevrah Ha-historit Ha-Yisrʾelit, 1969.
Semmel, Naava. *Eesraʾel* (IsraIsland). Tel-Aviv: Yediʿot Aḥaronot/Sifray Ḥemed, 2005.
Shaʾanan, Avraham. *Ha-sifrut ha-ʿivrit ha-ḥadashah li-zramayha—kerekh ḥamishi: ha-nosaḥ u-mitos ha-ḥipus b-nigudayhem* (Trends in modern Hebrew Literature—5: The nosaḥ and quest myth opposed. Tel-Aviv: Sifriyat Davar and Bar-Ilan University, 1997.
Shabtai, Aharon, ed. *Gavriel Preil: Mivḥar shirim u-dvarim ʿal yetzirato* (Gavriel Preil: selected poems and comments on his work). Tel-Aviv: Maḥbarot L-shirah, 1965.
Shabtai, Yaʿakov. *Ha-dod Peretz mamri: sipurim* (Uncle Peret takes off: stories). Tel-Aviv: Ha-kibbutz Ha-mʾuḥad, 1985.

Shaḥar, David. *Moto shel ha-ʾelohim ha-katan: sipurim* (The death of the little god: stories). Jerusalem and Tel-Aviv: Schocken, 1970.

Shaḥor, Sigalit. "Anan-laylah garah b-Rishon" (Night cloud lived in Rishon). *Yediʿot Aḥaronot,* "7 Yamim," 26 May 1995, 24–28.

Shaked, Gershon. *Ha-siporet ha-ʿivrit 1880–1970 [A]: ba-golah* (Hebrew narrative fiction 1880–1970 [A]: In exile). Tel-Aviv/Jerusalem: Ha-kibbutz ha-mʾuḥad/ Keter, 1977.

———. "Pninah tznuʿah shel sifrut: ʿal kamah mi-bʿayot ha-ysod ba-siporet ha-ʿivrit ha-'triviʾalit' beyn shtay milḥamot ha-ʿolam" (A modest literary pearl: concerning several fundamental problems of "trivial" Hebrew fiction during the interwar years). *Meḥkray Yerushalayim b-sifrut ʿivrit* 1 (1981), 5–28.

———. "V-halvai nitnah lahem ha-yekholet l-hamshikh" (Would that they could continue). *Tarbitz: rivʿon l-madaʿay ha-yahadut* 51, no. 3 (Nisan–Sivan 5742; 1982), 479–490.

———. *Ha-siporet ha-ʿivrit 1880–1980 (B): ba-ʾaretz uva-tfutzah* (Hebrew fiction 1880–1980 (B): In the Land and the Diaspora). Tel-Aviv/ Jerusalem: Ha-kibbutz Ha-mʾuḥad/Keter, 1983.

———. Ha-siporet ha-ʿivrit 1880–1980 (G) ha-modernah beyn shtay milḥamot ha-ʿolam mavo l-"dor ba-ʾaretz" (Hebrew narrative fiction 1880–1980: (C) the "moderna" between wars—introduction to "generation in the land"). Tel-Aviv/Jerusalem: Ha-kibbutz Ha-mʾuḥad and Keter, 1988.

———. *Sifrut az, kan v-ʿakhshav* (Literature then, here and now). Tel-Aviv: Zmora-Bitan, 1993.

Shakhevitz [Shaḥevitch], Boʿaz. *Yeʿarot mtohamim: epizodot ba-biyografiyah literariyah shel Shimon Halkin* (Abyssed forests: episodes in Simon Halkin's biographia literaria). Tel-Aviv: Katz Research Institute for Hebrew Literature, Tel Aviv University, 1982.

Shamir, Moshe. *B-kulmos mahir* (A quick pen). Tel-Aviv: Sfriyat Poʿalim, 1960.

Sharif, Bat-Sheva. "Sipuray Shimʿon Halkin" (The stories of S. Halkin). *Moznayim* 35, no. 5–6 (Tishrei–Kislev 5733; October–November 1972): 420–422.

Shavit, Zohar. "Ha-nisayon ha-koshel l-hakim merkaz shel sifrut ʿivrit ba-ʾAmerica" (The failed attempt to establish a center of Hebrew literature in America). *Migvan: meḥkarim ba-sifrut ha-ʿivrit uv-giluyeha ha-ʾAmericaniyim—mugashim l-Yaʿakov Kabakoff* (Migvan: Studies in Hebrew literature and its American manifestations—presented to Jacob Kabakoff). Ed. Stanley Nash. Lod, Israel: Makhon Haberman L-meḥkray Sifrut, 1988, 433–449.

Shenhar, Yitzhak. "Bisdeh sefer—naftulay elohim meʾet Ephraim E. Lisitzky" (In the book field—divine struggles by E. E. Lisitzky). *Gilyonot* 2, no. 10 (Kislev 5695; 1934): 361–363.

Shmeruk, Choneh. "L-toldot sifrut ha-'shund' b-Yiddish" (On the history of Yiddish "Shund" literature in Yiddish). *Tarbitz: rivʿon l-madaʿay ha-yahadut* (*Tarbitz: A Quarterly for Jewish Studies*) 52, no. 2 (Tevet-Adar 5743; January–March 1983): 325–354.

Shoʿer [Soyer], Avraham. *Dor holekh (sipurim)* (A generation goes: stories). 2 vols. New York/Tel-Aviv: Ḥaverim/Dvir, 1928.

Shoḥat [Schochatt], Refaʾel. *Kitvay Refaʿel Shoḥat* (Writings of R. Shohat). Ed. A. R. Malakhi. New York: Yedidim, 1942.

Silberschlag, Yitzhak (Eisig). *Bi-shvilim bodedim: shirim* (On lonesome roads: poems). New York: ʿOgen, 1930.

———. "Yehudah Halevi (poema)." *Gilyonot* 2 (1935): 308–318.

———. *Teḥiyah u-tehiyah ba-shirah: masot* (Wonder and renewal in poetry: essays). Warsaw: Avraham Yosef Stybel, 1938.

———. "Ha-shirah ha-ʿivrit ba-ʿolam he-ḥadash (Hillel Bavli)" (Hebrew poetry in the New World [Hillel Bavli]). *Aḥisefer.* Ed. S. Niger and M. Ribalow. New York: Keren Louis LaMed, 1943.

———. "Tzvi Sackler (Tzvi ʿn shalom)." *Bitzaron*, year 5, vol. 9, no. 4 (Tevet 5704; January 1944): 249–256.

———. *ʿAleh, ʿolam, b-shir* (Rise, o world, in song). New York: ʿOgen; Boston: Boston Hebrew College, 1946.

———. *Kimron yamay: shirim* (My days' arch: poems). Jerusalem: Kiryat Sefer, 1959.

———. "L-ʿEphraim E. Lisitzky ben ha-shivʿim va-ḥamesh: saba shel shiratenu ba-ʾAmerica" (To the seventy-five-year-old E. E. Lisitzky: grandfather of our poetry in America). *Hadoʾar,* year 39, vol. 40, no. 22 (11 Nisan 5720; 8 April 1960): 400.

———. "Kavim li-dmuto shel Hillel Bavli" (Outlines of Hillel Bavli's image). *Bitzaron*, year 22, vol. 44, no. 7 (225) (Av–Elul 5721; September 1961): 163–165.

———. "Ha-gorem ha-ʾanglo-saksi b-sifrutenu: magaʿim rishonim" (The Anglo-Saxon factor in our literature: first contacts). *Divray ha-kongress ha-ʿolami ha-rviʿi* (Fourth world congress of Jewish Studies). Vol. 2. (Jerusalem, 1968): 71–75.

———. *Igrotay el dorot aḥerim: shirim* (My letters to other generations: poems). Jerusalem: Kiryat Sefer, 1971.

———. "Hesped ʿal Sackler" (Eulogy for Sackler). *Hadoʾar,* year 53, vol. 53, no. 20 (21 Adar 5734; 15 March 1974): 308.

———. *Yesh reshit l-khol aḥarit: shirim* (There's a beginning to every end: poems). Jerusalem: Kiryat Sefer, 1976.

———. *Beyn alimut u-veyn adishut: shirim* (Between violence and indifference: poems). Jerusalem: Reuben Mass, 1981.

———. "Shlosh meʾot shanah la-shirah ha-ʿivrit ba-ʾAmerica" (Three hundred years of Hebrew poetry in America). *Bitzaron* 7, no. 26 (Spring 1985): 13–26.

Silkiner, Binyamin Naḥum. *Mul ohel Timmura: shivray poʾema* (Before Timmura's tent). Jerusalem: Asaf, 1910.

———. "Avtzan ish tam" (Avtzan the simple man). *Hadoʾar,* year 8, vol. 9, no. 42 (Rosh Hashanah 5690; 4 October 1929): 697–698.

———. "B-ʾarmon ha-melekh" (In the king's palace). *Hadoʾar*, year 9, vol. 10, no. 30 (3 Sivan 5690; 1930; 30 May 1930): 511.

———. "Motiv Kushi: me-ʿezvono shel B. N. Silkiner" (A Black theme: from B. N. Silkiner's bequest). *Hadoʾar*, year 13, vol. 14, no. 14 (24 Shvat 5694; 2 February 1934): 280.

Silkiner, Naḥum Binyamin. *Shirim* (Poems). New York: Ḥaverim; Tel-Aviv: Dvir, 1927.

Solodar, Avraham. *Shirim* (Poems). Ed. M. Ribalow. Chicago: Ha-histadrut Ha-ʿivrit B-Chicago, 1939.

Steiner, Moshe. "Parashat gvurah b-lashon ʿagah (b-shulay ha-maḥazeh 'b-ʿarvot ha-negev' l-Yigʾal Mossenson, hotzaʾat Twersky, Tel-Aviv, 5709)" (A heroic chapter in slang: at the margins of the play "on the plains of the Negev" by Yigʾal Mossenson, Twersky publishers, Tel-Aviv, 1949). *Bitzaron*, year 11, vol. 22, no. 5 (125) (Nisan 5710; April 1950): 60–62.

———. *Hagut ʿivrit ba-ʾAmerica* (Hebrew thought in America). Tel-Aviv: N.p., 1973.

———. "Shirah Kushit ba-ʾAmerica" (Black poetry in America). *Hagut ʿivrit ba-ʾAmerica* (Hebrew thought in America), 2. Ed. M. Zahari, A. Tartkover, and H. Ormian (Tel-Aviv: Brit ʿIvrit ʿOlamit/Yavneh, 1973, 310–323.

———. "Motivim indiʾaniyim ba-shirah ha-ʿivrit-Americanit" (Indian motifs in Hebrew-American poetry). *Divray ha-kongres ha-ʿolami ha-shishi l-madaʿay ha-yahadut* (Proceedings of the sixth world congress of Jewish studies). Vol. 3. Ed. Avigdor Shinʾan. Jerusalem: Ha-ʾigud Ha-ʿolami L-madaʿay Ha-yahadut, 1977, 503–509.

Steiner, Moshe, and Y. K. Miklishansky [Mikliszanski], eds. *Prozdor: mikraʾah l-veyt-sefer tikhon* (Prozdor: a high-school reader). Tel-Aviv: Maḥbarot L-sifrut, 1967.

Tabai (Tabak) A[haron]. "Beyn Sarah v-Hagar" (Between Sarah and Hagar). *Hed ha-kvutzah: Bitaʾon ha-kvutzah ha-ʿivrit b-Detroit* 11–12, no. 15–16 (5711–5712; 1951–1952): 42–44.

———. Yonah bi-mʿay ha-dagah" (Jonah in the belly of the fish). *Hed ha-kvutzah: bitaʾon ha-kvutzah ha-ʿivrit b-Detroit* 13–14, no. 16–17 (5713–5714; 1953–1954): 64–70.

———. "Plishtim" (Philistines). *Hed ha-kvutzah: bitaʾon ha-kvutzah ha-ʿivrit b-Detroit* 17–20 (5717; 1957): 57–63.

———. "Maʿaseh ba-ḥamishah avzay-bar" (A tale of five wild geese). *Hed ha-kvutzah: bitaʾon ha-kvutzah ha-ʿivrit b-Detroit* 22–24 (1962–1964): 49–52. Also appeared in *Hadoʾar*, year 42, vol. 43, no. 32 (6 Tammuz 5723; 28 June 1963): 601–602.

———. "Ester magedet (midrash agadah la-dor vla-dorot" (Esther foretells: a legend midrash for the generation and other generations). *Hed ha-kvutzah: bitaʾon ha-kvutzah ha-ʿivrit b-Detroit* 22–24 (1962–1964): 55–58.

Tamir, Noah. "Bi-sdeh sefer: b-ʾoholay khush" (In the field of books: in the tents of Cush). *Gilyonot* 30:1 (Kislev–Tevet 1954): 41–43.

Tarkov-Naʿamani, Yaʿakov. "Tziyon halo tishʾali . . ." (Zion, won't you ask . . .). *Hadoʾar*, year 28, vol. 29, no. 28 (Iyar 5709; 27 May 1949): 703–704.

———. *Rsisay ḥayim (mivḥar sipurim u-rshimot)* (Fragments of life: selected stories and sketches). New York: ʿOgen, 1951.

———. *Mivḥar sipurim* (Selected stories). New York: ʿOgen, 1972.

Tcharni [T. Carmi]. "Sfarim: ʿal 'medurot doʿakhot'" (Books: about "Dying campfires"). *Moznayim* 7(39), no. 3 (Sivan 5698; 1938): 395–398.

Toran, Ḥayim. "E. E. Lisitzky (l-vikuro b-Israel)" (E. E. Lisitzky: on the occasion of his visit to Israel). *Ha-poʿel Ha-tzaʿir* 45, n.d., 14–15.

Toran, Ḥayim, and Mordecai Robinson, eds. *Mi-Bialik ʿad Shimonovitch* (from Bialik to Shimonovitch). Vol. 1 of *Sifrutenu ha-yafah mi-Bialik ʿad yameynu* (Our literature: from Bialik to our times). Jerusalem: Aḥiʾasaf, 1944.

———. *Mi-Shneour ʿad Shoham* (from Shneour to Shoham). Vol. 2 of *Sifrutenu ha-yafah: mi-Bialik ʿad yameynu* (Our literature: from Bialik to our times). Jerusalem: Aḥiʾasaf, 1945.

Trainin, Avner. "Shir: l-Gavriʾel Preil, shanah l-moto" (A poem: for Gavriel Preil, one year after his death)." *Yediʿot Aḥaronot*, 17 July 1994, 35.

Ungerfeld, M. "Ngohot me-ʿarafel" (Brightness through the fog). *Ḥerut* (Elul 5717; 6 September 1957).

———. "E. E. Lisitzky." *Davar* 77, no. 11317 (24 August 1962): 7.

———. "Anshay midot la-mshorer E. E. Lisitzky" (Men of stature by the poet E. E. Lisitzky). *Ha-tzofeh* (16 May 1968).

———. "Ha-msaper vha-maḥazaʾi H. Sackler A"H" (The narrator and playwrite H. Sackler). *Hadoʾar*, no. 20 (21 Adar 5734; 1974): 308–309.

Wallenrod, Reuven (Reuben). *Ba-dyotah ha-shlishit: sipurim* (On the third floor: stories). Tel-Aviv: Dvir, 1937.

———. "B-ḥug mishapḥah" (In a family circle). *Sefer ha-shanah li-yhuday America* (The American Hebrew year book) 4 (1939). Ed. Menaḥem Ribalow. New York: Ha-histadrut Ha-ʿivrit Ba-ʾAmerica, 1939, 38–77.

———. "B-tzel ha-ḥomot" (In the shadow of the highrises). *Sefer ha-shanah li-yhuday America* (The American Hebrew year book). 6 (1942). Ed. Menaḥem Ribalow. New York: Ha-histadrut Ha-ʿivrit Ba-America, 1942, 296–329.

———. "B-layl pridah" (On farewell night). *Sefer ha-shanah li-yhuday America* (The American Hebrew year book) 7 (1944). Ed. Menaḥem Ribalow. New York: Ha-histadrut Ha-ʿivrit Ba-ʾAmerica, 1944, 271–282.

———. *Ki phanah yom: sipur* (For the day has waned: a story). New York: Ohel; Tel-Aviv: M. Newman, 1946.

———. *Drakhim va-derekh: pirkay masa* (Roads and a way: chapters of a journey). New York: Ohel; Tel-Aviv: M. Newman, 1950.

———. *Beyn ḥomot New York: sipurim* (Between New York's highrises: stories). Jerusalem: Mosad Bialik, 1952.

———. *B-'eyn dor* (Generationless). Tel-Aviv: Maḥbarot L-sifrut, 1953.
———. *Bayit ba-kfar* (A village home). Tel-Aviv: Dvir, (c. 1960).
———. "B-haray Catskill ma'arakhah A—maḥazeh mvusas 'al ha-roman 'ki phanah yom'" (In the Catskill Mountains, act 1—a play based on the novel "for the day has waned"). *Hado'ar*, year 42, vol. 43, no. 23 (11 Nisan 5723; 5 April 1963): 419–420; continued, act 2, vol. 43, no. 24 (2 Iyar 5723; 26 April 1963): 448; act 3, vol. 43, no. 25 (9 Iyar 5723; 3 May 1963): 467; act 4, vol. 43, no. 26 (16 Iyar 5723; 10 May 1963): 486; epilogue, vol. 43, no. 27 (23 Iyar 5723; 17 May 1963): 504.
———. "Traditziyot u-minhagim" (Traditions and practices). *Me-'otzar ha-sifrut ha-ḥadashah* (Modern Hebrew Literature). Ed. George L. Epstein and Max Zeldner. New York: Hebrew Publishing Company, 1965.
Wolfson, Tz. H. [Harry]. "Mul ohel Timmura (bikoret)" (Before Timmura's tent: criticism). *Ha-dror* 1, no. 6 (14 Tishrei 5672; 6 October 1911): 107.
"Yafyafuto shel kush b-'oholay shem" (The beauty of Cush in the tents of Shem). *Davar*, 16 October 1953.
Ya'oz Kest, Itamar, ed. *Mivḥar sifrutenu bi-shnat 5735* (Selected Israeli literature from 1975). Tel-Aviv: Misrad Ha-ḥinukh vha-tarbut/Yaḥdav, 1976.
Yehoshua, A. B. *Mar mani* (Mr. Mani). Tel-Aviv: Ha-kibbutz Ha-m'uḥad, 1990.
"Yovlot sofrim" (Authors' jubilees). *Hado'ar*, year 39, vol. 40, no. 13 (29 Tevet 5720; 29 January 1960): 227.
Zeitlin, Aharon. *Shirim u-pho'emot* (Poems and poemas). Jerusalem: Mosad Bialik, 1949.
———. "L-ha'arakhat shirato shel Hillel Bavli" (An appraisal of Hillel Bavli's poetry). *Hado'ar*, year 35, vol. 36, no. 13 (14 Shvat 5716; 27 January 1956): 249–250.
———. *Beyn ha-'esh vha-yesha: po'emah dramatit* (Between fire and salvation: a dramatic poema). Tel-Aviv: Yavneh, 1957.
———. "Dapim l-vikoret: ish v-sifro (he'arot b-shulay sefer-shirav shel M. S. Ben-Meir: 'tzlil va-tzel'" (Critical pages: a man and his book: comments at the margins of M. S. Ben-Meir's book, "Tzlil vatzel"). *Hado'ar*, year 38, vol. 39, no. 25 (7 Iyar 5719; 15 May 1959): 472.
———. "Asefah rabat-'am l-zikhro shel Hillel Bavli" (Large audience in memory of Hillel Bavli). *Hado'ar*, year 41, vol. 42, no. 9 (22 Shvat 5722; 19 December 1961): 139.
———. *Min ha-'adam va-ma'alah: shtay po'emot dramatiyot* (Above man: two dramatic poemas). Tel-Aviv: Yavneh, 1964.
———. *Ruaḥ mi-mtzulah: shirim u-pho'emot* (Spirit from the deep: poems and poemas). Tel-Aviv: Yavneh, 1975.
———. *B-'oholay sifrut* (In the tents of literature). Vol. 2 of *Beyn emunah lo'omanut: kerekh sheni* (Between faith and art). Tel-Aviv: Yavneh, 1980.
Zeldner, Mordecai, and G. L. Epstein, eds. *Me-'otzar ha-sifrut ha-ḥadashah* (From

the treasure of modern [Hebrew] literature). New York: Hebrew Publishing Company, 1965.

Zmora, Israel. "'Al shnay sifray shirah: a. Anshay midot, dmuyot v-havay shel tmol, po'emot, me'et E. E. Lisitzky" (Of two poetry books: a. people of stature, images and life of yesteryear, poemas, by E. E. Lisitzky). *Moznayim* 8, no. 4 (1–2 Adar 5719; March 1959): 271.

———. "Ephraim E. Lisitzky: bi-mlot lo 75 shanah" (E. E. Lisitzky at 75). *Moznayim* 11, no. 2 (Tammuz 5720; July 1960): 115–116.

———, ed. *Shiray rabbi Yehudah Halevi.* Kerekh 1, sefer 3 (The poems of Rabbi Yehudah Halevi, vol. 1, book 3). Tel-Aviv: Maḥbarot L-sifrut, 1946.

INDEX

Academy for the Hebrew Language, 182
Acco prison, 197
acculturation. *See* assimilation
Agnon, S. Y., 46, 141, 171, 196
Aḥad-Haʿam, 13
Aḥiʿever (Achieber), 15
ʿakedah, 170
Alabama, 45, 152. *See also* Montgomery
Aleichem, S., 2–3
Algonquin, 9
allegory, 23, 24, 67
Altalena, 197
Alterman, N., and "Magash ha-kesef" (The silver platter), 197
American Hebrew writers, statistics of, 6
Americanism. *See* Americanization
Americanization, 1, 3, 4, 6, 14, 30, 44, 54, 57, 65, 67, 76, 77, 92, 97, 102, 108, 110, 111, 113, 132, 136, 144, 159, 173, 175, 178–180, 181, 183, 190, 199, 219, 223, 224, 226, 238n27. *See also* assimilation
American Jewish Archives, 6
American River, 45
Amerikaniyut (*Ameriqa'iyut*). *See* Americanization
amphibrach hexameter, 16
anthropology, 53, 79
Antin, M., 6, 225
anti-Semitism, 24, 25
anxiety of influence, 26
Arab, 67, 207, 213, 287n74
Arabic language, 177
Aramaic, 41, 178, 180
"Ararat," 94–95
Arazi, R., 27, 52–53
Arieli (Orloff), L. A., 180–181, 183; "Emigrantim" (Emigrants), 181, 189, 202; "New York," 202
art, 35, 36, 49, 73, 78, 82, 140, 149, 165, 167, 168, 172–173, 215, 219
Asaf (publishing house), 14, 15
Ashkenazi Hebrew, 7, 175, 177, 182, 183–184. *See also* dialect
assimilation, 3, 8, 24, 36, 37, 66, 80, 90, 91, 96, 106, 111, 112, 131, 134–135, 136, 138, 153, 163, 164, 183, 188, 189, 190, 191, 192, 222, 227n2. *See also* Americanization
Atlantic Ocean, 88
Audubon, J., 86
Avinoam (Grossman), R., 4, 149, 215, 217, 228n11; "B-tzel sheḥor-ʿor" (In the shade of the one with the black skin), 149, 155, 173; "La-ruaḥ ha-ḥasudah" (To the kind wind), 217; "Mi-tokh yam va-layl" (From within sea and night), 217; "Viduyo shel Calev" (Caleb's confession), 149, 155–156
Aztecs, 93–94

Baʿal Shem Tov, Rabbi Yisra'el, 75
Babylonia, 97, 197

Balboa, 45
Balfour Declaration, 190, 193
ballad, 17, 118
Baltimore, 42
Bar-El, Y., 232n19
Bavli, H., 7, 15, 16, 81, 89, 91, 97–107, 118, 138, 203–204, 286n62; names of, 97, 253nn20–21, 263n35; "Bi-khfar Hodi" (In an Indian village), 98–100, 107; "Bi-vkhi mi-mekh yatzati" (Crying, I left you), 203–204; "Dike't oti" (You have crushed me), 203; "Dmuyot be-harim" (Mountain images), 98; *Masad*, 98; "Mormon msaper" (The tale of a Mormon), 98–100; "Mrs. Woods," 85, 100–106; *Nimim*, 98; *Ruḥot nifgashot* (Intersecting spirits), 97
Bellow, S., 5, 76, 181
Ben-Ami, S., 9
Ben-Avigdor, 14, 158
Ben-Meir, M., 156, 286–287n64; "Tfilat ishah Kushit" (A Black woman's prayer), 156
Ben-Yosef, R., 217, 227n11
Berdychevsky, M. Y., 147
Berkovitch (Berkowitz), Y. D., 2, 6, 184
Berlin (Germany), 198
Berlin, I., 138
Bernstein, L., 76
Bessarabia, 162, 163, 178, 187, 200–202
Bialik, Ḥ. N., 13, 30, 35, 53, 80, 111, 113, 176, 184, 192, 258–260nn9–10; "ʿAl saf beyt ha-midrash" (At the threshold of the house of study), 205; "B-ʿir ha-haregah" (In the city of slaughter), 81; "Ha-brekhah" (The pool), 81; "Mgilat ha-ʾesh" (Scroll of fire), 23; "Mtay midbar" (The dead of the wilderness) 16, 73
Bible. See *Tanakh*
Birobidjan, 200
Black as Jew, 116, 117, 139, 165, 173, 261n20, 274n61
Black Hawk, Chief, 95
Blank, S. L., 4, 7, 11, 110, 162–163, 178, 181, 183, 187, 200–202, 286n57; *Adamah* (Land), 201; "Adam v-khalbo" (Adam and his dog), 150–151; *ʿAl admat America* (On American soil), 162; *Bi-shʿat ḥerum* (A time of crisis), 162–163; *B-maʿarbolet ha-ḥayim* (In the whirlpool of life), 178; *Ee ha-dmaʿot* (The isle of tears), 160, 178–179, 181, 189; "Esh zarah" (Strange fire), 146; *ʿEtz ha-sadeh* (The tree of the field), 178; "Ish, ishah v-kof" (Man, woman, and ape), 161; "Maʿaseh b-Khushi" (The tale of a Blackman), 162; *Mister Kunis*, 160, 178, 179; *Naḥalah* (Patrimony), 201
blues, 118, 123, 124, 172, 260n14
Boston, 49, 111–112, 190
Brainin, R., 14, 22, 200
Brecht, B., 171
Brenner, Y. Ḥ., 14, 15, 171, 178, 180
Brind, M., 180, 181
Britain. *See* England; British people
British Mandate, 197
British people, 8, 25, 31, 32, 33, 36, 41, 92
Broadway, 36, 47
Bronstein, C., 5
Brooklyn, 2
Brooklyn Bridge, 83
Brooks, M., 5, 9, 76; *Blazing Saddles*, 9, 79, 174, 248n5
Brown, J., 133
Brown, S., and "Strong Men," 129
Buddhism, 9
Buffalo (New York), 9, 50, 73, 89, 94, 97

Bundists, 23
Burla, Y., 219
Byronic epic poetry, 22

Cahan, A., 225
Cajuns (Acadians), 154
Calafia, 44
California, 28, 41, 43, 44
Canaan, 90
Canada, 49, 50, 88
Canisius College, 97
Cape Cod, 87
Carmi, T., 149, 215, 217, 227n11
Catholicism, 25, 97
Catskill Mountains, 100, 102, 104, 106, 107, 255n42
Central Park, 81, 182
"Chain Gang Blues," 125–126
characterization, 22, 42, 44, 45–46, 71, 78, 95, 103–105, 107, 142
Chesapeake Bay, 28, 37, 42
children, 96, 101, 103–105, 140, 141, 142
China, 96
Chippewa, 70–71
Christianity, 23, 25, 26, 34, 41, 102, 119, 127, 150, 160. *See also* Catholicism
cigar store Indian, 42, 96
cinematic style, 19, 237n11, 251n3
City College, 159
Civil War, American, 100, 133, 153
classicism. *See* conservatism, linguistic and literary
colonialism, 23, 25, 28, 29, 32
Colorado, 43
Columbia University, 97, 154
Committee for the Hebrew Language, 182
Conquistadors, 20, 24, 25, 94
conservatism, linguistic and literary, 7, 8, 16, 17, 19, 23, 30, 48, 55, 116, 132–133, 140, 175–178, 182, 184–187, 192, 215, 220, 222, 226
Conversos, 85
Cooper, J. F., 91, 104
Corrothers, J., 98
Cortez, 45
cosmogony, 86
Cree, 67
Cuba, 25
Cullen, C., "Heritage," 129
Cyrillic alphabet, 180
Czernowitz, 175, 281–282n5

Daixel, Sheen, 79
Damesek, S., 142, 193, 268n9; "Bi-ymey nisayon" (Days of trial), 193; *B-gorali* (My fate), 141, 268n9; *Gam sham zarḥah ha-shemesh* (There, too, the sun shined), 193, 268n9, 268n18; *Mi-po umi-sham* (From here and there), 268n9
Days of Awe, 132
"De Gospel Train," 120–123
Delaware, 42
dialect, 7, 123, 129, 182, 183, 184
Dickens, 98
direct speech, 68
Dolitzky, M., 3, 13, 200, 219
Donner Party, 43, 44
Douglass, F., 133
Dropsy College, 215
Dubnow, S., 9
Du Bois, W. E. B., 98
Dunbar, P. L., 98
Dvir (publishing house), 14, 15
Dvořák, A., 9, 79

Eastern Europe, 81, 141, 176, 192
Eastern religions, 9
East River, 182
East Side, 96
Eddas. *See* Finnish Eddas
Efrat, I. *See* Efros, I.
Efros, I., 4, 6, 7, 16, 17, 21, 26, 27, 47,

50, 51, 66, 72, 92, 100, 102, 111, 112, 122, 181, 195–198, 212–217, 238n20; "ʿAl gesher ha-zahav" (On the golden bridge), 213–214; "ʿAl ḥof Manhattan" (On Manhattan's shore), 214; "ʿAl pnay ha-Yarkon" (On the Yarkon River), 214; "Bi-sfirat malkhut" (In sovereignty's sphere), 197; "Boker b-Tel-Aviv" (Morning in Tel-Aviv), 197; "Bo-ʾoniyah" (Aboard ship), 216; "Din" (Judgment), 197; "El ha-ʾaretz" (To the land), 214; "Ezra," 197; "Gvaʿot" (Hills), 214; "Gvurah" (Valor), 196; "Ilan" (Sapling), 215; "José," 213; "Ktarim" (Crowns), 214; "La-nehag ha-ʿivri bi-Khnaʿan" (To the Hebrew driver in Canaan), 214; "Malkhut" (Sovereignty), 196–197; "Marʾot ʿal ha-yam ha-tikhon" (Sights on the Mediterranean Sea), 212; *Meh ʿamok hu shatul* (*How deep he is planted*), 215; "Netzaḥ" (Eternity), 196; "Nginat artzi" (My land's melody), 195–196; "Seh" (Lamb), 216; "Shloshah shiray-yam" (Three songs of the sea), 216; "Shorashim" (Roots), 215–216; "Tohu" (Desolation), 216; "Vesuvius," 213; *Vigvamim shotkim* (Silent wigwams), 17, 19, 24, 25, 27, 28, 29, 31–48, 58, 86, 182, 237n17; "Yerushalayim" (Jerusalem), 196; "Yif koh ha-shvil" (The path is so attractive), 213; *Zahav* (Gold), 17, 27, 28, 33, 37, 43–47, 152
Efros-Scharfstein, Ghela, 31, 236n2, 238n18
Egypt, 8, 89, 115, 116, 117, 179, 197, 209
El Dorado, 44
Elisheva (Biḥovsky), 219
Ellis Island, 180, 181, 189
England, 8, 33, 42, 193, 220
Englander, N., 181
English language, 1, 9, 10, 41, 47, 54, 57, 79, 123, 151, 173, 178–180, 181, 183, 185, 188, 224, 226
English literature, 8, 16, 23, 49, 53, 86, 113, 158, 222
English people. *See* British
epic, 1, 23
Epstein, A., 98, 101, 102
Ethics of the Fathers, 75
Ethiopia, 145
etiology, 28, 55, 66, 74, 75, 87, 143
Europe, 2, 4, 5, 7, 10, 12, 14, 21, 23, 24–29, 32, 41, 47, 56, 65, 78, 79, 80, 83, 88, 89, 92, 95, 94, 104, 106, 107, 112, 114, 116, 122, 137, 147, 156, 175, 178, 179, 185, 188, 190, 191, 196, 198, 201, 206, 212, 218, 219, 220, 222, 223, 224. *See also* Eastern Europe
Even-Shoshan, A., 185

Faulkner, W., 171
Feinstein, M., 7, 210–212; "B-laylot kesef" (On silvery nights), 93; "Ha-rega ha-gadol" (The great moment), 211; "Libi v-gufi ba-mizraḥ" (My heart and body in the east), 211
Finnish Eddas, 54
First World War, 11, 19, 109, 114, 127, 179, 190, 191, 193, 198
folktales/folklore, 50, 53, 54, 57, 60, 61, 64, 65, 68, 72, 74, 75, 76, 79, 83, 86, 87, 88, 92, 124, 131, 140, 143; as songs, 54–55, 65, 119, 121, 123, 126. *See also* legends
Fort Hudson, Battle of, 133
French literature, 17
Fridland, E. D., 138
Friedland, Ḥ. A., 152, 161, 198
Friedman, D. A., 22
Frischmann, D., 219
"from within" (and "from without"),

10, 21, 44, 45, 57, 67, 85, 102, 110, 113–114, 162, 167, 243n23
Frost, R., 98, 144
Futurism, 82

Garden of the Gods, 43
Garrison, W., 133
Garsson, M. I., 13
Geles, Y. Y., 23
Germany (Germans), 79, 96
Gershwin, G., 5, 10, 76, 138; *Porgy and Bess*, 10, 79
Gibraltar, 212
Ginzberg, A., 181
Ginzburg, S., 3, 6, 16, 23, 80–84, 87, 154, 156, 157; "ʿAl nahar Hudson" (On the Hudson River), 80; "B-har beyt Columbia" (On the mountain of the house of Columbia), 154; "Joe," 144–145; "No-York," 23, 81–83, 154
Goldberg, A., and "Ha-mityaʾesh" (Despair), 193
Goldberg, I., and "Major Noah," 9
Goldfaden, 19
Goldman, Y., 289n103
Gold Rush (California), 28, 41, 43, 45, 152
Gomara, Francisco Lopez de, 55
Goodman, B., 138
Gordon, A. D., 201
Gordon, Y. L., 178, 184
gospel songs, 117, 119, 121, 122, 124, 148, 264n41
Grand Island (New York), 9, 94
Great Depression, 41, 48
Great Spirit, 20, 46, 60, 68–69, 72
Greenberg, U. Z., 219
Grossman, R. *See* Avinoam (Grossman), R.

Ha-dror, 22
Halevi, Y., 191, 205, 206–220, 287n74; "Ha-tirdof naʿarut," 218; "L-mi bakʿu" (For whom did burst out . . .), 209; "Tziyon halo tishʾali" (Ode to Zion), 209
Halevy, A. Z., 7, 11, 110, 146, 154, 156–158, 181, 195, 204–205, 271n24; "Ḥaveh b-tzur ha-dmi" (Hide in the rock of silence), 157; "Ha-yadekh tiktzar, moledet?" (Can't you help, motherland?), 204–205; "Lenox Avenue," 157; "Lo kam bi ḥazonekh" (Your expectations were frustrated), 205; "Mi-pnay artzi anokhi boreaḥ" (I flee from my land), 205; "Nofi ha-shavur" (My shattered landscape), 205; "Pitzʿay moledet" (Motherland wounds), 204; "Ptzuʿah at artzi" (You're wounded, my land), 205; "Tzabar" (Cactus), 205; "Tzemaḥ tzedek" (A shoot of righteousness), 157, 158
Halkin, S., 4, 6, 7, 14, 15, 16, 106–107, 110, 116, 146–149, 187, 194–195, 198, 215; *ʿAd Mashber* (Until breakdown), 151, 156, 163–166, 182; "Ba-ḥeder ha-pnimi" (The inner room), 182–183; "Ba-nekhar" (In the Diaspora), 194; "Bayit" (Home), 194; "B-ʾeretz zot" (In this land), 195; "Bi-shʿat bikur" (The visiting hour), 166; "El ha-kushit" (To the Blackwoman), 147, 150, 157, 173; "Hatavat ḥalom" (A dream made good), 166; "Pizmon Kushi" (A Black tune), 148–149; "Poh rav ḥori-ha-ʾaf" (Here anger abounds), 194; "Tarshishah" (To Tarshish), 195; "Yaʿakov Rabinowitz b-yarmut" (Yaʿakov Rabinowitz in Yarmouth), 194; "Yamim gdolim" (Great days), 194; *Yeḥiʾel ha-hagri* (Yeḥiʾel the Hagrite), 166; "Zar" (Stranger), 194

Harlem, 157, 158, 159, 166
Harlem Renaissance, 98, 114, 119, 138
Harrisburg (Pennsylvania), 89
Haskalah (and post-Haskalah), 3, 11, 12, 13, 19, 26, 30, 51, 62, 63, 64, 78, 118, 123, 133, 139, 140, 176, 177, 178, 181, 185, 187, 188, 201, 218, 219. See also *Ha-tzfirah;* maskil
Ha-toren, 15
Ha-tzfirah, 202, 285n55. *See also* Haskalah; maskil
Ḥaverim (publishing concern), 14, 15, 16
Hebrew month, 28, 37, 41, 45, 132. *See also* Ninth of Av
Hebrew Union College, 50
ḥeder, 3
Heine, H., 219
Hertzliah, 210–211
Heyd, M., 137, 271n22
Hiawatha, 60. *See also* Longfellow, H. W.: "The Song of Hiawatha"
Ḥibat Tziyon, 219
Histadrut ʿIvrit, 5
Holiday, B., 167, 172, 173
Holocaust, 2, 4, 42, 88, 113, 155, 161, 192, 193, 196, 197, 198, 204, 224, 238n20
Holtz, A., 101, 265n46
Homer, 54
Homo Americanus, 29, 166
Hudson River, 80
Hughes, L.: "Militant," 129; "The Negro Mother," 126
Humbolt Desert, 43
Hunter College, 47, 215

Imber, N. H., 13, 219
immigration/immigrants, 1, 2, 3, 6, 8, 11, 13, 54, 109, 134, 137, 159, 189, 190, 193, 198, 200
imperialism, 28, 79. *See also* colonialism
India, 154
Indian as Jew, 32, 72, 73, 75, 84, 91, 92, 95, 107
Indian summer, 94
Inquisition (Spanish), 24, 25, 85
Irish, 166
Isaacs, B., 94, 146, 180, 181; "Ba-maʿaleh uva-morad" (Ascent and descent), 202; "Bli shem" (Nameless), 202; "Shloshet ha-Manesim" (The three Maneses), 140–141
Italy, 146, 161, 166, 173

Jabbok River, 148–149
Jacobovitz, A. L., 22
Jamison, R., and "The Negro Soldiers," 130
Japan, 154, 155
jazz, 9, 118, 169, 171
Jeffers, R., 86; "Stinkers," 138; "Wounded Hawks," 138
Jerusalem, 14, 100, 203, 205, 207, 210
Jerusalem, Temple of, 85
Jesus, 130
Jew as Indian. *See* Indian as Jew
Jewish Theological Seminary, 50, 97
Jezreel Valley, 203
Johnny Appleseed, 50, 74, 88
Johnson, J. W., 127, 138; "The Black Mammy," 126; "O Black and Unknown Bards," 130; "Saint Peter Relates an Incident of the Resurrection Day," 129; "The Train Sermon," 131
Jonah, 82, 195, 204
Jordan River, 148

Kabakoff, J. (or Y.), 199
Kabbalah, 20, 127, 196, 197, 246n63
Kafka, F., 171
Kalevala, 16, 51, 54
Kaniuk, Y., 9, 167–173, 180; "Ha-msibah shel Charlie Parker"

(Charlie Parker's party), 168–172; *Sus'etz* (Rockinghorse), 171, 173; "Thirteen boiler-makers," 172
Kariv, A., 185
Katsika, 20, 21, 82, 83–84
Katznelson, B., 199
Keats, J., 144
kibbutz, 201
Klausner, Y., 9, 184
Kuloskap, 54

Lachower, F., 23
Lady Sings the Blues, 172
Lafitte, Jean, 154
Lake Oswego (New York), 196
Lakota, 10
Lamdan, Y., 56, 83–84, 198–199, 204; "Masada," 83–84
Landau, Y. L., 219
Last of the Mohicans, The, 104
"last of the Mohicans" (figure of speech), 91, 93, 95, 183, 221, 251n1
Latin alphabet, 180
Lawrence, D. H., 86
legends, 23, 53
LeGoff, J., 28
Leibushitzky, A., 219
Leland, 54
Lensky, Ḥ., 111, 257n5
Lexington (Kentucky), 153
Lincoln, A., 119, 126, 133, 153, 264n39, 266n69
Lindsay, V., 138, 265n46; "The Congo," 138
Lisitzky, E. E., 4, 7, 11, 15, 16, 19, 21, 27, 36, 37, 45, 49–76, 86, 87, 88, 92, 97, 100, 102, 108, 140, 144, 147, 149, 153–154, 176, 177–187, 204, 207–210, 214, 217, 218, 225; *Adam 'al adamot* (Man on earth), 187; "'Al ḥof Niagara" (On Niagara's shores), 56; "Amah khushit" (Black maid), 126; "Amen shaḥor guf ha-Kushi" (Yes, so black is the Black-man's body), 127–129; "America gam lanu" (America is ours, too), 134; *Anshay midot* (Men of stature), 177; "Ashdot Niagara" (Niagara Falls), 73; "Az ki usar el ha-'amud" (When he was tied to the stake), 126–127; "B-layl hitkadesh 'atzeret teḥiyah" (Consecration night at a revival meeting), 132; "Bo'akhah New Orleans" (Coming to New Orleans), 154; *B-'oholay khush* (In the tents of Cush), 27, 50, 56, 57, 110–136, 154, 184, 187; "B-'orḥam u-v-riv'am" (All their ways), 132; "Btulat ha-'ashadot" (Maiden of the falls), 56; "Divray masa mi-pi khohanim" (Priestly sermons), 129; *Eleh toldot adam* (In the grip of cross currents), 72, 73, 111–112, 117, 185; "Ezra hakohen" (Reverend Ezra), 116, 133; "Ḥasidim b-'umot ha-'olam" (The righteous of the world), 74; "Ḥatimah" (Conclusion), 134; "Ḥazon mi-laylah" (Nightly vision), 73; "Holekh l-masa'o Pete" (Pete's on his way), 119–120; "'Im 'erev" (At eventide), 72; "Israel ba-shitim" (Israel in Shittim), 118; "Ki ḥesed ḥafatzti" (For I seek kindness), 131; "Ki-tko'a shofar" (As the horn blows), 154; *Kmo ha-yom rad* (As the day has set), 29, 177; "Kna'anah" (To Canaan), 124; "Kol kri'at ha-rakevet" (The train's call), 124; "Kuvyustus Yupiter ḥozer bi-tshuvah" (Jupiter the gambler repents), 134; "L-'artzi" (To my land), 208–209; "Lo ra'ayah, lo ben v-lo bat li" (No wife, no daughter nor son have I), 124; *Mdurot do'akhot* (Dying campfires), 24, 27,

28, 29, 40, 51–53, 112, 239–240n4, 244n43; "Mrivay kohanim" (Reverend arguments), 154; *Naftulay Elohim* (Divine struggles), 67, 76, 230n26, 247n88, 265n52; "Negba" (Southward), 117; "Sfinat ha-yesha" (The salvation boat), 154; "Shir asir bi-'gdud-ha-kevel'" (A convict's chain gang song), 124–125; "Ushu ḥushu el ha-dovrah" (Hurry, scurry to the ferry), 124; "Va-tdaber Miriam b-Moshe" (So Miriam spoke of Moses), 117, 118; "Yehudah Halevi," 209–210
Lithuania, 97
London, 33
Longfellow, H. W., 10, 16, 40, 54, 59, 66, 86, 136; "The Song of Hiawatha," 10, 16, 27, 28, 30, 34–35, 40, 51, 52, 53, 55, 65, 110, 241–242n14
Long Island, 96
long poems, 13, 14, 16, 17–19, 23, 32, 33, 35, 40, 41, 56, 79, 92, 113, 152, 232n19
Lonnrot, 54
Lost Ten Tribes. *See* Ten Lost Tribes
Louisiana, 172. *See also* New Orleans
Lowel, A., 98
Lower East Side, 67
Luzzato, S. D., 206

Magellan, 45
magic, 55. *See also* myths/mythology
Maid of the Mist, 74
Maizlish, M., 211
Malakhi, A. R., 97, 102
Malamud, B., 5, 9, 76, 181; "Angel Levine," 9; *The People*, 9, 79; *The Tenants*, 9
Mammy songs, 124, 126
Manasseh ben Israel, 8
Mandelkern, 19, 219
Manhattan, 2. *See also* Brooklyn Bridge; Central Park; City College; East River; East Side; Harlem; Hudson River; Lower East Side; New York City; Williamsburg Bridge
Manito (Manitou or Manitu). *See* Great Spirit
Margalit, Y., 118
Markson, A. D., 13, 16, 232n17
Marquette, 49
Marranos. *See* Conversos
marriage, 12
Martha's Vineyard, 87
Maryland, 28, 31, 32, 42
Masada, 83–84, 249n14
maskil (or *maskilic*), 26, 27, 47, 62, 78, 131, 201. *See also* Haskalah
Masters, E. L., 98
matchmaking, 12
May, K., 79
McKay, C., 98, 126; "The Lynch," 126
Menaḥem Mendl of Kotzk, Rabbi, 75
Mendele Mocher Sforim (S. Y. Abramovitch), 30, 123, 141, 158, 176
metaphor, 23, 24, 29, 41, 42, 52, 56, 70, 80, 81, 83, 84, 86, 88, 93, 98, 101, 108, 121, 124, 140, 144, 151, 158, 160, 174, 214
metarealism, 58, 171
meter, poetic, 16, 54, 55, 100, 177
Mexico, 43, 85
Mexico City, 93
Michal (Lebenson), 184, 219
Michali, B. Y., 118
midrash, 69, 75, 86, 94, 129–131, 262n29
migration. *See* immigration
Mikliszanski, Ya'akov (Jacques), 6
Milwaukee (Wis.), 49, 117, 262n30
Mishna, 94, 178, 237n17, 252n13
Mississippi, 164

Mississippi River, 133, 148, 164
Missouri, 45
Mitzpeh (publishing house), 15
mlitzah, 118, 176, 185, 187
modernism/modernity, 1, 15, 19, 21, 49, 65, 77, 78, 82, 90, 98, 113, 121
Monterrey (Mexico), 85
Montesini, 8
Montgomery (Alabama), 156
Mormon, 89, 98, 102
Moses, 119, 130, 208, 210, 264n39
moshav, 201
Mount Adams, 87
Mount Hood, 87
Mount Saint Helens, 87
mulatto, 151
Muslim, 161
mysticism. *See* Kabbalah
mythic time, 34, 35, 87
myths/mythology, 16, 17, 22, 23, 25, 26, 28, 32, 33, 34, 37, 48, 53, 57, 59, 65, 66, 70, 75, 78, 81, 86, 88, 89, 90, 100, 104, 107–108, 138, 141, 168, 189, 206, 210, 225

Nanticoke, 37, 41
Nantucket, 88
narration, 37, 38, 40–41, 48, 68, 103, 106, 111, 131, 133, 141, 163, 167, 169, 170, 171, 172, 180, 187, 210
nationalism, 24. *See also* Zionism
Native American tribes, 91. *See also* Algonquin; Aztecs; Chippewa; Cree; Lakota; Nez Perce; Pawnee; Salish; Shawnee; Sioux; Snohomish
natural religion. *See* nature
nature, 19, 25, 27, 28, 30, 33, 35, 36, 70, 73, 77, 78, 80, 81, 82, 86, 87, 88, 90, 97, 100, 101, 102, 107, 139, 145, 147, 150, 160, 173, 174, 178
neo-romanticism. *See* romanticism
New England, 43–44, 45
Newman, M., 15
New Mexico, 98
New Orleans, 48, 49, 50, 114, 117, 130, 133, 208, 262n30
New York, 49, 80, 83, 95, 97, 98, 100, 102, 107, 157, 165, 167, 168, 172, 182, 204, 205, 210. *See also* Buffalo; Grand Island; Lake Oswego; Long Island; New York City
New York City, 81, 83, 96, 157, 158, 159, 166, 182, 214; as Jew-York, 165; as New-Nineveh, 155; as No-York, 155. *See also* Brooklyn Bridge; Central Park; City College; East River; East Side; Harlem; Hudson River; Lower East Side; Manhattan; Williamsburg Bridge
Nez Perce, 46
Niagara, 73, 94
Ninth of Av, 85
Noah, M. M., 8, 9, 10, 94–95, 193
North Carolina, 50
novel, 28, 33, 36, 37, 38, 39, 40, 225
nusaḥ, 30, 123, 176, 177

Odessa, 13, 80
ʿOgen, Y., 119
"Oh, Suzanna," 44
Oklahoma, 42
Ontario, 49, 50
Orloff, Arieli L. A. *See* Arieli (Orloff), L. A.
Orphic tale, 70
Other, the, 4, 10, 11, 24, 29, 32, 38, 48, 51, 54, 56, 65, 66, 67, 76, 77, 78, 79, 100, 102, 104, 106, 109, 110, 111, 113, 116, 135, 136, 142, 145, 149, 153, 161, 163, 173, 216, 224, 226
Ozick, C., 76, 181

Pacific Ocean, 20, 45
Palmaḥ, 167, 168
Paris, 198
Parker, C., 167, 168, 169–172

Parks, Rosa, 156, 271n21
Passover, 179
patriarchal culture, 12, 64, 98, 102, 106, 124, 186
Pawnee, 44, 67, 68
peace pipe, 68–69, 245n56
Penueli, S. Y., 187
Peretz, Y. L., and "Boncha the Silent," 150
Persia, 8
Persky, D., 4, 6, 15, 97, 177, 182
Pharaoh, 130
Philadelphia, 150, 161, 201
Philips, W., 133
Pichuto, Rabbi Moshe, 95
Pines, Y. M., 9
Pittsburgh, Pa., 5
Pocahontas, 104–105
poema. *See* long poems
pogroms, 21, 23, 126, 163, 192
Polish, 79
population statistics, U.S., 2
Poston, T., 156
Potok, 76
Preil, G., 29, 49, 93, 101, 138, 155, 181, 198; "Derekh ha-sahar bi-nharot" (The moon's way through rivers), 155; *Ha-ʿesh vha-dmamah* (The fire and the silence), 29; "Hamtanah la-maḥar ha-ʾatomi" (Waiting for the atomic tomorrow), 93; *Ner mul kokhavim* (Candle opposite stars), 29; *Nof shemesh u-khfor* (Sunny vista and frost), 29
primitivism, 28, 53, 54, 55, 64, 66, 78, 85, 88, 90, 95, 140, 146, 147, 148, 157, 173
prison songs, 124
Provincetown (Massachusetts), 32, 41
Prussia, 79
psychology, 68, 71, 72, 106, 138
Puccini, 37, 92
Puritans, 26, 45
Rabin, E., 230n26
Rabinowitz, Y. (I.), 3, 14, 108, 116, 144, 178, 187
Rachel (Bluwstein), 123
railroad, 119, 121, 123–124, 131, 133, 264–265n45
Rassler, B., 180
Ratosh, Y., 147
realism, 7, 11, 16, 28, 33, 35, 36, 37, 38, 48, 55, 57, 58, 59, 66, 70, 71, 72, 77, 78, 86, 98, 92, 94, 106, 109–110, 133, 135, 137, 138, 139, 140, 142, 150, 151, 152–174, 225
reception, literary, 21, 101, 239–240n4
Regelson, A., 4, 86–89, 92, 102, 108, 138, 161, 181, 198; "ʿAmud ha-sheḥafim" (A pillar of seagulls), 89; "ʿArafel b-kherem Marta" (Fog in Martha's Vineyard), 87–88; "Avaz afor" (Gray goose), 89; "Gesher ha-sela" (The stone bridge), 86, 87
Reḥovot, 15
revision, literary, 17–18
revolt, poetry of, 127, 154
rhythm, 54, 55, 61, 122, 123, 169–171
Ribalow, M., 5, 73, 101, 102, 191, 204, 231n14
Rimmon, Y., 219
Robinson, E. A., 113
Rocky Mountains, 45
romanticism (and neo-romanticism), 7, 10, 11, 16, 19, 21, 27, 29, 32, 35, 36, 45, 46, 52, 53, 56, 64, 66, 70, 71, 78, 79, 81, 82, 86, 89, 90, 93, 101, 109–110, 135, 139, 140–151, 155, 156, 157, 160, 206, 210, 215, 219, 222
Rome, 196, 213
Rosenzweig, G., 2, 13, 82, 191; *Talmud Yankaʾi* (Yankee Talmud), 2
Roth, P., 5, 76, 181
Rousseau, 78
Rubinstein, S., 29; *Nerot doʿakhim* (Dying candles), 29

Rumania, 162
Russia, 8, 16, 23, 180. *See also* Soviet Union
Ruth, 65, 144, 201

Sachem, 33, 37, 38, 41, 46. *See also* Sienkiewicz, H.
Sackler, H., 9, 163, 181; *Beyn eretz v-shamayim* (Between heaven and earth), 95–97, 193; *Mashiaḥ nosaḥ America* (Messiah, American style), 9, 94–95, 193, 252n16
Sacramento, 45
Sadan, Dov, 111
Salem, 45
Salish, 86
Salt Lake City, 89
Sandburg, C., 98
San Francisco, 43–44, 45
sanitization, 63, 64, 67, 75, 96, 123
San Juaquin River, 45
savagery. *See* primitivism
Schoolcraft, H. R., 65
Schulman, K., 9
Schwartz, A. S., 93, 152, 181, 203, 204, 218, 270n6; "B-lev yam" (In the heart of the sea), 218; "Moreh derekh be-harim" (Mountain guide), 93
Schwartz, I. J. (I. Y.), 110–111; *Kentucky*, 79, 92–93, 153, 270n6
Scotland, 85
Second World War, 88, 142, 163. *See also* Holocaust
Semel, N., 10; *Eesra'el* (IsraIsland), 10
Sephardic Hebrew, 175, 177, 182, 183, 186
sermon song. *See* song sermons
sexuality, 62, 64, 142, 145, 147, 151, 157, 162, 168, 174
Shaked, G., 158, 180
Shakespeare, W., 98, 113, 123, 184
Shamir, M., 123
Shapira, S., 219
Shavuʿot (Pentecost), 197
Shaw, G. B., 171
Shawnee, 60
Shenhod, S., 211
Shiḥor, S., 6
Shimoni, D., 219
Shlonsky, A., 123
Sholom Aleichem. *See* Aleichem, Sholom
Sienkiewicz, H., 79
Sierra Mountains, 45
Silberschlag, E. (Y.), 21, 24, 58, 110, 142–146, 181, 182, 198–199; "ʿAl kever shel Kushi" (On a Blackman's grave), 143–144; *Bi-shvilim bodedim* (On lonesome roads), 143; "Ha-ʾaḥavah" (Brotherhood), 143; "Ha-kinah" (The lament), 143; "Ha-ʿor ha-shaḥor" (The Black skin), 143; "Kokhavay knaʿan" (The stars of Canaan), 199; "Kol Cleopatra" (Cleopatra's voice"), 143; "Mexico," 93–94; "Mi-pi Kushim" (From the mouth of Blacks), 57, 142; "Mi-Polin ʿad America" (From Poland to America), 199; "Oznay ha-laylah kashuvot" (Night lends an ear), 146
Silkiner, B. N. (or N. B.), 7, 13–30, 37, 50, 51, 59, 66, 72, 97, 102, 108, 111, 112, 122, 187, 225; name of, 234n34; "Me-ʾagadot ha-hodim" (An Indian legend), 26; *Mul ohel Timmura* (Before Timmura's tent), 13–30, 32, 33, 35, 37, 46, 48, 77, 80, 92, 100, 176, 232n17, 233n27
Sinai, 74, 75, 94
Sinatra, F., 172
Sioux, 44, 174
skyscrapers, 181, 205
slavery, 115, 117, 119, 121, 124, 126, 134, 138, 150, 152, 153, 154, 155, 157, 173
Slutzk, 49, 115

Smilansky, M., 67
Snohomish, 74
Snunit, 184
Sobel, J., 13
Solodar, A., and "Himnon" ("Hymn"), 195, 196
song, 44, 110, 122, 123, 133, 171, 238n27; folktales as, 54–55, 65, 103, 118
song sermons, 124, 129–131
Soviet Union, 200. *See also* Russia
Spain, 20, 21, 24, 25, 31, 32, 33, 92, 94, 212
Spence, L., 68
spirituals, 117, 118, 119, 121, 122, 124, 130, 132, 148, 187, 264n41
squaw winter, 94
Statue of Liberty, 180
Stendhal, 171
Stern, N., 215
St. Louis, 43
Stowe, H. B., 116, 140, 153, 262n28
sunset, 29, 31, 33, 35, 43–44, 46, 106, 235nn52–53, 250n16
Sutter, 44
Syria, 8

Talbot County (Md.), 33
Talmud, 2, 49, 130, 132, 178, 184
Tanakh, 7, 16, 17, 60, 62, 64, 65, 69, 71, 75, 82, 89, 101, 107, 109, 117, 118, 123, 130, 131, 132, 133, 148, 153, 154, 155, 156, 158, 161, 170, 177, 178, 181, 187, 196, 197, 204, 205, 208–209. *See also* Jonah; Ruth
Taos (N.M.), 98–99
Tarkow-Naamani, Y., 84–86; "Bi-sʿor ha-saʿar" (As the storm blows), 84; "Shalom ʿal Israel" (Peace upon Israel), 85; "Tzlilay shkiʿah" (Sunset shadows), 85
Teḥiyah, 21, 30, 113, 140, 218, 241–242n14
Tel-Aviv, 197, 211. *See also* Yarkon River
Tel-Aviv University, 215
Ten Lost Tribes, 8, 29, 89, 95, 100, 253n18
Tennyson, 23, 184
Thoreau, H. D., 86
Todorov, T., 55
Tolstoy, 201
Tompkins Square, 96
Torah. *See* Tanakh
Transcendentalism, 86
translation, 10, 12, 14, 15, 57, 98, 137, 181, 182, 183, 238n27, 257n5
Tristano, L., 172
trochaic tetrameter, 16, 54
Truckee Flats, 45
Tschernichowsky, S., 35, 53, 54, 111, 113, 147, 192, 198, 241–242n14; "Levivot," 103
Tsfat, 203
Turkey, 8
Twain, M., 13

Ukraine, 215
Umatilla, 86

Venus, 73
vision quest, 55, 242–243n21
Volcani, Y. E., 15
Volhynia, 215

Walam Olum, 54
Wallenrod, R., 7, 32; "B-ḥug ishapḥah" (In the family circle), 161; "B-tzel ha-ḥomot" (In the shade of the walls), 160; "Hazayot boker" (Morning phantoms), 151; *Ki phanah yom* (For the day has waned), 29, 106–107
Wall Street, 41
Weingrad, M., 237n11, 251n3

Whitman, W., 86
Williams, M., 11
Williamsburg Bridge, 83
Wolfson, H., 22
women, 1, 12, 126, 143, 154, 156, 159–160, 163–165, 170–171, 172, 265n52. *See also* Mammy songs
Wordsworth, W., 144
World War I. *See* First World War
World War II. *See* Second World War

Yabetz, Z., 219
Yankee, 101
Yarkon River, 214
Yellowstone, 45
Yemen, 197
yeshiva, 3, 49, 73, 111
Yiddish, 2, 3, 5, 8, 79, 109, 111, 153, 158, 174, 175, 179, 180, 200, 224
Yizhar, S., 123
Yom Kippur, 94
Yosemite Valley, 43, 45, 98
Young Dog Band, 67, 245n50

Zamir, S., 177
Zangwill, I., and "Noah's Ark," 9
Zeitlin, A., 183, 198; "Ḥalomo shel ʿolam" (The world's dream), 198; "L-Zikhron Yaʿakov" (To Zikhron Yaʿakov), 198
Zionism (Zionist), 3, 4, 5, 7, 9, 21, 32, 40, 45, 84, 85, 93–94, 97, 175, 188, 190, 191, 192, 193, 194, 196, 199, 200, 201, 202, 204, 205, 206, 207, 212, 217, 218, 220, 222, 223, 226. *See also Ḥibat Tziyon;* nationalism
Zion Mule Corps, 193